Praise for Scott Anderson's

THE QUIET AMERICANS

"A story at once sweeping in its scope and fascinating in its particulars." —*The Washington Post*

"A darkly entertaining tale about American espionage, set in an era when Washington's fear and skepticism about the agency resembles our climate today." —*The New York Times*

"This intriguing book is an indictment. From its first page it argues that the CIA lost its way, in all senses, in the first decade of the Cold War.... [Anderson's] verdict is damning." —*The Economist*

"Absorbing.... Capture[s] in vivid detail the early days of the CIA and the origins of the Cold War." —*Rolling Stone*

"[A] richly researched, and deeply engaging history of the earliest forays of the Cold War.... [Anderson] shows how profoundly that era crafted the world we live in today." —CrimeReads

"In this sweeping, vivid, beautifully observed book, Scott Anderson unearths the devastating secret history of how the United States lost the plot during the Cold War. By focusing on the twisty, colorful lives of four legendary spies, Anderson distills the larger geopolitical saga into an intimate story of flawed but talented men, of the 'disease of empires,' and of the inescapable moral hazard of American idealism and power. It's a hell of a book, with themes about the unintended consequences of espionage and interventionism that still resonate, powerfully, today."
—Patrick Radden Keefe, author of *Say Nothing*

Scott Anderson

THE QUIET AMERICANS

Scott Anderson is the author of two novels and four works of non-fiction, including *Lawrence in Arabia*, an international bestseller that was a finalist for the National Book Critics Circle Award and a *New York Times* Notable Book. A veteran war correspondent, he is a contributing writer for *The New York Times Magazine*.

THE QUIET AMERICANS

THE
QUIET
AMERICANS

Four CIA Spies at the Dawn
of the Cold War

Scott Anderson

ANCHOR BOOKS

A DIVISION OF PENGUIN RANDOM HOUSE LLC

NEW YORK

FIRST ANCHOR BOOKS EDITION, MAY 2021

The Library of Congress has cataloged the Doubleday edition as follows:
Names: Anderson, Scott, author.
Title: The quiet Americans : four CIA spies at the dawn of the Cold War—a tragedy in
    three acts / Scott Anderson.
Description: First edition. | New York : Doubleday, 2020. | Includes bibliographical
    references.
Identifiers: LCCN 2019054799 (print) | LCCN 2019054800 (ebook)
Subjects: LCSH: United States. Central Intelligence Agency—Officials and employees—
    Biography. | Cold War. | Espionage, American—History—20th century. | Burke,
    Michael, 1918– | Wisner, Frank, 1909–1965. | Sichel, Peter M. F. | Lansdale, Edward
    Geary, 1908–1987. | Intelligence officers—United States—Biography. | Spies—United
    States—Biography.
Classification: LCC JK468.I6 A8435 2020 (print) | LCC JK468.I6 (ebook) |
    DDC 327.12730092/2—dc23
LC record available at https://lccn.loc.gov/2019054799

Anchor Books Trade Paperback ISBN: 978-1-101-91173-0
eBook ISBN: 978-0-385-54046-9

Author photograph © Robert Clark
Book design by Anna B. Knighton

www.anchorbooks.com

Printed in the United States of America
10   9   8   7   6   5   4   3   2   1

Contents

Author's Note

The Soviet Union's principal state security agency underwent nearly a dozen name changes during its seventy-four-year history, but was best known by two successive acronyms, the NKVD (People's Commissariat for Internal Affairs) and the KGB (Committee for State Security). In the interests of clarity, I have followed the example of most Cold War historians and adopted "KGB" as the primary acronym for most of the period covered in this book.

Somewhat more complicated is the usage of the acronyms OPC (Office of Policy Coordination) and CIA. For the first two years of its existence, from 1948 to 1950, OPC was regarded as quite separate from the CIA, even though it was "housed" within the Agency. This distinction blurred as the two organizations began to be integrated in late 1950, and disappeared altogether with their full merger in 1952. The end result, however, is that the same speakers or writers who might describe the OPC and CIA as two wholly separate (and often adversarial) bodies during the earlier period, will then use the acronyms interchangeably when referring to events in the later integrated period. I have attempted to delineate this changing relationship where necessary within the text, but some confusion might persist—as, indeed, it did for employees of both offices at the time.

THE QUIET AMERICANS

Preface

When I was a very young boy, my favorite day of the year was October 10. It was the mid-1960s and my family and I were living in Taiwan, where my father was attached to the American embassy. October 10 was the anniversary of an uprising in 1911 that led to the creation of the Republic of China, and it was celebrated in Taiwan by a massive military parade through the streets of the capital, Taipei. By great good luck, my father's office overlooked one of the main parade routes, as well as the vast square in front of the Presidential Palace that was the marchers' final destination. From his office window, I would watch transfixed as the square below gradually filled with soldiers wearing a riotous array of different-colored uniforms and standing at rigid attention. The highlight was when Chiang Kai-shek emerged onto a balcony of the palace to give a speech. It always ended with the same exhortation: "Back to the Mainland!" At this, artillery would thunder, a hundred thousand soldiers cheered as one, and great billows of propaganda balloons and homing pigeons carrying anti-communist messages rose into the sky, theoretically on their way to the enemy, Red China, just eighty miles away across the Formosa Strait. For a bloody-minded young boy, all of this was terrific stuff, better than Christmas. It took me a long time to realize that my father didn't actually enjoy these annual outings.

Like everyone else of my generation, my view of the world was fundamentally shaped by the Cold War. This shaping may have been more acute in my case due to the places where I grew up: South Korea, Taiwan and Indonesia. Korea and Taiwan were both regarded as frontline states in the Cold War, while by the time my family moved there, Indonesia was just emerging from a Cold War–inspired mass bloodletting that left at least a half-million dead.

One of the things I remember most from my childhood is that the threat of war, of a sudden attack by the communists, was always in the air. In South Korea, the government ruled under martial law, its army forever vigilant against the North Korean communists, massed just thirty-five miles up the road from the capital of Seoul. In Taiwan, Chiang Kai-shek went one better than martial law and declared a permanent state of siege. The entranceway to my elementary school was dominated by a large anti-aircraft gun on a swivel platform, two Republic of China soldiers constantly scanning the skies with binoculars for first sign of an incoming Red Chinese squadron. The result in both countries was soldiers everywhere: in the marketplaces, in the parks, passing by in long convoys of transport trucks during school field trips or family drives. Whenever I conjure an image from my childhood, there are usually soldiers somewhere in the frame.

I was alternately thrilled and terrified by all this. Once in Taiwan, when in the grip of the latter state of mind, when I couldn't sleep at night for fear that the communists might come before morning, I sought reassurance from my godfather, a tough-as-nails lieutenant colonel in Air Force Intelligence. When I asked how much advance warning we would have if the Red Chinese did attack, my godfather lit one of the sixty or seventy Camels he would smoke that day and gazed thoughtfully up at its coil of smoke. "About nine minutes," he said finally. "Why do you ask?"

I was too young to appreciate the cynicism of all this, to understand that much of what I was seeing was just so much political theater. The North Koreans weren't going to stream across the DMZ again, and the Red Chinese weren't going to invade Taiwan; by the 1960s, the East Asia front of the Cold War had long since settled into watchful stasis. Instead, what upholding the banner of anti-communism now meant in these places was that their military dictators need brook no opposition, could summarily crush even the slightest sign of domestic dissent. And so they did. In April 1960, my parents watched from a hillside above downtown Seoul as students protesting the dictatorship were machine-gunned by police. During the time we lived in Taiwan, Chiang Kai-shek's prisons were filled to bursting with tens of thousands of political prisoners. In the so-called Indonesian civil war, virtually all the killing had been done by one side, all the dying by the other, and rather than the advertised communist conspirators, the vigilante squads set loose by the military junta often found their victims among Indonesia's ethnic Chinese minority, the backbone of the nation's merchant class. In each one of these countries, the dictators' chief benefactor, the United States, could be counted on to steadfastly look the other way.

One reason I didn't grasp much of this at the time was because my parents didn't talk about it. Part of their reticence undoubtedly derived from their not wanting one of their children to blurt out an inconvenient truth at an inconvenient moment, but I'm sure another part stemmed from the fact that my father was part of the apparatus that kept these regimes in place. It must have been a strange and confusing experience for him—a farm boy from Fresno, California; a lifelong "yellow dog Democrat" with a hint of the socialist about him—but this, too, was something we never really discussed.

But perhaps it wasn't strange or confusing for him at all. By the 1960s, my father had been witness to a sweeping Red advance across the globe over the previous two decades. His liberal leanings aside, like virtually all Americans he regarded communism as an enslaving force, a cancer to be resisted. By virtue of his work with the American government—he was an agricultural advisor for the Agency for International Development, or AID—and the "frontline" postings he was given, he had the opportunity to personally engage in that struggle. I'm fairly certain he was not an intelligence officer but, like many American government employees posted abroad in the 1950s and 1960s, he often did double duty. In his soft-power role with AID, he assisted in agrarian reform schemes in a number of countries in Central America and East Asia, and distributed American emergency aid in the wake of natural disasters—noble work that also fit in nicely with the "hearts and minds" efforts to steer the rural poor away from communism. In his more hard-power role, my father also helped create rural paramilitary and "home guard" formations designed to watch for the unrest of leftist agitators and to monitor the political views of the local population. As often happens with such vigilante networks, most of those fostered by AID in the 1950s and 1960s ultimately proved more effective as vehicles for personal vendettas and score-settling than ideological policing, and certainly the fate of anyone denounced for their purported leftist views in places like South Korea and Taiwan couldn't have been a pleasant one.

Where it all truly began to turn, both for myself and for my father, was with the Vietnam War. By 1966, and accelerating through 1968, Taiwan became both a back-base and an R&R destination for soldiers serving in Vietnam, the streets of Taipei now filled with even more uniforms. Moving into our small American housing enclave above the city were the families of American officers stationed in Saigon, and the free-ranging game of Cowboys and Indians that we boys in the neighborhood had previously played was renamed Green Berets and Viet Cong. It didn't actually change the game that much, except that in the past the Indians sometimes won, and in the new version the Viet Cong never did.

This wasn't the impression my father came away with from his occasional work trips to Vietnam. Instead, the real war there seemed to be growing worse, and more unwinnable, all the time, and he would return from these trips with an uncharacteristic solemnity, a vague sadness that took him several days to shake. When finally we moved to the United States in 1969, my father's disillusionment was complete. He dragged me and my siblings along to the antiwar demonstrations on the Washington Mall, and vowed that if Vietnam was still going on when my brother and I reached draft age he would take us to Canada. It was a remarkable journey for a man who had been at Pearl Harbor, who had fought in World War II and spent his professional life promoting American influence abroad, but it was Vietnam, the staggering stupidity and directionless brutality with which that war was conducted, that finally caused my father to fully ponder both the waste and the wages of sin that accompanied the American crusade against communism. Rather than stay in Washington or accept another posting overseas, the day he turned fifty he took an early retirement from the government.

My passage to the same point took a good deal longer, but it was crystallized by an experience I had in the Central American nation of El Salvador in the spring of 1984.

By then, the Salvadoran civil war between leftist rebels and an American-backed right-wing government was entering its fifth year, and it had already taken the lives of some sixty thousand people. The vast majority of the dead had not perished in battle, but at the hands of death squads allied with—indeed, synonymous with—the government. In getting congressional approval for aid to the regime, the Reagan administration had performed all manner of political contortions to uphold the fiction that the death squads were somehow a separate and uncontrollable entity from the state—and that, anyway, the human rights situation in El Salvador was improving.

By the spring of 1984, the administration was actually correct about this last point. The monthly count of death squad victims had declined dramatically—possibly, as some critics charged, because the murder squads were simply running out of perceived enemies to kill—and the Reagan administration was touting those diminished numbers as proof that their policy was working, that a corner had been turned in El Salvador's "dirty war."

As an aspiring journalist, I visited the capital of San Salvador in late May of that year. One afternoon I was walking along the broad street that ran behind the El Camino Real hotel, the city's journalistic nerve center, when a nondescript van passed me and pulled to the curb perhaps a hundred feet ahead. The vehicle's sliding door was pulled back, and the body of a woman was thrown out onto the sidewalk. In my mind's eye, I can still see her: late twenties or early thirties, clad in a weathered floral-pattern red dress, lying with her back on the sidewalk and her bare legs extending into the road, her tied-together hands resting on her chest. I was the only person close by and as the van pulled away, I approached her with that odd half-hurrying, half-halting gait people seem to assume in such circumstances. I had only walked about halfway to the woman, a matter of maybe ten seconds, when a second van, this one marked as military, pulled up alongside her. Three soldiers scrambled out, and as one raised his machine gun to point at a spot just before my feet—pretty much a universal "don't approach" gesture—the other two hoisted the dead woman into the vehicle and climbed in after her. The soldier on the sidewalk then dropped his vigil to jump back into the van as it, too, merged into traffic. The entire transaction, from body-drop by "anonymous killers" to body retrieval by authorities probably took less than half a minute, a seamless little sleight-of-hand operation honed by long practice. That night in my hotel room, I watched the White House press spokesman on the evening news once again extol the great human rights progress being made in El Salvador.

For whatever reason, that incident by the El Camino struck me as many others had not, and it summoned to my mind a simple question: How had it come to this? How, in the name of fighting communism—or at least what some claimed was communism—had the American government come to tacitly sanction death squads, to support governments that would so brazenly murder its own people as to toss their bodies out on sidewalks in broad daylight?

I wouldn't say this question came to me as some kind of revelation. Instead, it was merely the culmination of a long personal journey, one that encompassed my own childhood experiences joined to all I knew about recent American history, about Vietnam and Chile and Guatemala. But something did change in me after El Salvador. From then on, the very phrase "anti-communist" took on a squalid quality when I considered the crimes done in its name, and I tended to consider those who gave themselves that label with much the same derision that I held for other lunatic fringes, the anti-fluoride or flat-earth crowds. This was a comfortable place to be in the mid-1980s, what with the Reagan administration cozying up to most any despot who called himself anti-communist, and I had a lot of company in my disgust.

Yet, even then, I was conscious of an essential contradiction in this outlook, something that didn't fit. Because when you really thought about it, most any right-thinking person *should* be anti-communist. Quite aside from its utopian pretensions in theory, what communism had displayed time and again in practice was a system tailor-made for the most cunning or vicious or depraved to prosper. Amid the blood-drenched history of the twentieth century, just two communist leaders—Joseph Stalin and Mao Zedong—had, through a combination of purges and criminally incompetent economic experiments, killed off an estimated sixty million of their own countrymen. If you added in the lesser lights of the communist world, its Pol Pots and Kim Il-sungs and Haile Mengistus, one could easily add another ten or fifteen million to the body count. Given this gruesome track record, shouldn't any right-thinking person be anti-communist in the same way that they should be anti-Nazi or anti–child molester or anti-polio?

But if anti-communism itself was not the issue, just when did its image become so sullied? While impossible to isolate to any singular event, I believe the answer to that question can be found in a fairly clearly delineated and brief stretch of American history, specifically that twelve-year span from 1944 to 1956 that comprised the first years of the Cold War.

The transformation that occurred in those twelve years of the American Century, both within the United States and in its standing in the world, is nothing short of staggering. In 1944, the United States was seen as a beacon of hope and a source of deliverance throughout the developing world, the emergent superpower that, in the postwar era envisioned by Franklin D. Roosevelt, would nurture democracy across the globe and dismantle the obsolete and despised rule of the European colonial powers. It was to be the end of the age of empire and, if Roosevelt's vision was achieved, possibly the end of war itself, with countries in the future settling their differences around the conference table of a powerful and transnational forum, the United Nations.

Just twelve years later, though, the United Nations was already beginning its long slow slide into irrelevance, and rather than dismantling the European colonial empires, in many places the United States was paying for their maintenance. Instead of fostering the spread of democracy, the United States was overthrowing democratic governments—in Iran, in Guatemala—that it deemed communist-tilting or otherwise unreliable. Even to opt for nonalignment between the competing superpowers was no guarantee of escaping American Cold War wrath in the form of economic embargoes or destabilization efforts; in the increasingly black-and-white view of the anti-communist crusaders in Washington, those who did not stand fully with the United States stood against it.

And at the end of this time span: humiliation. After years of trying to spur an anti-communist uprising somewhere in Eastern Europe, American Cold Warriors were finally handed one in Hungary in October 1956, only to have all their talk of "rollback" and liberation be exposed as meaningless rhetoric; the image of Soviet tanks rolling through the streets of Budapest to crush the revolution produced great bouts of hand-wringing in Washington, but nothing more. Ironically, at that very same moment, another anti-communist revolt, this one virtually unknown to the outside world, was taking place on the opposite side of the earth. Just as in Hungary, though, American strategists would decide there was nothing they could do to support the regional uprising against communist rule in the Southeast Asian nation of Vietnam. Finally in all this, in those same few fateful days of late October and early November 1956, Cold War myopia may have caused American leaders to miss a golden opportunity to start bringing that greater conflict to an end. Instead, the Cold War would drag on for another thirty-five years, avoiding the nuclear conflagration that so many feared, but sowing any number of lesser sorrows along the way: El Salvador, Angola, Cambodia and of course, Vietnam.

But along with the foreign missteps of those twelve years—indeed, helping to provoke them—there occurred within the United States a profound crisis of confidence, a kind of sustained and slow-motion hysteria. It took the form of a state-sanctioned witch hunt for alleged communist "fellow travelers," of mass loyalty pledges, of men and women seeing their professional lives destroyed by whisper campaigns accusing them of being "pink" or gay or otherwise suspect, all manipulated by an FBI director and a handful of politicians who saw great profit in the panic they induced. In the process, the purveyors of the Red Scare not only held up their own anti-communist cause to ridicule, but fueled a cynicism and distrust of government from which the United States has never truly recovered.

Much the same can be said of American standing abroad. To many around the globe, the image they held of the United States by the end of 1956 was that of one more empire in the mold of all those that had come before, one that lied and stole and invaded as empires are wont to do, never again that shining city on a hill so many had imagined just twelve years before. This perception, too, is not one that has improved with the passage of time.

Obviously, there are many ways to tell the history of the early Cold War, just as there have already been many books written on some aspect of it: accounts of the 1948–49 Berlin Blockade and airlift, for example, or exposés on the McCarthy era, the memoirs of countless diplomats and generals. The type of history I have always been drawn to, though, is that of people living at the ground zero of events, the stories of those with a direct and personal stake in a drama, rather than of politicians or scholars who experienced it from a higher, safer distance. Given this proclivity, I was struck by a comment made by a former CIA operations officer, Michael Thompson, in writing about covert operations conducted by the Agency during the Cold War. "There was no one else to undertake such tasks," Thompson wrote. "That the Agency was the one department of government uniquely designed to fight the Cold War was a source of strain as well as of pride among its members."

While I can't judge the veracity of the last part of that statement, the more I've thought of Thompson's assertion of the CIA's center-stage role in the Cold War, the more I am convinced he had it exactly right. It was the intelligence officers of both sides, what they did and didn't achieve, who provided the fuel for the nuclear arms race, who provoked the Red Scare, who drove nations into the orbits of East or West. It was spies who were the Cold War's first-line soldiers, its animating force.

With that in mind, I set out to find the stories of American intelligence operatives who had served on the very front line of the Cold War in those years when it ran the hottest, men who had run spy chains, cultivated defectors, who had lived double lives—and often at great personal risk. Through their personal stories and experiences, I believed, one might come to have a more intimate view into the Cold War, and to explore questions outside the scope of traditional history books: What did it feel like? Was there a singular moment when the contest turned? Ultimately— and on both a personal level and that of a nation—what was the price of winning, and was it worth it? This book is the result of that search.

It is primarily the story of four men: Michael Burke, Edward Lansdale, Peter Sichel and Frank Wisner.

At the outset of World War II, these four led very different lives, so different that it's hard to imagine a situation where their paths might have ever crossed. In the spring of 1941, Frank Wisner, born into wealth and privilege in the Deep South, was an attorney at a prestigious New York law firm. Michael Burke, a former college football star, worked the rough waterfronts of Brooklyn as a maritime insurance investigator, while nineteen-year-old Peter Sichel toiled as a stock boy for a wholesale shoe distributor. In San Francisco, Edward Lansdale, at thirty-three the oldest of the four, was a rising star in an ad agency.

What brought them together was World War II, and the roles they were assigned to play in it. Through a combination of both design and caprice—a language proficiency in one instance, a chance encounter on a city sidewalk in another—all found themselves attached to the Office of Strategic Services, or OSS, the first federal agency in American history devoted to gathering intelligence and conducting covert operations abroad.

Within the OSS, both the specialties and experiences of the four varied greatly. Considered one of the Agency's brightest lights, Frank Wisner took over a vast spy network in southeastern Europe that had been disastrously compromised. Michael Burke operated as a commando behind enemy lines. Peter Sichel proved such a consummate trader on the wartime currency black market that he was able to simultaneously fund an array of OSS espionage missions and to purchase the contents of an Algerian wine cellar for his private consumption. Edward Lansdale, by contrast, had a decidedly "bad war," shifted over to another branch of military intelligence and stranded in stateside postings for the duration.

At the war's conclusion, two of the men endeavored to stay on with the military—no small feat in a rapidly shrinking army—while the others returned to civilian life, to wives and young children. Very soon, though, a new conflict arose, the Cold War, and one by one, all returned to their wartime roots, not as members of the old OSS but of its much more powerful successor, the Central Intelligence Agency. For all four, this new contest came to define their lives, bringing adventure and intrigue and purpose, but also failed marriages, estranged families, the isolating burden of maintaining a double life.

Drawn to enlist in that struggle for an amalgam of reasons—patriotism, certainly, but also the thrill of danger, the sense of being a part of history—the four would also ultimately come to view their roles in the Cold War very differently. Two would leave the CIA in despair, stricken by the moral compromises they had been asked to make, or by their role in causing the deaths of others. Another, battling mental illness and haunted by a Cold War calamity he had tried to avert, would end up taking his own life. The fourth would make a kind of Faustian bargain, embracing governmental policies he knew to be futile in order to maintain his seat at the decision-making table, only to become a scapegoat when those policies failed.

This book is the chronicle of those four men. In its own way, it is also the chronicle of the greater tragedy in which they participated, of how at the very dawn of the American Century, the United States managed to snatch moral defeat from the jaws of sure victory, and be forever tarnished.

Act 1

THIS SAD AND BREATHLESS MOMENT

Now, at this sad and breathless moment, we are plunged in the hunger and distress which are the aftermath of our stupendous struggle.

—WINSTON CHURCHILL, March 5, 1946

1

OPERATION DOGWOOD

As Frank Wisner watched from a dark corner of the night-club, the diverted stage spotlight swept over the crowd until it found the man who had just stepped through the entranceway. He was in his mid-forties, bespectacled and wore a well-tailored suit. He was also clearly well known at the Park Hotel for, along with drawing the spotlight, his arrival caused the nightclub band to slide into a different jazzy number.

> *I'm involved in a dangerous game,*
> *Every other day I change my name,*
> *The face is different, but the body's the same,*
> *Boo boo, baby, I'm a spy!*

Wisner felt a growing irritation, directed less at the song than at the man being serenaded. His name was Lanning "Packy" Macfarland, and he was, in fact, a spy, the head of the Istanbul branch of the Office of Strategic Services (OSS), America's wartime intelligence agency. He was also the man that Frank Wisner, a fellow OSS officer, had made the 1,400-mile overland journey from Cairo to meet.

> *You have heard of Mata Hari,*
> *We did business cash and carry,*
> *Papa caught us and we had to marry,*
> *Boo boo, baby, I'm a spy!*

"Boo Boo, Baby, I'm a Spy" was a popular ditty in Istanbul in the spring of 1944, and with no group more so than the habitués of the Park Hotel bar. Located near the sprawling German consulate in neutral Turkey's largest city, the bar was the favored watering hole for officials of the Abwehr, the Nazi military intelligence agency. Naturally, that status also made it a destination spot for all the other spies circulating through wartime Istanbul, along with the assorted lowlifes—con men and arms merchants, prostitutes and pimps—inevitably drawn to such an underworld. Wisner had arrived early for his rendezvous with Macfarland and situated himself in a dark corner of the bar so as to avoid notice, a pointless precaution judging by the extravagant welcome given the American spy chief.

> Now, as a lad, I'm not so bad,
> In fact, I'm a darn good lover.
> But look, my sweet, let's be discreet,
> And do this undercover.

In Macfarland's defense, he may have simply accepted as absurd any notion that his Axis counterparts didn't know exactly who he was; as author Barry Rubin notes, World War II–era Istanbul practically survived on espionage: "Would-be spies for rent strolled up and down Istiklal Boulevard and around Taksim Square with its neo-baroque monument to the republic. They lounged in Istanbul's bars, dining places, nightclubs, and dance halls. . . . The music from the cafes and the bells of the crowded trolleys played accompaniment as men weaved through the streets trying to follow or evade each other."

> I'm so cocky, I could swagger.
> The things I know would make you stagger.
> I'm ten percent cloak and ninety percent dagger,
> Boo boo, baby, I'm a spy!

Certainly, Macfarland's own OSS colleagues had been little help in maintaining his cover as a banker with the U.S. government's Lend-Lease program, the wartime structure that funneled American weapons and matériel to its allies. Soon after setting up shop in the Istanbul Lend-Lease office, the frustrated spymaster had fired off a despairing cable to OSS Cairo: "Please, please, please! Instruct everyone to leave out any reference whatsoever to Office of Strategic Services in addressing envelopes. Today there came two more that bear this inscription."

The element of farce aside, the mission of the OSS in wartime Istanbul was deadly serious—so deadly serious, in fact, that by the time of Wisner's arrival in the city, Packy Macfarland had managed to compromise a whole series of intelligence missions and may have been instrumental in prolonging the course of World War II. Indeed, so calamitous was the workings of his Operation Dogwood, a spy network that extended throughout Eastern Europe but which had been thoroughly infiltrated by Nazi agents, that many details of the story still remain classified. What *is* known is that by the late spring of 1944, OSS leadership in Washington had become so alarmed by the dire news coming out of Istanbul on Dogwood that they scrambled to find an operative close at hand who might be brought in to stanch the bleeding. The man they chose was a thirty-four-year-old naval officer attached to OSS Cairo, Frank Gardiner Wisner.

It was a call Wisner had been awaiting ever since joining the military three years earlier. In that time, his lot had been to look over legal briefs and shuffle paper, to sit in a back-base office and collate the fieldwork of others. Now, by being dispatched to Istanbul, he was finally going into the field with the opportunity to accomplish something tangible, and he set to the housecleaning mission in Istanbul with a zeal. OSS higher-ups swiftly took note of the contrast between their two men in Turkey; just days after his arrival, Wisner was made head of the Secret Intelligence branch of OSS Istanbul, then shortly after named chief of the entire mission, with Macfarland bundled off to a posting in Yugoslavia where he could do little harm. At long last, Frank Wisner had arrived. The inauspicious trappings of his meeting with Macfarland at the Park Hotel notwithstanding, he was now on his way to becoming one of the most important and powerful figures of the American intelligence community in the twentieth century.

Childhood acquaintances of Frank Gardiner Wisner rarely recalled seeing him walk; he seemed to run everywhere. Even as a boy, he fairly crackled with a kind of impatient energy. In a photograph taken of him around the age of eight or nine and in which he is posing with two other boys, he appears to be practically bursting out of his Sunday suit, as if clothes are just another thing getting in his way, slowing him down.

Wisner was born in the town of Laurel, in the swampy, yellow pinelands of southeastern Mississippi. Even today, Laurel dubs itself "the town that lumber built," although "lumber" might more accurately be traded out for "the Iowans." In the early 1890s, a group of prospectors from eastern Iowa moved into the economically moribund Deep South town, and proceeded to both buy up vast tracts of the surrounding yellow pine forest, and then to build a state-of-the-art lumber mill. Among the newcomers was Frank Wisner's father, Frank George.

Their timing was propitious, for within a few years the lumbering of Southern Yellow Pine was experiencing a nationwide boom, making the Midwestern transplants in Laurel—along with the Wisners, there were the Gardiners and Eastmans—fabulously wealthy. According to one local historian, by the 1920s Laurel boasted more millionaires per capita than any city in the nation, and had converted the once scrubby little town in the pinelands into an unlikely architectural showcase, with a park designed by Frederick Law Olmsted Jr. and mansions lining its own Fifth Avenue.

At its heart, Laurel was a boomtown. As such, it had far more in common with, say, the mining settlements of Montana or the oilfields of California than with its Mississippi counterparts. In this most rigidly segregated state of the Deep South, blacks and whites worked alongside each other in Laurel's Eastman-Gardiner lumber mill, and there was a degree of racial intermingling virtually unheard-of elsewhere in Mississippi. In the black sections of town, the Iowans funded parks and streetlights and, in 1926, one of the first high schools for black children in the state, a development regarded as shocking, even subversive, by many Mississippi whites at the time.

All of this made Frank Wisner, born in Laurel in 1909, something of an oddity, a hybrid of two very different cultures. While his childhood bore all the hallmarks of the privileged white Southerner—he was raised by a black nanny, and black housekeepers tended to the expansive Wisner home on Fifth Avenue—his family had little in common with the Mississippi "aristocracy," those wealthy landowning families who traced their roots back to pre–Civil War days and who remained steeped in nostalgic notions of the Old South. Instead, from a very early age, Frank Wisner had his sights set beyond Mississippi. After graduating from the local high school at sixteen, he was dispatched to one of the South's better preparatory boarding schools, Woodberry Forest in Virginia, then sent on the obligatory grand tour of Europe prior to going to college. For his part, Frank Wisner never truly regarded himself as a Southerner except, his middle son, Ellis, recalled, on those occasions when outsiders denigrated the region. "That's when he got his back up," Ellis Wisner recalled. "If people made fun of it, that's when he became a Southerner."

This was a distinction lost on most of his future CIA associates. To them, Frank Wisner seemed the very epitome of the Southern gentleman—his colleagues invariably remarked upon his politeness and good manners, his soft rounded drawl—and, as a result, often ascribed stereotypes to him which didn't really apply.

Perhaps the most inapt was the stereotype of Southerners being laid-back, even a bit slow. Much to the contrary, by his adolescence, Wisner seemed propelled by a kind of edgy anxiety, the need to prove something to himself and to others. Along with being quite small for his age, he suffered a series of childhood illnesses that left him bedridden for weeks or even months at a time. This was undoubtedly an enormous worry to his parents—they had lost two children in infancy prior to Frank, and would lose another afterward—and might easily have resulted in a cosseted youth. Instead, these frailties appeared to spur a fierce self-discipline. On his college track team at the University of Virginia, Wisner was such a standout sprinter and broad jumper that he was invited to try out for the American Olympic team. "And that's where you see the conservativeness of the family come in," said Graham Wisner, the youngest of Wisner's three sons. "My dad was, I don't know, maybe the second or third fastest runner in the country, but his father said no. 'A gentleman does not do athletics when he should be going to law school and starting a career. A gentleman is serious.'"

Wisner obeyed his father's dictate, and instead turned his fire-at-the-heels sensibility to academics. After receiving his undergraduate degree at Virginia, he went on to its law school, one of the most demanding and select in the nation. There, he sat on the Law Review, finished third in his graduating class, and was inducted into UVa's most exclusive secret club, the Seven Society. To the surprise of no one, within weeks of his graduation in 1934, the newly minted attorney was hired on by a prestigious Wall Street law firm, Carter Ledyard.

At that juncture, it seemed Frank Wisner was determined to check off all the requisite boxes that marked the rites of passage of the successful, if utterly conventional, American man—albeit to do so a bit faster than most. Two years after he joined Carter Ledyard, he married his girlfriend, Mary "Polly" Ellis Knowles. Moving into a spacious apartment on Manhattan's East 57th Street, the couple soon had the first of what would ultimately be four children. By 1938, the twenty-nine-year-old corporate lawyer—most of his work was for the American Express Company—was already highly regarded in the tightknit Wall Street legal community, and well on his way to becoming a Carter Ledyard partner.

"He came up with very defined parameters of his own behavior," Graham Wisner explained. "This is what men of his class, of his time, did, what was expected of them."

And yet, for all his life's ease and privilege, it somehow didn't satisfy. Always keenly interested in politics and world affairs, Wisner closely monitored the march to war in Europe and, after the fall of France to the German war machine in 1940, became convinced the United States would eventually intervene. But "eventually" wasn't a word that sat well with the hard-driving lawyer; in early 1941, he told his startled Carter Ledyard colleagues of his plan to take a leave of absence from the firm and join the Navy. No doubt those colleagues tried to talk him out of the idea—after all, Wisner had a wife and now two young children to support—but instead, and under the weight of his considerable persuasive skills, ended up writing Wisner glowing letters of recommendation.

By that spring, the lawyer from Mississippi had received his naval commission—lieutenant, junior grade—and was assigned to the New York branch of the Office of Naval Intelligence, or ONI. He was there when Pearl Harbor was attacked that December.

But if Wisner had been prescient in enlisting before the United States came into the war, he quickly discovered the downside of leading a life of advantage. Taking note of his academic and professional pedigree, his ONI superiors immediately shunted Wisner into a managerial role—and in 1941, just as today, "managerial" was usually shorthand for sitting behind a desk. Matters didn't improve when he was transferred to the naval cable and radio censorship office for the New York district. While that posting came with the benefit of allowing Wisner to continue to live with his family, it was also mind-numbingly dull. "He had a joke about it," his eldest son, Frank Wisner Jr., recalled, "that in the Navy, they gave him command of a cutter. A paper cutter, that is, chopping up documents."

After enduring the censorship office for nearly two years and seeing no end in sight, Wisner desperately looked to transfer to any military branch that might offer something more interesting. His lucky break came when an old Carter Ledyard colleague passed his name on to another former corporate lawyer who had joined in the war effort, William Donovan. As unpromising as that might sound, Donovan was no typical lawyer and neither was the wartime agency that he headed. Instead, the sixty-year-old attorney from Buffalo, New York, had earned his nickname, "Wild Bill," through heroism on the battlefields of World War I Europe, and he was now President Roosevelt's handpicked spymaster, the director of the Office of Strategic Services.

The adjectives used to describe William J. Donovan tend to run to hyperbole: brilliant, charismatic, fearless, larger-than-life. A former CIA officer based in postwar Berlin offered a different one: "Exhausting. He was a wonderful man, with an extraordinary mind, but he just never damn stopped." Donovan occasionally visited Berlin in the late 1940s and early 1950s, and sometimes stayed in the CIA officer's home. "He'd keep you up till one or two in the morning peppering you with questions, and then he'd be up at seven and he would start in all over again."

By the time Frank Wisner's résumé landed on his desk in October 1943, Wild Bill Donovan had been a prominent figure on the American political landscape for the previous quarter-century. A very successful Ivy League–educated lawyer, he had first garnered notice in the early days of World War I when he vigorously lobbied for the United States to join the military alliance of Great Britain, France and Russia; what made this noteworthy was that, as an Irish Catholic Republican, Donovan was from an ethnic group that overwhelmingly favored neutrality in the conflict.

And the Buffalo attorney was no armchair hawk. As was still common among a certain type of wealthy men of the day, Donovan had helped sponsor the formation and upkeep of a troop of National Guard cavalry in his hometown, and maneuvered to have himself appointed its commander. When, in 1916, President Woodrow Wilson sent General "Black Jack" Pershing and the U.S. Army into northern Mexico in pursuit of the renegade revolutionary leader Pancho Villa, Donovan was thrilled when his troop was ordered to join the fray. Leaving his Buffalo law practice in the hands of associates, the thirty-three-year-old Donovan spent six happy, if fruitless, months galloping about the Mexico borderlands in search of Villa.

It was when President Wilson finally did take the nation into World War I, however, that Donovan found his moment of glory. As a battalion commander on the Western Front, he rallied his faltering troops in one battle by refusing to leave the field despite being badly wounded. Time and again, he braved murderous fusillades to personally lead frontal assaults against the entrenched enemy, contending that in no-man's-land his men required "some visible symbol of authority." On the strength of such heroics, Wild Bill Donovan was awarded both the Medal of Honor and the Distinguished Service Cross; even today, he remains one of the most highly decorated soldiers in American history.

After the war, Donovan became a power broker in New York legal circles and Republican Party politics. While maintaining his law practice in Buffalo, he was named the U.S. attorney for western New York in the early 1920s, then went on to hold senior positions in President Calvin

Coolidge's Department of Justice. In 1932, he ran for governor of New York, but it was a case of exquisitely poor timing; as with Republican candidates across the country, he was swept away in that year's Democratic landslide, a seismic political shift that also carried Franklin D. Roosevelt into the White House. After that defeat, Donovan rather receded from public view only to be rediscovered by Hollywood. In 1940, Warner Bros. had rolled out a patriotic James Cagney vehicle, *The Fighting 69th,* that glorified the exploits of Donovan's World War I regiment, with the role of Donovan played by matinee idol George Brent.

But what the general American public didn't know about Wild Bill's intervening years of obscurity was the curious, behind-the-scenes mission he had created for himself.

Since shortly after losing his 1932 governor's race, Donovan had thrown the better part of his energies into a series of extended visits to far-flung corners of the earth. Ostensibly these trips were to look after the varied interests of his law firm's clients, but they more closely resembled one-man intelligence operations, with the lawyer conducting lengthy interviews with resident journalists, industrialists and even heads of state. Donovan's successful 1935 meeting with the Italian prime minister, Benito Mussolini, led to his being given a VIP tour of the Italian battlefront in Abyssinia at a time when American military intelligence officers had barely an inkling of what was happening there. Of particular note were Donovan's visits to Germany, where Adolf Hitler had become chancellor in 1933. With his firsthand look at the new Nazi regime backed by incisive analysis, Donovan's accounts of these trips circulated to an ever-expanding mailing list of prominent Americans. By the late 1930s, these included President Roosevelt.

Just a year apart in age, Roosevelt and Donovan had overlapped at Columbia Law, and had frequently crossed paths in subsequent years due to their involvement in New York state politics; indeed, when Donovan ran for New York governor in 1932, he was vying to be Roosevelt's successor. Though the two remained political rivals—well into the 1930s, Donovan continued to rail against Roosevelt's New Deal policies—the president clearly respected Donovan's views on a wide range of foreign issues. He also saw an advantage to having a prominent and internationalist-minded Republican as an ally against the isolationist tendencies of that party. As the global situation steadily deteriorated in the late 1930s, as Hitler tightened his hold on Germany and the Japanese sought to expand their empire in eastern Asia, Donovan became an ever more trusted member of Roosevelt's "kitchen cabinet" of unofficial advisors.

This role took on vital importance in the summer of 1940, when Roosevelt sent Donovan on a fact-finding mission to Britain. The previous September, Poland had been jointly dismembered by Nazi Germany and the Soviet Union—allies under the Molotov-Ribbentrop Pact—leading Great Britain and France to declare war on Germany, and to the outbreak of World War II. The Anglo-French alliance only lasted until June 1940, when a massive German blitzkrieg brought France to its knees within a matter of weeks, leaving Britain to face the Nazi juggernaut essentially alone. That seemed a highly doubtful proposition, considering that the British Army had left a staggering percentage of its war matériel on the beaches of Dunkirk during its retreat from France. Certainly the American ambassador to Great Britain, Joseph P. Kennedy, felt the matter was decided. Having already scandalized London society with his anti-Semitic remarks, Kennedy further outraged his hosts by suggesting the British war effort was a lost cause and that Roosevelt should seek an accommodation with Hitler. Instead, the president sent Donovan to London.

Donovan's brief that July was to first determine if Britain had any hope of surviving the German onslaught and, if so, what war matériel a still neutral United States might provide it. Not surprisingly, desperate British leaders did everything possible to accommodate Roosevelt's emissary, ensuring that Donovan had access to whichever military or political officials he wished to meet, including the king and Prime Minister Winston Churchill. The charm offensive worked. Following Donovan's report to the president upon returning to Washington, armament transfers to Britain were steadily accelerated.

That trip was soon followed by a far lengthier expedition. Beginning that December and continuing into March 1941, Donovan embarked on an extraordinary tour of some of Britain's most sensitive military installations, both on the home front and in her outposts of empire in the eastern Mediterranean, followed by an extended jaunt through the Balkans and Middle East. Under Churchill's instructions, he was also given completely unfettered access to the records and methodology of Britain's domestic and foreign military intelligence services, MI5 and MI6, respectively. Donovan came back from that trip convinced of at least two things: first, it was only a matter of time before the United States was drawn into the war and, second, it better have a sophisticated intelligence apparatus in place beforehand so as to avoid the kind of surprise assaults that had felled Poland and France. With the avid support of his new-found British friends, Donovan urged on the president the creation of a new federal intelligence office.

Roosevelt wasn't so convinced. As incredible as it might seem given the national security state that exists today, in the spring of 1941, the United States still hadn't a permanent agency dedicated to the gathering of foreign intelligence. Instead, in times of war this was handled by the military's intelligence wings—the Army's G-2 and the Navy's Office of Naval Intelligence—and in times of peace primarily by the State Department.

This arrangement, so in contrast to the elaborate espionage apparatus of most European nations, could partly be explained by the United States' enviable geography, the historical lack of any potential adversaries on its frontiers who needed watching. But it also reflected a provincialism shocking in so powerful a nation. Until well into the twentieth century, what passed for American intelligence collection in even important foreign nations often consisted of whatever gossip American diplomats posted abroad chose to include in their dispatches; from less consequential regions, years might go by in which virtually nothing was added to the country files maintained by the State Department. Even international conflagrations barely stirred this national complacency. As an example, it was several months into World War I before the State Department saw fit to hire its first field intelligence officer to report from the Middle Eastern war theater, and not until well after the United States had entered that war before it thought to add a second.

Interestingly, American leaders often touted such ignorance as a virtue, and expressed their disdain for espionage in high-minded, moralistic terms; as Secretary of State Henry Stimson famously said in 1929 when ordering his department's code-breaking unit shut down, "gentlemen don't read each other's mail." By the late 1930s, tales of the murderous depredations of the Soviet Union's NKVD and Nazi Germany's Gestapo had the effect of further poisoning the American public to the notion of government spy outfits.

What's more, Roosevelt, ever the negotiator, surely knew that Donovan's proposal for an independent agency would encounter ferocious resistance within the government. The United States already had an embryonic domestic intelligence office in the Justice Department, the Federal Bureau of Investigation, and when it came to foreign and military intelligence, the State Department and G-2 and ONI would surely contest any rivals on their turf. Instead, the president chose to take a half-step; in July 1941, he announced the creation of a new federal position, the Coordinator of Information (COI), to be filled by William Donovan.

While that job title could hardly have been less inspiring, the stated purpose of the new office was little more so. As spelled out in its charter, the COI was to act as a kind of informational clearinghouse for the president and his senior executive officers, a central repository of intelligence generated by other federal agencies with an eye to avoiding duplication or redundancy. If this mandate was kept to its narrowest interpretation—and that was certainly the goal of COI's bureaucratic competitors—it made Wild Bill Donovan little more than a glorified librarian. But then came Pearl Harbor.

Beyond propelling the United States into World War II, the Japanese surprise attack on Pearl Harbor came as a shocking blow to the Roosevelt administration's image of preparedness, and to the collective American notion of the country's invulnerability. It also provided Roosevelt with the pretext to radically strengthen the government's intelligence-gathering capability. In June 1942, the Coordinator of Information office was subsumed by the Office of Strategic Services, an agency answering directly to the president and the Joint Chiefs of Staff, with William Donovan appointed its first director.

Given his intimate exposure to Britain's intelligence network, it was rather to be expected that Donovan would choose its foreign spy branch, MI6, as the model for the OSS. It went far beyond simple emulation, however. Building off their already close ties, senior British intelligence officials quietly worked hand-in-glove with Donovan and his closest aides in not only laying out the organizational structure of the new American spy unit, but even in designing its application forms and training regimens.

Beyond the organizational similarities, Donovan also sought to replicate the "league of gentlemen" collegiality of MI6, to inhabit the OSS with men of breeding and manners and high education. This gave rise to several derisive takes on the OSS acronym—"Oh So Social" was especially popular—while columnist Drew Pearson ridiculed the new spy agency as a preserve of Wall Street bankers. Contending that "it was easier to train an honest citizen to engage in shady activities than to teach honesty to a man of dubious background," Donovan countered: "You know, these bankers and corporation lawyers make wonderful second-story men [burglars]." Whatever the merits of that reasoning, four directors of the future Central Intelligence Agency, as well as many of the CIA's senior administrators, would get their intelligence start with the OSS. At the end of 1943, that included the standout young lawyer with the Mississippi upper-class background, Frank Wisner. That December, and only two months released from the purgatory of the Navy's cable and radio censorship office, the thirty-four-year-old lieutenant was dispatched to OSS regional headquarters in Cairo to take up his duties as head of the Intelligence Reports office.

But while the exotic climes of Cairo were obviously far more stimulating than a cubicle in a Manhattan office building, Wisner still felt at a remove from the action; after all, it had been over a year since Erwin Rommel's army was thrown back from the Egyptian frontier at El Alamein, and the war had only grown more distant from the country since. And even though the Cairo position was a fascinating and important one—the chief of the Reports Section was tasked with synthesizing the flood of intelligence communiqués coming in from the Middle Eastern and southeastern Europe war theaters and passing it on to Washington in usable form—it still meant Wisner was essentially deskbound as the United States entered its third year in the war. Into the first five months of 1944, he dutifully saw to his job of managing the reports coming in from the field, while strategizing on how he might get to that field himself.

In early June, it appeared Wisner's luck was about to turn when he was selected to join a small intelligence unit being dispatched to Syria. Those plans changed at the last minute, however, as the full scope of the disaster that was Operation Dogwood began to unfold in Istanbul, and OSS supervisors scrambled to find a repairman. Instead of to a strategic backwater like Syria, Frank Wisner was about to be thrust into one of the world's most fabled spy dens.

———

As President John Kennedy would famously remark of the CIA, it is in the nature of an intelligence agency that its "successes are unheralded and its failures trumpeted." This was most emphatically true about William Donovan and his Office of Strategic Services, which left a history of some remarkable triumphs—often only revealed decades later—punctuated by colossal blunders.

Some of these fiascoes simply came with the territory, the price of launching a start-up spy office amid a global conflict with little in the way of precedent to work from. Part of it, too, could be attributed to the total-war nature of that conflict. Put bluntly, at a time when hundreds of thousands were dying every month, and when units of soldiers might be sent onto beachheads in anticipation of 60 or 70 percent casualty rates, not a great deal of consideration was given to whether a particular espionage mission might fail, or what that could mean to the life expectancy of a handful of intelligence officers and their field agents.

But another reason for the haphazard quality of many OSS operations stemmed from the rivalry the upstart outfit engendered from other branches of the American military and intelligence community, and the bizarre set of restrictions it operated under as a result. Within the Army bureaucracy, so fierce was the antipathy of many field commanders, loath to subordinate their own G-2 intelligence units to an outside agency, that the Roosevelt White House simply left it up to individual senior commanders to decide whether or not to avail themselves of the OSS's services. To be expected, many chose the "not" option. In the European war theater, this created an absurd jumble where the OSS often worked extensively with one Army group on the battlefield, while having virtually no relationship with the Army group that was immediately adjacent.

This situation was replicated in the Asian theater, where the greatest opposition to OSS involvement came from General Douglas MacArthur, the supreme commander of Allied forces in the southwest Pacific. Given MacArthur's recent track record, his stance was more than a little ironic. In December 1941, he had been commander of U.S. forces in the Philippines when, just minutes after the Japanese attack on Pearl Harbor began, his headquarters was warned that a similar attack on his forces might be imminent. Inexplicably, MacArthur ignored the warning, leaving his air squadrons, still neatly parked on their airfields, to be destroyed when the Japanese attacked the Philippines nine hours later. Without air support, MacArthur's outnumbered forces had little chance when the Japanese launched their massive ground assault shortly after, ultimately leading to the greatest surrender of military forces in American history. Despite this ignominious start, and despite being on friendly terms with William Donovan—the two had served together in World War I—in 1942, MacArthur expressly barred the OSS from operating in territory under his Pacific command.

Joined to these strictures were those imposed by America's allies, Great Britain and the Soviet Union. Despite their mentoring role with the OSS, MI6 officers in the field often saw little reason to cooperate with, let alone defer to, the American arrivistes. Given Franklin Roosevelt's frequent disparaging pronouncements on European colonialism, this was especially true in nations or regions of the world that the British saw as falling within their imperial orbit, and where the Americans might promulgate a very different postwar political agenda. In the case of the Soviet Union, Stalin's deep suspicions of his Western allies made collaboration all but impossible, and an early Donovan bid to establish integrated intelligence teams went nowhere.

But Donovan was to face his most implacable—and as time would show, most durable—opponent from completely outside any military command structure. This was J. Edgar Hoover, the director of the Justice Department's still embryonic Bureau of Investigation. The two men had history going back to 1924, when Donovan had served as the assistant attorney general in the Coolidge administration, and Hoover was technically his underling. They had taken an instant dislike to each other then, and the intervening years had done nothing to soften either man's views.

With the creation of the OSS, however, the preexisting personality conflict was augmented by a bitter professional rivalry. Ferociously ambitious in his own stealthy way, Hoover had long harbored dreams of transforming his bureau at the Justice Department into a law enforcement and intelligence monolith with a global reach. By the late 1930s, he had achieved the first step by posting FBI agents at American embassies throughout Latin America. Not surprisingly, the FBI director saw Donovan's OSS as a clear and present danger to the fiefdom he was building, and lost no opportunity to try to poison President Roosevelt against his new spymaster. To keep the peace between the two men, Roosevelt came up with another bizarre compromise: while the OSS could operate in all other war theaters, subject to the approval of the various military theater commanders, the FBI would retain its intelligence-gathering role in Latin America, with OSS officers only allowed to operate there on Hoover's express permission. Similarly, while the OSS could maintain offices in the United States, any domestic intelligence operations were to be conducted by the FBI. Naturally, when this "solution" was announced it was accompanied by a great deal of talk about how the two agencies would work in close tandem but, given the animosity between their two directors, it's hard to imagine anyone believed it. Sure enough, wartime relations between the FBI and OSS were tortured at the best of times.

Another man might have felt chastened by all these restrictions, but not Wild Bill Donovan; indeed, his ability to improvise and to maneuver around bureaucratic obstacles might have been one of the chief reasons Roosevelt chose him for the intelligence post in the first place. Both by temperament and by the ever-expanding responsibilities of his office, Roosevelt had a strong preference for subordinates who displayed personal initiative, who would operate with minimal direction or oversight, and who would not bother him with the niggling details. William Donovan certainly fit that bill. In the months after the creation of the OSS, Donovan had set out to insert himself and his organization most anywhere he could, and in whatever capacity.

As a result, the OSS quickly took on a bewildering hodgepodge of functions around the globe, everything from traditional intelligence gathering in Central Europe, to the training of tribal insurgents in Thailand; from conducting commando raids in Italy, to beaming propaganda broadcasts into occupied Norway. At the same time, and despite Donovan's notions of creating a kind of gentlemen's club preserve, the myriad functions of the OSS predicated recruitment across an extraordinary array of backgrounds and personalities, everyone from elderly and deskbound academics (the research and analysis branch of Secret Intelligence), to Madison Avenue admen and Hollywood movie producers (Morale Operations), to the sort of hard-edged fighters (Special Operations) who might normally have found their way into a group like the French Foreign Legion. In the process, what was also created was an organization quite egalitarian for its time, where one's skills or aptitudes counted for far more than one's educational background, religious affiliation or even political sympathies.

At the same time, this throw-it-against-the-wall-and-see-what-sticks approach was bound to lead to some grand missteps, and few were grander than Packy Macfarland's Operation Dogwood.

Encouraged by Churchill, Donovan had first begun to focus on southeastern Europe as Nazi Germany's potential weak spot as early as the summer of 1940. At that time, most of the Balkan nations were still neutral, and the British had a military base of operations in Greece. That had been 1940, however. Three years later, the Germans had long since ousted the British from Greece, and the rest of the Eastern European nations were either occupied by German forces or ruled by Nazi puppet regimes.

For Donovan, however, this only made the Balkans interesting in a new way. Given the intricate tapestry of political rivalries that existed between the various Balkan states, as well as the array of homegrown partisan groups already waging guerrilla war against the Axis forces of Germany and Italy, the region was the perfect milieu for the spies, plotters and saboteurs who comprised the OSS. What's more, in the Balkans, Donovan didn't have to worry about bureaucratic turf wars: no American armies were anywhere nearby while, with the exception of Greece, the British could hardly claim any sort of imperial prerogative in the region. The OSS had begun operations there in early 1943 and, quite logically, established their regional headquarters in neutral Istanbul.

To head that office, Donovan had turned to Lanning Macfarland, a Harvard graduate from a prominent Chicago family who had risen swiftly through the ranks of the Northern Trust investment firm. How this qualified him for intelligence work was not altogether clear, except that Macfarland had proven his pluck as a World War I volunteer ambulance driver on the Serbian front, and kept in touch with many of his old comrades there.

In fact, Packy Macfarland seemed to display a most remarkable aptitude for espionage work. Soon after his arrival in Istanbul, he linked up with a Czech émigré engineer named Alfred Schwarz who had been living in Turkey for fifteen years and who, through his varied com-

mercial interests, enjoyed close ties to anti-Nazi officials and businessmen throughout the Balkans. With Macfarland's enthusiastic approval,
Schwarz, operating under the code name Dogwood, set out to create an
elaborate, multinational intelligence network for the OSS. In very short
order, Operation Dogwood grew to encompass at least sixty-seven agents
operating within a half-dozen spy cells—or "chains"—stretching across
the breadth of southeastern Europe.

Those agents stayed very busy, turning in a torrent of reports on everything from German troop movements and Ruthenia crop yields, to the
inner workings of Balkan palace intrigues. Most impressive of all, the
tentacles of the Dogwood chains extended into some of the most sensitive and far-distant offices of the Nazi war machine. Before long, the
information flowing into OSS Istanbul—and then on to Frank Wisner's
records branch in OSS Cairo—included precise locations for some of
Nazi Germany's most vital military installations. With that intelligence,
Allied bombers were able to target concealed ammunition depots and
communications centers, factories churning out everything from Mes-
serschmitts to ball bearings.

But there had always been some troubling aspects to the spying missions being run out of OSS Istanbul. By early 1944, amid the expanding flood of reports being generated by the Dogwood chains, some in
the OSS Cairo office began pushing Macfarland for details on Schwarz's
operatives, the steps he and his subordinates were taking to track their
veracity. Those requests grew in urgency after British intelligence officers warned OSS Cairo about bogus intelligence reports that were the
handiwork of known Abwehr agents, but which were virtually identical
to Dogwood reports. Macfarland and his associates continued to resist
explaining their methods, until there was revealed an astonishing fact:
not only had OSS Istanbul not vetted the Dogwood operatives, in most
cases they'd never even met them. Instead, by the terms of the original
deal made with Schwarz, only the Czech engineer was to have direct contact with his agents.

Through a hasty joint investigation by OSS and MI6, it was determined
that as many as eight of Schwarz's agents—and possibly even more—were
doubling for the Nazis. When Macfarland continued to balk, the MI6
commander in Istanbul ordered his men to end all contact with their
American counterparts, lest their operations be compromised, too.

But the postmortem on Dogwood suggested far worse. Through 1944,
the OSS had put out a series of peace feelers to anti-Hitler German officials, as well as to several Eastern European governments looking to
escape their alliance with the Third Reich. Each time, these missions were

sabotaged, and the common threads to most of them were Dogwood and Istanbul. Guided by information from Schwarz's chains, Allied bombers had repeatedly bombed factories or military installations in German-occupied Europe where subsequent aerial photography suggested little of value had been hit. At the same time, bomber squadrons had frequently been sent against "soft targets," only to find themselves flying into killing zones of marauding enemy fighters and antiaircraft gun emplacements. While certainly not all the aerial losses in the southeastern Europe war theater could be attributed to enemy disinformation, the clear inference was that, while Operation Dogwood had never been an OSS triumph, it might very well have been an Abwehr one.

For Macfarland's superiors, it was finally all too much. In early June 1944, the regional head of OSS, Colonel John Toulmin, chose Frank Wisner to try to save what he could of the Istanbul mission. It was at the start of that assignment that Wisner met up with Macfarland at the Park Hotel nightclub.

For weeks, Wisner worked nearly around the clock to try to reorganize the OSS Istanbul office, and to salvage the Dogwood intelligence network. He soon concluded that almost all of it was compromised, that he would now have to start over practically from scratch. This was a task that would elude him, however. Instead, just thirteen days after becoming head of OSS Istanbul, an event was to occur that would cast Frank Wisner into the very vortex of the war. It began on an otherwise quiet evening in late August 1944, with a radio broadcast by a twenty-two-year-old king.

2

A DEMON INSIDE ME

t was but a small memory lapse, a quite understandable one under the circumstances, but of the precise sort that has gotten soldiers killed since time immemorial: as Michael Burke crouched in the darkness of the French farm field, he simply could not remember the mission passphrase. That was a problem, because from what he could make out in the half-moon light, the three men steadily advancing in his direction were all carrying guns. When they drew close enough for Burke to determine they were whispering to each other in French, not German, he relaxed slightly and let out a soft call: "Alors, mes amies," or, "Hello, my friends."

This failed to produce the desired effect. Instead, the three men immediately dropped from sight, and Burke heard the metallic clack of a Sten submachine gun being readied to fire.

It was the predawn of September 9, 1944, and just minutes earlier Burke had been one of five Allied soldiers airdropped into this remote corner of northeastern France. Their orders were to make contact with a unit of rural French Resistance fighters, or *maquis,* fighting the occupying Germans in the vicinity of the village of Confracourt. Dropped into the landing zone with them were eleven metal canisters containing weapons, ammunition and a half-million francs' worth of gold coins.

Still unable to remember the passphrase, Burke next decided to go with the simple explanatory, reasoning that the three prowling men had almost certainly been brought out by the sound of the low-flying B-24 that delivered him. "I've just arrived," he called again in French. "From the plane."

This didn't impress his stalkers either—but then at last Burke remembered the code. "Le renard a corrou," he shouted, the fox has run. "Le renard a corrou!"

At this, the three gunmen rose up out of the blackness and, maquis after all, came forward to welcome Burke with hearty handshakes and backslaps. But as it turned out, the partisans of Confracourt were only expecting an airdrop of supplies that night, and knew nothing about plans for an Allied liaison team to join them. As a result, they had been completely baffled by Burke's presence—to say nothing of all his talk about running foxes. That glitch aside, Michael Burke was now where he so keenly wanted to be: in occupied Europe, behind enemy lines.

It had taken a great deal of effort on his part to get there.

At the start of his military service in Europe in 1943, Burke had been attached to the Special Operations branch of the OSS, a designation that had enabled him to take part in a series of commando missions in North Africa and Italy. In early 1944, however, and for reasons never explained, he had been transferred to the more back-base wing of the OSS, Secret Intelligence. He was also sent off to a rambling old mansion in southern England, Drungewick Manor, to undergo something called French Agent Training. While puzzled by the switch, Burke had initially managed to pass the time pleasantly enough. "We kept fit on the obstacle course," he wrote, "improved our language facility—all instruction and social conversation was in French—and at night we drank convivially at the Crown Inn in Chiddingfold."

It was at Drungewick in the spring of 1944 that Burke learned of a new OSS initiative being planned for the upcoming invasion of mainland Europe.

In the immediate aftermath of the D-Day landings, a select group of OSS officers was to be teamed up with British and Free French commandos, and parachuted into occupied France. Called the Jedburghs—the name's derivation remains a mystery—these three-man units would link up with French Resistance fighters to carry out sabotage and hit-and-run attacks behind the German front lines. The tricky part was that these teams—each would consist of two Americans or Britons, and one Frenchman—would have no easy way off the battlefield, but were to remain in place until the advancing Allied army reached their operating zone. If this didn't sound dicey enough, Adolf Hitler had made it more so. Stung by the success of partisan and guerrilla units operating throughout

German-occupied Europe, the Nazi leader had decreed that, even if in uniform, "irregular" commandos were not to be treated as prisoners of war, but instead summarily executed. OSS commandos operating with French Resistance units would certainly fit Hitler's criteria.

All of which made Jedburgh exactly the sort of scheme Burke wanted in on. The problem, he soon discovered, was that those OSS men being selected for the Jedburgh missions were drawn exclusively from his old branch, Special Operations, with none at all coming from his new one, Secret Intelligence. Testament to the grinding bureaucratic inertia of the modern army, there seemed absolutely no way for him to finagle an exception to this policy, or to countermand his transfer.

As the months at Drungewick slipped past, and then as D-Day came and went, Burke finally reached his breaking point. Writing to the chief of Secret Intelligence in OSS London, he pleaded to be released from the French Agent course and to become the first SI officer dropped into enemy-held France. Impressed, the colonel in charge finally granted Burke's wish.

The mission ultimately chosen for Burke in late August 1944 was a suitably perilous one. By then, with Paris liberated and the German army retreating slowly eastward, a formation of several hundred rural partisans, or maquis, had established a forest redoubt outside Confracourt in the eastern province of Haute-Saône. That redoubt was also right alongside one of the principal routes the withdrawing enemy was taking to reach Germany, and the maquis were now preparing to deny escape to as many as possible in pitched battle. To assist them, ten Allied commandos were dispatched to the Haute-Saône, clambering aboard two B-24 Liberators at an airfield in southern England on the night of September 8. Accompanying Burke on his plane were two French and two American army officers.

But the snafus attendant to the Marcel Mission went beyond merely failing to inform the maquis of the commandos' arrival. While Burke and his four comrades all made it safely to the rendezvous site, the second B-24 simply disappeared in the night. That left Burke and his colleagues as the sole Allied liaison officers in the Confracourt sector but, as it turned out, with no one in the outside world to liaise with. That's because the radio crystals the team needed for radio communication with OSS London were either lost somewhere in the French countryside, or had been aboard the errant B-24. It meant that for however long it took for the regular Allied army to reach Haute-Saône—a development that might not occur for weeks or months or, at least theoretically, ever— Burke and his comrades were on their own.

Burke soon gained a keen appreciation of this. On September 13, just four days after his arrival, the German forces based around Confracourt, tiring of the maquis' small-scale harassment attacks, launched an all-out assault on their foes in the forest. With Mark IV tanks in the vanguard, several thousand German troops converged on the outgunned and vastly outnumbered partisans from different directions. Although the advance stalled after a bitter battle, it was renewed the next day, and then the one after that.

By the evening of September 15, the situation in the encircled forest encampment was exceedingly grim. The Germans had gained the treeline, and were sure to start spreading through the forest under the cover of nightfall, and while some of the French partisans might be able to slip out of the noose and return to "civilian" life in classic guerrilla fashion, that was hardly possible for the uniformed commando team recently arrived from England. In light of this, the maquis commander gave the order for his men to stand and fight as best they could. Most recognized this as a death sentence. Nevertheless, Burke was to recall, all remained "cool and resigned. No one funked. Whatever their private thoughts, outwardly they were controlled and committed. Perhaps each expected his underground existence might one day lead to a place from which there was no exit, and each man dealt with it in his own way."

Except the Germans didn't attack that night. Instead, they pulled back into Confracourt, and early the next morning a courier under a white flag walked into the forest to deliver a message from the German commander. During the night, he had taken forty-six male villagers hostage and locked them in the Confracourt municipal hall; if even one more shot was fired from the forest, all the hostages would be killed.

Rather than be cowed by this ultimatum, the maquis commander sensed panic in his German counterpart. He decided on a counteroffer that, given his force's paltry size, amounted to a monumental bluff: if the Germans released their hostages and surrendered, they would be accorded prisoner-of-war status—never a given when fighting the partisans—under the protocols of the Geneva Convention.

The crucial question was who might leave the relative safety of the forest and walk across no-man's-land to deliver this audacious message. Burke swiftly volunteered, as did one of his American companions, Army Lieutenant Walter Kuzmak. By Burke's reasoning, the Germans were far more likely to take such an offer seriously if delivered by Allied soldiers in uniform, rather than by maquis "terrorists"—except that also depended on the German commander choosing to defy Hitler's order to summarily shoot enemy commandos. Armed with nothing but a white cloth on a stick, the two junior American officers stepped out of the forest and began the long, slow walk toward the village and the waiting Germans.

"I forced myself to walk erect," Burke recalled, "not to cringe at the gnawing thought of being zapped by a sudden fusillade, but my body tightened with attention, irresistibly gathering itself in. Kuzmak and I may have talked to one another, but if we did, I don't remember what we said."

Not for the first time, and certainly not for the last, Michael Burke was putting to the test a core conviction upon which many of his decisions in life were predicated: that bad things happened to other people, that he was going to come through all this just fine. Of course, this belief in personal immunity is one that a great many soldiers take into battle—army recruiters of the world rather count on it—and it tends to hold up well right up until the day it's proven wrong.

———

Many people have exciting and varied lives—and then there was Edmund Michael Burke. Star athlete, black ops commando, Hollywood screenwriter, ladies' man, spy. Some of the other highlights of his diverse résumé: maritime insurance investigator, baseball team president, media executive, circus manager. On a personal level, friends with Ava Gardner, Muhammad Ali and Eleanor Roosevelt; drinking buddy of Ernest Hemingway, Gary Cooper and Mickey Mantle. During one particularly hectic stretch in his spying days, his social circle included a lively group of aspiring filmmakers and an even livelier group of aspiring paramilitary assassins, and such were the demands of his profession that he often had to entertain both in the same day. Charismatic, suave and possessed of black-Irish good looks, in essence Michael Burke was James Bond before James Bond existed.

Not that everyone knew him by that name. During this same period, he was known to many as Randolph R. Northwood, and he was a movie producer in Italy or a political advisor in Germany or a businessman dabbling in the import-export trade in Greece. Amid the ever-changing subterfuges, however, there were certain constants. One was Burke's taste for the good life. Another was his disdain for the shoulder holster. In his opinion, that accessory was best suited for beefy men wearing shapeless suits, whereas to conceal a gun on his own slender and well-tailored frame, he found "the pocket of a trenchcoat or the barrel tucked into the waistband of my trousers suited me better."

In looking back at the fantastically improbable turns of his life, at the journey that would take him from a rural Connecticut childhood to the darkest corners of the Cold War espionage world, and then on to the most rarefied reaches of New York high society, Burke would modestly attribute most of it to dumb luck, to simply being in the right place at the right time; in fact, he would title his autobiography, *Outrageous Good Fortune*. There was clearly more to it than that, though, because no one enjoys good luck so consistently as did Michael Burke, basks in fortune quite so outrageous.

A more textured explanation emerges in the recollections of those who actually knew him. With remarkable uniformity, former friends and associates choose the same first adjective when describing him: "charming." Indeed, to one former CIA colleague, Michael Burke was simply "the most charming man I have ever met." If that sounds a tad hyperbolic, consider the assessment of one of his debriefing officers in World War II. Tasked to conduct spot interviews with scores, sometimes hundreds, of soldiers in rapid succession, it's hard to imagine a more world-weary bunch than military debriefing officers, but the one assigned to Burke in December 1944 was sufficiently impressed to jot down a word rarely seen on a debrief form: "delightful." On the most basic level, it seems that to meet Michael Burke was to like him—and not just to like him, but to like him so well as to want to help him along in life.

But behind his endearing demeanor there dwelt something a bit harder: a kind of hunger, a need to excel and impress. That hunger first displayed itself on the sports field, but it then carried to the battlefield, to situations where Burke not only risked his own life but those of others. In later years, it manifested in a unique talent for social climbing.

"Whenever my father walked into a room," recalled his eldest child, Patricia Burke, "he would immediately size up who was the most important or most famous person there. Before long, he'd be talking with them, and by the end of the night they'd be friends. He collected people, and the more famous or powerful the better. It wasn't that he was a glad-hander, exactly, but he just always wanted to be around people who were doing things, big things." She pondered for a moment. "I think from very early on, my father was looking for a bigger life than he'd been handed, to go beyond anyone's expectations of him."

This yearning might seem somewhat at odds with the ease of Michael Burke's upper-middle-class childhood. Growing up in an Irish Catholic family in rural central Connecticut in the 1920s, he would recall a Norman Rockwell–tinted youth, an idyll in which two sets of doting grandparents lived nearby, and where for his ninth birthday he was given his first pony. He was close to his two younger siblings, but especially to his father, Patrick Burke, a Yale-educated lawyer for a Connecticut-based insurance company, who frequently took his inquisitive eldest son along on business trips to Boston or New York. A standout athlete from an early age—he was equally talented in baseball, basketball and football—the young Burke further honed his strength and stamina by laboring in his uncle's tobacco fields during the autumn harvest.

His physical prowess also led to the first pivot point in his life when, at the age of sixteen, he was awarded a football scholarship to the prestigious Kingswood Preparatory School in Hartford. That scholarship not only granted him a degree of independence most any teenager would envy—Burke lived away from his family, in a boardinghouse near campus—but lifted him from the insular Irish Catholic world of his youth and squarely into one of the toniest bastions of New England WASP society. He distinctly remembered the celebratory party that a classmate threw at his home when Burke was chosen captain of the Kingswood football team.

"The front lawn was a full-sized golf course," he wrote, "and the garage held eleven cars, eight of them Rolls Royces. A long narrow building alongside the kitchen gardens contained the bowling lanes."

But what Burke most recalled from that party was a feeling of ineptitude, of being out of his depth. The moment of mortification came when his aristocratic classmates—still just sixteen- and seventeen-year-olds, after all—toasted his new captaincy with champagne. "I didn't know whether to sit or stand, drink or not drink. I felt like a great bloody clod and sat fumbling in confusion and ignorance, flushed with embarrassment, saved only by the casualness with which my new friends sailed past what for me was a painful social milestone. I had so much to learn."

But Michael Burke was determined to learn it. During his time at Kingswood, he carefully watched and listened and practiced until few would ever suspect that he hadn't been born into its refined social milieu. So well did he fit in, both socially and academically, that the Kingswood scholarship was followed by one to the University of Pennsylvania.

It was shortly after arriving at that Ivy League school in the summer of 1935, however, that Burke experienced his first major comeuppance. As a matter of course, he tried out for the U Penn football team, but the coaches were so little impressed with the running back from Connecticut that Burke was relegated to the Freshman B squad, the equivalent of sixth- or seventh-string. For a young man who had always been defined by his athleticism, it was a deeply humiliating experience—and it got worse. Through Freshman B's first game, and well into the second, Burke sat on the bench. Finally, just before halftime of that second game, he was rotated in to take the place of an injured player. When the ball was punted to him, Burke's need for respect translated into a kind of wrath.

"Anger and frustration exploded, I suppose," he remembered. "Some demon inside me slashed and cut and sprinted sixty yards for a touchdown. When the second half began I was in the starting lineup, fielded another punt, ran seventy yards for another touchdown. My mind recorded no details of the runs, only the desperate, half-crazed will that nothing should stop me."

After that game, Michael Burke was moved from Freshman B to varsity first-string. For the next four years, he was a standout Ivy League halfback, and might well have made the all-American squad save for an injury that left him severely visually impaired in one eye. Even with that injury, the powerfully built but remarkably nimble Burke so impressed scouts that he was given a tryout with the Philadelphia Eagles of the fledgling National Football League.

Burke would later claim that he was put off from joining the pros after noting the punch-drunk behavior of his prospective teammates, as well as the paltry wages: in the late 1930s, the NFL's basic pay scale was around $125 per game. Perhaps a more likely explanation was that, by the time of his tryout with the Eagles, he also had a wife to consider. In his junior year at Penn, Burke had met a visiting New York model named Faith Long and been instantly smitten. "She was a lively, gregarious, extroverted girl and looked the way a New York model should look." The two soon became lovers and, following a pregnancy scare, secretly married during the Christmas break of Burke's senior year. A few months later, in June of 1939, they "came out" to their families in a formal wedding.

But if Burke's life thus far had been a string of good tidings—a prep school scholarship leading to an Ivy League scholarship leading to a New York model wife—his fortunes now dimmed. In the summer of 1939, the U.S. economy remained in the doldrums from the decade-old Great Depression, and with the war clouds building over Europe—they would burst open that September—few companies were in the market for new college graduates with degrees in finance. With no other immediate prospects, Burke accepted an entry-level job with his father's employer, the Insurance Company of North America.

As a newly minted maritime insurance investigator, the twenty-three-year-old Burke was dispatched to work the New York City waterfront. At first, he found the work fascinating—certainly his physical presence gained him a degree of instant respect in the tough world of longshoremen—but it gradually palled as what he envisioned to be a temporary state of affairs took on the trappings of permanency, his time in the docklands dragging out for two years. All that changed on the first Sunday in December 1941.

He had just learned that Faith was pregnant. The couple was still trying to process that news when there came the Japanese attack on Pearl Harbor.

Perhaps surprising, given the part he was to eventually play in that conflict, Burke's first thought upon America's entry into World War II was to stay at home, held by the idea that his "proper" role was to continue on as a civilian in order to support his wife and now imminent child. The notion proved fleeting, though.

"I knew I must go," he wrote. "This was my generation's war. Simplistically, subjectively, I could not abide the thought of other people—my own friends perhaps—fighting to defend my wife and child while I sat safely home." It was a line of reasoning that didn't go over well with his pregnant wife. "Faith, like wives from the beginning of the world, could not comprehend why I had to go, why of my own free will I would leave a wife and an infant in order to risk death."

Except the American military seemed in no hurry to have Michael Burke risk death. By virtue of his college degree, he was eligible for an officers training program, but in the chaos accompanying the first rush to war, all manner of military appointments and inductions were hopelessly backlogged. His damaged eye certainly didn't help matters. Although registering with the Selective Service System right after Pearl Harbor, Burke hadn't heard anything four months later. Finally he hopped on a train to Washington, D.C., with an ill-formed plan: he would simply make the rounds of the different military branch headquarters until he found someone to sign him into an officers program.

In a lifetime of serendipitous turns, none was to prove more momentous than that which occurred during Burke's visit to Washington in April 1942. For several days, he dutifully visited various armed service recruitment centers, only to be constantly shuffled to different offices or told to come back at another time. It was at the end of another fruitless day, as he gloomily trudged back to his hotel, that a passerby on the street recognized him. The man was a University of Pennsylvania alumnus and he remembered Burke from his football playing days. After talking for a few minutes, the man mentioned that he was throwing a small dinner party at his home that night and invited Burke to come along. With nothing better to do, Burke accepted.

At that gathering, Burke's attention was drawn to one of the guests, a stocky but handsome, white-haired man in his late fifties. It was hard not to be drawn to him for, without apparent intent on his part, the man exuded a magnetism that made him the party's center of attention: President Roosevelt's Coordinator of Information, William J. Donovan.

Along with his varied other attributes, Donovan possessed a kind of photographic memory when it came to topics of special interest to him. In his college years, he had played quarterback for the Columbia University football team and remained devoted to the game. After exchanging a few words with Burke, a glimmer of recognition rose in Donovan's eyes.

"Didn't you play halfback at University of Pennsylvania?" he asked.

When Burke replied that he had, Donovan asked what had brought him to Washington. After the younger man explained the difficulties he'd been having getting himself placed in an officers training program, Donovan offered a simple solution: "Why don't you come and join us?"

The Coordinator of Information office (COI) had been created only nine months earlier, with a vague mandate to serve as a central clearinghouse for intelligence being sent to the president, its employees more akin to file clerks than soldiers. Still, it was better than anything else Burke had on offer. Rushing back to New York, he temporarily moved his pregnant wife into her parents' home, then returned to the nation's capital. On May 15, 1942, he showed up for his first day of work at COI headquarters, an imposing stone building on the corner of E and 25th Streets in northwest Washington. As he waited for his background check to go through, he toiled as a junior clerk while trying to convince himself he'd made the right decision by hitching his star to that of Wild Bill Donovan.

He certainly had. The very next month, it was announced that the COI was being replaced by the Office of Strategic Services. With vastly expanded powers, Donovan's OSS was to be the primary wartime agency in charge of foreign intelligence and would be comprised of two main—and very different—components: Secret Intelligence, or SI, was tasked to the collection and analysis of all manner of foreign intelligence with a long-range focus, while Special Operations, or SO, was to primarily operate on the battlefield, carrying out sabotage behind enemy lines, organizing and assisting partisan units, whatever the situation demanded. For Michael Burke, there was never a question which branch he was most suited for.

In July 1942, Burke at last received his commission as an ensign in the U.S. Navy, seconded to the OSS. That same month, his first child, Patricia, was born. Fatherhood did little to alter his determination to get to the front. As he wrote the head of OSS personnel that fall, "Anxious to do field work, and will go anywhere."

Once again, though, the United States seemed in no hurry to put Burke in harm's way. For the next year, he and his wife and their infant daughter shared a small apartment in Alexandria, Virginia, from which an increasingly dejected Burke made the daily commute to OSS headquarters.

The mission that finally secured his escape from this prosaic existence was an extraordinarily sensitive one. By June 1943, with Allied forces about to go ashore in Sicily, there were tantalizing signs that the Italian government might overthrow Hitler's henchman, Benito Mussolini, and switch to the Allied side. In such a scenario, the Germans would naturally try to grab whatever Italian military assets they could get their hands on, and the one asset the Allies were most fearful of was Italy's still formidable navy. The goal of Operation MacGregor was to get a message to a high-ranking Italian admiral urging him, when the coup against Mussolini came, to either scuttle his fleet or, better yet, sail it into Allied-controlled waters. Flown out from Washington and put in charge of getting that message to the admiral was Michael Burke.

For weeks, Burke and his OSS colleagues used the cover of darkness to race PT boats up to two hundred miles inside enemy-held Italian waters in an attempt to place a courier ashore under the Germans' noses; each time, and for a variety of reasons, the efforts failed. When at last they did get the courier ashore, they abruptly lost all contact with him. They were still trying to reestablish communication when, on July 25, Mussolini was overthrown and the new Italian government sued for peace. Just as Allied strategists had predicted, the Germans snatched whatever war matériel they could across Italy, but most of the Italian fleet eluded them; on the morning of July 25, it sailed into the Allied-held harbor in Malta and surrendered.

That made Burke's original Operation MacGregor redundant, but it was soon replaced by another. This time, he and his colleagues were dispatched to spirit another Italian admiral, this one the inventor of an advanced torpedo, out of his homeland and away from the Gestapo's grasp. While that operation certainly had its adventurous elements—for several days, the admiral and his wife were hidden away in a villa in the Tunis casbah as Burke stood guard against possible Nazi and Vichy French assassins—it was, frankly, more along the lines of a baby-sitting mission than the high derring-do Ensign Burke was looking for. In its aftermath, he set his sights on what was sure to be the next big milestone of the war: the invasion of France. After just a very quick visit home to his wife and daughter, on Christmas Eve 1943 Burke flew to London, home to the main OSS headquarters in Europe, and began lobbying to be sent out into the field again. Instead, he was transferred into Secret Intelligence and shunted off to Drungewick Manor.

═══

Pancakes and bourbon. While making for an exotic breakfast most anywhere, it was exceedingly so in 1944 war-rationed London. Yet, someone had thought to bring over a package of pancake mix from the United States, Ernest Hemingway was a veritable bloodhound when it came to finding whiskey in even the driest of climes, and so it was that on the morning of June 18, 1944, Michael Burke and his best friend in the OSS, Henry North, left their small, shared apartment in London's West End and made for the Dorchester Hotel. Already gathered in Hemingway's penthouse suite—and well into the liquid portion of the breakfast, from the look of things—were several of the famous writer's other friends, as well as his third wife, the war correspondent Martha Gellhorn.

It had been a month since Burke and North, both briefly back in the United States from their OSS London postings, had boarded a plane together for the return transatlantic flight. In wartime, that journey meant taking a flying boat out of New York that put down on the Shannon River in neutral Ireland, where passengers transferred to a conventional airplane for the short hop to the English capital. Since the flying boat typically arrived in Shannon at dawn, transiting passengers traditionally made for the airport dining room in order to gorge on the hearty breakfast to be had in ration-less Ireland, but utterly unobtainable in war-rationed London. On Burke and North's flight, however, one particular passenger, Ernest Hemingway, was having none of it. In the disembarkation hall, the writer bellowed that he was headed to the bar for a gin-and-tonic and was looking for company. Burke and North quickly fell in with the plan. It marked the beginning of a friendship with Hemingway, on his way to London to report on the war, that over the next month was lubricated by long boozy sessions at the Dorchester Hotel bar. So inseparable did the three men become that the writer announced the formation of a secret society, Hemingstein's Junior Commandos, with himself, Burke and North as its charter members. The pancake-and-bourbon breakfast on June 18 marked their latest reunion.

It came at a time of both frustration and high anticipation for Burke. Having recently made good his escape from the French Agent Training course at Drungewick, he was now awaiting word on the mission that would take him into occupied France. That wait had become excruciating; on June 6, twelve days earlier, Allied forces had stormed ashore at Normandy, marking the beginning of the western offensive into Nazi-held Europe, and already the first of the Jedburgh teams were being dropped behind enemy lines. No matter who he called or pleaded with, however, Burke's name didn't come up on the roster.

But the D-Day landings had triggered another change in the war in the West: the V-1 buzz bomb. Built and deployed in secrecy by Nazi scientists, Hitler had unleashed his vaunted "secret weapon" against London on June 12, and within days hundreds of the remote-guided missiles had rained down on the English capital, killing hundreds and reviving memories of the Blitz of 1940. As Burke and the others gathered in Hemingway's Dorchester suite that Sunday morning, a new wave of V-1s came in.

"We drank bourbon and had a clear view of the buzz bombs flying up the Thames through the clean spring sky," Burke wrote, "could hear their engines, sounding like distant backfire of motorcycles, cut abruptly to silence, as the bombs nosed and dove to earth. Where they struck, stone and steel, timber and tile blasted high into the air, hung for an instant of slow motion at the top of their arc, then plunged to earth in mad disarray."

Ernest Hemingway was a man given to a kind of private nonsensical language among his friends and, as the flurry of buzz bombs threatened to overwhelm the mood of the breakfast party, he urged his companions to "get out their Ignorers." In Burke's memory, they did, "more or less. That is, we ate and drank and kept one ear cocked to be sure the buzz bombs kept their distance."

But then one of the missiles broke the pattern, the distinctive whirring sound of its engine over the city growing ever louder—and, of course, louder meant closer.

"It came on and on at a determined, unhurried, throbbing, exasperating pace. Everyone rushed to windows. This one seemed bent on joining us for breakfast. Its nose, loaded with explosive, loomed larger and blacker.

"'Sweet Jesus!' cried Hemingway. 'We'll have to get out our Bulldozer Ignorers for this one.'"

Instead, the V-1 passed directly before the Dorchester and had just cleared Green Park when its engine died and it began its rapid descent. It struck on the far side of St. James's Park, passing neatly through the roof of the Guards' Chapel and into the main apse where the Sunday morning church service was under way. At least 110 churchgoers were killed in the blast, two hundred more wounded.

"We raced across the park to help," Burke wrote, "but the police and firemen, four years' experience in their kit, needed no amateur assistance."

It was a reminder, as if London needed one, that death in this war might come at any time. Just weeks later, Burke was told to prepare for his mission into France.

═══

No volley of German gunfire greeted Burke and Lieutenant Kuzmak as they neared Confracourt. In fact, there were no Germans there at all. Just as the two American officers reached the outskirts, they saw the last of the German troops boarding vehicles at the far end of the village and speeding away. Incredibly, the Germans had chosen that very moment to begin their retreat toward home. They had also spared the lives of their forty-six hostages, enabling them to join in that day's celebration of freedom. "[They] bore the look of men delivered by some godly stroke, pledging privately never to sin again," Burke wrote. "Presently, sung in a loud clear baritone, the 'Marseillaise' soared high and strong above the sounds of celebration. . . . A seven-year-old girl dressed in a pale blue school smock was in my arms. I sang along with her, and, deeply moved, wept too."

Days later, the vanguard of the U.S. Seventh Army reached Confracourt. Officially, that meant the end of Marcel Mission, and Burke and his two American companions were now to report back to London. Instead, they made an unusual decision. Rather than notify OSS London of their whereabouts—without radio contact, the lost team in Haute-Saône had been written off as dead or captured—the three officers, as well as a contingent of Confracourt maquis, simply "enlisted" with the Seventh Army's advance reconnaissance unit. For the next six weeks, Burke and the other Confracourt veterans carried out a series of ever-more perilous probes of the German lines. It was almost as if, having improbably cheated death in the forest, they wished to tempt it again. And death obliged; at least three of the maquisards in Burke's scouting unit were killed that month including Simon, one of the men who had first greeted him in the farm field in September and with whom he'd developed a close friendship.

For finally leaving before he, too, became a casualty, Burke had his best friend in the OSS, Henry North, to thank. In late October, North tracked Burke down in northeastern France and convinced him it was time to come in from the field. Out of gratitude for Burke's service, the reconnaissance unit commander arranged for a jeep and driver to take him to Paris, two hundred miles away. "I was grateful for the metallic whine of the Jeep's motor," Burke wrote, "grateful for the rhythmic roar of the Red Ball Express trucks barreling east with gas for Patton's tanks, grateful

for the slashing rain and slick roads that concentrated the driver's attention, leaving me silently withdrawn inside myself, alone with thoughts of
silenced friends."

On his first day in Paris, Burke was to have one of those back-base
experiences common to the frontline soldier in wartime. Craving a
hearty meal after two months in the field, the Navy lieutenant made
for the dining room of the Royal Monceau, an elegant hotel in the 8th
arrondissement that had been requisitioned by the U.S. Navy for officers quarters. Clad in his soiled field uniform, and still sporting a beard
and maquis beret, Burke was not only promptly ejected from the Monceau dining room, but ordered to report to a Navy captain for repri-
mand. Unimpressed by the OSS officer's recent exploits, the captain
upbraided Burke for failing to travel with his "undress blues" uniform,
and warned this lapse would keep him barred from the Monceau dining
room and sleeping quarters until remedied.

Instead, Burke made for a friend's couch, and then for the bar of the
Hotel Ritz. There, he was reunited with a stunned Ernest Hemingway.

"Christ, kid, they told me you were dead!" Hemingway shouted as
he waded across the crowded room in Burke's direction. Very swiftly,
room was made for Burke at the writer's table, and champagne ordered.
"They told me the kid was dead," Hemingway kept repeating to his other
companions.

Bravery and heroism are horribly overused words in our modern
vocabulary, clichés for an act of human behavior that is rarely examined
for its possible underlying motive. Certainly, it was brave, and perhaps
heroic, of Michael Burke to step out of the Confracourt forest into no-
man's-land, but it wasn't born of some moviehouse concept of courage.
Rather—and far more interestingly—it seemed rooted in a kind of guilt.
Years later, in placing himself back at that moment, Burke could offer
only a partial answer for his actions.

"I was doing it for myself, because of my expectation of myself," he
wrote. "Had someone else volunteered, had I hung back, and had that
other person died or succeeded, either way, I, by my own private measure, would have hated my guts forever for having finessed the risk. I
don't know why that is; it simply is. There are some spheres in which
reason does not penetrate at all."

It was also an impulse that suggested Michael Burke was likely to have
a very difficult time returning to civilian life.

3

A MAN CALLED TYPHOID

To those who heard the radio broadcast of Romania's King Michael on the evening of August 23, 1944, the import of his words had the effect of masking his youth. Earlier that day, the twenty-two-year-old monarch had summoned Romania's longtime dictator, General Ion Antonescu, together with the vice premier, to the royal palace and placed them under arrest. Now, Michael announced in a slow and solemn cadence, his nation, one of Nazi Germany's most dependable satellite regimes through four years of war, was switching sides. Already, those Romanian troops facing off against the advancing Soviet Red Army on the nation's northeastern frontier had been ordered to turn their guns around, to join the Soviets and attack the Germans beside them.

Exhausted and diminished from their bitter fighting retreat out of the Soviet Union, German military units in Romania were in no shape to take on a new enemy in their very midst. Beginning that night, and accelerating over the next several days, the Germans rapidly fell back before the Soviet-Romanian onslaught. Some remnants made good their escape northwest into Hungary, while others—some fifty thousand troops in all—were encircled and compelled to surrender. In Bucharest, the Romanian capital, the resident German military and political staff fled in disorganized bands, frantic to reach the frontier however they could. In one bold move, King Michael and the political leadership of Romania had achieved the once unimaginable: a sudden and complete break from the Nazi yoke.

One person elated by the news was OSS director Wild Bill Donovan.

Over the previous year, Allied bomber squadrons had repeatedly targeted the vast Romanian oilfields at Ploesti, vital to the Nazi war machine, but had suffered enormous losses in the process. Courtesy of a subclause in the German-Romanian treaty of alliance, those downed Allied airmen captured in Romania—over one thousand by best estimate—had been kept in local prisons, rather than sent to POW camps in Germany. With Romania now on the Allied side, the OSS could send in a team to organize the airmen's repatriation, an act sure to play well to the agency's public image and to win Donovan the gratitude of American and British air commanders.

But the OSS director had an even more compelling reason to get his people into Romania fast. From the very start of American involvement in World War II, Donovan had been one of those advisors to the president deeply leery of the alliance with the Soviet Union. That wariness partly explained why Donovan had been an early advocate of launching an Anglo-American offensive against Nazi Germany through southeastern Europe, lest the Soviet armies advancing from the east have the region to themselves. It might also explain why Donovan and his deputies had been so lax in policing Lanning Macfarland's disastrous Operation Dogwood, that perhaps the OSS director had been so desperate for some kind of presence in the Balkans—a presence that could impede the Germans in the short term, but the Soviets in the long term—that he was willing to take the chance of being played. But now, the doors to one of those Balkan nations, Romania, had been thrown open to the Allies, and it was the Soviets who were walking through them first. To the OSS director, what transpired over the next few weeks in Romania was likely to be a test run of what could happen throughout Eastern Europe as the German defensive lines crumbled and the Red Army poured into the breach.

On August 29, just six days after Michael's radio broadcast and with the German and Soviet armies still engaged in firefights throughout Romania, a nine-man OSS team from Italy flew into Bucharest. Its primary mission was to find and organize the repatriation of the downed Allied airmen. With the enthusiastic help of locals, as well as of Romanian and Soviet troops, the OSS team quickly found some 1,400 airmen—or considerably more than they'd been expecting—scattered across the breadth of the country.

While that mission garnered most of the attention, it was soon joined by a far more sensitive one. On August 31, a special Romanian air force plane left Istanbul with another contingent of OSS officers, including the man chosen to head its new command center in Bucharest: Lieutenant Commander Frank G. Wisner. In his order of instructions to Wisner,

Donovan had been blunt; one of the team's highest priorities was to "establish the intentions of the Soviet Union regarding Rumania."

If ever there was a man ideally suited to functioning in the chaos that was Romania in August 1944, it was the hyper-energetic Frank Wisner. And Romania at that moment was ideally suited to Wisner, too, a kind of spy's paradise.

The Germans had been so swiftly pushed out of Bucharest that they didn't have time to take their files or even destroy them, bad news for a war machine renowned for its love of paperwork. Bursting into the offices of the company that coordinated Romanian oil exports, Wisner and his men found comprehensive statistics on monthly oil shipments to Germany, enabling OSS analysts to determine almost precisely how much the Ploesti air raids had disrupted the flow of Romanian oil to the Reich. In the local Nazi Party headquarters in downtown Bucharest, OSS officers found completely intact party membership records—tens of thousands of names—while in the files of the departed German air attaché, they discovered the logbooks of those German warplanes previously based in Romania, revealing, noted historian Elizabeth Hazard, "the names and locations of plants where the planes had been manufactured and depots where they were sent for repairs. The information was of incalculable value to the U.S. Army Air Force bombing planners." As George Bookbinder, one of the OSS officers in the Romanian unit relayed to OSS headquarters: "This place is wild with information and Wisner is in his glory." That exuberance was apparent in a letter Wisner wrote home to his wife, Polly, in early September. "In a word," he wrote, "I have caught up with the war and I do not intend to get behind it again." Indicative of his mordant sense of humor, Wisner assigned the members of his small team code names derived from diseases or medical maladies. For himself, he chose Typhoid.

Considerably easing the OSS workload was the fact that just about everyone in Romania, beginning with King Michael himself, stood ready to assist their mission however they could. This friendliness was partly rooted in the political—the United States was already regarded by Romanians as the one power that might save them from Soviet domination—but it also stemmed from fear of the Red Army. In their advance through the nation, Soviet soldiers had gone on a looting spree, stealing or "requisitioning" whatever they could lay their hands on. As a result, wealthy Bucharesteans vied with one another to hand over to the Americans for safekeeping most anything of value—cars, gold, jewelry, even radios— and practically begged them to billet in their homes to avoid their mansions being taken over by the Soviets. Seeing no need to rough it, Wisner gladly accepted the offer of housing from Romania's beer magnate, Dumitru Bragadiru, and converted an entire wing of his enormous palace on Calea Rahovei into the local OSS headquarters.

Testament to their star status, even as the OSS continued to vacuum up intelligence on the departed Germans, they kept a busy social calendar. With Romania now effectively out of the war, senior Red Army officers along with Bucharest's upper class were in a relieved and celebratory mood, and most every night was marked by a gala party in one or another of the mansions along Kiseleff Boulevard. By virtue of Bucharest being one of the least war-damaged of the Eastern European capitals, well-stocked cellars were raided for these gatherings, so that the finest wines and cognac flowed freely. As another member of Wisner's OSS team, Robert Bishop, recalled: "Rumanian tables groaned under the load of plenty: an iced dish with fresh caviar from the delta of the Danube; sliced salami, smoked sturgeon, little meat rolls, all taken with sips of tuica, a mild prune brandy." And this was merely the cold buffet part of the meal; after that, Bishop explained, "the Rumanians sat down and really started eating."

As might be expected in such an atmosphere, rumors of romance soon blossomed. One source of gossip was of the very close relationship between Officer Typhoid and Princess Tanda Caragea, the beautiful twenty-four-year-old wife of Wisner's much older host, Dumitru Bragadiru. While never acknowledging that the two were lovers, the exotic Caragea—she was reported to be a descendant of Vlad Tepes, better known as Vlad the Impaler, or Dracula—did allow in a postwar interview that she had acted as Wisner's "hostess." As she wryly noted, the OSS chief wanted to meet people in Bucharest, and "when you're rich and above all a good-looking girl, you know a lot of people."

Eventually, the OSS team moved out of the Bragadiru mansion and into more spartan quarters, at least in part to rein in the ceaseless festivities. As Robert Bishop sniffed: "Eating, working, sleeping, drinking and loving other men's wives all under one roof while husbands and enlisted men were around was just a bit too much for some of us." (This seemed a particularly priggish comment coming from Bishop, considering that in a few months he would be hauled before an American military tribunal for smuggling his Romanian mistress—and purported Gestapo mole—into Austria.)

But quite beyond the hoard of German intelligence and the merry times to be had on Kiseleff Boulevard, Frank Wisner fully appreciated that in Romania he and his OSS colleagues were witnessing something utterly unique. For the first time since entering the war three years earlier, the Soviet Union was now an occupying force in a land where it had no territorial claim, and for the first time an American military unit was there to observe the Red Army in a peacetime, administrative role. Little wonder that William Donovan had been so emphatic in his instructions to Wisner about gauging Soviet intentions.

Easier said than done, though, because from what Wisner could discern in his first days in Bucharest, it appeared the Soviets weren't completely sure of their intentions themselves. On a personal level, the OSS commander developed an excellent rapport with a number of senior Red Army officers, but the topic of politics or the future of Romania rarely arose. It certainly didn't come up with soldiers in the streets, who, rather than an army of occupation, more closely resembled a mob of pillagers and rapists. Until the Soviet high command began to impose some measure of order, members of the OSS team frequently saw Red Army transport trucks trundling down the boulevards of Bucharest laden with stolen furniture, maneuvering through an obstacle course of drunken Soviet soldiers passed out in the streets.

Most Romanians were deeply concerned about the Soviets' ultimate plans—and with ample justification. Historical mistrust between the two nations dated back centuries, and the Romanians had done nothing to reverse that trend by joining forces with Nazi Germany; as Soviet officials frequently pointed out, after Germans themselves, Romanians had represented the largest military contingent in Operation Barbarossa, the Axis invasion of the Soviet Union. It also seemed a tad convenient that Romania's ideological conversion had come at the very moment the Red Army was massing on her border. Not surprisingly, the Soviets remained deeply wary of their newfound allies, allowing some Romanian military units to join them on the battlefield even as other units were disarmed and hustled off to POW camps.

What soon became apparent, however, was that Romania's future was not going to be decided in Bucharest, but in Moscow. Less than one week after King Michael's radio broadcast, the Soviet foreign minister along with the American and British ambassadors to Moscow went into conference in the Soviet capital to thrash out the terms of the Allied armistice with Romania. Those proceedings were watched by a much wider audience, for many viewed it as a prototype of the kind of peace settlements to come as other Axis-allied nations were conquered or switched sides, a litmus test for revealing the degree of cooperation or dissension between the Big Three allies on the matter.

The terms of armistice were announced in early September 1944. For those Romanians expecting the worst, their expectations were fully met.

Romania would formally cede the region of Bessarabia to the Soviet Union, a stretch of land the two nations had contested and traded since 1812. For the duration of the war, Romania would bear the cost of hosting the Soviet Red Army on its soil—over a half-million soldiers at the time—as well as the burden of putting some 200,000 of its own soldiers into the field under Soviet command. Most punishing of all was the war reparations bill: $300 million, to be paid in goods and services to Moscow over the next six years, but enough to keep the impoverished nation in a state of indentured servitude for far longer. Of course, servitude to Moscow, in the view of some cynics, was precisely the goal.

This wasn't all. While Romania's occupation would officially be under the supervision of something called the Allied Control Commission (ACC), composed of representatives from all three major Allied powers, actual authority would rest exclusively with the Soviets. While this might seem only logical—after all, it was Red Army soldiers, not American or British, who were now billeted across the nation—it provided the practical framework for the Soviets to begin reshaping Romania to their own specifications should they see fit. And the Soviets saw fit.

On September 12, 1944, King Michael's representatives signed the formal papers of armistice in a brief ceremony in Moscow. Almost immediately, Frank Wisner started sending alarmed cables to OSS headquarters. Citing a highly placed Romanian businessman he spoke with the day after the armistice signing, Wisner contended that "the Russians have apparently adopted the policy of undermining the King and present Government . . . with the result that the Government may be unable to function, and may fall."

The OSS commander wasn't shy about placing blame. "It is the feeling of industrialists and government officials that Roumania has been abandoned by the US and Great Britain."

That was mere prologue. Over the next three weeks, Wisner so forcefully and frequently bombarded OSS Washington with reports denouncing Soviet behavior in Romania that he finally drew a mild rebuke from William Donovan himself. On October 2, the OSS director urged Officer Typhoid to tone things down, and to refrain from any "speech or action that would evidence antagonism to Russia."

Wisner was not the sort of man to blithely pick a fight with his superior, but it was a measure of his indignation at what he was witnessing that he fired off a sharp defense of his team's analyses to Donovan. He also continued to report on the Soviets' actions in the darkest terms. On October 9, that included their issuance of arrest warrants for forty-seven prominent Romanians on accusations of war crimes; as Wisner pointed out, the list included a number of senior-ranking generals who had been instrumental in engineering Romania's switch to the Allies, but who were resistant to Soviet dictates. In late October came another Wisner report detailing how Red Army troops, in furtherance of the armistice's ruinous reparations terms, were systemically stripping the nation's oil refineries of its machinery and loading it onto railcars bound for the Soviet Union.

But most ominous of all, in Wisner's mind, was that taking place in the political sphere. According to some sources, within days of Romania's capitulation, hundreds of Soviet political commissars had been brought into Bucharest and dispatched across the country. Very soon, their robust efforts to marshal the political left—efforts that allegedly ranged from cajolery to bribery to death threats—led to the consolidation of Romania's small and splintered leftist parties into one grand alliance, the National Democratic Front (FND). With de facto leadership of the FND placed in the hands of the minuscule local communist party—by best estimate, its pre-1944 membership had numbered less than one thousand—the Soviets then began leaning on both the king and the serving prime minister to "broaden" the government's composition by bringing in FND ministers.

What Wisner observed firsthand over the next several weeks was just how quickly a government could be undermined and supplanted, the speed and relentlessness with which the Soviets operated. When the coalition government was reshuffled in early November, several conservative cabinet ministers were replaced with FND officials. The following month, the sitting prime minister was forced out in favor of a more Soviet-friendly leader; he gave the FND even more positions in the political leadership. With attention focused on the changes occurring at the top tier of government, few took note of a crucial change at the next level down. Appointed the new undersecretary of the Interior Ministry, a position that appeared modest on paper but which oversaw Romania's police and internal security forces, the head of the national communist party immediately launched a purge of the old guard throughout the country and their replacement with communist cadres. The effect of all this was bracing: between King Michael's August 23 switching-sides speech and the installment of a wholly Soviet-compliant government less than four months had elapsed.

In a few years, Hungary's communist strongman, Mátyás Rákosi, would coin a colorful term to describe the methods used to bring him and other Soviet allies to power in Eastern Europe: "salami tactics." Also known by the more graphic "death by a thousand cuts," it is the strategy of tearing away at an existing political framework from so many different and seemingly unrelated angles—the appointment of an unqualified but loyal functionary to a sub-ministry here, the annulment of a legal protection over there—that it leaves the opposition overwhelmed and flummoxed and unsure of where to make a stand.

Naturally, it has precisely the same effect on any external powers trying to counter such assaults. Is protesting a judge's shutting down of a regional newspaper really worth provoking a diplomatic incident? Is challenging a regime's intimidation tactics against a labor union worth the risk of an armed confrontation? The answer almost invariably is no, because left in the hands of diplomats, there is always some larger goal, some greater consideration, that is best served by making smaller compromises along the way; the end result, though, is that it can eventually become too late to make a stand anywhere. As World War II drew to a close, the laboratory where these salami tactics were being tested was Romania, and the first outsider to see them in action was Lieutenant Commander Frank G. Wisner.

Whether his warnings were having any effect back in Washington was an open question, however. While Donovan made sure Wisner's Bucharest reports were circulated at the highest levels of the State and War Departments, the most tangible responses were, like Donovan's missive of early October, requests for Wisner to tone things down. That admonition was reinforced in mid-November when Wisner was informed that the long-delayed American delegation to Romania's Allied Control Commission, the inter-Allied committee established to oversee the nation's political and economic restoration, was finally about to take up residence in Bucharest. Heading the delegation was a certain Cortlandt Van Rensselaer Schuyler, a brigadier general who had served out the war on the home front, and whose knowledge of Romania consisted of whatever he had gleaned while overseeing the U.S. Army's domestic antiaircraft unit training facilities. Despite this, Wisner was tersely informed that he and his OSS team would be wholly subordinate to Schuyler's command, and that their continued presence in Romania "would depend largely on extent to which you maintained cordial relations with Russians since [Schuyler] would not allow his work to be embarrassed or compromised." In the first test of U.S. policy toward Soviet machinations in postwar Eastern Europe, the diplomats—or at least the armchair-general version of a diplomat—were winning out over the spies.

Not that Wisner was so naive as to be shocked by any of this. After all, maintaining the wartime alliance with the Soviet Union had already required all manner of political and moral contortions by the Roosevelt administration. There was also the basic issue of facts on the ground. The Soviets had suffered dearly at the hands of Romania's previous,

Nazi-allied regime, in a theater of the war that the Americans missed altogether. Further, in November 1944, Wisner was one of perhaps fifty American servicemen in Romania in contrast to a resident Red Army contingent of at least a half-million. Under these circumstances, joined to the need to keep the Big Three alliance functioning with a minimum of rancor, the question of who would ultimately call the shots in Bucharest was already answered.

But along with this core truth, the longer Wisner stayed in Romania, the more he appreciated there was an even simpler—and in its way, far more frightening—explanation for what was occurring there, and likely to be repeated elsewhere. To a degree that few Western statesmen at the time wished to acknowledge, the future dispensation of postwar Europe was not going to hinge on a philosophy or ideology or even a geopolitical strategy, so much as on the whims and fevered calculations of a single man. His name was Joseph Vissarionovich Dzhugashvili, but he was better known by the nom de guerre he had bestowed upon himself and that derived from the Russian word for steel: Stalin.

═══

Late on a night in mid-September 1936, a portly forty-three-year-old man named Karl Pauker was dragged into the dining room of a dacha outside Moscow by two guards. As he vainly struggled with his captors, the terror-stricken Pauker shrieked: "For God's sake, call Stalin. Stalin promised to save our lives!"

From the other end of the dining room and surrounded by his entourage, Joseph Stalin watched this unfolding spectacle with unbridled glee.

Rather than being led to his own death, Karl Pauker was reenacting the last moments of a man named Grigory Zinoviev. Two weeks earlier, on the morning of August 25, 1936, Zinoviev and another senior Kremlin leader, Lev Kamenev, had been led into an execution chamber in the basement of the Lubyanka prison in central Moscow. As had happened many times before—and would occur countless thousands of times more—the two men had been tortured and then coerced into signing "confessions" of their purported plotting against Stalin, on the promise of clemency from the Soviet dictator. In the dacha dining room, Pauker, the head of Stalin's personal bodyguard and a kind of Kremlin court jester, was re-creating the moment when Zinoviev realized he had been tricked and was about to die. According to Stalin biographer Simon Montefiore, the jester also played on the murdered man's Jewish heritage to increase the scene's comic appeal: "Pauker, a Jew himself, specialized in telling

Stalin Jewish jokes in the appropriate accent with much rolling of 'R's and cringing. Now he combined the two, depicting Zinoviev raising his hands to the Heavens and weeping. 'Hear oh Israel the Lord is our God, the Lord is one.' Stalin laughed so much that Pauker repeated it. Stalin was almost sick with merriment and waved at Pauker to stop."

Naturally, all the others gathered in the dacha dining room that night, the dozen or so friends and party apparatchiks who composed Stalin's inner circle, howled with laughter right along with the *vozhd*, or leader. This included a man named Genrikh Yagoda. As Stalin's chief assassin, Yagoda had personally officiated over the executions of Zinoviev and Kamenev—in fact, he'd ordered the fatal bullets extracted from their brains to keep as souvenirs—and was undoubtedly gratified by the dictator's reaction to Pauker's little skit. Over the previous three years, Yagoda had officiated over the murders of thousands at Stalin's behest, but one could never be certain who or what might draw his distrust next.

With the exception of Stalin himself, what no one gathered in the Kuntsevo dacha that night in 1936 knew was that the dispatch of Zinoviev and Kamenev, once among the closest of Stalin's associates, was the harbinger of a purge so indiscriminate and sweeping it would become known as the Great Terror. Over the next two years, that killing spree would consume most of the communist party leadership, at least 35,000 senior military officers, and much of the Soviet Union's intellectual and artistic community. It would also destroy many of those assembled in Kuntsevo that night. This was to include both the court jester, Karl Pauker, liquidated in August 1937, and Genrikh Yagoda himself. Just weeks after the dacha party, Yagoda was stripped of his leadership role and cast into Lubyanka to await his own execution. Officiating over that March 1938 event would be Yagoda's replacement as master executioner, Nikolai Yezhov, a man so sadistic he would earn the nickname "The Poison Dwarf." Less than two years later, the Dwarf would have his own appointment in one of the Lubyanka murder rooms.

Even this slaughter of his intimates doesn't begin to capture the depths of Stalin's murderous paranoia or the depravity of his rule. Determined to leave no potential revenge-seekers behind, after eliminating his perceived enemies the Soviet dictator often killed the dead men's wives. After the liquidation of the wives, it might be the turn of their children, even infants, and then of his victim's extended families. In just this way, many notable Russian families were virtually scrubbed out of existence during Stalin's reign.

And just as with families, so entire professional classes and ethnic groups. Stalin's 1930 pogrom against Russia's small landholding peasants, or *kulaks*, led to the deaths by execution or starvation of an estimated one million. By sending troops to seize Ukrainian grain harvests amid the famine of 1932, Stalin was able to both feed the urban dwellers upon whom his rule depended, and to dramatically thin a Ukrainian population whose loyalty he suspected. The body count of the Ukrainian Holodomor: between three and eight million.

The butchery became self-perpetuating—and for simple reason. With the Terror inducing a kind of mass panic, citizens at every level of society rushed to denounce others before they themselves were denounced, with the sheer flood of those denunciations serving as "proof" in Stalin's mind that enemies were everywhere. And for all those with the license to pass judgment, whether one of Stalin's favored lieutenants or the headman of a provincial village, the prudent choice was to convict rather than exonerate, to kill rather than pardon, because only the living might cause problems down the road.

But until the mid-1930s, most all of this had been an internal horror, one that might appall the outside world but didn't greatly affect it. That changed when Stalin thrust the Soviet Union out of its own shadow and onto the world stage. Here, though, rests one of the first great divergences in opinion about Joseph Stalin. Was this outward turn meant to take advantage of Europe's growing chaos to expand the Soviet empire, or was it rooted in a kind of defensive posture against that chaos? In the future Cold War, conservative Western analysts embraced the first explanation, portraying Stalin as a rapacious opportunist who would stop at nothing in the pursuit of world domination. A more measured look, however, suggests the latter was probably nearer to the truth. Indeed, one of the bitterest ironies of the twentieth century is the degree to which the actions—and inactions—of the Western democracies in the 1930s and well into World War II could be seen as validating the worst fears of a paranoid sociopath like Joseph Stalin.

That pattern was first established with the Spanish Civil War in 1936, when the Western democracies did nothing to come to the aid of an elected Spanish government under attack by right-wing military mutineers. Instead, it was left to the Soviets to try to save Republican Spain—unsuccessfully it would turn out—against rebels being armed and advised by fascist Germany and Italy. In the face of such Western timidity, Stalin could hardly be confident of support from the democracies if the ascendant Adolf Hitler launched an attack on the Soviet Union, a war that the virulently anti-communist German leader had been advocating his entire adult life. Any lingering confidence was surely further eroded by the West's hand-wringing acquiescence to Germany's escalating offenses in Central Europe: the annexation of Austria in March 1938, and then of the Sudetenland seven months later; the takeover and dissolution of Czechoslovakia in early 1939. Each time, Britain and France sat back— and the United States did even less—and what a quick glance at the map revealed was that each one of these capitulations occurred on Germany's eastern flank, not its western. As the old joke goes, just because one is paranoid doesn't mean the world isn't out to get you, and by early 1939, Stalin might be forgiven for believing that the West was deliberately trying to fix the warmongering führer's attention in his direction, to save their own skins by throwing his nation to the Teutonic wolf.

So, time for a bold counterstroke. By entering into a nonaggression alliance with Hitler in the summer of 1939—the Molotov-Ribbentrop Pact—Stalin was at least able to buy himself some time. Mindful that Soviet-German friendship might falter in the future, he used that time to build up buffer zones by attacking and taking control of an assortment of the Soviet Union's neighbors: the eastern half of Poland; the Baltic states of Latvia, Lithuania and Estonia; swaths of Finland and Romania. Alas, these buffer zones proved of little help when Hitler betrayed the pact in June 1941 and launched his long-planned invasion of the Soviet Union, Operation Barbarossa.

Incredibly, for a man who appeared to trust absolutely no one, it seems the Soviet dictator harbored a lingering faith in his German counterpart—or perhaps he was merely stunned into paralysis by the idea of someone even more devious than he. For nearly eight hours after Barbarossa was launched on June 22, during which entire Russian armies were cut off and surrounded, Stalin clung to the belief that it was all just a "provocation," one that could be sorted out if only he could get Hitler on the telephone. But the führer wasn't taking calls. When finally Stalin was disabused of this notion, he disappeared into his Kuntsevo dacha and remained there, virtually incommunicado, for the next five days. Within a month of the invasion's start, the Soviet Union lost well over two million soldiers, most of its tanks and a third of its air force.

But if his pact with Hitler proved a disappointment, Stalin had been scarcely more pleased by the one that replaced it: his alliance with Great Britain and the United States. To be sure, the flood of American war matériel was critical in enabling the Red Army to withstand the German invasion and eventually reverse it, but both Britain and the United States seemed quite content to let the Soviets do the vast majority of the fighting and dying. Particularly enraging to the *vozhd* was what he saw as his allies' dithering in opening a second European front against the Germans to relieve pressure on his own armies. In the spring of 1942, an overly exuberant Winston Churchill had promised Stalin that such a front would be established by the end of that year, but when the British and Americans did open a second front that November, it wasn't in Europe at all but in the strategic backwater of North Africa. That was followed by an invasion of the almost equally inconsequential Italian island of Sicily in July 1943, and then by the unrewarding assault on the Italian mainland two months later. Indeed, it wasn't until the D-Day landings in northern France in June 1944, after the Red Army had for three years borne the full brunt of the Nazi war machine virtually alone, that one could begin to talk of a shared military burden at all. Even then, such a description was exceedingly generous to the Americans and British, almost insulting to the Soviets. After all, the 400,000 American troops who would ultimately die in the Europe and Pacific theaters of World War II represented less than one-twentieth of the estimated nine million Soviet soldiers killed on the Eastern Front, which in turn was just half of the estimated eighteen million Soviet civilians who perished.

In light of all this, as World War II drew to a close, even a paranoid like Stalin might be reasonably forgiven for nurturing another of his conspiracy theories: that his wartime allies were holding back, nibbling away at the margins of things before swooping in to take over once an exhausted Red Army was bled dry. To forestall that, and to avoid a future catastrophe along the lines of what she had just endured, the Soviet Union needed to have full control of its frontiers, to have a defensive bulwark in Eastern Europe against its historical enemies to the west. Romania became the first potential building block of that bulwark.

But however much Frank Wisner had pieced all of this together in the autumn of 1944, there was a further wrinkle to the Romanian situation of which he hadn't a clue. It centered on a secretive mission to Moscow by none other than British prime minister Winston Churchill.

A lifelong "anti-Bolshevik," Churchill had long harbored a far more distrustful view of Stalin than his American counterpart, Franklin Roosevelt. By the autumn of 1944, with Soviet hegemony in southeastern Europe rapidly becoming a fait accompli, the prime minister was determined to salvage what he could of British interests in the region. That goal put him on a flight to Moscow on the night of October 7, 1944.

Anxious to protect Britain's long-standing close ties with Greece, Churchill essentially offered to trade away Romania and Bulgaria to the Soviets in return for continued British primacy in Athens. Just in case his message got muddled in translation or diplomatic nuance, the prime minister sketched his proposal out on a piece of scratch paper. On what would eventually become known as "the percentages agreement," Churchill listed Romania, Greece and Bulgaria, and then wrote "Russia 90%," "Great Britain 90%" and "Russia 75%" next to each respectively.

Considering that Greece was an impoverished nation sliding into anarchy, while Romania was the largest oil producer in Europe, Stalin didn't need to ponder the offer for very long; taking up the sheet of paper, he made a quick check mark on it with a blue pencil and handed it back. Deal in hand, Churchill returned to London, but in his after-action report to President Roosevelt somehow forgot to provide details of his diplomatic side arrangement. It also left Frank Wisner to try to puzzle out on his own why Soviet officials in Bucharest were suddenly much friendlier to their British counterparts, and why those same British officials seemed increasingly sanguine about Soviet excesses in the country.

With any hope for an independent and democratic Romania thus secretly betrayed, it was really only a question of how soon and how harshly the fix would be administered. Wisner didn't have to wait long for answers.

Already warned about respecting the authority of the Allied Control Commission, Wisner endeavored to show deference to General Schuyler, and by all accounts was pleasant, even courtly, to the various Soviet officials who made the rounds of the Bucharest Christmas parties that December. In the first days of 1945, however, came an event that not only marked a pivotal moment for Romania, but was to forever be a haunting influence on the OSS commander.

On the morning of January 4, 1945, a Soviet military officer delivered to the American ACC delegation headquarters a declaration announcing that, in order to safeguard the nation from internal enemies and holdout Nazis, all able-bodied Romanian men and women of ethnic German origin were to be immediately rounded up. Once assembled, this group—some 100,000 Romanian citizens by best estimate—were to be relocated to work camps in the Soviet Union. To add a further note of insult, the edict had gone out on Allied Control Commission letterhead, technically making the United States and Great Britain signatories to the deportation order.

The American and British ACC delegates strenuously protested to the Soviet high commissioner for Romania, General Vladislav Vinogradov, but it was to no avail. As Vinogradov reminded his commission colleagues, their role in Romania was a purely advisory one, and on this matter, the Soviets weren't in need of advice. In the early morning hours of January 6, teams of Red Army soldiers deployed across Romania with lists of ethnic Germans to be taken into custody and transported to the Soviet Union. Learning of the chaotic scene unfolding at Bucharest's

Mogosoaia train station, a number of OSS officers, including Wisner and Robert Bishop, raced to the terminal. Bishop would later give a vivid, if slightly overwrought, account of what he witnessed: "The victims were driven between two lines of guards to a waiting train," he wrote. "As they passed a given point, they were counted again, and when their number reached thirty the next victim was stopped temporarily. The group of thirty was shoved into a box car. Sometimes husband and wife or parents and son or daughter were separated. That did not matter. The only thing that mattered was always to get thirty to a car—men, women, or youngsters—and as quickly as possible. Once they were inside, the sliding doors were shut. Iron bars banged into place and padlocks snapped. There was no time for protests or hysterics. Everything went with the speed and precision of a cattle-loading station."

As the expulsions got under way, General Schuyler, along with the American political representative in Romania, fired off urgent protests to Washington and to the overall leadership of the Allied Control Commission at their London headquarters. It had little effect, and the deportations of the ethnic Germans continued apace. Over the next several days, an estimated sixty thousand ethnic Germans, many of whom could trace their ancestry in Romania back to the twelfth century, were forced onto freight trains and sent off to the work camps.

What also accelerated was the Soviet dismantling of the Romanian government. Following violent street demonstrations in Bucharest in February, Stalin dispatched his deputy foreign minister, Andrei Vyshinsky, to Romania. In an icy meeting with King Michael, Vyshinsky demanded that Romania's increasingly fragile coalition government be disbanded, or face an outright Soviet takeover. A week later, a new Romanian government was formed with a communist hireling, Petru Groza, at its head. When Roosevelt called on the British to join him in denouncing the Soviet's strong-arm tactics, he received a coy response from Churchill that alluded to the deal he had cut in Moscow five months earlier. "We have been hampered in our efforts against these developments," Churchill wrote, "by the fact that, in order to have the freedom to save Greece, [British foreign minister Anthony] Eden and I at Moscow in October recognized that Russia should have a largely preponderant voice in Rumania and Bulgaria."

That was the beginning of the end for Romania. In subsequent months, opposition to the Groza regime was steadily marginalized, with more and more Romanian politicians, businessmen and civic leaders arrested or forced to flee abroad. By the next November, when anti-communist royalists staged a demonstration in downtown Bucharest, the Groza regime felt secure enough to dispense with niceties; asking the Red Army detachment based in the capital for assistance, soldiers opened up with machine guns, killing scores.

One person who didn't remain to witness any of this was Frank Wisner. In early February 1945, shortly after he had protested the deportation of the ethnic Germans in a series of cables to Washington, the OSS mission in Romania was radically scaled down and Wisner transferred out of the country. He took with him a memory of that morning at Mogosoaia train station that, according to friends and family, stalked him to his last days. As his wife, Polly Wisner, told a historian forty years later: "It was what probably affected his life more than any other single thing. The herding-up of those people and putting them in open boxcars to die on their way as they were going into concentration camps."

But if Romania was lost to the thrall of Soviet control, there were those within the Roosevelt administration determined to avert any further losses. One was OSS director William Donovan.

Already by February 1945, Donovan was anticipating the final collapse of Nazi Germany. When that collapse came, the OSS was sure to undergo two dramatic changes. The first would be a potentially enormous reduction in manpower, and the second would be a redeployment of most OSS officers who remained to the ongoing Asian war theater. Convinced that American troops might soon be facing off with the Soviets, however, Donovan sought to maintain a strong OSS presence in Europe for the foreseeable future. To help organize this effort, the director turned to two of his most promising junior officers: a thirty-year-old naval officer named Richard Helms who had been serving as the deputy head of Special Intelligence in OSS London and, senior to him, thirty-five-year-old Lieutenant Commander Frank Wisner.

Shortly after Wisner came out of Romania, he and Helms met in Paris and began working up a list of criteria for those few select OSS men they hoped to retain for OSS Europe. One candidate that they heard a great deal about was a twenty-two-year-old officer currently operating on the front lines in eastern France. His name was Peter Sichel, but he was better known throughout the spy agency by a nickname: the Wunderkind.

4

THE WUNDERKIND

Peter Sichel falls into what surely must be a tiny subset of ex-soldiers: those with fond memories of basic training. In his case, the good times got started when a drill sergeant at Camp Robinson in Little Rock, Arkansas, asked his newest batch of raw recruits if anyone spoke French. "Well, naturally, I raised my hand," Sichel recalled. "I was the only one who did."

Somewhat inexplicably, among the recent arrivals at Camp Robinson were two young French Canadian enlistees who didn't speak English. They also happened to be illiterate. Apparently to avoid the paperwork required to send the pair elsewhere, the Robinson staff chose to simply wait until another French speaker showed up. When Peter Sichel raised his hand, on the spot he was assigned to be the Canadians' minder. "I ended up, like Cyrano de Bergerac, writing and reading their love letters," Sichel recalled, "and in exchange they shined my boots, made my bed, polished my buttons, and did my kitchen duty. It was a very pleasant arrangement."

It was also only the first in a series of unlikely twists that, in less than five years, would transform Peter Sichel from a struggling immigrant teenager toiling in a New York City stockroom to one of America's most highly regarded early Cold War spymasters. While the acronyms of the spy agencies that employed Sichel were to change with dizzying speed—from OSS to SSU to CIG to CIA—his institutional nickname would stay constant: the Wunderkind.

If, in 1942, central Arkansas seemed an exotic destination for the way-

ward French Canadians, it was at least as much so for nineteen-year-old
Peter Sichel. Until the age of twelve, he had lived in the medieval and
picturesque German city of Mainz, the scion of a wealthy extended family of wine merchants. From its start in the mid-nineteenth century, by
the early 1920s, Sichel & Company had grown to become one of Germany's largest wine exporters, with branch offices in Bordeaux, London and
New York, and it was naturally assumed that Peter, born in 1922, would
join the next generation of the family business. That assumption was cast
into doubt when Hitler came to power in 1933.

Like many other German Jews, Peter's father, Eugen, was slow to take
the new chancellor seriously, dismissing Hitler's anti-Semitic rants as an
electioneering ploy. His mother, Franziska, saw things very differently,
however, and urged her husband to make contingency plans for the family's escape. In 1935, that led to twelve-year-old Peter and his older sister,
thirteen-year-old Ruth, being installed in English boarding schools and
entrusted to the care of a relative involved in the London branch of the
family's wine business. It was the start of an exodus. As the Nazi "racial
laws" and restrictions against Jews became steadily more repressive, the
extended Sichel family of Mainz began slipping out of Germany one by
one. By 1938, the last to remain—and now barred from leaving—were
Peter's mother and father. They ultimately made their escape by concoct-
ing a terminal illness for their daughter in England, and obtaining two-
week exit visas in order to visit their "dying" child.

But if the Sichel family had escaped the Nazis, it wasn't necessarily for
long. Having resettled in the city of Bordeaux in southern France, they
were there when Germany launched its blitzkrieg invasion of France in
May 1940. With Paris capitulating so quickly as to make flight impossible, the Sichels, like other foreign Jews caught out in the attack, lived as
refugees in the Vichy-controlled area of southern France. For a harrow-
ing nine months, the family maneuvered to find some means of escape
before the French quislings got around to handing them and thousands
of other trapped Jews over to the Germans. At last, in March 1941, the
Sichels managed to slip across the frontier into Spain. From there, they
made for Portugal, and passage on a steamer to New York.

Although gaining a chance to start over in America, the family had
lost virtually everything in their travails of the previous six years, and all
had to pitch in to make ends meet. For the teenaged Peter, that meant
taking a job at J. Einstein & Company, a shoe supply concern in midtown
Manhattan. "I worked my way *up* to stock clerk," he said. "That was a
promotion; I started out as an errand-boy."

He was still with Einstein & Company when Pearl Harbor was attacked on December 7, 1941. The next day, a Monday, Sichel went to the Army recruitment office to join up.

But whether due to his family's refugee status, or to the same chaos that had stalled Michael Burke's efforts, Peter Sichel's enlistment papers seemed to disappear into the bureaucratic ether. It wasn't until late 1942 that he was called up and assigned to the U.S. Army Medical Corps. In furtherance of that assignment, he was shipped off to Camp Robinson and a rendezvous with his two French Canadian wards.

The year-long delay in being called up was only the beginning of Sichel's frustrations with the American military. For the next six months, he was shunted about the American heartland as he awaited a permanent assignment—there was briefly talk of a specialized training course at the University of Wisconsin—until finally, during a protracted stay in Salt Lake City in the summer of 1943, he was visited by two men in suits.

The men seemed to already know a good deal about Sichel, and most especially about the time he had spent in the southern reaches of Vichy France prior to his family's escape; they asked about his familiarity with that region, as well as his facility with the French language. After a half-hour or so of such casual questioning, the visitors got to the point: would Sichel be willing to be parachuted behind enemy lines on an intelligence mission? If not thrilled by the prospect, Sichel's reply was matter-of-fact: "I am a soldier, and whatever I am commanded to do, I have to do."

Soon after, he was given a train ticket and orders to report to a building on 25th Street in Washington, D.C. It was only when he reached the building that Sichel realized he was being inducted into the OSS.

Yet, just what that entailed was to remain a mystery for some time. The very afternoon of his arrival at OSS headquarters, Sichel was herded onto a bus with a group of other young men and transported to a wilderness camp north of Washington known as Area B (and which today is the Camp David presidential retreat). There, the émigré anticipated undergoing the kind of rigorous training he had avoided at Camp Robinson, but he was soon set straight. "We were assigned rooms in a temporary building, and for the next three weeks, a number of other people and I were fed and housed, but not given any training, indoctrination or indication of why we were there. I spent my evenings playing poker with people who were much better at it than I."

Brought back to Washington, Sichel endured another long stretch of idleness until he at last reached his breaking point; storming into the OSS personnel office, he demanded to either be sent overseas or returned to the regular army. The complaining seemed to work. Days later, Sichel received his ship-out orders and was soon bound for the North African city of Algiers. If it lacked the cachet of being airdropped behind enemy lines, the position the OSS had chosen for him was still a beguiling one: special funds officer. It also marked the beginning of a career in covert operations that would ultimately bring the young German exile to the attention of a recruiting Frank Wisner and Richard Helms.

Along with all the other burdens it brings, waging war requires a great deal of cash. This is especially true with unconventional or guerrilla warfare, where fighters operating in open territory or behind enemy lines need to carry actual money to buy supplies, bribe officials or pay recruits. But not just any money, of course, only the currency used in that specific milieu, and woe to the infiltrating commando or spy who tries to conduct his or her trade with currency that is too old or too new or obsolete. As a matter of life or death, then, the spy needs an ample supply of whatever money is currently being used on the terrain he or she travels, and this is where the OSS special funds officer came into play.

Since war inevitably disrupts the flow of money, it often leads to a currency black market that bears no resemblance to the "legal" or official rates of exchange. The task of a special funds officer is to maneuver through this financial underworld in order to amass enough local money to fund local guerrilla operations, and to do so as cheaply as possible. This was both Peter Sichel's mission and his genius. For nearly a year, first out of OSS headquarters in Algiers and then in Allied-occupied Italy, he essentially functioned as a mobile currency trader, traveling about the countryside with a portable safe hitched to a small trailer behind his jeep. Within that safe there were often staggering amounts of gold or dollars or francs or lira. "So much money you wouldn't believe," he said with a grin. "Millions. Most of the time we didn't even know how much we had."

Sichel's greatest financial coup occurred toward the end of his tenure in Algiers.

In their haste to escape a rapid Allied advance across North Africa in the spring of 1943, the German high command left behind some 100 million newly minted francs in Tunis, the capital of Tunisia. That money had promptly disappeared into the Tunisian underground. By late 1943, the Allies were running low on usable francs—francs desperately needed by Resistance units operating in France—but their replenishment could only be obtained on the world market at the official, grossly inflated, exchange rate. Instead, Sichel was dispatched to Tunis with orders to buy up as many of the looted francs as he could find on the black market. To do so, and to convince the locals he was serious, he brought with him from Algeria a safe full of French gold coins. To give his mission the veneer of diplomatic respectability, he also took over the residence of the vacationing American vice consul, as well as the consul's servants, car and driver. Most crucial, though, was his linking up with a figure of shadowy repute named Max, "a Maltese Jew who ran a very popular bar called Chez Max on one of the main streets of Tunis."

Working with Max, and overcoming the locals' initial distrust, for the next several weeks Sichel made the rounds of a whole network of villages around the capital city, trading gold coins for the looted francs. By the time he was done, the special funds officer had obtained some 78 million francs, most still in their original printer packets, and at a fraction of the exchange rate being demanded by French officials.

Back in Algiers, Sichel's next task was to mix and "age" his enormous collection of francs, both to break up serial number sequences and to make the bills appear used. The latter process was surprisingly time-consuming. From past efforts, OSS special funds officers knew that simply spreading dirt on new money accomplished very little, that the best way to produce the needed scuffing effect was to scatter the bills over a floor and repeatedly walk on them for several weeks. Francs required an additional laborious step. By long tradition, French banks often bundled together higher-denomination notes by running a thin, single-prong "staple" through one corner of the bills. Thus, Sichel and his OSS colleagues were required to painstakingly "pinhole" their mountain of francs before they were ready for circulation.

It was also around this time that Sichel first came into contact with a dashing young Navy ensign named Michael Burke. Arriving in Algiers in late 1943 and about to embark on a high-stakes mission behind enemy lines in Italy, Burke was instructed to make for the local OSS special funds office to pick up a large quantity of Italian lira. His point of contact there was Peter Sichel. Although they were a study in contrasts—at twenty-three, Burke still had the physique of a University of Pennsylvania football star, and towered over the much slighter Sichel—the two hit it off immediately. "He was a wonderful man," Sichel recalled of Burke, "and an excellent drinking companion. I liked him immensely." He was fairly certain the affection was mutual. "Mike *had* to like me; I gave him lots of money."

And there was an altogether different reason that the former stock boy for Einstein & Company made for good company in Algiers in late 1943, one that would have caused Michael Burke and most any other self-respecting American soldier to hold Sichel in the highest esteem. It seems that during his black market negotiations in Tunis, Sichel's financial artistry not only enabled him to gather nearly 80 million francs, but to buy up the contents of an entire cellar of cognac and scotch, a cache which he then arranged to have hauled back to Algeria on military transports for his personal consumption and distribution. As he would blandly put it, the hoard "made our lives more pleasant in Algiers that winter."

It was but one example of the way in which Sichel consistently challenged Sherman's famous dictum about war being hell. In taking part in the invasion of occupied France in the summer of 1944, for instance, not for Sichel the hailstorm of lead that had greeted those wading ashore on Omaha Beach in Normandy. Attached to the U.S. Seventh Army, he instead arrived two months later in the French Mediterranean resort town of St. Tropez, part of the virtually unopposed Allied amphibious landing in southern France. Passage to that beachhead was aboard a U.S. Navy communications ship on which Sichel somehow arranged to be given his own stateroom. "The luxury of that cabin," he wrote, "as well as the food and service during the trip, with Philippine mess boys serving us at any time, day or night, was a welcome break"—although precisely what Sichel needed a break from was not entirely clear.

Nor was it clear just what function an OSS special funds officer might perform in St. Tropez in August 1944, considering that the German military units in the area, caught flatfooted by the Allied landing, were offering virtually no resistance as they fled to form a new defensive line far to the north. In lieu of more pressing matters, Sichel was detailed to track down OSS agents and Jedburgh commandos who had earlier been infiltrated into the region but remained unaccounted for. One of these was an OSS officer, Horace "Hod" Fuller, who had parachuted into the area two months previously. While the assumption was that Fuller was either dead or a POW, Sichel and a companion, Frank Schoonmaker, were told to take a vehicle from the Seventh Army motor pool and search the countryside for him.

Another man given this assignment might have been content to sign out a standard-issue Army jeep, but Sichel, aware of St. Tropez's reputation as a prewar playground for the European rich, instead made for that corner of the motor pool compound where requisitioned civilian vehicles were parked. And there, among the broken-down Citroëns and rusting Renaults, he spotted a 1937 Cord 812, not merely one of the most luxurious and extravagant sedans of the automobile Golden Age but, according to *American Heritage* magazine, "the single most beautiful American car" built in the twentieth century. In short order, the Cord became Peter Sichel's staff car.

"It was a marvelous drive," he said, "very smooth. We never did find Fuller, and we looked everywhere, but what a wonderful way to see the French countryside." Still, the memory of the Cord was a bittersweet one for Sichel for, after mere weeks of driving it around, Schoonmaker fell asleep behind the wheel one day and drove it into a tree. "I was able to get Frank to the hospital in time," he recalled, "but the Cord was a complete loss."

By late September 1944, matters grew a good deal more serious for Sichel when, rejoining the main OSS unit attached to the Seventh Army, he was sent up the Rhône Valley to the new front lines along the Moselle River. There he was to take on a completely different kind of mission for the intelligence agency, one that required both steady nerves and extraordinary acumen.

Since coming ashore in August, the Seventh Army had rolled through southern France virtually unchallenged before running up against the Germans' new defensive line on the Moselle, only a few miles from the German border. Ever since, that front had been essentially static, with both armies content to do little more than probe at the enemy. Other than a few inconsequential skirmishes—a village taken here offset by a farmhouse lost over there—the overall contours of the battlefield had barely changed for weeks, a welcome respite for frontline troops but a frustration for military intelligence officers.

Naturally, the primary function of OSS frontline units was to gather whatever information could be gleaned about enemy units on the other side of no-man's-land. In normal circumstances, this meant sneaking spies into enemy territory, as well as interrogating prisoners or friendly locals, but all these sources rather dried up on a "hard front" like the Moselle. An added complication was that the Seventh Army was now in Alsace-Lorraine, a region contested and traded between France and Germany since the 1870s. Whereas in the rest of France, most all locals would enthusiastically tell an American intelligence officer whatever they knew about the German occupiers, in Alsace-Lorraine, loyalties were more divided. Further, the predominant language along the Moselle was not French, but German. For one of the first times in the war, the espionage wing of the OSS was operating on a conventional battlefront where, whether out of fear or allegiance, the local population could not be trusted. This meant trying to puzzle out a new strategy that could answer two essential questions: how to get a spy across such a rigid and hostile front, and who to recruit for the mission?

In northeastern France, Peter Sichel's commanding officer, Henry Hyde, came up with a novel answer to the second part of that question: German POWs. In the months since the Allies first came ashore at Normandy, hundreds of thousands of German soldiers had surrendered across the breadth of France. Many of these were from units of so-called

Strafkommandos, or punishment squads, that German procurement officers had taken to forming up as they ran out of willing bodies from elsewhere to fling into battle. While some Strafkommandos were common criminals, many more were religious conscientious objectors or anti-Nazi malcontents; regardless of their background, few had any great desire to fight and die for the Third Reich, and had often seized the first opportunity to surrender. Surely, so the reasoning went, some of these dissidents, currently languishing in POW camps, might be willing to spy for the Allies if it helped hasten the end of the Hitler regime.

Skirting the clause in the Geneva Convention that forbids employing POWs for military purposes, Hyde had quickly won approval for his scheme from OSS higher-ups. Soldiers with the Army's Counter Intelligence Corps (CIC) were instructed to conduct a first screening of potential recruits in the POW camps, and to forward the names and files of any promising candidates to the Seventh Army's OSS unit. It then fell on the very small pool of German-speaking OSS officers in that unit—three, to be precise—to further question the candidates and decide whom to select. One of those three was Peter Sichel, who in early October 1944 was pulled from his new position as the Seventh Army OSS unit's paymaster and logistics officer. He was to now spend his days touring POW camps in search of willing spies.

Because the POW camps were still full of Nazi true believers, the approach to a potential recruit was done discreetly, with the candidate typically grabbed out of sight from his fellow inmates and whisked to an isolated spot—a storage room, the back of a covered truck—for interrogation by Sichel or one of the other OSS specialists. A great deal was decided at that first meeting. Above all, Sichel was trying to get a read on the kind of man before him for, even if he could be sure the prisoner was anti-fascist, it wasn't as if the OSS was making him a particularly attractive offer. After all, it takes a special type of soldier to risk torture and death in trying to sneak across a battlefield to betray one's former comrades. And what was to prevent such recruits from agreeing to undertake the mission, but to then rejoin their fighting unit or, more likely, simply go home and await war's end?

In an effort to separate the patriots from the opportunists, the OSS conducted surprisingly thorough background checks. In one case, for example, a potential recruit who claimed to be from a strongly anti-Nazi family mentioned that their next-door neighbors, a Jewish family, had fled to the United States in the late 1930s. After a search of several weeks, OSS officers in the United States traced down the Jewish family, who vouched for the POW's anti-Nazi credentials.

In Sichel's case, the vetting process was aided by a hidden talent. "I discovered I was very good at picking up accents," he explained. "There are dozens of different German accents, each quite distinct, and I found that after just a few minutes of listening to someone from, say, Munich, I could talk just like him. This helped to build a rapport. They felt they weren't just talking to a fellow German, but to someone from the same background, the same place."

Once chosen for the infiltration project, the POW was taken to the OSS unit's operational command center. There, the recruit underwent training, studied maps of that section of the front he would be operating in, and tutored on a plausible cover story should he be stopped on the other side. At the command center, the POWs were joined by a number of civilian prospective agents, including several women. One of the latter, a German army nurse named Maria, had previously been the mistress of a Gestapo officer and proved an especially popular addition to the team. As the author of an official CIA history of the Moselle missions delicately explained, Maria "was accustomed to being around soldiers and never claimed to possess the highest moral standards. While at the SSS [Strategic Services Section] training areas, she ingratiated herself to agent and ally alike in a random and physical fashion."

There was one crucial feature of the POW infiltration missions that predicated all others: this was the decision that the German soldiers would go across in their own uniforms and under their own names. This negated any need for that most perilous accoutrement to a spy's life—the creation of a false identity—and lessened any dangers from a missing documents standpoint. The typical German soldier in World War II carried a formidable array of official papers with him, but any that had gone missing since a recruit's capture could be easily replicated in one of the OSS forgery labs. There was also little concern that a German sentry or Abwehr agent might question why a soldier whose unit had been stationed hundreds of miles away suddenly found himself on the Moselle River. The German retreat from France had been so swift and chaotic that different units were jumbled together all along the line, making a soldier's presence in any one spot nearly as plausible as anywhere else.

Of course, that still left the question of precisely *how* to get the spies across no-man's-land, and how to get them back. Initially, Hyde opted for the same tactics that had been used in Italy and western France: after frontline troops had probed for a weak or unguarded spot along the enemy line, the agent would be brought up and, under the cover of darkness, slip his or her way across. Along the more tightly controlled Moselle front, however, this approach proved unworkable, with several agents paying with their lives. Instead, the OSS tried something far trickier, and seemingly even more dangerous.

Taking advantage of the pattern of small advances and retreats that marked the Moselle battlefield, the OSS devised a scheme whereby a POW agent was brought up to near the front line, and then carefully hidden: in a barn cellar, for example, or in a hole dug deep in the woods. Once they were concealed, the Allied army unit holding that sector would fall back a short distance, ceding the ground to the enemy. After the advancing Germans had passed over the agent's hiding place, he would emerge and, clad in his old army uniform, innocently make for the rear. By prearranged timetable, and hopefully after sufficient time for the desired intelligence to be gathered, the agent returned to his original hiding spot and awaited the American counterattack that would recover the ceded ground.

It was a brilliant ploy, and so masterfully executed by Sichel and his colleagues that, of some thirty agents sent across the Moselle line, only two were lost.

But also lost was an OSS officer of unusual pedigree. By odd coincidence, at almost the very moment that Michael Burke was being reunited with Ernest Hemingway at the Ritz Bar in Paris in the autumn of 1944, the writer's eldest son, John "Jack" Hemingway, deployed alongside Peter Sichel in the Moselle sector, fell prisoner to the Germans.

As a junior member of the Seventh Army OSS unit, Jack Hemingway had been sent up to the front to assist Sichel and his partners in the infiltration operation, although what kind of assistance he might provide was subject to debate. "Jack was the most beautiful, dumbest man I have ever met," Sichel recalled. "A very sweet guy, and not a bad bone in his body, but you wouldn't trust him to bring in the mail."

At the end of October, Hemingway and an OSS colleague had been scouting the location for a future "agent drop" when they stumbled straight into a unit of German mountain troops. Within seconds, both Americans had been shot, with Hemingway taking rounds to his right arm and shoulder, and taken prisoner. It wasn't long before the Germans learned one of their captives was the son of the famous writer and, with Ernest Hemingway enjoying a surprisingly large fan base within the Nazi leadership, Jack spent the remainder of the war in the relative comfort of some of Germany's better prisons. "I saw Jack after the war," Sichel recalled, "and I asked him, 'Jack, what the hell happened up there?' He just sort of laughed about it."

Along with the ground infiltration operations, the need for intelligence from deeper inside Germany led the Seventh Army OSS unit to send some of their agents across on "tourist missions." These involved parachuting agents up to fifty or sixty miles inside enemy territory, who would then go on a "walking tour" along a prearranged route. Told to take meticulous note of any installations they passed of military interest, the tourist spies then relayed their findings to high-flying communications planes by means of an ingenious and compact two-way radio, known as a Joan-Eleanor, that allowed for "in the clear" conversations while being virtually impossible for the enemy to track.

In recalling his involvement in the Moselle infiltration scheme, Sichel was very proud of the fact that all the spies he recruited held up; not one of them defected or simply took advantage of his freedom to make for home. And even though two of those recruits were killed, in similar OSS operations across Europe, the mortality rate was often over 50 percent. "And those guys knew those odds going in," Sichel said of his agents, "that there was a very good chance they would be caught and executed. And not just executed, but tortured to death—what the Germans did to traitors or spies was horrific—but they did it anyway. They were a good bunch of people, true German patriots."

This peculiar line of work—recruiting spies; slipping them across no-man's-land; waiting to see if they returned—was to be a prominent feature of Sichel's life for the next fifteen years. He received a first hint of that in late January 1945, when he was briefly pulled off the Moselle front to attend a series of OSS conferences in London and Paris. Initially, a chief topic of conversation at these meetings was how the agency might combat a new threat that, by most accounts, lay in wait for the American army once it crossed into Germany: the Werewolves. For months, rumors had circulated through Allied headquarters telling of bands of Nazi fanatics organizing into guerrilla cells to wage a terror campaign against the enemy invaders. Even with the regular German army defeated, it was feared, continuing attacks by roving bands of Werewolves might extend the war for months, even years.

At the OSS strategy sessions, Peter Sichel was dismissive of the Werewolf threat. When asked why, his answer was simple: "Because they're Germans. Germans don't do insurgencies. They need a leader to tell them what to do. Once you get the Nazi leadership, trust me, resistance will collapse. They'll all want to be your friend and tell you how little they did for the Nazis."

In the near future, Sichel would be proven right. After Nazi Germany formally surrendered in early May 1945, only a handful of isolated and small-scale attacks were directed at the Allied occupiers, the vaunted Werewolves proving largely a myth.

But of all the back-base meetings Sichel attended as the war wound down, the one that most stood out took place in Paris in early February, shortly before he was scheduled to return to the front. It began with a summons from a pair of senior OSS commanders on a recruitment drive.

Even with the passage of over seven decades, Sichel vividly recalled the two men who sat across from him in that Paris office. Although only in their early thirties, they bore insignia indicating they were in the senior ranks of the OSS. One was tall and urbane, with an old-world manner about him. This was thirty-one-year-old Richard Helms, most recently the deputy head of Secret Intelligence in OSS London, and a future director of the CIA. The other, stocky and intense and clearly in charge, was thirty-five-year-old Frank Wisner.

Sichel sensed a kindred spirit in Helms. "He very much had a European manner about him: calm, soft-spoken. He had been raised in Paris, you know, and educated at a Swiss boarding school, so almost at once there was a familiarity between us. We became close friends, and remained so for the next fifty years."

He found Frank Wisner much harder to read.

"He was extremely polite, and obviously very intelligent, but there was a kind of tension, a nervousness, about him. And he was a Southerner, of course. I hadn't really been around many Southerners at that point, so it was hard for me to square his energy level, his dynamism, with this soft accent, this gracious quality of his."

But as their talk on that February afternoon progressed, Sichel was most struck by the passion with which Wisner spoke. This was especially true when Wisner recounted having witnessed the Red Army's deportation of the ethnic Germans of Romania the month before. "He was very emotional about that. You could see right away that this was a man who felt things deeply, who wore his heart on his sleeve. That's not something you see very often among people in this line of work and . . . well, frankly, it troubled me a little."

Pressed to explain, Sichel groped for something more. "Frank took things personally. And in this business, you can't ever take it personally."

At that Paris meeting, Wisner and Helms explained why they had summoned Sichel. By early February 1945, the German last-gasp offensive into the Ardennes, better known as the Battle of the Bulge, had foundered and British and American forces were now pushing toward the western reaches of Germany itself. On the opposite side of Germany, a massive Soviet offensive in late January had brought the Red Army to just forty miles east of Berlin. Even with the issue of the Werewolves still a topic of concern, it was now clearly only a matter of time—and probably not much time—before the Third Reich collapsed. In anticipation of this, William Donovan was quietly working to ensure that a number of his top field officers were not demobilized or sent on to Asia, but remained in Europe, there to form the nucleus of a peacetime OSS station in Germany. Wisner and Helms were among the first chosen for this mission, and they in turn were selecting others. Having received glowing reports about Peter Sichel from both OSS and regular army commanders all the way from Algiers to eastern France, the Wunderkind from Mainz was a prime candidate.

Sichel readily agreed to stay on in Europe until the end of his service—whenever that might be—and to resist any efforts to transfer him to Asia. "I was a first or second lieutenant," he recalled, "totally innocent, and here these guys were above me in rank, much more sophisticated, and American-born. I was flattered, frankly. I mean, they asked me for the dance, and I was willing to dance."

While Sichel may not have fully thought it through, there appeared to be a certain illogic to this initiative of Donovan's. After all, the OSS was a wartime agency, and since in early 1945 the war against Japan was expected to continue for many months, even years, reason dictated that the OSS's best and brightest not be left lolling about a peacetime Germany, but rather dispatched to Asia forthwith. The unspoken truth of the matter, though, is that William Donovan was already preparing for the new contest that, in his mind, seemed all but certain to occur in Europe after Hitler's demise, that between the Soviet Union and the Western allies. If this contest did come to pass, the kind of espionage work Peter Sichel was just then performing for the Seventh Army in northeastern France would have extraordinary currency indeed.

———

By the time the U.S. Seventh Army crossed into southern Germany in early March 1945, its attendant OSS detachment numbered over one hundred officers. Chosen to head one of its vanguard units was twenty-two-year-old Peter Sichel.

For their push into the German heartland, Sichel's OSS team was given two broad directives. The first was straightforward. Working off lists of names and accompanying photographs, in each town and village the Seventh Army passed through, OSS officers were to search for any high-ranking Nazi officials who might be trying to hide or slip away, along with a number of scientists who had worked in the regime's various weapons programs.

The second directive was a good deal more enigmatic.

"Uranium," Sichel said. "Uranium mines, uranium storehouses, factories where it was being refined; we were told to watch out for anything like that. Also any large stores of metallic calcium. At the time, I had no idea what that was about—none of us did—but when you're in the Army, you just do what you're told and don't ask questions."

What it was about, of course, was atomic weapons, and even if few people had any inkling of such a thing in early 1945, the issue had already carved the first fissure in the West-Soviet military alliance.

In the late 1930s, scientists began to achieve a series of breakthroughs in the field of nuclear physics that, if theory held, might have tremendous application in the arenas of both energy and weaponry. As with so much of cutting-edge science and technology at the time, many of the leading pioneers in nuclear research were German, and this included a number of German Jews. It is one of the great ironies of history—an irony for which the world should be eternally grateful—that the malignant anti-Semitism of Adolf Hitler had caused most of these German Jewish scientists to flee abroad by the mid-1930s, thus ending Germany's lead in nuclear research and development. While Hitler continued Germany's atomic program, and his scientists continued to amass the uranium necessary to build a workable weapon, the führer increasingly directed the Nazi arms industry to concentrate their development efforts on rocketry, convinced that this would more quickly yield the "secret weapon" that might save his regime. Obviously, he was wrong on all counts.

By early 1945, scientists and analysts involved in the United States' own top secret atomic weapon program, the Manhattan Project, were fairly confident they were well ahead of whatever the Nazis might be working on in the field, but naturally wanted to be absolutely sure. As American troops pushed into western Germany, advance intelligence units like Sichel's OSS detachment were alerted to be on the lookout for any telltale signs of the Nazi atomic program, even as they were not told why.

But if Sichel's men didn't grasp the reason behind the hunt for Nazi uranium and metallic calcium, another American advance team did. Known as the Alsos Mission, and including scientists versed in the work of the Manhattan Project, the highly secretive unit had operated at the vanguard of the Allied army since shortly after D-Day, roving over the vast battlefield in search of both potential German atomic weapon facilities, and of several dozen scientists known to be involved in the German development program. Led by a colonel of Russian extraction named Boris Pash, Alsos operatives had extraordinary authority to go wherever they wanted whenever they wanted, and to commandeer regular army units for their purposes if necessary.

But this wasn't the full story behind the Alsos Mission either. From the very inception of the Manhattan Project, President Roosevelt directed that, while British and Canadian scientists would be invited to collaborate on the venture, knowledge of the work being done, including that at the main testing facility of Los Alamos in New Mexico, would be limited to the smallest handful of senior Allied officials possible. This shroud of secrecy produced some curious anomalies, including the fact that while the British and Canadian prime ministers knew of the Manhattan Project, the American vice president did not.

Also kept in the dark—at least so American and British leaders believed—was the third principal member of their alliance, the Soviet Union. Although it had long been known that the Soviets were pursuing their own atomic program, the consensus of American and British scientists in early 1945 was that they lagged far behind—and those officials privy to the secrets of the Manhattan Project were intent on keeping it that way. In actuality, a British scientist involved, Alan Nunn May, had been passing information to the Soviets as early as 1943, and even if his material wasn't detailed enough to accelerate the Soviets' own atomic program, it was enough to keep them generally apprised of progress at Los Alamos.

All of this resulted in the kind of unspoken cat-and-mouse paradox that would become such a regular feature of the Cold War about to descend. By striving to keep their Soviet ally in the dark about the Manhattan Project—knowledge the Soviets were surreptitiously gleaning on their own—the Americans and British were also stoking the suspicions of their ally as to their ultimate intentions, and the longer this failed secrecy was maintained, the deeper those suspicions became. At the same time, the Soviets couldn't protest their exclusion from the atomic club, because that would tip the Americans and British to the fact that they had already penetrated their wall of secrecy through spying.

Where this became quite fascinating was in how it played out on the German battlefield. If either side—and that term in itself has significance, since it points to the cleavage already forming in the alliance—was to appear overly anxious to take possession of Germany's uranium stores, it might alert the other side that their own atomic program was sufficiently advanced as to appreciate the need for it. To forestall that, as World War II drew to a close, both the Americans and the Soviets were operating highly specialized and highly secretive search teams in a race to grab up German atomic scientists and facilities before the other could, without ever acknowledging that such a race existed.

But just as in the Cold War to come, this complex reverse-psychology game was capable of playing out with very tangible and very tragic consequences. Such was the case with the German city of Oranienburg on the mid-afternoon of March 15, 1945.

Located just ten miles north of Berlin, Oranienburg until that time had largely escaped the massive Allied bombing runs that had turned so many German cities to ash. This was because earlier smaller-scale bombing attacks had largely destroyed Oranienburg's few objects of military value—a couple of factories by the Havel River, a small railroad junction—leaving little to recommend it for more. Just a few weeks earlier, however, Allied aerial spotters had determined that one of the factories by the river had been retrofitted to process enriched uranium. Something else worried American atomic scientists even more: by mid-March, advance units of the Soviet Red Army were just a few miles outside Oranienburg as they began their encirclement of Berlin. Desperate to prevent its uranium stores from falling into Soviet hands, General Leslie Groves, the director of the Manhattan Project, ordered Oranienburg to be bombed anew. Not to the scale it had been struck in the past; this time, the city was to be wiped out.

Over the span of forty minutes on the afternoon of March 15, over six hundred American B-17 bombers dropped 1,500 tons of high explosives on the center of Oranienburg, obliterating the city and marking it as the site of one of the greatest concentrations of conventional explosives in world history. That wasn't the worst of it, however. Most of the bombs dropped on the city were equipped with a recently developed time-delay fuse. In contrast to the traditional explode-on-impact bomb, the detonation of these depended on the speed of an internal chemical reaction that triggered their firing pins, a process that might take several minutes or hours or even days. Or decades, as it turned out. Due to a peculiarity of Oranienburg soil composition, hundreds of the bombs dropped in March 1945 failed to explode at the time, but have done so intermittently ever since, killing residents and earning Oranienburg the title of "the most dangerous city in Germany."

The city might also bear the title of first victim of the Cold War for, when the Red Army entered Oranienburg a few days later, they found a place reduced to dust. Even the enriched uranium pile was gone. Of course, Soviet leaders knew precisely why the Berlin suburb had been destroyed, but to protest would have tipped the Americans and British that the Soviets understood what had been stolen from them. Instead, and in keeping with the strange rules of the shadow game now being played between the Allies, they kept quiet.

Of all these complicated machinations at the dawn of the Cold War, Peter Sichel was totally unaware. He would soon gain an education, though, and he would prove a quick learner.

5

THE MAN WHO COULD DISAPPEAR

By September 22, 1945, a seemingly never-ending procession of naval ships passed under the Golden Gate Bridge into San Francisco Bay. They were bringing home the first of several million American soldiers who had served in the Pacific theater of World War II, officially ended just three weeks earlier. Given the exuberant celebrations that accompanied these homecomings—ship horns sounded incessantly across the bay at all hours of the day and night—probably very few took notice of a loaded troopship, the USS *Uruguay*, that cast off from a San Francisco pier that day and headed in the opposite direction. On board were some 4,500 servicemen being dispatched to peacetime duty in East Asia. Among them was a slender thirty-seven-year-old Army major named Edward Geary Lansdale, a former ad agency executive with a pencil mustache and a peculiar—one might even say unnerving—glitter to his eye.

To use a phrase popularized during World War II, Lansdale had not had "a good war." Very much the opposite, in fact. Although he had rushed to enlist after the Japanese attack on Pearl Harbor, doctors discovered a dormant thyroid condition that, combined with his age and domestic situation—he was a married father of two in 1941—all but precluded him ever seeing active service. With that path effectively barred, Lansdale had maneuvered his way into a stateside position with the Office of Strategic Services, but even if his work there was important to the war effort, it reduced the adman to what combat troops derisively termed "a Remington raider," a soldier in name only, his command post a desk and a Remington typewriter. It clearly rankled; for the rest of his life, Lansdale would subtly round the edges of his wartime service, implying that he'd seen active service.

Yet, from this most unpromising of starts, on the day he climbed aboard the *Uruguay*, Edward Lansdale was about to become one of the most celebrated and influential military intelligence figures of the coming Cold War, a theorist who painstakingly studied and then sought to emulate the enemy. So vast was his impact that he would serve as the thinly disguised protagonist of one best-selling book, *The Ugly American,* and quite possibly of a second, *The Quiet American,* and be named by a CIA director as one of the ten greatest spies in modern history. On a darker and more exotic note, he would be portrayed in the 1968 film *Ombre sur Angkor,* starring Prince Sihanouk of Cambodia, as the murderous CIA villain, Colonel Mansdale. Director Oliver Stone would tread the same conspiratorial ground in his movie *JFK,* even as he coyly denied that his General Y, the evil mastermind of the plot to assassinate President Kennedy, was a Lansdale stand-in. "I consciously backed away from the Lansdale business," Stone dissembled, "but obviously it would have been someone *like* a Lansdale." With the possible exception of Henry Kissinger, it's hard to think of a modern figure involved with American foreign policy quite so polarizing, simultaneously "a freedom fighter among freedom fighters . . . a Lawrence of Asia," and a man for whom "assassinations and exterminations are as often as the meals he takes every day."

But if, in September 1945, there were few indications of Lansdale's impending importance and notoriety, there were even fewer suggestions of it in his background.

The second of four sons born to an automobile industry executive and his stay-at-home wife, Lansdale had led a peripatetic childhood, as his restless, entrepreneurial father hopped from one auto-related company to another. By the age of fourteen, the boy had already been uprooted and dropped into new homes across America at least a half-dozen times, until the family finally settled in rapidly growing Southern California in the early 1920s.

In 1927, Lansdale—"Ed" to family and friends—graduated from Los Angeles High School and entered UCLA, but beyond an inchoate interest in writing, no career path truly compelled. Through college he had the habit of signing up for classes that interested him rather than those that might bring him closer to a marketable degree. He also proved less than a stellar student, distracted by an array of extracurricular activities and his holding down a variety of odd jobs. Ironically, considering it was Lansdale's knack for communicating with foreigners that would later set him on the path to fame, the insurmountable stumbling block toward his getting a degree was UCLA's foreign language requirement. As he explained to biographer Cecil B. Currey, he had absolutely no aptitude in that sphere, and retained little beyond some Spanish cusswords and a few French phrases he remembered from kindergarten. "I'm a typical American that way."

Because of that language requirement, and still with no career goal beckoning, Lansdale dropped out of UCLA just a few credits short of graduation. Provided the names of a couple of newspaper editors by a family friend, he instead struck out for New York City in the autumn of 1931 with hopes of becoming a journalist.

But 1931 was a bad time to enter almost any profession, let alone journalism. With the country in the grip of the Great Depression, American papers were firing, not hiring; in fact, one of the New York newspapers that Lansdale considered among his most promising prospects shuttered just as he got there. With the help of another family friend, Lansdale landed a job as a file clerk in a railroad administration office that, although stupefyingly dull, at least enabled him to stay on in New York until something better came along.

Shortly after, at the age twenty-four, Lansdale began dating a strikingly pretty young woman named Helen Batcheller, a secretary at a hardware company similarly struggling to make it in New York. The two soon married but, as noted by Currey, it was an unlikely pairing from the start: "Lansdale was a handsome young man, outgoing, with a sometimes raucous sense of humor, who sincerely enjoyed the company of other people. Helen was a serious girl, sober and quiet, most comfortable when the two were alone." Years later, according to Currey, when the youngest Lansdale brother, David, asked Ed what had been the initial attraction to Helen, his brother offered a spare and rather pitiful answer: "We were both very lonely."

In his free time away from the railroad office, Lansdale tried to break into the New York literary world, at whatever level that world would take him. He wrote plays, satirical articles, humorous cartoons. Nothing worked. With his writerly aspirations going nowhere, he eventually lost heart and was lured back to Los Angeles by his eldest brother, Phil. Working in the advertising department of a Los Angeles–area chain of men's clothing stores called Silverwoods, Phil was looking for an assistant and offered his younger brother the job at the princely sum of $15 a week, along with the use of an apartment. Even though the pay was a fraction of what Lansdale was making at his New York clerking job, in the summer of 1935 he and Helen packed up their few possessions and moved across the country.

And it was in advertising that Ed Lansdale seemed to discover his calling. For the next two years, he worked under his brother at Silverwoods, but used the time to closely study and analyze most every aspect of the advertising business. By 1937, he decided to strike out on his own, and he and Helen moved to San Francisco. After apprenticing at one of the city's smaller advertising firms and proving himself a natural, Lansdale was recruited away by the Leon Livingston Agency, one of San Francisco's most successful. From then on, everything clicked together nicely. By the summer of 1941, the Lansdales had moved to a pleasant home in the bedroom community of Larkspur, and Helen was raising their infant son, Ted, with a second child expected that November. As for Ed, he was earning some $5,000 a year at Livingston—nearly seven times what he'd made at Silverwoods—and working on ad campaigns for such high-profile local clients as Wells Fargo and Levi Strauss & Company. At long last, the thirty-three-year-old Lansdale had arrived: funny, spirited, and with that pencil mustache that gave him a passing resemblance to Clark Gable, he charmed clients and coworkers alike.

Then came Pearl Harbor.

Along with millions of other American men, Lansdale joined in the stampede to enlist. He had undergone several years of ROTC training in high school and at UCLA, and he hoped that would ensure a junior officer's assignment. Working against him, though, was both his age and the colloid goiter that showed up in a routine medical exam. Despite his insistent appeals, Lansdale's Selective Service classification was downgraded to III-A, making it highly improbable he would ever be called up for frontline service.

But with the war on, Lansdale found it intolerable to simply continue as before. Through friends in New York, in the summer of 1942 he managed to finagle a position with the San Francisco branch of the newly created Office of Strategic Services, with the job title of intelligence agent. Since no one could quite tell him what an intelligence agent was meant to do, Lansdale rendered his own interpretation and decided it made him a sort of free-ranging detective, a field investigator at liberty to wander—both physically and academically—wherever his inquiries might take him. This also marked the genesis of what Ed Lansdale would become, a kind of cultural anthropologist in the field of human conflict.

Drawing on his former aspirations as a journalist, Lansdale took to tracking down and questioning people who had traveled to offbeat places in Europe and Asia that might be of interest to American field command-ers as they fought for territory seized by Germany and Japan. This was augmented by exhaustive interviews of recent émigrés or refugees. When not acting as a gumshoe, Lansdale was likely to be at the San Francisco central library, poring through obscure scientific or technical journals as he pursued specific matters of potential military value. As his eldest son, Ted, explained: "He quickly found that, by asking the right questions of people, he could gather all kinds of useful information. 'You were in Hong Kong? Can I see your photographs?' He'd pinpoint different land-marks, different topographical features that might be important for war planners. It was the same with the library research. He always said it was incredible how much intelligence you could piece together from open sources. You just had to know where to look."

Lansdale's surviving notebooks of the time give a hint of his wide-ranging interests and investigations. In one, he identified a certain Charles Nordhoff as knowing "a great deal about fishing methods around Tahiti . . . should know about crews and commercial methods there." Colonel Guillaume Cognac, the French governor of Cochin China, was a shady character who was so paranoid about anti-French secret societies that "he heard the grass grow," while François Bernardini, the owner of a café in the Arab quarter of Fez, was extremely well informed about com-ings and goings in that Moroccan city, but had to be approached in just the right way: "Very touchy personality. A Corsican. Mention Monguio." In the search for potentially useful information, no angle was too obscure to pursue, no detail too trifling to note down.

Greatly aiding Lansdale's sleuthing was his personality. Possessed of an easy manner with people, along with a genuine curiosity in their stories, sources tended to quickly trust and confide in him. He appeared to have a special skill in talking with Asian Americans. Even before World War II, many Asian Americans routinely suffered abuse at the hands of Anglos, and that situation had inevitably grown far worse since Pearl Harbor. In Edward Lansdale's relaxed and solicitous manner, however, there seemed to be a singular lack of prejudice, a quick acceptance of cultural differ-ences. Even without a shared language, Lansdale soon became the go-to guy in the San Francisco OSS office when it came to questioning Koreans or Japanese or Filipinos.

Lansdale's OSS superiors took note of his doggedness, and then so did the regular Army. When at very long last his officer's commission came through in February 1943, he was made a first lieutenant and seconded to the Army's own unimaginatively named intelligence agency, the Mil-itary Intelligence Service, or MIS. This didn't represent a break with the

Victorious Red Army soldiers plant the Soviet flag atop Berlin's Brandenburg Gate on May 2, 1945. Within months of the fall of the Axis powers in World War II, an exhausted world was descending into the grips of a new global conflict: the Cold War.

A young Frank Wisner in his own version of a cowboy outfit. Despite a series of debilitating childhood illnesses, a fiercely determined Wisner grew into a star athlete and academic overachiever—on his way to becoming America's preeminent Cold War spymaster.

Married and the father of two young children, in 1941 the thirty-two-year-old Wisner appeared destined for a life of conventional success as a highly regarded Wall Street lawyer. Instead, on the eve of America's entry into World War II he cast it all aside to join the navy as a lieutenant, junior grade.

William "Wild Bill" Donovan, the director of America's wartime intelligence agency, the Office of Strategic Services (OSS). With the OSS, Donovan sought to emulate Britain's MI6 well-heeled "club of gentlemen" with the recruitment of the likes of Frank Wisner, but he also brought in "men of action" based on personal whim.

Outrageous good fortune: Michael Burke, a maritime insurance investigator desperate to join the war effort, was invited into the OSS after a chance encounter with Donovan at a Washington dinner party. Surviving a series of perilous commando missions, including being air-dropped behind Nazi lines in France, Burke was sustained by the naïve belief that bad things only happened to other people.

In wartime Cairo, Wisner was marooned behind a desk and far from the action. His luck changed in 1944 when he was dispatched to Turkey to try to salvage one of the worst Allied intelligence fiascoes of World War II.

In Romania in the fall of 1944, Wisner was one of the first American soldiers to observe firsthand the actions of the Soviet Red Army in liberated Europe. Despite getting along well with individual Red Army commanders, as shown here, Wisner sent increasingly alarmed secret cables to Washington warning of Moscow's imperialist designs in the region.

During his wartime tenure in Romania, Wisner enjoyed a flirtatious relationship with his hostess, Princess Tanda Caragea. Rumors of a romance with Caragea were to haunt Wisner for decades to come, a handy weapon for his Washington rivals to keep the future spymaster in check.

In a life marked by improbable highs and lows, none were quite so dramatic as those experienced by Burke in the fall of 1945. In a matter of weeks, he was transformed from a down-and-out war vet wandering the streets of New York with a broken heart to a highly paid Hollywood script consultant, dating starlets and hobnobbing with the likes of Gary Cooper, pictured here. Then, almost as swiftly, it all went terribly wrong again.

Berlin: Ground zero of the close of one war and the start of a new. In their wholesale looting of occupied Germany, Soviet soldiers had a special obsession with grabbing watches. Before releasing this iconic photograph of Red Army soldiers atop the German Reichstag, alert Kremlin censors first airbrushed out one of the *two* watches adorning the lower soldier's wrists.

In their pillaging of Berlin, the Soviets organized Trummerfrauen, or "rubble women," into bucket brigades to sift through the ruins to find anything of value. Streetcar rails, salvageable bricks—even door hinges and nails—were then loaded onto railroad cars and shipped east.

Peter Sichel, who escaped from Nazi Germany as a teenager, was dubbed "the Wunderkind" within the OSS, renowned for his ability to work wartime currency black markets. To confront the veritable army of Soviet intelligence officers and informants in postwar Berlin, Sichel was put in charge of the primary U.S. covert intelligence unit in the city. The unit consisted of a mere nine officers, and Sichel had just turned twenty-three.

A former ad agency executive with a hint of the rogue about him. Already in his thirties and with a medical condition, intelligence officer Edward Lansdale spent World War II stranded stateside. When he was finally dispatched to the postwar Philippines, his Madison Avenue-inspired ideas to "sell" the American way of life abroad would make him one of the most influential—and unlikely—counterinsurgency experts in the unfolding Cold War.

As a communist and anti-American insurgency gained strength in the Philippine countryside, Lansdale became determined to make contact with its renegade leader. To do so, Lansdale enlisted the help of a local female journalist, Pat Kelly, whom he knew to be in secret contact with the communists. To complicate matters, Landale and Kelly also began a romance that would last their lifetimes.

Luis Taruc, the commander of the Huk communist insurgency in the Philippines, and the man Lansdale hoped to meet.

OSS, though. Instead, contractually tied to the two agencies, Lansdale spent the next two years working for both OSS and MIS. This habit of wearing two hats was one the former advertising executive would repeatedly employ in the years ahead, and it was to prove very useful in leaving people forever guessing where his true affiliations lay.

Well into 1944, Lansdale continued his investigations for the OSS and MIS, with his intelligence-gathering forays taking him throughout the American West. In Salt Lake City, he met with a former Mormon missionary to Germany who passed on rumors of a Krupps munition factory built completely underground in the German town of Neubrandenburg. With the help of a renowned ichthyologist, he compiled a master list of the poisonous fish of the South Pacific. All the while, Lansdale was sought out to produce specialized training manuals for incoming OSS agents— somewhat odd considering that he'd never received any OSS training at all. "Maybe they thought I didn't need it," he later theorized.

So varied and endlessly fascinating was the work that it largely ameliorated Lansdale's disappointment at not being dispatched to the field. It similarly eased the separation from his family when, following the shuttering of the MIS San Francisco office in June 1944, he was transferred to New York City. He was still at that post when Japan surrendered in August 1945.

It is an old truism that what soldiers know of a war is often limited to what they see of the battlefield directly before them, that all else is mysterious or unimportant. In August 1945, almost the precise opposite was true of Edward Lansdale. Instead, due to his distant, bird's-eye view of a war that had spanned the planet, a view augmented by a thousand disparate interviews and insights, he was a kind of armchair field marshal, removed from the fog of the battlefield but able to see the greater historical and political currents at play. From that vantage point, what was utterly apparent to the former adman was that at the very moment one global conflict had ended, a new one was taking form. Already by that summer, signs of this new conflict were appearing across Europe, as the Soviets and their local communist allies sought to exploit vacuums of power. What perhaps Lansdale saw more clearly than most by virtue of his West Coast orientation was that a very similar phenomenon was about to play out in Asia.

With one great difference. In Europe, the Soviets had established a position of preeminence by liberating, at horrendous cost to themselves, the eastern half of the continent. In Asia, by contrast, the Soviets had only joined the war against Japan after the dropping of the atomic bomb on Hiroshima. To be sure, they had then taken maximum advantage of the situation—on the same day as the atomic blast in Nagasaki, a Red Army group had invaded Japanese-held Manchuria, followed a week later by a second advance into northern Korea and Japan's Kuril Islands—but there simply wasn't time for the Soviets to plant their flag as they had done in Europe. Still beyond their reach, and destined to remain that way with Japan's surrender, was well over 90 percent of the Asian continent.

But any American officials who found comfort in that statistic were overlooking another crucial difference between the European and Asian war theaters.

Despite the comic book narrative of good-versus-evil that was fed to the wartime American public about Germany and Japan (perhaps due to its military incompetence, Allied propagandists could never gin up much animus for fascist Italy), one of the more extraordinary features of World War II was the ability of both Axis powers to initially generate a popular appeal beyond their own national borders. This was especially remarkable when one considered that both Nazi Germany and Imperial Japan were rabidly nationalistic and peddled a mythology that touted their racial and cultural superiority. Yet, in their blitzkrieg advance into the Soviet Union in 1941, the Germans had been enthusiastically welcomed by many locals, with crowds lining roadways and city streets to applaud and urge them on. Largely unknown to the American public— certainly footage of it never found its way to moviehouse newsreels—the Japanese invaders met a similar reception as they marched into Saigon and Jakarta. While both fascist powers had almost instantly squandered these reservoirs of goodwill under a torrent of cruelty and mass murder, what had sparked the appeal in the first place?

In a word, hatred, but hatred spawned from disparate sources. In the Soviet Union, that hatred was largely a response to the brutality of the Stalinist regime, strengthened in the "lesser" republics—in places like Latvia or Ukraine—by resentment over their domination by ethnic Russians. In Asia, what initially rallied many locals to Japan's side was hatred of their colonial overseers, of being lorded over by the British or the Dutch or the French. So despised were these colonial masters, and so anxious were Asians to be rid of them, that Tokyo's cynical sloganeering about anti-imperialism and the Greater East Asia Co-Prosperity Sphere had found fertile ground.

All of which meant that, as they maneuvered for advantage in the new postwar era, the Soviet Union and the "Western democracies" each had a colonial problem on their hands that the other side might exploit. This posed only a limited danger for the Soviets in Europe, considering that Stalin had repeatedly displayed a willingness to slaughter restive populations, and was surely ready to do so again. For the Western imperial powers, however, impoverished after six years of war and now facing unrest in their far-off Asian colonies, the perils were stark and the options narrow: either placate their subjects by shedding colonialism's most odious aspects; begin dismantling it altogether; or resist change and wage battle with local insurgencies in which anticolonialist communist formations were sure to be in the vanguard.

Franklin D. Roosevelt had clearly anticipated this situation. In speeches going back to before the war, he had argued that the way forward for the United States was to be seen as an anticolonial force, as the Western power that wished to foster peaceful and democratic change in the developing world even at the expense of its imperial friends in Europe. Early indications, though, were that this message hadn't been taken on board by his successor, Harry Truman. Shortly after assuming office, and over the strenuous objections of most of his closest foreign policy advisors, Truman had blithely acceded to continued French rule in the Southeast Asian nation of Vietnam despite a growing and communist-led anti-French insurgency there.

Where all this got even trickier was that, in the eyes of many Asians, the United States was already an imperial power in its own right, as exemplified by its rule of the Philippines. Ever since wresting the islands from Spain in the Spanish-American War of 1898, the United States had exerted total control over the Philippines. And much like the European colonizers in the region, the Americans came to dominate most every aspect of the economic and political life of their new possession, a domination codified by a series of one-sided treaties and rule by a resident American governor-general.

At the same time, control of the Philippines had been a deeply contentious issue in the United States from the very outset—for good reason, many saw it as empire-building, making the United States "no better than the Europeans"—and American diplomats had begun grooming the islands for independence as early as 1916. In fact, an official transfer of power was fast approaching when the Japanese invaded the Philippines in 1941. This went a long way toward explaining why the conquering Japanese never received the warm welcome accorded them in some other "liberated" Asian countries, and why the Filipino insurgency against them was so spirited.

To a strategist like Edward Lansdale, it was only logical that the first litmus test of American influence in postwar Asia would come in the place where that influence was already the strongest. If, in the coming contest with the Soviet Union, the Americans could come up with a plan to keep the Filipinos to their side, then it might serve as a model that could be transported elsewhere in Asia. Conversely, if the Americans couldn't figure out the Philippines, they were going to be in very deep trouble all across the continent.

Lansdale was given a chance to explore this theory firsthand. Just days before the atomic bomb was dropped on Hiroshima, he had at last been informed that he was being dispatched to the front, part of the massive army being assembled for the upcoming invasion of the Japanese home islands. His particular role in that enterprise was to join the Army intelligence (G-2) staff in the Asian country that would soon make him famous: the Philippines. Hiroshima ultimately nullified the invasion of Japan, of course, but not Major Lansdale's marching orders. It was those orders that put him aboard the USS *Uruguay* in San Francisco Bay, just as most every other American soldier was coming home.

———

As he traveled about the Philippines in the spring of 1946, a young Filipino army officer named Frank Zaldarriaga took note of a striking pattern. Attached to the psychological warfare bureau of the U.S. Army's Office of War Information, Zaldarriaga was attempting to take the pulse of his country, so recently freed from Japanese occupation, and that meant not just getting out of the capital city of Manila, but venturing into some of the more remote reaches of the Philippine archipelago. Wherever he went, though, it seemed there was always someone around to ask the question: "Do you know Lansdale?"

In fact, Zaldarriaga *did* know Ed Lansdale, but the prevalence of the question underscored just how vast a network of friends and acquaintances the American intelligence officer had established within mere months of his arrival in the Philippines. "He could make a friend of everybody but Satan, I think," Zaldarriaga said. "This man was a legend. Wherever I went, he was [already] known."

It could be argued that, as the new deputy chief of staff of Army intelligence in the Philippines, it was rather Lansdale's job to get out and talk to people, but that hardly explained the energy and exuberance he brought to the task. Instead, Lansdale in the Philippines appeared to be one of those rare instances of an outsider having an almost preternatural affinity for a foreign culture. Far beyond any job description, the intelligence officer seemed to regard it as his personal quest to experience and understand the Philippines as well as any foreigner might. Nor was his ubiquity limited to the hinterlands, where the presence of a gringo might naturally be remarked upon. Already by early 1946, the thirty-eight-year-old Army major so recently arrived from San Francisco was known to most of Manila's power class—its newspaper editors and politicians, its industrialists and union leaders—and was a fixture of the expatriate community's social circuit.

One person who came to know Lansdale quite well during this period was a Reuters correspondent named Peter Richards. From observing Lansdale in social settings, he noted an intriguing trait in the intelligence officer. "He made friends with everybody," Richards explained, "but the secret of his success is that he was a man who could disappear. He wasn't in the room, but he was. You get ten people in a room and he could make himself completely disappear. . . . That was one of his biggest assets. He was camouflaged."

A future CIA colleague of Lansdale's, Rufus Phillips, described him in almost precisely the same terms. "His manner wasn't flamboyant at all. He was a listener. He would skillfully get people talking to each other, and then he'd kind of recede. He was often the quietest guy in the room."

This ability to vanish into the background, to be quiet and to observe, was something others would remark upon throughout Lansdale's intelligence career, but it was joined to another quality almost as rare. Perhaps stemming from his earlier aspirations in journalism, he was also a keen student of body language, often focusing less on what people said than how they said it, and had a knack for forging ties that didn't rely on verbal communication. "The look in your eyes and your shoulders and your hands tell a lot when you're really concentrating," he explained. "People can tell whether you are interested or not just by your attitude and the attention you pay. . . . I've had to depend a great deal on a look of empathy, a physical look, and an ability to try to communicate without words."

The end result was a talent for developing an almost instant rapport with whomever Lansdale stood across from. "Ed operated at a genius level in terms of being able to understand people," Phillips observed, "of establishing a bond with them almost immediately. He had a very informal manner, so it wasn't like some American official was talking to you. He very quickly got on a different plane entirely with people."

All of this made Lansdale a natural fit in the famously easygoing Philippines, and it enabled him to extend his circle of friends well beyond Manila's English-speaking elite. Jumping into his Army-issue jeep and heading into the bush, he routinely ventured into regions of the country where only Tagalog, the Filipino official language, was spoken—and often even beyond the reach of Tagalog. Years later, Lansdale fondly remembered a long "conversation" he held with a tribal leader of the Negrito aboriginal minority despite their having only a single word—"okay"—in common. As he occasionally half-joked, some of his "best friends" he'd never actually spoken to.

But also aiding Lansdale in his Philippine travels was a characteristic fairly typical of the American abroad: a certain cheerful guilelessness, an uncomplicated amiability built on the belief that, so long as one is friendly with strangers, that treatment will be reciprocated. While a Briton abroad might *suspect* he is loathed, and a Frenchman knows full well that he is, the very idea is so alien to many Americans as to never cross their mind. Ironically, the sheer innocence of this outlook can be quite endearing and, thus, self-fulfilling.

In his memoir, *In the Midst of Wars,* Lansdale recounted the time he was steering his jeep along a back road in Pampanga province, a region known for its anti-American sentiment, when he came into a village where a young man was haranguing the residents on the evils of Yankee imperialism. Rather than beat a retreat, Lansdale parked his jeep, climbed onto its hood, and thought to compete with the speaker by shouting: "What's the matter? Didn't you ever have an American friend?" As the crowd turned in his direction, Lansdale—alone and wearing his American military uniform—began having second thoughts. "I kicked myself mentally for giving in to such an impulse among hundreds of people living in hostile territory."

But, as the intelligence officer may have intuited from previous encounters, any hostility evaporated. Within moments, the crowd had gathered around to pepper him with friendly questions, "naming Americans they had known and liked, and asking if I was acquainted with them." Among those vying for Lansdale's attention was the very man who had been shouting anti-American slogans minutes before. "It was a long time before I could get away from the gossipy friendliness."

What Lansdale may have also intuited, however, was that such solicitousness—redolent as it was of the "little brother" mind-set common to colonized peoples everywhere—was unlikely to last much longer. That's because by mid-1946, the Philippines was about to explode.

6

THE SENTINEL

The air was clammy, and smelled of mold and soiled clothes; more than one visitor likened it to a poorly ventilated men's locker room. Between the low ceilings and dim lighting, the warren of small rooms induced a powerful sense of claustrophobia, especially if one thought too long about this complex being thirty feet underground, or that ten feet of solid concrete stretched above one's head. Even if Adolf Hitler had escaped the gallows he so richly deserved, there could be at least some small measure of consolation that it was within this dank underground tomb, void of all sunlight and reeking of diesel fumes from overworked generators, that he spent the last three months of his life.

One of the first Americans to tour that infamous bunker beside the Berlin Reichschancellery was OSS Lieutenant Commander Frank Wisner. It was right around May 8, when the last remnants of Nazi Germany officially surrendered to the Allies.

In almost every room, papers and broken furniture lay strewn about, scattered by souvenir collectors, but left largely intact was a cramped exterior sitting room. Against one wall was a cloth-covered patterned couch, with a spread of blood over the armrest and cushion at one end. It was here, Wisner was told, that Hitler had shot himself in the head after he and his mistress, Eva Braun, bit into cyanide capsules. So damp was the underground lair that, even a week later, the blood on the couch was wet to the touch.

It was three months since William Donovan had selected Frank Wisner to head up the Secret Intelligence branch of the OSS that was to operate in peacetime Germany. Wisner had spent that time in careful preparation. After a month-long furlough home, he had returned to Paris in mid-March and, together with his newly appointed deputy, Richard Helms, continued putting his future team together.

It was undoubtedly the chaos of the moment, joined to force of personality, that had enabled Wisner to bluster his way past Soviet army checkpoints and enter Berlin just days after the Nazis' last stand there; at the time, the American front lines still lay some fifty miles to the west. He entered a twilight world of smoke and dust and ruin, of a once modern and cosmopolitan place collapsed into primitiveness, all made eerier by a blanketing silence. In Berlin's famous network of parks, most all trees and shrubs had long since been cut for firewood or shorn by artillery fire, and scattered about were the high dirt mounds of mass graves. More graves dotted the median strips of the city's once grand boulevards, the location of the dead marked by homemade crosses or, more often, by simple shards of metal or twisted pipe stuck upright in the dirt. The hush that lay over the city was occasionally interrupted by the crack of gunfire, sustained bursts suggesting reprisal killings or vigilante justice, a single shot perhaps denoting another suicide to add to the thousands that had already occurred. Many of those Berliners who were trapped by the Red Army's encirclement in mid-April and who had survived all the bombs and artillery shells and tank fire before the city's fall, remained concealed in cellars or in nooks carved from the ruins, hiding now from marauding gangs of looters and Red Army soldiers.

To Frank Wisner, one of the very few Americans to have now observed the Red Army's conduct in two conquered cities, the mistreatment he had seen visited on the residents of Bucharest paled to nothingness when set against that being inflicted on the survivors in Berlin. If not excusable, it was at least predictable. Not only was Berlin the capital of the regime that had unleashed unspeakable suffering upon the Soviet nation, but Red Army soldiers had been explicitly exhorted for years to take vengeance when the German downfall finally came. As that end drew near, Ilya Ehrenburg, one of the Soviet Union's most famed propagandists—in a 1943 manifesto, he had admonished Red Army soldiers that, "if you have not killed at least one German a day, you have wasted that day"—was positively ecstatic. "German towns are burning. I am happy. Germany, you now whirl round in circles, and burn, and howl in your deathly agony; the hour of revenge has struck."

If the days of killing were now ending, those of rape and robbery were just beginning. It was a crime spree tacitly encouraged by Stalin himself, who suggested that it was quite understandable, "if a soldier who has crossed thousands of kilometers through blood and fire and death has fun with a woman or takes a trifle." By some estimates, as many as two million German women would be raped in Soviet-occupied Germany during the first three months of peace, with at least 100,000 victims in Berlin alone. In a famous memoir entitled *A Woman in Berlin: Eight Weeks in the Conquered City,* the anonymous writer described how she and other Berliner women frantically sought to attach themselves to senior Soviet officers, the only somewhat reliable method of escaping gang rape at the hands of their subordinates. As for looting, by early May Soviet engineers were already dismantling entire German factories for shipment to the Soviet Union, while individual Soviet soldiers scoured the city for trophies. They had a curious obsession with watches. The most iconic photograph of Berlin's fall, that of Red Army soldiers planting the Soviet flag atop the roof of the Reichstag, had to be retouched prior to release in order to airbrush out one of the *two* watches being worn on one of the soldier's wrists.

Frank Wisner had probably been at war long enough to refrain from making a lot of pious judgments about all this; if not to the same scale as the Red Army, American and British troops had certainly left their own trail of rape and robbery across Western Europe. Yet, before his May visit to Berlin was over, the OSS commander was to be given another reminder of some essential division in the alliance that had defeated Germany, between its American and British components on the one hand, and its Soviet component on the other. It happened toward the end of his tour of the Führerbunker.

Following his erstwhile guide, Wisner climbed the stairs out of the bunker and emerged into an enclosed garden pitted by artillery fire. Just beyond the bunker doorway, he was shown a blackened depression in the ground—Wisner likened it to a shallow trench—alongside of which were scattered a number of gasoline cans. It was here, he was told, that the bodies of Hitler and Braun were brought after their suicides to be burned.

But there was something about the cremation spot that puzzled the OSS man. He was familiar enough with the properties of fire to know that it took intense and prolonged heat to fully cremate a human body, especially to break down its teeth, and an open, gasoline-fed fire like that in the Chancellery garden was unlikely to have been sufficient. Most suspiciously, the trench was void of ashes. "I have always believed," Wisner wrote sometime later, "that the Russians removed and took back to Russia for the most careful examination and analysis whatever grisly objects they may have discovered in the trench—and so as the result they have a good deal of knowledge which they have never seen fit to share with their former allies."

As history would show, Wisner had it exactly right. Immediately after capturing the Führerbunker, a Soviet investigative team swept up the remains found in the trench—they included a sizable section of jawbone with teeth attached—and spirited them to Moscow. In short order, Hitler's charred remains were positively and indisputably identified. Yet, for reasons clear only to him, Stalin chose to withhold this information—and not only from his American and British allies, but even from his most senior military commanders in the field. Rather than be allowed to savor their moment of victory, those commanders were exhorted to find the "fugitive" Hitler, and periodically chastised by Stalin for their continuing failure to do so. The full story of Hitler's end—and the fragment of jawbone that conclusively proved it—would not be revealed to the rest of the world until decades later.

But if Frank Wisner had suspected something was missing from the funeral pyre story, the more baffling question at the time was why? Contradicting his own soldiers in Berlin, what possible motive did Stalin have for withholding knowledge of Hitler's death from those who had fought alongside him for four years and who shared that very goal? For Wisner, a man trained in the law, who tried to deduce the logic behind actions, the lack of any clear-cut answers to this question was the most disquieting aspect of all.

In the weeks ahead, he and other American intelligence officers would be faced with an ever-expanding series of similar riddles about their Soviet ally, even as their ability to answer them sharply diminished; just days after Wisner's visit, Soviet authorities cut off access to Berlin. The ban effectively remained in place for the next two months.

Perhaps Frank Wisner sensed such a shutdown was coming. While passing through the ruined Reichschancellery after his tour of the bunker, he hastily grabbed up whatever souvenirs he could comfortably carry. These included a sketchbook and "several fistfulls [sic] of German Iron Crosses and decorations of lesser distinction."

━━━

For many months prior to Wisner's tour of the Führerbunker, global events had assumed an inevitable, if utterly ghastly, quality. The noose around Nazi Germany steadily tightened as the Allied armies of the Soviet Union, Great Britain and the United States closed on Berlin from all sides. In Asia, the war with Japan was also in its death throes, even if the agony looked to continue for some time. Already, though, enough of the fires of war were going out, enough of the survivors emerging from the ruins of the most colossally destructive conflict in human history, that the broad parameters of a postwar world could be discerned in the gloom. Then, at about 12:30 on the afternoon of April 12, while sitting for a portrait in the living room of his presidential retreat in Warm Springs, Georgia, Franklin Roosevelt came forward slightly in his chair and slapped his right hand to the back of his neck. "I have a terrific pain in the back of my head," he said. They were the president's last words. Less than an hour later, he was declared dead from a cerebral hemorrhage at the age of sixty-three.

With the war in Europe just days away from ending, and with so many millions anticipating the final hours of the Axis leaders, that it should be the American president who was suddenly felled came as a shock to people everywhere. It should not have. Within the president's inner circle, it had been well known for many months that Roosevelt's physical decline was both dramatic and accelerating. One government official who had seen him in February described him as looking "sort of dead and dug up." When considering the absolutely crucial juncture of history during which this deterioration was occurring, it is an eternal mark against that circle of intimates, as against Roosevelt himself, that they steadfastly did nothing to prepare for the eventuality of his passing. Instead, all the burdens and responsibilities of the most powerful elected position in the world abruptly descended on a man who, up until then, had been so peripheral to the running of the nation that the sum total of his private meetings with President Roosevelt consisted of two chats of less than fifteen minutes each. As Harry S. Truman confided to a group of journalists the day after he assumed the presidency, "when they told me yesterday what had happened, I felt like the moon, the stars and all the planets had fallen on me." In contemplating the small, unprepossessing man now standing in Roosevelt's place, that sentiment was shared by many others.

Raised on a farm in rural Missouri, Truman didn't enter politics until his late thirties, and only then after he had failed at or lost interest in a whole range of other professions: law clerk, storeowner, door-to-door salesman of automobile club memberships. He was a product of the Kansas City political machine—a hack, in layman's terms—but one so lowly that the machine only reluctantly backed Truman in the 1934 Democratic primary for a Missouri Senate seat after several more attractive candidates had begged off. To the surprise of most everyone, and largely thanks to a Democratic sweep in the 1934 national elections, that November saw the obscure Jackson County judge packing his bags for Washington as Missouri's junior senator.

Following a lackluster first term in the Senate, Truman only won his 1940 reelection primary when two Democratic challengers split the opposition vote, and then barely squeaked past his Republican rival in the general election. In his second term, Senator Truman finally gained a small measure of national notice when he chaired a committee investigating fraud and abuse in the defense industry, but this was enough to draw the attention of Democratic Party bosses. As Roosevelt set to run for a fourth presidential term in 1944, those bosses, fearing his popularity was waning, felt Roosevelt should offset his liberal Northeastern roots by having a moderate conservative on the ticket, and convinced him to drop his current vice president, populist Henry Wallace, in favor of Truman. Delegates to that summer's Democratic convention were clearly baffled by the move—on the eve of the voting, the only delegates committed to Truman were from his home state of Missouri—but through fierce backroom arm-twisting and deal-making, support gradually swung his way.

Not that this suggested any great bond on the Democratic ticket. Roosevelt and Truman reportedly appeared together only once on the campaign trail, and not again until their victory celebration on election night. During his ensuing three months as vice president, Truman was told little about the inner workings of the White House, and nothing at all about the atomic bomb research being conducted in the Manhattan Project. Little wonder, then, that on April 13 he should feel the planets had fallen on him.

Little wonder, as well, that in the first onslaught of responsibilities thrown at him, Truman largely tried to base his actions around a simple tenet: what would Franklin do? When it came to the conduct of the war, and America's relationship with its chief Allied partners, this precept at least provided the new president some guideposts to work within, as minimal as those guideposts were. Both an outspoken anti-imperialist and an ardent anti-communist, Roosevelt had obviously set those convictions far to one side in allying with Great Britain and the Soviet Union in 1941. Once in that arrangement, though, the president had stuck to a core principle: whatever political differences existed among the Big Three—and clearly they were vast—they would have to wait and be sorted out in the war's aftermath, that until the Axis was destroyed, nothing could be allowed to come between the Allies and their common purpose.

Across the war years, a number of tantalizing proposals had been floated to Roosevelt that promised American gain, but at the expense of the alliance—and almost invariably, at the expense of the Soviet Union in particular. These included the Hungarian government's 1944 attempt to forge a separate peace with the United States, to the exclusion of the Soviets, and any number of overtures from different German military commands in the last days of the war with offers of a stand-down of German forces on the Western Front so that they might continue fighting on the Eastern. Each time, Roosevelt had flatly rejected these proposals, not wavering from his stance that all surrenders must be unconditional and with the concurrence of all three Allies, that there would be no repeat of the backroom dealings and betrayals that had carried Europe into two world wars. Even if Roosevelt's rigidity on this score sometimes exasperated his counselors and his more morally dexterous British partner, Winston Churchill, it lent a rectitude to his dealings that he hoped would have a reassuring effect on an ever-suspicious Joseph Stalin.

As for why Roosevelt felt it so vital to keep Stalin to his side, there were two primary reasons, one quite high-minded, the other brutally self-interested.

The first was Roosevelt's dream of creating a United Nations, an international deliberative body that might address the world's crises so as to avert the sort of catastrophe it had just endured. This was essentially a reprise of Woodrow Wilson's League of Nations concept after World War I, but just as that idea had foundered on American isolationism, so Roosevelt's United Nations scheme would mean little if the Soviet Union—the world's newest superpower—stayed out.

And then there was Japan. Despite incremental progress on the Manhattan Project, well into 1945 American war planners envisioned at least another year of fighting, and as many as a million more Allied casualties, before Japan was beaten. "Allied" in this context was a misnomer, since thus far the United States had borne nearly the entire cost of fighting the Japanese in both blood and treasure. Far more appealing to President Roosevelt was the casualty breakdown in Europe, where the Soviet Red Army had suffered upward of 90 percent of all Allied casualties; in the cold rationale of war, if whole new legions of young men had to die defeating Japan, much better they be from Minsk than Chicago. Just as with his United Nations proposal, Roosevelt persistently tried to win from Stalin a promise that, once the conflict in Europe was concluded, the Soviet Union would join the continuing fight in Asia.

In return for Soviet commitments on these two matters, Roosevelt was willing to trade away a great deal—and in the eyes of his critics, he most certainly did. Over the course of two summit conferences of the Big Three leaders, first in Tehran in late 1943 and then in Yalta in February 1945, the broad, if tremendously vague, outlines of a postwar Europe began to take shape. Yes, borders might have to be redrawn slightly, and certain populations resettled, and of course it was vital that the Soviet Union should finally have secure and defensible borders, but beyond this was a general consensus among the Allies that out of the ashes of World War II would emerge a European constellation of peaceful and democratic states free of the thrall of imperial powers or their spheres of influence. Naturally, nothing could be firmly fixed as far as elections or interim governments at these early stages, but all would be worked out in the natural course of events.

It's doubtful that a single British official at either Tehran or Yalta fully trusted in these breezy platitudes—certainly Prime Minister Churchill didn't—and it's hard to believe American officials were any less skeptical. Save possibly one: Franklin Roosevelt. Even as late as Yalta in February 1945, when the Soviets' power-grab tactics had already been put on full display in Romania, the president seemed determined to publicly cling to a view of his Soviet counterpart so sanguine it suggested an almost willful naïveté. Famously illustrating this was the recollection of William Bullitt, Roosevelt's former ambassador to the Soviet Union. Having lived in Moscow through the Great Terror, Bullitt was forever urging the president to take a harder stand against Stalin, but was constantly rebuffed. "I firmly believe," Bullitt paraphrased Roosevelt in his memoir, "that if I give Stalin all he asks for—noblesse oblige—then he will be satisfied and not ask for more."

It is conceivable that Roosevelt actually believed this. Certainly, this was to be the accusation leveled by American conservatives in the near future when they came to regard the arrangements made at Tehran and Yalta as a colossal sellout of Eastern Europe, an eternal disgrace built on the gullibility—in a darker version, the culpability—of Franklin Roosevelt and his inner circle. Consistently missing in these right-wing attacks, however, was any coherent idea for what Roosevelt might have done differently. Theoretically, the Americans could have threatened war if the Soviets didn't live up to the agreements, but how would that have worked on a practical level? In Romania, for example, well over a half-million Red Army soldiers were still garrisoned in the country at war's end, matched up against perhaps two hundred American troops. If it came to a shooting match in the streets of Bucharest, how was that going to play out? Straighten Stalin out by imposing economic sanctions? When placed on an extreme totalitarian state like Stalin's Soviet Union, economic sanctions tend only to strengthen the grip of the regime over the masses, since soldiers and secret police are always the last to go hungry.

Instead of naïveté, Roosevelt's actions suggest that he simply hoped for the best. He tried to pin down Stalin when he could at Tehran and Yalta, but he was playing a very weak hand, and everyone—Stalin included—knew it. So, extend the game, play for time, and maybe the cards would improve.

And in fact, by early April 1945, the cards *were* improving. At the top secret Los Alamos facility in New Mexico, scientists were now very close to having a working prototype of an atomic bomb, a weapon so astoundingly devastating—at least in theory—that it might cause the Japanese to sue for peace far sooner than projected. That, of course, would nullify Roosevelt's need for the Soviets to come into the war in Asia, and if that core requisite went by the wayside, the president would have far more negotiating clout when next the Big Three leaders met. In concert with Roosevelt's extraordinary ability to charm, to bend others to his will, it all might have been enough to cause Stalin to soften his acquisitive designs in Eastern Europe. Then came April 12, and instead of Franklin Roosevelt sitting across from Winston Churchill and Joseph Stalin at the next Big Three conference, it would be Harry Truman.

That conference got under way on the afternoon of July 17, at a faux-Tudor mansion known as Cecilienhof in the Berlin suburb of Potsdam.

Despite Truman's reputation for plainspokenness and modesty—a reputation, incidentally, far more firmly affixed today than when he was alive—he was actually a complicated man. Possessed of the provincial's acute sensitivity to perceived condescension, he had a reflexive disdain for cultural elites—he especially disliked the mostly Ivy League–educated diplomats, the "striped pants boys" he called them, he had inherited from Roosevelt—and this often manifested in obstinacy; in Truman's world, the more his learned advisors tried to push him in one direction, the more apt he was to do the opposite. He tended to mask his insecurities behind a facade of utter certainty, so that once he made up his mind on an issue, he rarely wavered or reconsidered. He also had a country-store notion of how to deal with people, a belief that the best way to come to an understanding with a rival was to sit across a table from him, speak plainly and look him in the eye. Understandably, the thought of such a man going into negotiations with Churchill and Stalin, two of the century's greatest political gamesmen, caused many of the career American diplomats who accompanied Truman to Potsdam to shudder with dread.

Their fears would hardly have been allayed if they'd been privy to Tru-

man's self-satisfied musings after his first meeting with the Soviet dictator. "I can deal with Stalin," he wrote in his journal. "He is honest—but
smart as hell." Of the three assertions contained in those twelve words,
the new president would soon be proven wrong about the second one
and, as events would show, wrong about the first, as well.

For the next two weeks, the Big Three leaders conferred and parried
with one another at the Cecilienhof. As the time dragged on, Truman
gradually cooled toward Stalin; he seemed to grasp that what he'd first
perceived as blunt forthrightness in the generalissimo—a title Stalin had
given himself just before coming to Potsdam—was actually obduracy.

Truman continued to push the Soviet leader for the same two commitments that had been of such importance to Roosevelt at Yalta—that
the Soviet Union would join the war against Japan, as well as a postwar
United Nations organization—even as news Truman received on his first
day in Potsdam had the potential of rendering the first issue moot. In
the predawn of July 16, scientists in New Mexico detonated a prototype
of the atomic bomb, and its massive destructive force surpassed most all
expectations. The success of that test fueled a growing optimism among
American war planners that, once a few such bombs had been dropped
on Japan, it might bring the conflict to a quick close.

Yet, beyond pursuing those two issues, Truman soon became aware
of just how limited his options were to compel Stalin to do much of anything. In July 1945, Great Britain and the United States were demobilizing
soldiers at the rate of several thousand every day, while simultaneously
crating up much of their arsenal in Europe for redeployment against the
Japanese. By contrast, at least four million Red Army troops remained in
Eastern Europe. In essence Truman at Potsdam faced the same dilemma
Roosevelt had faced at Tehran and Yalta, that if cajoling Stalin failed, and
Britain and the United States tried threats, just what did they have to
back them up? As a result, and despite Truman's periodic outbursts of
annoyance with Stalin, there was a feeling of fait accompli about the Pots-
dam proceedings.

One of the most tragic outcomes was the fate of Poland. Since the slic-
ing up of Poland by Germany and the Soviet Union in 1939, Great Britain
had housed a Polish government-in-exile in London, and a quarter-
million Polish soldiers fought on the side of the Allies during the war.
Helping spur them on was a promise from Churchill that an independent
and democratic Poland would be established at war's end. At Yalta, Stalin
brushed that promise aside and, with Poland still completely occupied
by the Red Army, installed an interim puppet government of his choosing. Even worse, at Potsdam the *vozhd* finalized a Polish dismemberment

he had first proposed at Yalta. In defiance of its historical boundaries, Poland's eastern border was to be pulled back 120 miles, giving the Soviet Union ten million new citizens and some of the nation's best farmland, while Poland's western frontier would be extended ninety miles into Germany to incorporate some six million new inhabitants there. In one fell swoop, this redrawing of the map provided the Soviet Union with a vast and wealthy buffer zone on its western frontier; detached Prussia, the heartland of German militarism, from the German nation; and ensured that a war-shattered Poland would become little more than a Soviet vassal state.

But the reconfiguring of Poland was only part of Stalin's master plan to solve Europe's "German problem" once and for all. For these redrawn boundaries to work, he had argued at Yalta, populations had to shift so that different peoples could be joined to their own kind. In practice, what this meant was a "de-Germanization" policy that, over the next several years, would see the flight or forced expulsion of some twelve million ethnic Germans from their homes in Poland, East Prussia and Czechoslovakia, at a cost of at least a half-million dead. When the Americans and British feebly protested this scheme at Potsdam, Stalin breezily suggested such population transfers were already happening naturally. "Whenever the Germans see us coming," he pointed out, "they run anyway."

But amid the sad and ponderous deliberations at Potsdam, there came two remarkable moments. The first occurred on the evening of July 24 when, at the end of that day's meetings, President Truman casually walked around the large round table in the Cecilienhof banquet hall to chat with Stalin. So impromptu was this encounter that Truman wasn't even accompanied by his translator, but instead let Stalin's perform the duties.

In reality, though, everything about that encounter was carefully choreographed, for it was the moment Truman was to tell Stalin of the existence of the atomic bomb. Indeed, American and British diplomats had spent days debating the precise words—vague but substantive—that the president should use. Nor was this chat between the leaders quite as private as it appeared. Several Western officials in the banquet hall, including Churchill and his foreign minister, Anthony Eden, were cued to what Truman was about to say and, while feigning engagement in other conversations, carefully watched for Stalin's reaction.

After brief pleasantries, Truman let drop that the United States had developed "a new weapon of unusual destructive force." The comment appeared to barely register with Stalin, who only nodded and replied that he hoped the Americans would "make good use" of it. Since the *vozhd* displayed no great interest in the news, American and British officials agreed, it surely meant he hadn't deduced that Truman was referring to an atomic bomb. Over the following days, those officials quietly congratulated themselves on the narrow diplomatic needle that had been threaded: Stalin had been provided with an excellent clue, and he had only himself to blame for failing to pick up on it.

In their collective relief at that moment, few considered an alternative explanation for Stalin's reaction: that the *vozhd* didn't ask questions because he already knew the answers, and he didn't pursue the matter because this would have increased the odds of his allies figuring that out. On that same evening of July 24, according to a Soviet general at Potsdam, Stalin sent an urgent coded message to Moscow informing his own team of atomic scientists of the American breakthrough and demanding they speed up their work.

The other surprise at Potsdam occurred in something like slow motion. On the eve of the conference, Great Britain had held parliamentary elections, the results of which were greatly delayed by the need to count the ballots of servicemen scattered across the world. Consequently, it wasn't until midway through the proceedings that, to the slowly dawning shock of most everyone, it became clear that Churchill's Conservative Party had been routed by the Labour opposition. In the last days of Potsdam, then, it was not Churchill, a man beloved for having shepherded his nation through the war, who sat across the negotiating table from Stalin and Truman, but a diffident and uninspiring Labour politician—"a sheep in sheep's clothing," in Churchill's description—named Clement Attlee.

This startling development underscored a more profound one. Over the previous five years of war, the fate of the planet had largely rested in the hands of six men gathered into two opposing camps: Roosevelt, Churchill and Stalin on the Allied side; Hitler, Mussolini and Japanese prime minister Hideki Tojo for the Axis. This had remained true right up until April 1945. By the end of that month, however, three of those six— Roosevelt, Mussolini and Hitler—were dead. Now, a fourth, Churchill, had been cast from power, and in just a few more weeks, Hideki Tojo would be as well. In short, of the six men who controlled the world's destiny in spring 1945, by that autumn only one remained: Stalin.

As had been mapped out at Yalta, in the summer of 1945 Germany was divided into three zones of occupation by the Big Three allies (a fourth occupation zone, administered by France, was created soon after). Berlin was similarly divided by the conquering powers, even though the city lay completely within the Soviet occupation zone.

While the military administration in the American zone was centered in the city of Frankfurt, the headquarters of OSS Germany was located in a sprawling champagne factory on the outskirts of the city of Wiesbaden, twenty-five miles away. The site had several features to recommend it. Unlike Frankfurt and most other cities in the American zone, Wiesbaden and its infrastructure had suffered relatively little damage in the war, with the Henkell Trocken factory scarcely touched. This enabled senior OSS officers to travel to other areas in the American sector as needed, but to otherwise enjoy the comfort of the richly appointed corporate headquarters building. The site came with the added benefit of allowing these officers to end their workday with a dip into the crates of Henkell champagne, some of Germany's finest, that were stockpiled in adjacent warehouses.

It was from here, beginning in May 1945, that Lieutenant Commander Frank Wisner and his deputy, Richard Helms, set to the task of organizing the Secret Intelligence unit of OSS Germany. Their immediate supervisor and overall director of OSS operations in Germany was Allen W. Dulles, a pipe-smoking and professorial former Wall Street lawyer. As OSS station chief in wartime Switzerland, Dulles had fostered relationships and subterranean alliances with a whole host of German generals and government officials involved in plots to overthrow Hitler, and had very nearly succeeded in brokering the surrender of German forces in Italy. Those various efforts had all come to naught, but his résumé of wartime escapades, so closely resembling a pulp novelist's conception of a spymaster's life, had been enough to cement Dulles's reputation as something of an OSS poster boy; along with Wisner and Helms, he was destined to be a dominant influence in the American intelligence community for the next twenty years.

With his characteristic energy, Wisner set to the task of developing a network of field intelligence units throughout the American sector. Operating under the control of these units, long chains of spies and informants reached into an astounding array of Germany's economic and political structures. The American spymasters were greatly aided by the fact that the fallen Reich lay prostrate, that men and women were ready to perform any task, and trade any information, for a bar of soap or a packet of cigarettes—the Fatherland's new de facto currency. Even so, the results were remarkable. Despite working with an ever-shrinking staff of administrators and case officers—the end of war in Europe was already translating into mass demobilization orders—by August 1, Wisner had seen to the creation of ten SI field units across the length of the American zone, and those units had generated nearly three hundred separate field reports. In the following month, the units compiled over seven hundred more.

Yet, Frank Wisner grew increasingly dissatisfied with the material being produced. The problem, from his standpoint, wasn't quantity or even quality, but content. While it may seem odd to an outsider, an intelligence agency is basically a specialized service provider, its clients being the various other governmental agencies to which it passes information; indeed, the modern-day CIA uses this precise terminology of "client" and "product" in describing its function. And just as with any other kind of service provider, an intelligence agency needs to furnish those products that its clients want or think they need, or suffer the consequences. In the summer of 1945, the information most desired by the OSS client base—both governmental agencies back in Washington, and the various American military formations in Germany—tended to be of very local and immediate concern: the status of the vaunted Nazi underground diehards known as the Werewolves; the hunt for fugitive war criminals; the movement of refugees. Already in Frank Wisner's estimation, however, the principal focus of SI Germany shouldn't be on the remnant issues of a defeated Germany, but on the growing threat of an empire-building Soviet Union. This view clearly wasn't shared by others, considering that in the first mission directive sent to OSS Germany from headquarters in June, not one of the twenty intelligence priorities listed were directed at the Soviets.

The true task before Frank Wisner, then, was to get Washington and the local American military command to redirect their attention from the small-bore to the macro-view—in essence, to "sell" them on a product for which they had yet to appreciate a need. Ironically, Wisner's effort was partially aided by fallout from the Potsdam conference. With the Soviet crushing of Poland's bid for democracy, there were finally some in the American political and military hierarchy who saw the need to take a harder line against their erstwhile ally, even if they remained in the minority. Incredibly, though, even at this late hour, there were those among the "striped pants" crowd at the State Department who saw no need for intelligence work at all; as one special assistant to the secretary haughtily opined to a colleague, maintaining "clandestine operators in a foreign country against which we are not at war . . . would be honoring the totalitarians by imitating them."

Wisner was also contending with a collective sense of exhaustion. "The dilemma was, it's the end of the war and we're finished fighting," Graham

Wisner said. "Based on what he'd seen in Romania, my father was kind of the canary in the coal mine about what the Russians were doing, but you can only scream so loud in a country that's tired."

By late summer, Wisner took matters into his own hands. In unusually blunt language for a man with a tendency to write in legalese, the SI Germany chief informed OSS headquarters that, from then on, his primary intelligence-gathering efforts would be directed at the Soviets—and not just in Germany, but in Soviet-occupied Poland and Czechoslovakia, as well. Wisner also passed word of this fundamental shift in priorities to his Secret Intelligence units in the field.

The immediate effect of this wasn't that dramatic. Although the new emphasis met with the approval of some senior military officers, as well as a smattering of diplomats at State, from what Wisner could discern of the Truman White House, Soviet policy continued to consist of little more than the hope of making nice with Stalin. And far from an expanded OSS mission in Germany—something Wisner and Helms and Dulles argued for every chance they got—the SI chief spent much of his time just trying to hold on to the few good men he had amid a succession of memos from Washington demanding further staff reductions. So overwhelming was the workload and so precarious SI's status that, in late August, Wisner pleaded that his own scheduled transfer from the field be delayed; given the twenty-hour days that he and the rest of the team at Henkell Trocken were already working, he simply didn't have the time to mentor a replacement. On this matter at least, OSS Washington relented; in early September, Wisner's tour of duty in Germany was extended to the end of the year.

At almost the same time that Wisner received his tour extension, there occurred a curious event far distant from Germany that, the SI chief fervently hoped, might at last serve as a wake-up call to Washington. Pun intended, since what was to prove one of the most devastating intelligence breaches of the early postwar era was made possible by the nocturnal cries of a young child.

By long-standing policy, Soviet embassy personnel were normally required to all live in one secure legation building, the better for the resident KGB officers to surveil them. An exception was made in the case of Igor Gouzenko, a low-level ciphers clerk at the Soviet embassy in Canada, when his colicky infant son so disturbed other embassy officials with his nighttime crying that the family was allowed to move to a private apartment. Venturing from that apartment one night in early September 1945, the clerk slipped into the embassy and, with a key to the safe, made off with a stack of top secret documents. So ill-formed was Gouzenko's plan to defect that he first made for an Ottawa newspaper office. Workers there redirected him to the Department of Justice, where a night guard told him the office was closed and to come back in the morning. Despite an ensuing tragicomedy of blunders that nearly led to Gouzenko being grabbed by Soviet security officers—so desperate were some Canadian government officials not to annoy the Soviets that they even debated handing him back—the ciphers clerk and his wife and troublesome son were finally taken into protective custody and whisked to a Canadian army base for interrogation.

Over the next few days, Gouzenko laid out before astounded Canadian intelligence officers—soon joined by their American and British counterparts—the story of an elaborate Soviet spy ring that had been in operation across Canada and the United States for years. The ring involved dozens of spies and informants, and its activities ranged from industrial espionage, to monitoring émigré communities, to unlocking some of the most closely guarded military secrets the Soviet's wartime allies possessed; as was soon determined, these spilled secrets included details on the Manhattan Project. Ultimately, the Gouzenko affair would lead to the arrest in the West of over three dozen on charges of espionage, and would be cited by many as the opening salvo of the Cold War.

For a man like Frank Wisner, here at last was prima facie evidence of the kind of Soviet skullduggery he had been warning about since Bucharest; surely now those in Washington with the capability to act would do so. As for the type of action required, the answer seemed utterly obvious: not just a wartime OSS, but a peacetime one as well. And not an OSS shaved down to a nub, as was happening currently, but a greatly expanded one.

But what Wisner didn't know that September was that, largely for reasons of personal animus and ambition, a number of powerful figures in Washington were quietly working to make sure none of that happened. Within this group was a man without equal when it came to the bureaucratic knife fight, and for whom bringing down OSS director Donovan had become something of a personal crusade.

═══

The FBI director's office was an expansive and softly lit room, with large quartered windows overlooking Pennsylvania Avenue. The select few who gained admittance to that sanctum may have detected something a bit peculiar about it, however. To compensate for J. Edgar Hoover's short stature—he stood just five-foot-seven—his desk and armchair sat on a raised platform of several inches, so that most any seated visitor to the office was compelled to physically look up at him. It might be expected that such an intimidation technique, combined with the director's forbidding stare, would cause such a caller to become tongue-tied, except that an audience with Hoover actually required very little in the way of discourse. "As soon as you paused for breath," recalled FBI agent Robert Lamphere, "the Director would take over the conversation, and from then on all you'd be able to do would be to agree with whatever he was saying. . . . He spoke in a rapid-fire fashion with a good command of the language but given to repetition."

In the nearly half-century since his death, the image of J. Edgar Hoover has congealed in the minds of many Americans, and especially of those on the political left, into that of a conniving and power-mad martinet, a ruthless schemer who utilized the cause of anti-communism—and his file cabinets full of blackmail-worthy material on American political leaders—to maintain the FBI as his personal fiefdom for forty-eight years. In actuality, a more accurate portrait of Hoover and the absolutely profound effect he had on the United States during the early Cold War is a good deal more nuanced.

Despite what his detractors might claim, anti-communism was no cause of convenience for Hoover. He truly did regard it as a kind of virulent virus set loose on the land, and battling it as a primal struggle between the forces of good and evil, darkness and light. Where matters get complex is in trying to gauge when Hoover's actions were motivated by that cause and when they were spurred by baser aspects of his personality: his obsession with both secrecy and self-promotion; his grasping for ever more authority; his no-quarter attacks on those he saw as opponents or competitors. A prime and early example of that complexity was his relationship with William Donovan.

The two men took an almost instant dislike to one another from the moment they met in Calvin Coolidge's Justice Department of the mid-1920s, where Donovan was technically Hoover's boss. The passage of years did nothing to cool their hostility.

Part of it came down to temperament. Donovan was a charismatic bon vivant, while Hoover was a socially awkward loner. Wild Bill's catholic fondness for women was legend, whereas Hoover, a lifelong bachelor, was never romantically linked to a woman and lived with his mother well into his forties. Testament to both Hoover's puritanical streak and his penchant for conspiracy, he reportedly began compiling a dossier on Donovan's romantic peccadilloes as far back as the 1920s.

Having failed to block the ascension of Donovan as OSS director in

1942, the FBI director remained vigilant for any signs of OSS encroachment onto his turf throughout the war, and howled with protest whenever it occurred. He kept count of the number of leftists and communists employed by the OSS—Hoover didn't buy Donovan's explanation that in wartime it was expertise, not political orientation, that mattered—and made sure the Roosevelt White House was kept apprised of his rival's ideological laxity. As might be expected, he was also ready to pounce when it became clear that Donovan hoped the OSS would continue as a permanent, peacetime agency.

In November 1944, one of Donovan's closest aides, Otto Doering, prepared a detailed proposal for President Roosevelt entitled *"The Basis for a Permanent U.S. Foreign Intelligence Service."* Anticipating the end of World War II, the paper emphasized the very changed global environment the nation would soon face. If isolationism had once been an option for an American president, no more; now, between the uneasy alliance with the Soviet Union, a war-ravaged Europe, and a dizzying array of independence movements clamoring to throw off the bonds of colonialism in the developing world, the United States had no choice but to engage across the planet. That meant, Doering argued, having the same sort of permanent foreign intelligence agency that nearly every nation in Europe had utilized for over a century, and that the United States had employed for the previous three years in the form of the OSS. In a nod to the agency's critics, a peacetime OSS would not engage in domestic intelligence, nor would it have a law enforcement function.

If William Donovan thought these assurances would mollify his opponents in Washington, he was soon set right. Sent around to a number of government departments, including the twelve other branches that dealt with foreign intelligence or domestic security in some way, the Doering proposal was thoroughly savaged by most everyone on the circulation list, including the departments of War, Navy, Justice and State. But Donovan's proposal did far more than just roil the bureaucratic waters; it provided his enemies with an early warning of his ambitions, and a road map with which to attack him. None saw this more clearly, or was more prepared to leap to that attack, than Hoover.

Lending an urgency to his mission, the FBI was just then floating a proposal of its own through the corridors of Washington. While it shared with the Doering paper much of the same rationale in calling for a permanent foreign intelligence-gathering capability, a key point of divergence was that this mission would be taken on by the FBI while the OSS was tossed into the dustbin of history. The paper duel between the rival agencies, each maneuvering for support, continued for several weeks—but then matters turned ugly.

In early February 1945, a journalist with the ultraconservative McCormick-Patterson newspaper chain named Walter Trohan penned the first of a series of "exposés" on the OSS. Under banner headlines, readers of the *Chicago Tribune* and the *New York Daily News* were warned that a "super Gestapo agency" was in the works, one that would "pry into the lives of citizens at home" and generally wreak havoc with the American way of life. What soon became clear, courtesy of Trohan's carefully cropped quotes, was that someone had leaked the top secret Doering paper to him. A furious Donovan never doubted for a moment that Hoover was responsible, an accusation lent credence when it was found that a copy of Doering's paper in the FBI director's office had gone missing.

Through the winter and early spring of 1945, Donovan had painstakingly tried to regain his footing, and to win over some of his less strident critics in the administration and Congress. He especially worked his allies in the Roosevelt White House. The effort appeared to be paying off—right up until Roosevelt's death on April 12.

As with the head of every other "war office" hoping to reinvent itself for the coming peace, Donovan was thrown for a loss by the ascension of Harry Truman. Whatever stratagems he had developed to play to Roosevelt's favor—the deceased president loved hearing spy tales of high drama and derring-do—were unlikely to have much sway with the impatient and no-nonsense Truman. Donovan soon had bigger problems on his hands, though, when he was blindsided by another poison-pen assault.

Just weeks after assuming the presidency, a fifty-nine-page report on the OSS landed on Truman's desk. Purporting to be a fair and balanced account of the agency's track record in the war, the report, written by a low-level White House military aide named Richard Park, was instead little more than a compendium of dirt and gossip gathered by its rivals, "a cut-and-paste collection," in the words of one Donovan biographer, "of accusations of petty graft, rule infractions, scandalous behavior, and communist infiltration in the OSS, with practically every complaint the FBI, Pentagon, and State Department had ever lodged against the agency included." Just as with the earlier Trohan articles, suspicions about the origin of some of Park's accusations led straight back to Hoover's FBI.

Its salacious—and in many cases, demonstrably false—charges aside, the Park Report underscored once again the irony inherent to the intelligence world, that failures become known while success remains secret. Donovan had undoubtedly added to the failure column—and multiplied his circle of critics in the process—by the scattershot approach with which he had plunged the OSS into all manner of operations around the globe, a policy all but guaranteed to yield some spectacular fiascoes. The report, coming just days before Congress was to decide on the OSS budget for the coming fiscal year, surely figured in the outcome; Donovan's request for $45 million was slashed to $24 million.

But what may ultimately have done in William Donovan was a couple of quirks in his personality. Displaying little interest in or talent for bureaucratic gamesmanship, he was going up against a man, J. Edgar Hoover, who was a consummate master of it. Prone to boredom if he sat still too long, Donovan was forever disappearing from Washington on long fact-finding missions, often to very remote places, giving his enemies ample time and a clear field in which to plot against him. In short, Donovan seemed to lack both the calculation and the focus necessary to best a stealth fighter like Hoover, a man possessed, as an aide memorably put it, of "a terrible patience."

Also, Harry Truman just didn't like Donovan. For a self-proclaimed simple man with a prickly demeanor and scant charisma, there was something about the charming and larger-than-life OSS chief that undoubtedly grated. It didn't help that the Ivy League–educated spymaster occasionally assumed a somewhat professorial manner, a habit sure to get under the skin of a boss who had dropped out of Spalding's Commercial College in Kansas City. This antipathy was reflected in the fact that, despite Donovan's repeated requests, Truman didn't see fit to have a first meeting with his intelligence chief until fully a month after he had assumed office, and then spared Donovan a mere fifteen minutes. It was also reflected in Truman's decision to not even show Donovan the courtesy of a face-to-face explanation when, on the afternoon of September 20, 1945, he signed a presidential directive ordering the immediate dissolution of the OSS and dismissal of its director. Instead, Donovan received a perfunctory, boilerplate letter in which the president thanked him for his "capable" leadership. Ten days later, the OSS ceased to exist.

As Truman and his underlings were quick to point out, this didn't mean the end of American foreign intelligence gathering. By that same presidential directive, the OSS Research and Analysis unit was transferred to the State Department, while its Secret Intelligence and Counterintelligence wings were to be absorbed by the War Department. As some Truman apologists would have it, this meant the shutdown of the

OSS was really more of a streamlining procedure, a way to cut costs and improve efficiency at a time of shrinking need—certainly not the gutting that many OSS veterans charged.

But this is a rather specious claim. Whether in government or private business, office reorganizations are invariably touted as efficiency moves, when just as invariably—as anyone who has experienced one can attest—their short-term effects are redundancy and paralysis. Naturally, the extent of these ill effects correlates to the amount of thought and planning—or lack thereof—preceding the move; when it came to the OSS, what possible urgency was there to shutter an agency in a mere ten days, especially one whose officers and bureaus were scattered across five continents? Finally, mergers such as that outlined by Truman's directive, with disparate OSS units being absorbed by either State or War, are never simply a matter of moving one set of workers into desks adjacent to another set. Instead, the teams being absorbed are almost always broken up and dispersed between different branches, and the "newcomers" to an existing agency—in this case, those migrating from a defunct OSS— inevitably have less influence than the resident old guard. In the opinion of many, Truman's decision to shut down the OSS, coming at the very moment the Soviet Union was relentlessly pushing for advantage across Europe, represented an astonishing act of unilateral disarmament.

Defense hawks sputtered with outrage. British officials were said to regard it as a grievous mistake. Then there was the reaction of Rudyerd Boulton, a celebrated ornithologist who had been with the OSS since 1942, when he heard the news: "Jesus H. Christ, I suppose this means that it's back to those goddamned birds."

Few were more shocked than the chief of Secret Intelligence-Germany, Frank Wisner. For six months he had worked himself to the point of exhaustion building an extensive intelligence network throughout the American occupation sector. At one stage, he had been just days away from going home to a reunion with his wife and young children, but had instead begged his superiors for permission to stay on, arguing that the work was too important to endure even the temporary slowdown that his leaving would entail. His subordinates and their agents had filed hundreds upon hundreds of intelligence reports, often at extraordinary personal risk, and yet for far too long it had all seemed to fall on deaf ears. Now, with the shuttering of the OSS, that deafness would only worsen, no matter what fine claims the administration made.

Still, Wisner endeavored to soldier on. The final straw, according to an oft-told story, came when he requested funds to buy two hundred bicycles so that his couriers and spies could get around more efficiently and safely—and, of course, gather intelligence more quickly. When Washington rejected the request, Wisner handed in his resignation.

Returning to New York, on March 29, 1946, Wisner was officially released from the United States Navy. Three days later, on the morning of Monday, April 1, he walked through the doors of 2 Wall Street, and took the elevator up to the offices of the Carter Ledyard law firm, there to resume the lucrative career he had set aside five years before.

It seems that, despite Bucharest and Berlin, despite running spy chains and exploring Hitler's bunker, he imagined he was simply going to return to proofreading contracts and managing custody accounts. Perhaps another type of man could have managed such a return, but not Frank Wisner.

7

A LUSH LAWLESSNESS

Peter Sichel flew into Berlin's Tempelhof airport on the morning of October 1, 1945. Waiting for him on the tarmac was the deputy head of OSS Secret Intelligence-Germany, Richard Helms, along with a car and driver.

During the drive into the city center, Sichel stared out at the ruins. Over the past six months, he had seen the effects of Allied bombing on a number of German cities, including on his hometown of Mainz—his childhood home there had simply been erased—but nothing quite prepared for the utter devastation of Berlin. Although much of the debris had now been cleared, in some respects the German capital felt more desolate in October than it had at war's end in May. This was because the Soviets, acting on the ruinous war reparations settlement agreed to at Potsdam, had used the interim to strip the city of virtually anything of value. Automobiles, generators, furniture—even silverware and door hinges—had been loaded onto freight trains and hauled to the Soviet Union; shortly before Sichel's arrival, the Red Army trophy squads had ripped out the streetcar tracks in their sector of the city and sent the steel rails east. A measure of order was established in July, when American, British and French troops arrived to divide the city into four occupation zones, but even then the work of clearing and stripping the city continued. One of Peter Sichel's most vivid first memories of Berlin was of the Trümmerfrauen, or "rubble women." Throughout the German capital, women had been recruited to help clear the city's ruins, and while some worked in bucket brigades, passing pails of debris hand to hand to consolidate smaller piles of rubble into larger ones, others used hammers and chisels to meticulously chip the mortar off reusable bricks. The work of the Trümmerfrauen began in the early morning and continued until sunset. "Everywhere you went," Sichel recalled, "you heard the tapping of their hammers."

With Richard Helms running the official, overt branch of OSS Berlin, Sichel was being brought in to take over its clandestine wing. By coincidence, he arrived on the very day that OSS ceased to exist. As of that morning, he and Helms were now members of something called the Strategic Services Unit, or SSU, created by President Truman ten days earlier. Thus far, the change had meant little to Berlin base other than the temporary hiring of a few local office workers; for the past several days, these clerks had been working their way through stacks of old OSS letterhead one sheet at a time, crossing out the name of the defunct organization and rubber-stamping them with the new.

As Helms explained during the drive into the city, Sichel's first order of business was to clean up the covert Secret Intelligence team in Berlin, better known within the OSS/SSU by its code name of the Peter Unit (the commonality with Sichel's first name was coincidental). Almost all its members, Helms believed, were thoroughly involved in the black-market trade—and little wonder. As a writer on postwar Germany noted: "On the Berlin black market ten packs of cigarettes, which an American soldier could obtain for 50 cents in a PX, had the purchasing power of $100. A cheap Mickey Mouse watch might be worth as much as $500." One GI who served in the city in the immediate postwar period told of a comrade who bought a beautiful villa for fifty cartons of cigarettes. "The villa is still owned by his widow," the ex-GI wrote fifty years later.

The reach of corruption extended even into the car in which they were traveling: the young enlisted man who was their driver, Helms softly told Sichel, was already worth hundreds of thousands of dollars. "You're going to have to get rid of all of these people," Helms said, "because otherwise you are never going to be able to run an intelligence unit."

Sichel may have been uniquely suited for the task. After all, any junior officer possessed of the financial creativity to buy a wine cellar in Algiers and to claim a Cord 812 luxury sedan as his personal squad car was apt to know a thing or two about pulling off fiddles. He also didn't have to wait long to begin the housecleaning. At the reception held to mark his arrival at the OSS base that morning, Sichel noticed his new deputy covetously eyeing his wristwatch. "He told me he could get me $1,500 for it," he recalled. "And this was on my first day, my first hour, there!"

Rather than hand over the watch, Sichel told the man he could either have an investigation conducted of his finances, or resign from the SSU effective immediately. It marked the beginning of a thorough purge that the new SI chief carried out over the following days. "I dismissed a lot of them," Sichel said, "and then brought in my own people. Within a few weeks, I felt I had control of the situation enough that we could get down to business."

What that "business" entailed was a herculean task. In Berlin in October 1945, Peter Sichel stood at the very epicenter of history, the proving ground where the future arrangement of the postwar world, of whether the United States and the Soviet Union were to remain allies or become foes, was likely to be revealed. Berlin was also unique in that, as the one "open city" in a divided Germany, the intelligence agencies of either side could employ legions of local spies to unobtrusively gather information on the other. This wasn't to say the odds were evenly stacked. In the Soviet sector of Berlin was an espionage apparatus composed of hundreds, probably thousands, of intelligence officers attached to an alphabet soup of spy agencies—NKVD, GRU, MGB—with networks that reached into every neighborhood, every street, of the city. Facing off against them in the American sector was a complement of Army counterintelligence officers whose numbers were rapidly dwindling amid the ongoing demobilization drive, and the nine operatives who comprised the clandestine Peter Unit of SSU Berlin. The new commanding officer of that unit, Peter Sichel, had just turned twenty-three.

———

For a long time after the end of World War II, Berlin retained its den-of-thieves atmosphere, a place of "lush lawlessness," as one senior American spymaster described it. The Tiergarten, the city's once grand central park, remained a muddy, crater-pocked open-air market, where occupation soldiers could buy antiques, Persian carpets and grand pianos, in exchange for food, drugs, forged documents—and, of course, cigarettes. So established were American cigarettes as Berlin's de facto currency that few people actually smoked them anymore; instead, they were traded back and forth in unopened packs or in small bundles held together with string.

For an agency like Peter Sichel's Strategic Services Unit, this made the recruitment and payment of spies both very easy and very cheap. Keeping SSU Berlin in operational funds was no more burdensome than periodically dispatching an officer to the PX or Army Exchange Service—government-run emporiums that sold goods to American servicemen at below-stateside prices—to buy a few cartons of cigarettes to be handed out as wages. Indeed, a 1948 audit would find that the base's entire operating budget over the previous two years came to considerably less than $500 a month. (The same audit noted that SSU Berlin's greatest single expenditure during this period was for "operational liquor.")

The free-for-all environment did have its drawbacks. SSU officers soon learned to never leave their vehicle unattended on a Berlin street lest they return to find it stripped. Similarly, while Peter Sichel trusted the officers he brought in to run the Berlin base, as well as most of the local hired staff, he had far less faith in the American army enlistees detailed to guard the base perimeter at 19 Föhrenweg, all of whom presumably were up to their epaulettes in the black market and looking to grab any tradable item they could find. The Gold Rush atmosphere also came at the cost of any respect the average Berliner may have once had for the American soldier; as a February 1946 SSU report acidly noted, to the average Berliner, "an American is just a Russian with his trousers pressed."

The larcenous impulse even extended to the upper reaches of the American military. On the same day in January 1946 that Peter Sichel was to hand over command of Berlin base to his newly arrived superior, Dana Durand, a contingent of MPs swarmed into the SSU compound to impound all their vehicles. They did so on orders from Brigadier General James Edmunds, the chief of administration in the American sector. When Durand confronted Edmunds, the general freely admitted he had ordered the raid in order to appropriate the SSU's three top-shelf Buick sedans. "Within two hours after my arrival," Durand reported, "I secured the return of our motor pool, and convinced Gen. Edmunds that the Buicks were the inalienable property of SSU. The crisis was over, but Gen. Edmunds was hardly one to forgive and forget such a defeat."

On the level of intelligence gathering, however, this collapse of the economic order also posed enormous challenges. Put simply, in a place where a local resident could be "bought" for a packet of cigarettes, and where being an informant was just about the only steady work going, how to ever trust in the information one was receiving? Through that autumn of 1945, Sichel carefully culled the existing Peter Unit agent chains, shedding those he deemed unreliable and establishing "backstops" for those he kept. This was most frequently done by employing three or four—or even a half-dozen—spies to all report back on the same matter; duplication was the easiest way to establish corroboration and, given Berlin's black-market economy, it wasn't as if this safeguard cost much.

During this same period, a directive from Frank Wisner in Wiesbaden made clear who was to be the principal target of these intelligence-gathering missions: the Soviets. By then, the worst excesses of the Soviet occupation, the rapes and freelance lootings, had been curbed, but throughout their occupation zone in Berlin—as in their larger zone of occupation in eastern Germany—the Soviets were steadily tightening their political and economic control. It was vital, Wisner commanded, that individual SSU units monitor and chronicle these efforts, so that a counterstrategy might be devised.

Due to their frontline status, this dictate naturally fell most directly on the Peter Unit in Berlin, even if the unit was provided with hardly any more resources to carry it out. By March 1946, Sichel had finally managed to procure an SSU officer who spoke Russian, a first, but the output of his horribly overworked operations chief was still hampered by the lack of a secretary who could type or take shorthand. The unit had even been required to appeal to the local American military hierarchy for special permission to wear civilian clothes, a development that, as Sichel dryly noted in a report to his superior, "has greatly helped the security of our operations."

By then, however, with Dana Durand assuming much of the managerial duties of running Berlin base, it enabled Sichel, staying on as Durand's deputy, to become more directly involved in actual espionage. On a personal level, Sichel generally got along with Soviet officials—ironically, the lingua franca between them was German—but it was readily apparent that their local actions were being dictated by orders from behind the scenes, that real power now lay with the political commissars. Throughout the Soviet occupation zone, those commissars were stage-managing civic leadership at even the municipal and village level, marginalizing political centrists and conservatives when necessary, while simultaneously engineering the rise of whatever local communists were available. With Sichel's new spy chains steadily extending into the farthest corners of that occupation zone, the more obvious it appeared was the Soviets' intention to fully take over.

But not at all obvious to the general in charge of the U.S. administration in Germany, deputy military governor Lieutenant General Lucius Clay. A career military man, if something of a backbencher—with an engineering background, his most notable achievement in World War II had been overseeing the rebuilding of a captured Cherbourg harbor—Clay was deeply suspicious of the work of American intelligence units, and just as deeply committed to working in harmony with America's Soviet allies. Making matters much worse, from Sichel's perspective, the breakup of the OSS left intelligence units like his with no easy way to maneuver around a hostile general like Clay. To the contrary, under Truman's reorganization, the Strategic Services Unit was now attached to the War Department—and in occupied Germany, that meant Lucius Clay.

"He was our biggest problem," Sichel said. "For a long time—for far too long a time—he had the idea that we could work with the Soviets, that as long as we didn't antagonize them, they would be reasonable and accommodating."

Sichel came to see that he was caught in something of a catch-22 with the general. Naturally, most all of SSU Berlin's agents and informants were Germans, but German antipathy for the Russians was so thoroughly established—indeed, it had been a major contributor to both world wars—that the more a report sent to Clay was critical of the Soviets, the more likely the general was to dismiss it out of hand as embittered German propaganda. In hopes of finding a way around this impasse, the young SI chief decided to take a very narrow focus, to methodically and dispassionately look at one small aspect of Germany's changing political climate.

Sichel was uniquely qualified to do so since, as a German expatriate, he had been able to assume a semi-overt role in the higher reaches of Berlin society soon after his arrival, the sympathetic American official to approach if one needed a favor or had information worth passing along. "Of course, if anyone ever asked directly if I was intelligence, I would laugh it away," Sichel said. "'I'm just ordinary Army.' But this is the way things worked then; people knew privately what was never stated officially."

Through these ministrations, by the beginning of 1946, Sichel had built up a network of well-placed informants within Berlin's business and political communities. He had something else, as well: the Crown Jewels. This was a loosely affiliated group of anti-fascist Germans who, during the war, had schemed to either overthrow Hitler or to broker an early surrender to the Western Allies. The common bond between them was that their principal conduit to the West had been the OSS station chief in neutral Switzerland, Allen Dulles. Many of the Crown Jewels—Dulles had coined the term—ended up being executed by the Gestapo, especially in the wake of the failed assassination attempt on Hitler in July 1944, but those who survived into the postwar era represented a kind of aristocratic, if mostly destitute, fraternity. Before leaving Germany, Dulles had given Sichel the names and files of the Crown Jewels, and asked him to look out for them as best as he could.

"This wasn't about using them as assets, per se," Sichel explained, "but these were the good Germans, the ones who had risked everything against Hitler, so if some small thing could be done to help them, why not? And yes, as well, they were well connected."

With the help of Dulles's Crown Jewels, Sichel forged close ties with two key political operatives in the Soviet-occupied sector of eastern Germany, one a member of the socialist party, the other a high-ranking official with the Christian Democrats (CDU). From these sources, he gained a detailed account of how pliant party lieutenants were being wooed—or threatened—by Soviet commissars to overthrow their parties' existing, Soviet-resistant leadership. The Soviets' tactics weren't subtle. In the province of Saxony, Soviet political commissars ordered local CDU officials to turn against their national leadership, "hinting at possible arrest if latter would not play ball, and promising long-desired CDU newspaper, cars and real estate in case of compliance." The situation bore some similarities to what Frank Wisner had first observed in Romania a year earlier, except there matters had been obscured by the fog of war and the ad hoc nature of the provisional government. This time, Sichel and his SSU colleagues were able to show the effort was deliberate, methodical and relentless. It also didn't hurt that Sichel was a native German speaker. On December 21, 1945, for example, the wunderkind from Mainz sensed something off about the front-page article in *Die Neue Zeit* announcing the surprise resignation of a top conservative CDU leader; sure enough, a bit of sleuthing revealed that the awkwardly worded article had been forced on the newspaper by the Soviets with the command that it "be printed by [the] editor without change."

Knowing that time was of the essence, through the cold dreary days of January and February 1946, Sichel stayed up nights putting together a damning report for his superiors. At least initially, it didn't go at all well. When the incendiary paper landed on his desk, General Clay immediately summoned its author to his office to explain himself. Despite intense and harsh questioning by the general's deputies, and despite the menacing stare of General Clay himself, the twenty-three-year-old Sichel refused to back down or soften his analysis. At last, having failed to intimidate the young SI chief, Clay's underlings ushered the troublemaker from the office.

But there had been another ticking clock animating Sichel's anxiety to complete his work that winter. In March, he would have enough service "points" to go on inactive duty status, the first step toward quitting the army. That status also meant a trip home to New York. As Sichel informed both Dana Durand in Berlin and SSU headquarters in Washington, once he got to New York he had every intention of filing his termination papers and mustering out; after nearly four years as a soldier and being away from his family since 1942, he was anxious to get on with his life. Not that there was much mystery where that life would take him: as a scion of the Sichel family of Mainz, he would assume his place in the family's four-generation wine business. Still, bowing to the entreaties of his SSU superiors, Sichel agreed to make his trip home with an open mind, to at least entertain the idea of returning to Berlin.

During his first few days in New York, Sichel simply tried to reorient himself to the frenetic, thrumming city that had once been his home. Surely adding to his disorientation was that he had come from Berlin, a city hollowed out and made ghostly by war.

Quite beyond the physical contrasts, though, the young captain was caught off guard by the mind-set of his family and friends. With the war over, everyone was naturally eager for a return to normalcy, to pick back up all those livelihoods and relationships that had been so disrupted. Yet, to Sichel, the general obliviousness to the continuing turmoil in Europe, the deepening tensions with the Soviet Union, possessed an almost willful quality. "Their attitude was, 'everything's just fine now, right?'" he recalled. "It was like they didn't want to know. And when I tried to talk to them about it, they didn't want to hear."

This head-in-the-sand attitude wasn't unique to Sichel's personal acquaintances, but extended to the highest levels of the American government. One working to counteract it was Sichel's ultimate superior at SSU, Colonel William Quinn.

As it turned out, Sichel's damning report on the Soviets' strong-arm tactics in eastern Germany had made it past Lucius Clay's desk and been disseminated by Quinn to senior officials in Truman's White House, as well as in the War and State Departments. Learning its author was just back in New York, the SSU chief summoned Sichel, still technically on active duty, to Washington. There he was subjected to an exhausting round-robin of interviews with some of the highest officials in the Truman administration. "I think with almost everyone, there was this initial psychological resistance to hearing it," he remembered. "We had just finished with this awful war, we don't have even a moment to catch our breath, and now we're right on to the next one. Gradually, though, they came around. I think almost all of them, especially the senior people at State, they already had a sense by then of where we were headed."

And the longer his stay in the U.S. extended that winter, the more Sichel reappraised his own immediate future. This partly stemmed from disapproval at how his older relatives were running Sichel Companies, the realization that he would be under their authority if he returned.

Another part, though, had to do with the resistance his Soviet sector report had encountered. As Sichel well knew, there were American intelligence officers in Germany who were simply counting off their days, who had neither the interest nor the wherewithal to penetrate the Soviet system as he had done. There were also apple-polishers who might have buried the report's unpopular findings, or produced precisely what General Clay and his supporters in the administration wished to read. If Sichel hadn't been there, first to compile the report and then to defend it, who would have been?

And there was at least one more factor at play. "Berlin was exciting," Sichel said. "What I was doing there, it was exciting and it was important."

Rather than submit his termination papers with the Army, in April 1946 Peter Sichel flew back to Berlin and to the espionage unit operating out of 19 Föhrenweg.

===

Talk of spy rings or agent chains didn't come anywhere close to capturing the reality of the Soviet intelligence apparatus. The more Sichel grappled with it, other descriptors came to mind: a culture; a way of life.

At least initially, the Soviets' informant networks in Berlin had been rather slow to build out—they simply lacked the necessary reach into German society—but by early 1946, their tentacles were everywhere. "You walked down a Berlin street, and they had you every step of the way," Sichel explained. "The shopkeeper, the postman, the garbage collector, everyone reported to them. Anywhere you went, anyone you saw in the open, you had to assume it was being reported back to the NKVD. Coming from a noninformant culture, we just had no experience with that."

Another huge Soviet advantage was that they played the long game. "They don't think in terms of quarters, the way we do. They think in terms of years, even decades." In testament to that approach, it wasn't until many years later that the Western powers realized the Soviets had used the open-city status of Berlin in the early postwar years to flood the West with thousands of "sleeper agents"; some were never activated, while others remained dormant until called to service in the 1960s or even 1970s.

And then, of course, there was simple brutality, and the fear it engenders. On the flimsiest of pretexts, a Berliner living in the Soviet sector who displeased the authorities could be arrested as a "war criminal" and sent off to the gulags. It wasn't as if those living in the Western sectors were much safer. By early 1946, so many residents had been grabbed off the streets of the American and British sectors, wrestled by thugs into waiting sedans which then sped east, that Berlin had won the nickname "Kidnap City." Joined to the ever-changing and ever-creative horde of freelance opportunists and fraudsters circulating through the Berlin shadow world, and it was devilishly difficult for an American intelligence officer to determine which end was up.

Yet, if there is one eternal truism about a battlefield it is that, as a matter of survival, soldiers quickly adapt to whatever terrain they find themselves on. So it was that even in the early days of the Berlin spy war, and despite the vastly greater forces arrayed against them, there were times when SSU Berlin could prove just as clever and ruthless as their adversaries. One such episode involved using one entrapment artist to double another.

In the autumn of 1945, one of Sichel's deputies had begun running a former lawyer and Abwehr intelligence officer named Karl Krull. Given the code name Agent Zig-Zag, Krull's main function was to track down any of his former Abwehr colleagues who were hiding in Berlin, all of whom were on the Allies' automatic-arrest list, and to lure them into the open where they could be grabbed by American authorities. As Richard Cutler, the junior SSU officer put in charge of running Krull, recalled: "Zig-Zag set about his task with surprising zest. In almost no time, he discovered two or three targets."

Those caught were given a stark choice: go to prison or become spies for the Americans. That was the straightforward part. As the entrapment scheme extended, Sichel's team discovered that some of the men they collared were already spying for the Soviets. These were carefully converted into double agents and released back onto the streets of Berlin, but now passing information to the Americans as well.

But through his double agents, Zig-Zag soon learned the Soviets were running an almost identical entrapment scheme in their sector, employing another former lawyer/Abwehr officer named Hans Kemritz. Mirroring Krull's modus operandi, Kemritz lured his former Abwehr comrades to his law office in East Berlin, where they found a KGB arrest party awaiting them. Those snatched by the Soviets had a rougher time than those grabbed by the Americans; while some of Kemritz's victims were given the option of becoming Soviet spies, many others were executed or shipped off to the Siberian gulags. So effective was Kemritz in his sting operations that he became one of the KGB's most prized assets in Berlin, with his control officer, a certain Captain Skurin, enlisting his help in an ever-greater number of operations. All of which gave SSU Berlin an idea.

"We considered Kemritz to be a potentially valuable double agent," Cutler wrote. "The more targets he fingered for Skurin, the more he was asked to nominate and locate. He could help us learn more about this Captain Skurin, whom we came to believe was a key figure in anti-American espionage."

And, of course, if the SSU could double Kemritz, they could start feeding Skurin bogus intelligence. Once Skurin acted on bad intelligence enough times to arouse his superiors' suspicions, he might be recalled to Moscow—and to an appointment in the Lubyanka execution rooms—or he might opt to escape that fate by fleeing into the loving embrace of the SSU. Either way, doubling Kemritz was the way to neutralize Skurin.

At great risk to their own operative, SSU Berlin dispatched Zig-Zag to confront Kemritz and attempt to turn him. Perhaps figuring that his own life expectancy would be improved by having an escape hatch to the West, Kemritz readily agreed to turn double for the SSU, who gave him the code name Agent Savoy. In short order, Kemritz, the Soviets' asset, was passing along to Krull, the Americans' asset, copies of all the reports he was providing to the KGB. The SSU had hit the mother lode. "Savoy is the outstanding double agent under our control at present," SSU Berlin reported in a top secret memo to headquarters in July 1946, "and continues to supply excellent material." By then, so central had Kemritz/Savoy become to Skurin's myriad operations that Cutler estimated Kemritz was providing "90 percent of the information gathered by SSU about Soviet intelligence in Berlin."

All things come with a price, though, and in Agent Savoy's case it was a steep one. To keep the double running, it was obviously vital that Skurin maintain full confidence in Hans Kemritz, and that meant allowing Kemritz to continue to lure victims to East Berlin. While the SSU checked over Skurin's hit list beforehand to warn off anyone they wished to protect, at least seventeen German citizens, fourteen men and three women, made the fateful trip into the city's Soviet zone at Kemritz's invitation and into the KGB's hands.

But there was at least one more peculiar wrinkle to the Zig-Zag/Savoy saga, a somewhat bizarre one. Due to their contentious relationship with General Clay, SSU Berlin never told the American military government about Hans Kemritz, let alone that their double agent was privy to the inner workings of Soviet intelligence; the worry was that, once informed, the appeasing Clay would order Savoy shut down. As a result, when the wives of some of Kemritz's disappeared victims appealed to officials in Clay's administration and were promised justice, the SSU not only professed to know nothing about the matter, but kept Kemritz in the Soviet zone to avoid his possible arrest by American authorities. In the same vein, some of the fifteen aliases that the SSU worked up for Krull/Zig-Zag during his hugely successful counterintelligence career were designed less to protect him from Soviet spy-trackers than from American military investigators in Clay's administration. "We just couldn't take the chance of their compromising the operations," Sichel said of the American military authorities who were technically his superiors. "We took the attitude that, until our relationship with Clay gets better, let's try to have as little contact as possible."

Or at least contact of a certain kind. In a case of poetic justice, when Clay forbid the SSU from using the cover of the military government to carry out clandestine operations, Sichel and his colleagues managed to secrete an operative in the upper ranks of the provost marshal's office. That mole then tipped off the SSU about impending Military Police raids that might ensnare one of their agents or interfere with their own covert missions.

"It can get quite complicated," Sichel said, with considerable understatement.

But beyond the goldfish bowl existence of Berlin, already by early 1946 were growing signs that Lucius Clay's view of the Soviets was falling out of favor, that in light of their steadily tightening grip in eastern Germany and elsewhere in Eastern Europe, it was time for the Western powers to assume a more confrontational posture. This sentiment received a tremendous boost in mid-February when the Canadian government, having sufficiently overcome its initial timidity in the face of Igor Gouzenko's revelations, announced the arrest of nearly two dozen of its citizens on charges of spying for the Soviet Union. It was with Gouzenko that, for the first time, the Western powers had an inkling of just how pervasive and deep the Soviet spy apparatus ran—and if this held true in Canada, how much more so in Great Britain and the United States?

Then, shortly after the arrests in Canada, there began to circulate in the upper reaches of the American government an incendiary document known as "The Long Telegram." Written by an anonymous American diplomat identified only as Mr. X (in actual fact, the author was George Kennan, the number-two man at the American embassy in Moscow), the 5,500-word paper was ostensibly meant to explain the Soviet Union's opposition to the newly created World Bank. Instead, the Long Telegram was a carefully considered, but utterly scathing, critique that bore down to the very nature of the Soviet system.

"We have here," Mr. X/Kennan wrote, "a political force committed fanatically to the belief that with the US there can be no permanent modus vivendi, that it is desirable and necessary that the internal harmony of our society be disrupted, our traditional way of life be destroyed, the international authority of our state be broken, if Soviet power is to be secure." As for how the United States might confront this existential threat, Kennan was equally blunt: while the Soviet system was "impervious to the logic of reason," it was "highly sensitive to the logic of force."

Just weeks later, this warning was echoed in a public forum by former British prime minister Winston Churchill during a visit to the United States. As President Truman sat impassively behind him, Churchill took to the stage of Westminster College in Fulton, Missouri, to deliver what would instantly become known as "the Iron Curtain speech."

"From Stettin in the Baltic," Churchill orated, "to Trieste in the Adriatic, an iron curtain has descended across the continent. Behind that line lie all the capitals of the ancient states of Central and Eastern Europe. . . . All are subject, in one form or another, not only to Soviet influence but, to a very high, and in some cases increasing, measure of control from Moscow."

A new threshold was crossed in early June 1946 when President Truman requested a comprehensive analysis of Soviet armed forces in eastern Germany in order to gauge if they were planning an offensive. Known in military and intelligence circles as an "order of battle," or OB, report, such surveys convey a clear message that an adversarial footing has been reached. That was certainly the case with Operation Grail, but it was a mission much easier asked for than accomplished. At the time, the SSU had precisely one agent reporting from inside the Soviet Union, and he was nowhere near a position of prominence to judge the Kremlin's intentions or access Soviet military plans. The "border" between eastern and western Germany was effectively closed, barricaded and heavily policed. This meant the major burden of conducting Grail fell to the one SSU unit that was in the Soviets' backyard and couldn't be blocked: Berlin.

To oversee the massive undertaking, Sichel turned to one of the more unusual residents of 19 Föhrenweg, a soft-spoken Austrian émigré in his late thirties named Henry Sutton. "Sutton was a socialist," Sichel explained, "a trade unionist who was extremely well read on communist ideology, but totally opposed to it. He was a heavyset guy who I think had no sex life at all, but who had an endless capacity for work. He worked endlessly, day and night, and very methodically, like an Austrian bureaucrat." Considering the time pressures placed on Operation Grail, Sutton was exactly the sort of workaholic Sichel needed. "He was my man in charge of running the spy operations. I had a very close relationship with him, and he was a good spymaster."

In quick order, Sutton unspooled spy chains across the breadth of Soviet-occupied East Berlin and eastern Germany, a miniature army of "tourists"—spies posing as commuters and tradesmen and travelers— taking note of the Red Army barracks being built over here, the expanding or diminishing Red Army truck park over there. By the end of summer, Sutton's chains of spies and informants ran to well over 250 people. "At that stage," Sichel recalled, "we could assure Washington that the Soviets had no intention of advancing. They didn't have the backup. They hadn't made any logistical preparation for starting to march. That was the pre-liminary analysis, but Washington wanted more."

But there was something about Operation Grail that made Sichel increasingly nervous. Not only were Sutton's chains getting very long but, in many cases, basic operational security wasn't being observed, with agents routinely crossing paths with one another, even at times sharing the same accommodations. When Sichel pressed Sutton on this, the Aus-trian became defensive. "His response was that we had these enormous demands to get OB information quickly, and this was the only way to do that. And the truth is, with the amount of people we were running, there was no way to keep it totally secure."

Something else concerned Sichel. The backbone of Sutton's oper-ations, and the hands-on overseers of most of his chains, were former German military officers—and if there was one feature that had always typified the German officer class it was arrogance. Fittingly for a people inculcated with the idea that they were a superior race, time and again during World War II, German intelligence had missed security breaches on their part, blinded by an unshakable belief in their own cleverness. The most famous example was their steadfast refusal to suspect that their sophisticated Enigma encryption system had been compromised by the British, despite numerous indications this was the case; in their minds, the enemy simply wasn't capable of besting German ingenuity. This sense of superiority especially held against Russian Slavs, a race that centuries of German literature depicted as irredeemable primitives—never mind that, in 1946, these primitives had just thrashed Germany in a war. "So, being Germans, the agents running these chains were just very confi-dent," Sichel explained. "Maybe they would have been more careful if they had been working against us or the British, races they respected, but against the *Russians*?"

The curtain came down in the last days of 1946. One of Sutton's best operatives was a former German army captain who had put together a long chain of subagents by recruiting from his old military unit; he coordinated their work from a safe house in Berlin's American zone. Just around Christmas, the ex-captain was contacted by one of his agents, saying he needed to meet with him in the Soviet zone as soon as possible. Both Sichel and Sutton sensed a trap, and ordered the man not to go across. "Well, he went anyway," Sichel said, "and that was it. The Soviets grabbed him, and then they rolled up his entire chain."

But not just the army captain's chain. While Sichel and Sutton stood helplessly by, over the next few days one Operation Grail network after another simply vanished, its members rounded up by KGB counterintelligence teams that had undoubtedly infiltrated the rings weeks or even months earlier.

In recalling those grim days of late 1946, Peter Sichel grew troubled. "The Soviets just rolled them up," he said softly. "We were devastated. Devastated. A lot of people went to the gulags—or worse—because of that." Then the old spymaster gave a slow shrug. "Well, you learn by doing. And we did learn. But we lost a lot of people in the process."

By coincidence, almost simultaneous to the liquidation of Henry Sutton's spy chains, there came the downfall of Hans Kemritz/Agent Savoy. It was the result of a mistake far too ridiculous for fiction.

Discovering that Kemritz had been surreptitiously making carbon copies of his KGB reports, his KGB control, Captain Skurin, subjected the lawyer to a harsh interrogation, at the end of which he demanded Kemritz retrieve and hand over his folder of carbon papers. A frightened Kemritz hastily did so, only to belatedly remember that in the same folder he had placed several reports meant for his other patron, the SSU. With his unmasking imminent, an SSU team whisked Agent Savoy out of East Berlin and put him on an army flight to Heidelberg, en route to an eventual exile in Uruguay. Even without Savoy as bait, the SSU tried a number of times to turn Captain Skurin, but never succeeded.

As for Agent Zig-Zag/Karl Krull, the man who had been instrumental in doubling Kemritz, he continued to work entrapment schemes for American intelligence well into 1947. In fact, so effective was he in tracking down and neutralizing his former Abwehr colleagues who were spying for the Soviets that, by deductive reasoning, the Soviets began focusing on Zig-Zag as the cause of their steadily mounting casualty rolls. In response, the SSU merely changed the game, giving Krull a new identity each time he ran a Soviet spy to ground. "He simply disappeared," Cutler explained, "only to pop up later with a new name, job, and residential quarters."

Finally, with a Soviet hit team close on his trail, Zig-Zag was bundled out of Berlin. He went on to a new, and presumably calmer, career selling carpeting at a Sears, Roebuck store in Bergenfield, New Jersey.

Staying on in the Berlin shadow world, Peter Sichel remained ever-vigilant to seize on any opportunity that might play to his advantage. One such prospect arose when a drunken Soviet colonel accidentally ran into his car, causing minor damage. "He begged me not to report it," Sichel said, "since he would get into enormous trouble. I didn't, and out of gratitude, the next day he sent me a kilo of coffee."

As precious as coffee was in postwar Berlin, the SSU man was after rather bigger game. Tracking the Soviet colonel down in the Soviet sector, Sichel attempted to recruit him as a spy. The effort failed. "Coffee was one thing," Sichel said, smiling at the memory, "high treason another. But hell, I had to try."

8

THE QUIET AMERICAN

On the morning of March 29, 1947, Edward Lansdale received a message from a friend of his in the Philippine army, a certain Major Napoleon Valeriano. For the past several weeks, units of the army had been closing on a principal stronghold of the Huk rebels battling the government, a jungle-covered dormant volcano named Mount Arayat. By that morning, the encirclement of the mountain was complete and soldiers were advancing up Arayat's steep slopes, steadily tightening their noose around the trapped enemy. Valeriano wanted Lansdale to come up to the battlefield to "see the fun." Throwing some gear into his Army-issue jeep, Major Lansdale set out for the front, some sixty miles north of Manila. He didn't make for Valeriano's headquarters, though.

Leading the fight against the Huks was a paramilitary constabulary force known as the Military Police Command, or MPC, and by March 1947 it had a well-deserved reputation for take-no-prisoners brutality. After a year and a half in the Philippines, Lansdale had seen the MPC "in action" quite enough already. "I didn't want to be around MPC," he wrote of that trip to Arayat. "I have broken bread and shared cans of beer with folks on both sides of this squabble, and I couldn't square with myself if I had to sit and listen to the orders being issued to kill people I knew."

Instead, as he approached the battle zone that evening, Lansdale found a small gravel road and traveled down it until he came to a suitable camping spot on an outer flank of the mountain. Stringing some mosquito netting between his jeep and a tree, he lay in his sleeping bag and gazed at the silhouette of Arayat, "a sort of silvery dark gray in the moonlight." At about ten, he saw the first artillery flashes on its slopes, followed moments later by the rumble of the explosions, a barrage that continued with fluctuating intensity until dawn. "I slept most of the night," Lansdale recounted, "except for the heavier firing when I awoke long enough for a cigarette and to wonder if there were any Huks on the mountain and what a bad spot they were finding themselves in."

Then again, Lansdale probably knew both the MPC and the Huks well enough at that point to figure the rebels were long gone from Arayat, that with their American-supplied artillery shells the MPC was simply blowing up empty jungle (perhaps indicative of the army's inability to catch the Huks by surprise was the code name they'd given their Mount Arayat offensive: Operation Arayat). When the sun finally came up that morning, the American intelligence officer had his "breakfast"—a warm Coke, followed by a warm beer and a cheese sandwich—and, deciding he'd seen enough, headed out of the war zone.

Precisely a year earlier, in March 1946, Lansdale had composed an intelligence report in which he described the leftist Huk rebels as "true disciples of Karl Marx" who imposed a "reign of terror" in the territory they controlled. In the year since, however, he had come to a fuller appreciation of the incestuous corruption of the Manila ruling class, and the cruelty of a land tenancy system that kept rural peasants in a state of perpetual servitude. He had also come to realize that it was in those regions of the countryside where this system was most entrenched, maintained by an unholy alliance between large landowners and a terrorizing local police force, that support for the Huks was both broad and very real. By March 1947, when he wrote to friends about the army assault on Arayat, the easy "reign of terror" certitude of his earlier missives was gone, replaced by a kind of weary recognition that matters were far more nuanced. "Agrarian reforms seem to exist only on paper," he wrote of the Philippine countryside, "and I suppose armed complaint is a natural enough thing after the guerrilla heritage of most of these folks."

Even if Lansdale himself was not fully aware of it, he was already coming to grasp the complexity of the Philippines, to see the legitimacy of the grievances of "the other side," and the grave danger to its influence if the American government didn't also. He was already becoming "the quiet American."

When Edward Lansdale walked down the gangplank of the USS *Uruguay* in Manila harbor on October 19, 1945, he had entered a country that stood at the most crucial juncture in its history.

Since being taken from imperial Spain in the Spanish-American War of 1898, the Philippines had existed as a de facto American colony, one maintained along the lines of the long-established European model. On the one hand, that had meant schools and hospitals and roads. On the other, it had meant rank economic exploitation and the swift crushing of any aspirations for self-determination; in the failed war for independence that followed the American takeover, some twenty thousand Filipino and four thousand American combatants were killed, figures that dwarfed the estimated quarter-million Filipino civilians who died in an attendant cholera epidemic.

But the idea of an overt American imperium never sat particularly well with the American public, and a broad range of pressure groups, extending from progressive liberals to isolationist conservatives, consistently agitated for an end to their nation's role in the Asian islands. By a 1934 act of Congress, the date for Philippine independence was set to occur in ten years' time.

That plan was thrown off course by the outbreak of World War II, and the ruinous three-year Japanese occupation of the Philippines that followed. That occupation also revealed a deep fault line in Filipino society. While much of the established oligarchy that controlled the islands' economic and political life entered into collaboration with the Japanese, very few ordinary Filipinos were taken in by Tokyo's talk of a Greater East Asia Co-Prosperity Sphere. Instead, many took up arms against the invaders, spawning one of the largest guerrilla resistance movements against the Axis powers in World War II. The Japanese response took the form of razed villages and massacres, a traumatized and starved population. The capstone to this brutality occurred in the war's closing days when a Japanese army trapped in Manila by the encircling Americans went on a murder spree, raping and killing tens of thousands of residents and leaving most of the city in ruins.

Despite this devastation, the United States chose to only slightly delay Philippine independence, rescheduling it for July 4, 1946, or just nine months after Lansdale's arrival. Several complications lay in the path to this event, however, and most of them stemmed from the fact that, for all its talk of Filipino liberty and self-governance, the American government appeared determined to keep the islands firmly in its thrall.

The vehicle to do so was known as the Bell Trade Act. In return for

$800 million in desperately needed American reconstruction funds, the act included a proviso that effectively ceded to American corporations the right to develop "all agricultural, timber and mineral lands of the public domain," along with "all forces and sources of potential energy, and other natural resources of the Philippines." In essence, the price for independence and reconstruction aid was to be economic bondage.

As to why a Philippine government would ever accede to such a terrible deal, the Americans could rely on another feature of its colonial rule. In wresting control of the Philippines from Spain, the United States had also inherited an entrenched local elite. In return for maintaining its privileged place in society, this resident oligarchy could naturally be relied upon to uphold American interests—just as it had previously upheld those of Spain and, more recently, Japan. Getting Filipino approval of the onerous provisions in the Bell Trade Act merely depended on putting the right member of the Manila ruling class into the Malcañang presidential palace.

In the Philippine national elections of April 1946, held just three months before independence, two men vied for that position. Both had been government ministers prior to World War II, but while Sergio Osmeña had fled the nation to lead a government-in-exile, Manuel Roxas had served in the Japanese puppet administration after being captured. If that seemed a blot on a presidential candidate's résumé, it failed to take into account the patronage system of Philippine politics. Roxas enjoyed the support of the Philippine sugar barons, who stood to make out very handsomely under the Bell Act and who could also deliver the votes of the hundreds of thousands of tenant farmers who worked their estates. Perhaps even more significant, Roxas could rely on the help of a man who still cast a very long shadow over the island nation: General Douglas MacArthur. In the run-up to the April 1946 elections, the American general who had lost the Philippines to the Japanese in 1942 made it clear that Manuel Roxas, his collaboration with the Japanese notwithstanding, was his man.

From his office at military intelligence headquarters in Manila, Major Lansdale had cast an increasingly jaundiced eye on all this. While he had come to know Roxas quite well, he was little impressed with the man—although his opinion may have been colored by Roxas's irksome habit of bumming cigarettes from him. More to the point, Lansdale felt the United States stood poised to squander an enormous reservoir of goodwill among the Filipino population if it ignored the legitimate grievances and worsening conditions of the poorer classes. The contrasting sides of this Filipino coin—an abiding affection for the United States alongside a growing anti-American sentiment—had become increasingly stark to Lansdale in his travels through the country, and it coincided with the rise of a third force in Philippine politics: the Huks.

Among the guerrilla groups that had fought the Japanese, one of the most committed was a militia called the People's Anti-Japanese Army, known by its Tagalog acronym of Hukbalahap, or simply the "Huks." An avowedly leftist formation led by a charismatic former tailor named Luis Taruc, by war's end the Huks had taken control of much of central Luzon, the largest and most populous of the Philippine islands. They did so by launching attacks on vulnerable Japanese military units, and by waging an assassination campaign against Filipino collaborators. The results weren't pretty: by 1945, it was estimated that the Huks had killed as many as twenty thousand fellow Filipinos.

While waging such "soft target" warfare might make sense from a tactical standpoint—it's usually much easier to kill an enemy collaborator than an enemy soldier—it often leaves a guerrilla group open to charges of gangsterism. Wealthy enemy collaborators, for example, might be invited to buy their safety by means of a generous "contribution" to the guerrilla effort, while the residents of a village might have to provide food or money or hideouts in return for protection. This awkward fusion of "popular struggle" with underworld tactics is a common feature in many guerrilla wars, and it was displayed in a number of areas that the Huks controlled during World War II. It was also a feature that dovetailed perfectly with the postwar narrative of Huk criminality that the Manila ruling classes wished to promote to their American benefactors. Nervous over the Huks' leftist orientation and the influence they might exert in a post-independence Philippines, the transitional American administration took largely at face value the claims of Manila politicians that the Huks were a communist front, leading Washington to exclude them from receiving the postwar compensation it granted other partisan groups that had fought the Japanese. That exclusion also signaled to the wealthy landowners of central Luzon that they could unleash the local constabulary, along with their auxiliary private militias, against the Huk "bandits" to wrest back their holdings. Through the late months of 1945 and into early 1946, precisely the time when Edward Lansdale was first traveling throughout the Philippines, central Luzon was wracked by tit-for-tat killings between the landlords' hired guns and the Huks.

Then something somewhat unexpected happened: the Huks joined the political process. Having banded together with other leftist groups under a banner called the Democratic Alliance, six Huk leaders, including Luis Taruc, won election to the national Congress in April 1946. At the same time, the hard-line Manuel Roxas was elected president, a not altogether surprising outcome considering the boosterism of American officials. It set the stage for a showdown.

While the Philippine Congress approved most provisions of the Bell Trade Act on the eve of independence, the clause that favored American companies required the approval of fully three-fourths of Congress. That posed a problem for Roxas and his American backers because a bloc that included the Democratic Alliance was large enough to defeat the measure. To get around this, Roxas, alleging voter intimidation, simply stripped nine opposing congressmen of their seats, including most of the elected Huks. The charges were baldly absurd—in Luis Taruc's case, he had garnered thirty times more votes than his closest competitor—but with Congress thus reduced in size, Roxas had the precise number of votes he needed to ratify the agreement.

To anyone of the Filipino left, the arc of betrayal—and of American manipulation—was now complete. The quislings who had served the Japanese occupiers were returned to power, there to do the bidding of their American colonial masters once more, while those who had fought against the Japanese and for true independence were marginalized. In May 1946, shortly after Taruc and his colleagues were denied their congressional seats, a Huk unit ambushed a police convoy in central Luzon, killing ten policemen. Three months later, after a prominent Huk activist was kidnapped and murdered by local police, Taruc and other Huk leaders went into hiding to join the "armed struggle." With remarkable speed, the Philippines stood at the precipice of civil war.

On Independence Day, Major Ed Lansdale sat in a Manila reviewing stand to hear President Roxas express his fealty to the United States in the loftiest of terms. In one of his more flowery supplications, Roxas averred that the Philippines was ready to follow "in the glistening wake of America, whose sure advance with mighty prow breaks for smaller craft the waves of fear," leaving some in the audience to wonder if Roxas actually grasped the definition of independence.

As the Huk rebellion widened across central Luzon that summer, Lansdale became determined to make contact with them, to discern for himself where all this might lead. Above all, he wished to meet the man who stood at the center of the revolt, Luis Taruc.

Lansdale had a good idea of who might be able to make that happen. She was a thirty-one-year-old Filipina journalist named Patrocinio Kelly. In her column in *The Advocate* newspaper, Kelly sometimes quoted the fugitive Taruc, suggesting the two had some covert means of communication. But along with the foreseeable complications of an intelligence officer using a journalist as a go-between to a rebel commander, there was an added one: like a fair number of other American servicemen in Manila, Lansdale was thoroughly infatuated with Patrocinio Kelly.

Although she was well known among the expatriate community of Manila in 1946, few might have guessed at the difficult circumstances and recent tragedy in Kelly's life. To the contrary, the vivacious and pretty journalist was rarely seen without a smile, seemed in perpetual good spirits. In actual fact, Patrocinio—"Pat" to most all who knew her— was already a widow. Just before the onset of the war, she had married a Filipino of Irish extraction, James Kelly, who had died of tuberculosis during the Japanese occupation. That left Pat a single mother to an infant child. At war's end, Pat Kelly had left her young daughter to be raised by her extended family in her hometown of Tarlac, while she set off for Manila and a future in journalism. By the time Ed Lansdale met her in 1946, Kelly, along with being a correspondent for *The Advocate,* was also working as a reporter for a U.S. Army radio station and a regular visitor to Clark Air Base north of Manila.

By all accounts, Kelly cut an impressive swath among the young, unmarried American officers stationed at Clark, cheerfully conceding to an interviewer years later that she rarely lacked for male companion-ship. "I had a great time," she said, laughing. But some in the American expatriate community questioned if there wasn't more to Kelly's dalli-ances than simple romance. Many harbored suspicions that she was a Huk operative.

Not a completely outlandish supposition, considering that Kelly's fam-ily was from a province in the heartland of the Huk insurgency. What's more, she had attended the same high school as Luis Taruc, and Taruc had gone on to marry one of her closest childhood friends. Lending further credence to the theory was the frequency with which Kelly quoted the fugitive Huk leader in her articles. For her part, Kelly would later admit that she maintained a "war correspondence" with Taruc, but insisted she hadn't been a spy. "I wasn't that interested. . . . I was too young to be interested in those things."

Dismissing this protestation of innocence was Ed Lansdale. "I knew she was . . . helping [the Huks] out from time to time," he told biogra-pher Currey. "[She was] sympathetic towards them as individuals and carrying messages." He even gave Pat Kelly a playful nickname: "The Huk Tease." This, however, was the very reason Lansdale had initially sought Kelly out and, amid a budding romance, he put it to her bluntly: could she take him to Taruc? He was startled when Kelly readily agreed to try to arrange a meeting.

Jumping into Lansdale's jeep, the two set out for the "Huklandia" territory of central Luzon, a region increasingly unsafe for Philippine government officials, let alone for an American military officer. With Kelly directing the way, they made for a particular Huk stronghold about a three-hour drive from the capital, but their efforts to find Taruc proved fruitless. They had no better luck on several subsequent journeys into Huklandia—although of course, failure may have been Pat Kelly's intention all along.

But if not with the rebel leader himself, Lansdale did begin making contact with the Huks, both on forays with Kelly and on solo ventures of his own. One technique he developed was to ascertain where the army was planning to conduct its next anti-Huk sweep—embargoed information for most, but easily obtainable for a senior American intelligence officer. Then, having long since observed the Philippine security forces' ineptitude in the field, Lansdale simply positioned himself on the path the Huks were most likely to take in their inevitable escape. Time and again, as Huk formations slipped away from a theoretically encircling army, they found the same smiling and friendly American major waiting for them at the head of the trail. As for why he would take such a risk, Lansdale, taking the guileless American exemplar to the extreme, figured his best defense was his complete lack of one.

"I was one person sitting there and they were an armed group. I would smile and give them something else to think of fast." Two items he always remembered to bring were drinks and cigarettes; in the Philippine heat, everyone was always thirsty and, like soldiers the world over in the 1940s, most every Huk smoked. "They'd come up and say, 'yeah, I'd like a cigarette' instead of shooting me. You don't kill a guy laughing, being nice to you."

Over the course of these impromptu meetings in the bush, Lansdale got to know a number of Huks, both rank-and-file cadres and midlevel commanders. Over shared cigarettes and shared meals, he explored why they had taken up arms in the first place, what might induce them to set them down again. In the process, he began developing a far more shaded view of the conflict, one reflected by his ambivalent reaction to the army's assault on Mount Arayat in March 1947.

What didn't at all change was Lansdale's abiding and free-ranging fascination with the Philippines, his endless curiosity for understanding how it worked. This wasn't isolated to its conflicts. Shortly after observing the Arayat firefight, he had been on his way home one night when he noticed a gambling game going on at a little *sari sari,* or corner store. "Gambling is against the law," Lansdale recalled, "so I stopped and asked a few questions. The folks were sort of surprised at my questions, explaining that it was a wake and gambling was okay at wakes. I felt a little foolish when they pointed out that I was leaning on the rough, box-like coffin while talking to them."

Ironically, it was Lansdale's growing popularity in the Philippines that was to upend, at least temporarily, his career in military intelligence. In the summer of 1947, General MacArthur, as overall commander of U.S. Army forces in the Far East, took note of the increasingly anti-American tilt of most Philippine newspapers amid the ongoing Huk revolt, and moved to take remedial action. After asking around and discovering that Ed Lansdale was just about the only American most Filipinos in Manila knew and liked, the general ordered the G-2 officer transferred over to the Army's Public Information Office. For Lansdale, the transfer was a mixed blessing. On the one hand, it meant a promotion from major to lieutenant colonel, and a commensurate rise in salary. On the other, it meant he was now a public information officer (PIO), and as he himself noted, it was common knowledge that "public relations was the lowest form of life in the army."

Still, Lansdale endeavored to make the best of it, and over the next year he transformed the Public Information Office from a career-hobbling Siberia into one of the most vital and visible components of the American military presence in the Philippines. He did so by moving his office from American military headquarters to downtown Manila, where he organized regular breakfast meetings with local newspaper and magazine editors, most of whom had never even met the previous PIO. This was joined to a charm offensive in which he got to know most every journalist assigned to cover American military- or policy-related issues. In short order, coverage of the American presence in the country, once largely restricted to crime-beat accounts of off-duty GIs drinking and whoring in Manila's red-light district, expanded into flattering accounts of the work the American military was doing in the areas of postwar reconstruction and civil engineering.

The cost of such exposure, though, was an endless and overwhelming social calendar. As Lansdale related to stateside friends, there were three kinds of parties in Manila—army, government and moneyed—and as the U.S. Army PIO, he was obligated to attend all three varieties. That frequently meant he had to put in appearances at five or six different functions a night. Even worse were the dinners. "Being PIO means that you go on everyone's dinner list," he complained, "someplace down the table between the hostess' embarrassing cousin from Cebu and the Vietnamese representative. It means, too, a coat and tie in a climate worthy of a T-shirt and shorts only."

Around this time, Lansdale's résumé underwent another significant change. Under the National Security Act of 1947, the old Army Air Corps was made an independent branch of the military, the U.S. Air Force. Speculating that this new branch might be more receptive to innovative thinking than the tradition-bound Army, Lansdale arranged to transfer himself in. The move may have also been rooted in cold calculation. In 1947, the U.S. Army was still being radically cut in size, whereas any newly created government body like the Air Force was more apt to face expansion. Whatever the impulse, that September Lansdale took a cut in both pay and rank—he was back to being a major—to become the newest member of the U.S. Air Force.

At about the same time, there came another transformation in Lansdale's life, a particularly complicated and bittersweet one.

After great bureaucratic wrangling, he arranged to have his wife, Helen, and their two young sons join him in Manila in late 1947, marking the first time in nearly four years the family had actually lived together. After the Christmas break, the boys were placed in the Manila American School, and Lansdale began introducing Helen around to some of his many friends in the Philippine capital.

Matters soon turned contentious. Part of Helen's quick and deepening disenchantment with the Philippines appeared to stem from her husband's frequent absences, both his nightly social circuit commitments and his longer forays into the countryside. Most of all, though, it was rooted in suspicions of his infidelity during their long time apart, suspicions that centered on one woman in particular: Patrocinio Kelly.

Whether born of intuition or of information supplied by the Manila gossip mill, Helen Lansdale had it exactly right. As revealed in a long loveletter correspondence obtained by writer Max Boot, Lansdale and Kelly had become lovers shortly after their first meeting in 1946, and remained so throughout Lansdale's tour in the Philippines. The relationship was both intense and, given Lansdale's marriage, star-crossed. "You're the one person I want to share my life with," he wrote Kelly during one of their times apart. "I'm just not a whole person when I'm away from you, and cannot understand why God brought us together when I had previous obligations unless He meant us for each other."

As Dorothy Bohannon, the wife of Lansdale's closest friend in Manila, would later confide to a biographer, relations between the Lansdales eventually deteriorated to the point that Ed resolved to divorce Helen and marry Pat. He only changed his mind, according to Bohannon, when Kelly turned down his marriage proposal. "She didn't want to hurt anybody," she explained. In an alternate version, Ed did ask for a divorce, but Helen refused to grant it; given the messiness of a contested divorce at the time, he then decided to simply stick it out for the sake of their two boys. And stick it out he did. Although rarely living together, Ed and Helen Lansdale would stay married until Helen died in 1972. One year after her death, Ed would finally marry Pat Kelly.

Amid this personal turmoil, and along with maintaining his public relations duties, Lansdale continued to monitor the ongoing bush war between the government and the Huks, a conflict that in early 1948 continued to ebb and flow through central Luzon with neither side able to gain a firm advantage. Then, on the afternoon of April 15 of that year, President Manuel Roxas, the man almost singlehandedly responsible for provoking the Huk insurgency in the first place, dropped dead of a heart attack; perhaps fittingly for this most fervid of American supplicants, his death occurred at Clark Air Base just hours after he had delivered a laudatory speech to American servicemen. Lansdale had been with Roxas earlier that same day, part of the president's press corps entourage, but about all he could find to say by way of eulogizing the fallen leader was, "now that I've switched to Chesterfields, he didn't bum Camels from me as he used to do."

Few expected much from Roxas's successor, Vice President Elpidio Quirino, a lawyer and career politician. To most everyone's surprise, though, Quirino extended negotiations with the Huks, then swiftly pushed an amnesty program through Congress. The peace process culminated in a meeting between Quirino and the Huk leadership at a schoolhouse in a remote corner of Bulacan province on July 11, 1948. Despite having no official role in the proceedings, Lansdale got himself invited.

He described the setting in a letter to friends. "The place was a grammar school, unpainted since 1941, with two big rooms and a porch. It perched up above the flooded rice fields on one-story high timbers. A faded blue sign with white letters said 'San Roque Grammar School.' About 150 people were crowded on the porch, all straining and pressing towards the middle where a plump and effete president of the Philippines stood talking to a quick and wiry guerrilla chieftain." That chieftain was Luis Taruc, the tailor-turned-revolutionary who Lansdale had unsuccessfully sought to meet for the previous two years.

Quirino took to the microphone to declare that the amnesty he had pushed through Congress, and which was now scheduled to end in just one month's time, offered a golden opportunity to end the nation's civil strife, an opening for the Huks to lay down their arms and return to civilian life without penalty. Taruc, Lansdale noted, told those assembled "that he believed the government was now sincere, that his people should come in and register as requested, that Huks were going to continue pressing for land reforms and that Americans and their capitalistic agents should be driven from the Philippines. Great cheers."

For Ed Lansdale, that morning at the San Roque schoolhouse represented a watershed moment. Not only had he finally set eyes on Luis Taruc but, far more importantly, he now anticipated trying to implement some of the ideas for rapprochement and reform that he had been mulling over ever since beginning his clandestine dialogues with the Huks two years before. With President Quirino willing to try a different approach, there suddenly was the opportunity to transform the Philippines into a kind of laboratory for nonviolent political change in Asia. Major Lansdale very much wanted to be a part of that process.

But perhaps the new Air Force officer had been a bit too strategic in his career planning, for while it is often true that the creation of a new bureaucracy necessitates more hiring, it's also true that more hiring necessitates more training instructors. Just weeks after attending the reconciliation meeting between Quirino and Taruc, Lansdale received the ghastly news that he was being transferred to the Air Force's new intelligence training school at Lowry Air Base in Colorado, there to become an instructor in something called economic intelligence.

Lansdale tried every maneuver he could think of to scuttle the transfer, but it was to no avail. That November, he and Helen began packing up the scant possessions in their Manila home for the voyage back to the United States; in evidence of the rift between the couple, it was already decided that Helen and the boys would not follow Ed to his Colorado posting, but remain in California.

But as much as he dreaded the journey home and the job awaiting him at the other end, this wasn't to be the end of Ed Lansdale's association with either the Philippines or the Huks. To the contrary, a clue to his future involvement was revealed that day at the San Roque schoolhouse. As the ceremony drew to a close, after Quirino's eloquent appeal for the Huks to "take up a peaceful life," and after Taruc had urged his followers to accept the government at its word, Lansdale thought to try to quantify the day's success by wandering over to the weapons collection point and tallying up just how many guns had been turned in. The counting didn't take long; the answer was zero.

9

A WORLD BLOWING UP

From his well-appointed office at Carter Ledyard on Wall Street, Frank Wisner tried to readjust to the civilian world. He had returned to the white-shoe law firm after his discharge from military service in March of 1946 but, as with many returning war veterans, found a certain tedium to everyday life after his adventures in the field. This was not eased—and, indeed, may have been exacerbated—by the fact that Wisner and his wife, Polly, now had two young children underfoot in their Park Avenue apartment.

But Wisner's postwar disaffection had deeper root than merely missing the action. First in Romania and then in Germany, he had been eyewitness to the Soviets' repressive tactics in consolidating their grip over the local population. The American response, in the lawyer's opinion, had run the gamut from energetic hand-wringing to fatalistic acceptance to tacit complicity. Like many in the intelligence community, he had been appalled by Truman's decision to dissolve the OSS, regarding it as essentially clearing the field for the Soviets at one of history's most crucial junctures.

"He absolutely perceived a continuum of threat," Wisner's eldest son, Frank Jr., said. "In his view, Stalin's Russia was predatory. The gobbling up of Eastern Europe wasn't the creation of some cordon sanitaire between West and East that Stalin was going to respect, but a jumping-off point before he went farther west. The Russians had designs well beyond, they had a mobilized force that vastly exceeded ours, and they were damned good at what they did. Even at that point, this was all very clear in my father's mind. Very clear."

By the time Wisner started back up at Carter Ledyard there were stirrings that at least some within the Truman inner circle had begun to grasp the nature of the Soviet threat: there was the "Long Telegram" out of Moscow by Mr. X/George Kennan, followed by the tacit sanctioning of Churchill's portentous Iron Curtain speech in March. Even here, though, hawks like Wisner felt the administration was being too coy by half. After all, why the game over the identity of Mr. X? Obviously, so that the administration could take a sounding on Kennan's combative treatise, but without lending it the imprimatur of official approval. And why did a former British prime minister give the Iron Curtain speech and not the sitting American president? Truman had sat on the stage with Churchill, had surely read his address beforehand, and yet took pains to neither endorse nor disavow its message afterward. To observers like Wisner, it encapsulated the myopia of the new administration, that while the Soviets continued their march of conquest, Truman and his advisors busied themselves by leaking anonymous missives and crafting tiptoe theatrics. The new president seemed to labor under the illusion that there was still time to maneuver and parry and reason with the Soviets when, in Wisner's view, time was the one commodity Truman absolutely did not have.

Not that the president's political opponents seemed any wiser to the situation; in fact, the Republican Party appeared to be falling even more under the sway of isolationists and America Firsters. In the midterm elections in the autumn of 1946, Republicans seized control of both the House and the Senate for the first time in sixteen years, but they did so on the promise of a massive tax cut and a radically smaller government; barely mentioned was the need for a change in foreign policy. "The world is about to blow up in our faces," columnist Joseph Alsop wrote shortly after the Republican congressional sweep, "and the damned fools in Congress behave as though there were nothing worse to worry about than their richer constituents' difficulty in paying their taxes."

And still, the torrent of grim news from abroad continued. In sham elections held in Romania in November 1946, the communist bloc of parties won 70 percent of the vote; the United States and Great Britain protested the charade, but otherwise did nothing. The following month, Vietnamese nationalists under the banner of the communist-led Viet Minh launched an all-out offensive against French colonial forces that had reoccupied their country, sparking the beginning of what would become known as the First Indochina War. As the year of 1947 began, elections in Poland saw the communists, a minuscule political party just

two years earlier, win 394 of 444 parliamentary seats after most opposition candidates had either been arrested or struck from the polls. In
Hungary, the secret police of a newly installed Stalinist regime rounded
up opponents on the pretext of a purported coup plot. All of this may
have been distant or abstract to some, but not to Frank Wisner. In January
1947, he received a letter from a Romanian woman he had worked with in
Bucharest and who was now trying to find some way to escape. "My dear
Commander," she wrote, "I do not think it is necessary to explain to you
that in all events we are completely washed up where our future in this
country is concerned."

Perhaps most painful to Wisner, the chance of the United States being
able to counteract any of this was fading all the time. By the start of 1947,
the three million American troops in Germany at war's end had been
cut to a mere 160,000, and on their way to being halved again. In that
same time frame, the 9,000-man-strong OSS of which Wisner had been
a proud member was shaved to an SSU husk of about 800.

If not to actually effect change, Wisner at least had an outlet for his
frustrations through his membership in the Council on Foreign Relations (CFR), then as now one of the nation's most renowned foreign policy think tanks. At the Council's stately headquarters on 68th Street in
Manhattan, Wisner attended as many talks and panel discussions on the
European situation as his obligations of job and family would allow. It
was also where he socialized with many of his old OSS colleagues, including Allen Dulles, the new president of CFR and the former OSS station
chief in wartime Switzerland. After briefly serving as OSS chief in postwar Germany, Dulles had returned to civilian life and, like Wisner, gone
back to his old Manhattan law firm—in his case, the equally prestigious
Sullivan & Cromwell. Also like Wisner, Dulles chafed at the Truman
administration's inaction before the Soviet threat. Peter Sichel picked up
on their anxiety when he had lunch with the two during a brief visit to
New York from his posting in Berlin. "They were both chomping at the
bit," Sichel recalled. "The OSS had been the highlight of their lives, and
they were desperate to get back into the game."

And then, in February 1947, there finally came the jolt that shook the
administration from its torpor. It took the form of a short note to the new
secretary of state, George C. Marshall, from the British ambassador to
the United States, and it concerned the situation in Greece.

Building on its historically close relationship with Athens, Great Britain had taken the lead in supplying the Greek government with weapons and logistical support when a long-simmering civil war with leftists
had reerupted in March 1946. Backed by the communist governments

in neighboring Yugoslavia and Albania, by the following winter the estimated 25,000 fighters of the outlawed communist group—known as the
Democratic Army of Greece, or DSE—were steadily gaining the upper
hand, having taken their fight to most every corner of the country.

Throughout that year, the British had periodically dropped hints to
Washington that, with Britain's own postwar economy in a shambles and
its treasury coffers dwindling toward empty, they couldn't afford to sub-
sidize the Greek regime indefinitely. By February 1947, the time for hints
was over. In the note to Marshall, the British announced they had no
choice but to cut off all financial and military assistance to the Athens
government in six weeks' time. If Greece was to be "saved" from communist control, the Americans would have to step into the breach—and
immediately. And it wasn't just Greece. The situation was also dire in
neighboring Turkey, where the Soviets were asserting territorial claims
and applying intense pressure on the Ankara government to bow to their
demands.

The British memo had the effect of convincing Truman that the time
for diplomatic protests and toothless entreaties had ended. On March 12,
he gave an address to Congress in which he urged the authorization of
$400 million in emergency aid for the embattled regimes in Greece and
Turkey. In what would soon become known as the Truman Doctrine, he
also outlined a containment policy against communist expansion, a vow
that the United States would come to the defense of imperiled democracies around the world.

More action followed. In June, the Truman administration put forth
a proposal for a breathtakingly ambitious scheme to revive the war-
shattered economies of Europe through eliminating trade barriers and
providing a massive infusion of American financial aid and loans. Soon
to become known as the Marshall Plan in honor of the man who would
be its chief administrator, Secretary of State Marshall, participation in the
plan was offered to most all the nations of Europe, as well as to the Soviet
Union. Stalin rejected the offer, regarding it as a Trojan horse for the
spread of American influence, but it placed the newly installed communist governments of Eastern Europe in the awkward position of having
to choose between potentially bolstering their economies or displaying
their further obeisance to Moscow. All chose the latter.

But of all the newly muscular steps taken by the Truman administration to confront the Soviets, none were to have such a direct effect
on Frank Wisner as the National Security Act of 1947. The basis for the
American intelligence apparatus that still exists today, the act called
for the establishment of a National Security Council (NSC) that would

advise the president on intelligence and foreign policy matters, as well as for the creation of a permanent foreign intelligence-gathering bureau in the federal government. This bureau, directly answerable to the president and his or her National Security Council, was to be named the Central Intelligence Agency.

All quite straightforward thus far, but amid the seventeen pages of dreary bureaucratese that comprised the National Security Act, there appeared a curious subclause. It was tucked away in Subsection D of Section 102, and it noted that, in addition to its more clearly defined responsibilities, the CIA might be tasked "to perform such *other functions and duties* related to intelligence gathering affecting the national security as the National Security Council may *from time to time* direct [emphasis added]." With no further explication of what either "other functions and duties" or "from time to time" meant, it could be construed that the new intelligence agency had the prerogative to conduct *any* action the NSC deemed necessary, and at *any* time. As history was to show, this was precisely the interpretation that the architects of Truman's emerging Cold War policy would adopt.

As the newly assertive program outlined by the Truman Doctrine and the National Security Act took form, administration officials began looking around for the best men—and in 1947 Washington, it was invariably men—to direct it. They soon took note of Frank Wisner. Early that autumn, the lawyer was offered a position with the State Department, that of deputy assistant secretary of state for occupied areas. The ponderous job title aside, the post would make Wisner one of the overseers of American policy in Germany and Japan, at a time when both war-ravaged nations were being buffeted by Soviet designs.

Still, having been burned once by the Truman administration during his time in Germany, Wisner initially balked at the job offer and reportedly only relented after a personal appeal from Undersecretary of State Dean Acheson. Even then, cognizant of "the many pitfalls and possibilities of 'sudden death' which exist in connection with any form of government service," Wisner only asked his law firm for a one-year leave of absence. With that in hand, in October 1947 he made the move to Washington.

Even more than Acheson's appeal, it may have been the counsel of his old OSS colleague Allen Dulles that finally took Wisner back into public service. During one of their how-to-save-the-world conversations in New York, Dulles had advised Wisner to "find an inconspicuous slot in the government and start building up a network for political warfare from within." As the take-charge Wisner had himself discovered, first in

Romania and then in Germany, government positions were often just as big or as small as their occupant chose to make them.

Even Wisner, though, may have been unprepared for the enormity of what was coming his way. A hint of it came just months after he had assumed his post at State. It happened in Berlin, and it at least peripherally involved one of Wisner's old colleagues from OSS days: the Wunderkind, Peter Sichel.

═══════

By way of explaining the odd episode that occurred in Berlin in March 1948, Peter Sichel quoted the famous proverb from Shakespeare's *Henry IV*, about wish being father to the thought. "Meaning that we all have this tendency to look for information that confirms our beliefs," he said, "and to ignore what conflicts with them. When it comes to intelligence, it's very hard to give somebody information he doesn't want to hear, and the more senior they are, the worse it is. This was General Clay's problem. He was a very bright man, but he wished so much to be able to run Germany with the Four Powers in agreement, that his wish became his thought. It was almost an ideology." The old spymaster gave a wry smile. "And what happens to ideologues when they finally see they were wrong? They go completely the other way. That always happens, you know."

At the beginning of 1948, there were few signs that General Lucius Clay, now the chief American military governor in Germany, was headed for a political crisis of faith. To the contrary, he seemed just as determined as ever to find common ground with the Soviets—which meant maintaining the short leash he had imposed on American intelligence units in Germany. The previous summer, Clay had cavalierly decided to consolidate all the Military Police installations scattered through Berlin's American sector into a single central barracks. "The effect of this order," a 1948 CIA report stated, "as pointed out to [Clay] in advance by all the American law-enforcement and intelligence agencies, has been to denude of police protection the highly exposed areas bordering the Russian Sector, and to invite abductions and other Russian forays into our sector. General Clay admitted that he was taking a 'calculated risk.'"

That decision followed on an earlier pact—"a gentlemen's agreement" it was called—that Clay had made with his Soviet counterpart to promptly hand over to the Soviets any of their "delinquent" citizens found in the American zone. With the Stalin regime already in the process of executing or sending to the gulags many of the hundreds of thousands of its citizens who had been repatriated at the end of the war, the Clay-Sokolovsky agreement was obviously a virtual death sentence for any Soviet deserter handed over. Peter Sichel and his team flouted the edict whenever they could, hiding Soviet deserters from Clay's minions until they could be interrogated and smuggled out of West Berlin, but it naturally served as a massive impediment in trying to entice Soviet officials to defect.

In another sphere, however, Sichel's unit had at last gained some maneuvering room from the general, thanks to yet another bureaucratic reshuffling in Washington. In 1946, the SSU had been folded into a new organization, the Central Intelligence Group (CIG), only to have that appellation disappear with the 1947 National Security Act; with that, the veterans of OSS/SSU/CIG were now members of a new and independent branch of the federal government, the Central Intelligence Agency. Whatever other changes this reorganization might portend—and in early 1948 that was all still being thrashed out in Washington—for Sichel and the others at Berlin base it meant they were now freed from Army control, and from the direct oversight of General Clay.

At the same time, tensions were intensifying across the region. In December 1947, a meeting of the Big Three foreign ministers in London collapsed in acrimony over the issue of how to reconstitute a partitioned Germany. As always, the effects of this deepening rancor were most nakedly felt in Berlin, where Soviet troops launched a harassment campaign of conducting laborious identification checks on British and American trains entering the city. That marked the start of a steadily intensifying Soviet effort to slow the flow of people and goods into Berlin's Western enclaves, leading the intelligence team at Föhrenweg, now known as CIA Berlin, to warn that it appeared the Soviets were planning to force the Western powers from the city altogether.

In February came one of the most aggressive moves to date. With the clear assistance of Moscow, the communist minority in Czechoslovakia's elected government forced a constitutional crisis that brought down the ruling coalition, and the swift installation of a Soviet puppet regime. Two weeks after the parliamentary coup, the only non-communist left in the government, Foreign Minister Jan Masaryk, jumped or was thrown to his death from his apartment window. The coup in Prague, just two hundred miles south of Berlin, marked the end of democratic rule in the last of those Eastern European nations liberated by the Red Army; from Poland in the north to Bulgaria in the south, all were now Soviet satellites.

Still, even with this latest provocation, there was little to immediately account for the alarming "eyes-only" cable that Lucius Clay sent to the Joint Chiefs of Staff on March 5. "For many months," Clay wrote, "based on logical analysis, I have felt and held that war was unlikely for at least ten years. Within the last few weeks, I have felt a subtle change in Soviet attitude which I cannot define but which now gives me a feeling that it may come with dramatic suddenness." While a shocking statement, even more remarkable was that it seemed to be based purely on a hunch, as Clay himself admitted. "I cannot support this change in my own thinking with any data or outward evidence in relationships other than to describe it as a feeling of a new tenseness in every Soviet individual with whom we have official relations. I am unable to submit any official report in the absence of supporting data but my feeling is real."

The Clay missive triggered alarm in the Pentagon, especially since it came from someone previously viewed as almost a Soviet apologist. Inexplicably, the generals initially chose to keep the information to themselves, so that CIA Berlin, surely the group best positioned to evaluate Clay's apprehensions, didn't learn of it until a full week later. Awareness came in the form of a directive for the base to conduct an immediate appraisal of Soviet military intentions, in order to answer three stark questions: "Will the Soviets deliberately provoke war in the next 30 days? In the next 60 days? In 1948?"

Peter Sichel and Dana Durand dispatched their subordinates and their agent chains to compile a new order of battle report on the Red Army, much as had been done two years earlier in Operation Grail. The same pattern soon emerged. "It actually isn't that difficult," Sichel explained. "You put agents out to look for troop buildups, ammunition dumps. Most of all you look at the railways. A modern army can't start a war without first organizing the railroads, because neither the guns nor the tanks can move very far without them. To start a war, you need to gather up the trains, and that hadn't happened."

On March 16, a terse, top secret memo from the CIA director landed on President Truman's desk. A snap analysis had "produced no reliable evidence" of an imminent Soviet attack, Director Roscoe Hillenkoetter wrote, before archly adding that this conclusion was based on "the weight of logic, as well as evidence."

There was unmistakable irony in all this, that a panicked American general was being talked off the ledge by the very intelligence officers whose warnings he had assiduously ignored for the previous two and a half years. But the March crisis spurred by Clay's cable also underlined a frightening new feature in U.S.-Soviet relations. With nerves increasingly on a hair-trigger, and with the two armies mere miles apart in Germany, just how easy might it be for some unforeseen event or circumstance—a military convoy making a wrong turn into hostile territory, a precipitous order issued by a rattled officer—to propel the whole delicate standoff into outright war?

———

In late April 1948, some six weeks after General Clay's "March crisis" had been defused, Frank Wisner left Washington for an extended tour of the American occupation zones in western Germany and Austria. Rather than as the intelligence officer he had been three years earlier, he did so as the deputy assistant secretary of state for occupied areas.

By the time of that trip, Wisner's pessimism over the state of the world had lifted somewhat. Thanks largely to a massive infusion of American aid, the government of Greece had inflicted a string of military defeats on the communist-led DSE rebels, and although that insurgency was still a long way from being extinguished, the panic previously gripping Athens had abated. Galvanized by the Soviet's blatant intervention in Czechoslovakia that February, both the Republican-controlled Congress and American public opinion were rapidly swinging in support of the Marshall Plan and of an international American military presence, presaging a reversal of the radical downsizing regimen that had been in place since the end of World War II. Most heartening of all was the news out of Italy. At the beginning of 1948, it had appeared the Italian communist party was on track to triumph in the upcoming parliamentary elections, a sufficiently alarming scenario to cause the Truman administration to dispense with an American tradition of noninterference in the elections of other democratic states. Through the instrument of its new intelligence arm, the CIA, the administration had secretly poured money into the Italian electoral process in support of moderate and center-right parties, while conducting a covert media scare campaign warning Italians of the catastrophe to accompany a communist victory. The effort was a great success, helping to usher in a conservative government and to limit the communist vote tally in the April elections to a mere 31 percent. It was close on the heels of this good news from Rome that Wisner set out on his tour of western Germany.

While officially there in the capacity of a diplomat, one of the chief purposes of Wisner's trip had to do with what was known as political warfare, to determine how the State Department might serve as a marshaling force in the struggle between the United States and the Soviet Union in Central Europe. In fact, Wisner had already floated one proposal on the topic to some of the top foreign policy power brokers in Washington.

As both a student and eyewitness to recent European history, Wisner contended that, in the deepening contest with Stalin, a great deal could be learned by studying how the Germans had managed to rally so many non-Russian Soviet citizens to their side during their invasion of the Soviet Union in World War II. The motives for these Ukrainians and Latvians and Estonians weren't hard to discern—hatred for the murderous regime in Moscow; fear of domination and forced assimilation by the Soviet Union's ethnic Russian majority—and Wisner pondered whether there was a way to update these animosities and cultural fissures for American purposes. As he was to tell an aide, Washington "should stop thinking of the Soviet Union as a monolithic nation and investigate the internal strains."

On earlier visits to Western Europe, Wisner had taken special note of the hundreds of thousands of Soviet émigrés living there in permanent exile. Some dated their exile to the 1917 Bolshevik Revolution, while many more had been displaced in World War II and remained in refugee camps scattered through the region. The latter were joined by hundreds of thousands more from those countries in Eastern Europe now controlled by the Soviet Union. An outlook that virtually all of them shared was a virulent anti-communism. In contemplating this expatriate community, Wisner saw a potential nucleus for "encouraging resistance movements into [sic] the Soviet World and providing contacts with an [anti-communist and indigenous] underground."

Wisner had a ready-made forum for expounding his ideas since, in addition to his official State Department position, he served as one of State's representatives on a high-level interdepartmental security council known as the State-Army-Navy-Air Force Coordinating Committee, or SANACC. In mid-March, and just as the panic triggered by Lucius Clay's cable from Berlin was starting to abate, he had set before his SANACC colleagues a proposal entitled "Utilization of Refugees from the Soviet Union in U.S. National Interest." Soon to be given the far snappier code name of Operation Bloodstone, the plan's aim was to "remove present deterrents and establish inducements" for defection by high-ranking Soviets, as well as to employ Soviet refugees to "fill the gaps in our current official intelligence, in public information, and in our politico-psychological operations." As noted by intelligence historian Christopher Simpson, this hazy last term was "a euphemism for covert destabilization and propaganda operations."

Its opacity notwithstanding, Wisner's proposal swiftly ran into opposition from the newly created CIA. After first being savaged by a lower-level agency official, the attack on Bloodstone was taken up by the CIA director himself, Admiral Roscoe Hillenkoetter. As Hillenkoetter wrote the head of the National Security Council, "during the past three years, CIA (and its predecessors) has systematically explored the potential intelligence value of the numerous anti-Communist and anti-Soviet groups in Central and Eastern Europe." In the process, he continued, enough information had been collected on these groups "to permit a sound evaluation of their possible value to the US Government for the purpose of propaganda, sabotage and anti-Communist political activity."

Alas, that evaluation was not a positive one. Hillenkoetter's CIA operatives had found all the émigré groups to be fractious and scheming, with their greatest goal being to preserve their tapline of outside funding. Of the five specific objections he listed to Wisner's proposal, perhaps most damning was the last. After noting such groups were a primary target for Soviet spies, Hillenkoetter wrote, "CIA has sufficient evidence at this time to indicate that many of these groups have already been successfully penetrated by Soviet and satellite intelligence agencies."

But against all the CIA director's sober-minded doubts there stood an institutional imperative: the need to do *something*. Especially in the wake of the coup in Czechoslovakia, there was a mounting consensus among Truman's senior policy advisors that a much stronger stand against the Soviets had to be taken, that the administration could no longer simply be reactive to events, but needed to act preemptively and even, in situations that permitted, offensively. In a catch-all phrase, that meant covert action: quietly funneling money to anti-communist politicians, as had just been done in the Italian elections, but also lending aid to those groups willing to conduct espionage operations within the Soviet bloc, perhaps even to those seeking to destabilize a Soviet-allied regime.

This was certainly the view of the man who had come to be seen as the intellectual guide of Truman's Soviet policy: George Kennan. Building off the reputation he had gained as the author of the "Long Telegram," in 1947, the forty-three-year-old Kennan had created and taken leadership of the State Department's Policy Planning Staff, an august body designed to serve as a kind of internal think tank and strategy board. In that capacity, Kennan had increasingly come around to a belief that containment against Soviet expansionism—the idea for which he will always be remembered—was not enough, that what was needed was a kind of below-the-radar offensive capability to chip away at the Soviet behemoth. In this, Frank Wisner's Operation Bloodstone proposal was very much along the lines of Kennan's own thinking; as early as September 1947, he had written Secretary of Defense James Forrestal calling for the creation of a "guerrilla warfare corps," suggesting that while the American public might be reluctant to endorse the sorts of "irregular" methods already being used by the Soviets, there were times when "it might be essential to our security that we fight fire with fire."

Yet, Kennan also saw something of a built-in paradox to all this. Obviously, the State Department would need to assert a great deal of control over something like Bloodstone, since its activities could directly affect foreign policy. At the same time, State needed to be sufficiently removed from such a mission's seamier aspects so as not to befoul its ongoing and overt diplomatic function. What was required, then, was to park such an organization outside of State, but in a place where State could still control it.

By the spring of 1948, Kennan had increasingly settled on where this new top secret outfit should be housed: in a nice touch of irony, considering his heated objections to the Bloodstone proposal, it was to be Roscoe Hillenkoetter's CIA. Kennan had also decided on who should head it: Frank Wisner. Indeed, one of the hidden agendas of Wisner's travels through Central Europe that April and May was to sound out some of his old OSS colleagues who had stayed in the game on just how such a new agency might best be put together.

In light of the institutional opposition that Bloodstone had drawn, neither Kennan nor Wisner imagined an easy go of things with this new and far more ambitious scheme. Once again, though, an external crisis would have the effect of sharpening opinions and propelling events forward. Once again, that crisis would come in Berlin.

━━━

On June 18, 1948, Soviet troops temporarily blocked rail and road traffic into the Western zones of Berlin. It was in retaliation for an announcement made by the Western powers earlier in the day that they would soon introduce a new deutsche mark in their German occupation zones, a move the Soviets had been fiercely opposing for months. Three days later, and despite both protests and threats from Soviet-controlled eastern Germany, the Western powers introduced the new currency anyway. On June 24, the Soviets struck back, severing all road and rail connections into western Berlin until further notice. The next day, they cut off all food and electricity supplies as well. It marked the beginning of the Berlin Blockade, a Soviet campaign months in the planning and meant to choke the Western enclaves of the city into submission.

For at least the first few weeks, it seemed the Soviet gambit might work, with the rest of the world watching and waiting for Berlin to capitulate.

Instead, Western air force commanders hastily organized an extraordinary airlift effort. Over the next eleven months, the three airfields in Berlin's western sectors became the busiest air terminus in the world as American and British military transport planes flew over a quarter of a million relief flights into the city, bringing food, clothing, even milk and coal, to ensure the survival of its two million residents. Rather than a humiliation, the Soviets had handed the West a massive propaganda coup. Around the world, newspapers and radio stations provided regular updates on the "siege of Berlin," while iconic photographs of Berlin children cheering the incoming planes made very clear who were the aggressors, who the rescuers.

Along with bad press, the Berlin Blockade came at enormous local cost to the Soviets, as one resident of the city at the time, Peter Sichel, quickly perceived. "Up until then, Berliners saw the Americans as occupiers," he said. "Better behaved than the Red Army maybe, but still occupiers, and they resented us for it. The blockade changed that. They saw that we were all in this together, that we were trying to keep the city alive, and so we went from this relationship of considerable animosity to them seeing us as their allies. This was specific to Berlin—it was much less true in other parts of Germany—but this was a dramatic change. The blockade was one of the greatest mistakes the Soviets committed."

It also made the American spymaster's job in Berlin a good deal easier. With residents in the Western zones developing an even greater resentment of the Soviets—on top of their earlier plundering, the Soviets were now causing them to be hungry and cold—a whole new raft of potential recruits were brought into the Berlin spying game. "Most of them were still doing it for money or some kind of favor," Sichel said, "but now they could also tell themselves they were working for the right side, the good side. That is no small thing when you're recruiting agents."

What the Berlin Blockade also proved was that, for all the advantages Soviet intelligence enjoyed over its Western counterparts in Europe—manpower, sleeper cells, vast networks of informants—it was hobbled by two great liabilities.

The first, and most obvious, was the unpopularity of the Soviet system. Throughout Eastern Europe in the late 1940s, those living under the tightening control of communist regimes had begun voting with their feet, and nowhere was this truer than in the Soviet zone in Germany where contrasts to the West were most readily visible. While Western propaganda liked to portray this exodus as rooted in a yearning for freedom, probably an even greater motivator was economics; the West promised a better and easier life, and its economic vitality relative to the

East was becoming more pronounced all the time. The lure of eventual settlement in the West was bait that Western intelligence agencies could dangle before prospective agents for which the Soviets had no answer.

The second great liability was fear. While Stalin had injected an element of paranoia through much of Soviet society, within the intelligence services it permeated down to the lowliest field officer. Given the *vozhd*'s obsession with having spies everywhere, one could never be sure which intelligence report might land on his desk, only that he heartily disliked bad news. As a consequence, officers at every level of this vast enterprise constantly second-guessed themselves, driven by the knowledge that any analysis that smacked of defeatism, or suggested the West had outsmarted the Soviets in some way, might earn its author a recall to Moscow, possibly followed by a trip to the gulags or the Lubyanka murder rooms. The hidden costs of this culture of fear was evident in the run-up to the Berlin Blockade. In the stream of enciphered cables from Soviet intelligence commanders in Germany to the Kremlin had been the nearly uniform conviction that such a blockade would force the Western powers to either drop the currency reform or quit Berlin; either way, they constantly told Moscow, the Soviets couldn't lose—which, of course, was precisely what Stalin wanted to hear. That the West might turn the tables by organizing an airlift sufficient to "save" Berlin was something that virtually no one in the Soviet military or intelligence hierarchy appeared to have considered, or at least been foolish enough to commit to paper.

Anxious to find some way out of the public relations disaster they had created, the Soviets finally negotiated an end to the blockade in May 1949. On the day it ended, hundreds of thousands of Berliners took to the streets of the Western sectors in celebration, while a redeemed General Lucius Clay—whatever his other shortcomings, he had been the airlift's masterful architect—was given a hero's welcome. For the Soviets, the repercussions were severe and lasting. That April, the United States and Canada and nine Western European nations signed the North Atlantic Treaty, a mutual defense pact that would shortly lead to the creation of NATO. Then there was Germany. Since the end of the war, the four occupation powers had endlessly wrangled over proposals to reunify the nation. With the Berlin Blockade, this notion was such a dead letter that, less than two weeks after its lifting, there came the creation of the Federal Republic of Germany—West Germany—a union of the American, British and French occupation sectors, and the exclusion of the Soviet. Faced with this fait accompli, five months later the Soviet sector was reconstituted as the German Democratic Republic, or East Germany. That division—it would last for the next forty-one years—was an apt symbol of the worsening Cold War.

Well before that, however, the Berlin Blockade had provided an impetus for another extraordinary event. It was a meeting held in a suite of the Old Executive Office Building, the seven-story monolith immediately next to the White House on Pennsylvania Avenue.

—————

On the morning of August 6, 1948, five men strode along the marble corridors of the Old Executive Office Building, and made for the wood-paneled office of Sidney Souers. A former admiral, Souers had assumed the position of executive secretary to the National Security Council with the passage of the National Security Act the year before. Among his visitors were some of the most influential members of the American foreign policy and intelligence leadership in the Truman administration. They included CIA director Roscoe Hillenkoetter; the head of the State Department's Policy Planning Staff, George Kennan; and Deputy Assistant Secretary of State for Occupied Territories Frank G. Wisner. While its awkwardly worded minutes would offer scant clue, that meeting was to prove one of the most profoundly important conclaves in modern American history, one that would fundamentally shape the nation's future foreign intelligence apparatus and trigger consequences that continue to reverberate today.

The reason for the gathering was a top secret directive formulated by the National Security Council seven weeks earlier. Known as NSC 10/2, the directive stated that, in recognition of "the vicious covert activities of the USSR, its satellite countries and Communist groups" in attacking American interests, the NSC had concluded that "the overt foreign activities of the US Government must be supplemented by covert operations." As to what sort of activities fell under the covert operations rubric, NSC 10/2 was expansive: "propaganda; economic warfare; preventive direct action including sabotage, anti-sabotage, demolition and evacuation measures; subversion against hostile states, including assistance to underground resistance movements, guerrillas and refugee liberation groups, and support of indigenous anti-communist elements in threatened countries of the free world." If any of the very small handful of government officials given access to NSC 10/2 found it overly aggressive, their dissent was soon overwhelmed; precisely one week after the directive was first disseminated, the Berlin Blockade had begun.

Dominating the meeting was the man who had spent many months pondering how this new covert operations capability might be put into practice: George Kennan. Imperative, in his view, was that it be conducted by a semiautonomous organization, but one that took its direction primarily from the departments of State and Defense, since its activities would be "essentially an instrument of foreign policy." Where this got a bit tricky was that, as spelled out in NSC 10/2, the sort of hostile covert operations being contemplated had to be performed in such a way that "if uncovered the US Government can plausibly disclaim any responsibility for them."

This, of course, was only logical. In the arena of diplomacy and statecraft, there were sure to be situations in which the State Department would want no association with a group whose overseas activities included sabotage and subversion. Similarly, a Defense Department with bases and military advisory teams scattered across the globe might want to keep its distance from an outfit committed to aiding underground resistance forces and guerrilla groups. But how to maintain plausible deniability over a branch of government?

First, by denying its very being. Given the forgettable name of Office of Special Projects—soon to be changed to the even more forgettable name of Office of Policy Coordination, or OPC—it would be more than two decades after that 1948 meeting before this new agency appeared on any publicly available governmental flow chart, or even officially acknowledged to exist. Second, by hiding it within a preexisting entity. This is where the Central Intelligence Agency came in. Since its creation the year before, the CIA's niche in the federal government was largely that of rarefied think tank. While it encompassed some field intelligence units like Peter Sichel's team in Berlin, the bulk of its employees were academics and technical experts from the old Research and Analysis wing of the OSS. At the same time, the CIA was the recipient of that wonderfully vague subclause in its charter that enabled it to perform "other functions and duties" such as the National Security Council directed "from time to time." What could possibly meet the definition of "other functions and duties" better than covert operations?

And the CIA beckoned with another highly attractive feature: unvouchered funds. "Because the CIA's work was highly classified," Peter Sichel explained, "it bypassed all the usual financial oversight mechanisms of Congress. So, by being placed within the CIA, OPC was able to both hide its own funding and siphon money off from the parent organization. Kennan was smart: 'follow the money.'"

But this was only the starting point in building out the plausible deniability framework and, from a standpoint of bureaucratic smoke-screening, the formulation of OPC was a feat of sheer magnificence. As outlined in NSC 10/2, this new covert action unit would be "created within" the CIA, but would "operate independently of other [CIA] components." Further, while the CIA director would be "responsible" for this addition to his agency, he wouldn't have actual control over it; instead, he would share authority with representatives from the departments of State and Defense in a kind of consultative triumvirate. Just in case this wasn't slippery enough, it was further decreed that in times of war—"or when the President directs"—the OPC would sidestep this overseeing triumvirate, and instead answer to the military Joint Chiefs of Staff and their war theater commanders. Somehow meant to keep track of all this was the man Kennan had chosen to head the OPC, Frank Wisner.

While this "understanding" appeared to assign lanes of responsibility, however confusedly, between State, Defense, CIA and the Joint Chiefs of Staff, it actually achieved the precise opposite—which may have been the intent all along. At the August 6 meeting, Kennan stressed that, since he was to be accountable for the OPC's performance, "he would want to have specific knowledge of the objectives of every [covert] operation" in cases that involved "political decisions"—except that at no time was "political decisions" defined. Similarly, CIA director Hillenkoetter, having already gone on record saying he wanted no "political responsibility" for the new office, nevertheless requested that "he be kept informed in regard to all important projects and decisions"—except that defining what was important would be left to the discretion of the OPC.

If forced to make a guess out of this tangle, one might reasonably surmise that the greatest responsibility for this new agency rested with its creator, George Kennan—except that was to overlook a crucial facet of Kennan's personality. Whatever his brilliance or admirable traits in other arenas, when it came down to protecting his own reputation and career, Kennan was, for want of a more decorous term, a two-faced weasel. A clue to this was contained in a note he had written to the undersecretary of state, Robert Lovett, five weeks before the August 6 gathering, in which he put forward a list of six candidates who might head the new covert operations office. "I have placed Wisner at the head of the list," Kennan wrote, "on the recommendations of people who know him. I personally have no knowledge of his ability, but his qualifications seem reasonably good."

This appraisal surely would have been a surprise to Wisner, considering that not only did he and Kennan have frequent contact through their work at the State Department but, with both couples traveling in the same close-knit Washington social circle, George and Annelise Kennan had been guests in the home of Frank and Polly Wisner. It would also have come as a surprise to Paul Nitze, Kennan's successor as head of the Policy Planning Staff, who recalled that the two men were very close friends. But Kennan's slipperiness would only grow in the years ahead, especially once the OPC became a source of controversy. In fact, so energetically would Kennan seek to disassociate himself from his own creation that, years later, he would shamelessly tell a biographer that when it came to the OPC, "I scarcely paid any attention to it." As Wisner's eldest son and namesake, Frank Wisner Jr., charitably put it, Kennan possessed "at best, a mixed memory" of that period in his life. Indeed, in penning his sprawling, two-volume memoir, Kennan, the architect of "plausible deniability," evidently chose to put that precept into practice when it came to his stewardship of the OPC and his long association and friendship with Frank Wisner; over the span of nine hundred pages, neither OPC nor Wisner are ever mentioned.

What took place on August 6, 1948, then, was a fascinating bureaucratic shell game, one in which six government officials representing six different branches of government sought to simultaneously assert and shirk responsibility for the new covert action agency they were creating, eager on one hand to shape its charter, but even more eager to escape any fallout from its future "dirty deeds."

Instead, the burden of all of this awesome power was to fall upon one man: Frank Wisner. As intelligence historian Richard Immerman would note, through either cowardice or a lack of foresight or some combination of the two, those gathered in Sidney Souers's office that August morning had crafted an almost completely autonomous agency and ensured that, as its chief, "Wisner was accountable to virtually no one."

Several years earlier, Allen Dulles had advised Wisner to "find an inconspicuous slot in the government and start building up a network for political warfare from within." On August 6, 1948, Wisner went one better, not just finding that inconspicuous slot, but helping build it to his specifications. To be sure, though, there was a catch. As the cravenness of George Kennan forewarned, if and when things went wrong, Frank Wisner would be quite on his own.

10

AN END TO NORMAL THINGS

A lot of soldiers returning from war face difficult readjustments to civilian life—and then there was Michael Burke. Even in a lifetime marked by extraordinary highs and lows, the string of setbacks Burke experienced in 1945 was so unrelenting that he could be forgiven for feeling cursed.

If asked to choose the singularly darkest moment, he might have picked the afternoon in late September that he spent drinking at the Pierre Hotel bar on Manhattan's Fifth Avenue. He had just come from a meeting with his wife on a bench in Central Park.

Four months earlier, with the war in Europe just ended, Burke had been granted an extended leave from his post with OSS London to return to New York and deal with an unspecified "family problem." That problem was his six-year marriage to Faith Long. There had been signs of a rift in the marriage for some time, but by May 1945 those signs took the form of another man—a wealthy French glove merchant, of all things—with whom Faith and daughter Patricia were now living. At the end of that furlough, Burke had returned to London and tried to put the matter out of his mind, deciding it was something to be dealt with down the road. By September, he had run out of road.

On the Central Park bench, Faith asked for a divorce. As Burke was to recall: "Her scheme, she confided in her gay, thoughtless way, was to marry Jean, divorce him five years hence and come away with a settlement on which she and Patricia and I could live happily ever after. She was neither dismayed nor diverted when I said it was a depraved idea, urged her to hurry along to Reno for the divorce, and said goodbye. She kissed me on the cheek . . . a scene to hurry through without tears and be gone, unencumbered. She left behind a faint scent of Shalimar." Shuffling away from that meeting, he had walked aimlessly through Central Park until he came to the Pierre Hotel bar.

But the breakup with Faith was merely the latest grim tiding to come Michael Burke's way. After ending his commando stint with the French maquis in November 1944, he had been detailed to the Secret Intelligence operations desk at OSS London headquarters, overseeing the airdrop of agents into Germany and occupied northern Holland. It was while walking into OSS headquarters one morning in February that he was handed a terse cable informing him that his younger brother, Robert, a Navy pilot, had been killed in the South Pacific. Just twenty-one, Robert left behind a widow of the same age.

The news had sent Burke into a lost wander through the streets of London, one that finally led to one of his and Ernest Hemingway's old haunts, the bar at the Dorchester Hotel. There, a young woman out with a group of girlfriends and their RAF pilot dates noticed his sadness, and coaxed the story out of him. At the end of the night, the woman announced she was taking Burke home with her, and it said something about the times that whichever airman she'd originally been paired with didn't protest. "I could speak with her about [Robert's] good young days and she perceived a hurt too deep for tears. . . . Often I wished I might have seen her again. Or even known her name."

As he tried to come to terms with his brother's death, Burke could find some small consolation in knowing that, at war's end, he would at least have a job to step into in the United States, a distant prospect for many of the millions of soldiers about to be demobilized. So meticulous and careful had Burke proven on the Secret Intelligence operations desk—over the course of forty-six airdrops, he and his partner had delivered eighty-six agents into enemy territory with just one known fatality—that he had come to the attention of the senior OSS command. As with every other branch of the U.S. military, a peacetime OSS was slated to be radically reduced in size, but a place had already been reserved for Michael Burke. In fact, the incoming head of OSS New York, Robert DeVecchi, was so impressed by the Navy lieutenant from Connecticut that in late August he had passed over a slew of higher-ranking candidates to choose Burke as his future deputy. Just weeks later, though, and mere days before that fateful meeting with Faith in Central Park, all that had vanished when President Truman abruptly shut down the OSS. Now, with no other job possibilities on the horizon, Burke had joined the tens of thousands of other returned war veterans walking the sidewalks of New York, and every other American city, looking for work. As a final indignity, Burke was doing so while staying in a dingy, cheerless room at the University of Pennsylvania Club in midtown, about the only place in Manhattan he could afford.

But as he drank at the Pierre bar, Burke was also gripped by a more generalized melancholy, one familiar to many who return from war, but which can't be easily explained to civilians, let alone to home-front loved ones. Along with its horrors, war is thrilling, exhilarating, it propels the prosaic concerns and nagging chores of everyday life into inconsequence. At least this had been the case for Michael Burke. In London, he and his partner in the Secret Intelligence operations office, Rob Thompson, had rented an apartment near Sloane Square and proceeded to cut a swath through the city's bars and nightclubs, as well as its men-deprived womenfolk. By Burke's accounting, it seemed most every night ended in a drink-hazed dawn in some far-flung corner of London, where invariably at least one person was trying to find a misplaced bottle, room key or undergarment. As he would recall of that time: "Sleep seemed wasteful of good living."

Even the occasional German V-1 or V-2 missile that buzzed overhead before plummeting to explode somewhere in the city only seemed to add to London's vitality.

"They gave a strange edge to normal things," Burke said of these attacks. "To have lived in London in late 1944 and 1945 was to have been very lucky."

Now, as he drank whiskey and soda at the Pierre, Burke saw that all of this was gone forever. Taking its place was a sad remembrance of all else he had lost in the war: his brother, a number of comrades-in-arms, and just hours earlier, his marriage.

Finally paying his bar bill, he stumbled out to the street. "'Where now?' I asked myself. I had no answer but to board a double-decked Fifth Avenue bus, climb to an empty wooden bench at the rear of the open topside, and ride to Washington Square and back again in the mild September twilight. . . . At the moment survival in civilian life was my most ambitious hope. . . . I hadn't a clue where to begin, but some inner voice, impatient with my mood, told me I could not ride the Fifth Avenue bus forever."

When at last Burke returned to his bleak lodgings at the University of Pennsylvania Club that night, he found a telephone message waiting for him. It was from a former OSS comrade named Corey Ford, and he wanted Burke to call him back.

A writer best known for his satirical essays in the 1930s, Corey Ford had joined the OSS in 1943, and he and Burke became friends during their wartime postings in London. Helping cement that friendship was Ford's helpful advice after Burke had confided his own vague aspirations of becoming a writer. By September 1945, Ford had coauthored a recently released sensationalized history of the OSS entitled *Cloak and Dagger*. Where Burke came into the picture, Ford explained on the phone, was that Warner Brothers had just bought rights to *Cloak and Dagger,* and they needed a technical advisor to help with the script. Recalling his friend's interest in writing, Ford wondered if Burke might be the man for the job. Oh, and along with a suite at the Beverly Hills Hotel, the one-month gig paid $600 a week, which was not only twelve times the average American income, but exactly $600 a week more than Burke was currently earning.

Any interest, Ford asked? In less than forty-eight hours, Michael Burke had wrapped up his commitments in New York and climbed aboard the Super Chief luxury train for the five-day journey to Los Angeles.

While there are many variations of the American Dream, within weeks Burke was living its particularly pleasant Southern California version: driving around in a convertible sports car, being paid large sums of money for no discernible reason, drinking cocktails on the beach with Hollywood celebrities.

Not that there weren't some shaky moments. When he first showed up at the Warner Brothers lot to serve as technical advisor to the *Cloak and Dagger* screenwriters, Burke had been deeply intimidated. In fact, for the first several weeks, he barely uttered a word at the daily story conferences that were attended by the producer, Milton Sperling, and the famous German director, Fritz Lang. "From the beginning," Burke remembered, "I sat on the perimeter waiting to be asked a question while Sperling and Lang and first one team of writers and then another pair who replaced them argued, shouted and despaired over a series of rejected story lines."

With little progress being made on the script—each story idea seemed more absurd than the previous—Burke's one-month assignment soon stretched to two, and then beyond. That, of course, was just fine with Burke until he began to worry the stalled project might be canceled altogether. At last, he got up the courage to throw out a plot idea of his own, one loosely based on his commando rescue of an Italian admiral in southern Italy. At the next story meeting, a thoroughly dispirited Milton Sperling only half-listened as Burke launched into his idea, but gradually perked up. Finally, the producer leapt from his chair. "You sonofabitch," he shouted at Burke in apparent anger. "You've been holding out on us!"

When he understood that Sperling was about to press-gang him into being a scriptwriter, Burke demurred, pointing out that he was only a technical advisor.

"You're now a writer!" Sperling shouted again, then turned to yell at someone in the outer office. "Get him a new contract!"

And so, Michael Burke, Hollywood screenwriter, was born—and along with that, entry into the imagined life of movie-world glamour. Except not so imagined; in Burke's case, pretty true-to-life. In short order, he was hanging out at the Malibu Beach home of writer Irwin Shaw, dating an aspiring actress, and palling around with Robert Capa, Ingrid Bergman, Gene Kelly and Ava Gardner. And that was only during his off-hours. Once filming of *Cloak and Dagger* got under way, he became friends with the leads, Gary Cooper and Lilli Palmer, as well as with director Lang. Eventually, someone on the set noticed that not only was Michael Burke a bona fide former OSS commando, but he looked exactly like a Hollywood version of one. Over his alleged protests, Burke was given a screen test and then written into a *Cloak and Dagger* scene as an OSS officer (the scene was ultimately cut).

But Burke's fortunes were to turn even brighter when, at a 1946 New Year's Eve party, he met a beautiful twenty-two-year-old woman named Dorothy "Timmy" Campbell. Totally smitten, Burke soon handed back the car he had borrowed from a sometime girlfriend, to cruise the streets of Los Angeles with Campbell in her pale gray La Salle convertible. The ultrasophisticated Campbell—she worked as a fashion coordinator for Goldwyn Studios—also set out to "civilize" her new boyfriend, turning Burke on to jazz and poetry and ballet. It had been less than four months since Burke had drowned his sorrows at the Pierre Hotel.

And then there was the moment when everything about Michael Burke's radiant new life came together as one. In 1945, he had been recommended for a Navy Cross for his perilous missions in eastern France, but it wasn't until July 1946 that the backlogged medals office finally caught up to him. Although the filming of *Cloak and Dagger* was long over, Warner Brothers wasn't about to pass on free publicity, and they arranged for the award ceremony to be held on the studio lot. Squeezed into a lieutenant's uniform taken from Cary Grant's old wardrobe room, Burke was brought out onto a soundstage to have the medal pinned to his chest while the local French consul general and assorted Navy brass applauded. Also looking on were Burke's fiancée, Timmy Campbell, and his new friends, Gary Cooper and Lilli Palmer. Could a life possibly glow any brighter?

But Michael Burke may have been around the film industry long enough at that point to have picked up on a truism of the trade: when good things happen to writers in Hollywood, it's a sure sign that trouble is on the way.

It was the spring of 1948 and Michael Burke, not yet two years removed from his gala medal ceremony on the Warner Brothers lot, was unemployed and essentially broke.

Just before the release of *Cloak and Dagger,* Burke had discovered that, despite their effusive praise for his work on the film, Warner Brothers had limited future need for his writing skills—"limited" in this case translating to "none at all." The same held true for the other Hollywood studios and directors he approached. After several months of futile door-knocking, he decided to head back to New York City and pursue his new dream of making it as a writer. Specifically what kind of writer wasn't solidified—along with screenplays, Burke wrote short stories, and was interested in journalism—just that success needed to happen fairly soon. In that same summer of 1946, he and Timmy married, and almost immediately their first child together, Doreen, was on the way.

But just as Michael Burke once seemed to have a golden touch, so now everything he reached for turned to cinders. His screenplay about the spurned wife of King George IV looked set to go into production with Twentieth Century–Fox—right up until the day it wasn't. Snowbound in a small cottage on the Hudson River during the Great Blizzard of 1947, Burke feverishly worked up an idea for a radio drama centering on a secret agent called Solitaire. That project also appeared to be a done deal until it, too, was suddenly scuttled. In desperation, he teamed up with an old OSS colleague from his Italian commando days, Marcello Girosi, to write subtitles and liner notes for a series of Italian films and operas being distributed in the United States. It was hardly enough to make ends meet, however, and by early 1948, Burke was so broke that when someone stole his infant daughter's stroller from in front of their Manhattan apartment, the cost of replacing it posed a severe burden. By that spring, the family's financial situation was so dire that Burke was forced to swallow his pride and borrow money from his father. As he would later describe it, "the move from Hollywood to New York was a plummet down a mine shaft."

But as might be expected from the roller-coaster nature of his life, poverty was about to look quite a bit different for Michael Burke than it did for most people. This gentler face of destitution was made possible through the connections of his wife, Timmy.

During a stint as a Warner Brothers publicist, Timmy had become close friends with an actress, Faye Emerson, who went on to marry Elliott Roosevelt, one of Franklin and Eleanor's sons. By 1948, the newlyweds had taken up residence at Top Cottage, a bungalow President Roosevelt built for himself on the family's magnificent Hyde Park estate just north of New York City, and they frequently invited Michael and Timmy Burke up from the city for visits. The president's widow, Eleanor, took a quick liking to the handsome young couple and their little daughter and, after learning of their straitened circumstances from her son, invited them to spend the summer on the estate. Given use of one of the old cottages on the compound, as well as a car, the Burkes soon found themselves included in the Roosevelt family social whirl.

"He was basically couch-surfing," explained his eldest daughter, Patricia, "but surfing on the very best couches."

The matriarch of the Roosevelt clan came to like Michael Burke so well that he became something of a confidant. He recalled one afternoon at the Hyde Park pool when, with the shallow end teeming with her various young grandchildren, the sixty-four-year-old Eleanor executed a graceful dive off the diving board, then swam over to where Burke sat at the pool's edge. "I really hate diving," she told him in a conspiratorial whisper. "I do it only to set an example for the children."

While that summer of 1948 at Hyde Park was a welcome respite from the quietly desperate life he had been leading ninety miles to the south, Burke was also acutely aware that summers eventually end. As he contemplated his return to the "real world," and with no sign that his hoped-for career as a successful writer would come to fruition, he grimly concluded that he really only had two skills to fall back on: football and guerrilla warfare. The problem was, he was now too old for football, and there was no market for former guerrilla fighters. Or was there?

The caller from Washington was vague to the point of evasiveness. He explained that he was calling on the recommendation of a man named Frank Lindsay, one of Burke's old OSS comrades, and it was in connection with a possible job opportunity. But the caller much preferred to discuss things in person, and was willing to come to New York to do so; might Burke know of a "discreet, quiet place" where they could meet?

As dubious as all this sounded, Burke was hardly in a position to decline. It was several months since he and his family had summered at the Roosevelt estate in Hyde Park, and his economic situation had grown only bleaker in the interim. About the only paid writing gig he had landed was working up a script for a technical training film on alternating electrical current, a project unlikely to shake the New York literary scene. Beyond that, "rejection slips piled up like autumn leaves, and every day now was closing down with a taste of failure." With a touch of irony considering his stalled aspirations, Burke suggested to the Washington caller that they meet in New York City's most legendary literary watering hole: the Oak Room of the Algonquin Hotel on 44th Street.

On the appointed day, Burke was met in the Oak Room by two young men in suits who sat with their backs to the wall. One had fine blond hair and wore gold rim glasses, while the other had a nervous habit of constantly touching an expensive leather briefcase set on the banquette beside him. Burke sized him up as the flunky. "You knew that all his life he would be the aide, the second man, the one who carried the briefcase."

Martinis were ordered. For some time, the conversation meandered along in pleasantries, the two well-dressed strangers giving scant hint of either their affiliation or their reason for coming. Finally, the blond asked a peculiar question: what might Burke know of Albania?

Not much, it turned out. "My mind's eye darted around the Adriatic and the Mediterranean trying to fix just where Albania was," he recalled. "The last time it had crossed my mind was in a college political science class: Mussolini had stomped over Albania and King Zog had fled carrying a bucket filled with the Crown Jewels. That was 1939. Ten years later I could remember nothing else about Albania." This didn't seem the moment for such candor. Instead, Burke muttered a simple but portentous: "Oh, yes."

That was good enough for his visitors. After a second round of martinis was ordered, the blond man finally passed on a few salient details, revealing that he and his companion were representatives of a new branch of the federal government that was attached to, but not exactly a part of, the Central Intelligence Agency, a branch so secretive it didn't officially exist at all. While it's unlikely Burke was told the name of this shadowy unit—Frank Wisner's Office of Policy Coordination—his visitors did let on that it was dedicated to conducting covert action against the communist enemy throughout the world.

That is where Albania entered the picture. By early 1949, the communist government of Josip Broz Tito in neighboring Yugoslavia had broken with Stalin and the Soviet bloc. Whatever this might mean for Yugoslavia's future, it also meant that communist Albania was now geographically isolated from the rest of the Soviet satellite nations, hemmed in by Yugoslavia and Greece on three sides, and by the Adriatic Sea on the fourth. What's more, the dictator of Albania, Enver Hoxha, was a mercurial and despotic leader, and there were persistent reports that he faced widespread opposition in the conservative and clannish mountain nation. Where Michael Burke fit into this Albanian civics lesson, the men in the Oak Room explained, was that they wanted him to start a revolution there.

"I gazed into the dark wood behind their heads striving to look reflective, to give the appearance of weighing their proposal. . . . I reined in my eagerness, masking the fact that I would have agreed to unseat Stalin had they asked. Wiser, I thought, to allow them the satisfaction of persuading me over lobster salad, escalope de veau, [and] two bottles of Sancerre."

But Burke was too strapped to play it cool for very long—and it became even harder once he learned some of the details of his prospective job.

His principal mission for the OPC would be to oversee the infiltration of anti-communist Albanian partisans into their homeland, with their recruiting done in consultation with leaders of the Albanian émigré community. Since most of those émigrés lived in Italy, the operation would require Burke and his wife and young child to leave their cramped Greenwich Village apartment and relocate to a villa in Rome. To compensate for this inconvenience, as an OPC contract agent, Burke would receive an annual salary of $8,000, or almost three times the average American income at the time. It got better. Since Burke would be traveling a great deal and not have a normal work schedule—he wouldn't be going into an office every day, for example—to avoid suspicion, he needed to live a sufficiently opulent lifestyle as to be seen as a man of some means. To accomplish this, he would also be given a tax-free living allowance of $7,000, an almost incalculable sum in Italy's slowly recovering economy. When Burke broke the news to his wife that afternoon—"probably I was somewhat vague about the specifics," he noted—Timmy was ecstatic.

This still left one crucial matter. Obviously, Burke needed some kind of cover story to mask his activities in Italy, but when he raised this point with the Oak Room emissaries it drew nonplussed stares. He assured the men he would come up with his own false front.

Easier said than done, because just what kind of profession would allow Burke to live and entertain lavishly without requiring too much in the way of actual work, or the need to eventually show some kind of end product? The answer came to him in a flash: movie producer. After establishing a corporate bank account and a backstop New York City address, Burke contacted a Warner Brothers executive he knew and announced he was moving to Rome to try to break into the then-burgeoning Italian film industry. The Warner executive offered to consider any projects that might seem promising, thus unwittingly becoming Burke's chief reference should anyone in Italy question his bona fides.

With a stack of business cards identifying him as the head of Imperial Pictures, that August, Michael Burke headed for Rome. Just in case the movie producer bio proved lacking, also in his luggage was a new .380 Colt automatic. "I could feel my adrenaline flow stepping up," he was to recall, "rising to the old lure."

Act 2

HEARTS AND MINDS AND DIRTY TRICKS

It's not enough to be *against* communism;
you have to be *for* something.

—EDWARD LANSDALE, March 29, 1960

11

THE MIGHTY WURLITZER
AND THE ROYAL DWARF

On the evening of April 13, 1948, a Czech engineer named Jan Prosvic received a visitor at his apartment in Prague. The stranger called himself Johnny and, after a bit of circuitous conversation, revealed he was an agent of the U.S. Army's Counter Intelligence Corps, or CIC. It had been just seven weeks since the communists seized power in Czechoslovakia, and Johnny had learned through the underground grapevine that Prosvic was being targeted by the new government; if Prosvic wished to escape to the American occupation zone in neighboring Germany, Johnny was there to help him do so.

As detailed by historian Igor Lukes, there was reason for the CIC to be interested in helping Prosvic, and even better reason for Prosvic to seize on Johnny's offer. An accomplished engineer, Prosvic was a founder of one of Czechoslovakia's leading manufacturers of household electrical appliances, and his wealth made him precisely the sort of person the new regime looked to go after. In fact, that process was already under way. With the coup not even two months old, Prosvic had already been stripped of the ownership of his company and, just days before Johnny's visit, picked up by Czech security forces and harshly interrogated.

Despite these ominous signs, Prosvic had little desire to flee his homeland. His wife, Jirina, perhaps thinking of the future of their four young children, was even more adamant on the topic. After thanking Johnny for his offer, the couple sent the CIC man on his way.

Over the next several days, the Prosvics received a number of anonymous telephone calls informing them that they were in imminent danger from the regime. These warnings still didn't dissuade the couple from rebuffing Johnny a second time. It was only on the CIC man's third visit, and after more anonymous calls, that the Prosvics finally appreciated the peril they were in and accepted his offer.

On the night of April 23, Johnny drove the couple, along with their two eldest daughters, to Kdyně, a small town a hundred miles southwest of Prague and close to the border with American-occupied Germany. There, Johnny handed the family off to a local police chief. After the Prosvics paid a smuggler's fee of 70,000 Czech korunas (several years' income for the average Czech), the policeman escorted the family through a series of Czech security roadblocks, then led them on foot around a small lake until they came to a border marker fixed in the ground. In the darkness, the policeman pointed out a lighted building a short distance away: it was a forward United States Army post, just inside Germany.

At the outpost, the Prosvics were met by German border guards. Explaining they had fled Czechoslovakia, the family was brought inside the compound and taken to a conference room where they were greeted by an American army officer named Tony. After congratulating the Prosvics on their escape and giving chocolate to the girls, Tony began to debrief the couple, typing their answers in the form of an affidavit required by American authorities of those seeking political asylum. During the interview, the Prosvics took note of framed portraits of Presidents Roosevelt and Truman on the office walls, a spread of recent American magazines on a coffee table.

But from its celebratory beginnings, the interview steadily grew tense. The source of that tension appeared to be Tony's deepening disappointment at the couple's replies to his queries about the Prague underground scene. The fact was, though, that Jan and Jirina Prosvic were quite apolitical, had never been part of an anti-communist movement, and knew no one who was. The engineer and his wife were just as unavailing in providing the names of people who had helped the family plan their flight, or of others who might wish to escape. Ultimately, Tony became convinced the Prosvics weren't prospective defectors at all, but rather provocateurs sent by the Prague regime, and angrily ended the meeting. "We have no interest in Czech Communists," he announced. Drawing a pistol, he then led the stunned couple, along with their daughters, to a waiting car. Hustled inside, within minutes the Prosvics had been driven back across the border and delivered to Czech police.

Trapped by the asylum petition they had signed, the Prosvics paid dearly at the hands of the Czech judicial system. Jan Prosvic was banished to a penal labor camp, while the once affluent family had both their

Prague apartment and their countryside villa confiscated, leaving them destitute. For all those Czechs who learned of the grim fate of the Prosvics, here was a cautionary tale on the potential calamity to befall those who would betray the homeland—as well, of course, as those who would trust in the Americans.

Except it was all a lie. In truth, the Prosvics had never met any American officials, nor had they crossed the German border. Instead, they were victims of an elaborate entrapment scheme conducted by the Czech secret police code-named Operation Kamen, and everyone they had come into contact with—from Johnny, to the policeman in Kdyně, to the "German" border guards, to Tony—were in on it. Johnny's real name was Josef Janousek and both he and Tony, aka Amon Tomasoff, were actually agents of the Státní bezpečnost (StB), the Czech internal security agency.

As detailed by Lukes, Czech authorities ran Operation Kamen for the next three years. In some cases, they followed the same script used on the Prosvics, with the "Americans" turning back would-be escapees for being insufficiently anti-communist. At other times, once their interviews with Tony were completed at the outpost, defectors were told to walk farther on into "Germany" where they would be received and processed by other American officials; somewhere along this walk they would be "detected" by Czech border guards and arrested. So convincing were the Kamen actors that many of their victims remained convinced even years afterward that their capture was a result of their own carelessness, that they had made contact with the West but then become disoriented in the forest. Most cunningly, the StB even floated a photograph through the Prague underground of a defector being interviewed by Tony in the "German" border outpost, providing "proof" that an escape route existed as encouragement for others to follow suit. Whatever the game's variation, what all the failed defectors had in common was being pumped dry for information—first by Tony the American, and then by their post-Tony StB captors—for the names of others who were disloyal or might be tempted to flee. With those names, "CIC officers" like Johnny lined up their next batch of prey. Before Kamen was shut down in 1951, according to Lukes, the scheme had netted hundreds of victims, resulting in nearly three hundred prison sentences, twenty life sentences and ten executions.

The stunning efficacy of operations like Kamen underscored the formidable odds Western intelligence agencies faced as they squared off against the Soviets and their satellite regimes in postwar Eastern Europe. In 1945, the West had been forced to cede physical control of the region due to the sheer numbers of Soviet soldiers and commissars on the ground. By 1948, that disadvantage was being mirrored in the spy war sphere by an opponent that, from a standpoint of guile and ruthlessness, had no equal. At first glance, it might seem remarkable that a deception as sophisticated as Kamen had been organized and launched within mere weeks of the communist coup in Czechoslovakia. Except that the StB was emulating nearly identical stings that the Soviet KGB and their East German acolytes had been running in Berlin over the previous three years, which in turn took their inspiration from entrapment schemes the KGB's forebears had run in the 1920s.

But operations like Kamen were merely one facet of a fantastically calculating security apparatus that extended throughout the Soviet orbit. As far back as the 1920s, and continuing into the 1980s, the KGB and its precursors routinely sent across to the West "dangles," or false defectors, and then meticulously built out their bona fides. One technique they often used to accomplish this was to have the "defector" betray some of his spy colleagues in the field. For a regime that, during Stalin's reign, routinely recalled and executed its own intelligence officers for no other cause than their "Western taint," it was a small step to sacrifice a batch of their less-important operatives in the West if it helped cover the tracks or burnish the credentials of a more important one.

Joined to such callousness was a culture of paranoia and scrutiny of which Western authorities could hardly conceive. Well into the 1930s, Soviet internal security agencies retained in their archives samples of the typescript of *every* typewriter in the Soviet Union. Woe to any dissident who thought to type up an anti-state tract, for the typescript archives "enabled the KGB, using technical procedures, to determine the origin of any typed text."

Further, in the Soviet government—and by extension, in her Eastern European satellites—information could be quarantined to a degree unimaginable in the West. To cite one example, even though the deployment of American Jupiter nuclear missiles to Turkey in 1961 was a state secret of the highest order, certainly scores, and probably hundreds, of American officials were involved in some aspect of the mission. By contrast, when Soviet premier Nikita Khrushchev chose to install nuclear missiles in Cuba the following year, the group tasked to prepare the groundwork consisted of precisely four Soviet generals and a colonel. "Throughout the early planning stage, no secretaries were used to prepare final typed texts. A colonel with good penmanship wrote the proposal that the Defense Council adopted." Even when that proposal was forwarded on to the Soviet defense minister and Khrushchev for final approval, it remained in its handwritten form.

On top of all this was a police state and informant culture that permeated down to the shop floor and the nuclear family. At the time of East Germany's demise in 1989, it was estimated that 1 out of every 165 residents were full-time employees of the Stasi internal security agency, with their work supported by a far greater network of part-time workers and informants. Throughout the Soviet bloc were innumerable documented cases of siblings turning in siblings, children informing on parents. If the distinguishing characteristic of Nazi Germany's intelligence agencies was institutional arrogance, the chief characteristic of Soviet intelligence would seem to be the precise opposite, an inferiority complex so deep-rooted as to fuel an unslakable paranoia. Of course, the perils of arrogance are clear if one's goal is world domination, but if one's goal is to maintain a police state, paranoia would hardly seem a handicap at all.

And just how to ever do battle against such a system? While a vast array of men and women in Western governments and intelligence agencies and think tanks grappled with that question in the late 1940s, the burden fell disproportionately on the shoulders of a single man: OPC director Frank G. Wisner. He brought a unique outlook to the task. As *New York Times* journalist Harrison Salisbury noted, "Frank Wisner was the key to a great many things, a brilliant, compulsive man . . . a man of enormous charm, imagination, [the] conviction that anything, *anything* could be achieved and that he could achieve it."

Franklin Lindsay was in Paris when he got the call in the autumn of 1948. Frank Wisner was circumspect on the phone, only allowing that he was "doing some very interesting things," and asked Lindsay to come see him the next time he was in Washington. When that meeting came a few weeks later, Wisner explained that he was putting together a top secret outfit called the Office of Policy Coordination. He wanted Lindsay to come in as one of his "senior people."

The two men knew each other from World War II, and though separated in age by seven years, came from similar upper-class backgrounds. Lindsay, the younger of the two, was from a well-to-do Boston family and had obtained an engineering degree at Stanford. As a junior Army officer during the war, he had ended up in Cairo, where he fell in with a group of OSS officers. "I suspect they thought that, 'Well, anybody who has an engineering degree must know how to blow up bridges,'" he recalled. "So they proposed that I transfer to OSS." Lindsay soon did so, and a few months later was parachuted into northern Yugoslavia as a liaison officer to the partisans. He subsequently met and became friends with fellow OSSer Frank Wisner in wartime London.

When he got the call from his old comrade in 1948, however, Frank Lindsay had long since left the service, and was very happily living in Paris and working on the Marshall Plan. Far more sedate than Wisner, he also wasn't convinced the OPC job was a good fit—at least what he understood of it from the few details he could wring from Wisner—and he put off the forceful lawyer as best he could. That only lasted until Lindsay met with his immediate boss, Marshall Plan administrator Averell Harriman. Somewhat to Lindsay's surprise, Harriman counseled that other people could do the Paris job, but that the OPC posting was unique; he had to take it.

Lindsay's initial misgivings undoubtedly grew when he arrived at OPC headquarters in Washington. It consisted of a few grim and badly constructed wooden buildings set down in a swampy stretch of land near the Reflecting Pool, part of a series of structures thrown up along the edge of the National Mall as temporary office space during World War II but never taken down. The shabbiness extended to Wisner's personal office, a spare room with peeling linoleum floor tiles and the most utilitarian of government surplus furniture. Lindsay also discovered that the nickname given OPC headquarters, the Rat Palace, wasn't hyperbole, but derived from the throngs of rodents that roamed its rooms in search of any food carelessly left out. What *was* hyperbole had been Wisner's talk of bringing Lindsay on board as one of his "senior people," considering that, at the time, the entire office consisted of three or four employees. "He designated me as head of operations," Lindsay recalled, "whatever operations was."

Throughout his life, acquaintances tended to use rather conflicting adjectives in describing Wisner, as a man both charming and intense, a wonderfully engaging storyteller but impatient; "cool yet coiled," is how one CIA colleague described him. These seeming contradictions were most especially on display as Wisner launched into his recruitment drive for OPC. The former lawyer tended to work with rolled-up shirtsleeves, and many called into his Rat Palace office were to comment on how his soft Deep South accent with its suggestion of an easygoing manner was undercut by his habit of rhythmically clenching and unclenching his fists, causing his forearm muscles to constantly flex.

Another OSS veteran who received a summons to the Temporaries—or "Tempos"—on the Mall was writer and future Watergate conspirator E. Howard Hunt. Having served in India and China during the war, Hunt had never crossed paths with Wisner, and his first impression was of a "stiffly postured" man, but one who appeared to be "perpetually smiling to himself about something he knew and you didn't." After brief pleasantries, Wisner gave him a quick rundown on his OPC start-up.

"It'll be something different, maybe something up your alley. OPC won't just gather intelligence." Wisner then went in for the kill, the bait that few OSS veterans could resist. "We'll be what America needs in this Cold War, an action arm. You're a man of action. Aren't you, Hunt?" E. Howard Hunt had swiftly signed on, too.

By Lindsay's account, Wisner had been promised a three-year shake-out before OPC took on any major operations. That quaint notion went by the wayside almost immediately, overwhelmed by the rush of events: the Berlin Blockade; a rapidly deteriorating situation in China. Instead, the OPC was expected to immediately launch its campaign against Soviet and communist expansion or, as laid out by the National Security Council, to "undertake the full range of covert activities incident to the conduct of secret political, psychological, and economic warfare." Added to this vague and sprawling charter was something called "preventive direct action," a euphemism for paramilitary operations including demolitions and sabotage.

Certainly, Wisner was offered no respite from the man who had been the prime mover behind the OPC's creation (until he forgot that he was): George Kennan. After reading over Wisner's fantastically ambitious plans for the 1949 fiscal year, Kennan sent a somewhat frosty note to the OPC head in early January: "In my opinion, this presentation contains the minimum of what is required from the foreign policy standpoint in the way of covert operations during the coming year. . . . As the international situation develops, every day makes more evident the importance of the role which will have to be played by covert operations if our national interests are to be adequately protected."

An easy pugnacity for Kennan to assume since he had already ensured his own invisibility in such matters. As he had reminded the undersecretary of state two months prior to that goading note to Wisner, "a cardinal consideration in the establishment of Wisner's office . . . [is that] this Department should take no responsibility for his operations."

But if ever there was a man equal to the colossal task ahead, it was Frank G. Wisner. In his conception, "intelligence was about doing things, not finding out about things," and to that end, the OPC would engage the communist enemy on most any conceivable battle front, a gamut that ran from the cerebral and cultural, to the violent and revolutionary. This effort would come to be known as the Mighty Wurlitzer, a vast and ever-adaptive apparatus that, over time, was to extend its reach into a bewildering array of political and social spheres around the world. An underground guerrilla force called the Ukrainian Insurgent Army would have association with the Wurlitzer, but so would the Boston Pops Symphony Orchestra; the AFL-CIO; and an outfit called the Crusade for Family Prayer. Put on the OPC payroll—although often completely unaware of it—were blues musicians, Third World colonels, avant-garde poets, and university professors. Perhaps inevitably, the man sitting atop this fantastically eclectic structure, Frank Wisner, would earn the nickname "the Wiz."

"There was nothing else in my father's life that he cared as much about," recalled Wisner's son Graham. "He was totally devoted to this sense that we are a force for good in the world, and that we have to go out into the world and propel that good however we can. A nuanced question these days, but my father absolutely believed it."

Many of the OPC's initial forays occurred in Western Europe and on the cultural front. As an internal CIA history of the OPC noted, in the late 1940s groups with "political aspirations contrary to those of the Communists had few resources to advance their cause." Along with making clear where those resources needed to come from—the United States—the CIA warned of what would happen in their absence, "that the [Soviets'] Cominform might proceed unhampered in its program to envelop the world with Communist ideology."

Curiously, these first anti-communist efforts in Western Europe displayed a high degree of sophistication, bearing scant resemblance to the kind of hectoring and sophomoric propaganda the CIA would later often employ elsewhere. This undoubtedly reflected the social and political refinement of Wisner and the mostly Ivy League graduates he gathered around him at OPC headquarters, but it also revealed a considered awareness that, at least in the urbane circles of Western Europe, their approach had to be less about combating the appeal of communism head-on than in co-opting it. After all, conservatives were already "in the bag" and, thus, essentially irrelevant to the hearts-and-minds campaign Wisner sought to wage; the real battle was for the middle and the left. To this end, a 1950 OPC creation, the Congress for Cultural Freedom, drew the participation of an array of left-of-center intellectuals and such luminaries as Tennessee Williams, Bertrand Russell and historian Arthur Schlesinger Jr. In Berlin, the OPC sponsored art exhibitions and traveling musical troupes, the goal being to subtly illustrate the importance of freedom of creative expression and, by extension, the superiority of the American "way of life." One of the OPC's more enduring contributions was its involvement in the founding of *The Paris Review* in 1953. Destined to become one of the leading literary quarterlies in the Western world over the next half-century, few of the writers who appeared in the *Review*'s pages—a list that included the likes of Jack Kerouac, Samuel Beckett and Jean Genet—might have guessed that two of its three founding editors, writers George Plimpton and Peter Matthiessen, were on the OPC payroll. It would be little exaggeration to say that, in the late 1940s and early 1950s, one of the principal sources of funding for cultural and artistic projects in an economically prostrate Western Europe was the CIA's Office of Policy Coordination. And, as spy agencies go, the OPC had a pretty discerning eye; as historian Hugh Wilford notes, "the CIA's tastes in literature were predominantly highbrow and modernist. Much the same could be said, it seems, of the visual arts." All the while, the OPC was also funneling money to Western European think tanks and labor unions and youth leagues, vying for influence at the leftward end of society wherever they might make inroads.

All well and good for Western Europe. When it came to Eastern Europe, the OPC went in for a more boisterous set of initiatives. In both displaced persons camps and Western capitals, OPC officers sought to forge ties with leaders of émigré groups living in exile from their communist-controlled homelands. Such figures were seen as potentially useful in the conduct of psychological warfare in their native countries and, if a future opportunity arose, as the military vanguard of "preventive direct action." Toward that goal, in 1949 the OPC created the National Committee for a Free Europe (NCFE), a political front headed by Wisner's friend and former OSS colleague Allen Dulles, and designed to serve as an umbrella for Eastern European anti-communist émigré groups. It was soon joined by the American Committee for the Liberation of the Peoples of Russia, or ACLPR.

Even here, though, the OPC's schemes contained a strong element of what has come to be known as soft power. From an old OSS base outside Frankfurt, the ACLPR initiated Radio Liberty, which beamed Russian language broadcasts into the Soviet Union. From its own installation outside Munich, the NCFE's well-funded Radio Free Europe targeted the Eastern European satellite states, and was soon broadcasting in over a dozen languages. From a stockpile of surplus weather balloons left over from the war, Wisner came up with the idea of filling them with propaganda leaflets and floating them across the Iron Curtain. "A trial project took place over a two-week period in 1951," noted a history of the propaganda radio stations. "The prevailing west-to-east wind patterns carried the hydrogen-inflated balloons sailing over the border of West Germany, where they dropped their payload of more than eleven million leaflets on Czechoslovakia."

What most all these disparate endeavors had in common was plausible deniability, the lack of evidence of direct American support. This, too, reflected a mature reading of European sensitivities, an awareness among those manning the Mighty Wurlitzer that it would be self-defeating should the agency's role become known. One can well imagine that a playwright like Tennessee Williams might be chagrined to learn that at the Congress for Cultural Freedom he was in the service of an OPC front group, but how much more enraged some French leftist intellectual learning the same about his contributions to *The Paris Review*? Similarly, if it was leaked that Radio Liberty and Radio Free Europe were organs of American intelligence, Moscow's regular accusations of such would be instantly confirmed.

To remain as the unseen hand, the OPC ran its funding through all manner of innocuous-sounding political front groups, legitimate labor unions, even highly prestigious charities and arts institutions; both the Whitney Trust and the Museum of Modern Art frequently served as conduits for OPC funds. As for how the OPC amassed all this funding in the first place, that was the result of a fairly ingenious shell game, its ability to tap into a little-known cash source within the American government known as counterpart funds, set-aside accounts meant to cover administrative costs of the Marshall Plan. These accounts gave OPC access to a cache of "unvouchered funds" that some have estimated ran to as much as $200 million a year. Starting in 1949 and extending well into the 1970s, counterpart funds served as a crucial means for the CIA—and during its quasi-independent years, the OPC—to fund clandestine foreign operations throughout the world with virtually no oversight from any direction. "[The CIA] could do exactly as it pleased," recalled Tom Braden, a senior CIA operations officer in the 1950s. "It could hire armies; it could buy banks. There was simply no limit to the money it could spend and no limit to the people it could hire and no limit to the activities it could decide were necessary to conduct the war—the secret war."

The appeal of all this could be seen in who the OPC managed to recruit. Between its anything-goes ethos and its willingness to get creative, the secret agency attracted many former OSS officers who, frustrated either by world events or the dullness of their civilian lives, leapt at the chance to rejoin the fray. It also didn't hurt that OPC was a most generous employer, as Michael Burke could attest. At the same time, this generosity provoked a good deal of tension and jealousy within the other branches of the CIA. While Wisner was warned against poaching from the "regular" CIA staff or their operatives in the field, OPC offered such markedly higher salaries and payouts that, rather like using a salt lick to hunt deer, the quarry simply came to him. As the hottest show in town— albeit one that didn't officially exist—the OPC ballooned in size. By the end of 1949, the three or four employees Frank Lindsay had encountered upon his arrival at the Tempos a year earlier had multiplied to over three hundred officers operating out of five foreign stations with a budget of nearly $5 million. Within another three years, that would mushroom to forty-seven foreign stations, a permanent and contract staff of over six thousand, and a budget of $84 million.

But one of the most remarkable features of the Mighty Wurlitzer in its early years was just how few people truly grasped the breadth of its oper- ation. In addition to Frank Wisner and Frank Lindsay, both of whom routinely toiled sixteen hours a day at their Tempo desks, those OPC offi- cials with a good sense of its myriad operations around the globe could probably be counted on two hands—and even that estimate may be high.

One who did was a man named Carmel Offie. If largely unknown today, Offie remains one of the most unlikely and intriguing figures ever to reach a position of prominence in the American government, a consummate charmer, schemer and scoundrel who earned the nick- name the Royal Dwarf for the behind-the-scenes power he wielded. Making his modern-day anonymity more surprising is that most every- one even peripherally connected to the American intelligence world of the late 1940s seemed to have a favorite Carmel Offie story, a distinct Offie memory. To a journalist who knew him well, Offie was "exception- ally witty, wonderful in the salons of Georgetown, and extraordinarily sinister." Frank Wisner's eldest son, Frank Jr., remembers the weekend family gatherings of the OPC senior leadership at Offie's mansion on Woodley Road, during which he and the other young children would be parked in a television room to watch cartoons. "Periodically, our parents would send Offie in to entertain us," he recalled. "My God, what were they thinking?!" An OPC officer who frequently battled with Offie could never shake the image of their last encounter, the Royal Dwarf sprinting across the tarmac of an airfield in Europe with silver candelabras tucked under each arm. "That sort of summed up Offie for me," Frank Holcomb told writer Burton Hersh. "He'd got something someplace, and he was bringing it back." In Berlin, Peter Sichel heard frequent mention of the mysterious savant who appeared to be everywhere at once, the OPC's ultimate fix-it man. "He was very well known but, from what I can recall, no one ever said a good thing about him. Except Wisner. Wisner seemingly loved him." Asked if he ever met Offie, Sichel wistfully shook his head. "No. It is a lack in my life."

A small and exceedingly odd-looking man—few who met him could refrain from noting his physical repulsiveness—Offie, born in 1909, was one of at least eleven children born to an Italian immigrant laborer and his illiterate wife in the scrubby steel town of Sharon, Pennsylvania. Despite the harshness of his upbringing, the young Offie was clearly both brilliant and ambitious, and his first ambition was to get the hell out of Sharon. His improbable ticket to do so was stenography. In 1926, the seventeen-year-old Offie, having taken a stenography class at a local business school, decamped for Washington and a job as a clerk at the Interstate Commerce Commission. After arranging a transfer to the State Department and clerking for several years at the American embassy in Honduras, Offie returned to State Department headquarters in Washington. There, coworkers marveled at his ability to write two memorandums simultaneously with a pen in either hand, while effortlessly slipping between the several foreign languages—he would eventually be fluent in at least five—that he had taught himself.

Offie's true ascendancy began in 1934, helped along by a wealthy diplomat and close friend of President Roosevelt's named William C. Bullitt. Appointed the first U.S. ambassador to the Soviet Union in late 1933, within months Bullitt had become so overworked in Moscow that he pleaded with the State Department to send him a personal secretary. Answering the call was Carmel Offie.

Implausible as it might seem, these two extraordinarily different men—Bullitt a Philadelphia blue blood voted "most brilliant" of his Yale class, Offie a working-class high school graduate nearly twenty years younger—became inseparable in Moscow, so much so that, within six months, the ambassador promoted his secretary to vice consul. As Bullitt told President Roosevelt, Offie "is more useful to this mission than any [other] man."

Their odd-couple partnership only expanded when Bullitt was transferred to Paris in 1936, as did Offie's circle of admirers. In a matter of weeks, the former stenographer had become the darling of Parisian aristocracy. As Bullitt informed the president that October, "Offie was the guest of honor at Maxim's at a dinner given by the Marquis and Marquise de Polignac, who are the greatest snobs in France. Inasmuch as the Polignacs habitually ignore everyone from this Embassy, including the Ambassadors, I think you will agree with me that [Offie] is already going fast and far." But Offie had higher to climb on the social ladder; before long, he was the favorite bridge partner of the Duchess of Windsor, Wallis Simpson, and an intimate of the Comtesse de Portes, the mistress of the French prime minister. "More than ever," Bullitt wrote Roosevelt in the summer of 1940, "Offie is the power behind the throne."

By then, Bullitt and Offie were so conjoined in people's minds that whispers around the State Department held they were lovers. While this may not have been true—the twice-married Bullitt also had the reputation of being a serial womanizer—it was lent credence by Offie being as close to openly gay as was permissible in 1930s American officialdom. Above all else, Carmel Offie was a consummate collector of favors, an opportunist who seemed to possess a preternatural skill for gaming the system and knowing just whom to flatter. During his tour in Moscow, he reportedly used embassy funds to buy expensive Russian fur coats, then used the diplomatic pouch to distribute them to senior State Department officials in Washington. In Paris in the late 1930s, he lined up attractive women as "dates" for the visiting sons of Joseph Kennedy, the ambassador to Great Britain, Joe Jr. and Jack. Especially frequent recipients of Offie's attentions were President Roosevelt's personal secretaries, Missy LeHand and Grace Tully.

"I merely want to drop you this line to tell you that I shall take care of the antique cigarette box in the next few days," he wrote Tully from Paris on May 30, 1940. This was only the latest of many presents Offie had showered on the president's secretaries over the years, but notable this time was that he was writing just as the invading German army was closing on the French capital, a matter he alluded to at the note's end. "We still have no food problems or anything like that, but I have just been reading that during the 1870 crisis, the people of Paris were calmly eating dogs, cats, etc. Do you suppose Mary [another Roosevelt secretary] would send me a can of pears if things get bad?"

Throughout the war, and even as his new position as a military intelligence officer took him from one devastated battle zone to the next, Offie somehow always managed to find the time to procure a rare Oriental carpet for one friend, a nice bottle of contraband perfume for another. He was also adroit enough to switch mentors when Bullitt fell out of favor with Roosevelt, attaching himself instead to Robert Murphy, the State Department's liaison to the Allied military high command. He had much the same effect on Murphy as he'd had on Bullitt; when Murphy was named the chief U.S. political advisor in Germany at war's end, an extremely powerful position, he not only took Offie with him, but made him his deputy. Somewhat incongruously considering the mores of the time, battle-hardened American generals across occupied Germany were soon vying for the counsel and political wisdom of the flamboyant former stenographer from western Pennsylvania.

Having already come to loathe communism from his time in Moscow—Offie had been posted there during the run-up to Stalin's Great Terror—this sentiment hardened into a visceral hatred during the three years he spent in Germany and observing the Soviet subjugation of Eastern Europe firsthand. It was a sentiment that found common ground with Frank Wisner when he went looking for an OPC fix-it man in the summer of 1948.

Wisner's timing was impeccable for, just that spring, Offie's freebooting ways at the State Department had finally caught up to him when inspectors discovered he was using the German diplomatic pouch to move large amounts of currency around Europe; this came on the heels of persistent rumors about contraband diamonds, black-market trading, war profiteering, and some nasty business about commandeering a military plane to transport three hundred Finnish lobsters. While Offie managed to talk his way out of those missteps, he saw that his days at State were numbered, and resigned that summer. By happy coincidence, though, what State viewed as gross violations of diplomatic norms, Frank Wisner apparently regarded as entrepreneurship; that September, he brought Offie into the OPC as one of his very first hires, giving him an office immediately adjacent to his own.

Much as had Bullitt and Murphy, Wisner soon came to so rely on Offie as to consider him irreplaceable, and while the OPC director largely manned the home front, it was his indefatigable aide who stayed in constant motion, holding strategy sessions with OPC officers in Munich one day, delivering a suitcase of cash to an Italian labor leader the next. When in Washington, Offie was in the habit of getting up at 4:30 to call the OPC bases in Europe to get a jump on the latest news and to compile lists of that day's tasks for his underlings by the time they reached the office. Indeed, when it came to keeping track of the vast and varied range of OPC actions around the globe—a range constantly growing in both number and scope—no one, not even Frank Wisner, was Carmel Offie's equal.

Of course, such sway has a way of becoming noticed, and of fostering enemies. Of Offie, an awed observer once remarked that "either he was going to be Secretary of State some day or his body was going to be found floating down the Potomac river." Within a very short time of his arrival at OPC, an ever-growing number of people were determined to see that, at least figuratively, he suffered the latter fate. One such nemesis was to be found in an office a mere stone's throw away from the Rat Palace, in the Department of Justice building at 950 Pennsylvania Avenue.

═══

While many officials in Washington were alarmed by the creation of the OPC in 1948, and even more by its rapid expansion thereafter, none was in a greater position to do something about it than FBI director J. Edgar Hoover. What remains a point of debate is how much of Hoover's opposition to the upstart agency derived from personal animus—just as he had despised William Donovan, he developed an instant and abiding dislike for Frank Wisner—and how much from a genuine belief that the outfit was undisciplined and a danger to the republic. To all but the most rabid of Hoover defenders, the evidence tilts heavily toward the first explanation.

Having once vanquished Donovan and his OSS in 1945, Hoover actually enjoyed fairly amicable relations with Donovan's immediate successors. That largely derived from the intelligence chiefs assuming a posture of deference. Reportedly, little pleased the FBI director more than when Colonel William Quinn, the SSU chief, came calling to ask for his help in vetting his staff. "The Donovan days are over," Hoover is said to have crowed to Quinn. "And to have you as his successor come to me for help is just taking all the steam out of my hatred."

The fuzzy feelings ended abruptly in the run-up to the National Security Act of 1947. As he had done in vanquishing the OSS two years earlier, Hoover lobbied President Truman for the FBI to assume the mission of international intelligence gathering. Once again, he was denied. Worse, Truman had created the autonomous Central Intelligence Agency, and then ordered the FBI to relinquish its Latin American intelligence operations to the new agency. So enraged was Hoover and his bureau loyalists by the move that many FBI field offices in Latin America destroyed their intelligence files rather than hand them over to their CIA successors. Then came the creation of the Office of Policy Coordination.

From the outset, the FBI director set out to hobble "Wisner's weirdos" however he could. Considering that the OPC's mandate was to battle communism, the weapon Hoover took up to combat it was more than a tad ironic: anti-communism. In fact, though, a double irony was at work for, even before OPC came into being, it was hard to identify anyone who, through overreach and incompetence, had inflicted more damage to the anti-communist effort in postwar America than J. Edgar Hoover.

Always obsessed by the "Red Menace," in the closing months of the war Hoover had the FBI conduct a massive surveillance operation against the leadership of the Communist Party of the United States, or CPUSA. Dispensing with such niceties as search warrants and probable cause, FBI agents compiled dossiers built on nothing more than rumors passed on by neighbors or enemies, illegally wiretapped the telephones of CPUSA leaders, and burgled their offices and homes, making any evidence gathered useless in court.

Then, in November 1945, a thirty-seven-year-old woman named Elizabeth Bentley sat down with FBI agents to tell an astounding story. For the past seven years, Bentley said, she had been a courier for two different Soviet spy networks in the United States. In this role, she had collected microfilms and purloined documents from a host of American communist fellow travelers—she would ultimately implicate over one hundred individuals, including some thirty federal employees—and passed them on to Soviet agents. The effect of Bentley's revelations was electrifying, at least on Hoover; the day after the FBI's first in-depth interview of Bentley, he fired off a top secret memorandum on the matter to the Truman White House.

The Truman response was utter silence, understandable perhaps considering the FBI director had long since earned a reputation of overselling the "Red threat" as a means to bolster his own standing and the bureau's budget. Having failed to excite Truman, the FBI went back to the basics, subjecting Bentley to a grueling battery of interviews during which she steadily gave up ever more names. As the outline of the alleged spy ring expanded, Hoover shifted scores of agents onto the case—some estimates range as high as 250 agents—to initiate intensive surveillance on those Bentley accused.

The result of Hoover's clean-cut G-men trying to tail communist spies might have been predicted. So badly was the FBI surveillance operation conducted that the spy ring's Soviet control officers realized almost instantly that they'd been compromised and shut down nearly their entire North American network. For all their massive dragnet, the FBI succeeded in observing one suspect dump some communist literature in a neighborhood trash can, and another conduct evasive maneuvers to see if he was being followed. Hoover's second Bentley report to the White House, this one running to 108 pages and naming dozens of alleged spies, garnered no greater response than the first.

But Hoover possessed an ace card. A consummate behind-the-scenes intriguer, he had long maintained a cache of secret documents that existed outside the bureau's official records system. Into Hoover's

"Personal/Confidential" file went compromising reports—and often just unconfirmed gossip—on congressmen and senators and presidents, as well as on his bureaucratic rivals. As need dictated, Hoover would quietly slip copies of these files to reliable journalists or politicians for dissemination, under the strict caveat that neither he nor the FBI ever be identified as their source. In the spring of 1946, frustrated on how to move against the Bentley spy ring and getting no satisfaction from the administration, Hoover used his existing back channels to pass along investigative files to sympathetic newsmen—the syndicated columnist Drew Pearson was a favorite—and conservative congressmen.

His timing had been perfect for, amid the ongoing Soviet clampdown in Eastern Europe, the talk of Red spies running amok played into a growing narrative that the Truman administration was "soft on communism." While other issues played a more determinative role, such fears contributed to the overwhelming Republican wave election that fall that saw them gain control of both the House and Senate.

Those elections also set the stage for the greatest windfall in FBI history: Executive Order 9835. While he would later call it one of his biggest regrets, Truman signed 9835—better known as the Loyalty Order—in March 1947 to try to forestall an even harsher measure from being enacted by the newly seated Republican Congress. Meant to expose "subversives"—shorthand for communists—in the federal government, the order called for an initial screening of all federal workers in a joint effort by the FBI and the Civil Service Commission. Those deemed potential risks would be investigated further and, if warranted, dismissed once their appeals were exhausted. But Hoover had argued for a far stricter set of regulations, and was furious at Truman's dilution of FBI authority by making the Civil Service Commission the lead investigative agency. In a move quite without precedent, just days after the Loyalty Order was announced, the director appeared before a congressional board, the House Un-American Activities Committee (HUAC), to deliver an overtly partisan attack on the political left and, by oblique extension, on the Truman administration.

Charging that the American communist party was indisputably a Soviet fifth column, Hoover went on to suggest the political left was its enabler. "I do fear," he offered with mock concern, "for the liberal and progressive who has been hoodwinked and duped into joining hands with the Communists." To inoculate himself from counterattack, Hoover pointed out that anyone brave enough to stand up to the communists "becomes the object of a systematic campaign of character assassination." Both he and his HUAC allies could expect this campaign of calumny to begin shortly, since "the basic tactics of the Communist Party are deceit and trickery."

It was an astounding performance, and one for which the outmaneuvered Truman had no answer. It also marked the start of communism being used as a political wedge issue to divide Democrats and Republicans, liberals and conservatives, a fissure that would only deepen and grow more bitter in the years ahead. It was also effective. The Republican-controlled Congress quickly reconfigured Order 9835 so that the FBI was its chief administrator, and removed many of the safeguards Truman had inserted to prevent unlawful dismissals. Incredibly, under the rewritten Loyalty Order those accused of being security risks would have no intrinsic right to confront their accusers, or even to necessarily know the specific charges leveled against them.

The Loyalty Order catapulted J. Edgar Hoover and the FBI to the forefront of the American national security complex. Never mind that the end result was decidedly paltry: of the more than two million federal workers screened over the next six years, fewer than three hundred would be dismissed as security risks, with not one of those linked to actual espionage. In that same period, the number of FBI special agents nearly doubled, from 3,600 in 1946 to over 7,000 in 1952, with almost all that gain attributable to the administrative demands of Order 9835. Inevitably, the order also spurred a bandwagon effect—after all, to stand in opposition to such a patriotic exercise must mean a politician or labor union official or schoolteacher had something to hide—so that similar vetting procedures were soon instituted in both local governments and private companies. So absurdist did the phenomenon become that, by the early 1950s, a New York City resident seeking a permit to fish in the city's reservoirs had to sign a loyalty oath. Most importantly for Hoover, however, he now had carte blanche to launch investigations of his enemies, whether they were to be found in the CIA or the OPC or any other federal office.

In 1947, federal prosecutors tried to resurrect the Elizabeth Bentley case by empaneling a grand jury to hear her testimony, along with the denials of some of those she accused. Once again, the effort foundered when, with the FBI unwilling to detail their supporting evidence, much of it illegally obtained, the grand jury refused to bring indictments. In a novel twist, prosecutors then retrofitted their case to target the leadership of the American communist party.

On July 20, 1948, the federal grand jury handed down indictments against twelve members of the CPUSA leadership. The next day, readers of the *New York World-Telegram* were treated to the story of Elizabeth Bentley, "the Red Spy Queen," beneath a banner headline. Having converted the brunette and rather frumpy Bentley into a "svelte striking blonde" the tabloid newspaper went on to describe how she had been at the center of a vast Red spy ring that robbed the federal government of "much of its top secret information."

Days later, Bentley took her star turn before the House Un-American Activities Committee in a packed Capitol Hill committee room. Following her, another defector, a journalist and ex-communist named Whittaker Chambers, took the stand to buttress Bentley's claims and to provide his own supplementary list of "secret communists" working for the government. His most shocking testimony centered on a former high-ranking State Department official named Alger Hiss, who, according to Chambers, had been a spy ring confederate of his in the mid-1930s.

Cynics might be forgiven for suspecting that the timing of the Bentley-Chambers HUAC hearings, coming a mere three months before the 1948 national elections, had a political component. If incipient concerns over the Red Menace had aided the Republicans in the 1946 midterm elections, it seemed likely those same concerns, now vastly amplified, would prove a death knell for Harry Truman's electoral chances in 1948.

Consequently, the FBI director could not have been pleased by the news that came trickling in during the early morning hours of November 3. Against all odds, Truman had not only slipped past his Republican opponent, Thomas E. Dewey, giving Hoover's nemesis four more years in the White House, but a reverse wave had given back to the Democrats control of both the House and Senate.

But the shocking news of that November hardly discouraged Hoover and his allies in Congress from continuing to use the banner of anti-communism to battle Truman. To the contrary, they were to now redouble their efforts and, helped along by a series of external events, escalate the campaign against their opponents into what would amount to an intergovernmental civil war. For Hoover, there were no greater foes in this coming clash than the upstart agency that had robbed him of the chance to head an international intelligence office, the CIA, or that agency's peculiar offshoot occupying the grim prefab buildings down on the National Mall: Frank Wisner's Office of Policy Coordination.

The clash would give rise to another great irony in the life of J. Edgar Hoover. In the late 1940s, legal overreach by his bureau had prevented the prosecution of a vast and very real Soviet spy ring; among the scores of bona fide spies identified by Bentley, only two would ever face trial, and on charges that had nothing to do with spying. On the heels of that fiasco, Hoover had redirected the Red Scare to focus on domestic communist party members, almost none of whom would ever be linked to actual espionage. That's because the KGB had taken the obvious precaution of ordering its actual spies to stay well clear of the party.

And so to the next ring of irony. With that perverse formulation in place, Hoover would now set out to destroy the careers of many of those who were actually at the forefront of formulating strategies to curb Soviet influence around the world. This would include some of Frank Wisner's closest friends and coworkers, as well as Wisner himself. The first prominent victim within the OPC was to be the Royal Dwarf, Carmel Offie.

12

OPERATION RUSTY

For over seven decades, Peter Sichel has been plagued by a recurring nightmare. "It is not something you discuss," he explained softly, "and certainly I would never tell it to my wife, but all my life I have had this dream where I am one of those boys . . . you know, one of those boys in the extermination camps. And I am lying there with them, in one of those rows of beds, one row on top of another, and we are all just there, waiting for our turn to die." He paused, glanced about his living room. "And you know, there is always this feeling of guilt among those who survive: 'Why you? Why did you live when the others didn't?' " For a moment, Sichel appeared shaken, distraught, but then, in the blink of an eye, it was gone, he had straightened in his chair and mentally shifted to someplace else. "Well, as I said, this is something you don't discuss—and certainly you don't let it carry into your professional life."

Easier said than done. The Sichel family of Mainz had both the foresight and the means to escape Nazi Germany, but not so much of German Jewry. Of a prewar population of some 500,000, a mere 30,000 German Jews remained in the country by war's end, and while about half of that greater number had also managed to escape, forever erased were the touchstones of a Jewish community that dated back over a millennium, its businesses and synagogues and schools, even its cemeteries. Maintaining a degree of detachment was surely even harder for someone like Peter Sichel, considering that he had been on the ground when the full horror of the Final Solution was finally revealed. On April 29, 1945, he had been just a few miles away when advance units of the U.S. Seventh

Army liberated the Dachau concentration camp outside Munich. Sichel heard from stunned OSS colleagues of what they found there: thousands of corpses scattered across the camp and an adjacent railway siding, thousands more inmates on the verge of death, too weak from starvation or disease to do anything but stare out from the wooden pallets where they lay. Sichel felt no urge to go to Dachau himself. "I didn't need to see it," he said. "I already knew."

In light of all this, and that Sichel himself had twice escaped the death grasp of the Nazi regime—first in Germany and then in Vichy France—it becomes even harder to comprehend the psychological fortitude required of him as he set to building out his agent networks in postwar Berlin, knowing full well that most all the men and women he was recruiting had once sworn fealty to that regime. The moments Sichel found most trying, though, were when his prospective German assets tried to initiate "The Conversation."

"I never told them I was Jewish, of course, but even so, they all wanted to tell me, 'I was one of the good Germans. I was always opposed to Hitler. I hid Jews in my basement and—.'" Sichel raised his hand. "'Stop. Stop. I don't want to hear it. I'm not interested. That is between you and your own conscience. You either were a good guy or a bad guy, but be sure to be a good guy from now on. This is a new day.' That was my principle."

This emotional asperity undoubtedly contributed to Sichel earning a reputation as an outstanding spymaster in Cold War Germany, his ability to view the contest he was now engaged in as a kind of chess game where impulses of sentimentality or revenge or hatred could only work against him. It also explains his detached recollection of that day in late October 1948 when he and Dana Durand, the overall head of CIA Berlin, were called to a meeting at the new headquarters of CIA Germany in the city of Karlsruhe.

Initially, Sichel assumed it was one of the routine gatherings of senior CIA officers from around the region held most every month. Instead, the leadership of CIA Germany had been brought to Karlsruhe to discuss a top secret initiative known as Operation Rusty, and to debate the fate of an organization so controversial that, among the handful of American officials aware of its existence, it was most often referred to simply as "the Org."

The person at the center of the Org was a slight, slope-shouldered man with pointy ears named Reinhard Gehlen. Belying his elfin appearance, through most of World War II, Gehlen had been Hitler's spy chief for the Soviet Union, only losing the führer's favor when he concluded that the war with Stalin was unwinnable and had the temerity to say as much. In the last days of the Reich, a demoted Gehlen, convinced that the Soviets and their Western allies would soon be adversaries, quietly set to work on his own escape plan. Persuading his superiors that his Soviet intelligence files should be moved south for safekeeping, Gehlen and a few trusted lieutenants bundled up their most important papers and placed them in some fifty airtight and waterproof metal cases. As the Reich collapsed around them, Gehlen and his underlings then secreted those cases in a number of remote locations in the Bavarian Alps. At war's end, the spy chief surrendered to the American army and offered his captors a deal: in exchange for safety and immunity from prosecution for himself and his former comrades in the Foreign Armies East (FHO) intelligence unit, the Americans could have his files. Better yet, the Americans could employ Gehlen and his FHO colleagues, and thereby inherit a ready-made intelligence network as they pivoted to the contest with the Soviets. Gehlen's officers quickly ingratiated themselves with U.S. Army intelligence (G-2) commanders, offering to be their eyes and ears within the local community. Thus was the Gehlen Organization, its activities given the code name Operation Rusty, born.

From its modest beginnings, the Org grew exponentially—and very much in tandem with the growing Western perception of a Soviet threat. By the late autumn of 1947, the headquarters of Gehlen's outfit occupied a sprawling walled compound outside the Bavarian town of Pullach, just south of Munich, while its various regional branches employed hundreds of former German intelligence officers. Adding to the unit's success, Germany was still home to hundreds of thousands of refugees living in displaced persons camps, the vast majority of them from Soviet republics or those Eastern European nations now dominated by the Soviets. With their informant networks in these refugee populations, the Org was able to boast to its American paymasters of highly placed spy chains running clear across the eastern half of the continent and into the Soviet Union.

By late 1948, however, due to the ongoing slashing of the American military budget and a G-2 intelligence apparatus that was winding down its operations in Germany, the point was reached where Operation Rusty had to be either shuttered or taken over by another intelligence branch. The meeting in Karlsruhe that October was to debate whether the CIA should inherit the Org from the U.S. Army.

The proposal was soundly rejected by all the CIA officers present. None were more vehement than Peter Sichel. "I was adamantly opposed for three reasons," he explained. "First, I simply didn't believe Gehlen had the kind of assets in the Soviet zone that he claimed; this was 1948, and no Russian was going to work for the Germans. Maybe they had well-placed Romanians or Bulgarians, but Russians? No way. Second, I didn't trust in their security arrangements, which meant they were probably thoroughly infiltrated by the KGB. And third, there was absolutely no accountability. Gehlen's people had a vested interest in passing on cooked intelligence because they were getting a paycheck from the Americans, and those paychecks would stop if the intelligence stopped. That meant we had to monitor them very closely." Instead, the Org shared an alarming feature with the disastrous Dogwood chain of 1944, in that Gehlen often refused to tell his Army G-2 controls who his agents were. "It was the typical German: 'Trust us, we know what we're doing,'" Sichel said. "It was an absurd arrangement."

The absurdity was multifaceted. In a milieu where everyone was desperate to make a living, and where information was a marketable commodity, informants had every incentive to supply whatever material, no matter how erroneous, might bring them reward. Likewise, the informant's case officer had little reason to question too closely, since his performance was largely judged by the number of chains he was running and the amount of raw intelligence he brought in. Worst of all, this kind of "checkbook espionage" created a system tailor-made for the Soviets to penetrate and manipulate. All this had been hard enough for Sichel to contend with just in Berlin, but Operation Rusty meant replicating the dynamic regionwide. For his part, CIA director Roscoe Hillenkoetter had personally argued for Rusty to be shut down in the summer of 1947, a recommendation he repeated shortly before the meeting in Karlsruhe.

Interestingly, none of these objections, neither those made by Sichel and his colleagues at Karlsruhe nor those aired previously, hinged on the issue of morality—although it surely must have crossed some minds.

A hugely disproportionate share of German atrocities in World War II occurred on Soviet soil, a monstrous catalogue of slaughter not only of Jews and communist officials, but of any Slav *Untermenschen,* or subhumans, they found disagreeable. Tasked with collecting and organizing German military intelligence from that same blood-drenched corner of the battlefield, it was utterly absurd to imagine Reinhard Gehlen and his FHO colleagues weren't aware of the war crimes being committed there by the Einsatzgruppen and other Nazi murder squads.

An equally unsavory air clung to many of those Soviet and Eastern European émigré groups that were Rusty's purported eyes and ears within the Soviet bloc. In recruiting agents from among the refugees in Germany's displaced persons camps, the Org naturally sought to find legitimate anti-communists, and the quickest way to verify that was to choose from those who had fought against the Red Army in their homelands a few years earlier. Practically by default, this meant choosing men who had fought *with* the Germans—and, as was very well known by 1948, the Germans had often employed their local allies as extermination squads in their advance through Eastern Europe and the western Soviet Union. Just as the Gehlen Organization surely included in its ranks those with direct knowledge of the wartime atrocities committed in the East, so some of the Soviet and Eastern European émigrés hired on by the Org surely played a role in perpetrating them.

Yet, to the degree any of this represented a moral quandary, a simple counterargument could be made: what was the alternative? In those parts of Europe under Soviet control in 1948, whatever moderate or democratic centers that once existed had been at least twice and in many cases three times "burned over," its members first decimated in the Stalinist pogroms of the 1930s, then by the invading Germans, and then by the counterattacking Soviets again. As historian Timothy Snyder calculated in his aptly named study, *Bloodlands,* "between them, the Nazi and Stalinist regimes murdered more than fourteen million people in the bloodlands" of Eastern Europe and the western Soviet republics in a mere twelve-year period. The desperate and stateless men in Germany's displaced persons camps, having already proved their anti-communist mettle, were the only potential allies close at hand. The same could be said of Gehlen and his Org confederates, for if one intended to wage a serious fight against the Soviets, the obvious choice was to turn to those who had already done so. As future CIA director Allen Dulles was to glibly say about Gehlen: "He's on our side and that's all that matters. Besides, one needn't ask him to one's club." If not with the same supercilious tone, this view was undoubtedly shared by those gathered in Karlsruhe; their objections to inheriting Operation Rusty were rooted in pragmatism, not morality.

Yet, a new sense of urgency had gripped American policymakers by late 1948. Close on the heels of the brazen communist coup in Czechoslovakia in February had come the Berlin Blockade, the Soviet attempt to starve the Western powers out of the city that in October was still continuing. In China, the Nationalist forces of Chiang Kai-shek were lumbering toward disaster at the hands of the communist Red Army of Mao Zedong. For the most proactive of American officials hoping to halt communism's spread, a conviction was growing that it was time to try anything and everything that might work.

Second, those hard-liners now had a powerful ally in Frank Wisner and his new Office of Policy Coordination. Indeed, it was the OPC that was driving this latest reappraisal of Operation Rusty, spurred by an awareness that walking away from the Gehlen Org now probably meant

walking away from it forever. Given the still desperate European economy, if the Army shut down the spy agency, those Org officers and agents
let go would have to find new jobs and professions, and were highly
unlikely to come back if it was decided to reconstitute the agency at some
later date. Even worse, facing financial destitution, some of those operatives would undoubtedly shop their files and résumés to the Soviets. For
Wisner, the choice was clear.

And there was a final factor at play, one quite banal but rooted in the
covetous nature of bureaucracies everywhere. Put plainly, in Operation
Rusty Frank Wisner was being asked to either acquire or forgo a dramatic expansion of his office's reach and authority. What would any self-
respecting bureaucrat do in such a situation?

But perhaps what was most remarkable about the CIA's momentous
decision to assume Rusty was the utterly offhand manner in which it was
carried out.

One of those present at the Karslruhe meeting—although quite bewildered as to why—was a thirty-one-year-old former military intelligence
officer named James Critchfield. Hired by the CIA just months earlier,
Critchfield had only been in Germany a few weeks and was under the
impression that he had been sent there to establish a Soviet intelligence
processing unit at the CIA's Munich office. At no point during his training or intensive briefings in Washington had there been any mention of
Operation Rusty. Indeed, Critchfield probably would have remained a
mere mystified onlooker at the Karlsruhe gathering were it not for the
intercession of CIA Berlin base chief Dana Durand.

"Dana was all right," Peter Sichel recalled, "but frankly, more liked
than respected among his colleagues. That's because he was intensely
political. He saw everything through the prism of what was likely to benefit or cause problems for him personally."

True to form, at the Karlsruhe meeting, Durand voiced his opposition
to taking on Rusty by allowing that "it was a job that would not enhance
anyone's career." At the same time, the station chief was loath to voice his
opposition too strongly lest it incur fallout from higher-ups. In hopes
of gumming up the works without appearing to do so, Durand reverted
to that classic delaying tactic of office workers everywhere: he suggested
someone write up a report. He further suggested that this task fall to the
man in the room least able to protest, the newly arrived and very junior
James Critchfield.

"I had every reason to ask that I not be given this task," a flabbergasted
Critchfield later recalled. "I was new to the CIA. . . . I was not an OSS
veteran with a background in German operations." Most incredibly, he

was being asked "to investigate a German intelligence organization about which I had been given virtually no background information."

Under the circumstances, all sterling credentials for the job. Just days after the meeting, Critchfield was ordered by CIA headquarters to singlehandedly conduct a crash evaluation of Operation Rusty, and "to recommend at the end of four weeks of investigation whether the German organization should be liquidated or continue to receive support from the U.S." One month later, a thoroughly exhausted Critchfield submitted his report and, in contrast to all his CIA colleagues at Karlsruhe, urged that the CIA assume control of Rusty. That minority view held sway; at the end of December 1948, Frank Wisner was informed by secret memo that "it has been agreed in principle that Operation Rusty will be taken over—lock, stock and barrel—by CIA."

What the dissenting CIA officers in Germany didn't know was that the OPC had long since forged close ties to a number of Rusty operatives anyway. In fact, even before the Karlsruhe meeting, Frank Wisner was arranging the emigration of one of Reinhard Gehlen's chief deputies to the United States under an assumed name, there to become a key OPC advisor on Eastern European affairs. The alias was necessary because the man was wanted by the Soviets for war crimes.

———

On October 19, 1948, the State Department's George Kennan sent a friendly note to Frank Wisner. "Dear Frank," it began, "I am glad to learn that your efforts to bring Gustav Hilger to this country for work with CIA has been successful. . . . I regard him as one of the few outstanding experts on Soviet economy and Soviet politics. He had [*sic*] not only a scholarly background on Soviet subjects but has had long practical experience in analyzing and estimating Soviet operations on a day-to-day basis. I hope the Department of State may be provided with copies of any studies which Mr. Hilger produces under your direction."

The subject of the letter, sixty-two-year-old Gustav Hilger, had an unusual pedigree, a German citizen who had spent nearly his entire life in first czarist and then Soviet Russia. Despite being educated as an engineer, in 1923 he had won appointment to the German embassy in Moscow due to his fluency in Russian and extensive contacts in the Kremlin. It was in that position a decade later that he met and developed a friendship with a young rising star in the American legation to the Soviet Union, George Kennan. The friendship lasted until Kennan was transferred from Moscow in 1937.

In his absence, Gustav Hilger's résumé became a bit more checkered. In his counselor role with the embassy, Hilger served as chief interpreter for Hitler's foreign minister, Joachim von Ribbentrop, in the secret negotiations leading to the Nazi–Soviet concord, the Molotov-Ribbentrop Pact, of 1939. After that accord collapsed with the launching of Operation Barbarossa in 1941, Hilger's diplomatic status led to his being deported to Germany, where he served as Ribbentrop's chief advisor on Soviet affairs for the rest of the war.

Like other high-ranking German officials, Hilger took pains to surrender to American soldiers at war's end. Considered a "prisoner of high value," he was taken to the United States for extensive questioning by Army intelligence, then returned to Germany in 1946. There, he found work with the Gehlen Organization as a Soviet analyst, a secure enough position for American authorities to feign ignorance as to his whereabouts when the Soviets petitioned for Hilger's arrest on charges of war crimes. Two years later, after determining that Hilger remained in danger of kidnapping or assassination by the Soviets, getting him out of Germany and into the United States became a CIA concern. Kennan urged Wisner to employ him as an OPC advisor, and Wisner was glad to do so.

But how to get Hilger into the country with an international arrest warrant hanging over his head? The CIA's answer was to just play dumb, to avoid learning those unpleasant details of a person's life that might undermine the concept of plausible deniability.

To Gustav Hilger's later good fortune, he had never joined the Nazi party, so there was scant reference to him in the Nazi party records housed in the American-controlled Berlin Document Center. What's more, already in his mid-fifties when World War II began, Hilger spent the war essentially sitting behind a desk in the Soviet department of the Foreign Ministry, a locale that enabled him to profess ignorance about any nastiness that may have occurred on the battlefield.

As much as this strained credulity—how could any senior German Foreign Ministry official tasked to Soviet affairs not know of the atrocities being committed in Operation Barbarossa?—the idea was demolished altogether by Hilger's receipt signature on a series of activity reports from the Eastern Front in 1941 and 1942. In unambiguous language, these papers included status reports from SS murder squads operating in conquered Soviet territory, even listing how many Jews, communists and "bandits" had been executed during that reporting period. At the very least, it meant Hilger had full knowledge of the slaughter being perpetrated on the Eastern Front. It also cast George Kennan's comment that

Hilger had "long practical experience in analyzing and estimating Soviet operations on a day-to-day basis" in a rather different light.

But only if one chose to see that light. Instead, by dismissing the charges laid out in the Soviet arrest warrant as propaganda, and by not seeking out the activity reports that had crossed Hilger's wartime desk, the American intelligence community could continue to hold the German out as a respectable scholar. Ultimately, the CIA cut ties to Hilger in 1953 when Carmel Offie observed that his reports contained very little new, and that he was trading on the "ancient history" he had gleaned during his service to the Third Reich. As for Kennan, that grand master of forgetfulness, he would later write of Hilger: "I do not recall having had anything to do with, or any responsibility for, bringing him to this country; nor do I recall knowing, at the time, by what arrangements he was brought here."

But such associations had set the Agency on something of a moral slippery slope: if it was permissible to employ those Germans who knew of the Holocaust while it was occurring, what of those who played a more direct role? And if it was possible to overlook the shady background of a man like Gustav Hilger by simply not digging too deeply, what about dealing with someone whose notoriety was impossible to ignore? Soon after taking control of the Gehlen Org, the CIA found its own uncomfortable answer to these questions in the form of a man named Otto Albrecht Alfred von Bolschwing.

From an aristocratic and staunchly conservative family in Prussia, Bolschwing had been an early recruit to the Nazi Party. Once Hitler came to power, he steadily rose through the ranks to become a deputy of Heinrich Himmler in the Reich Main Security Office, or RHSA; Bolschwing's specific area of responsibility was in the RHSA branch that focused on "the Jewish problem." In 1937, he came up with a detailed proposal to drive the Jews out of Germany through terror tactics, and to rob them as they left.

So radical were Bolschwing's politics that he was destined to be one of the few Nazis whose zealotry actually got him in trouble with the leadership. As chief SS intelligence officer in Romania in 1940, he encouraged leaders of the Iron Guard, a rabidly anti-Semitic paramilitary group, to attempt a coup against the existing German-allied government. The Iron Guard revolt of January 1941 was put down, but not before Iron Guard Legionnaires had rampaged through the Jewish quarter of Bucharest, burning synagogues and murdering residents with a display of sadism that managed to shock even resident SS officers. For his behind-the-scenes role in the coup attempt, done in defiance of Berlin policy, Bolschwing was hauled back to Germany and spent several months in detention.

The Prussian aristocrat was to spin this brief imprisonment into a very helpful postwar fiction, "proof" that he had opposed the Nazi regime and been persecuted as a result. Much to the contrary, after his Romanian hiccup, Bolschwing continued his rise in the Third Reich hierarchy, ultimately becoming a deputy to the chief logistician of the Holocaust, Adolf Eichmann. At war's end, he escaped into American-occupied Austria where he linked up with a number of his exiled Iron Guard friends, before joining the Gehlen Org in 1947. Through that affiliation, Bolschwing became a familiar figure to those American army officers managing Operation Rusty, although not necessarily in a good way; finding the Prussian unreliable and devious, the Org control officers were eventually warned "not to use subject in any capacity."

But that had been 1947. By 1949, with Rusty now being managed by the CIA—and given the new code name of Operation Odeum—Bolschwing's areas of expertise dovetailed with several initiatives the CIA was pursuing in collaboration with the Gehlen Org. In particular, the Org had recruited a group of old Romanian Iron Guardists, led by a man named Constantin Papanace, that the CIA hoped to use for espionage operations in their communist-controlled homeland. To augment that effort, the CIA also wanted to tap into Bolschwing's intelligence network in Austria. In a report outlining the Prussian aristocrat's potential, James Critchfield, now the CIA's chief liaison to Odeum, was unequivocal. "We are convinced that Bolschwing's Romanian operations, his connections with the Papanace group, his internal Austrian political and intelligence connections, and last but not least, his knowledge of and probable future on Odeum's activities in and through Austria make him a valuable man whom we must control."

This the Americans set out to do. In February 1950, Bolschwing was hired away from Gehlen and put under direct CIA supervision. Given the intriguing code name of Agent Unrest, Bolschwing's handlers were soon describing him in glowing terms. "He is unquestionably an extremely intelligent person," one of his control officers wrote, "an experienced intelligence operator, a man with an unusually wide and well-placed circle of friends, acquaintances, and sources, and a man whose grasp of the political-intelligence field throughout the Balkans, and to a lesser degree in Western Europe, is of a high order."

As for Agent Unrest's Nazi pedigree, this could be conveniently forgotten; one after another, Bolschwing's American supervisors were content to accept the false history that Bolschwing had concocted for himself in the war's aftermath, a stirring tale of an anti-Nazi activist cast into prison for reasons of conscience.

Except matters hit a snag. Shortly after his move from the Org to the CIA, the Austrian government launched an investigation of Bolschwing, and asked American officials to conduct a check of his wartime background by looking through the Nazi Party files at the Berlin Document Center, or BDC. Given Bolschwing's ties to the CIA, this request wended its way through the American bureaucracy in Berlin until it landed on the desk of Peter Sichel.

As was to be expected of such a committed Nazi, a check of BDC records on Bolschwing set off alarm bells, news that Sichel forwarded on to the CIA team overseeing Agent Unrest in Pullach. Sichel soon received a curious follow-up: Pullach now wanted CIA Berlin to either withhold Bolschwing's file from the Austrian government or, in the deliciously Orwellian jargon of bureaucratese, to produce a "negative file."

On April 24, 1950, Sichel responded to his colleagues in Pullach by pointing out the absurdity of such a move, explaining that the Document Center files on Nazi membership and former German intelligence officers were so complete that to go back to the Austrians with a "negative file" could only arouse suspicion. "On top of this," he wrote, "the persons you are dealing with are so well known and their background so well publicized in the past that I deem it improbable that you can protect them from their past history."

As for the idea of giving Bolschwing a new identity, Sichel went a good deal further. "At the end of the war we tried to be very smart and change the name of several members of the SD [Security Service branch of the SS] and Abwehr in order to protect them from the German authorities and the occupation authorities. In most cases these persons were so well known that the change in name compromised them more than if they were to face a denazification court and face the judgment that would have been meted out to them."

In closing, and despite his admonition, Sichel offered to withhold Bolschwing's file if this was still what CIA Pullach desired. It was, and the CIA never passed on Bolschwing's file in the Berlin Document Center to the Austrian government.

This wasn't to be the end of the story, however. Suspecting the CIA was stonewalling, the Austrians asked at least two other American investigative agencies in Germany, the U.S. Counter Intelligence Corps and the Army's Criminal Investigation Division, or CID, to intercede on their behalf for the Bolschwing file. Not only were these agencies similarly fro-

zen out, but the Austrians' persistence finally led the CIA to request the
CID's help in blocking them.

But for all their effort in recruiting and shielding him, Otto von
Bolschwing also soon proved a disappointment to the CIA, more interested in producing run-of-the-mill historical analysis pieces about the
Balkans than in exploring the potential for clandestine operations in
the region. By the beginning of 1952, having concluded there was little
chance Bolschwing "will ever develop into a first class agent," CIA Pullach transferred him back to his adoptive hometown of Salzburg, Austria,
and foisted him on the CIA unit there.

The Prussian was to get the last laugh. As some of his case officers
long suspected, Agent Unrest's greatest passion had always been less
about conducting espionage against the Soviets and more about trying
to gain American citizenship—and with the CIA having once hired the
war criminal, the Agency was now on the hook for disposing of him. In
1953, Bolschwing's employers went about the delicate task of preparing
his immigration papers while skirting the issue of his Nazi background.
The solution CIA lawyers came up with was to expunge mention of his
Nazi Party membership from his official records; if Bolschwing were
directly asked by immigration authorities, they advised, he "should admit
membership, but attempt to explain it away on the basis of extenuating
circumstances."

The ploy worked. For the next quarter-century, Bolschwing and his
family lived quietly in a Sacramento suburb, before finally coming to the
attention of the Office of Special Investigations (OSI), the Nazi-hunting
unit of the U.S. Justice Department, in the late 1970s. Destined to be
the highest-ranking German war criminal ever prosecuted by the OSI,
Bolschwing was stripped of his American citizenship in late 1981 for having lied on his immigration application, just weeks before his death from
brain cancer.

The links that the CIA forged with former Nazis in the late 1940s were to
ultimately hurt the Agency in a variety of ways.

For one thing, those links played perfectly into the hands of Soviet
propagandists eager to declaim their American opponent as in league
with "fascists" and "Hitlerites." For ordinary Soviet citizens, survivors
of the savagery of German forces in World War II, every unmasking of
an Otto von Bolschwing conveyed the message that their government's
accusations against the West held the ring of truth.

Those ties also cast a blot on the CIA's image—and by natural extension, that of the United States—that has never been dispelled. In the more than six decades since their employment with the CIA, scores of books have detailed the "Nazi connection" to the Agency, some claiming the number of war criminals involved ranged into the hundreds, even the thousands. In fact, the Justice Department's Office of Special Investigations—certainly no apologist for the CIA—tallies the list of German Nazi war criminals employed by the Agency over the years at probably less than a dozen, while also pointing out that nearly all of these were "inherited" from other branches of government, as was the case with both Gustav Hilger and Otto von Bolschwing. No matter; in the public imagination, even those infamous figures with whom the CIA had no apparent connection, the Klaus Barbies and Josef Mengeles of the Nazi netherworld, are now firmly fixed in many minds as having been agency assets. It's highly doubtful the CIA will ever get out from under this cloud; rather like a thief who admits to having robbed dozens of people, but certainly not hundreds, so an institution arguing it employed "only a handful" of Nazis is already playing a losing hand. As CIA historian Kevin Ruffner has noted, "In its quest for information on the USSR, the United States became indelibly linked to the Third Reich."

But perhaps the greatest damage the Nazi connection inflicted on the CIA rests more in the psychological realm, as the "gateway sin" that paved the way for other sins to follow.

At the end of World War II, American officials blithely announced a sweeping purge of Nazi Party members in their German occupation zone, effectively disenfranchising all of them from participating in the nation's reconstruction. That decree went by the wayside almost immediately when planners were confronted with the impossibility of rebuilding a shattered and starving land while excluding the 8.5 million citizens who had previously maintained it. Instead, the denazification courts which had proposed to judge an entire society very quickly limited their focus to only the most notorious of Nazi Party members, while giving everyone else essentially a free pass. Most observers would probably find this a reasonable compromise, even if it enabled some hideous characters to escape justice.

Carried a step further, as the CIA and other Western spy agencies set to do battle against the Soviets in Central and Eastern Europe, could they really be expected to refuse the services of the former Nazi enemy who also happened to know the new enemy best? Again, all but the most pious would probably support their hiring, even if it meant enjoining the services of a man like Gustav Hilger, one of the paper pushers of the Holocaust. But what of the next step, of working with someone like Otto von Bolschwing, a man who didn't just move paper but who devoted his energies to making the Final Solution happen?

And then on to the next step, not just accepting intelligence gathered by such triggermen—a shameful endeavor perhaps, but at least a rather passive one—but now going into direct alliance with them, now actively enlisting them to carry out operations against the new enemy? In just this way, the crossing of one moral threshold, often for the most practical of reasons, can ease the crossing of the next, and what becomes exceedingly difficult when one is living in the midst of it all is to determine just where lies the line not to be crossed. A simple matter to determine in hindsight, perhaps—at least so the sanctimonious believe—but not at all at the time, and this was the path, more an erosion, where the CIA found itself at the end of the 1940s. It was an erosion that would accelerate and take on new forms in the years ahead, but it began in the late 1940s amid the ashes of the Third Reich.

One person intimately caught up in this moral maelstrom was Peter Sichel. In our first meeting, he stated, "I never knowingly helped a Nazi war criminal," and he said this with the strong and steady voice of complete conviction. Yet, as Sichel himself would undoubtedly acknowledge, the operative word in that sentence was "knowingly," for many were the times when he had chosen to avert his gaze, when he had refused to engage in The Conversation. And then, of course, there was his signature on the papers outlining a scheme whereby Otto von Bolschwing might escape justice, a scheme which seemed to strain against, if not break through, whatever line of conscience Sichel drew in his mind.

When gently pressed on the matter, Sichel professed to have no memory of the Bolschwing memo, before offering that, as chief of station, "papers often went out on my signature that I never even saw. That happened many times, but. . . ." He trailed off, as if finding the tinge of defensiveness in these words embarrassing. "It was a war," he started again. "We all believed that and, like all wars, that one was dirty. And I was young. I was young and I still believed things that, even a few years later, I no longer believed." Sichel gazed thoughtfully about his living room, as if searching for something more to say. Then he shrugged. "That's all."

13

RIPE FOR REVOLT

No sooner did Michael Burke arrive in Rome in August 1949 than he turned to the first item on his to-do list: getting rid of the shoulder holster for his .380 Colt automatic. As he later explained, the holster "was more difficult to conceal than the gun itself, and not the kind of thing you tossed into the hotel wastebasket for the maid to find." Waiting until nightfall of his first day in the city, Burke left his hotel and strolled to a nearby park, where he made for a dark stand of pine trees. After making sure he wasn't being observed, he found a garbage can and buried the troublesome accoutrement under the surface rubbish.

He discovered that his preference for the waistband method of weapon storage was shared by his new colleagues. Days later, when he met with his Albanian co-conspirators for the first time, each man pulled a pistol from his belt and set it on the long conference table before taking their seat.

They were a rough-cut bunch, and none more so than a man in his late fifties named Abas Kupi. A tribal chieftain from the mountains of central Albania, Kupi arrived at the OPC safe house last, accompanied by his bodyguard-interpreter. After warmly shaking Burke's hand, he set out his own pistol, then took the seat of honor reserved for him at the far end of the conference table.

The deference shown Kupi by the other Albanians may have stemmed from his reputation. Considered a consummate conciliator of the feuds that had always bedeviled his remote mountain homeland, Kupi was known to lock himself and a rival inside a hut for days, the two emerging only when a rapprochement had been reached. On other occasions, if the disagreement proved intractable or Kupi was pressed for time, these summit meetings were reportedly brought to speedier resolution, with a single gunshot echoing from the hut and Kupi emerging alone. As Burke would recall of his first meeting with the tribal chief, "I liked him from the start, and grew fond of him as our enterprise progressed."

Belying its humble setting—the safe house was in a drab apartment building in a working-class neighborhood of Rome—that meeting in August 1949 inaugurated one of the most audacious schemes to arise in the early Cold War: the OPC plot to strike back at the expanding Soviet constellation by attacking its satellite regime in the Balkan nation of Albania. The undertaking, which would grow to become the largest and most expensive covert action undertaken by the United States in the early 1950s, had already been given a sufficiently ominous-sounding code name: Operation BGFIEND or, as it was more commonly known, simply Fiend.

The genesis of Fiend had occurred in somewhat roundabout manner. Like many of OPC's early initiatives in Europe, it took its cue from the British.

In the later days of World War II, the British had sought to hasten the end of German control in the Balkans by providing military advisors and supplies to the various partisan bands operating in Yugoslavia and Albania. In both countries, the British deemed that the communist partisan groups were the most committed to actually fighting and, in the whatever-it-takes ethos of the time, helped them gain preeminence over rival factions in both training and weaponry.

Britain soon had reason to regret that policy. By war's end, the communist partisan leaders of both countries—Josip Broz Tito in Yugoslavia, Enver Hoxha in Albania—seized power and allied themselves with the Soviets. Worse, when the civil war in neighboring Greece flared anew in 1946, both regimes offered assistance and sanctuary to their Greek communist brethren. Impoverished Britain had been compelled to rush their own advisors and weaponry to their embattled ally in Athens, before convincing the Americans to take over the financing of the costly rescue mission in 1947. Raising the stakes further were reports of a Soviet submarine base being built in the Albanian port city of Vlore, a development that would allow Stalin to threaten the balance of power throughout the eastern Mediterranean. Taken all together, both London and Washington had ample reason to wish to see the end of the Hoxha regime in Tirana.

By late 1948, the odds of making that happen had dramatically improved. The previous summer, Tito had broken with Stalin and taken

Yugoslavia out of the Soviet camp of satellite nations. He had also begun shutting off aid to the Greek communists, causing the tide of war there to turn inexorably against them; in the near future, the last remnants of the beaten rebel army, the DSE, would straggle out of Greece and into an Albanian exile. When viewed on a map, the sudden precariousness of the Hoxha government was plain: Albania was now physically cut off from its Soviet bloc allies, hemmed in on one side by the Adriatic Sea, and on the other three by its now hostile neighbors of Yugoslavia and Greece.

That precariousness was internal, as well. Despite tightly policed borders, reports seeping out of Albania told of an already impoverished nation sliding toward disintegration, with a host of different armed bands ensuring that government control in many regions barely extended beyond principal towns. Clearly, if an opportunity existed to pluck a nation from the Soviet galaxy, it was Albania. In describing its fragility, Western observers tended to reach for fruit metaphors: "a ripe peach hanging at the end of a branch," one opined, while the OPC desk officer overseeing operations in southeastern Europe was convinced that in Albania "we had only to shake the trees and the ripe plums would fall."

In early spring of 1949, OPC and MI6 put the final touches on their separate proposals to initiate subversion campaigns against Hoxha—the British opted for the rather more decorous-sounding Operation Valuable—and agreed to coordinate their efforts so as to not trip over each other in the field. Frank Wisner was especially enthused, regarding the joint effort as a "clinical experiment to see whether large rollback operations would be feasible elsewhere."

That June, Wisner and Carmel Offie took the OPC plan to George Kennan's Policy Planning team at the State Department and the National Security Council. As with the British Operation Valuable, Fiend called for infiltrating commando teams into Albania for the initial purpose of gathering intelligence, but plans turned steadily more aspirational after that. As was bluntly stated in the Fiend mission statement, the minimum goal of the operation was to curb Albanian support for the communist guerrillas in the still lingering Greek civil war. The maximum goal was to overthrow the Albanian government.

"This operation is not a large one by modern standards," Wisner explained in a top secret twelve-page briefing paper, "and even with complete success it will not be decisive in the cold war. Nevertheless, I believe it deserves your attention at this time for three reasons." While his first two reasons were clear enough—Fiend had "obvious military implications," and would serve as a shakeout cruise for similar operations in the future—his third was a good deal more calculating. "We hope [Operation Fiend] will develop typically and will demonstrate the wisdom of the National Security Council in placing all United States clandestine operations in OPC under centralized control." In other words, the OPC director was looking to Fiend to justify his office's existence—which, of course, also meant he would be loath to abort the operation under all but the most dire of circumstances. Not that Wisner anticipated such problems. "Albania is ripe for revolt. All that is necessary is leadership, subsidy money and eventually some arms. . . . If we have great success we shall have eliminated a pocket of communist imperialism and dealt the Soviet Empire a blow that will resound behind the iron curtain."

Kennan and the National Security Council liked what they heard and approved the scheme. Immediately after, OPC chief of operations Frank Lindsay had dispatched an underling to track down the man who he felt would be ideal for overseeing the project's day-to-day operation: Michael Burke. In very short order, Burke decamped for Rome and just the sort of double life he had described in his failed spyworld radio play of three years earlier: head of Imperial Pictures by day, contract agent for the world's most secretive spy agency by night.

As he conferred with his new Albanian friends in the OPC safe house, Burke surely sensed that he was venturing into a culture unlike any he had previously known. While a ruggedly beautiful land, Albania was also one of the poorest and most technologically primitive nations in Europe; in 1949, electricity was still a rarity, and in great swaths of the country-side the only modes of transportation were foot or horse cart. And while many Eastern European émigré groups were already notorious in the eyes of British and American intelligence agencies for their fractiousness, the Albanians gave balkanization a whole new meaning. In a place where allegiance to family and clan was vastly stronger than to state, and where many tribal chieftains could trace their authority back to the Dark Ages, the hills of 1949 Albania remained the stomping grounds of armed bands perpetuating blood feuds begun decades, even centuries, earlier.

Despite the language barrier, Burke was made aware of these divisions at that first meeting with his co-conspirators, with some of those in the room barely deigning to speak to others. Indeed, those gathered around the safe house conference table represented in microcosm the larger schisms that ran through Albanian society, and underscored the frantic patching work performed by American and British officials to smooth them over.

The reason for this patching was clear. To maintain plausible deniability, both Fiend and Valuable called for the infiltration squads that would penetrate Albania to be composed solely of Albanian nationals, with their OPC and MI6 administrators remaining outside the country and in the background. Those infiltration squads were to be drawn from among the multitudes of Albanian émigrés still living in refugee camps scattered across Germany and Italy, and they were to be personally selected by the men sitting around the conference table with Michael Burke. Where this got tricky was that the Albanian "community" was actually an amalgam of different tribal and regional factions, with whatever political organization that existed between them, as one observer noted, "originally established for the primary purpose of destroying the others." For Fiend and Valuable to have any chance of success, these divisions needed to be papered over, and through the spring and summer of 1949, American and British officials had toiled to forge an Albanian political front group that—at least in theory—could serve as a kind of coalition junta. As with so many other wearisome tasks at OPC, much of the burden of this mission had fallen to the ubiquitous Carmel Offie, an ordeal he would recall as "not particularly inspiring or pleasant."

But if there was one thing Offie had learned over his varied career, it was that even the most ancient and bitter rifts between peoples might be soothed by a sufficient outlay of cash. So it was that in late August, and almost precisely coinciding with Burke's arrival in Rome, a new group calling itself the National Committee for a Free Albania (NCFA) held a press conference in Paris. While making no mention of the OPC funding that had led to its creation, the NCFA announced it was an umbrella organization drawn from a range of Albanian political factions, brought to unity for the stated purpose of battling the Hoxha regime. Unfortunately, it seems few of those in the intended home audience heard the news; in addition to radios being a great rarity in Albania, both BBC and Voice of America reportedly broadcast their coverage of the press conference well before Albania's electricity had been turned on for the evening.

It was the local representatives of the newly formed NCFA that Burke met with on that night in Rome, a group that faithfully mirrored the factional percentages of the parent organization: 40 percent loyalists to the exiled Albanian monarch, King Zog I, who had fled the invading Italians in 1939; 40 percent republican nationalists; and 20 percent drawn from so-called Independents. This same formula was to be replicated in the selection of commandos. As Burke explained to those at the safe house, their task now was to circulate among their followers in the refugee camps in search of volunteers for the perilous infiltration missions, with those chosen to undergo rigorous training under Burke's overall supervision.

The OPC contractor had few illusions about the challenges that lay before them, starting with the lack of reliable information coming out of

Albania. Burke suspected that, like war-displaced refugees everywhere, those gathered in the Rome safe house were wildly overconfident about the reliability of their contact chains within Albania, and of the readiness of the general populace to rise up in revolt. In essence, what was being attempted was the formation of a national underground movement from wholly outside the targeted nation. That meant somehow sneaking small teams of operatives into a tightly controlled police state, where they were expected to gauge the potential for revolution, make contact with whatever local resistance groups might exist, and see to the recruitment of new fighters, all while being tracked by an internal security army intent on capturing or killing them. "If the results were positive," Burke wrote with suitable vagueness, "a larger body of men would be recruited for paramilitary training and would be infiltrated in commandolike units at some propitious time."

If it all seemed a bit desperate and unlikely, the summer of 1949 was a desperate time. In China, the disintegration of Chiang Kai-shek's regime was now so complete that the Truman administration had quietly written him off, recognizing that the end was near. In June, Enver Hoxha had tried and executed his chief rival in Tirana, just one of a number of show trials occurring throughout the communist sphere and further decimating whatever was left of moderate opposition. At the end of August, there came the greatest shock of all when the Soviets detonated their first atomic bomb, a landmark achievement that the CIA had predicted was as many as two years away. In the march of bad news through the first years of the Cold War, American leaders had at times consoled themselves with the knowledge that, in the very worst-case scenario, the atomic bomb represented their ultimate trump card over the Soviets. Now that trump card was gone. Given the ever-darkening outlook elsewhere, how not to pursue Operation Fiend if it bore even a small chance for success?

At that first meeting with the Albanians, Burke later maintained, he spelled out the odds stacked against their enterprise. He was also keenly aware that, while he and the OPC might hold the purse strings, in no way were those men signing on to do battle for the American cause, nor was he their boss. Rather, their cause began and ended with Albania, and Burke, the youngest man in a room filled with warriors who had been fighting their entire lives, would have to win their respect. "That would take longer," he wrote, "but, I told myself, it could be won as they discovered I was not new to covert operations, not obtuse about the political conflicts among them, and not clumsy in human relations."

A few weeks after that conference, Burke's personal life considerably brightened when he was joined in Rome by his wife, Timmy, and their young daughter, Doreen. Making use of the OPC's generous living allowance, the family moved into the top floor of a magnificent villa at 11 Via Michele Mercati, near the Borghese Gardens, owned by the Contessa Carasotti. There, the couple transformed their rooftop terrace, with its spectacular view of the Rome skyline, into a vast hanging garden and playground where Doreen steered her tricycle amid an obstacle course of flowerpots and tree boxes.

If the Burkes' living arrangements in Rome were dazzling, their social life soon became so, as well. The handsome and outgoing young couple gathered about them a circle of good friends, many of them drawn from the burgeoning Italian film world—an altogether natural fit for Timmy, the former Goldwyn Studios dresser, and only slightly less so for her husband, the head of "Imperial Pictures." "Often a number of us breakfasted together at a popular sidewalk café," Burke wrote, "taking orange juice, espresso and brioche in the midmorning sun. It was an amorphous group to which passers-through added and subtracted themselves and regular members departed and arrived in the normal course of their trade. Consistency would have been abnormal and the irregularity of my own life blended conveniently into this rhythm."

Indeed. Prior to coming to Rome, Burke had meticulously plotted and committed to memory every aspect of his cover story, quite conscious that "half-covers" like his, in which one's real name was retained but attached to a false biography, were often far easier to slip up on than a "full-cover." He had also been leery of drawing too close to the Rome film crowd, worried over potential questions about his ties to a production company no one had ever heard of, and which didn't seem to actually produce anything. Fortunately, though, Burke discovered the Roman cinéastes were, much like their Hollywood counterparts, a profoundly self-absorbed lot. "I was mildly surprised at how incurious people were and how very easy it was, when it suited my purpose, to direct attention away from myself simply by asking the right question of other persons and being a good listener, or at least appearing to be." For all the scrutiny it garnered from his new social circle, Michael Burke's "career" with Imperial Pictures might have stretched out indefinitely.

All the while, the OPC contract officer maintained covert contact with his Albanian co-conspirators, stealing away to the far corners of Rome for quiet conferences, the sorts of meetings where notes weren't taken and everyone arrived and left separately. He also found the villa at 11 Via Michele Mercati, set one hundred yards back from the street and with its grounds surrounded by a high stone wall, an ideal place for his "clandestine friends" to come and go unnoticed.

It wasn't long, though, before these meetings took on a new element of solemnity, a realization that they were playing at a deadly game.

Far ahead of the Americans in their planning, the British officers running Operation Valuable had begun training their Albanian commandos—their trainers called them "pixies" on account of their short stature—at a military base in Malta even before Burke arrived in Rome. In October 1949, the British began slipping commando teams into southern Albania during nocturnal runs of a leased sailboat named, appropriately enough, *Stormie Seas*. By the end of the month, they had put some thirty pixies ashore in this fashion.

When the commandos began filtering out of Albania and into Greece a few weeks later, however, they painted a bleak picture. One four-man team had been wiped out, while nearly all the others had been forced to run for their lives from the Albanian *Sigurimi*, or internal security police, from almost the moment they went ashore. Far from gathering meaningful intelligence or forming conspirator cells, the survivors were lucky to just get out with their lives. That wasn't all. Once the pixies were debriefed, it became clear that, in most every case, the *Sigurimi* had been cued to their arrival; one commando even reported encountering villagers who already knew his identity, his name having been provided by secret police circulating through the area days beforehand. The inescapable conclusion was that, somewhere along the line, the Valuable landings had been compromised.

The news provoked Frank Wisner to call a meeting of those senior officials in Washington most directly involved with Valuable/Fiend in mid-November. These included the two men with the most direct day-to-day involvement in the Albanian enterprise—they were often referred to as its "co-commanders"—an OPC official named James McCargar and his British counterpart, a thirty-seven-year-old MI6 man named Kim Philby. Although Philby was a newcomer to the group—it had been a little over a month since he'd arrived in Washington to assume the role of chief MI6 liaison to the American intelligence community—the *Stormie Seas* landings were a British undertaking, so he naturally assumed something of a leadership role at the November conclave.

Much of the meeting was taken up with the question of how to plug the obvious security breach in the Albanian operation, and whether, in light of the dismal track record of the *Stormie Seas* commandos, Operations Valuable and Fiend should continue to be pursued at all. Philby

Churchill, Stalin and the new American president, Harry Truman, at the Potsdam Conference, July 1945. At their first meeting, Truman would breezily decide Stalin was honest and a leader "I can deal with." He would soon rethink both assertions.

Wisner, second from right, arriving in American-occupied Germany, 1948, as a senior State Department official overseeing policy in the region. Alarmed by communist expansion in Eastern Europe, Wisner had again quit his Wall Street law firm to join State, and was already laying the groundwork for a covert action agency to confront the Soviets. Created in late 1948 with Wisner in charge, the innocuous-sounding Office of Policy Coordination was so top secret that its existence wouldn't be officially acknowledged for decades.

Peter Sichel in early Cold War Berlin. Against the vast Soviet intelligence apparatus in the German city, the embryonic CIA unit scored some small victories amid colossal failures. In December 1946, a CIA "chain" of more than two hundred agents and informants disappeared virtually overnight, rolled up by a KGB that had thoroughly infiltrated the network.

Berliners watching the arrival of relief planes during the Soviet blockade of the city, 1948-49. Stalin hoped the blockade, one of the first nakedly aggressive acts of the Cold War, would force the Western powers out of the city, but it instead proved a Western propaganda coup.

To Peter Sichel, it was one of the greatest mistakes the Soviets ever made: "For the first time, Berliners saw us as allies, not occupiers."

The unscrupulous Lucien Conein, also known as Three-Fingered Luigi, headed up the CIA's "disposal unit" in Berlin and was a master at smuggling defectors and Agency assets out of the Soviet zone. In 1954, he would join Lansdale in Vietnam and win a new nickname: the Thug.

A resurrected Michael Burke on the terrace of his villa in Rome, 1949. As the field coordinator for the OPC's ultra top-secret Operation Fiend, Burke led a complicated double life, masquerading as a film producer by day while conspiring with Albanian anti-communist commandos by night.

By 1950, Burke was running the OPC's biggest overseas station, in charge of all covert operations and infiltration missions out of the American sector of Germany. The strain of constantly making life-or-death decisions registere[d] on his face, his boyish good looks of jus[t] a year or two earlier fast receding.

Many in the CIA, including Michael Burke and Frank Wisner, felt personall[y] betrayed by the 1951 unmasking of seni[or] British intelligence officer Kim Philby a[s] a Soviet spy. A prodigious drinker with [a] charming upper-class stutter, Philby ha[d] ingratiated himself with the most senio[r] ranks of the CIA and been privy to the inner workings of a staggering array of anti-Soviet covert operations.

Perhaps inflicting even more damage on the early CIA than Philby was the backroom scheming of FBI director J. Edgar Hoover, pictured here with his bureau deputy and lifelong companion, Clyde Tolson (right). Hoover wanted the FBI to take on the role of international intelligence agency and never forgave either Truman or the CIA for thwarting that plan. He nursed a special animus for Frank Wisner.

A consummate backstabber, Hoover secretly used Red-baiting Senator Joseph McCarthy to do his dirty work for him, passing along confidential FBI files on his enemies that McCarthy would then use in public attacks. McCarthy's chief henchman was a young lawyer named Roy Cohn (right), who would later be memorably characterized as "the worst human being who ever lived."

In a circuitous attack on Frank Wisner, the FBI gave McCarthy the file on one of Wisner's most trusted—and certainly most colorful—aides, Carmel Offie. When Offie was targeted by McCarthy for being a closeted homosexual, Wisner staunchly defended his deputy until higher-ups forced his resignation. Despite having already destroyed Offie professionally, a vengeful Hoover kept the former CIA official under intermittent FBI surveillance for the next twenty-one years.

As the communist insurgency in the Philippines worsened, Lansdale identified an obscure Filipino congressman, Ramon Magsaysay, as a possible savior. With the CIA's help, Magsaysay was appointed secretary of defense, with Lansdale as his chief advisor.

To reform an inept and corrupt military, Magsaysay and Lansdale paid surprise visits to army installations throughout the Philippines, firing ineffectual commanders and promoting ambitious ones. Magsaysay's habitual shabby appearance, as shown here, meant Lansdale frequently had to convince doubting army sentries that his companion *really* was the national defense secretary.

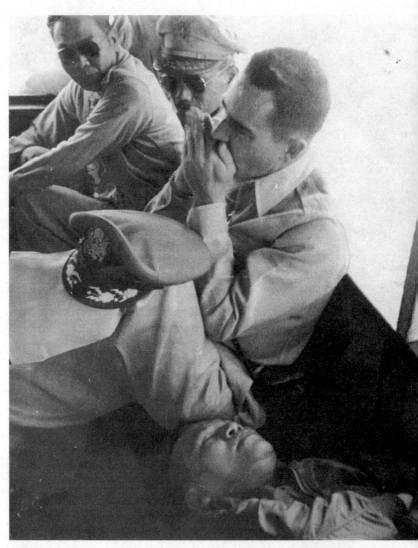

Lansdale playing the harmonica while Magsaysay (foreground) naps beside him, aboard a naval patrol boat in the Philippines, 1952. So close were Lansdale and Magsaysay that the American intelligence officer often likened their relationship to that of brothers. Others had a more cynical view, regarding Lansdale as Magsaysay's behind-the-scenes puppet master.

posited that, while there was obviously a leak somewhere in the operational apparatus, the most likely culprit was someone within the fractious and notoriously loose-lipped NCFA leadership. As a remedy, he suggested that the NCFA be largely kept out of the commando-selection process, and given only the vaguest information about operational timetables. The MI6 man further suggested that, while he saw no reason to shelve the infiltration program, perhaps they needed to set more modest goals until they devised new strategies to counter the *Sigurimi.* Wisner concurred with these proposals, as well as with deemphasizing the idea of actually overthrowing the Hoxha regime. Given the pervasiveness of the Albanian internal security system and the lack of any appetite for committing American or British troops into a possible war, probably the most prudent course in the short term was to accelerate the propaganda campaign against Tirana and use the infiltration squads primarily for intelligence gathering.

All this represented a very abrupt about-face. Just the previous month, the National Security Council had issued a top secret directive, NSC 58, outlining a strategy "to reduce and eventually to cause the elimination of dominant Soviet influence in the satellite states" of Eastern Europe. When it came to Albania in particular, a CIA paper of early October 1949 was even more explicit, stating that current U.S. policy "has as its objective the restoration of Albanian independence through the overthrow of the Moscow-controlled regime and its replacement by an enlightened government."

The change of course also placed Michael Burke in an extremely awkward spot. To the idea of pushing the NCFA leadership to the operational sidelines, the men Burke was dealing with in Rome were senior representatives of that organization, and would not take easily to being marginalized. Even more to the point, all the Albanians involved with Fiend were operating under the assumption, actively promoted by Washington and London, that they were working toward the overthrow of the Tirana regime. How to now turn around and tell them that what they were actually working toward—and in the case of the commandos, risking their lives for—was something that, at least for the foreseeable future, was infinitely more modest? The short answer was to not tell them at all. Although Michael Burke himself may not have been fully aware of the extent of the change in objectives, senior American and British officials simply chose to keep the NCFA leadership in the dark over their scaled-down agenda.

To the extent that Burke *did* grasp any of this, it would have been especially galling since Operation Fiend was slated to be a far more compli-cated undertaking than Valuable—and when it came to covert operations, more complicated almost always meant more perilous.

Due to Albania's provincialism and ubiquitous secret police, it had always been an article of faith that the pixies should be infiltrated into their home districts; that way they would be maneuvering over famil-iar ground and, if put to flight, more likely to find shelter among family or friends. This stricture had been followed in the Valuable landings of October 1949—those commandos were all from southern Albania and near where the landings occurred—and even then, their survival had been a near thing. By contrast, most all the Fiend recruits were from the mountainous interior of central and northern Albania, which meant that sea landings would be tantamount to suicide.

Instead, Fiend called for the far riskier approach of airdropping com-mandos at selected landing spots throughout the Albanian interior. In pursuit of plausible deniability, this meant a clandestine airplane flying out of a clandestine airfield, and ideally situated so close to the Albanian frontier that such "ghost flights" might barely register on even friendly radar. But this plan raised a whole host of security soft spots. A mysteri-ous boat trolling the high seas was one thing; how to hide an airplane and paratroopers and a flight crew?

The logical staging ground for such an undertaking was Greece. That also happened to be the adopted home of a man who, more than anyone else Michael Burke could think of, might find answers to those questions. Shortly after receiving a directive from Washington calling for tighter operational security, Burke made the quick flight from Rome to Athens. Mindful of maintaining his cover, and of choosing the kind of accommo-dations a successful American film producer might seek out, he checked into the five-star Grand Bretagne Hotel near Syntagma Square. He then set out to find Horace "Hod" Fuller.

A renaissance man much like Burke himself, Fuller had quit his Ivy League school to become an ambulance driver in France in 1940, then joined the Marines when the United States came into the war. Wounded at Guadalcanal, he had finagled a transfer into the OSS and parachuted into Nazi-held southern France. He and Burke had caroused in London together, and become fast friends. As Burke noted in his memoir, Hod Fuller would be his choice if forced "to pick one man in the world to have alongside me in a live-or-die situation"—and there was a good chance Operation Fiend would produce just such a scenario.

But Fuller was also a maverick and a man of extraordinary resource-fulness, as evidenced by the fact that he was the very same missing OSS commando that Peter Sichel, requisitioning the Cord 812 from the Seventh Army motor pool, had unsuccessfully scoured southern France in search of back in the autumn of 1944. As was subsequently revealed, the reason Sichel didn't find Fuller at the time was because Fuller didn't want to be found. Instead, marooned in a region of southern France that the occupying Germans had already vacated, and apparently deciding the war could be won without him, Fuller had used part of the cache of gold coins dropped with him to buy a French farm and settle in among the local population. Unfortunately—and this was to be a source of some lingering resentment for the former Marine—Fuller had been uncovered and returned to active service just before he could bring in the autumn harvest.

When Burke finally tracked him down, Fuller was busily restoring an old boat that had been raised from the bed of a Greek harbor, with vague plans of becoming an itinerant Mediterranean sailor. Perhaps to heighten the sense of historic moment, Burke lured his friend back to Athens and waited until they were watching a sunset from atop the Acropolis before launching into his Fiend sales pitch. After hearing out his friend's plan, Fuller decided that maybe his vagabond days could wait awhile; on the spot, he agreed to sign on as the logistics officer for the Greek segment of Operation Fiend. "Afterward," Burke recalled, "we went down the hill to a tavern to toast our adventure with ouzo."

It is almost a cliché of the spy world that the demands of the profession—the leading of a double life, the inability to share its details—tend to fray marriages until they come apart. In Rome, Michael and Timmy Burke found the opposite. "Keeping the two lives compartmentalized was in fact an interesting mental exercise for us," he wrote. "Between Timmy and me, it created a special kind of closeness, not self-conscious, not dissected by tedious analysis or even talked about. . . . Given the persistent optimism that nothing untoward would happen to me, clandestine activity spiced more than menaced our lives."

It was a secret world that ultimately brought Timmy into the mix, at least in a small way. As recalled by Burke's daughter Patricia, during one of her father's periodic absences from Rome as he planned for Fiend, Timmy received a message from one of his field agents, with the request that it be relayed to headquarters right away. Unable to reach her husband, and with no instructions on what to do in such a situation, Timmy simply called the American embassy and asked to be put through to the CIA desk officer. In the wake of that snafu, a system was established whereby Timmy could receive or pass messages to a female courier during "chance" encounters while dog-walking or in the ladies' room of the Excelsior Hotel. So frequent did these meetings become that the CIA Rome desk officer eventually gave the strikingly pretty Timmy her own playful code name: Mrs. U. R. Darling.

As the pace of the Fiend prep work intensified, Burke's double life in Rome began to tilt heavily in one direction: less time eating brioche with his film-world friends, and more talking shop with his Albanian co-conspirators. One detail he didn't spend much time pondering was any issue of the morality of the enterprise he had joined, either of the plot to subvert a foreign government or of the backgrounds of the men he was now in alliance with. As in many other parts of Europe, World War II in Albania had been a vicious, obscene affair, with different partisan groups often switching from fighting the Axis armies to joining with them in order to attack one another. During the war, most every Albanian political faction or partisan commander—and that included Burke's new friend, Abas Kupi—had at some point made a pact of convenience with the Axis, had murdered civilians and tortured prisoners. But just as with Peter Sichel in Berlin, none of that was important now. "Given the black-and-white definition of the Cold War," Burke wrote, "there was no shilly-shallying about morality. Who is not with me is against me."

Besides, he genuinely liked the Albanians. In fact, so comfortable did he become in their company that, during a brief lull in Fiend preparations, he decided to host a grand dinner at his home in their honor.

"The shutters of the tall glass doors that formed one side of the sitting room were drawn closed for security," he recalled. "We drank brandy, and cigar smoke mingled with that of the smoldering candles. The good food and wine and the sociable talk had eased the normal tensions of their émigré life and the political wariness among them. Their clothes, cheap and ill-fitting, looked the more forlorn against Contessa Carasotti's elegant period furniture, the rich marble floor and the high molded ceiling of her villa. Yet their manners were gracious and even courtly in an Old World way."

Even in such an elegant setting, though, the Albanians didn't forget that danger lurked everywhere and that, the spirit of pan-Albanianism aside, one still had to watch one's back. At around midnight, they took turns rising from their chairs to leave the villa on Via Michele Mercati in spaced intervals. "One by one, they kissed Timmy's hand and vanished down the gravel drive, through the high iron gate and into the moonless night."

By March 1950, the demands of Operation Fiend planning kept Burke in almost constant motion. The reason was simple enough. Due to Fiend's ultra-top-secret status, its component parts were scattered over a half-dozen nations and carefully walled off from one another, and it fell to Burke, as one of the only officials with a grasp of the entire picture, to maintain contact with all of them. Liaising with the British and their Operation Valuable team meant frequent trips to London, while conferring with the Albanian émigré leadership meant stopovers in Paris. Along the way were logistical planning sessions with Hod Fuller in Athens, meetings with OPC colleagues at military bases and safe houses across West Germany, and excursions to those displaced persons camps where Fiend volunteers were being recruited. It was exhausting and exhilarating and it never let up.

Other than Burke, full knowledge of the Albanian enterprise was largely limited to just four members of the Western intelligence community, those officials who comprised the joint British and American coordinating team based in Washington and known as the Special Policy Committee (SPC). During a stopover in London in March, Burke learned that Harold "Kim" Philby, the MI6 liaison to American intelligence and the British SPC member most involved in the committee's day-to-day deliberations, happened to be in town on a quick visit, and wished to meet with him. Burke leapt at the offer, no doubt thankful for an opportunity to speak freely about the mission that had come to consume his life with someone fully in the know.

Always an adept social networker, Burke may have had another motive for wanting to meet the MI6 man, for Kim Philby, not yet forty, was already something of a legend in the upper reaches of the Anglo-American intelligence community. The son of a famous British intelligence officer, St. John Philby, who had made a name for himself in the Arabian Peninsula, Kim began his intelligence work for the British government in the late 1930s when, after graduating from Cambridge, he went to cover the Spanish Civil War for *The Times* of London. In a particularly astute move, he attached himself to the Nationalist, or Francoist, side of the conflict when the vast majority of foreign journalists—then as now tending to be a liberal lot—flocked to the more sympathetic Republicans. His standing among the Nationalists had been solidified in late 1937 when the press car he was traveling in was destroyed by a Republican artillery shell; of the four journalists in the car, only Philby survived. Thus bloodied, Philby gained the acceptance and confidences of those in General Francisco Franco's inner circle, confidences he then passed on to his government's Secret Intelligence Service (SIS).

In World War II, Philby's freelance status with British intelligence became official. Recognized as both brilliant and acerbic, he steadily rose through the ranks of SIS—soon to become better known as MI6—and was so highly regarded that he became one of the lucky few to be retained through successive postwar personnel cuts. After first heading the British intelligence office in Turkey, a vitally important post, in late 1949 he had been awarded the plum assignment of MI6 representative to the United States.

It was a perfect fit. Taking up his Washington duties that October while posing as a first secretary at the British embassy, Philby soon gained entree to a rarefied media and diplomatic social circuit that included such luminaries as George Kennan, Secretary of State Dean Acheson, and *Washington Post* publisher Philip Graham. By all accounts, he was a particularly favorite dinner and drinking companion of both Frank Wisner and James Jesus Angleton, the head of the CIA's Office of Special Operations, who had become friends with Philby during the war. To James McCargar, Philby's American "co-commander" on the Albanian Special Policy Committee, the Briton's appeal was thoroughly understandable. "He had a stammer and a good stock of anecdotes—an excellent combination," McCargar recalled. "He had charm, warmth and an engaging, self-deprecating humor. He drank a lot, but then so did we all in those days."

By the time Michael Burke encountered him in London that March, there was growing talk in both British and American intelligence circles that it was merely a matter of time before Kim Philby, already in the top ranks of MI6, became its chief.

At their meeting, Burke and Philby fell into easy conversation, much of it, of course, having to do with the ongoing preparations for Operation Fiend, and Burke was struck by the Briton's deep familiarity with operational matters. Not that they agreed on all things. In particular, Philby shared none of Burke's affection for Abas Kupi, the tribal chieftain from central Albania. To the well-bred Philby, the "whiskered and habitually armed to the teeth" Kupi was just an old rascal, of the sort that traditionally caused Britishers of his class to go weak at the knee. "I had no doubt that he could equal the feats of his ancestors in raiding unarmed caravans or sniping at heat-stricken Turkish infantrymen plodding hopelessly through the gorges," Philby later commented. "But I never shared the bemusement of the British gentleman at the sight of a tribesman. I am sure that tribal courage is legendary only in the sense that it is legend."

When Philby suggested they continue their discussions over dinner, Burke gladly accepted. They decided on Wheeler's, a famed seafood restaurant in Mayfair, where, along with sole, the two men consumed a prodigious amount of Meursault. The longer the evening went on, the more Burke liked Philby—and it wasn't just the wine talking. "His considerable charm was disarming," he remembered, "his slight stutter sympathetic, his face almost handsome in a neglected way. He gave the appearance of wasting no more time shaving or combing his hair than he did with his clothes, which were unfashionable and unpressed. Entirely likeable and very much at home in and on top of his profession."

That affection was clearly reciprocated for, after dinner, Philby announced he was going along to a nearby gentlemen's club to say hello to his father—the legendary St. John was in town on a rare visit—and invited Burke to join him. At the club, Burke walked into a classic upper-class British scene, with the elder Philby and his friends gathered about a dinner table in a wood-paneled room sipping port. Even the awkwardness of the Philby father-son embrace spoke to pedigree. "Personal diffidence and English good form inhibited a fuller expression of the affection one sensed they felt for one another," Burke recalled. "We stayed for no more than a quarter of an hour and St. John Philby said he expected that two young men had more stimulating things to do with the young night and we were dismissed."

Determined to keep their revelry going, the two new friends then went on to an after-hours club Philby knew.

While it might seem curious that Burke, writing of that evening some thirty years later, should recall it in such detail, there were two possible explanations. Ever since the OSS was created in 1942, the British intelligence community had tended to gaze upon its American counterpart rather like a hapless little brother—perhaps more, like a rich-but-clueless cousin. In his meeting with Kim Philby, however, Burke detected none of the condescension or put-upon forbearance he'd sensed so often before in his British colleagues. Instead, he was at last being treated as a peer, being listened to—and by one of the leading lights of MI6.

The second possible explanation was that, in the near future, the OPC contract officer would have reason to wrack his memory, to try to recall every word that had passed between him and Kim Philby.

14

FINDING "OUR GUY"

For a man already gaining a reputation as a keen strategist, by October 1949 Edward Lansdale was anxiously trying to bring that talent to bear on his own life. At the time, he was one of ninety-eight students enrolled in an academic instructor training course at the Air Force Special Staff School in Selma, Alabama. At the conclusion of the course, students were to receive a numerical ranking, a standing that would determine who was offered a permanent teaching position somewhere in the American military training hierarchy, and who was not. Having determined that, at a minimum, the top ten students would be retained, Lansdale sought to position himself well out of that danger zone.

"'I'd like to be in the middle someplace,'" he recalled thinking. "I'd figured it out. I'd carefully missed questions and everything. 'I can afford to miss so many on this exam,' and I was sure I'd gotten down into the middle of the percentile group."

A long trail of misfortune had led Lansdale to his predicament in Selma.

In the summer of 1948, he had received orders in Manila to return to the United States and take up a new position as an instructor at the Air Force's intelligence training school at Lowry Air Force Base in Denver. With all efforts at evading the assignment coming to naught, Lansdale had taken up his post at Lowry that February. He was in time to experience one of the coldest and snowiest winters to strike the Rockies in decades, a torturous ordeal for someone who'd just spent four years in the tropics. Greatly adding to the bleakness of his existence, his estranged wife, Helen, chose to stay in California with their two young sons.

Having never regarded himself as any kind of educator, Lansdale clung to the hope that, upon observing his performance in a classroom, the Lowry administrators would conclude the same thing and hastily arrange his transfer. This hope was soon dashed. "After preparing and giving one series of lectures," Lansdale recalled, "I was dismayed to learn that some of my superiors had concluded that teaching was my true calling."

From there, matters simply spiraled downward. Despite Lansdale's unconventional teaching methods—he encouraged discussion and debate in the classroom—Lowry administrators found he was such a favorite among the cadets that they greatly increased his class assignments. They also decided he should undergo specialized instructor training. It was in furtherance of that mission that the forty-one-year-old Air Force major found himself at the Special Staff School in Selma, Alabama, in the summer of 1949.

Even more than a disinterest in teaching, it was that Lansdale desperately wanted to return to the field, and to one field in particular: Asia. Just before he had left the Philippines, the Huk rebellion, having briefly shown promise of peaceful resolution, had roared back to life. By 1949, a three-year-old communist insurgency in French Indochina had only grown bloodier, with no resolution in sight. That conflict was now joined by a similar insurgency against the British in their colony of Malaya. Certainly, the greatest upheaval had taken place in China. After twenty-one years of intermittent civil war, the communist armies of Mao Zedong were on the verge of finally vanquishing the Kuomintang forces of Chiang Kai-shek. Over the course of five months in late 1948 and early 1949, the Chinese Red Army had annihilated three different Kuomintang armies totaling well over a million soldiers in the conquest of northern China, and had now turned its attention to the south. Indeed, even as Lansdale saw to his studies at the staff school in Selma, newspaper headlines were telling of Chiang Kai-shek's final defeat on the Chinese mainland, and the beginning of a Kuomintang exodus to the island sanctuary of Taiwan.

Yet, even with the grim news out of China, events in Asia barely registered with the American public and little more so with the Truman administration, thoroughly preoccupied as it was with the ongoing contest with the Soviets in Eastern Europe. It was almost by default, then, that Lansdale saw Asia as where he *had* to be, the place where he could both make the greatest contribution to the global anti-communist effort and have the freedom of action to test some of his nascent counterrevolutionary theories. There was also a strong personal component to this wish; with his marriage to Helen now largely existing only in name, he longed for a reunion with Pat Kelly. "These months away from you seem like an unpleasant dream," he wrote her in February 1949, "and my life has lost so much of its flavor that I've crawled into myself with you."

Before any such reunion, though, he needed to escape the groves of military academia once and for all, and by October 1949 the first step to accomplishing that was to sabotage his standing at the Special Staff School.

But Lansdale apparently either underestimated his own abilities or badly overestimated those of his colleagues, for when the final class rankings in Selma were posted, the results were dire: rather than landing in the safe middle range—well behind the classroom stars, but far enough ahead of the dullards to escape suspicion that he'd thrown the game—Lansdale had placed third. Naturally, his superiors back in Colorado were delighted to learn their candidate had been adjudged "exceptionally capable," the highest ranking possible, their hunch about his academic aptitude now confirmed.

At this distressing juncture, Lansdale had reason to recall a letter he had received seven months earlier. It had been from his former commanding officer in the military intelligence unit in Manila, Colonel George Chester. Chester had always thought extremely highly of Lansdale, and his letter was tantalizingly cryptic. "Looks more than ever as if I'll go to Washington and in[to] something of our mutual interest—I don't mean PRO [public relations officer]. You may get a note, or a call from someone there. If you do, you'll know the impetus came from here. Don't know too much definite myself, but I think you'd like it, and I'd surely like to have you with me again."

Neither a note nor a call had come, but after receiving his grades at the Special Staff School, an anxious Lansdale detoured to Washington to explain his predicament to Chester. It was a wise move; within days of his return to Lowry, Lansdale was visited by an Air Force colonel he didn't know.

If George Chester had been enigmatic in his letter, the visiting colonel was hardly less so. About all he imparted to Lansdale was that Chester now worked for a branch of the government dedicated to manning the front lines of the new "cold war" developing between the United States and the Soviet Union, an agency so top secret that even its name was classified. Considering that Chester had recommended his former subordinate in the highest possible terms, might Lansdale be interested in joining up? By mid-November 1949, the Air Force officer was on his way to Washington, there to become the newest contract hire of Frank Wisner's Office of Policy Coordination.

At least initially, Lansdale could be forgiven for concluding there was little to choose between his posting at Lowry and his new one in Washington. As in Colorado, his wife declined to make the move east with their two boys, so Ed took up bachelor's quarters at the Fort Myer army base in Alexandria. Most every workday he made the two-and-a-half-mile walk through Arlington Cemetery and over the Memorial Bridge to OPC headquarters, the eyesore collection of Tempos in the shadow of the Lincoln Memorial. In his small, dingy office in M Building, he became one more member of the rapidly growing staff of OPC analysts and covert action specialists who labored under the watchful eye and mercurial enthusiasms of Frank Wisner.

At first, the newcomer from the Air Force—Lansdale had recently regained his rank of lieutenant colonel—was detailed to the same task that commanded the attention of nearly the entire OPC staff: how to confront the Soviet Union and its growing sway in Europe and, increasingly, the Middle East. "Most of my staff colleagues in Washington," he recalled, "were focused on the moves of Stalin and on the Soviet strategy of manipulating the urban intelligentsia and proletariat into undertaking revolutions in countries friendly to us." From his time observing the Huks, however, Lansdale was more interested—or at least it was where he felt he might contribute something original—in the Asian corollary to this revolution-making process.

That process was almost the precise reverse of that in Europe. Rather than a top-down revolt led by industrial workers and an educated urban class—the Russian Revolution was a prime example of this scenario—the Asian model worked from the ground up and tended to gain its initial impetus in the countryside. As Lansdale described it, it was the concept of "a poor man's war that would start with rural farmers as guerrillas, a bucolic force that would become a conventional army as it met with success until, finally, it would be able to swallow up the cities and complete the conquest of a country."

When Lansdale arrived at OPC, the world had just seen a vivid illustration of this in China. Through the final stages of the Chinese civil war, Mao Zedong's communist cadres had largely avoided trying to control urban centers in favor of systematically consolidating their hold in the countryside. In the face of conventional military offensives from Chiang Kai-shek's Nationalists, the Red Army gave ground and allowed their enemy to overextend itself. The result by late 1948 had been a constellation of Nationalist-controlled urban islands marooned amid a "red sea." Thus, even as Chiang Kai-shek continued to think he was winning because he controlled most of the population centers, his impending defeat was both inevitable and likely to be swift.

But just why had Chiang lost the countryside, and what was the "secret" of Mao's success there? In truth, it was no secret at all, but rather an essential point that Lansdale had gleaned from studying Mao's writings: land reform.

For centuries, much of China's best farmland had been in the hands of a small cabal of landlords and aristocratic families, with most everyone else reduced to lives of impoverishment and the indentured servitude of tenancy farming. By simply promising to dismantle this system—and never mind the practical issues involved—Mao went a long way toward winning over China's rural peasantry, who were the overwhelming majority of the population. This same promise had a devastatingly corrosive effect on Chiang Kai-shek's armies. Largely composed of conscripts from this same poor rural class, it didn't take long for many Nationalist soldiers to conclude they were being asked to fight and die in the service of their oppressors, with the result that hundreds of thousands deserted at the first opportunity or switched sides when the Red Army closed in.

But it wasn't just China. Much the same dynamic was now evident in other Asian countries, including the Philippines. Land reform had always been the core rallying cry of the Huks, and it was surely no coincidence that the rebels had found their greatest pool of support among the very poorest—and landless—peasants of central Luzon. While somewhat obscured by the anticolonial sheen of the communist-led revolts in French Indochina and British Malaya, there, too, the issue of land reform was an animating factor.

Incredibly, though, at the start of 1950, few American intelligence officers had read Mao's teachings; Edward Lansdale may have been one of the very first. Even more remarkable, in light of the recent communist takeover of China, many American Cold War analysts still failed to appreciate the radically different approach to revolution-making of the Soviet and Chinese models. "There were a lot of differences that way," Lansdale noted, "and the people back here [in Washington] weren't looking at them that way at all."

One effect of Mao's victory was to spur a heated round of finger-pointing in Washington, the beginning of a bitter debate that would gain force over the next several years over the question of "who lost China?" Another effect was to impress upon Frank Wisner and his OPC deputies that, whether they liked it or not, their Cold War battleground had now expanded to Asia. In this atmosphere, Lansdale's request to be moved off the OPC's Soviet planning desk for the embryonic Far East desk was quickly accepted.

But where to focus his energies? It was obviously too late to "save" China, and any unsolicited American engagement in Indochina or Malaya was complicated by the United States' alliance with France and Britain. That left the country Lansdale had already come to regard as a second home. "The more I got into Cold War problems," he told biographer Cecil Currey, "the more I got to worrying about the Philippines."

Those worries were hardly misplaced, for the situation there seemed to be growing worse by the day. From his Tempo office on the Washington Mall, Lansdale stayed abreast of the torrent of bad news coming out of Manila. "It was filled with reports of Huk successes," he wrote. "Towns had been looted and burned. Constabulary barracks in six provinces were being attacked frequently. Ambushes on the highways were becoming commonplace, as were kidnappings and murders of local leaders in the provinces."

On the OPC Far East desk, Lansdale made devising a strategy to defeat the Huks his chief priority. Easier said than done, however, for amid the blizzard of ill tidings from abroad vying for the attention of official Washington, there was scant constituency—which meant scant resources—for bearing down on a small and still geographically contained Asian "bush war." Tasked to devise simple and inexpensive schemes that could supplement the American aid already flowing to the Philippine military, Lansdale came up with the idea of holding a seminar for Filipino officers undergoing training in the United States on methods they might employ to counter "the political-military tactics of the Huks."

Put more plainly, Lansdale was talking about psychological warfare and, in particular, a strain of it that would come to be known as "hearts and minds." Rather than stay isolated in large well-guarded firebases, he counseled, Filipino troops needed to move in small units among the people, and rather than combat the Huks with firepower alone, these troops should engage in the sort of civic action projects—digging wells, refurbishing schools—that might gradually win over the support of local communities. In the spring of 1950, Lansdale put on his psychological warfare seminar for several dozen Filipino officers, with instruction delivered by whatever American psy-ops veterans of World War II he could round up. "We had no funds to support the seminar," Lansdale recalled, "just an available conference room in the Pentagon and much goodwill. We met for two days. I didn't know it at the time, but this was to be the extent of my own formal education in psychological warfare."

Despite the seminar's success, the new OPC man appreciated it was a small beginning. Specifically, inculcating junior officers with the precepts of psy-ops was of very limited value if there weren't also structural changes in the Philippine political and military establishment—and there were few signs of that occurring. Despite his earlier overtures to the Huks, Elpidio Quirino had proved a lackluster president, with little interest or ability in addressing the societal inequities that helped fuel the Huks' appeal. Similarly, the Philippine military leadership operated on the crony system and was staggeringly inept, the kind of calcified hierarchy unlikely to empower junior officers or embrace new ideas.

It was while trying to puzzle a way through this knot of problems in his new Washington home that Lansdale met a visitor from the Philippines. From outward appearances, there was precious little to suggest their meeting would be of any great import—Ed Lansdale was an OPC neophyte working at a backwater desk, while the Filipino was a junior congressman from a minor province—but from that encounter was to be forged one of the most consequential political friendships of the day, one that would not only alter the course of events in the Philippines, but create an enduring touchstone in the history of the Cold War.

═══

Ed Lansdale had put out a standing invitation to his old friends in Manila to call on him should they ever visit Washington, and many took him up on the offer. In March 1950, it was the turn of Mamerto Montemayor, a lieutenant colonel in the Philippine army. Montemayor had come to Washington to lobby for greater benefits for Filipino veterans who had fought on the American side in World War II. He was joined in this endeavor by a forty-two-year-old congressman named Ramon Magsaysay. When Montemayor suggested the three of them join up for dinner, Lansdale, still new to the capital and with time on his hands, gladly accepted.

What first drew Lansdale's attention was Ramon Magsaysay's physique. At nearly six-foot, he was unusually tall for a Filipino, with the calloused hands and dark complexion of someone used to manual labor and life outdoors. In this, he stood in marked contrast to most of the other Filipino politicians—slight, refined, with the light skin denoting them as members of the mestizo mixed-race aristocracy—whom Lansdale had dealt with over the years.

Magsaysay also had a far more interesting background than that typically found among the Manila elite. Just six months older than Lansdale, he had grown up in a small town in the Zambales province of western Luzon, the second of eight children born to a blacksmith and school-teacher. Despite the "barefoot" legend that would later be built around him, his family was fairly middle-class by Philippine standards. Proving an uninspired student—Magsaysay attended two different colleges but failed to graduate from either one—by 1941 he was leading a pleasant if utterly unremarkable life, the thirty-three-year-old branch manager of a regional bus company and the doting father of three young children. His life was turned upside down, however, and his true calling revealed, with the Japanese invasion of the Philippines that December.

Following Japan's swift conquest of Luzon, Magsaysay joined a guerrilla force led by some of the few American officers to have escaped capture at Bataan. Proving a natural leader of men, the onetime mechanic steadily rose through the guerrilla ranks to ultimately become the commander of a force numbering in the thousands. In early 1945, his unit helped clear the Zambales coastline of Japanese troops prior to the landing of American troops there, an offensive that both minimized American casualties and hastened Philippine liberation. Capitalizing on his war-hero status, Magsaysay was elected to the Philippine Congress in 1946, and won easy reelection two years later. In recognition of his wartime service, he was made chairman of the congressional National Defense Committee, and selected to serve as chief negotiator in efforts to wrest greater benefits from the United States for Filipino war veterans, the mission that brought him and Lieutenant Colonel Montemayor to Washington in March 1950.

At their dinner, Lansdale and Magsaysay immediately hit it off. "They discussed problems besetting the Quirino government including the attitudes of the Philippine armed forces toward fighting Huks," wrote Cecil Currey. "They found that their evaluation of various Filipino generals were similar. As they tested their ideas on one another, they discovered they were in essential agreement."

So much in agreement, in fact, that at the conclusion of their meal, they returned to Lansdale's billet at Fort Myer to continue their conversation. Eventually, Lansdale brought out his portable typewriter and began typing up Magsaysay's answers to his steady stream of questions. When he was done, Lansdale later told his biographer, he compared his Magsaysay notes to a memo he had recently penned on how to salvage the situation in the Philippines. "The sequence [of priorities] was the same as the program I had just sold the U.S. policymakers," Lansdale said, "and in the same language."

Exhilarated, the next morning Lansdale briefed both his supervisor on the Far East desk and Frank Wisner on his meeting with Magsaysay. He also arranged a luncheon for the following day to introduce the Filipino congressman to his OPC superiors, as well as senior officials from the State Department and Air Force.

That gathering took place in the dining room of the Hotel Washington, one block from the White House. Attendees may have been struck by how much the Filipino's recommendations for confronting the Huk insurgency mirrored those that Lansdale had been advocating in recent weeks. This was hardly coincidental for, as Lansdale would later admit, he had carefully tutored Magsaysay on what to say ahead of time.

At the conclusion of the luncheon, the much impressed senior staff of OPC discussed between themselves what action might be taken, whether they should throw their support behind Magsaysay in hopes of advancing his political career, or to try and propel him into a leadership position in the Philippine military. Either way, it raised the question of just how overt their assistance should be. Ultimately, Wisner and his OPC lieutenants decided on a go-slow approach that carried their organizational credo of plausible deniability to a new level, "to provide Magsaysay with quiet OPC support, arranged in such a way that he would not be privy to its source."

If such a strategy smacked of imperial hubris, so, too, did Lansdale's reappraisal of the Huk problem as a result of his meeting with Ramon Magsaysay. "I decided he should be the guy to handle it."

In the near future, Lansdale would be the American point man in making that happen, a campaign that would ultimately pluck both him and Magsaysay from obscurity and cast them onto the center stage of the Cold War in East Asia.

15

WITCH HUNT

Locust Hill Farm is located a short distance outside the town of Galena on Maryland's Eastern Shore, a 340-acre spread of corn and alfalfa fields, wood copses and marshland. The main home, a two-and-a-half-story brick structure built about 1790, sits on a slight rise and is surrounded by a cluster of barns and worksheds, along with an enormous old corn-crib.

Frank Wisner bought Locust Hill in 1946, shortly after returning from Germany. While working at the Carter Ledyard law firm in Manhattan, he would make the four-hour drive down to the farm whenever he could sneak away, both to check in with the resident caretakers, and to tend to the large vegetable garden he planted just behind the main house. After moving to Washington in 1947, Wisner's commute to Locust Hill could take even longer until the Chesapeake Bay Bridge was opened in 1952.

Clearly, buying a large working farm in such an isolated place was not the most practical idea for so busy a man, but Locust Hill was Wisner's refuge, the place where he was returned to the land and could relax. Granted, relaxation looked different for him than for most people; not for him whiling away an afternoon in an easy chair with a good book. An avid duck-hunter, no matter the weather he was likely to go to the blinds he'd built in Locust Hill's marshlands with several of his shotguns. Changing out of his city clothes, he could happily spend all day walking the fields with the caretakers, or stowing corn or hay in the barns with the farm's conveyor belt.

But even at Locust Hill, Wisner could never quite escape Washington.

It took practically nothing to be investigated for subversion by the FBI in the late 1940s: a baseless rumor spread by a hostile neighbor or ex-husband; membership in an organization advocating civil rights for blacks; putting one's name on a petition for increased school funding while ignorant of the fact that the leader of the petition drive had once rented an apartment to someone whose uncle was suspected of being a communist. Nothing was ever too absurd, too tangential.

Naturally, the odds of being the target of such an investigation spiked for anyone whom J. Edgar Hoover perceived as an enemy or a potential threat. Among the many hundreds of men and women who, in the FBI director's estimation, fell into these categories was the man in charge of the international covert operations and intelligence unit that Hoover had once coveted for himself: the OPC's Frank Wisner.

If it was inevitable that Wisner should fall under Hoover's scrutinizing gaze, it began innocuously enough. In order to visit atomic weapons facilities, the OPC chief, like every other American official, first had to submit to an Atomic Energy Commission (AEC) background check. Those checks were conducted by the FBI.

The bureau's investigation of Wisner in the spring of 1949 looked to be a pro forma exercise; indeed, with tedious regularity, all of the nearly one dozen former or current government officials contacted by the FBI both praised Wisner for his service to the country, and held that any doubting of his loyalty or patriotism was ludicrous.

But FBI special agents did happen upon one interesting tidbit: Wisner's wartime relationship with a princess in Romania. As the young and lovely bride of a Romanian brewing magnate, the exotic Princess Tanda Caragea had played hostess to Wisner in their Bucharest mansion in late 1944 and early 1945. According to rumors circulating through the Romanian capital at the time—and coming to the attention of the FBI four years later—those hostessing duties had extended to the Tanda bedroom. Even for a puritanical moralist like Hoover this was hardly disqualifying material, and Wisner quickly received his AEC clearance. The problem was, the story of his purported wartime dalliance was now part of his FBI file, there to reside as a potential weapon of personal destruction should the need ever arise. In a few years' time, the FBI director would perceive just such a need.

In the meantime, though, Hoover had many more targets to pursue, and in the late 1940s, just as earlier, he could turn to select politicians to both do his bidding and cover his tracks. Of these none were more immediately useful than a junior congressman from Southern California named Richard Nixon.

With the FBI continuing to undermine the prosecution of espionage cases, either because of its illegal methods in gathering evidence or in refusing to reveal its sources, Hoover became especially incensed in 1948 over the case of Alger Hiss, a former high-ranking State Department official. In dramatic congressional hearings, ex-communist Whittaker Chambers testified that he and Hiss had been part of the same communist cell in the 1930s, a charge Hiss stoutly denied and which, with the statute of limitations long passed, posed little legal threat in any event. With Hiss looking to go scot-free, his FBI file was secretly passed to Nixon, who led a two-year crusade against the former diplomat, culminating in his conviction for perjury. Congressman Nixon parlayed his role in bringing down Hiss into a Senate seat, and ultimately the vice presidency.

The Hiss case played to the benefit of J. Edgar Hoover, as well, proving once again the utility of extralegal back channels to smite the foe when legal avenues were closed. Even the torturously slow process that led to Hiss's fall played to the director's advantage; the longer such cases stayed in the public eye, the more dire the perception of the communist threat, and the more secure the position of Hoover and the FBI as frontline defenders against that threat.

But merely retaining power had never been enough for Hoover. It had always been about amassing more, and with the sudden rise of Senator Joseph McCarthy in 1950, Hoover was able to launch a vastly expanded attack on those he deemed enemies. Inevitably, this would include the CIA and the covert action unit housed within it, Wisner's Office of Policy Coordination.

McCarthy leapt to national prominence in February 1950 after his speech at a Lincoln Day dinner in Wheeling, West Virginia, in which he claimed to have the names of 205 State Department officials who were members of the communist party. The reckless fiction and demagoguery of this assertion provided the template for the congressional hearings that soon followed. Democrats on the committee, including its chairman, Millard Tydings, anticipated the proceedings as a public humiliation of McCarthy, a laying bare of his lies, but it didn't quite work out that way.

Through the first few days of the hearings, begun on March 8, McCarthy seemed utterly out of his depth, stumbling his way through his opening testimony, losing his temper in response to Tydings's needling, at one point admitting he couldn't remember the names of half the people on his list. Gradually, though, he gained his footing, his delivery became more assured, his accusations more specific. As would eventually be revealed, the abrupt change stemmed in large part from a mysterious outside source of information.

In the days leading up to the hearings, McCarthy had frantically reached out to his anti-communist colleagues in the House, to like-minded officials in government agencies, even to private citizens for any leads they might have to buttress his claims. Rescue came from two directions: the newspaper magnate William Randolph Hearst, and FBI director Hoover. As Hearst would later confide to muckraker columnist Jack Anderson, "Joe never had any names. He came to us. 'What am I gonna do? You gotta help me.' So we gave him a few good reporters." In short order, McCarthy could rely on a stable of a half-dozen well-connected and archconservative investigative journalists on loan from the Hearst Corporation and other right-wing newspaper syndicates.

McCarthy received an equally vital boost when he asked Hoover for advice on hiring an investigator to search for his State Department Reds. His timing was excellent. Shortly before, Hoover had been forced to dismiss one of his favorite bureau investigators, a ten-year veteran named Donald Surine, for consorting with a prostitute. Within days, Surine was the head of McCarthy's investigative team and, according to Hoover biographer David Oshinsky, leaning on his former colleagues in the bureau to hand over whatever State Department dirt they had.

By mid-March, McCarthy's Senate office was receiving a steady stream of unmarked envelopes containing anonymous reports, many consisting of little more than unverified gossip, about various alleged communists or communist sympathizers in the State Department. The origin of this incriminating information was all but untraceable since none of it appeared on official letterhead. Instead, all the material had been retyped onto plain typing paper or index cards. This allowed McCarthy's stable of journalist assistants to claim the reports came from their anonymous sources, and not from Surine or the FBI.

The sleight of hand didn't fool many people in the bureau, and it caused a good deal of resentment among some senior officials. To Robert Lamphere, one of the bureau's chief specialists on espionage cases, feeding information to McCarthy undercut the legitimate hunt for communist spies in the government because "McCarthy lied about his information and figures. He made charges against people that weren't true." This served to discredit the counterintelligence effort by inviting ridicule, a point that seemed lost on McCarthy's most powerful patron. "All along," Lamphere noted, "Hoover was helping him."

But McCarthy was even more clever in attaching his crusade—already a "witch hunt" to his liberal enemies—to one that had been gaining traction for some time: the targeting of gays employed by the federal government.

In the immediate postwar period, Hoover and other archconservatives had forcefully argued that, because of the homosexual's "perverted" lifestyle and his or her need to keep it secret, gays were uniquely susceptible to blackmail and, thus, unique security risks in sensitive government posts. Hoover's militancy on this point came despite—and perhaps because of—long-standing rumors of his own homosexuality, centering on his relationship with his lifelong companion and bureau deputy, Clyde Tolson. Capitalizing on a security-risk rider attached to its 1946 appropriations bills, the State Department quietly began purging gays from its ranks the following year. With passage of the 1947 Loyalty Order, the practice had spread to other government branches. And just as with the other investigatory demands created by the Loyalty Order, the principal agency tasked to ferret out and build cases against suspected gays was the FBI.

Few seemed to ponder the self-fulfilling nature of this equation, that if people are liable to be fired for their sexual orientation—or for any personal characteristic, for that matter—naturally they will try to conceal that orientation. The act of concealment then makes them more susceptible to blackmail and, ergo, greater security risks.

But what made the so-called Lavender Scare especially pernicious was that there was essentially no way to refute a charge once made. After all, someone accused of being a card-carrying communist could, at least theoretically, clear their name by proving they weren't a party member, but when it came to aspersions cast on one's sexuality, how to ever establish one's "innocence"? Except of course, it rarely got to that point. So taboo was the topic of homosexuality in mainstream America of the late 1940s and early 1950s that even just a rumor was usually enough to send its target, gay or straight, rushing to the exits so as to avoid the disgrace that would accompany the rumor's airing. Completing the circle of paranoia, such capitulations increased the fear of others who might be targeted, and lent further credence to the idea that both communists and gays represented mortal threats to the federal government and, by extension, the American way of life.

Where all of this was to first become evident—the symbiosis between the Red and the Lavender Scares; the coy, backhanded arrangement between McCarthy and the FBI—was in the Tydings Committee conference room on an afternoon in late April 1950. For J. Edgar Hoover, that day's proceedings finally provided the chance to chip away at the power and influence of Frank Wisner.

It was a masterful pivot. By the afternoon of Tuesday, April 25, 1950, the hearings into McCarthy's claims of communists in the State Department were well into their seventh week. As had occurred so often over those weeks, McCarthy was engaged in another acrimonious debate with Millard Tydings. The committee chairman had repeatedly ridiculed the Wisconsin senator for his fluctuating numbers of alleged communists, and a seething McCarthy had just as often hurled new accusations in response. After reminding the committee of McCarthy's prior claim of 205 communists in the State Department, Tydings that afternoon pointed out that McCarthy's suspect list now totaled just 81. "Where are the 205 card-carrying communists?" he sneered. "Was that a reckless statement?"

At that point, and with the intercession of a supportive Republican colleague, McCarthy turned the tables on his tormentor, pointing out that he had recently given Tydings the "complete criminal record" of an unnamed State Department employee. "This man has now been assigned to the Central Intelligence Agency," McCarthy announced. "I was extremely curious to know why the Central Intelligence Agency had not discharged him, but the fact that he is in the State Department explains that." Employing the stilted language of Senate tradition, he then essentially accused Tydings, a Maryland senator, of being the criminal's protector. "Is the Senator aware of the fact that I gave the complete police record of this man to the Senator from Maryland, this man who was a homosexual? . . . This man is still in an extremely sensitive position, being paid by the American people some ten or twelve thousand dollars, and yet, so far as I know, the Senator from Maryland has not done one single thing to get him off the Government payroll."

The man McCarthy was alluding to was Carmel Offie. As for Offie's "complete criminal record," it consisted of a 1943 Washington, D.C., police report noting his arrest for propositioning an undercover policeman on a stretch of Vermont Avenue known to be a gay cruising spot. Offie had pled guilty to the scaled-down charge of disorderly conduct and paid a small fine, but now, seven years later, the incident was to destroy his career.

Attacking Offie benefited both Hoover and McCarthy. For the FBI director, it enabled him to discreetly go after someone very close to Frank Wisner, tarnishing the OPC chief in the process. Even better, since the damning evidence was a local police report, it kept the FBI out of the picture and Hoover's hands unsullied. For the same reason, McCarthy could deflect the growing suspicion that he was being fed information by the FBI. In fact, though, Offie's police report had surfaced amid an FBI investigation of another State Department official on suspicions of homosexuality, Charles Thayer, in which the bureau had enlisted the help of one Roy Blick, the head of the morals squad of the Washington, D.C., police. By coincidence, Blick had been a junior officer in the morals squad in 1943, and was the very man who had arrested Offie on Vermont Avenue. On March 4, 1950, an FBI field officer had sent Hoover an update on the Thayer case, alerting him that it now appeared they might have two homosexuals on their hands. When Hoover ordered another investigation, this time of Offie, the news "somehow" reached McCarthy's ear, enabling him to add Offie to his list of "security risks."

The heat had been turned on very quickly, and long before McCarthy's April 25 attack. Already by March 10, the CIA's liaison to Congress was tipped that "McCarthy was considering charging an employee of this Agency with homosexual practices." Days later, the Wisconsin senator gave Offie's name to the Tydings Committee, which immediately passed it along to CIA director Hillenkoetter to take action. That action, most all assumed, would be Offie's swift dismissal. When, three days later, that had yet to happen, a call came into CIA headquarters from Capitol Hill inquiring "whether a certain homosexual [Offie] was presently employed in this Agency." It was telling that this call didn't come from McCarthy's office, but rather from that of Congressman Richard Nixon. Clearly, McCarthy and Hoover were marshaling their forces for an assault on the CIA; the only true puzzle was why the normally pliant Hillenkoetter wasn't yielding.

But it wasn't the CIA director who was obdurate, it was Frank Wisner. In fact, from the moment he first learned of the building attack on Offie, Wisner resolved to defend him.

Part of it undoubtedly came down to pragmatism. Carmel Offie had been one of Wisner's very first hires at OPC, and had worked just as tirelessly as the chief in carrying out its agenda. Even more to the point, in March 1950, the National Security Council was putting the finishing touches on a new top secret policy directive, NSC 68, that was slated to dramatically expand the OPC's mission. If Wisner had been grossly overworked in the past—and he had—NSC 68 promised to push him even closer to the breaking point, and among the very few people he felt he could rely on to share that burden was Carmel Offie.

The OPC director was also enough of a bureaucratic infighter to divine that Offie was only the surface target of McCarthy's attack. The real target was himself and the OPC, the move against Offie the opening gambit in an effort by McCarthy and Hoover and whoever else rallied to their flag to cut away at the Office of Policy Coordination in any way they could. Today it was Offie's reputation and loyalty that was being besmirched, but in the guilt-by-association strategy that was already a McCarthy trademark, it would next be the people who had worked with Offie, and then the coworkers of the coworkers. If ground was ceded at the beginning, Wisner believed, the capitulations might never stop.

But what the OPC chief also sensed in the effort against Offie was the stirrings of a new front in the culture war. While very conservative on foreign policy matters, Wisner skewed to left-of-center when it came to social issues. "I don't think my father could have cared less about Offie being gay," Wisner's youngest son, Graham, said. "To him, it was all about 'are you with me in this crusade?' He wanted the most effective people who could throw off their Americanisms and be able to understand how this war was changing, so if you're gay or a woman or black, it's irrelevant. Offie was effective, and that's all that mattered."

This outlook generally held throughout the upper reaches of both the CIA and the State Department, composed as they were largely of men—and in 1950, it was still almost all men—of socially tolerant backgrounds who had been educated at Ivy League schools grown increasingly inclusive. As such they had little in common with the kind of nativist reactionaries, most from the South or Midwest, who rallied to Joe McCarthy's side. Indeed, from top to bottom, Washington's so-called Georgetown set of well-heeled socialites and policy wonks, and of which Frank Wisner was a standing member, was almost universally appalled by McCarthy's bombastic and cruel methods, and regarded him as both a buffoon and national embarrassment. This was certainly Wisner's view, and he was determined not to knuckle under to such a man.

His eldest son, Frank Jr., suggested another, simpler reason for his father's resistance. "I think a lot of it came down to honor," he said. "He had been raised with this very strict code of personal honor, and it was that you stand by your friends, you don't throw them over just because it's expedient to do so."

Throughout March and into April, Wisner stood by Offie, and gamely tried to rally his allies to come to his assistant's aid. In this effort was joined the glowing appraisals of senior government officials who had benefited from Offie's acumen in the past—and not just State Department diplomats, but high-ranking military officers who had worked with him during World War II or in postwar Germany. Typical was the view of Lieutenant General Clarence Huebner, the tough-as-nails chief of staff of American forces in occupied Germany, who found that Offie had an "almost unparalleled" understanding of the complexities facing the United States in postwar Europe. "Offie embodies a mind that is brilliant and active to an outstanding degree," Huebner wrote. "His friendly gregarious personality and his companionable ways have endeared him not only to his work associates, but to all the rank and file with which he comes in contact."

Against this, however, were growing signs that the Offie controversy was starting to hurt both the Truman administration and the CIA. In early April, the House Democratic majority leader John McCormack sought out the CIA's congressional liaison to issue a stark warning. From information he had received, McCormack said, Republican congressional leaders were planning to use the Offie case to launch a concerted attack on the CIA. If that happened, the "Agency's friends would be completely defenseless and would be unable to defend the Agency." Clearly, McCormack counseled, Offie had to go.

But still Wisner would not relent. By mid-April, the situation had become so fraught that CIA director Hillenkoetter took the matter up with the president. The dam finally broke on April 25 when McCarthy executed his sly pivot on Tydings, excoriating his nemesis for doing nothing about the highly paid criminal who "spent his time hanging around the men's room in Lafayette Park," a reference to another popular gay meeting place in 1940s Washington.

The effect of McCarthy's semipublic assault on Offie made any continuing defense of him untenable. That same afternoon, Hillenkoetter brought Wisner into his office and informed him that his loyal lieutenant had to go—and immediately. Before the end of the day, one of McCarthy's Capitol Hill allies, Senator Kenneth Wherry of Nebraska, took to the floor for the "privilege" of announcing that "within the last 30 minutes I have been informed by the head of a Government agency that the man against whom the Senator from Wisconsin made a charge on the Senate floor this afternoon has finally resigned." Turning to McCarthy, Wherry then burbled: "I am proud to be associated with a man who is doing his level best to clear this country of Communists and moral perverts in the Government."

Drawing on his prodigious network of contacts, Wisner managed to get Offie transferred from OPC into a far less sensitive post at the American Federation of Labor. By the summer of 1950, the improbable tenure of the former stenographer from Sharon, Pennsylvania, atop the highest reaches of the American intelligence community was officially over.

Offie's downfall was the herald of a particularly cruel phenomenon to sweep the country in the 1950s, one often overlooked. By making gays equal security risks to communists, by merging the Red Scare with the Lavender, "homo-hunters" like McCarthy and Hoover ensured that untold thousands of Americans saw their careers destroyed. Indeed, for every person blacklisted or forced from jobs in the more famous Red Scare, many more times their number were victimized in the concurrent Lavender Scare. Further, the damage lasted a lifetime; thanks to a change in Civil Service rules partly spurred by Offie's case, federal office managers were required to give a specific reason for an employee's dismissal, making it "increasingly difficult for a gay worker to resign without a permanent tag of 'perversion' or 'homosexuality' on his or her record." In all this, Carmel Offie was Exhibit A, a test case in the destructive power to be unleashed when two panics were joined.

The fall of the Royal Dwarf foretold another feature of the American political landscape in the years just ahead. Just as the list of Red Scare targets had inexorably spread beyond actual card-carrying communists, so the pool of those deemed disloyal would expand beyond alleged Soviet spies and moles to include government officials who had merely stood in history's path, who could be blamed for "losing China" or "surrendering at Yalta." In one of American history's great perversities, this vendetta, carrying with it the tinge of hysteria, would ultimately tarnish many of those who, like Carmel Offie, had been in the very vanguard of the fight against international communism. In a strange mirroring of Stalin's distrust of those "tainted" by their time in the West, in the very depths of what was to come in the United States, mere past exposure to the Soviets—attending wartime Allied conferences, for example, or having served at the American embassy in Moscow—was often enough to cast a pall of suspicion that lasted a lifetime. Here again, Carmel Offie was a harbinger. Though he left the OPC in 1950, on the personal orders of J. Edgar Hoover, Offie would remain under FBI investigation as a potential security risk for the next twenty-two years, with the last notation in his bureau file made just two days before his death.

But this element of vigilantism in the late 1940s and early 1950s was to engender an even more destructive force on the American political scene, a schism that has never truly healed. For a generation of American liberals, the grotesque excesses of the Red and Lavender Scares, joined to the spectacle of men like McCarthy and Nixon profiting from them, produced a permanent distrust and cynicism of the political system. In this worldview, Alger Hiss was an innocent man railroaded by his persecutors, as were many of the other government officials forced out in disgrace; even Julius and Ethel Rosenberg, the Soviet spy couple convicted of espionage in 1951 and executed two years later, were sent to the gas chamber on flimsy—and quite possibly, doctored—evidence.

In one of the terrible ironies of mid-century America, however, a sat-isfactory answer to many of these polarizing controversies actually lay close at hand at the time. That these answers were withheld from the American public was, once again, the handiwork of Hoover's FBI.

In 1943, a U.S. Army cryptology unit had begun studying an assort-ment of encrypted cables that had passed between Moscow and some of the various Soviet diplomatic and trade missions scattered about the United States. While the cables' codes were initially thought to be unbreakable—the Soviets used a system called the one-time pad that was supposed to produce a unique code for every message sent—by late 1946, cryptologists had deciphered enough fragments of the cables to reveal something astonishing: the broad outline of a vast range of espionage operations that the Soviets had conducted in the United States during the war years, complete with the code names of some three hundred domestic operatives and their KGB control officers. Dubbed the Venona Project, the effort to decrypt the cables was to lead to one of the most remarkable—and in a roundabout way, destructive—counterintelligence coups of the twentieth century.

The true breakthrough with Venona came when Robert Lamphere, the FBI espionage specialist, was brought onto the project in late 1947. With his access to the FBI's investigative files, Lamphere was gradually able to match some of the Venona code names to individuals on the bureau's subversive watch list or those fingered by the likes of "the Red Spy Queen," Elizabeth Bentley. Ultimately, the Venona decrypts yielded proof beyond all reasonable doubt that Alger Hiss had, in fact, been a Soviet spy, as had Julius Rosenberg and most of the other Red Scare "martyrs" of the late 1940s and early 1950s.

Except in the interim, Hoover had chosen to take his obsession with secrecy to a wholly new level. So sensitive did he consider the Venona Project that he decided virtually no one outside the cryptologists crack-ing the codes, along with perhaps a half-dozen FBI officials and Britain's intelligence liaison, Kim Philby, should know of their existence. Among those kept in the dark was the director of the CIA, the secretaries of State and Defense and, most incredibly, President Truman and his attorney general. At the same time, Hoover refused to submit Venona-gleaned evidence in espionage trials, ensuring that, just as with the earlier Eliza-beth Bentley cases, prosecutions collapsed or defendants were convicted on only trivial charges, which further ensured that a large segment of the American population believed the whole process to be a sham. Instead, the American public wouldn't hear a thing about Venona for over a half-century, not until 1995, and by then it was far too late; even if there was now a convincing answer to the controversies that had fueled the nation's Red Scare schism, the distrust built up over a half-century remained. It was a distrust that cut both ways. Writing about Venona shortly after their public disclosure, Cold War historian Thomas Powers noted that "the defensive response of many American liberals not only was wrong on the facts, but also exacerbated the suspicions of the right, making it easier for demagogues to argue that progressive causes and treason somehow went hand in hand."

Of course, one might argue that the profound secrecy surrounding Venona was unavoidable, a necessary precaution to prevent the Soviets from learning their code had been broken. This was certainly J. Edgar Hoover's ultimate rationale. The argument loses some of its luster, though, when one takes into account that, despite the extraordinary restrictions Hoover imposed on who should know about Venona in its early days, this select group managed to include at least two Soviet spies, both of whom alerted Moscow to the breach no later than the autumn of 1949. In sum, when it came to the greatest American counterintelligence coup of the early Cold War, the KGB learned of it at least three years before the CIA and forty-six years before the American public.

———

Having lost the battle to save his lieutenant, Frank Wisner plunged back into the endless onslaught of work at OPC headquarters. In spring 1950, the flood was especially unrelenting.

In April, the National Security Council circulated the working draft of its new directive, soon to be known as NSC 68, outlining a radically more aggressive stance toward the Soviet Union. In language approaching the apocalyptic, the NSC 68 authors portrayed the contest with the Soviets as nothing short of that between the forces of good and evil, of freedom and slavery. If that didn't sufficiently alarm, hinging on the issues now before the country, the authors warned, was "the fulfillment or destruction not only of this Republic but of civilization itself."

Its overwrought language aside, what was patently clear to Wisner was that with NSC 68 the OPC was about to be called upon as never before: more covert operations, more recruitment of anti-communist fighters, more destabilization efforts against the Soviet bloc. The problem was, OPC didn't have the manpower. As Wisner explained to the National Security Council in a top secret brief in early May, the difficulty of "inducing physically, intellectually and psychologically qualified American personnel to abandon their present activities and enlist in the cold war imposes a significant limitation on the capacity to plan and conduct covert operations." What's more, the OPC chief pointed out, the ability of the government to maintain plausible deniability of covert operations diminished in direct proportion to the scale of the operations and the amounts of money involved. Even by hugely ramping up both the size and budget of the OPC as called for in NSC 68—and which Wisner naturally supported—the only way out of this twinned dilemma was for the Agency to increasingly rely on "indigenous personnel" in covert missions.

That memorandum hinted at a curious shift in Frank Wisner. In the view of many of his colleagues, the OPC director had never seen a proposal for a covert operation that he didn't like, was willing to try most anything in his crusade to stem the communist tide. Now, quite suddenly, a note of caution seemed to be entering his outlook, an awareness that at times the scalpel was more effective than the cleaver. Certainly, his ultimate goal hadn't changed, and it wasn't as if he were arguing against an expansion of the OPC's reach, but for perhaps the first time, he was edging toward a more moderate voice in the debate, suggesting the need to keep both missions and expectations reasonable.

By the following month, however, all thoughts of caution would evaporate when, early on the morning of June 25, 100,000 soldiers from communist North Korea poured across the 38th parallel into Western-allied South Korea. It was the beginning of the bloodiest conflict since World War II, and the first truly global crisis of the Cold War.

It also caught the United States completely off guard. Within three days, the North Korean army, backed by Soviet-supplied tanks and warplanes, had seized the South Korean capital of Seoul and sent a decimated and hopelessly outgunned South Korean army into headlong retreat. At huge cost in both blood and treasure, American troops rushed in from nearby Japan managed to slow the enemy advance and establish a defensive perimeter in the southeastern corner of the country, long enough for a United Nations force under American leadership to be dispatched. Within three months, battlefield fortunes had completely reversed, with the North Korean attackers now fleeing north before the United Nations juggernaut, but set in motion was a seesaw conflict that would last three years and result in the deaths of over one million.

What the Korean War would also do is render moot any last hope that some kind of rapprochement with the Soviet Union could be forged. For the first time, communist forces had sought to seize a Western-allied nation by force of arms, and they had done so with the clear approval and assistance of the Kremlin leadership. To many who had been on the dissemination list of NSC 68 back in April 1950, that directive's tone had reeked of extravagant and dangerous hyperbole. After June 1950, no more. Now, there would be no second-guessing over controversial covert operations, no moralistic hand-wringing over the often distasteful methods and personalities employed in the anti-communist effort. Now, in the arenas of spycraft and subversion and proxy fighters, it was to be all-out war with very few rules, and residing at center stage of those varied arenas would be Frank Wisner's OPC.

16

OPERATION FIEND

B y October 1950, the launch date for Operation Fiend was finally drawing near. On the 12th of that month, the sixteen commandos chosen for the mission's first wave were taken out of the main Albanian training camp in central Germany. Brought to Munich, they were then loaded into a closed U.S. Army transport truck and driven to an isolated estate in the Bavarian foothills, near the Austrian border, there to undergo two weeks of intensive final drills. In anticipation of their arrival at the Fiend staging ground in Greece, a large safe house was rented on the outskirts of Athens. Nearby, another safe house became home to a six-man Polish flight crew, members of the wartime Polish RAF, who had been flown in from London; it was they who would make the perilous flight across Albania to deliver the commandos to their drop zones. Thirty minutes to the northwest of Athens, an unmarked Douglas C-47 Dakota obtained from the U.S. Air Force sat parked on a remote rural airstrip.

As the launch date approached, life became even more frenetic for Michael Burke, a blur of secret meetings and coded messages and air travel. Under his cover of being a producer with the fictitious Imperial Pictures, he crisscrossed Western Europe, checking and double-checking that all components were in place and ready to go. Yet, despite all the meticulous planning, at this eleventh hour there suddenly arose an odd complication. It involved an amorous Italian policeman.

Returning to his home in Rome late one night from yet another foreign trip, Burke found a distraught Timmy awaiting him. As his wife explained, earlier that evening an Italian policeman had tried to force his way into their Via Mercati villa, evidently hoping to "make himself available" to the attractive and frequently alone American lady. Burke was still calming Timmy over the encounter when the couple heard approaching footsteps in the stairwell, followed by a light rapping on their door; apparently adhering to the theory that persistence is rewarded, the amorous policeman had returned.

The man was understandably chagrined when the door was opened not by the object of his affections, but by a powerfully built former college halfback, and he surely grew more disappointed when that former halfback chose to hurl him down the marble staircase, followed by another bodily heave out the front door. The following morning, two Italian policemen showed up at 11 Via Mercati with an arrest warrant for Burke for assaulting their colleague.

While there is probably never a good time to become entangled in the notoriously slow Italian legal system, it would seem especially important to avoid when one is in the final planning stages of a complex and top secret commando operation to subvert a foreign government. In the company of a lawyer from the American embassy, throughout that day and well into the next, Burke shuttled between various Roman police departments and courtrooms, under constant threat of being held over in jail until a trial could be scheduled. Interspersed with these tense meetings, he recalled, "I hurried from one [Operation Fiend] rendezvous to another, tying an operational knot here and there in case I had to spend time in the slammer." At last, Burke was allowed to make a "statement of contraction"—essentially a formal apology—and the assault case was shelved.

But even with the Italian legal system brought to bay, there continued to be those moments in the autumn of 1950 when it seemed as if Michael Burke were living inside a particularly implausible movie. With the launch of Fiend looming, in late October he and his wife took a quick vacation to Sorrento, an exquisite resort town on the coast below Naples. A hidden motive for the excursion was for Burke to determine if he was under surveillance—he wasn't—and afterward he couldn't decide what had been the trip's highlight, the nighttime tour of Pompeii by flashlight, or watching Orson Welles perform magic tricks at the home of actress Gracie Fields. Within days of their return to Rome, Burke slipped out of town for Athens and his Operation Fiend comrades.

In the early postwar years, one of the great vulnerabilities of a complicated covert operation like Fiend was the difficulty in maintaining secure communications between the various actors involved. In the era before satellite phones and computer links, all long-distance communication was done via a small handful of mediums—landline telephones, wireless radio, telegrams—and conducted either "in the clear" or after ponderous encoding. Naturally, the more chatter going back and forth meant the greater risk the operation would be compromised. This went a long way toward explaining why Michael Burke was constantly shuttling across the European continent month after month—physical contact remained the only truly secure link—and why individual actors in such a scheme often functioned with enormous day-to-day autonomy. Of course, this also explained how a mission coordinator, only able to meet with his various operatives intermittently, could suddenly walk into a crisis he never anticipated. This is what greeted Burke when he flew into Athens at the end of October.

If there is a first cardinal rule to operating safe houses it is to never place more than one group of agents or conspirators in the same installation at the same time. The reason is obvious: to maintain operational security, one group should not be in a position to know—and thus potentially betray—the identity or the mission goals of another. In Athens, this most elemental of strictures had been disregarded.

The Fiend first wave consisted of four Albanian commando teams, each given a different mission, comprised of four men each. Since the sixteen men had undergone final training together at the Loeb estate in southern Bavaria, so the reasoning apparently went, wouldn't it be simpler to keep them together in Greece until they went operational? To that end—or perhaps merely to save money—someone somewhere in the chain of command had chosen to rent a single large house on the outskirts of Athens, one big enough to house all sixteen commandos along with several of their "handlers."

In addition to violating the first rule of safe houses, this arrangement also overlooked the fact that the Albanian commandos were drawn from different political and regional groupings, some of which were historically in conflict with others. This meant that if one group balked about going ahead, the others were very likely to follow suit, either because misgivings in such circumstances are infectious, or because those still ready to go now had to worry about betrayal by those staying behind. This was precisely the situation Burke found when he stepped into the Athens safe house, with two of the commando groups flatly refusing to go forward, and the other two strongly tilting that way. After fourteen months of scrupulous and exhaustive planning, the CIA contract officer faced the very real prospect that it had all been for naught.

But even as Burke pondered the arguments he might use to persuade the Albanians, part of him couldn't fault them at all. When pulled out of the main Albanian base camp to start their specialized training in Bavaria, the sixteen commandos hadn't even been told where they were going. As was later explained by Xhemal Laci, the Albanian liaison between the commandos and the émigré leadership in Rome: "The Americans wanted it to remain secret that the men were leaving on a mission. They were afraid it might reach the ears of the communists. So they told us to tell them that they were just being moved to another company. We felt sad after they had left. They were all volunteers. We felt that we ought to have treated them in a manly manner and told them the truth."

There was also the matter of the operation's objective, one that had been simultaneously scaled back and vastly expanded. In Fiend's original inception the chief aim of the first wave of commandos was to basically take a look around: to get a sense of conditions in the country, to gauge the possibility of forming counterrevolutionary cells that might be activated at a later date, and to then quickly get out. But as so often happens in these situations, the more other branches of the American intelligence and defense communities were apprised of Fiend, the longer the wish list grew, so much so that by the time the commandos reached Athens, their mission more closely resembled that of itinerant statisticians. As historian Nicholas Bethell noted, "they were also told to collect information about the political balance in each assigned area, to discover how many supported communist power and how many were opposed, to estimate the level of industrial development and standard of living. They were to note the location of military units, arms dumps and particularly anti-aircraft defenses as well as the state of local communications—width of roads and density of traffic."

But the mission goal had changed in another strange way, as well. Similar to Fiend, the original aim of Britain's Operation Valuable had been for the infiltrated pixies to conduct rudimentary spying and distribute propaganda. By the pixies being immediately forced to flee for their lives, these objectives clearly hadn't been met, but in analyzing the shortcomings of Valuable, OPC officials chose only to scale back their near-term political goal, recognizing that actually overthrowing the Albanian regime was a distant prospect. This assessment had not been shared with their Albanian émigré allies, and certainly not with those men about to risk their lives to that end. To the contrary, as outlined in a May 1950 OPC memorandum, the Albanian volunteers were now going to "operate as small guerrilla bands" with the dual mission of "organizing the nuclei of resistance and the creation of operational intelligence nets." In this way, they would lay the ground for "an insurrectionary apparatus." How all this was to happen when earlier volunteers had been hunted from the moment they touched ground wasn't specified.

As a first step toward this goal, the commandos would be dropped from an airplane at night into one of the most heavily policed nations on earth, furnished with only light weapons. For communicating to the outside world, they would be wholly dependent on their bulky wireless radio transmitters, but no rescue mission would be launched if they radioed that they were in trouble; rather, in the event of capture or death, they would be disavowed. Just in case the Albanians needed another reminder of how completely isolated they were to be inside, Burke had brought with him for distribution a packet of so-called L-pills, cyanide ampules that, when bitten into, ensured death within seconds. As a final indignity—and it isn't clear the commandos were ever told this either—due to the stringent demands of operational security, none of those who survived their ordeal inside Albania would be allowed to return to Germany, but instead were to be resettled in a third country.

But perhaps what most crystallized the commandos' misgivings were the actual logistics of their proposed infiltration. In hopes of evading Albanian radar, the C-47's Polish flight crew was to fly in at so-called treetop level, staying at most only a couple of hundred feet above the ground. Just before the designated drop zones, the pilot would spike the plane up to about eight hundred feet, where the commandos would have a matter of mere seconds to bail out before the C-47 dove back down to treetop level. Such LALO (low altitude, low opening) jumps were terrifying and extraordinarily dangerous for even the most seasoned of paratroopers, let alone for anyone who hadn't actually jumped before; incredibly, the parachute training the commandos underwent in Germany had consisted only of simulations. Little wonder they were having second thoughts.

For Michael Burke, here was a moment like no other, one in which his abilities at leadership and persuasion were put to the greatest test. After a long night of discussion, of Burke listening to the Albanians' concerns and addressing them as honestly as he could, nine of the commandos, grouped together in two squads, agreed to forge ahead.

But even having made that decision, those choosing to proceed must have been a remarkably unsuperstitious bunch, for the bad omens surrounding Fiend kept multiplying.

To get the commandos to the airfield, Burke's fix-it man in Greece, Hod Fuller, had purchased an old transport truck: "Secondhand," Fuller told Burke, "maybe third." At the Athens safe house on the night of November 3, Burke and Fuller loaded the nine commandos and their jump gear into the back of the truck for the thirty-minute drive to the airstrip in Eleusis—only to find the truck wouldn't start. Behind the wheel, Fuller repeatedly turned the ignition key, but nothing.

Burke was instantly and unpleasantly reminded of a mission report he had recently received from his British counterpart in Greece, Patrick Whinney, who was running his own Albania commando operation. Opting to infiltrate a new group of commandos into Albania by land, the British-led group had set out across Greece for what was slated to be a two-day journey to the frontier but which, due to a transport truck that constantly broke down, turned into a seven-day ordeal. To Burke, it seemed utterly bizarre that two different commando missions—first Pat Whinney's, and now his—should be plagued by balky vehicles, until a dark thought came to him. Turning to his colleague at the wheel, he asked Hod Fuller precisely where he had obtained the truck.

"I bought it from Pat," Fuller replied.

At last, after some fifteen long minutes, the truck started up and the team set off for the airstrip and their rendezvous with the flight crew. Under the cover of nightfall, the C-47 lifted into the sky, bound for Albania. A few hours later, though, it was back and with the commandos still on board. In the faint light of a half-moon night, a darkness deepened by the lack of electricity in Albania, the crew had been unable to find the drop zones. Five days later, the team flew out again, only to return with the same result. A third attempt was scheduled for the night of November 11.

This time bad luck took on wholly new form. Grinding the decrepit transport truck up the same country lane they had traveled so often before, Burke and Fuller were startled to spot a wooden sawhorse barrier straddling the road ahead, a half-dozen Greek soldiers gathered to one side. Burke had no idea what it could mean. Was it a trap of some kind? Even if pure coincidence, how to explain two foreign men driving a military-style transport truck in the middle of the night, let alone the nine armed guerrillas with their jump- and combat gear in back? As they approached the barrier, Burke made a snap decision.

"Christ, Hod, we can't stop now! Gun it!"

A decidedly relative command considering their mode of transportation. In a scene bearing scant resemblance to its rendering in countless thriller movies, the old truck gradually picked up some faint semblance of speed, enough to roll through the flimsy barrier and trundle on into the night, but all performed so slowly that the Greek soldiers looking on reacted more with puzzlement than alarm, the destruction of their barrier leaving them "shouting and confused" rather than reaching for weapons.

Burke fervently hoped that, this time, the mission finally went off, especially since, while reversing the truck toward the C-47's cargo bay, its entire transmission system fell out from beneath the hood.

After helping load the parachutes and field gear into the cargo bay and saying goodbye to the nine commandos, Burke watched the plane ascend into the black sky and then turn off its running lights. For the next several hours, he and Fuller tensely waited for the C-47's return. When at last it did, it was with word that this time all had gone perfectly. The first phase of Operation Fiend was a success.

But Burke's jubilation soon faded away. On subsequent nights, the plane's Polish crew crisscrossed those areas of eastern and northern Albania where they had dropped the commandos in hopes of picking up a radio transmission. No message came. As each day passed with still no word from the men inside, Burke was plagued by an inevitable specula- tion of what that silence might mean: "the silence of the dead."

———

If there were any lingering doubts that the new CIA director was a mark- edly different man from his predecessor, they were dispelled on the day Walter Bedell "Beetle" Smith summoned the Agency's senior leadership to study the new organizational chart he had devised. Like most organi- zational charts, the old one had been a devil's spawn of boxes and arrows and crisscrossing dotted lines, but in Smith's revision, drawn on a black- board at the front of a conference room, this tangle had been reduced to precisely three boxes: Plans, Intelligence, and Administration. After a brief presentation, Smith asked if everyone understood the proposed revamping and agreed with it.

One of Frank Wisner's OPC deputies, Kilbourne Johnston, apparently didn't grasp this was a rhetorical question, and allowed that there was one point on which he disagreed.

"Goddamn you, Johnston." Smith pounded the conference room table. "You don't disagree with me, do you understand that?"

It went no better when someone else suggested it might be helpful if Smith had his new organizational chart reproduced and distributed for further study. As it was a mere three boxes, Smith felt this unnecessary, and shared his feelings with the attendees. "I will not reproduce that god- damn chart," he thundered, "and you can sit here in silence until you have committed it to memory!" He then imposed a long silence in order for his underlings to do just that, finally broken with, "have you got it?" Like chastened schoolchildren, the others answered "yes" in unison.

His impolitic personality aside, most of those involved in the American intelligence community of 1950 not only welcomed Beetle Smith's arrival at CIA, but considered it long overdue. From almost the day of its creation in 1947, Truman and his national security advisors had been aware of inherent structural problems with the CIA, issues that only worsened with the advent of the OPC the following year and its bizarre a-part-of-but-not-really status. Two different committees were formed to study the Agency and make recommendations for its reorganization. The more important of the two, headed by Frank Wisner's friend and former OSS luminary Allen Dulles, had outlined a whole roster of potential reforms and submitted its findings to the National Security Council in early 1949. The Dulles Report was praised for its incisiveness and clear thinking, and then put on a shelf to gather dust.

One of the CIA's biggest problems, immediately apparent to any outside analyst at the time and still not fully resolved today, was the built-in paradox of housing intelligence gathering and covert operations— "thinkers" and "doers" in the most simplistic characterization—within the same organization. To be fully effective, the intelligence analysts of the first group needed a free-wheeling, university-like environment, one that allowed for dissent and peer review, while the covert operations of the second group often required a militarist, do-as-you're-told approach. This division was undoubtedly exacerbated in the early CIA-OPC construct by the outlooks of the two men at its top. While appreciating the strange new contours of the Cold War and the unorthodox tools required to wage it, Roscoe Hillenkoetter could never quite shake the old-fashioned military man's disdain for covert operations. On the other hand, Wisner stood ready to launch them most anywhere under any guise, a hot-button approach whose motto might be "do something, even if it's wrong." There was also the contrast of personality between the low-pulse Hillenkoetter and the hard-driving Wisner. As a State Department official surveying the scene lamented in the summer of 1949, while there was a clear need for some kind of intermediary between the two intelligence chiefs, "it is obviously impossible to get a man big enough to be over Wisner and small enough to be under Hillenkoetter."

As with so many other reorderings of the American government in the early 1950s, the final spur for change came with the Korean War. In the aftermath of the June 1950 North Korean attack, rumors of Hillenkoetter's imminent demise began circulating in Washington. They were confirmed when Truman announced General "Beetle" Smith would be replacing him that autumn.

A career Army officer, the fifty-four-year-old Smith had served as Dwight D. Eisenhower's chief of staff during World War II, where he earned a reputation as the Allied commander's hatchet man. That only added to his repute as a perpetually irritable and brusque figure, an appraisal subsequently confirmed by most any CIA officer who requested a meeting with him. Whereas the Missouri-born Hillenkoetter had been unfailingly polite to subordinates, those calling on Smith were apt to be met by a glowering stare and the general's preferred form of greeting: "What's your problem?"

Similarly, Smith could be less than tactful in rejecting proposals he disagreed with. To one CIA official in the habit of advocating for more propaganda balloon programs in Eastern Europe, the director advised: "if you bring one more balloon project to me, I'll throw you out of my goddamned office."

But the general, most recently the U.S. ambassador to the Soviet Union, had come to the CIA with the express mandate of knocking the Agency into shape, and that's what he set out to do; as he told Truman upon accepting the post, "I expect the worst, and I am sure I won't be disappointed."

He arrived at a time of devastated morale within the Agency, which had borne the brunt of blame for failing to foresee the North Korean invasion. This was an assessment actively promoted by General Douglas MacArthur, the commander in chief of American Forces in the Far East, whose zone of responsibility included Korea. It certainly didn't help that this latest communist surprise had come so closely on the heels of the shockingly swift "fall" of China to Mao's Red Army, followed by the CIA's failure to predict the detonation of the Soviet Union's first atomic bomb. Just five days before that blast in August 1949, the Agency had predicted it wouldn't occur until mid-1950 at the earliest, and most likely not until 1953.

When it came to Korea, however, this apportioning of blame took no notice of an inconvenient fact about MacArthur's leadership. Just as he had done with the OSS in his Western Pacific command during World War II, MacArthur in Japan had fiercely resisted allowing the CIA to operate within his domain—and with similarly disastrous results. It also ignored the fact that the CIA actually *had* raised the alarm about Korea. In February 1949, amid discussions of further reducing the small American army garrison in South Korea, the CIA had warned the National

Security Council in a top secret report that such a move "would probably in time be followed by an invasion, timed to coincide with Communist-led South Korean revolts, by the North Korean People's Army." Dissenting from this view was the U.S. Army's own military intelligence unit, which contended that the North Korean army "does not have, of itself, the preponderance of strength over South Korean military forces which would be required to insure victory in an armed struggle." In light of such confidence, American troop levels in Korea had been scaled back to less than five hundred.

This historical whitewash partly came down to bureaucratic primacy. In 1949 and 1950, the CIA was still the poor stepchild of American national security agencies, and when it came to taking control of the Korea narrative the vainglorious MacArthur and his Pentagon allies easily outflanked the passive Roscoe Hillenkoetter. As the new CIA director, Beetle Smith was determined to put an end to that.

Smith also didn't need a commission report to alert him to the most glaring problem with his new posting, one that neatly played into the CIA's role as foreign policy fall guy. It was the fact that the Office of Policy Coordination, by far the largest and best-financed branch of the CIA, somehow didn't fall within the Agency's zone of responsibility at all. Instead, it existed in a kind of free orbit, theoretically answerable to the departments of State and Defense but, given the plausible deniability clause in the OPC charter, actually not answerable there either. Instead, State and Defense could simply disclaim any knowledge of OPC's actions whenever it suited them. The end result was supremely paradoxical: Frank Wisner and his OPC were simultaneously a power unto themselves without precedent in the American government but also, should matters go awry, everyone's patsy. Not that the finger-pointing stopped there; given how Washington politics worked, blame naturally floated up the chain of command to the CIA director.

Within days of arriving at the Agency that October, Smith convened a meeting with the National Security Council where he insisted that OPC come fully under the control of the CIA, meaning himself, and that State and Defense be relegated to a peripheral, consultative role. So forceful was Smith's presentation—because he also made clear that he neither needed nor wanted this goddamned job anyway—that Truman ordered an immediate restructuring along the lines Smith demanded. Pressing home the point further, Smith then directed Wisner to spell out the new lines of authority to the secretaries of State and Defense in a memorandum to go out on Wisner's own letterhead; that way, there could be no protestations of confusion or misunderstandings down the road. This was made clear to Wisner, as well. "Frank," Smith said, "from now on, OPC is working for me."

Smith moved more slowly on another fundamental issue confronting the CIA, the interagency friction in the field between the upstart OPC and the preexisting Office of Special Operations. To many in the OPC, the OSO "librarians" were timid and pedantic, engaged in the careful work of university researchers rather than of operatives on the fluid front lines of the Cold War. To many in the Office of Special Operations, the OPC "cowboys" had a habit of plunging headlong into dubious missions heedless of consequences, missions that might inadvertently sabotage a preexisting OSO operation. In many CIA stations around the world, tensions reached a point where the resident OSO and OPC units barely acknowledged one another.

In his commission report, Allen Dulles had advocated integrating OSO and OPC under one directorate, but Smith, perhaps mindful of the chaos that such reorganizations invariably sowed in the short term, thought better of it. Instead, he appointed a CIA second-in-command, along with a deputy director for plans (DDP) who would have oversight over Wisner's covert operations. To fill this latter post, Smith strong-armed Allen Dulles himself. (In a subsequent reshuffling in the summer of 1951, Dulles was moved up to CIA deputy director, while Wisner assumed Dulles's vacated position as DDP.)

Although this technically made Wisner the fourth-most powerful official in the CIA, there was no getting around the reality that his wings had been clipped. No longer would he be able to launch a covert operation somewhere in the world on his own volition; now Beetle Smith and Allen Dulles would be constantly looking over his shoulder, with the former more than willing to give Wisner hell if he felt so inclined.

Smith did feel so inclined on many occasions. According to an official CIA history of his tenure at the Agency, Smith tended to store up the worst of his wrath for Dulles and Wisner, as he often felt the pair were working behind his back. The difference between the two was that Dulles could shrug off Smith's tirades, even find them amusing, while the more emotional Wisner took them very much to heart. "Wisner was always shaken," the CIA history acknowledged. "He likened an hour with General Smith to an hour on the squash court—and he did not mean by that to suggest that he enjoyed it."

That said, having his wings clipped may have come as something of a relief to Wisner, for there had always been a willy-nilly quality to OPC that must have been exhausting. As one historian wrote, "rather than coherent, planned growth, there were bursts of wild activity as Wisner plunged off in one direction or another in search of a mission for OPC." The situation wasn't helped by Wisner's obsessive attention to detail. "There was never any sense of delegation," Tom Braden, a senior CIA official in the 1950s, recalled. "He made every decision. Frank wasn't just a hard driver, he was a nervous driver."

What's more, it wasn't as if Beetle Smith's arrival led to a diminishing of the OPC's mission. Much to the contrary, the Korean War had spurred a sweeping American call to arms. Just five days after the war's start, the Truman administration announced plans to double the defense budget for fiscal year 1951, and to expand the size of the U.S. military from 1.4 million soldiers to over three million, a dramatic reversal of the down-scaling that had been under way since 1945. The CIA and OPC saw an even greater boost in funding. Over the next two years, the number of OPC field bases would grow from seven to forty-seven, its permanent and contract personnel from a few hundred to some six thousand, while the number of individual covert missions would multiply a staggering sixteen-fold. As counterinsurgency expert William Corson wrote, it reached a point where it was "almost impossible for anyone except Wisner to render an accurate statement about how many operations were underway at any given moment—and he was too busy with other problems to carry out such a census."

Nor was much thought given to accounting. With funding multiplying at a dizzying rate, OPC simply couldn't spend it all. According to one CIA official, when Frank Lindsay submitted a proposed budget of $80 million for his division in the coming fiscal year, Wisner replied: "Why don't we round that out and make it $100 million."

While all this might strike some as overkill on the Truman administration's part, it appears less so when one considers the staggering tumult of the time. To cite one example, in the four-week period surrounding Beetle Smith's assumption of the CIA directorship, U.N. forces poured across the 38th parallel in pursuit of a now routed North Korean army; communist China invaded Tibet; a French garrison of six thousand troops was virtually wiped out by Viet Minh guerrillas in Vietnam; and the Polish government arrested some five thousand dissidents for anti-state activities in a twenty-four-hour dragnet. As Frank Wisner surely appreciated as he tried to keep track of the hailstorm of events occurring around the globe, the era of covert operations and proxy war wasn't likely to end anytime soon, and having a degree of direction from above might allow him to more tightly focus his energies.

By the close of 1950, Wisner was zeroing in on two places in particular in which to expand that proxy war: Poland and Ukraine.

At the end of World War II, a Polish underground army had waged brief but bitter guerrilla war against their Soviet "liberators." For two years, a group called Wolność i Niezawisłość (Freedom and Independence), or WiN, had attacked Soviet military and political personnel based in their homeland, staged hit-and-run attacks on municipal authorities, and conducted an assassination campaign against Polish collaborators and informants. To counter WiN's successes, Poland's communist government and its Soviet overseers had launched a carrot-and-stick initiative, offering amnesty to WiN members who laid down their weapons, in concert with a ruthless infiltration and ambush operation against those who didn't. It worked. By the end of 1947, WiN had been all but wiped out.

Or so the West thought. Then, in 1949, a senior WiN commander named Stefan Sieńko managed to get word out to the West that the organization was very much alive after all; not the guerrilla army of tens of thousands as before, perhaps, but still a hard-core nucleus of some 500 active fighters, backed by as many as 20,000 partially active reservists and another 100,000 ready to take up arms in the event of war. Lending further credence to Sieńko's claim was an August 1950 CIA intelligence report telling of large-scale fighting in a region south of Warsaw. By that autumn, OPC had begun a small-scale airdrop effort to assist WiN fighters in the Polish countryside, but Wisner wanted to do much more.

A similar opportunity was presenting itself in neighboring Ukraine. The historical animus between Russians and Ukrainians went back centuries, and had not been improved by Stalin's murderous Holodomor famine, in which millions of Ukrainians were starved to death in the early 1930s. Under the sponsorship of Nazi Germany in the late 1930s, Ukrainian nationalists had built out an army of some thirty thousand fighters, the Ukrainian Insurgent Army, or UPA, by the eve of Germany's 1941 invasion of the Soviet Union. Marching into their homeland alongside Hitler's war machine, the UPA temporarily ran afoul of their sponsors by declaring Ukrainian independence, before managing to return to Germany's good graces just in time to share in its defeat at the hands of the Red Army. In the postwar aftermath, thousands of former UPA soldiers ended up in the displaced persons camps of Germany where, like so many other Eastern European exiles, they nurtured hopes of one day returning to their homeland to root out the communists.

That may have seemed a forlorn pipe dream, except for an intermittent trickle of Ukrainian resistance fighters who made their way into western Germany in the late 1940s, with reports of hundreds, perhaps thousands, of UPA fighters still holding out in the forests and marshes of their homeland. An internal CIA report compiled in November 1950, just after Beetle Smith took over, largely confirmed the news. With a well-established and tightly defended underground network, the CIA report found, the UPA was not only conducting retaliatory raids on communist party installations but, emboldened by success, establishing new commando cells all the time. This was precisely the sort of thing Frank Wisner wanted to hear. "In view of the extent and activity of the resistance movement in Ukraine," he wrote on January 4, 1951, "we consider this to be a top priority project."

Of course, the very first step in such an ambitious scheme was to find someone capable of keeping track of it all. To that end, in December 1950 Wisner sent for a man already running infiltration missions in the field, one of OPC's brightest lights.

═══

In early December, some three weeks after seeing off that first group of Albanian commandos, Michael Burke's dark fretting about their fate was interrupted by a summons to OPC headquarters in Washington. Exhausted by the endless machinations that had attended Fiend, he decided to make a vacation out of the trip and, in keeping with the style in which he now traveled, booked passage to New York for himself and his wife and young daughter aboard the *Liberté* luxury passenger ship.

Once in Washington after the holidays, a series of conferences at the Tempo buildings culminated in Burke being led into Frank Wisner's office. It was his first encounter with the OPC director and, for reasons Burke couldn't quite identify, he found him somewhat off-putting; he would later describe Wisner as "an intellectual smoothie." He had a much better rapport with the other man brought into the meeting, his old OSS comrade and now head of OPC's Eastern Europe operations, Frank Lindsay.

If Burke surmised that being called into conference with the OPC's top leadership meant his job was about to get bigger, he was correct. A very great deal had changed in Washington since his last visit, and it could be distilled down to one word: Korea. That conflict had also recently turned much worse for the United States. In late November 1950, the Chinese Red Army had poured across the Yalu River to save their North Korean ally and caught the U.N. forces led by General Douglas MacArthur by surprise. On the very day that Burke met with Wisner and Lindsay that January, U.N. forces were in headlong retreat from territory they had taken just weeks earlier.

What had also changed with Korea was a fundamental shift in Washington's Cold War rhetoric; instead of "containment" of world communism, the talk now was becoming of "rollback" and "liberation." That meant pursuing an offensive approach toward the Soviet Union, to destabilize and even peel away some of those nations in its thrall. This was no longer the "clinical experiment" of Albania; now, it was time to provoke opportunity whenever and wherever it seemed possible.

As Wisner informed Burke at their meeting, OPC was about to dramatically expand their infiltration efforts in northeastern Europe, and especially in Poland and Ukraine. The staging point for these missions was to be in Germany, and Wisner wanted Burke to assume operational command. This would entail Burke's transfer from Rome to Frankfurt, as well as a change in his status from OPC contract worker to permanent employee.

Burke quickly accepted the offer, and soon received both his new code name, Randolph R. Northwood, and a top secret memorandum outlining his duties. "It shall be your responsibility as Chief of FJNADIR [OPC covert operations in Germany] to control and direct the operation and administration of FJNADIR Headquarters and subordinate stations." The memorandum then provided some detail about Burke's new position, specifically that he was to see to the organization, command and supervision of all OPC personnel operating in Germany unless informed otherwise by "Harold S. Whiting," alias Frank Wisner.

Somewhat to his own surprise, Michael Burke was not intimidated by the massive scale of obligations he was assuming. "Looking back," he later wrote, "I find it curious that I had no qualms whatsoever about taking charge of what was then the CIA's largest and most comprehensive field operation." Then again, this expanded mission fit very nicely into the image Burke had of himself, and how he wished to live his life. "I was not looking for a quiet corner. On the contrary, I was eager for a new level of responsibility. . . . On a purely subjective level, I knew this was where I should be."

What the new assignment also meant was an end to his field supervision of Operation Fiend. With another OPC contract officer in Rome taking over the Albania project, Burke stayed on in Washington to be tutored on the parameters of his German mission, and to forge closer links with those at headquarters to whom he'd be reporting.

It wasn't all cramming at the office, however. The resident intelligence community of Washington was famous for its frequent dinner and cocktail parties, and during their extended stay in the capital, Michael and Timmy Burke were invited to a great number of them. The "largest, jolliest and wettest" party, in Burke's memory, was that held on the evening of

February 24, 1951, at a fine Federal-style house at 4100 Nebraska Avenue, in the northwestern reaches of the city. It was the home of Kim Philby, the MI6 liaison to the American intelligence community, with whom Burke had spent a very pleasant evening of dinner and drink in London the previous March.

Far more drink flowed on that February night, and through the tastefully appointed downstairs rooms of Kim and Aileen Philby's home circulated some of the most important people in the nation's capital: diplomats from the British embassy, of course, but also senior officers from the State Department, the CIA and the FBI, officials with whom Philby had regular contact on work-related matters, but who had also become social friends. While Michael Burke's invitation to this august gathering may have stemmed from the quick camaraderie he and Philby had developed back in London, it surely didn't hurt that, with his promotion, he was now very much a rising star within the OPC.

Burke so enjoyed himself that night that he and Timmy, along with a friend named Ken Downs, ended up being the last to leave the party. The group was chatting with the Philbys on the house porch waiting for a taxi when there occurred a humorous mishap. As Burke was to recall: "Downs, still carrying one more martini for the road, fell from the porch into a thick hedge, landed flat on his back, and held up his glass triumphantly to show that he hadn't spilled a drop. The Philbys and we cheered him extravagantly from the top step. We all hugged one another in semidrunk camaraderie, rescued Downs from the bushes, and left the Philbys awash in bonhomie. It was that kind of party."

In April, the Burkes finally left Washington for Rome and the villa on Via Mercati, there to pack up their belongings for the move to Germany. On May 3, his Albanian co-conspirators in Operation Fiend threw a grand going-away party for Burke, a multi-course Balkan meal liberally layered with liquor. At the conclusion, his hosts presented him with a large folded parchment. Painted on the cover was Albania's national symbol, a two-headed eagle, and an inscription from "the Sons of the Eagle." On the inside page, the Albanian resistance leaders thanked the OPC officer for "your many acts of kindness, your devotion to our cause and your continuing efforts on our behalf."

Burke would treasure that parchment—it would be one of the very few personal mementos preserved in his personal papers six decades later— but it may have also served as a kind of penance; on the day he received it, one of the two teams of commandos who had gone into Albania six months earlier still hadn't been heard from.

For a man like Frank Wisner, both privy to and a participant in the innermost workings of the American government, the turn of domestic politics after the outbreak of the Korean War took on an appalling cast. Although he had voted for Truman in 1948, he was hardly a diehard supporter, forever critical of his 1945 decision to shut down the OSS and his early laxity in perceiving the Soviet threat. That said, the vehemence of Truman's political opponents in attacking him at a time when the nation was at war in Korea struck many, including Wisner, as reckless bordering on treasonous.

Those attacks reached their nadir in April 1951, after Truman dismissed Douglas MacArthur as commander of the forces in Korea. Among the American far right, the general was transformed into a martyr to the treacheries and incompetence of the Truman administration, the "Old Soldier" being sacrificed on the altar as a scapegoat. Joseph McCarthy joined in, decrying that the Reds had brought MacArthur low.

As exemplified by Frank Wisner's personal experience, in the annals of American history, a less-deserving martyr could scarcely be found. Building on the incompetence he'd displayed in the Philippines in World War II, MacArthur had managed to escape blame for being caught out by the North Korean invasion courtesy of the bold flanking attack he had launched against the communist invaders three months later. Just like that, the landing at Inchon had shifted the tide of the war and recast MacArthur as the savior of Korea, a standing only slightly tarnished by his continuing bungling in the conflict. The most catastrophic of these was his blithe disregard of warnings in late 1950 that Chinese forces were massing on the North Korean border for a counterattack, an assault that abruptly shifted the fortunes of war yet again and led to the deaths of thousands of American troops.

Wisner's own association with the general had preceded these fiascoes. After being constantly rebuffed, in April 1950 Wisner had flown out to Japan to meet with MacArthur and personally plead for the OPC to be allowed to operate in his Far East zone of responsibility. The general had at last given his grudging approval, but only after lecturing Wisner that the place in Asia his agency should really be focusing on was not Japan or Korea, but the Philippines. That May, the OPC established its first station in Japan, but it had yet to place anyone on the ground in Korea when the invasion came the following month. It underscored a remarkable pattern in the career of Douglas MacArthur. In less than a decade, the United States military had been disastrously blindsided in Asia on four occasions: the 1941 Japanese attacks on Pearl Harbor and the Philippines; the North Korean invasion of the South in June 1950, followed by the Chinese military intervention there of five months later. Save for Pearl Harbor, MacArthur had been the on-site commanding officer for all of them. No matter; the demands of demagoguery often require the swift recasting of heroes and fools, and so it was with the glorification of Douglas MacArthur.

But if domestic politics cast a gloom over Frank Wisner, it was joined by a personal component. No matter how much he might remind himself that Beetle Smith was rude and demeaning to everyone, he couldn't help but take the CIA director's barbs personally; it was certainly not the way Wisner treated his staff, nor how he'd been treated by superiors in the past. "Beetle Smith, I just don't think he liked Frank," his wife, Polly Wisner, told an interviewer. "Smith was very, very intelligent, very tough and quite a mean man." In the remembrances of several close friends, Wisner frequently thought of resigning during the first months of Smith's tenure, only to be repeatedly talked out of it.

At the same time, Allen Dulles's elevation over him rankled. After all, Wisner had given up his lucrative law career for government service three years before Dulles came into the CIA, only to see Dulles leapfrog past him in the Agency hierarchy. "Between trusted colleagues that slight could be managed," Polly Wisner said, "though to the end of his career, Frank's respect for Allen was mixed with a degree of sadness and rivalry."

A rivalry also underscored by profound personality differences. There was a glibness and superficiality to Dulles very much in contrast to Wisner's passionate and emotional nature. And whereas Wisner had a circle of close friends to whom he was fiercely loyal, the professorial Dulles was far more aloof, a man with "a million warm acquaintances," as a colleague would put it, but no real friends. Put in the starkest terms, those who knew Wisner felt his actions were dictated by a sense of honor and fairness, even if they didn't always trust his judgment. By contrast, as biographer Peter Grose would memorably put it, Allen Dulles "learned to deal comfortably in perfectly bad faith."

Another pressure was Wisner's work itself. Further belying his reputation as the ultimate Cold Warrior, the OPC chief became increasingly alarmed by the lack of any coherent strategy behind the expansion of covert operations, and of the absurdly optimistic results other branches of the government expected from them. In early 1951, American military leaders seized on the notion of "retardation," whereby the OPC was directed to develop large-scale guerrilla warfare units in Eastern Europe that could be activated in the event of war—never mind the tremendous difficulty in fostering and keeping alive such units even in small-scale. By May 1951, Wisner had become so irked by this climate of wishful thinking that he wrote a memo to the National Security Council demanding more concrete guidance. The eventual response, NSC 10/5, was another airy directive that covert operations should be used to inflict "maximum strain on the Soviet structure of power" through the use of indigenous underground resistance groups.

Wisner found some release from these frustrations by socializing with the MI6 liaison, Kim Philby. The two frequently met for lunch and shop talk, complemented by strategy planning sessions with other senior CIA officials down at the Tempos. In the alcohol-infused environment of the intelligence world at the time, Wisner was a near match to Philby when it came to drinking prowess and, as Philby would fondly remember, these meetings "would end by Wisner or whoever producing bourbon from his office bar, after which we would debate the wisdom of again abandoning our wives for another regular-guy evening on the town."

Certainly, when it came to surveying the domestic American political scene, the Cambridge-educated Philby was just as aghast of a backwoods crudity like Joe McCarthy as Wisner. Where they might have diverged slightly on that score was in their levels of cynicism. Where to Wisner, McCarthy was a threat to the very fabric of American society, to Philby he was a nonentity, a useful fool to J. Edgar Hoover who could be employed to maintain the nation's spy fever and thereby boost FBI funding. The Briton felt he had received sly confirmation of this during his first meeting with Hoover when he asked him "point-blank" about McCarthy. " 'Well,' said Hoover in reply, 'I often meet Joe at the racetrack, but he has never given me a winner yet.' "

As for why the FBI director would speak belittlingly of McCarthy to Philby, it was probably because, by early 1951, Hoover had already decided he no longer needed him. He had to cope with the hated Truman until the next presidential elections, but the little man from Missouri was now clearly a lame duck—Truman's approval rating would eventually decline to an unprecedented 22 percent—so what did Hoover gain by continuing to feed his undisciplined attack dog? Instead, the Venona decrypts were offering up bona fide communists and spies with regularity, enough to ensure the Red Scare's survival.

Yet, if the FBI director had been a more curious—or less smug—man, he might have given thought to a couple of lingering mysteries surrounding his crusade against the Reds. In the wake of Elizabeth Bentley's disclosures in November 1945, Hoover had cast a dragnet of over two hundred agents to surveil the scores of suspects she eventually named, yet not one of them had been caught in an act of espionage. Precisely the same pattern had developed among those uncovered by Venona. It was a strange coincidence and it suggested one of three possibilities: that the suspects were actually innocent (which Hoover knew to not be true); that all had previously severed their ties to the Soviets (equally unlikely); or that they had been tipped off at the outset of the FBI investigations. This third scenario was both the most likely and most alarming, for it meant there was a mole somewhere in the very inner circle of the counterespionage effort. Most likely, perhaps, but there is no evidence that Hoover ever seriously considered it.

For many, many years, Kim Philby had carried an image of how it would end. It wouldn't be the result of some special task force methodically charting facts, building a chronology. Nor, he was quite certain, would it come from carelessness on the controllers' part or betrayal from within. Instead, it would occur when someone allowed their mind to wander, when they were stuck in traffic, perhaps, or staring into a shaving mirror. All at once, the thought would pop into their head—not even a full thought at first, a mere wisp of something—to be followed by a moment of shocked wonderment, disbelief. Maybe they would even tell themselves it was absurd and try to push it from their mind, but the idea wouldn't leave, and then there would come a cascade of remembrances, the litany of odd happenstances and missed moments accumulated over the years, and then it would all start falling into place, the truth unfurling like the lifting of a fog. All this Kim Philby took as a virtual certainty; the only question, he had told himself, was, "How soon? How late?"

There had been so many close calls. The first had come in 1937 with the defection of a Soviet spymaster named Walter Krivitsky. Over the course of his interviews with Britain's MI5, Krivitsky supplied the names of over ninety Soviet intelligence officers or agents working around the world, including over sixty in Britain alone. He also recounted that, shortly before his own defection, the KGB had plotted the assassination of Spain's General Franco by employing one of its foreign assets who had managed to insinuate his way into the fascist leader's inner circle; Krivitsky didn't know the asset's name, only that he was "a young Englishman, a journalist of good family." MI5 hadn't immediately pressed Krivitsky on the matter, and by the time anyone's curiosity was aroused, he wasn't taking any more questions; on February 10, 1941, Krivitsky was found dead with a gunshot wound to the head in Room 532 of the Bellevue Hotel in downtown Washington. After a cursory examination by a medical examiner unaware of Krivitsky's background, his death was ruled a suicide.

An even closer call had come in Istanbul in 1945 when Konstantin Volkov, a high-ranking intelligence officer attached to the Soviet consulate, told a British diplomat that he wished to defect. At a follow-up meeting several days later, Volkov offered to provide the names of hundreds of Soviet spies, both in Turkey and Great Britain, in return for asylum; to whet his listener's appetite, he added that at least seven of these spies were in British intelligence or the Foreign Office, including one who headed "a department of British counterintelligence." Getting Volkov safely out of Istanbul was considered so high-priority that MI6 headquarters dispatched one of its senior men to facilitate his defection: this was the head of Section IX, the unit devoted to Soviet counterintelligence, Kim Philby. But Philby was slow in reaching Turkey, and by the time he got there, Volkov was missing. British authorities soon had reason to suspect the worst, when it was reported that two heavily bandaged and sedated figures strapped to gurneys had been hurried onto a Soviet transport plane at Istanbul airport bound for Moscow. As would only be confirmed decades later, those "patients" were Konstantin Volkov and his wife, Zoya; once in Moscow, the couple was taken to the KGB's Lubyanka headquarters to be tortured, then led into one of the basement murder rooms.

Along the way there had been a host of subtler threats, chance encounters with people from the past, coincidences that might have appeared less coincidental if anyone had bothered to puzzle them out. Soon after arriving in Washington, Philby had been passing down a State Department hallway when he bumped into Teddy Kollek, an old acquaintance visiting from Israel. An Israeli intelligence officer and future mayor of Jerusalem, Kollek had known Philby and his first wife, Litzi Kohlman, in Vienna in the 1930s, and knew both to be dedicated communists.

"What is Philby doing here?" Kollek asked a senior CIA official afterward. When told Philby was the MI6 liaison in Washington, Kollek was stunned. "Don't trust him," he said, a warning that went unheeded.

But even if they harbored suspicions, neither Teddy Kollek nor anyone else could have possibly imagined the magnitude of it all, or for how long it had been going on.

As is often the case, Philby's double life was initially of a nature that many people, especially those of a liberal bent, might have found little fault with. In the Spanish Civil War, General Franco and his fascist followers had mutinied against a democratically elected government, and often followed up their victories on the battlefield with mass executions of their foes. As a journalist and firsthand witness to the Francoists' murderous excesses, Philby probably considered it a moral responsibility to pass along what he knew to his own government, as well as to that one foreign power, the Soviet Union, that had come to the aid of the Spanish Republic.

Moral considerations were only slightly more complex when it came to providing information to the Soviets during World War II. True, Stalin had helped precipitate the war by initially going into an alliance with Hitler, but then the Soviets had borne the brunt of defeating the Nazis, losing some twenty-five citizens for every American or British war dead. In light of this suffering, it might almost be considered a patriotic duty to pass along to Moscow those secrets being selfishly withheld by their American and British allies. This was certainly the core rationale of many Western wartime spies for the Soviets, including Julius and Ethel Rosenberg, and it most likely was for Kim Philby, as well.

But even though their pasts often caught up to them, most of the Americans and Britons who had passed secrets to the Soviets during the war quit in its aftermath, and especially once the Cold War set in. Not so the Cambridgean with the charming stammer. Instead, Philby redoubled his efforts, as did most of the other four members of the British spy ring that would come to be known as the Cambridge Five.

Of the five, by far the most important to the Cold War Soviets—and most devastating for the West—were Philby and Donald Maclean, a senior official in the British Foreign Office who, in 1944, was attached as second secretary to the British embassy in Washington. After serving four years there, Maclean returned to London, leaving Washington shortly before Philby arrived as MI6 liaison to the CIA and FBI. No two spies ever attained such positions of influence and trust. Between Philby and Maclean, in the seven-year span from 1944 to the spring of 1951, the Soviets gained access to many of the most closely guarded secrets of the Western alliance, including inner details of the American atomic weapons program, the order of battle formations of NATO forces in Europe, even top secret cables between the American and British heads of state as they strategized over Soviet policy.

Despite all the previous close calls, the unraveling finally began with Venona. By early 1950, the cryptologists on the Venona Project had determined that one of the most prolific mid-1940s spies for the Soviets had been attached to the British embassy in Washington—this was Maclean—and for help in identifying him they naturally turned to the new senior British intelligence officer in the capital, MI6 liaison Kim Philby. Almost instantly upon being shown the Venona decrypts, Philby realized that the spy code-named "Homer" was Maclean. In what must have been a disquieting moment, he also recognized "Stanley" as himself. That February, Philby warned the KGB that it was now probably only a matter of time before their spy ring was cracked.

Throughout his tenure in Washington, Philby kept a nervous watch on the progress of the Venona Project. By May 1951, he knew his time was nearly up. With the cryptologists rapidly closing in on Homer's identity, Philby frantically tried to figure out a way to get a warning to Maclean in London without implicating himself in the process. The plan went awry when Guy Burgess, another member of the Cambridge Five and the man Philby dispatched to warn Maclean, instead decided to join Maclean in fleeing to Moscow.

When the two eventually surfaced in the Soviet capital and were revealed as spies, two things were immediately apparent to American investigators. First, Maclean had run because he learned the Venona net was closing on him. Second, while Burgess had obviously tipped off Maclean, he was only the messenger, since Burgess had no access to Venona. But that wasn't true of the high-ranking British embassy official who was not only a close friend of Burgess's, but who had put him up in his Nebraska Avenue home for the past year: Kim Philby.

Within days of the Maclean-Burgess defection, the Americans demanded Philby be dismissed, but with insufficient evidence to bring charges, MI6 could do no more than force his resignation. Even then, many of Philby's former MI6 colleagues stoutly refused to believe the accusations, deeming it inconceivable that "one of their own"—Oxbridge-educated, upper-class—could be a traitor; as one Philby supporter had earlier noted, "I knew his people." Instead, it wouldn't be for another eight years, not until the winter of 1963, that Philby would finally be fully unmasked. At the time, he was living in Beirut as a journalist and, much as with Donald Maclean, he jumped just as British interrogators were closing in. At a subsequent press conference in Moscow, he admitted to having been a spy for the Soviets since 1934, earning for himself the dubious honor of being the most highly placed double agent in the history of the Cold War.

Long before that Moscow press conference, the reverberations of Philby's treachery were profoundly felt—and nowhere more so than in the halls of CIA headquarters. For Frank Wisner, Philby's betrayal took personal form. He had considered the MI6 man a friend, had frequently dined and shared confidences with him. That one of the very top spymasters of the American intelligence community had been taken in by a double agent was a bitter pill to swallow. "I can't recall him ever talking about it," Wisner's middle son, Ellis, said, "but it must've been devastating. It *had* to have been."

Even more devastating was the damage assessment that followed, as investigators tried to determine precisely what Philby had access to, what he might have compromised. The grim fact was that he'd had access to most everything, could have compromised practically any British or American or joint intelligence operation since 1945.

From this conclusion, a rather predictable phenomenon occurred: Kim Philby swiftly became an institutional dumping ground, the traitor-within responsible for sabotaging a whole roster of intelligence missions of recent years. In some cases, such as Valuable/Fiend in Albania, suspicion was at least warranted—after all, the man had served as the operation's supervisory co-commander—but in others, the defrocked MI6 man was blamed for botched ventures that he may not have even known about, and certainly not at the close-in operational level required to facilitate ambushes in the field. To the old maxim of success having a hundred fathers while failure is an orphan, Kim Philby offered a new twist, a hundred failures fostered by one father.

This vigorous blame game played perfectly into the hands of the Soviets, for now their Western adversaries had to question the security of their closest secrets and the integrity of their covert operations throughout the world. It is surely no coincidence that even in the brief period of "archival glasnost" that accompanied the collapse of the Soviet Union in 1991, one set of KGB files never fully opened to the outside world were those detailing Kim Philby's disclosures. Given the nature of the current Russian government, it's hard to imagine they will be seen anytime soon.

But the scapegoating of Philby soon led to another, even more questionable, thread of logic. This one held that, if the MI6 liaison had been the great betrayer of clandestine missions, then with him out of the picture, operational security was now restored. Which meant that, far from shutting down those covert missions that had failed in the past, the West could now expand them. The fallacy—and the tragedy—of this logic would soon become apparent.

17

WAR AS A PRACTICAL JOKE

Roused from his sleep on the deck of the Philippine naval destroyer, Ed Lansdale peered up to see a soldier standing over him with a submachine gun. The man had come to deliver a warning.

Earlier that day, Lansdale and the new Philippine defense secretary, Ramon Magsaysay, had been in the Luzon countryside observing an army operation against the Huk guerrillas. Deciding to return to Manila that evening, they had hitched a ride on a navy destroyer making an overnight run to the capital, only to learn the ship was also transporting the armed forces chief of staff, General Mariano Castañeda, along with a bevy of the general's senior aides. A war hero, Castañeda had further burnished his reputation by physically shielding the Philippine president during a 1947 hand grenade attack. He also happened to be a bitter enemy of Lansdale's traveling companion, Ramon Magsaysay.

With not enough staterooms for all the traveling dignitaries, Lansdale and Magsaysay had magnanimously ceded the more comfortable sleeping quarters to Castañeda and his staff, while they threw some blankets down on the destroyer's deck. But, as the soldier who woke Lansdale explained, the general and his men hadn't gone to sleep; instead, they were gathered in a wardroom belowdecks for a bout of drinking. As the night wore on, a recurring topic of conversation was their loathing for the two men sleeping topside. Finally, General Castañeda drew out his pistol and announced he was going up to shoot Lansdale, "the interfering bastard behind all the changes being made." It was then that the soldier raced up to the destroyer deck to raise the alarm.

Figuring that a shootout between the nation's two highest-ranking defense officials might make for unwanted headlines, Lansdale commanded the soldier to stand watch over the still sleeping Magsaysay while he went below to confront Castañeda. When he entered the wardroom, he was met with baleful stares. To break the icy silence, he asked Castañeda for a drink, since, "I heard you're going to shoot me and it might be my last one."

At this, Castañeda laughed, breaking the tension, and poured out a drink for Lansdale. "I'm not going to shoot you" he said, "although you deserve it; we've known each other too long. I'll wait, since somebody else is bound to shoot you sooner or later."

Lansdale took a seat at the table, and for the next hour, he and the general thrashed out their differences, even as Castañeda's aides continued to cast dagger-eyes at the American interloper, the source of so many of their problems.

The seeds for that confrontation had been planted some three months earlier, in August 1950, when a senior State Department official named John Melby was led into the inner sanctum of the Philippine presidential palace in downtown Manila. Melby was there to meet President Elpidio Quirino and, while meant to be a courtesy visit, he came with a sizable hidden agenda.

It was five months since Ed Lansdale had met Philippine congressman Ramon Magsaysay in Washington, and ferried him around to meet some of the senior State Department and CIA officials involved with East Asian affairs. Since that time the situation in the Philippines had worsened, with the Hukbalahap rebellion, once isolated to central Luzon, spreading dramatically. With the Korean War going badly, the Americans felt a desperate urgency not to let another Asian government fall to the communists, and they weren't subtle about it. Quirino had already relented to make use of the services of one Lieutenant Colonel Edward Lansdale, who was to return to Manila as a psychological warfare advisor, but he balked at Melby's request that Magsaysay be made defense secretary.

"I don't want any trouble," Quirino told Melby, a tacit admission of the complex web of alliances and sinecures and featherbedding that kept the Manila oligarchy fed and happy.

In the face of Quirino's resistance, Melby was blunt. "Well, all I can say," he told the president, "is if you don't do it, there will be no more

American aid. No more military aid. I'm prepared to recommend that it be cut off."

Quirino blinked. Days later, Magsaysay was the new defense secretary. Once word of Magsaysay's appointment reached OPC headquarters in Washington, Lansdale was given mere hours to put his affairs in order, pack up, and catch a flight to Manila.

He traveled with an ambitious agenda. In the words of biographer Cecil Currey, Lansdale was "to provide counsel and support to the new secretary of national defense, influence the revitalization of the Philippine Army, help the government make progress in its war against the Huks, urge political reform upon the host government, and see what he could do to help Filipinos have an honest election in the November 1951 balloting."

It promised to be a busy time in Manila, for to accomplish all this, Lansdale was given just ninety days. Making his mission even more implausible, his support staff numbered precisely two: his closest friend from his first Philippines tour, counterinsurgency expert Charles "Bo" Bohannon, and a communications specialist on loan from the U.S. Army named Alger "Ace" Ellis. The inclusion of the second man hinted at the proconsul role Lansdale was about to assume; with Ellis's help, the forty-two-year-old Lansdale would have an independent and secure communication link to OPC headquarters, one which neither the American embassy nor the resident CIA station chief in Manila could track. Not that Lansdale anticipated interference; despite his lowly official rank and title—a lieutenant colonel serving as a temporary security advisor to Quirino—"embassy officials were supposed to cooperate with Lansdale almost without question, up to and including the ambassador."

———

Both from his past travels and from his professional study, Ed Lansdale thought he knew the Philippines quite well by the summer of 1950. He was perplexed therefore when, flying into Manila early that September, he began hearing radically conflicting narratives about what was taking place there, the tale of two nations.

Within days, he met with both President Quirino and the American ambassador, and at these and other high-level meetings Lansdale heard a surprisingly upbeat assessment of the security situation. Among the Philippine political leadership was general agreement that the Huks consisted of a few thousand malcontents roaming the countryside with little popular support; while capable of spreading fear with their ambushes and hit-and-run attacks, they certainly posed no great threat to the state. This view was seconded by officials at the American embassy and the U.S. military command, with one embassy official pegging the number of active Huks as low as one hundred. As Lansdale soon determined, however, this consensus among American officials may have been less rooted in reality than in the fact that they were only talking with their Filipino counterparts; incredibly, American government personnel, both military and civilian, were barred from venturing into the countryside on orders of the commander of the resident American military advisory group.

Lansdale drew a vastly different picture in talking with old friends among the Philippine military intelligence apparatus and the Manila news media. From them, he heard ominous reports that Huk ranks had swelled to as many as fifteen thousand fighters who could rely on the auxiliary or home front support of hundreds of thousands, perhaps millions, of their disaffected countrymen. Not only did the Huks enjoy de facto control over great swaths of the Luzon countryside, they were now exerting their authority in many of Manila's poorer suburbs; at the present rate, Lansdale was told, it was only a matter of time—and probably a short time—before the Huks could meet and militarily defeat the Philippine army on the battlefield. In response, the army and government-supported vigilante squads were waging an ever more indiscriminate terror campaign in suspected Huk strongholds, a campaign that, as so often happens in such circumstances, was degenerating into outright criminality.

The American advisor was given a stark example of the pall of anxiety descended on Manila when he called on an old publisher friend. As the two of them sat in the man's living room, Lansdale casually asked why everyone in Manila seemed so frightened.

"He looked startled at the question," Lansdale recalled, "and shook his head no. Silently, he got to his feet, beckoned me, and walked out of the door."

Without a word between them, the two left the house and walked to a clump of bushes at the farthest corner of the garden. Only then did the publisher speak, and only in an angry whisper. "I had alarmed him by asking about the fear," Lansdale wrote. "Anybody could have bugged his place with a hidden microphone or have had a listener under the window of the room. In addition to himself, he had a family who could be kidnapped or killed." As for precisely who posed such a danger, the publisher explained it could come from either side, either the increasingly emboldened Huks or the increasingly brutal goon squads being operated by the Quirino regime.

But in fact, the Philippines had become the tale of three nations, as Lansdale discovered when, flouting the American military's travel ban, he ventured into the countryside to visit the site of a recent Huk attack.

The insurgents' raid on Camp Makabulos had occurred shortly before Lansdale's return to the Philippines, and been particularly shocking. In broad daylight and over a period of hours, a Huk raiding party had stealthily spread throughout the village adjoining an army camp, while the garrisoned soldiers remained completely unaware. When the Huks launched their surprise assault, they killed some thirty soldiers and civilians, most of them patients or visitors at a military hospital. They also broke into the local jail, freeing nearly fifty prisoners, then dragged the district army commander from his home to publicly execute him in the street.

But in interviewing local residents in the attack's aftermath, Lansdale received a jolt. The majority view was that the dead soldiers and the murdered commander got exactly what they deserved, because they weren't "defenders of the people," but rather their violators. What's more, they were in the service of a corrupt regime that had stolen the 1949 elections to ensure that power and wealth remained with the privileged few. "Of course the people were joining and helping the Huks," Lansdale wrote, paraphrasing what he was told. "The Huks were right. The only thing left for the people to do was to use bullets, not ballots, to get a government of their own."

The incident in Makabulos exemplified the vicious cycle now playing out across Luzon and, increasingly, across the Philippines as a whole. Due to the corruption of the government and abuses by its soldiers, a civilian population had stood by as rebels prepared an assault. Having been caught off guard and badly beaten in that assault, the surviving soldiers knew it could only have been launched with the connivance of the local civilians. Now, the soldiers would regard those locals as enemy supporters, spurring the next round of abuse, which would then ensure the success of the next insurgent attack.

But if there was anyone who might begin to untie this Gordian knot, Lansdale believed, it was Ramon Magsaysay.

The new defense secretary lived very differently from his governmental peers, as Lansdale discovered when Magsaysay invited him to his house for dinner. Instead of the palatial mansions set behind high walls that were the usual habitations of the Manila elite, the Magsaysay homestead was a simple bungalow in a middle-class district near downtown. Also, a district infiltrated by the Huks, as Lansdale deduced from the plethora of idle young men with hard stares lingering in the surrounding streets.

Counseling Magsaysay that the area was unsafe—if he insisted on staying there, it would only endanger his wife and their three children—Lansdale finally convinced the new defense secretary to at least temporarily move into the same house that he and his support team were occupying in a secure corner of a nearby American army base. That house, though, was very small, and so it came to be that in September 1950, the sleeping quarters of the defense secretary of the United States' most important ally in Asia, and of the chief American intelligence advisor to the president of the Philippines, consisted of a shared bedroom in a nondescript tract house on an American army base in the Manila suburbs.

Not that a lot of sleep was to be had. As Lansdale would later recall: "Each night we sat up late discussing the current situation. Magsaysay would air his views. Afterwards, I would sort them out aloud for him while underscoring the principles or strategy or tactics involved. . . . Between present circumstances and the achievement of our goals lay the Communist party and its guerrilla army aggressively dominating the scene, the ills in Philippine society that provided soil for rebellion to flourish, and a government military force that we felt was largely out of touch with reality or with the people it must defend."

In Magsaysay—"Monching" as he was known to friends—Lansdale had found a man just as dynamic and impatient as himself. Prior to Lansdale's appearance on the scene, the Philippine high command had insisted that Magsaysay check in with them beforehand if he wished to visit any military installations—for security reasons, they said—with the result that all was spruced up and made shiny before the secretary's arrival. Once Magsaysay and Lansdale teamed up, they began flying and driving around the country together on the spur of the moment, often without escort, popping in unannounced at army garrisons or outposts for impromptu inspections. There was often a comic aspect to these trips, stemming from Magsaysay's fondness for loud aloha shirts and floppy sun hats; as a result, the uniformed Lansdale often had to vouch for the defense secretary's bona fides at entrance gates. Once that confusion was cleared up, however, these spot inspections had a bracing effect, with Magsaysay prone to summarily dismissing any officer he deemed lax or corrupt. "The early fall days of 1950 found the bamboo telegraph full of news about Magsaysay's surprise visits to unlikely places," Lansdale wrote, "as well as the consequences of each visit. The troops in the field started behaving as though the secretary of national defense might show up on the scene at any moment to praise or chastise them for what they were doing."

In their plans to remake the Philippine military, Magsaysay and Lansdale had one factor strongly in their favor. Prior to Lansdale's arrival, American officials had leaned on President Quirino to reform the Philippine Constabulary, the 24,000-man rural paramilitary force that bore the brunt of fighting the Huks. Notorious for doing the bidding of local governors and landlords, the Constabulary had proved useless in that mission, but quite effective in terrorizing the civilian population. Under Quirino's restructuring, seventeen thousand Constabulary members were incorporated into the national military, while the remaining seven thousand were stripped of their .50-caliber machine guns and armored cars and sent back into the provinces to be the civilian policemen they had ostensibly been before. With the Constabulary thus muzzled, it would now be possible to rein in some of the government's worst human rights abusers.

But only if Ramon Magsaysay was given any actual say. Working behind the scenes, Lansdale lobbied the American embassy and military advisory team to put a new squeeze on Quirino, this time to radically expand the defense secretary's powers. In short order, Magsaysay had the authority to fire and promote as he saw fit, and to order court-martials of those accused of corruption or brutality. While this reform drive had a salutary effect on the morale of the army rank and file—and spurred a gradual improvement in the public's opinion of their nation's soldiers—it also drew bitter opposition from the military high command, as evidenced by the confrontation between Lansdale and General Castañeda on the navy destroyer.

But if the military leadership held out hope they might gradually marginalize their new defense secretary, that prospect was fairly demolished by a spectacular feat Magsaysay pulled off just six weeks into his tenure.

On the very day he became defense secretary, Magsaysay had held a secret meeting with a high-ranking Huk ideologue grown disenchanted by the group's increasingly indiscriminate attacks. Over a series of subsequent clandestine meetings, Magsaysay tried to get the man to "defect" and, while those efforts were unsuccessful, the dissident did let slip the arrangement by which the Huks' urban leadership communicated with one another. With an astounding lack of prudence—although in itself a reflection of the impunity with which the rebels now felt they could operate—the Huks employed a single courier to collect and deliver messages between their Manila commanders. After surveilling this courier for several weeks, on the early morning of October 18, 1950, raiding teams from the Philippine military intelligence agency launched a massive dragnet; caught up in the net were over one hundred Huk operatives, including top members of their urban Politburo. Also captured were

documents detailing plans for an all-out offensive against the government, one in which Huk advance teams would fan out from Luzon to
foment rebellion across the Philippines. So confident were the rebels of
ultimate victory that, according to Lansdale, they had even set a date for
their complete takeover of the nation: May 1, 1952.

While the October raid dealt a severe setback to the Huks, it also fairly
neutered the army's opposition to Magsaysay. Their new defense secretary, civilian though he was, had now been personally instrumental in
delivering a more grievous blow to the rebels than the military had been
able to inflict in four years.

The Huks naturally took note of this, as well. Learning that the new
defense secretary was living in a bungalow on the American military
base, they began sending in "trigger squads" to kill him. Lansdale and
Magsaysay, along with a handful of the secretary's most trusted bodyguards, remained on high alert against these assassination attempts,
which, as Lansdale blandly recalled, led to firefights "from time to time in
the small hours of the morning." Since most of the adjacent homes were
occupied by American officers and their families, it wasn't long before
the bungalow occupants were treated to frosty stares from other residents and that label of notoriety common to housing developments the
world over, that of problem-neighbor. "We tried to be quiet about these
skirmishes in the suburban setting," Lansdale lamented, "but we must
have made too much noise."

———

If Ed Lansdale had ever idly pondered the worst place to be caught out
in a firefight, a strong contender was revealed to him on the morning of
February 6, 1951: a streambed. Since streams always flow through lowest
land, it necessarily means that whoever is shooting at you commands the
higher ground. There is also often thick vegetation along a stream bank,
so that sound is distorted and visibility limited. Adding to Lansdale's dis-
quiet on that particular morning was the impossibility of determining
if the closest gunfire was friendly or hostile, since both sides were firing
American weapons.

Earlier that day, he and Magsaysay had awoken in their shared bedroom to the news that a battle between the Philippine army and a Huk
formation raged on a sugar plantation some thirty miles to the north.
Without bothering to arrange an escort, the two men had jumped into
Lansdale's jeep and, with the American intelligence officer behind the
wheel, raced off for a firsthand look. They were just approaching the edge

of the battleground, skirting the front on a dirt road, when Lansdale tried to ford a stream too quickly. In the geyser of water kicked up, the jeep sputtered and died.

Reverting to his training as a mechanic, Magsaysay, in his trademark aloha shirt and floppy sun hat, waded into the water to lift the jeep hood. With a rag, he methodically dried the inner chambers of the carburetor, then turned to the spark plugs. It was a time-consuming process, and must have seemed more so given the sound—a "din" as Lansdale would remember it—of gunfire echoing through the trees. For want of anything more useful to do, Lansdale stood guard on the stream bank as the defense minister saw to his labors, but at some point it must have surely crossed his mind that this was a strange way to spend his forty-third birthday.

With the stalled jeep finally back in operation, the two men continued on to the army's field command post. From the battalion commander, they learned that a group of Huks was trapped in a nearby cane field, cut off from escape by his flanking soldiers. Through that morning and into the afternoon, the shooting continued as the Huks tried to find a way out of the trap. One by one, though, the rebels began heeding the army's call to surrender and emerged from the canefield with their hands raised.

For anyone witness to previous battles between the Huks and the army, there were a couple of anomalies to this scene. Foremost was the notion of the Philippine military actually trapping anyone at all. Over the previous five years of desultory combat with the Huks, the army's standard tactic had been to advance in a line until they encountered resistance, at which point the infantry halted while artillery and warplanes shelled and bombed the rebel-held territory into a scorched wasteland. The problem was that, like guerrillas everywhere, the Huks didn't *hold* territory in the face of an advancing army, but rather melted away to return at a more propitious time. Luis Taruc, the Huk military commander, estimated the total number of his men killed over the years by the army's "search-and-destroy" operations at about twelve; instead, he wryly professed to be saddened "to see thousands of government troops and civil guards cordoning off our campsite and saturating, with every type of gunfire, the unfortunate trees and vegetation."

Equally remarkable was the idea that the Huks would heed an army offer of surrender, or that the army would honor it. In the past, trapped combatants of both sides usually committed suicide or fought to the death, knowing capture meant only a longer and more painful end.

Together, these two battlefield features epitomized the radically changed face of the Philippine battlefield in a matter of mere months—

but it didn't end there. Over a time span of less than two years, the Philippines was to be the site of one of the most rapid collapses of a guerrilla insurgency in military history, a reversal for which the two men in the flood-prone jeep could claim a good deal of the credit.

With the assistance of American military advisors, Magsaysay dismantled the army's previous cumbersome structure to create so-called Battalion Combat Teams, or BCTs, 1,200-man units each with its own arsenal of heavy weaponry, but mobile enough to respond quickly to trouble. And rather than sit in military compounds waiting for the Huks to attack, the new Philippine army took to constant patrols in the countryside and the deployment of small ambush teams in areas where Huks were known to operate. One officer was to remember the countless hours he and his soldiers spent crouched on the edge of provincial cemeteries waiting for local Huks, most of them still tied to the country's ancestor-worship traditions, to visit the graves of their relatives.

But perhaps the greatest innovation was also the simplest: the payment of a living wage. For years, the starting salary for a Filipino soldier had been 30 centavos a day, about 15 U.S. cents at the official exchange rate, a slave wage that all but required him to "forage." That meant demanding or stealing food from civilians or falling onto the payroll of the local oligarch. By raising the soldiers' salary over threefold, and simultaneously letting it be known that the days of robbing from the citizenry were over, Magsaysay raised both the morale of his army and its image in the court of public opinion.

Lansdale's personal contribution was most keenly felt in the arena of psychological warfare, in devising battlefield tactics that had nothing at all to do with firepower or flanking maneuvers. Even this, though, was a collaborative effort, with many of those tactics the outgrowth of a kind of military salon that Lansdale officiated over in the living room of the army base bungalow. It was a forum for military officers to share notes on which counterinsurgency tactics appeared to be working, which had backfired.

Largely stemming from these informal strategy sessions, there developed a multilayered carrot-and-stick approach to the Huk insurgency. On the carrot side of the ledger, the once thieving army would now engage in "civic action." That meant being rousted from their provincial barracks to assist in public works: to dig wells, repair schools, at times even to help in the harvesting of crops. This was to not only give the soldiers a newfound understanding—and respect—for the civilians among whom they lived, but to nurture the idea that the military was truly the "people's army." Once that idea took hold, Lansdale believed, it was the Huks who would be seen as the outsiders and oppressors.

At the same time, Magsaysay came up with a set of inducements for the rebels to lay down their arms, initiatives ranging from amnesty to integration in the military. In the most highly touted campaign, the government established a model settlement where, alongside retired army veterans, surrendering Huks would be given title to a patch of land and the chance to start life anew. To great fanfare, the first settlement was established in February 1951. Word of the initiative quickly spread to those Huks still in the mountains, so that by mid-1951, Lansdale wrote, hundreds of surrendered rebels were petitioning to join the land grant program.

But along with the carrot, so with the stick—or, as Ramon Magsaysay defined it, "all-out friendship or all-out force." A bounty was placed on the heads of Huk leaders, with the death or capture of a local rebel commander worth 5,000 pesos—about five times the average farmworkers' annual income—and the payout climbing to as high as 100,000 pesos for a top leader. A double agent operation was launched in which soldier-volunteers went undercover to join local Huk formations; in time, several of these plants rose through the ranks to become senior rebel commanders, all the while reporting back to the army.

Lansdale augmented these efforts with his talent for, and broad-minded approach to, psychological war. As he explained: "Conventional military men think of combat psywar almost exclusively in terms of leaflets or broadcasts appealing to the enemy to surrender. Early on, I realized that psywar had a wider potential than that. A whole new approach opens up, for example, when one thinks of psywar in terms of playing a practical joke."

In areas where the army built up sufficient intelligence on a local Huk unit, low-flying military spotter planes with loudspeakers trolled over the forest to make threats against some insurgents by name, with the broadcasters then thanking their anonymous—and fictitious—"friends" among the rebels for the information. Rather than simply arrest arms traffickers who were supplying the Huks with weaponry and ammunition, the army introduced booby-trapped matériel into the arms pipeline, faulty rifles or hand grenades primed to blow up in a Huk's hands. One of Lansdale's favorite psy-war anecdotes from the Philippines was the oft-told "vampire story."

An enduring superstition in Philippine society is that of the *asuang*, a vampire-like creature who lives in the mountains and attacks its human prey at night. In one Luzon village where a Huk unit was firmly ensconced on an adjacent mountain, an army psy-ops team was brought in to spread rumors that an *asuang* lived on that same mountain. "Two nights later," Lansdale recalled, "after giving the stories time to circulate among Huk sympathizers in the town and make their way up to the hill camp, the psywar squad set up an ambush along a trail used by the Huks. When a Huk patrol came along the trail, the ambushers silently snatched the last man of the patrol, their move unseen in the dark night. They punctured his neck with two holes, vampire-fashion, held the body up by the heels, drained it of blood, and put the corpse back on the trail."

When the superstitious Huks found the body of their slain and blood-drained comrade the next day, they swiftly abandoned their mountainside camp, never to return.

But even all of this, Lansdale understood, played mostly on the merely tactical level. As such, it would prove meaningless unless the core issue—restoring the Filipinos' faith in their government—was honestly addressed; as the psy-ops warrior was later to say, "it's not enough to be *against* communism; you have to be *for* something."

In November 1949, Elpidio Quirino and his Liberal Party had swept into power in elections regarded as the most fraudulent in the nation's history. To Lansdale, then, the road to political redemption in the Philippines of 1951 had to begin with ensuring the integrity of the midterm Senate elections being held that November. To this end, he helped devise a plan, secretly backed by millions in CIA funds, in which Filipino civic organizations would act as electoral watchdogs. Magsaysay's troops would also be enlisted to guard the ballot boxes. All this placed Lansdale in an odd position, considering that he was still officially detailed as President Quirino's personal intelligence advisor, and it was Quirino and his Liberal cronies who could be expected to most energetically try to hijack the elections.

For those back at CIA headquarters, the Philippine election operation represented a kind of hybrid mission, a combination of the kind of political front group initiatives it was then pursuing in Western Europe, while reminiscent of the Agency's covert involvement in the Italian elections of three years earlier that had helped thwart a communist victory. Should there be any moral qualms over interfering in another country's electoral process, the Philippine mission was actually a good deal more virtuous than the Italian; after all, the CIA technically wasn't taking sides in the Philippines, but simply working to ensure her elections were clean. Of course, such high-mindedness was helped along by the fact that there was absolutely no chance the true undesirables, the Huks, might win. For this, the Agency had their man in Manila partially to thank.

During a raid on a Huk propaganda cell, the Philippine army had captured an old typewriter and mimeograph machine that the insurgents had been using to produce communiqués and run off leaflets for distribution in the area. It gave Lansdale an idea. Gathering up a stock of flimsy paper of the sort that the impecunious Huks might use, and adopting the revolution-speak rhetoric of which they were fond, the intelligence officer worked up a "Huk directive" decrying the upcoming elections as a fraud and insisting they be boycotted. According to Lansdale, the counterfeit was then "secretly placed into Huk propaganda channels. . . . In the following days, the Politburo and the whole Huk apparatus adopted the slogan 'Boycott the Election!' and carried out a vigorous campaign using the arguments I had provided them." While Lansdale exaggerated the role he played in provoking it, the Huks' call for a nationwide election boycott proved a disastrous misstep for a rebel force that could ill afford one.

The November elections came off without a hitch, virtually free both of violence and charges of fraud. Further evidence of their honesty was the fact that Quirino's Liberal Party lost every contested Senate seat. For Lansdale and the CIA, the outcome reaped a windfall. With one quick stroke, many Filipinos had their faith in the political system restored, while also strengthened was the perception that the nation's army—as well as the man who led it, Ramon Magsaysay—were the guardians of that system. At the same time, by boycotting the elections, the Huks had not only neatly shut themselves out of the political process, but earned the label of opponents of democracy.

In truth, though, by then the Huks were already on their way to being a spent force, with both the incidence and severity of their attacks having fallen off dramatically. This was partly due to a catastrophic decision by Huk leaders to launch larger-scale and more conventional attacks on the army, a shift that might have worked when the Huks retained the prerogative of slipping off into the jungle, but not against the newly formed BCT units with their envelopment attacks. In one battle after another, the Huks were surrounded and eliminated. In other areas, small mobile army teams relentlessly pursued holdout Huk bands, pushing them ever further into the remote hills and away from the population centers that provided their sustenance.

Also accelerating their decline was psy-war. Fearful of potential spies in their midst, more and more rebels took advantage of the government's amnesty program to surrender—and, of course, to pass on information on those who remained behind. And, as so often happens with fighting groups, once the Huks' fortunes on the battlefield began to fail, so did their judgment. Individual commanders increasingly turned to "popular justice"—execution—of suspected traitors. The central Politburo reprimanded and then marginalized Luis Taruc, undoubtedly the Huks' most accomplished guerrilla leader, for his "excessive humanism." With astounding speed, the revolution was devouring its children, and the numbers showed it. When Ed Lansdale arrived in Manila in September 1950, the most reliable estimates were that fifteen thousand Huks were under arms at any given moment, supported by a reserve force of about fifty thousand. By the close of 1951, that number had been cut nearly in half, and was falling further all the time. As William Pomeroy, an American fighting with the Huks, was to note as the rebel force came apart: "There was a time when the forest was wholly ours, and we lived in it as within a fortress. . . . There is the sensation, now, of being in a vise."

In this spreading calm, it seems that Edward Lansdale began to ponder a broader role for himself in his adopted country. After all, it wasn't as if the Philippines' problems would end with the Huks' decline. There was still poverty and corruption and extreme economic inequity, all those issues that were a breeding ground for future social unrest, and that begged to be tackled by a good and honest government, something the Philippines had yet to truly experience. At the same time, Lansdale noted, "to the people, Magsaysay rapidly was becoming *the* government, *the* leader who cared about what was happening to them and who would try to right any wrongs." In sum, if the Philippines would soon no longer need the services of an American counterinsurgency expert, what about those of an American kingmaker?

To many observers, it appeared Magsaysay was a creation of Ed Lansdale. Whether the charismatic defense secretary was giving an impromptu speech in a provincial town or being interviewed by foreign journalists about the Huks, he often used remarkably similar language and phraseology to the American who seemed to always be positioned quietly off to his side. Yet, to what degree, if any, Lansdale was Magsaysay's puppet master is a difficult question to answer. Lansdale himself gave radically different answers to the assertion over the years. In a long 1962 letter to a Filipino biographer of Magsaysay, Jose Abueva, he took to task those Filipinos who claimed Magsaysay was essentially a Lansdale creation. "They are quite mischievous in doing this," he wrote, "and apparently are either jealous of Magsaysay or of his friendship with an American, or perhaps they simply didn't understand the critical days in which they lived. Magsaysay needed no help in 'making an image.'"

In more personal correspondence, however, and especially with fellow Americans, Lansdale could be downright patronizing. After reading the draft of a book by journalist Robert Shaplen that was somewhat critical of Magsaysay, Lansdale allowed that, while Magsaysay "did need some hand-holding," he hoped Shaplen would tone down his critique because "the Philippines is hard up for decent heroes."

Most frequently, and especially in any public forum, Lansdale adopted the stance that he and Magsaysay were so like-minded—"like brothers," he often said—and so often in each other's company, that it was only to be expected that they might start sounding alike.

But amid the claims and counterclaims, one particular moment would seem to offer a certain clarity. It occurred on an airplane flying between El Paso and Mexico City in late June 1952.

By then, Ramon Magsaysay was riding a wave—more, a tsunami—of support among his countrymen for his role in safeguarding the 1951 elections, and Lansdale had coordinated a triumphant tour of the United States that included a meeting with President Truman. It's fairly obvious the intelligence officer had a grander vision in mind: to promote Ramon Magsaysay as the potential next president of the Philippines, and to introduce him to those American officials who could help make it happen.

After the U.S., it was on to Mexico City, where Lansdale had arranged for Magsaysay to deliver the keynote address at the annual convention of the Lions Clubs International, a very powerful business group in the 1950s. During the flight, Lansdale happened to glance over to see that Magsaysay was reading through the speech he would give at the convention—except that it was not the speech Lansdale had prepared for him. Instead, it was the product of one of Magsaysay's journalist friends back in Manila, a hackneyed screed full of the extravagant hyperbole and pretentious turn of phrase of which Filipino politicians were traditionally so fond. When Lansdale asked why he was reading that speech, Magsaysay said he'd decided it was the one he would deliver at the Lions Clubs.

"No, it isn't," Lansdale replied. "You're going to read the speech I gave you."

Despite his general amiability, Magsaysay possessed a stubborn streak, and the more Lansdale pressed him on the matter, the more Magsaysay insisted he was going to deliver his friend's speech. Their argument escalated to the point where Lansdale stepped over to snatch the offending manuscript from Magsaysay's hands and, turning his back on the defense secretary, proceed to tear it to pieces. When Magsaysay rose from his seat and pushed Lansdale, the intelligence officer wheeled around with a roundhouse punch to the jaw.

"I slugged him real hard," Lansdale recalled, "and he went down."

Under the shocked gaze of fellow passengers, Lansdale helped Magsaysay to his feet. He then turned to the others in their traveling party and offered in half-contrition: "It's only because we're like brothers that we can argue like this. It's only because we're so close."

If Magsaysay added any comment of his own at that moment, it wasn't noted by those present. At the Lions Clubs convention in Mexico, he gave the speech Lansdale had prepared for him.

18

TOSSING THE DICE

D ue to the difference in time zones, news of the invasion of South Korea had reached CIA Berlin late on the night of June 24. As with every other intelligence and military unit in the Western world, the news instantly triggered alarm bells, but those bells rang especially loud in Berlin.

"If this was the prelude to something larger," Peter Sichel explained, "the beginning of a general Soviet offensive, the consensus was that Berlin would almost certainly be next."

That fear was seemingly well founded. In light of both the scale of the North Korean attack and the advanced Soviet-supplied weaponry employed in carrying it out, it was clear that, at the very least, Stalin had signed off on the invasion, perhaps even ordered it. If there was to be a second target, where else but Berlin, that nettlesome Western outpost in the heart of East Germany that the Soviets had already tried to choke off in the 1948–49 blockade?

No grand offensive came, of course, and once the initial alarm had passed, Sichel found something almost reassuring about life in Berlin in the post-Korea environment. "It might sound strange," he said, "but at least now there was a kind of clarity. After Korea, there were no more what-ifs, no more thoughts of, 'oh, maybe we're judging Russia too harshly, maybe there's still a way we can come together.' None of that. Now it was a pure war. Hopefully not a shooting or a nuclear war, but a war nevertheless."

But a war in which it appeared the United States was doomed to stumble in the dark, forever caught by surprise so long as it stayed on defense and tried to predict what the Soviets might do next. This had everything to do with the nature of their foe—and specifically, with the personality of Joseph Stalin. In the case of the other great belligerent of the twentieth century, Adolf Hitler, there had at least been a method to his madness; in *Mein Kampf*, Hitler had outlined many of his plans for European conquest and then pursued them. With Stalin, by contrast, there was no blueprint. If there was a discernible pattern at all to his actions it was that he would take whatever path might amass even more power to himself, to grab whatever he thought he could get away with. Even this, though, was hardly a guide. Testament to the *vozhd*'s ever-changing ambitions and fears and rages were the heaped bodies of most everyone who had once been an intimate. Put simply, Stalin made it up as he went along and, given the homicidal power structure he had forged in the Kremlin, there was no one and nothing to save him from his worst ideas.

Adding to this opaqueness, in 1950 the United States didn't have a single mole anywhere near the senior Kremlin leadership. It was also five years away from having the sort of advanced spy planes that could reliably chart the vast territory of the Soviet interior for signs of impending trouble, troop buildups or new missile silos. All of which meant that, as had been true since the beginning of the Cold War, the best place to gain a peek behind the Iron Curtain was in the one spot where a gap remained: Berlin.

For those operating out of the CIA base at 19 Föhrenweg, trying to gain that peek was a rarely satisfying exercise. From intensive debriefing of Easterners who managed to cross into West Berlin, the CIA was able to compile at least a pointillist portrait of some aspects of life in the Soviet bloc—a new factory being built here, a ministerial reshuffle over there—but this rarely rose above the level of general knowledge. Obviously, this was augmented with more specialized research by analysts back in Washington, but for anything more substantive, CIA officers in the field had to hope for defectors from Soviet military or intelligence agencies. Not only were such individuals few and far between, but the extreme compartmentalization of the Soviet security apparatus meant any one defector's knowledge was likely to be quite limited.

"KGB officers rarely spoke with each other about their operations," Sichel explained. "It was forbidden, so unless a defector was very high up, you would only get what he had been directly involved with. So just a very small slice of the overall picture—and naturally, even that ended, his operations shut down, the minute he came across."

Far better was to foster an ongoing relationship, to bribe or blackmail a Soviet official into passing secrets on a continuing basis or, best of all, to recruit a malcontent "defector-in-place," someone who had ideologically turned against the regime but was willing to stay and spy in his position with the promise of extraction at some future point. For obvious reasons, defector-in-place coups were very rare and, much like the bribery and blackmail routes, highly susceptible to KGB playback schemes.

For Peter Sichel and his fellow OSO officers in Berlin, this whole delicate dance, its steps learned over the past five years of spy-versus-spy skulking, threatened to be overwhelmed in the wake of the Korean War by the sudden rush of OPC teams into the city. "That's when things really accelerated," Sichel said. "All of a sudden, we were being flooded by all these bright-eyed young fellows, all ready to strike a blow against communism."

In contrast to the intense friction between the Office of Special Operations and the Office of Policy Coordination in many CIA stations around the world, Sichel described interactions between the two branches in Berlin prior to 1950 as collegial and complementary. This was partly thanks to Sichel's close relationship with the first OPC chief dispatched to the city, a Jewish émigré like himself named Michael Josselson, but also helping foster a cooperative spirit was Berlin's frenetic pace, with the sheer number of covert operations being run overwhelming any thought of assigned lanes. "It was quite haphazard," Sichel explained, "without any real method to it at all. The same guy who was the control for an agent network could also be in charge of putting on an art show or sending up propaganda balloons. That was how the CIA operated in those days."

In the wake of Korea and NSC-68, however, the OPC began running exponentially more infiltration missions into Eastern Europe, and the launch site for many of them was Berlin. "We didn't trust them being able to find secure agents," Sichel said of the OPC newcomers, "and we found them sloppy in running checks. They were supposed to check their people with us, but we weren't sure they always did. It quickly reached the point where I had to put up a wall between our operations and theirs—I never told them anything—because the people they took on were a possible threat to us."

One joint OSO-OPC endeavor that Sichel became personally involved with centered on a Russian émigré organization called the National Alliance of Russian Solidarists, or NTS. Through the late 1940s, Sichel and his OSO colleagues in Berlin used the local NTS branch both to conduct low-level espionage missions and to try to "turn" fellow ethnic Russians in the local Soviet bureaucracy. By early 1951, though, Sichel was increasingly troubled by the laxness of NTS security, a cavalier attitude that made them prone to Soviet penetration. This was joined to a kind of romantic fatalism about the struggle they were waging. "NTS agents did not despair when one of their number fell into Soviet hands," recalled David Murphy, the OPC chief in Munich at the time. "Rather, they chose to believe that one more Russian patriot had penetrated the enemy's defenses." Also working against NTS was its close and preexisting links to British intelligence, which meant all CIA operations had to be coordinated with MI6, another security soft spot.

By the spring of 1951, Sichel set out to find another Russian émigré group to work with. On David Murphy's recommendation, that led him to an outfit with the unwieldy name of the Union of the Struggle for the Liberation of the Peoples of Russia, or SBONR. OPC Munich had started working with SBONR at the beginning of 1951 to good result, so that May Sichel arranged for a contingent to come to Berlin.

"That was when I met Bill for the first time," he recalled. "He was their case officer, and he brought these guys up from Munich personally." Sichel was referring to a recent OPC hire, a twenty-six-year-old Russian-speaker from New York named William Sloane Coffin. "Well, you couldn't help but notice Bill," Sichel said. "He was handsome, strong, and just a brilliant mind—probably one of the more brilliant people I've ever known." The old spy chief paused, slowly shook his head. "Very sad what happened to him, a tragedy, really."

True to Sichel's description, William Coffin was destined to be one of the more remarkable—and sorrowful—figures to pass through the ranks of the CIA in the early Cold War.

———

Nestled below forested foothills just north of Frankfurt, Bad Homburg has long had the reputation of being one of the loveliest towns of central Germany. First gaining recognition for its purportedly restorative waters during the European health spa craze of the mid-1800s, a string of elegant hotels and a world-class casino made it a preferred destination for Germany's aristocracy and leisure class. This status was further secured in 1888 when Kaiser Wilhelm II declared his home there an official imperial summer residence.

The town experienced another heyday after World War II when, having escaped the aerial bombardments that obliterated most of nearby Frankfurt, Bad Homburg became a residence of choice of those foreign agencies and officials tasked with rebuilding Germany. One of its finest homes was that which stood at No. 2 Viktoriaweg, a sprawling neo-

Tudor mansion that, along with its own impeccably landscaped grounds, fronted on Bad Homburg's serene main park, a place where swans drifted about a shallow lake and centuries-old trees shaded pebbled walkways.

Due to the severe shortage of comfortable housing in the extended Frankfurt area, employees of the American occupation administration were assigned to requisitioned homes, with the more coveted sites naturally reserved for those in the bureaucracy's upper tiers. In the case of No. 2 Viktoriaweg, in the summer of 1951 it was awarded to a new arrival in Bad Homburg, a special advisor to the U.S. High Commissioner for Germany named Randolph Northwood.

This bestowal undoubtedly caused a good deal of grumbling among the American expatriate community since Northwood, a mere civilian in his mid-thirties and of modest job title, had somehow managed to leapfrog past a host of older and far more prominent officials in the housing queue to win the Viktoriaweg keys. What few in this community knew, however, was that Randolph Northwood—also known as Michael Burke—was actually the new OPC director of covert operations in Germany, a position that, under the peculiar guidelines of the American military occupation, gave him a ranking equivalent to that of a brigadier general. For the next four years, the Burke family, expanding to four in 1952 with the birth of a second daughter, Michele, enjoyed an almost regal existence in the Viktoriaweg mansion. It was, Northwood/Burke would later recount, "an uncommonly agreeable place in which to live a dual life."

On most every weekday, while Timmy tended to the house and their eldest daughter, Doreen, was packed off to a local kindergarten, Michael Burke made the short commute down to the offices of CIA Frankfurt, occupying one wing of the requisitioned I. G. Farben headquarters complex on the northern edge of the city. Burke was now overseeing the largest OPC covert field operation in the world, a job with staggering responsibilities. "I inherited a large disparate body of Americans with varying skills and talents," he recalled, "dispersed in a dozen locations through West Germany and in Berlin, a myriad of ongoing operations of varying quality, and hundreds and hundreds of indigenous men and women agents ranging from individual couriers to organized resistance movements."

With the individual CIA-OPC stations seeing to the nuts and bolts of their individual operations, Burke assumed more of an overseer's role, making sure the various units didn't inadvertently trip over each other— a problem inherent to covert operations—and implementing broader policy directives transmitted from Washington. Of the latter, one of the more ambitious was the so-called stay-behind program. Throughout Germany—as well as other Western Europe nations—the CIA established a network of secret arsenals, caches of weapons hidden in farmhouse basements and remote mountain chalets that, in the event of attack by the Soviet Union, would be distributed to trained cadres to slow the enemy advance. Burke spent a good deal of his time advising the CIA-Germany stations on how to amass and where to hide their arsenals, while also trying to grapple with a built-in paradox: so secret was the stay-behind program that local governments usually weren't informed (a situation that would cause the CIA great embarrassment when exposed in 1990), which begged the question of how the stay-behind fighters and their hidden weapons were supposed to find one another in an emergency.

This was only the home-base side of OPC operations. From its various stations in Germany, usually tucked inside U.S. Army bases or High Commission offices for cover, the OPC ran a blizzard of covert operations against the Soviet bloc, everything from disinformation campaigns to leaflet drops to agent infiltrations. These operations ranged across nearly 90 degrees on the compass, from Poland and the Baltic states to the northeast, across to Ukraine and the Soviet Union, and on down to Czechoslovakia and Hungary to the southeast. Given the OPC's anything-goes mandate, this meant that in any given week, Michael Burke might be asked for help in seeing to the logistics of an anti-communist political rally in Berlin, to aiding in the extraction of a blown agent chain in Hungary, to vetting potential recruits for infiltration missions into the Polish countryside. What he slightly chafed against was that most of his work didn't carry him into the field, as had been the case with Operation Fiend, but kept him moored behind a desk at I. G. Farben.

"Mine was a command function, if you will, carried out with the advantage of having myself experienced all levels of clandestine action and therefore equipped to direct others knowledgably and to share their dangers vividly if vicariously. The climate of tension for me came not from fear of an assassin lurking in a dark street or a secret police raid in the middle of the night, but from the constant awareness that those and other threats were built into the lives of our agents."

From both his own experiences in World War II and his involvement with Fiend, Burke believed he had developed a kind of intuitive sense of when to go forward with a mission and when to abort. He was to remember one proposed operation into Czechoslovakia, a cross-border infiltration that both the recruited agents and their case officer were keen to launch. Burke argued for its cancellation, but was overruled. Shortly after, the mission was compromised, the infiltration team eliminated. In the postmortem, Burke's overall superior in Germany, General Lucian Truscott, asked what had alerted him. "Finger feel," Burke replied. "A sixth sense you learn in the street."

Of course, it was more than that. In that particular case, Burke had carefully gone through the mission file several times and, if unable to fully articulate why, had detected something amiss. What he also knew was that the judgment of the case officer in such circumstances was usually worthless, that more often he was part of the problem. "A case officer tends to fall in love with an operation, tends to fall in love with his principal agent, and not notice the warts." This phenomenon frequently placed Burke in the position of doubter when all others involved with a mission strained to push ahead.

He especially assumed this role when it came to agent airdrops. In the case of a botched overland mission into a nation adjacent to West Germany, in Czechoslovakia or Hungary, for example, there was often at least the chance of rescuing an infiltration squad. That simply didn't apply to agents dropped hundreds of miles behind the Curtain, and to be compromised on such a mission meant survival depended on one's wits alone. The staggering amount of work involved in preparing for such an operation also tended to further cloud judgment, those involved naturally loath to see their endless months of physical and psychological training and counseling go for naught.

By the time Burke took over in Germany, there was a new factor to consider: the treachery of Kim Philby. Like most everyone else in American intelligence who came into contact with the British traitor, Burke had been thoroughly charmed by Philby, had never for a moment suspected his duplicity. While Philby's exposure may have shaken Burke's confidence in his own ability to spot deceit, far more profound was the shadow it cast over all the Eastern European infiltration missions. The MI6 liaison had been privy to the inner workings of Valuable/Fiend, and even if that wasn't true of the OPC's cross-border operations elsewhere, Philby had surely known their broad outline: what parts of a country were being targeted; where the commandos were trained; the approximate numbers and budget involved.

Yet against all this, the imperative to do something, the pressure to strike back against an expanding and ruthless communist empire by any means possible, an insistent urgency that started with the White House and OPC headquarters in Washington, and extended all the way down to the starry-eyed volunteer and his case officer in the field. And the fact was, the cross-border incursions, including the aerial missions, were meeting with some surprising success.

One operation that preceded Burke's arrival in Germany, the airdrop campaign to assist the WiN insurgents in Poland, showed special promise. Beginning in November 1950, OPC Germany had dropped a steady supply of agents, weapons and wireless radios to the Polish rebels, and the reports it received back indicated they were resources well spent: all across the country, anti-communist resistance was building, more insurgent cells forming. The success continued under Burke's tutelage, so much so that after one particularly pleasing field communiqué from a WiN operative, Frank Wisner crowed that the rebels needed only anti-tank weapons "to drive the Red Army out of Warsaw."

If not as spectacular, the news out of Ukraine was similarly encouraging. Folded into an ongoing penetration project code-named Operation Red Sox, in late 1949 the first of what would eventually be dozens of Ukrainian volunteers had been parachuted into areas of the country where units of the Ukrainian Insurgent Army (UPA) were known to be operating. Under the Red Sox mantle, by the summer of 1951, émigré commandos were also being infiltrated into Byelorussia, the Baltic States and Russia itself.

Where the news was most discouraging was in Burke's initial theater of operations: Albania. Through the first half of 1951, there had been several more espionage missions into the country, some by air and others by foot, but to uniformly little purpose; time and again, the commandos were quickly put to flight by the relentless *Sigurimi,* with only the luckier ones managing an escape into Greece.

But if Burke were to ever grow disheartened by the occasional losses these exercises incurred, he surely reminded himself that this was a war, and that in all wars there were both casualties and setbacks. What's more, it wasn't as if they were simply tumbling people out of airplanes and hoping for the best. The British Secret Intelligence Service (SIS) had been operating virtually identical infiltration missions into the Baltic states since shortly after the end of World War II, running supplies and agents out of Sweden to a variety of resistance groups. Those SIS missions were still ongoing in the summer of 1951 and, Burke reasoned, if it was all just pointless, if there was simply no hope that such sacrifice was making any difference, surely the British would have discovered it in Latvia or Estonia by now.

At moments of doubt, he would also remind himself of what he and OPC were there to do: "to harass and counter the Soviets by all special means—paramilitary, sabotage, black propaganda, political action—to turn loose among the chickens as many foxes as we could possibly get away with."

If Carmel Offie, the stenographer from Sharon, Pennsylvania, represented one extreme end of the OPC socioeconomic spectrum, William Sloane Coffin Jr. resided squarely at the other. Born into a fabulously wealthy and cultured New York City dynasty—his great-grandfather had been cofounder of W. & J. Sloane Company, the department store to Manhattan's elite, while his father was president of the Metropolitan Museum—Coffin had attended exclusive private schools through most of his early years until, at age fifteen, his strong-willed mother decided he was a musical prodigy. Taking him out of school, she moved with him to Paris so that he could study with some of the continent's greatest pianists. The investment paid off; in 1943, the nineteen-year-old was accepted into the prestigious Yale School of Music.

But William Coffin didn't fit the stereotype of the bookish musical virtuoso. Rather, he was gregarious, adventurous and a natural athlete, a young man of action who yearned to be at the center of things—and in 1943 there was a war on. He dropped out of Yale and joined the Army. With his fluency in French and near fluency in Russian, courtesy of his Paris-based piano tutors, Coffin was made a liaison officer with military intelligence; for a brief period, he even served as General George Patton's chief Russian translator.

"He was extremely impressive," Peter Sichel recalled. "Even though he tried to come across as a regular guy—and in a lot of ways, he was a regular guy; he drank, he chased women—you quickly picked up on the fact that this was someone quite extraordinary."

But also, as Sichel came to learn, a man haunted by a dark episode in his past.

Coffin's charmed life was turned upside down in early 1946, when he was posted to a Displaced Persons (DP) camp outside the German town of Plattling. The camp held several thousand Soviet men of combat age, most of them taken captive by the Germans during the war, and now slated to be repatriated to the Soviet Union under the terms of the Yalta agreement. This was a fate most were desperate to avoid. Some had switched sides to fight alongside the Germans, while others had joined or been press-ganged into Nazi labor battalions. Still others had simply defied the odds and survived their bestial treatment in German POW camps. Whatever their particular circumstances, in the eyes of Stalin, such men were either traitors or cowards, and by the beginning of 1946, the fate awaiting many of them once returned was well known: passage to either the gulags or to the closest execution pit. William Coffin had already been given a glimpse of what happened to Soviet soldiers whose loyalty was suspect. Shortly after the end of the war, he had been attached to a frontline American unit when a Red Army soldier wandered into their camp from the nearby Soviet line. As the unit's sole Russian speaker, Coffin was detailed to return the would-be deserter to his unit, but when he pulled up to the Soviet picket line, a drunken Red Army officer simply pulled the man from Coffin's jeep and shot him in the head.

Despite that experience, at Plattling, Coffin played the role of Judas goat, the designated chief interpreter for a U.S. Army screening committee deciding which of the camp inmates would be forcibly repatriated. Over the course of several weeks, several thousand unsuspecting inmates were brought before the committee where a cajoling Coffin endeavored to get them to talk freely about their background and, in the process, essentially hang themselves. By the time the process was over, some two thousand men were marked for repatriation. When the Plattling "raid" came early on the morning of February 24, 1946, there were enough American soldiers on hand to prevent those being deported from rioting or committing suicide, but none could harbor illusions about what they were party to. As journalist Nikolai Tolstoy related, after handing their prisoners over to the Soviets, "the Americans returned to Plattling visibly shamefaced. Before their departure from the rendezvous in the forest, many had seen rows of [prisoners'] bodies already hanging from the branches of nearby trees."

With Plattling, Coffin carried a burden of guilt that would haunt him for the rest of his life. But a guilt that perhaps could be partially expiated by a return to the Cold War battlefield. After leaving the military in 1947, Coffin had finished his degree at Yale and then enrolled in Manhattan's Union Theological Seminary with plans of becoming a minister. Instead, with the outbreak of the Korean War, he contacted his brother-in-law, Frank Lindsay, and announced he wanted to join the CIA. With his near fluency in Russian, the CIA was happy to oblige, and in November 1950 dispatched him to OPC Munich. In short order, Coffin was assigned case officer to the SBONR émigré organization, a role that led him to accompany the SBONR team to Berlin and to his meeting with Peter Sichel.

"He was very gung ho to join in the fight," Sichel recalled. "There were quite a few men like him around at that time—patriotic, idealistic, ready to take up the great crusade."

Despite its advance billing, the SBONR team Coffin brought to Berlin proved a disappointment. As David Murphy, the OPC chief in Munich who had forwarded the team, was to recall, the team leader "had little sense of operational security yet resented all efforts to moderate his behavior. He showed no aptitude for clandestine activities—a potentially fatal shortcoming in a city as dangerous as West Berlin."

After the exposure of Philby and his double agent cohorts, there was even less patience for working with potential security risks, and by that October, CIA Berlin had sent the SBONR team back to Munich. About the only benefit Peter Sichel could point to from their five-month stint in Berlin was his new friendship with their case officer, Bill Coffin.

Sichel saw little of Coffin over the next several months for, in the wake of the SBONR misadventure, the Russian-speaking OPC officer was given a new, highly sensitive task: touring those DP camps in the American sector that housed Ukrainian and Russian émigrés in search of potential new OPC recruits. But this was no longer about sending teams to turn Soviet officers in East Berlin, or to conduct quick espionage incursions behind the Curtain. In line with the new directive from Washington for bolder action, Coffin was looking for men willing to be parachuted into Ukraine to join the anti-communist guerrillas there, and into Russia to serve as deep-cover, lone-wolf agents.

Of the various men Coffin recruited, he seemed to draw especially close to a twenty-year-old Russian exile he would call Serge. "Although poorly educated," Coffin wrote in his memoir, "he had native intelligence, and his clear eyes and steady gaze reinforced the impressions his words conveyed of a man who was reliable, courageous and, in a quiet way, idealistic. He was built like a middleweight boxer."

Once Serge was recruited, he became part of a fantastically labor-intensive project, one that would consume his life for the next half-year. During that time, Coffin and other CIA specialists took turns putting their new recruit through the exhausting regimen required to build a successful deep-cover spy, one in which the physical demands, extreme though they were, paled beside those of the psychological.

Because of the Soviet Union's all-pervading internal security apparatus, any émigré agent using their real name in Ukraine or Russia would quickly be caught, their status as missing "enemies of the state" inevitably showing up on one list or another. Instead, the CIA had to build an entirely new persona for Serge, starting from his childhood and continuing up to the present day, narratives that needed to be memorized to the smallest detail. Over and over, Coffin and his assistant, Andrei, grilled the young Russian until his cover story could hardly be considered a fiction any longer but the fully integrated biography of a new person, one confirmed in every way by the counterfeited documents Serge would carry.

The training also carried constant reminders of the odds stacked against the future spy. For four hours a day, Serge practiced typing out

Morse code on the wireless radio he would be taking, while his instructor carefully studied his technique. Most every wireless radio operator develops his or her own distinctive transmission style, called "fisting," so that a very alert recipient of those transmissions can detect if another person has assumed the operator's identity. Most ominously, Serge was made to memorize those encoded clues—innocuous words or deliberate small typos or even a slightly too-long pause between two words—that would indicate to his handlers back in Germany that he had been captured and was transmitting under duress.

Understandably, given their months of constant contact, Coffin developed a strong bond to his recruits, a relationship built on deep trust and a keen awareness of the dangers that lay ahead. He described how that bond played out on the day he received Serge's dispatch orders. That night, the two of them and Andrei held an intimate drinking party at their Munich safe house. "With only three of us," Coffin recalled, "it was hardly a boisterous affair. But we felt close, having been through so much together. Serge's nervousness was barely discernible. More obvious was the quiet dignity that seemed to emanate from him, a dignity which came from the sense of purpose the mission had given his life."

Accompanying Serge to the secret airfield from which he was to fly out, Coffin spent an entire day quarantined with him in an isolated Quonset hut, the two playing endless games of cards as they waited for H-hour. When at last it came, Coffin escorted his young recruit into the unmarked spy plane, only leaving when the jumpmaster ordered him out.

The following day, Coffin got the news he had been anxiously awaiting. Shortly after parachuting into the darkness of the Russian countryside, Serge had sent out his first radio message: he had landed, all was well.

———

On the mid-morning of September 21, 1951, Michael Burke left his home in Bad Homburg for the thirty-mile drive to Wiesbaden. During the trip, he noticed the morning ground fog still hugging the lowlands and gentle river valleys that he passed. The fog was normal for this time of year in central Germany, but it had seemed especially thick the past few days, and this troubled him. Then again, it may have been that he simply needed to focus all his collective worries upon one in particular.

Burke was on his way to the U.S. Air Force base outside Wiesbaden. Once there, he would either cancel or give the go-ahead for the first secret overflight behind the Iron Curtain that he was personally overseeing since arriving in Germany four months earlier. The chief reason for his direct involvement was that this proposed overflight would extend across a far greater stretch of hostile territory than most any attempted previously. In Operation Fiend, overflights entailed crossing over, at most, about one hundred miles of Albanian airspace, with similar forays across the German or Greek borders to adjacent Soviet bloc nations ranging up to perhaps twice that. Even those flights to supply the Ukrainian guerrillas, usually routed through Turkey and then over the Black Sea, were designed to minimize the amount of time when the spy plane, rarely flying more than two hundred feet above the ground, was vulnerable to enemy radar and air defenses. But there were precious few ways to minimize the dangers facing the mission of September 21: a flight across the breadth of the western Soviet Union in order to drop a shipment of agents and sophisticated electronic eavesdropping equipment on the outskirts of Moscow. Even by charting a circuitous route to reduce air time over the Soviet Union—looping up toward Sweden and then coming in over the Baltic Sea—meant traversing six hundred miles of enemy airspace to reach the drop zone, and then six hundred more miles to get out. Given transport airplane speeds in 1951, that translated into a total of at least six hours. Professional airmen Burke had consulted gave little chance of the plane making it through the Soviets' radar screen, let alone making it back.

Testament to the gravity of the mission, when Burke reached the Wiesbaden command center, he found a cluster of quiet men—Air Force intelligence officers, the spy plane's Polish flight crew, the infiltration commandos—waiting for him. Once he took a seat in the cramped room, the intelligence officers began running through the latest information available on the risks the mission team might face. "I listened very carefully as briefing experts laid out the disposition of Soviet fighter aircraft, the [Soviet] radar warning system as they then knew it, the weather forecast—all pertinent to the route the crew proposed to fly."

Once the briefing was over, the room took on a heavy silence, all waiting for Burke's decision. The former OSS commando had been involved in enough of these sorts of operations in the past to know that, no matter how thorough the preparations or how current the intelligence, it was essentially a crap shoot—either the mission worked or it didn't—but he still carried the soldier's superstition about disaster striking at the last possible moment, when everyone's guard was down. This is what caused him to focus on the ground fog. The spy plane was scheduled to return to Wiesbaden the following morning, but if the fog was as thick then as it was now, it might be difficult for the pilot to find the runway. In the autumn of 1951, these overflight missions behind the Iron Curtain were one of the most closely guarded secrets of American intelligence and if, because of fog, the spy plane crashed upon its return or—nearly as bad— was forced to divert to a public airfield, they would be secret no more.

As if unconsciously stalling for time, Burke asked the chief Air Force briefing officer if there was any other information beyond what they'd already discussed that he should consider. The officer thought of one more thing: the weather forecast for the following morning called for ground fog.

But Michael Burke may have been searching for another, broader reason to abort.

While the aim of this particular mission was relatively modest, the ultimate goal of all these overflights and all the airdrops of supplies and weapons to rebel groups behind the Iron Curtain was anything but: to foment rebellion. That had been made patently clear to Burke in the instructions he'd been given at that very first meeting with the OPC representatives at the Algonquin Hotel: "create a revolution in Albania."

It was also clear why they had come to him. In World War II, Burke had worked both ends of the OSS airdrop missions, parachuting into France to link up with the maquis guerrillas in 1944, then helping to put together similar missions from the OSS operations desk in London. No wonder Frank Lindsay had thought of him when they needed someone to oversee Fiend, and why Frank Wisner turned to him to supervise the missions out of Germany; Michael Burke had already lived exactly what OPC was trying to do.

Except this wasn't World War II. To the contrary, Burke was increasingly coming to realize, believing that the current campaign might fuel internal rebellion actually required that the lessons of the commando-partisan operations of World War II be ignored.

In most Nazi-occupied countries of Western Europe, whatever partisan formations existed only became a factor on the battlefield when the arrival of Allied armies was imminent. Nowhere was this truer than with that most vaunted of partisan forces, the French Resistance. Despite the popular notion of a France united in undermining the rule of their German conquerors, in reality, the Resistance was little more than an intermittent and low-grade pest to the Nazis until their numbers suddenly swelled in June 1944. What happened that June? D-Day happened. A similar phenomenon occurred with partisan groups in Denmark, Holland and Czechoslovakia. If thoroughly understandable, the reticence of subdued populations to rise up against their subjugators before tangible help is near at hand didn't bode well for those partisan groups hoping to spark a popular uprising in the Soviet bloc, when their Western benefactors were not promising or even contemplating such help. Indeed, many of the pixies who survived their experience in Albania reported being mocked by locals when they couldn't produce their American allies. In essence, a handful of airdropped commandos or military advisors might help guide the actions of an ongoing rebellion, as Burke and his comrades did in the Haute-Saône, but they were not going to be the spark that started or expanded a rebellion.

And that wasn't the worst of it. In almost every Nazi-occupied country that broke with this pattern in World War II, where partisans proved a formidable fighting force without substantial outside assistance, a very different pattern had emerged: communist leadership. In Yugoslavia, Tito's communist partisans proved a far more effective fighting force than their non-communist colleagues, even with minimal supplies or logistical support coming from the West. The same was true of Enver Hoxha's communists in Albania, and with even less outside support. Clearly, the communist partisans had been able to develop and rely on a grassroots infrastructure that their non-communist competitors lacked, and it begged the question of why the opposition should fare any better now in those places where the former communist partisans were in power. To Michael Burke's knowledge, this was a question never asked about Albania, and it wasn't being asked now about the rest of Eastern Europe.

Certainly, recent developments in the Cold War suggested it should be. Just two months before Burke's briefing at Wiesbaden, in July 1951, twelve Fiend commandos had parachuted into central Albania—and directly into a *Sigurimi* security net. Six were killed outright, while four others died after being surrounded in a house that was then set on fire, choosing to be burned alive rather than surrender. The two survivors were captured and cast into prison, joining several other Fiend commandos captured previously. The losses in Albania paled next to those in Korea and China. In early 1951, OPC teams had begun training hundreds of Korean commandos to be infiltrated into the North, and hundreds more Chinese volunteers to stir insurrection in Manchuria. While those operations were still ongoing in September 1951, initial reports told of a colossal failure rate, with nearly 100 percent of the infiltrators quickly caught and killed.

This didn't mean that Burke was turning against the whole concept of working with partisan groups behind enemy lines. Certainly, the continuing reports of unrest and outright warfare in Poland as a result of the reconstituted WiN guerrilla group spoke to the possible efficacy of such actions, as did similar news from the Baltic states. Reports from Ukraine were likewise encouraging. But how long would even these successes last without the commitment of outside forces? Yes, in World War II, partisans had risked their lives to fight for the liberation of their homelands, but most had done so with at least the prospect of victory in sight. The partisans of WiN in Poland and of the Forest Brotherhood in Lithuania were similarly risking all, but how long would they continue with no reasonable prospect of ultimate success?

But these were issues to be pondered at one's leisure, not in the moment when a decision had to be made. At the Wiesbaden command center, after hearing the prediction of ground fog in the morning, Burke recalled, "I sat quietly for a few moments, drawn within myself." He once again ran through a mental checklist of pros and cons. "The overflight had been prepared sensitively and meticulously. Nothing had been left to chance but chance itself." On the other hand, "by some mishap or through Soviet alertness, we could lose the crew and the agents, killed or captured." In such a scenario, an international incident would be ignited, the American facade of plausible deniability stripped away before the entire world.

But none of these thoughts were new to Burke either, but rather the same train running the same circuit. He thought of a gambling analogy: "You can rattle the dice next to your ear just so long. Then you lay them down quietly and walk away. Or you suck up your gut, roll them out across the table and watch for the number that comes up. It seemed to me the moment had come to toss the dice."

To those silently gathered in the Wiesbaden briefing room, Burke finally looked up. "Okay," he said, "we'll go." Turning to the Air Force briefing officers, he added, "And thank you, gentlemen, very much."

When he got home that evening, Burke found he couldn't sleep. Instead, he spent the night sitting out on his terrace waiting for the dawn. As it neared, he gazed into the morning fog, and tried to judge for himself how soon it might burn away. Abruptly there came the shrill ring of the phone in the living room. Burke leapt for it, and from the other end received the news he had been waiting to hear: the mission was a success, the agents had jumped, the plane had returned.

Burke hadn't been aware that his wife, Timmy, was also awake, not until she came into the living room to bring him a cup of coffee. "Is it all right now?" she asked.

"Yes, it's okay now," he said. "Until next time."

In May 1952, Peter Sichel packed up to leave Berlin, his home of the past seven years. The official reason for his departure was that he had married his girlfriend, a German woman named Cuy Höttler, and a long-standing CIA stricture held that an officer married to a foreign national couldn't be stationed in the spouse's country of origin. In Washington, Sichel was to assume the position of CIA head of operations for Eastern Europe. It was a significant promotion, made more so by the fact that the full integration of OPC with the rest of the CIA, debated and delayed for years, was finally nearing completion.

Agency regulations aside, Sichel was more than ready to leave Berlin. Part of it came down to the unrelenting tension of working at the very epicenter of the Cold War. Like many of his colleagues, Sichel had developed the habit of turning to alcohol as a stress-relieving mechanism, and he feared it was catching up to him.

But it was more than the booze or Berlin. He was increasingly dispirited by the more aggressive posture the Agency had assumed over the previous two years, the greater risks it was asking of its agents. This was especially true of the long-distance infiltration schemes that had expanded exponentially since 1950 and that so often ended in failure, the volunteers killed or captured or simply vanished.

It also had to do with the company the CIA now kept. Sichel found particularly repellent the Agency's embrace of Ukrainian exiles joined under the banner of the Organization of Ukrainian Nationalists, or OUN. Sichel was not some pious naïf. He had understood the need to work in Germany with former members of the Nazi regime. He had even accepted the need to work with some of the more unsavory émigré leaders, men who had embraced fascism and collaborated with the Germans in the war. But the OUN was a step too far, its past crimes too well documented, its plans for a future "liberated" Ukraine sure to include more of them. "They were Nazis, pure and simple," Sichel explained. "Worse than that, because a lot of them did the Nazis' dirty work for them."

During World War II, OUN militias under the banner of the Ukrainian Insurgent Army, or UPA, had joined with the Germans during their sweep into Ukraine, and frequently served as their executioners of Jews and communist party officials. While the OUN ran afoul of the Nazi hierarchy by unilaterally declaring Ukrainian independence, resulting in its leadership being temporarily imprisoned in Berlin, the organization gained a new lease on life as the war turned against Hitler. Rejoined to the German war machine, UPA battalions had launched a terror campaign in the disputed border region between Poland and Ukraine, murdering tens of thousands of Poles in emulation of the *Lebensraum* (living room) aspirations of their German benefactors. After the war, the OUN exiles had split into two bitterly opposed factions and extended their assassination campaigns to include each other. Even though previously deemed a terrorist organization by American military authorities, by 1949 the CIA had cultivated close ties with one of the OUN factions, while the British backed the other.

Throughout the Soviet bloc, communist propagandists derided their exiled opponents as "fascists" and "mass murderers," and when it came to the OUN and UPA the propagandists had it just about right. Was this really the best the United States could do in promoting an alternative to communist rule, Sichel asked himself? Did it really serve American interests to validate the accusations of its enemies?

If this was a question of morality, another issue that troubled Sichel had to do with both feasibility and honor.

After establishing a network of secret stay-behind forces in Western Europe in the early 1950s, the CIA began to attach the stay-behind concept to some of their infiltration missions into the Soviet bloc. Since the scope of these missions wasn't on a scale that might lead to a regime's collapse, so the new line of argument went, their real function should be to create a stay-behind capability, to recruit a pool of indigenous anti-communist fifth columnists who, in the event of an actual East-West shooting war, could conduct sabotage and harassment operations behind the Soviet's front lines. Sichel had long since gained a reputation as an agency naysayer—he had been derisive of the postwar Werewolf threat, he had ridiculed the Gehlen Organization's claim of having moles in the Soviet hierarchy—and he built on that reputation with the stay-behind discussions.

"This became a big subject," he recalled, "and there was all this talk of building up a stay-behind in East Germany. I thought it was a complete waste of time. In order to do a stay-behind, you have to create caches where you put in money, arms, communications equipment, and then you have to recruit people to use that stuff if it's needed. We had no ability to do any of that in East Germany, and no [West] German had the ability to do it either, so it was a total waste of time and it exposed people unnecessarily. But it sounded good—that was the thing—and when something sounds good, it's hard to argue against."

But even if this was to be the retrofitted purpose of the infiltration operations, what galled Sichel was that this bit of news wasn't being shared with the émigré groups or with the volunteers being sent in. Instead, they were still being told that all was in the service of liberation, of overthrowing the communist regimes. That message was reinforced by the constant drumbeat of rhetoric now emanating out of Washington, and by the names of the CIA's various front groups; after all, it was the American Committee for the Liberation of the Peoples of Russia, not the American Committee for the Creation of Stay-Behinds.

"I thought that was disgraceful," Sichel said, "because we were essentially lying to these people. We were getting them to risk their lives for a lie."

But what Sichel also saw was the mechanics that kept all this going, a closed circle of motive and reward and double-speak. Whether or not the administration truly believed they could destabilize the Soviet satellite states, they needed to maintain the rhetoric that they could as a warning to the Kremlin. The émigré leaders actively promoted the notion of destabilization, perhaps because they actually believed it, but perhaps also because it was the one sure way to keep them and their organizations on the CIA payroll. In turn, the Agency's budget was predicated on how many missions it was pursuing around the globe, and how effective those missions might be in undermining Soviet rule. In this, there was a natural bias for covert action. "One boasted of intelligence, but what rings the cash register is clandestine operations," Victor Marchetti, a former high-ranking CIA officer, explained to an interviewer, "and within clandestine operations it isn't spying: it's covert action—overthrowing governments, manipulating governments."

Where in all this was a cautioning force, one that looked out for the foot soldiers on the ground bearing the actual—and often fatal—cost?

But beyond issues of morality and honor, Sichel's deepening doubts about the infiltration schemes also turned on simple reasoning. As well as any Westerner alive, the OSO officer knew how quickly and thoroughly the Soviets could button up a society. He had watched them do it in East Germany, and he had read endless eyewitness accounts of how they had done it through the rest of Eastern Europe. In drawing from only his own experience, and in considering only that one spot of Soviet bloc territory he knew best—East Berlin—he tried to imagine how long any kind of anti-communist "action cell"—that is, a unit of fighters—might last in hostile territory before being run to ground by the security forces and wiped out. Days? Hours? Certainly not weeks, and this despite Berlin still being a relatively open city (the Berlin Wall wouldn't be built until 1961) populated by hundreds of Western intelligence officers who might lend such a unit support. How much more difficult, then, to maintain a guerrilla force in a hermetically sealed police state, a place where great reward was promised to those who informed on "traitors," and where outside support was limited to the occasional furtive airdrop? To Sichel, it could only mean that those guerrilla groups still circulating in Eastern Europe and the Soviet Union were able to do so because the state was allowing it.

Shortly before his departure from Berlin, Sichel got together with Bill Coffin, and shared these various thoughts over a long evening's conversation. Although the two CIA officers were only two years apart—Sichel was now thirty, and Coffin twenty-eight—the gulf of their respective experiences on first meeting had made the difference seem more like decades. That gulf was considerably narrower now after Coffin's year and a half in Germany, but Sichel still sensed something of the romantic in his colleague, the need to believe in a higher and noble cause. This was compounded by a lingering streak of guilelessness. At the time, Coffin was running Ukrainian OUN agents into East Berlin and then, hopefully, to parts further east, but despite having worked extensively with the group since arriving in Germany, the OPC man seemed to have little inkling of its sordid past, Sichel's disquisition on the topic striking with the force of revelation. It was much the same when Sichel broadened his critique to the infiltration operations in general.

"I very bluntly told Bill that I considered them a crime. You're sending people into these Soviet-controlled areas—Poland or Ukraine or wherever—with the idea that they're going to start resistance groups or meet up with ones already there. But it's impossible that these resistance groups can exist under the Soviet security system. Look at Berlin. You can't walk down the street without the Soviets counting your steps, and you're going to go into the countryside and be part of a guerrilla group? It's a dream. It can't work. You're just sending people to their deaths."

Sichel took his argument one step further: to the degree such groups *did* exist, it was because the KGB and its Eastern European clones wanted them to exist. They were serving as catchment basins in which the regimes' enemies, both internal and external, could be concentrated and safely confined until the state was ready to scoop them up.

Sichel's words undoubtedly caused Coffin to think of the Russian volunteer he had grown close to, Serge. It was now several months since Serge had set off on his nighttime run to Russia, but after that first brief radio message, there'd been no further word from him. When at last Coffin responded, it was to mutter something that, even nearly seven decades later, left Sichel amazed.

"He became very quiet, very troubled, and finally he said, "'I never thought about that.' Can you believe it? Absolutely brilliant man, one of the smartest I've ever known, but 'I never thought about that.'" Sichel shook his head. "A lovely guy, but a total innocent."

Unbeknownst to Sichel, at that very same moment, his apprehensions over the infiltration missions were being mirrored by one of the highest-ranking officials in the CIA. This was Frank Lindsay, the man who was married to William Coffin's sister and who had also recruited Michael Burke into the Agency three years earlier.

Due to his wartime experiences with the OSS in Yugoslavia, Lindsay had always taken a particular interest in the OPC's Balkan missions, and especially with Operation Fiend; in fact, along with Kim Philby, he had been a member of the four-man task force that monitored the mission from Washington. As a result, he'd read the parade of grim situation reports coming out of Albania with mounting dismay, a parade that had culminated in an OPC status report in November 1951. By then, it was determined that of the forty-nine Fiend commandos sent into Albania, at least four had been captured, eight were dead, and nine others were presumed dead; of all forty-nine, only two were still in-country and active. An OPC review at the same time blithely noted that "the apparent ease with which [Albanian] security forces have been able to capture and ambush our teams suggests that we have overestimated our agents' survival capabilities," a problem the writer attributed to "a lack of high caliber agents." As for the missing commandos from the drop Michael Burke had overseen in November 1950, they finally surfaced in January 1952. They had spent the previous year recruiting and training a group of sixteen fighters along the Yugoslav-Albanian border, but all but two of those cadres were now dead.

Lindsay's reservations deepened further when, during a fact-finding mission to Western Europe in the summer of 1952, he put a series of questions to a Russian émigré leader whose organization was involved in the infiltration missions.

In conjuring how an ideal infiltration might play out, Lindsay posited an absolutely best-case scenario to the émigré. "Imagine you have the perfect agent in place in an important place in the Soviet Union," he said. "Just imagine the best possible man you can think of. Personal characteristics. Intelligence. Imagine that he is adequately documented, in a place where he can move around. Essentially, everything you could wish for. How long before he could feel confident enough to recruit the first person into his resistance cell?"

The émigré thought about it for a moment. "Something like six months," he replied.

Lindsay carried the scenario one step further. If this ideal agent was able to build up a cell of ten operatives, what were the odds that at least one of his recruits was a Soviet penetration agent? The émigré leader didn't have to think about this question nearly as long. "About 50 percent," he replied.

"I guess that was sort of the break point," Lindsay recalled. "I'd been building to this and thinking about it, but . . . [to hear] this from a fellow who was promoting and leading a group that was trying to do this . . ."

A couple of simple back-of-the-envelope calculations explain Lindsay's reaction. In the émigré's estimation, it would take the ideally situated and perfectly trained undercover agent five years to build up a ten-person cell, at which point there was a fifty-fifty chance he had been compromised. It would then take five more years to double the size of his cell, whereupon his odds of being uncovered would rise to 75 percent. With each subsequent ten-person, five-year interval, his chances of survival were halved again until, well before his group could even form a platoon—about forty-five men—those chances were approaching zero. Of course, the agent could decide to speed things along by having his original ten conspirators each go out and recruit ten more, but here the odds became even more dismal, exactly the same as flipping a coin and having it come up heads ten times in a row.

As Lindsay later recounted, that conversation with the Russian exile crystallized "all the things that were beginning to worry me." When he returned to Washington, he announced his resignation from the CIA. Before leaving, though, he set to work on a paper that would lay bare his grave concerns about the Agency's Eastern Europe operations.

While Michael Burke and Peter Sichel and Frank Lindsay had all soured on the CIA's infiltration schemes for a rather similar constellation of reasons, it was Sichel's theory—that the Soviets were tacitly allowing the guerrilla groups to operate—that was the most conspiratorial. Even he, though, didn't appear to carry his suspicions to the ultimate, most disturbing, possibility: what if the guerrilla groups didn't actually exist at all?

═══

For those CIA officers who had trained the Polish volunteers, the voices broadcast over Radio Warsaw on the evening of December 27, 1952, were unmistakable. Absolute proof came in the form of photographs released over the next several days. Arrayed on tables before the somber-faced "defectors"—WiN volunteers who had come to realize they were engaged in "criminal, anti-Polish activity" and surrendered to the authorities— were weapons and ammunition and wireless radios, some of the accoutrements of rebellion that the OPC had dropped into Poland over the previous two years. That triumphant broadcast represented the mission's final collapse, the last rounding up of those anti-communist insurgents of Poland's Freedom and Independence movement, or WiN, in which the CIA had placed such high hopes, who had once seemed poised to take their rebellion to the very streets of Warsaw.

Except, as the Radio Warsaw broadcasts over the next several days made clear, there never had been a WiN—at least not in recent memory. In actual fact, the Polish resistance group had been eliminated as a fighting force some five years earlier, its few remaining members reduced to fugitives hiding out in the forests. As for Stefan Sieńko, the WiN commander who in 1948 had put the word out to the West that the insurgency was alive and well, he had been an agent of Polish intelligence from the beginning, as were the WiN "volunteers" lamenting their past criminality on Radio Warsaw. This meant that all the airdrops into Poland that Michael Burke had approved over the past two years, all the volunteer commandos with all the weapons and the gold and the eavesdropping equipment that had accompanied them, had floated directly down into a trap, their arrival on the ground met by teams of KGB officers and Polish security forces. And after each such overflight, the same message was sent back to the West from "WiN": another great success, send more weapons, more money, more men.

And it didn't end with Poland. As would gradually come to light, almost all the resistance groups in Latvia, Lithuania and Estonia were either hoaxes or thoroughly controlled by the KGB, their actual members long since dead or captured or turned.

In Ukraine, it was less an outright hoax than the sort of scheme Peter Sichel had outlined: of placing one's internal enemies in a box, and then ensuring that all the aspiring troublemakers from abroad fell into that same box. While it was true that a very large and powerful anti-communist insurgency had fought Soviet forces in Ukraine to a near standstill, that had been in 1947. In the intervening years, the KGB and the Red Army had steadily annihilated the Ukrainian Insurgent Army through ambushes, infiltration schemes and collective punishment search-and-destroy missions. In March 1950, with the UPA already decimated, the KGB had tracked down and killed its fugitive leader, leaving the group rudderless. That occurred ten months *before* Frank Wisner, heartened by reports of ever-expanding UPA activity and strength, declared Ukraine to be a top OPC priority and initiated Operation Aerodynamic. By April 1952, the campaign to airdrop supplies and weapons to the UPA insurgents had become one of the OPC's biggest covert operations in Western Europe.

That same month, a Red Army field report to the Kremlin stated that the UPA was now so inconsequential that, by best estimate, the entire organization consisted of less than three hundred people banded together in several dozen isolated cells, with most of them reduced to living in underground caves. Nevertheless, buoyed by Soviet disinformation, the CIA continued with Aerodynamic for two more years.

True to its maverick status within the Soviet bloc, the Albanian regime came to the deception game a little later than the others. Through 1952, its security forces continued to ambush the incoming Fiend commandos, killing some and chasing the rest into Greece, before finally putting together their own sting in mid-1953. Their target was a legendary anticommunist leader who had already survived over a dozen forays into Albania, but who fell for an appeal sent out by wireless from one of his most trusted lieutenants. The lieutenant had long since been captured by the regime, and the commander parachuted directly into a *Sigurimi* trap. By the time Operation Fiend was finally shelved, it was estimated that up to two hundred pixies had been killed, accompanied by the retaliatory execution of as many as one thousand of their relatives.

Taken together, it suggested that the Western intelligence agencies may have had it all wrong about Kim Philby's hidden agenda during his days in Washington: instead of reporting back to Moscow on when the next group of infiltrators was arriving so that they could be stopped, perhaps he had been monitoring the West's reaction to the KGB's various deception schemes in order to ensure the doomed commandos kept coming.

By leaving for his new posting in Washington, Peter Sichel missed the final ruin of his friend and colleague, William Coffin. That came on a morning in early June 1953, in a CIA safe house outside Munich.

Just days earlier, Coffin had seen off his latest group of infiltrators, four Russian volunteers bound for the outskirts of Moscow. He was in the safe house living room when a German news bulletin came over the radio quoting a report in that morning's *Pravda* that a group of four spies had just been captured near Moscow. The Soviet newspaper went on to identify the four men in Coffin's team by name, both their aliases and their actual ones, the names of the CIA officers who had trained them— Coffin was the mysterious "Captain Holliday"—and even the address of the Munich safe house where the spies had prepared for their mission. It was the same safe house where Coffin was listening to the news bulletin. "Although stunned," he recalled, "we hadn't a moment to lose if we were to get out before any German reporters or anyone else came to visit. The wife of one of the men captured was with us. I can still see her running around the house helping us pack, while the tears poured down her cheeks."

It marked the beginning of the end for Coffin. He had joined the CIA at least in part to atone for his role in the shameful 1946 incident at Plattling, but instead had found only further tragedy, been complicit in operations all but certain to fail. A year earlier, his favorite volunteer, Serge, had gone off on his mission to Russia, never to be heard from again, and now four more men Coffin regarded as friends were gone, too, bound for the gulags or the KGB execution rooms. Shortly after, he abruptly resigned from the CIA. "It destroyed him," Sichel recalled of Coffin's tour in Germany, "just totally destroyed him. When I next saw him, he was a changed man."

Returning to the United States, Coffin enrolled at Yale Divinity School, and eventually became the university's chaplain. An avowed liberal and social activist, he was to become famous as an early and highly passionate critic of American involvement in the Vietnam War, as well as of the CIA.

Yet, even with the Radio Warsaw broadcast that exposed the WiN hoax in December 1952, there remained one last slender chance that future such tragedies might be avoided.

The timing of that broadcast was not at all coincidental, but rather meant to send a warning to the incoming administration of Dwight Eisenhower that continuing the CIA's infiltration operations into Eastern Europe was folly. The incoming president and his advisors were unlikely to heed such a warning from the enemy, but they might be more impressed by the same message coming from the man who had once overseen those operations, Frank Lindsay.

Following his dispiriting talk with the Russian émigré leader in the summer of 1952, Lindsay concluded that the CIA's infiltration missions were indefensible; he said as much in the long position paper he prepared for the new administration that autumn before he left the CIA. "I thought a memorandum ought to go to the NSC with sort of, 'This is our experience, what we've learned up to now,'" Lindsay recalled to an interviewer. "I was trying to convey, 'Think this over before you push it too far.'"

Even allowing for the dulling effect of bureaucratese, Lindsay's memorandum was remarkably blunt: "The consolidated Communist state, through police and political controls, propaganda and provocation, has made virtually impossible the existence of organized clandestine resistance capable within the foreseeable future of appreciably weakening the power of the state." What's more, Lindsay continued, the West simply lacked the tools to alter that status quo to even the most limited degree.

As a courtesy, Lindsay first showed his damning analysis to Frank Wisner, the man who had brought him into the Agency. Rather to Lindsay's surprise, Wisner was sympathetic to his arguments and reasoning. Wisner also suggested Lindsay take the memorandum to Allen Dulles, then the deputy director of the CIA and who, as a lifelong establishment Republican, enjoyed very close ties to the incoming administration. On a Saturday morning shortly before Eisenhower's inauguration, Lindsay was summoned to a meeting with Dulles at his Georgetown home to discuss the memorandum.

"He went over it, line-by-line," Lindsay remembered, "and every once in a while, he'd explode with, 'Frank, you can't say that.' And then we'd fight over the wording of that. And I probably compromised more than I should have."

Lindsay rationalized these compromises as the price to ensure that Dulles would forward his analysis on to the National Security Council and to his contacts in Eisenhower's inner circle, but this was merely taken on faith; as Lindsay himself later acknowledged, "I don't know whether [Dulles] ever sent it to the White House."

It seems clear that Dulles did not. Years later, when Lindsay thought to track down his old report, he found no record of it in the CIA archives. A watered-down and unclassified version was eventually found in a folder at the Eisenhower Presidential Library, but a folder so obscure it all but confirmed that the president never saw it.

In its absence, Eisenhower took up his campaign pledge to bring new vigor and aggressiveness to the anti-communist cause, to not just continue the subversion and infiltration operations begun by Truman, but to expand and accelerate them. Just as with its domestic offshoot, the Red Scare, the American crusade against international communism was about to take on new and even more tragic form.

Act 3

CROWDING THE ENEMY

This is the kind of time when we ought to be *doubling* our bets,
not reducing them. This is the time to *crowd* the enemy—
and maybe *finish* him, once and for all.

—JOHN FOSTER DULLES, 1953

19

AN ALARMING ENTHUSIASM

O n November 28, 1952, FBI director J. Edgar Hoover sent a top secret memorandum to his counterpart at the CIA, Walter Bedell Smith. It concerned the CIA deputy director for plans, Frank Wisner. If by circuitous route, the questions raised in the memorandum trod what was becoming very familiar ground: Wisner's wartime association with Princess Tanda Caragea of Romania.

The genesis for this inquiry had been set in motion six months earlier when the assistant director of the FBI, Louis Nichols, had received a letter from an official with the Anti-Defamation League (ADL) leveling a series of accusations against Wisner. While the nature of those charges and the identity of the accuser remain unknown—the FBI file on Wisner is heavily redacted—what is known is that Nichols, the third-ranking FBI official after Hoover and Clyde Tolson, requested that the writer resubmit his complaints on plain, nonletterhead, paper; in this way, the origin of the charges couldn't be traced. Nichols then suggested to Hoover that, while the letter seemed part of a concerted campaign targeting Wisner, perhaps a loyalty investigation of the CIA man was in order.

This coincided nicely with a recent lengthy report out of Austria updating the situation of the exiled Princess Tanda. According to that report, Caragea had led a most checkered life since the end of World War II, trading out husbands and lovers with some regularity as she flitted between various exile homes in Western Europe. Long rumored to have been a spy for a variety of intelligence agencies, both communist and non-, Tanda and her mother were now reputedly running an "intelligence shop" out of their latest exile home in the Austrian town of Dornbirn. What any of this may have had to do with Frank Wisner wasn't altogether clear, but joined to the complaints from the ADL official, it had been enough for the FBI liaison to the CIA to request a meeting with Director Beetle Smith in late May 1952. At that meeting, Smith dismissed the idea of an ongoing Wisner-Caragea link out of hand, and suggested that the accusations against his deputy were the result of a feud within the Romanian émigré community between two prominent exiles.

There the matter seemed to rest, only to be resurrected by Hoover's letter to Smith on November 28. In that letter, the FBI director once again raised the possibility of a continuing Wisner-Caragea association, this time citing information received from an anonymous "informant of known reliability." But Beetle Smith was having none of it; three weeks later, he sent a terse "eyes only" note back to Hoover stating that CIA investigators had determined that not only did Wisner have no "knowledge of espionage activities on the part of Tanda Caragea," but the two hadn't even been in contact since 1945. In closing, and in response to Hoover's request for secrecy, Smith wrote: "I have not informed Mr. Wisner of your memorandum nor of this report."

Hoover probably wasn't too bothered by this brush-off. That's because he had already accomplished what was surely his motive in raising the matter: to cast aspersions on Frank Wisner at the very moment he was a leading candidate to assume one of the most powerful positions in the American government.

Despite the initial tensions between them, over the previous two years Wisner and the irascible Smith had settled into a close working relationship at the CIA, even, according to some, a friendship. Smith had come to appreciate the probity of the man. Yes, Wisner was a lousy administrator—as one CIA historian remarked, he'd be hard put to administer a dinner for two—but there was a core integrity about the Mississippian that made him a reliable and trustworthy lieutenant. Smith had observed this time and again during the complicated merger of OSO and OPC into one integrated unit. With that merger dragging out for over a year—it wasn't fully completed until August of 1952—it was a situation tailor-made to provoke inter-office battles for primacy, yet Wisner had gone out of his way to smooth the process. That was exemplified by Wisner's relationship with his Smith-appointed deputy, Richard Helms, who had come from OSO and was innately leery of clandestine operations. Smith wanted Helms to serve as a counterweight to Wisner's impulsive tendencies, and rather than fight over decisions as one might predict, the two had settled into an easy partnership, with Wisner frequently deferring to Helms's judgment to scrap a mission.

Somewhat ironically, that balance was most often disrupted by the man Smith had appointed above Wisner, Allen Dulles. Dulles was so enamored of covert action and of being regaled with tales of high adventure from the field that among the residents of the Tempos he had won the nickname the Great White Case Officer. In fact, by the summer of 1952, Dulles was often urging covert missions that Wisner was reluctant to approve. As Smith belatedly realized, placing Dulles in a supervisory role over Frank Wisner and covert action created the very situation he'd meant to avoid by appointing Helms.

The CIA director's qualms about Dulles ran deeper than policy. Brilliant though Dulles was, there was a smugness to the former corporate lawyer that Smith found infuriating. More than that, though, a moral slipperiness, a certain streak of cunning that, to the CIA chief's mind, made Dulles less than reliable. In Beetle Smith's estimation, Frank Wisner was the sort of man who would stay loyal to the end, Dulles for as long as he perceived personal benefit.

Just three weeks prior to Hoover's November 28 memorandum to Smith, Dwight Eisenhower, Smith's former military superior, had been elected president. It was an open secret in Washington that Smith hoped to be promoted to chairman of the Joint Chiefs of Staff in the new administration (instead, Eisenhower made him undersecretary of state), but he also wanted to leave the CIA in good hands. To that end, he was reportedly lobbying the president-elect for Wisner to be named his replacement, while even more energetically lobbying against Allen Dulles. Given Hoover's vast network in official Washington, it surely wasn't long before he caught wind of Smith's petitioning efforts.

Hoover didn't approve of anyone as CIA director, of course—if he had his way, the whole outfit would simply disappear into some sinkhole—but choosing between Smith's most likely successors, Wisner or Dulles, came down to the least-bad choice. Hoover had loathed Wisner from their first meeting, and felt only slightly less hateful of Dulles. That animosity appeared to stem from a 1949 study of the American intelligence community that Dulles had conducted for President Truman, in which he pointedly never sought the FBI director's counsel. "It is outrageous," Hoover wrote at the time, "that the FBI should be excluded."

On the other hand, by the end of 1952, Hoover had a voluminous file on Allen Dulles, much of it detailing his marital infidelities. If the threat of exposure didn't keep him in line, Hoover could turn to Allen's older brother, John Foster. Eisenhower's closest foreign policy advisor and soon to be his secretary of state, John Foster Dulles was a rock-ribbed, fiercely anti-communist Republican, who could probably be relied upon to lean on his younger and more liberal brother if necessary. When it came to Wisner, however, a far less political man than Dulles and, thus, likely to be less pliant, Hoover had no obvious strings to pull to keep him in check. What he did have, though, was whispered gossip about a seven-year-old relationship with a Romanian princess. It wasn't much, but Hoover had brought men down with far less; on November 28, he sent his memo on Wisner to Bedell Smith.

In doing so, Hoover was letting both Smith and the incoming administration know that he had deemed Wisner unacceptable as the next CIA director. Left unsaid but implicit in the note was the warning that, should his judgment be ignored, there was a good chance Wisner's FBI file might find its way into the hands of one of the more aggressive statesmen on Capitol Hill—someone like Senator Joseph McCarthy, for example. In this way, the Eisenhower administration could face a public relations fiasco before it even took office. While Hoover's poison-pen correspondence was almost surely enough to scuttle Wisner by itself, his deviousness didn't end there; by getting Smith to agree to secrecy, Hoover both concealed his role as dagger-wielder and denied Wisner any chance to defend himself. It was essentially a variation of the FBI-administered loyalty board investigations in which the accused were denied the right to face their accusers—and just as effective.

With Wisner out of the running—and for reasons he would never learn thanks to a security classification placed on Hoover's letter for the next fifty-seven years—in January 1953, Eisenhower chose Allen W. Dulles to be the next CIA director.

———

Even as he appreciated Eisenhower's core appeal to the American public, Frank Wisner, both a registered Democrat and a member of the "Georgetown Set," had undoubtedly watched the ex-general's ascension to the presidency with mixed feelings.

As an "internationalist," Wisner had always regarded the isolationist cabal in the Republican Party as dangerously naive, and been hugely relieved to see them marginalized by Eisenhower. He also had nothing but contempt for nativist demagogues like Joe McCarthy and, despite a certain bashfulness in addressing the matter, rather imagined the worldly and fair-minded Eisenhower did, too. What's more, the core goals of the incoming administration—moderate social and economic domestic policies combined to a more robust stand against communism abroad—were very much ones the CIA deputy director had long supported.

That said, there were aspects of the new administration that surely gave Wisner pause. Those reservations undoubtedly began with the man Eisenhower had chosen to be the next secretary of state, John Foster Dulles.

Like his younger brother, John Foster had been a prominent New York corporate lawyer with a long-standing interest in foreign affairs. Unlike the affable and morally agile Allen, however, John Foster seemed to have inherited the severe, absolutist sensibility of their Presbyterian minister father. Ponderous in manner and given to self-satisfied pronouncements, both American and foreign officials tended to find a conversation with John Foster a tedious and one-sided exercise; as British statesman Harold Macmillan acidly quipped of him, "his speech was slow, but it easily kept pace with his thoughts."

To Peter Sichel, John Foster was a figure of pure malevolence. "He was a terrible man. Evil, totally evil." The old spymaster lowered his voice to a conspiratorial whisper. "You know, he went to church every Sunday. Never trust a religious man."

Nowhere was John Foster's moralistic rigidity more on display than when it came to the Soviet Union. To the elder Dulles brother, the fight against communism was a starkly black-and-white affair, a primal struggle between good and evil, between freedom and slavery. These weren't platitudes or propaganda catch-phrases to John Foster, but truths so enduring and self-evident they required no examination.

Sooner than anyone might have imagined, how all this might play out was put to the test when the new administration faced its first great foreign policy trial. That trial was to reveal a great deal about the internal dynamics of the Eisenhower White House, as well as the surprisingly cautionary role that Frank Wisner would increasingly assume.

⸻

The call came in at about two in the morning of Wednesday, March 4, 1953, the forty-third day of the Eisenhower presidency. Roused from his sleep, Frank Wisner was instructed to make for Allen Dulles's home on Q Street, just a few blocks from his own Georgetown residence. The two were soon joined there by several other senior CIA officials. The topic of conversation was Joseph Stalin.

Three mornings earlier, an attendant at Stalin's dacha outside Moscow had found the dictator sprawled on the dining room floor, barely conscious and unable to speak. In a fitting irony for a man who was just then orchestrating a purge of the medical community under the pretext of a fictitious "Doctors' Plot," no doctor was summoned for the next nine hours. Instead, a clutch of Stalin's most trusted lieutenants, a group known as The Four, spent the day tiptoeing into the room where he lay to gauge his condition, too paralyzed with fear or distrust of each other to do anything more. When medical help finally arrived, it was determined that the *vozhd* had suffered a cerebral hemorrhage, from which there could be no recovery. Without a source anywhere near the senior Kremlin leadership, the CIA knew none of this until a news flash on Stalin's condition was aired on Radio Moscow on the morning of March 4, still the middle of the night in Washington.

Among those gathered at the new CIA director's home, there was much conjecture on who among The Four would take the reins of power when Stalin died. Most placed their bets on Georgi Malenkov, Stalin's right-hand man for nearly thirty years, while others liked the odds of the secret police chief, Lavrenti Beria. Despite serving as Stalin's chief executioner since 1938, Beria had improbably transformed himself recently into a moderate seeking to ease tensions with the West. Garnering far less attention was the newest member of The Four, a short, chubby and unprepossessing functionary named Nikita Khrushchev. It was emblematic of the early Cold War, and of the perpetual state of unease that was its hallmark, that as the leader of the Soviet Union lay on his deathbed, the highest officials of the American intelligence community had the same level of insight as to what was happening inside the Kremlin as any Russian with a radio.

At the Georgetown conclave, Wisner steered the conversation to a more immediate concern: the proper mien the Eisenhower administration should assume as Stalin slipped away. The Russian people had a complex relationship with their *vozhd,* despite his murderous ways. Yes, Stalin had exterminated millions, but he had also led the nation to victory over Germany and wrenched the Soviet Union into the modern age, had transformed it into a superpower even as the "superior" European empires foundered. The atheist doctrine of the communist system aside, after a quarter-century of incessant beatification, the misshapen little Georgian had been elevated to something close to a living god. Paralyzing fear and swelling pride, revilement and adoration: Stalin engendered a range of emotions in his countrymen as contradictory as the man himself.

No such complicated relationship existed in the Soviet satellite nations of Eastern Europe, however. There, outside of the small ruling cliques beholden to him, Stalin was almost universally despised. In navigating between these two opposite camps at a moment of such high emotion, Wisner felt it vital that the administration make no statements that could inflame the situation, to neither enrage the Soviet people by disparaging their dying generalissimo nor give the Eastern Europeans false hope that their situation was about to fundamentally change with his passing. As noted by Dulles biographer Leonard Mosley: "[Wisner] was convinced that the Soviet satellites in Europe were in a volatile mood, and any rash talk from Washington could set a match to the fire. *And it was too early,* Wisner insisted. If the satellite peoples rose up in revolt now, the Red Army would crush them. . . . The CIA needed time to organize its clandestine forces and get arms dumps and commando forces ready to exploit the situation."

Allen Dulles not only agreed with Wisner's analysis, but arranged a predawn meeting with his brother, John Foster, so that Wisner could make the pitch directly. It worked. By the time Eisenhower was awakened with the news about Stalin shortly after 6 a.m., State Department officials were already cobbling together a sympathetic statement that the president would release later that day. "At this moment in history," it began, "when multitudes of Russians are anxiously concerned because of the illness of the Soviet ruler the thoughts of America go out to all the peoples of the USSR."

The gesture was keenly appreciated, especially in the wake of Stalin's death the following day. This was reflected in the remarkable eulogy given by Georgi Malenkov, the new Soviet premier and heir apparent, in which he vowed to strive for "peaceful coexistence" with the West, and offered that all outstanding security issues between the superpowers could be settled by negotiation. It was a message that, in its unadorned directness, would have been unthinkable mere days earlier.

It also dovetailed with an overture Eisenhower had been planning to make on his own. Since even before Stalin's death, the president had contemplated making a sweeping offer that might dramatically alter superpower relations, a call for both nations to take tangible steps to lessen their mutual suspicions and scale back their financially ruinous arms race so as to divert funding into the building of schools and hospitals. Eisenhower even toyed with the idea of proposing a summit meeting between the Soviet and Western heads of state, something that hadn't occurred since the Potsdam Conference in 1945.

But when Eisenhower finally gave his "Chance for Peace" speech in mid-April, over a month after Stalin's death, it had undergone a number of radical final-draft revisions. Despite its soaring rhetoric, gone was the conciliatory talk of the two powers sitting down as equals, replaced by a whole series of hoops the Soviets first had to jump through; to at least one American diplomat, the preconditions demanded of the Soviets essentially amounted to unilateral disarmament.

One who noticed was Winston Churchill, who had regained the British prime ministership in 1951. Upon reading the final version of "Chance for Peace" and seeing that all mention of a summit had been excised, Churchill proposed to meet with the new Soviet leaders on his own. That drew a quick rebuke from Eisenhower. "I feel that we should not rush things too much," he wrote Churchill. "Premature action by us in that direction might have the effect of giving the Soviets an easy way out of the position in which I think they are now placed."

Churchill was flabbergasted. While there was no more devout anti-communist than the British prime minister, there had always been a tactical suppleness to Churchill's dealings with the Soviets, and he had perceived the same in his first conversations with Eisenhower. What had happened since then?

In brief, John Foster Dulles happened. Since Stalin's death, the secretary of state had vehemently opposed extending any kind of peace feeler to the Soviets, insisting that they make the first move. Somehow Malenkov's repeated calls for negotiations didn't qualify. "I can say we have evaluated these speeches," John Foster sniffed at a March 20 press conference, "but we do not receive any great comfort." While steadily paring back most every olive branch contained in the proposed "Chance for Peace" speech, Dulles had then replaced them with ever more aggressive demands, leading at least one biographer to conclude that his ultimate purpose was "to foreclose any possibility of serious negotiation" with the new Soviet regime. That suggestion was reinforced when, two days after Eisenhower delivered his revised "Chance for Peace" speech, John Foster appeared before the same audience of newspaper editors to declaim that the only way to deal with the Kremlin was to apply more pressure.

For the first time, though certainly not for the last, those who dealt with the new president were struck by the degree to which Eisenhower submitted to John Foster's counsel, the alacrity with which he would reverse course on the advice of his secretary of state. In the estimation of a disgusted Winston Churchill, who positively loathed Dulles, "it appears the president is no more than a ventriloquist's doll." An alternate theory holds that the famously cautious Eisenhower knew exactly what he was doing, but used Dulles as a foil.

As to the reason for John Foster's obduracy, it was as plain and absolute as the man himself: the United States was winning. Why else would the Soviet Union, a dictatorial behemoth intent on enslaving the planet, suddenly be mewling about peaceful coexistence? It could only mean the behemoth was running scared. Just as obvious, in Dulles's view, was the source of that fear. At one end of the spectrum it was the United States' enormous nuclear weapons stockpile and its expanding network of military alliances around the world, and at the other it was the recruitment and support of anti-communist "freedom fighters" on the Cold War's front lines. All of that was about to pay dividends and Moscow knew it, so why should Washington settle now for the half-loaf of peaceful coexistence when so much more, perhaps even a complete Soviet collapse, lay just around the corner? In short, the conciliatory talk from the new Kremlin leaders was not an opportunity at all, but a Trojan horse designed to undermine America's newfound resolve as it approached the moment of final victory.

Within this oddly contradictory construct of John Foster's, that of a Soviet Union bent on world domination while also teetering on its last legs, most any Soviet action could be interpreted as proof of their malevolent intent, or of their panicked desperation, or of both at the same time. An accommodating gesture out of the Kremlin? A trick to seduce the naive before it pounced, or a gambit to cover up the feebleness that lay at its core. A Soviet deescalation of a crisis? Proof that the Reds were in headlong retreat or clever enough to take one step back in order to sneak two steps forward. It was all trickery and aggression and weakness, the Soviet Union was a great, godless monolith in a footrace between global mastery and utter collapse, and should the annihilation of Western civilization be averted, it required the eternal vigilance and unyielding resistance of the forces of good.

With excitement over the "Chance for Peace" speech soon dissipating, so did the belief that Stalin's death really carried much significance at all. Even Peter Sichel, recently returned to Washington from his Berlin posting, took note of the prevailing sentiment. "I don't recall anyone thinking of it as a watershed moment," he said, "or believing that anything would fundamentally change as a result. I think quite soon after, the judgment was that we were in for more of the same."

And if nothing had fundamentally changed in Moscow, so administration thinking went, then there was also no reason to fundamentally change how the United States confronted its rival. Instead of change, there would now just be more: more infiltration operations, more propaganda balloons, more destabilization efforts, more of everything.

All of which cast Frank Wisner in a peculiar role as the young administration set to planning a new roster of covert operations against the enemy. Certainly, no one had ever accused Wisner of being soft on communism, but after a long string of setbacks in OPC's operations against the Soviet bloc, he had steadily developed a more chastened approach to combating it. As he was well aware by the spring of 1953, over the previous four years it had been the OPC's soft power endeavors around the world, its broadcasts over Voice of America or its political conferences held under the guise of front groups like the Congress for Cultural Freedom, that had probably made the greatest impact on the international anti-communist effort. By contrast, the OPC's "hard power" initiatives—its commando airdrops into Korea, the myriad cross-border infiltration missions into Eastern Europe—had been almost uniformly futile. Wisner had first expressed doubts about the viability of Operation Fiend as early as the summer of 1952, and his pessimism about these sorts of missions had been further deepened by the revelation of the WiN hoax in Poland that December.

That pessimism was plainly evident in a top secret year-end progress report he had penned just days after the WiN story broke. Citing "the brutal efficiency of the Soviet security organizations," Wisner asserted that throughout the Soviet orbit, the state's blanketing control was such that it "reduced the opportunities for penetration, and seriously threatened existing successful operations." A year or two earlier, the deputy director likely would have closed on an upbeat, hopeful note. No longer. "Our difficulties have increased rather than decreased," Wisner concluded. "Furthermore, I am frank in stating that I cannot envisage a significant betterment of this situation."

Yet, it was precisely these sorts of aggressive operations that were most favored by the new administration, and it raised the question of how and from where a cautionary note might register. Surely not from President Eisenhower, who regarded such operations as an inexpensive alternative to military action. Given his animus for all things communist, John Foster Dulles had long argued for a more offensive approach toward the Soviets—and the more bellicose the better. Nor was a moderating influence likely to be exerted by the CIA's new director, Allen Dulles, the Great White Case Officer himself.

As improbable as it would have seemed mere months earlier, it appears that Frank Wisner was sufficiently spooked by the reflexive militarism of

men like John Foster Dulles that he saw his role within the new administration as that of a kind of brakeman. This was hinted at by the placat-
ing tone he had urged as Stalin lay dying, but it was laid bare just three
months later when the Eisenhower administration faced its first true foreign crisis. This time, it wasn't about the parsing of words or speeches, or
shadowboxing over who should make the first overture. This time, lives
were on the line.

On the morning of June 16, 1953, laborers on a building site in East Berlin were told that unless they fulfilled their state-mandated work quota,
they would receive a cut in their monthly pay. Rather than be cowed, the
approximately three hundred construction workers walked off the job.
As the strikers strode down a main boulevard of the city, they were joined
by other disgruntled laborers, and then by workers from all walks of life.
By the time the crowd converged on the Council of Ministers building on
Wilhelmstrasse, their number was conservatively estimated at five thousand. It marked the largest demonstration in a Soviet bloc nation since
communist rule had been consolidated.

The protest shouldn't have come as a complete shock. Under the burden of a Soviet-directed military buildup, joined to crushing war reparations still being paid to Moscow eight years after the end of World War II,
East Germany's standard of living was now dwarfed by that of West Germany. Despair was spurring a staggering exodus of East Germans to the
West, an average of nearly one thousand refugees per day.

With Stalin's demise in early March, many East Germans seized on the
hope that there might finally be a lessening of the grinding demands of
the state, of the shortages that left citizens scouring empty store shelves
for the most basic necessities. Consequently, it was remarkably tone-deaf
when, in late May, the governing Council of Ministers announced a radical solution to the country's economic crisis: an increase in both taxes
and the price of retail goods, joined to an across-the-board 10 percent
increase in work output quotas.

The first intelligence agency in East Germany to pick up on the depth
of the people's fury was the resident Soviet KGB. So disquieting were
their reports that, in early June, the Kremlin summoned the East German leadership to Moscow. There, in one of the odder incongruities of
the Cold War, Soviet leaders upbraided their East German counterparts
for their heavy-handedness, and ordered them to liberalize both economically and politically. After some foot-dragging, the German junta

grudgingly did so, but it was too late to forestall the construction workers' wildcat strike on June 16.

For the East German government, the situation swiftly deteriorated. Whereas the initial strikers fashioned banners asking for raises and work quota reductions, by the time the vastly larger crowd reached the Council of Ministers building, new banners demanded free elections and an end to collectivization. That afternoon, with government leaders refusing to meet with protesters, calls went out for a nationwide strike the following day.

A few years earlier, East German authorities might have been able to quarantine the disturbance to a single Berlin neighborhood, but that was before the American government's radio station, RIAS (the initials stood for Radio in the American Sector), began beaming its mix of news and entertainment and soft-sell propaganda across nearly the entire nation. By 1953, well over half of East Germans regularly listened to RIAS, far surpassing the listenership of the state-run stations. As a result, RIAS was the perfect vehicle for spreading the word about the June 17 general strike.

But some hoped for far more than a strike. After tracking the startling events in East Berlin throughout the 16th, Henry Hecksher, the second-in-command of CIA Berlin, sent an urgent cable to CIA headquarters. In anticipation of violent clashes between the East German security forces and the masses of demonstrators expected to take to the streets the following morning, Hecksher sought permission to distribute weapons to the protesters.

When Hecksher's cable came into headquarters in Washington that night, the two men with the authority to act on the request, Allen Dulles and Frank Wisner, were both out of the office and not immediately reachable. Instead, the cable landed on the desk of Wisner's newly appointed deputy for Eastern Europe, John Bross. Aghast at the prospect of the CIA distributing guns to demonstrators who might soon be going up against Soviet T-34 tanks, Bross worked up his own draft rejection of Hecksher's request even as he frantically tried to track down his superiors. At last getting hold of Wisner and explaining the situation, Bross was supremely relieved when the deputy director fully endorsed his position. As Bross would later recall, Wisner commanded, "'give support and offer asylum, but don't issue guns.' With twenty-two Russian divisions in East Germany, [issuing guns] was the same as murder."

The scope of the June 17 national strike surpassed most everyone's expectations—or, in the case of East Germany's rulers, their worst nightmares. East Berlin was virtually paralyzed by the sheer number of protesters who took to the streets, but so were towns and cities all across the country. Emboldened by their own numbers, the protesters also escalated their demands and now called for the government to step down at once.

The regime of Walter Ulbricht had a different idea. Early that morning, some twenty thousand Soviet troops were ordered out of their barracks to take up strategic positions throughout the country. By midday, with the protests quickly taking on the form of a nationwide rebellion, some of those troops began shooting. By nightfall, scores of East Germans were dead—some estimates ran as high as three hundred—and the uprising effectively crushed. Over the following week security forces launched a massive dragnet, arresting thousands of dissidents and initiating a crackdown that would soon transform East Germany into one of the most repressive of the Soviet bloc nations. In the face of the regime's brutal countermeasures, Wisner's decision to not distribute weapons appeared a wise one, that doing so would have achieved little more than increasing the body count. As he wrote in a situation report the following day, in his view, the CIA had "hit pretty close to the right line," in its response to the crisis. With the situation still extremely tense, though, he urged that the Agency "should do nothing at this time to incite East Germans to further actions which will jeopardize their lives."

But that was not at all how many Eisenhower administration officials saw it. Chief among them was the president's psychological warfare advisor, C. D. Jackson, a former Time-Life executive and OSS commander who had served as one of Eisenhower's chief speechwriters during the election campaign. Fond of quoting Thomas Jefferson on the need to nourish the tree of liberty with the blood of patriots, in Jackson's view the United States had lost a sterling chance to strike a blow against the Soviets: even if arming the East Berlin protesters didn't change the outcome, adding more martyrs to the cause would have made for good propaganda. If slightly less stridently, that opinion was shared by Allen Dulles. "It was the one time that I saw Allen angry and disappointed in me," John Bross recalled. As for C. D. Jackson, "he writhed in fury for weeks afterward."

No one was more regretful of the missed opportunity, or felt more vindicated in his hard-line stance, than John Foster Dulles. Here was final proof, he told the National Security Council the day after the uprising had been quelled, that all the recent peace gestures of Soviet Foreign Minister Vyacheslav Molotov—"undoubtedly the ablest and shrewdest diplomat since Machiavelli"—were designed only to destroy the unity of the Western powers at this crucial juncture, and to give the Soviets breathing room to do their evil best. "This is the kind of time when we ought to be *doubling* our bets, not reducing them," he expounded at a cabinet meeting a few weeks later. "This is the kind of time to *crowd* the enemy—and maybe *finish* him, once and for all."

＝＝＝

Even before making that pronouncement to the cabinet, John Foster Dulles had presided over a meeting in his State Department office that, to his mind, might set the nation on a course to do exactly that. Among the small handful of officials in attendance were Frank Wisner; John Foster's brother, Allen; and a thirty-six-year-old CIA officer named Kermit "Kim" Roosevelt Jr. In an interesting bit of juxtaposition, it had been just eight days since East Germans had taken to the streets to demand a democratically elected government, whereas those gathered in the secretary of state's office on June 25 were contemplating the overthrow of one.

Kim Roosevelt led the discussion. A grandson of President Theodore Roosevelt, the Groton- and Harvard-educated Kim had served with the OSS during World War II, and gone on to compile the Agency's official two-volume history. An Arabist, he had been an early recruit to Wisner's OPC, and one of a handful of CIA officers detailed to the Middle East at the beginning of the 1950s. He soon made his mark there. After failing to cajole the Western-pliant but fabulously corrupt Egyptian King Farouk into implementing reforms—in a nod to Farouk's ever-expanding girth, the CIA mission won the nickname Operation Fat Fucker—Roosevelt had encouraged a group of junior Egyptian army officers plotting his overthrow. The result was the Free Officers coup of July 1952, in which a young and charismatic colonel named Gamal Abdel Nasser soon came to the fore. By the following year, and with the action-oriented Eisenhower administration now in office, Kim Roosevelt was ready to make his next mark on the region.

This time, the target was Iran. Since 1951, the oil-rich nation had been the site of a fitful power struggle between its hereditary monarch, Shah Reza Pahlavi, and its elected prime minister, a liberal populist named Mohammad Mossadegh. With broad support, Mossadegh had instituted a host of social and economic reforms, including the nationalization of the British oil consortium, the Anglo-Iranian Oil Company, that had maintained a stranglehold over Iran's economy since the early 1900s. The move had placed Mossadegh on a collision course with both Great Britain and the shah. After trying unsuccessfully to force Iran into reversing course with economic sanctions, in the summer of 1952 London leaned on Shah Pahlavi to invoke a parliamentary maneuver stripping Mossadegh of his office. That gambit failed in spectacular fashion, and in the year since, the shah had become increasingly scorned by Iranians as a Western lackey even as Mossadegh's image as a nationalist and protector of the common man was burnished.

Long regarding Iran as essentially one of their vassal states, the British weren't about to let the populist in Tehran trammel their privilege unchecked. Having consistently failed to interest the Truman administration in schemes to be rid of Mossadegh, the British thought to try their luck with Eisenhower. Now they had a potent new card to play: the Red one.

Relations between Mossadegh and Tudeh, the Iranian communist party, had never been good, with Tudeh having once accused Mossadegh of being "an agent of American imperialism." That was before they had thrown their support to him during the oil nationalization showdown. Since the American government regarded Tudeh as little more than a Soviet fifth column, the British reasoned that perhaps a more effective strategy for getting Washington on board the anti-Mossadegh train was to suggest the Iranian leader was falling under Tudeh's sway. If that seemed a bit farfetched—Mossadegh had long since gone on record as an anti-communist—the British put forward the notion that Tudeh would take the country into the Soviet bloc once Iran's economy ran aground and Mossadegh lost power. While these arguments had induced little more than yawns from the Truman administration, they worked wonders on its replacement. Just two months after becoming secretary of state, John Foster Dulles approved a joint Anglo-American plan to destabilize the Iranian government. The new scheme called for the shah to again dismiss Mossadegh, but this time to swiftly name a Western-friendly replacement, one the British-trained army would support and who could be trusted to revert the nation and its oil fields to the pleasing status quo of the past.

In the three months between that initial accord and the meeting in John Foster's office, the pace of events had quickened. In May, the CIA station in Tehran began a "black propaganda" operation against Mossadegh, spreading rumors through media back channels and the bazaari gossip mill that he was in the pocket of the communists and planning to take Iran into the Soviet orbit. Key officials in the Iranian military, as well as in the shah's inner circle, were apprised of the coup plans and of the prospective roles they were to play. With everything set, in late June, Kim Roosevelt flew to Washington to brief the handful of men who would decide whether the anti-Mossadegh conspiracy, Operation Ajax, was to be scrubbed or given the final go-ahead.

According to most accounts, everyone in John Foster Dulles's office that afternoon heartily approved of Ajax, save one. That voice of hesitation was Frank Wisner.

Over the previous five years, the CIA deputy director had watched as the Middle East region, once a geopolitical backwater, had mushroomed in importance. Part of that was oil, of course, but with the steady diminishing of the French and British imperial powers that had long held sway there, a power vacuum was developing—and all vacuums are eventually filled by something. Across the region, Western-accommodationist monarchies were under threat from a younger generation of Arab nationalists and it behooved the United States, Wisner believed, to make connections and win these emerging leaders to the Western camp. That was already complicated by American support for the state of Israel, declared in 1948 over the ferocious opposition of most all the Arab world, but to even begin to counteract that, it was vital for the United States and the CIA to be on "the right side" of larger historical currents. This meant keeping a certain distance from Britain and France as they desperately tried to cling to their colonial prerogatives, and aligning as much as possible with the voices of change. That had been achieved in supporting the Free Officers in Egypt, but the proposed coup in Iran was in pursuit of the precise opposite. Wisner had opposed anti-Mossadegh schemes when they had come up in the past, fearing they would fan anti-American sentiment in the region, and he saw nothing in the revamped Operation Ajax to change his mind.

But it's doubtful that Wisner's dissent much concerned Kermit Roosevelt, who had always held a rather jaundiced view of the man who brought him into the CIA. As he was to later write of Wisner: "He was opinionated, but I had no confidence in his judgment." The CIA deputy director was "congenitally inclined to see things his way."

Besides, Roosevelt surely knew which men in that room were in charge in the new Eisenhower era. At that June 25 meeting, both John Foster and Allen Dulles endorsed the plan. The president gave his final approval shortly after.

Eisenhower and the Dulles brothers might have been less enthusiastic of Operation Ajax if they'd actually taken a good look at Shah Mohammad Reza Pahlavi. Despite the high-blown honorifics attached to his title—King of Kings and Shadow of God on Earth were but two—Pahlavi was a distinctly unimpressive figure, a nervous and frail fellow in his early thirties whose dark eyes bore a perpetual slightly stricken look. Those who knew the Iranian royal family were invariably far more impressed with Reza's twin sister, Ashraf, a quick-witted and forceful woman held to be the true power behind the Peacock Throne. Certainly, one factor the CIA and their British co-conspirators hadn't taken fully into account when launching Ajax was the shah's inveterate timidity. For weeks he dithered over their entreaties to sign the decree dismissing Mossadegh. When at last he did in mid-August, and only after being browbeaten by his sister, the shah took the precaution of fleeing the country. By the time his edict was announced and Mossadegh's enraged supporters were taking to the streets in protest, the Shadow of God on Earth was safely on his way to the plush confines of the Excelsior Hotel in Rome.

He had left behind a nation in tumult. Even as the shah's designated new prime minister, an army general, declared himself in charge, Mossadegh and his followers refused to submit, and gradually gained the upper hand in the streets of the capital. By August 18, three days into the attempted coup, CIA headquarters concluded that Ajax was a failure, and ordered its officers in the field to start shutting the operation down. For his part, Kermit Roosevelt grimly awaited word of the final collapse while drinking sloe gin rickeys and listening to Broadway show tunes in a Tehran CIA safe house.

But then, a touch of the bizarre. After several Iranian newspapers published the royal decree dismissing Mossadegh, a rent-a-mob was mobilized to chant their loyalty to the shah. The hired hands were gradually joined by spontaneous crowds of genuine pro-shah demonstrators—in essence, launching a second coup attempt. This time it was Mossadegh who blinked as his support within the military began to collapse. By the end of that next day, August 19, pro-shah army units controlled the capital, and Mossadegh and his ministers were under arrest. With the dirty work completed by others, Shah Pahlavi sheepishly returned from his Rome sanctuary.

As the shah once again consolidated his hold on his nation, aided by a declaration of martial law and mass arrests of Mossadegh supporters, Kermit Roosevelt returned to Washington and a hero's welcome. In the Oval Office, he recounted the implausible events in Tehran to a rapt audience of the president and his closest foreign policy advisors. Against all odds, and at a cost ultimately tabulated at a few million dollars, the CIA had thwarted communist encroachment in a vitally important nation, and restored the rule of a Western ally. At least that was the official story; as one high-ranking but cynical CIA official later noted, in reality, the administration had "confused" nationalism for communism.

Among those in the Oval Office that day to hear Roosevelt's post-action report was Secretary of State John Foster Dulles. So immobile was he during the presentation, leaning back in an armchair with half-lidded eyes, that Kermit Roosevelt initially thought he had fallen asleep. Then he looked more closely and saw that Dulles's eyes were gleaming. "He seemed to be purring like a giant cat."

And purring for very good reason. For Dulles and other hawks in Eisenhower's retinue, the timing of Operation Ajax's improbable success could not have been more propitious, for it came at the very moment the administration was putting the final touches on a bold new foreign policy strategy. It was called New Look, and what had just occurred in Iran exquisitely illustrated how one aspect of it was meant to work.

The core premise of New Look was that the need for the United States to retain a large standing army to deter its enemies had been mooted by the changed nature of war in the atomic age. Instead, deterrence could be maintained by concentrating resources on the far cheaper alternatives that existed at either end of the war-making spectrum: unconventional warfare at the "low" end of the scale, nuclear warfare at the "high."

In this first category were the sort of covert operations the CIA had been conducting for years, and that had so neatly brought down the Mossadegh government in August. By looking for weak spots in the enemy's armor, and by employing proxy forces to exploit them whenever possible, the United States could wage battle on many fronts and in many guises, at little cost. At the same time, the United States could deter communist aggression in regions that it deemed vital to its national security—Western Europe, for example—not by keeping a vast standing army in the field, but by the far more expedient route of threatening "massive retaliation." It was this core tenet of massive retaliation in the event of war—a nuclear strike in other words—upon which everything else in New Look rested.

If some found this worrisome, not the president; to the former general, atomic bombs were just another tactical weapon in the nation's arsenal, to be employed "exactly as you would use a bullet or anything else." As historian John Gaddis points out, there was a certain cold logic to this. Since a Western army couldn't numerically match that of the Soviet Union, let alone that of China, "to rule out nuclear use altogether would be to invite a non-nuclear war that the West could not win." The alternative then, as euphemistically laid out in the top secret New Look directive known as NSC 162/2, was for the West to amass "the capability of inflicting massive retaliatory damage by offensive striking power."

Of course, given the tit-for-tat nature of the Cold War arms race, once Eisenhower started talking about massive retaliation and first-strike options, it was inevitable that Soviet leaders would do likewise—but what could possibly go wrong with that?

———

In its first seven months in office, the Eisenhower administration had been compelled to quickly respond to three unfolding and profoundly important foreign dramas: the death of Stalin; the East German Uprising; Operation Ajax. For any of the hawks within that administration who were keeping count, CIA deputy director for plans Frank Wisner had been on the wrong side of all three. Belying his reputation as the ultimate Cold Warrior, his had been a voice of worry and caution at a time when reward awaited the bold.

Given the rapid sequence of these dramas, it was perhaps inevitable that those hawks tended to fuse the lessons derived from each, to draw together their disparate strands into a coherent whole.

In the death of Stalin, followed by the only slightly slower death of the "Chance for Peace" initiative, was the message that nothing had fundamentally changed in the Cold War. The core battle between the Soviet Union and the United States was not about personalities but systems, capitalism versus communism, Free World against captive, so it mattered little whether the man atop the Red Square reviewing stand was a murdering sociopath or a genial diplomat.

What *had* changed was the ability of the Soviet system to rule through fear. That was surely the lesson to be derived from the West's lost opportunity in the East German Uprising—and since the connection between that revolt and the passing of Stalin was so apparent, it meant there was apt to be more such upheavals in the post-Stalin era just dawning. While it had missed out in East Germany, the Free World needed to be vigilant in watching for such future cracks in the Soviet bloc, and to swiftly turn them to advantage.

From Iran came the simplest, most pleasing lesson of all, that by lending support to the right foreign leader and by working through the right proxy forces, the United States could bolster those regimes it regarded as allies, and be rid of those it didn't. For the first time, the United States had wrested back control of a nation falling into the Soviet camp, and it had done so for what, in the greater scheme of things, amounted to pocket change.

In fact, though, history was to show the utter fallacy of almost every one of these "lessons" and largely vindicate the cautious approach Frank Wisner had begun to advocate.

In the immediate aftermath of Stalin's death, Soviet rule lay in the hands of a junta—but juntas have a way of never lasting that long, inevitably a new strongman emerges. By failing to appreciate the intense competition taking place between Kremlin moderates and hard-liners—and there weren't just four men who counted in this calculus, but at least seven or eight and arguably as many as twenty—the hawks around Eisenhower robbed the administration of having much influence over the eventual outcome. To the contrary, by insisting that nothing had changed with Stalin's death, and by deriding the concept of "peaceful coexistence" in favor of a continued policy of confrontation, they undercut the moderate faction within the Kremlin and bolstered the militants. In the estimation of President Eisenhower's ambassador to the Soviet Union at the time, Charles Bohlen, by misplaying the aftermath of Stalin's death in 1953, the United States may have missed a golden opportunity to dramatically alter the course of the Cold War.

This insistence on viewing Soviet leadership as unchanging and inherently brutal also left administration hawks blind to the most intriguing aspect of the East German Uprising: that to a very large degree, the crisis had been precipitated by the severity of the East German regime colliding with the newfound *liberalism* of the Soviet one. The Kremlin leadership had summoned their East German colleagues to Moscow on the eve of the rebellion to upbraid them for the harshness of their rule, and to urge they scrap their austerity programs—advice the East Germans had failed to heed in time. As incredible as it might seem—and completely unthinkable to a man like John Foster Dulles—it suggested there was a faction within the new Kremlin leadership ready to not only act as a liberalizing force in the Soviet Union but across the greater Soviet bloc, a profoundly important development should Washington take notice. Far from taking notice, the hawks saw only the "lost opportunity" of failing to rush weapons into the East German tempest.

But to even entertain the notion of "opportunity lost" when it came to East Germany required an almost willful shortsightedness. Glided over amid the postmortem hand-wringing of men like C. D. Jackson was any appraisal of the actual logistics involved, of precisely how a small CIA unit in Berlin was meant to covertly gather up caches of weapons on a moment's notice, let alone identify those it should pass them to. It also meant ignoring the most basic truism revealed by the revolt. Given the smothering internal security apparatus that existed throughout the Soviet bloc, and that Frank Wisner had bluntly described in his year-end progress report, any future rebellion would, by necessity, be just as spontaneous as what had occurred in East Germany—which also meant impossible to predict or plan for. Given this, if either superpower moved to intervene in such a rebellion, overwhelming advantage lay with the one able to get there first and with the most guns. Anywhere within the Soviet bloc that meant the Red Army.

Even the seemingly unalloyed success of the Iranian coup was to ultimately play out very differently than the hawks imagined—and in both the short and long term. Just as Wisner had feared, the coup against Mossadegh and the CIA's obvious role in it was to fuel a deepening animosity for the United States throughout the Middle East, one that would only grow more virulent in the years ahead. In Iran, this was to culminate in the 1979 revolution that at last cast Reza Pahlavi from power, replaced by a fundamentalist Muslim theocracy that would be a thorn in America's side for at least the next forty years.

More immediately, the coup in Iran was to trigger a quick and disastrous boomerang effect on American policy in the region. Far from Mohammad Mossadegh grooming his nation as a Soviet satellite-in-the-making, a CIA after-action report would conclude that Moscow actually had no appreciable relations with the deposed Iranian prime minister at all. Instead, it was only after Operation Ajax that the Kremlin fully keyed to the idea that a whole new East-West playing field lay in the Middle East, and began jockeying for influence there. In a fitting irony, one of the first Arab leaders they would woo away from the American camp was Kim Roosevelt's friend in Cairo, Colonel Gamal Abdel Nasser.

But of all the misreadings achieved by the Eisenhower administration in its first year in office, none were to have more profound consequences than the fallacies that lay at the heart of its New Look doctrine.

Former military man that he was, Eisenhower seemed to exemplify the old cliché of generals always fighting the last war, for by the time the New Look doctrine was adopted in October 1953, the very notion of "tactical" nuclear weapons had become an anachronism. A year before, the United States had detonated Ivy Mike, a hydrogen bomb nearly one thousand times more powerful than those dropped on Hiroshima and Nagasaki. The Soviets had followed suit with their first hydrogen bomb test in August. In just a few more months, the United States would detonate the thermonuclear bomb known as Castle Bravo, which would release twice as much destructive energy as all the conventional bombs exploded in World War II; within a few years, Castle Bravo would be dwarfed by a Soviet bomb almost four times more powerful. Collectively, it meant there was no such thing as a tactical nuclear bomb; that in fact, it had already become a weapon so astoundingly destructive that its use would threaten the very existence of the planet.

Also shattered was Eisenhower's theory that, as a deterrent, nuclear weapons somehow offered a cheaper alternative to the traditional standing army of the past. To the contrary, New Look helped spur a nuclear arms race between the superpowers that would culminate in a stockpile of atomic weapons enough to annihilate the world many times over, and nearly bankrupt both countries in the process. When Dwight D. Eisenhower took office in 1953, the supply of American nuclear weapons numbered about 1,100; by the end of his presidency, it had grown twenty times over to approach 22,000. The absurdist end result, noted military analyst and historian Townsend Hoopes, "was to make the United States progressively more dependent on a nuclear capability it could not safely or rationally use."

But there were far more immediate downsides to the New Look doctrine. Specifically, the standing threat of both superpowers to resort to "massive retaliation" to protect regions vital to their national security meant that the entire rest of the world, all those nations and regions that did *not* fall within this national security rubric, were now about to become the new playgrounds of the Cold War. This would soon manifest in the form of assassinations and coups and proxy wars across the breadth of Asia, Africa and Latin America that would continue into the 1980s.

And still something else: what of those regions that the superpowers *did* deem vital to their national security, specifically the rival blocs of nations of Western and Eastern Europe? With New Look, these blocs were now off-limits to the enemy, and any effort to subvert their status meant to flirt with the tripwire that could initiate "massive retaliation" and trigger nuclear holocaust. Thanks to New Look, the Cold War and its European battle line were now immovable, locked in place.

The problem was, it seems no one in the Eisenhower administration had figured this out yet. Incredibly, there is scant evidence that anyone involved in formulating New Look ever fully pondered this obvious result of the "massive retaliation" precept. The consequences of this oversight would become apparent in three years' time in the streets of Budapest.

20

RED SCARE REVIVED

Both during and after his presidency, Dwight Eisenhower benefited from the image of being an avuncular, grandfatherly man, the reluctant statesman who somehow rose above partisan politics. Upholding that image requires overlooking his craven conduct when it came to confronting the character assassination tactics of Senator Joseph McCarthy.

As he campaigned for the presidency in the summer of 1952, Eisenhower made no secret of his contempt for McCarthy to his inner circle, especially when the Wisconsin senator began excoriating General George Marshall. Marshall had quite literally made Eisenhower's military career, plucking him from the oblivion of being a fifty-one-year-old barracks officer when the United States entered World War II, to engineering his appointment as commander of the European theater of operations less than two years later. Yet, Eisenhower did not publicly defend Marshall against McCarthy's attacks during the 1952 campaign, heeding the advice of Republican Party advisors that to do so might cause a rift within the party. On several later occasions, Eisenhower was to say he deeply regretted his decision, but it isn't the considered judgments of hindsight, but actions actually taken that show the true character of a person. What Eisenhower's conduct revealed was that, for all his carefully honed image of humility and integrity, the future president was an intensely ambitious creature, one willing to compromise on the most basic precepts of personal honor if it might play to his political advantage.

One who had looked beyond the public facade and taken the new president's measure was FBI director J. Edgar Hoover. If candidate Eisenhower hadn't stood up to McCarthy despite being on a glide path to the White House, it was highly unlikely that a President Eisenhower would, dependent as he was on a razor-thin Republican majority in Congress to get his policies enacted. All of which meant that, courtesy of Eisenhower's timidity, Joe McCarthy, so recently perceived as in eclipse, was headed for a renaissance at the beginning of 1953, and that the Red Scare he had come to personify would not only continue but intensify. And just as before, J. Edgar Hoover suddenly had every incentive to try to harness the coming McCarthy whirlwind to his own purposes.

As Eisenhower assiduously looked the other way, McCarthy went about the task of rebuilding his power base in the new Congress. A vital first step was his taking over the chairmanship of the previously obscure Senate Committee on Government Operations. While many of McCarthy's Senate colleagues heaved a sigh of relief at seeing the Wisconsin firebrand relegated to this legislative Siberia, they apparently failed to take note of the committee's investigative function and its loosely worded mandate to examine "government activities at all levels." With its subpoena powers, McCarthy turned the committee's investigative arm, the Permanent Subcommittee on Investigations, into his most powerful platform yet in perpetuating the Red Scare. Much of that power derived from the brutal effectiveness of its chief legal counsel, a twenty-five-year-old Department of Justice wunderkind named Roy Cohn. On J. Edgar Hoover's personal recommendation, Cohn moved over to McCarthy's Senate subcommittee in January 1953. At his insistence, he was joined there by another twenty-five-year-old, his close friend G. David Schine, as an unpaid "chief consultant."

Physically, the two young men could hardly have been more different: Cohn, slight and short with a streetfighter's curdled face; Schine, tall and fair-haired and extraordinarily handsome. By most all accounts, the contrasts extended to the cerebral. Where even Cohn's detractors conceded his brilliance—having graduated from Columbia Law School at the age of twenty, he'd been forced to wait a year to take and pass the New York bar—Schine seemed a far dimmer bulb, apparently gaining admission to Harvard largely on the strength of his being heir to the family fortune of the Schine Hotel Corporation. What the two had in common was a ferocious anti-communism and a knack for rubbing people the wrong way. A *Harvard Crimson* reporter who in 1954 conducted an exhaustive search of Schine's collegiate contemporaries could find just three people willing to say something nice about him, with one of those being Schine's personal valet. For his part, Roy Cohn would be memorably credited in a Broadway play as being "the worst human being who ever lived."

None of which was to bother Joe McCarthy in the slightest. To the contrary, he keenly appreciated the prosecutorial firepower he had gained with Cohn and Schine, and the use for which Hoover hoped to see them employed. In a message clearly designed to be passed on to the FBI director who had made the arrangements possible, McCarthy informed Cohn shortly after his hire that "nothing interested him more" than finally going after the CIA. In the Wisconsin senator's hands, that assault was fast in coming.

━━━

When Peter Sichel arrived in Washington in the summer of 1952 to take up his new position at CIA headquarters, he became aware of a curious anomaly to his life. For nearly a decade, he had been a spy in loyal service to a country he actually didn't know very well, having only lived in the United States in that brief period between when he and his family escaped Vichy France and when he had returned to Europe with the OSS. The greatest adjustment was settling into Washington—still something of a sleepy Southern city in 1952—and a predictable work routine, so different from the endless crises and round-the-clock tensions of Berlin. Moving into a comfortable home at the northern limits of the city with his new wife, Cuy, Sichel joined a carpool with four other CIA officers who lived in the same leafy neighborhood. Each morning, the five men would talk shop during their half-hour drive to CIA headquarters down by the Reflecting Pool.

At headquarters, Sichel, the new chief of operations for Eastern Europe in the Secret Intelligence branch, worked in close proximity to the two men who had persuaded him to remain with OSS Europe back in 1945, Frank Wisner and Richard Helms. "This was really when Dick Helms and I became close friends," Sichel recalled. "We saw each other every day, and he was someone whose judgment I implicitly trusted." His interactions with Wisner were a bit more removed. "I saw him often in social settings and work settings, and we became good colleagues. He had that amazing Southern charm, you know, but quite aside from that, he was just a very nice man."

Sichel was less generous in describing Allen Dulles. Courtesy of his position in the senior ranks at CIA headquarters, Sichel was a close observer of the internal power struggle that followed Eisenhower's election, and that ultimately led to Dulles being chosen as director. "That never should have happened," Sichel said bluntly. "Allen was a great guy in a lot of ways, but he carried himself with this air that caused everybody to think he was much more capable than he was. He really wasn't. He would have made an excellent headmaster somewhere, but he never should have been put in charge of the CIA."

Sichel's specific complaint was that Dulles was a bad administrator, and had no interest in improving. "He loved all the spy stuff, running agents, and he loved to hear about operations in detail, but that wasn't his job. His job was to run an agency, and he didn't know how to do that. [Bedell] Smith was a son of a bitch, but he knew how to run an agency. Even Frank [Wisner], who didn't know the first thing about management, would have been better, because he would have applied himself."

Yet, very soon after Dulles took over at the CIA, a series of events would cause Sichel to see the director in a much more favorable light—if still not for his managerial skills, at least for his courage.

A rejuvenated Joe McCarthy came after the CIA almost immediately. In mid-March 1953, less than two months after the change of administrations and not even one month since he had officially assumed the CIA directorship, Allen Dulles was called to appear before McCarthy's subcommittee. There, he was handed a list of twelve CIA employees the senator deemed security risks. This hardly seemed likely since, upon the most cursory of checks, it was determined only two of the twelve were still CIA employees, while others were completely unknown to the Agency. Incensed that his time was being taken up by McCarthy's frivolous provocations, Dulles reportedly carried his complaints all the way to Eisenhower.

But McCarthy just couldn't stay away from the CIA. By the following month, Dulles was concerned over rumors that the senator was about to target his friend and deputy, Frank Wisner, based once again on innuendoes over Wisner's wartime association with Tanda Caragea. As an internal FBI memo of late April 1953 noted, "reports about Wisner's past activities are again circulating in Washington and Senator McCarthy allegedly has taken an interest in Wisner's past." Left unsaid in the FBI memorandum was the fact that the origin of these reports was almost certainly the FBI itself.

While the assault on Wisner was defused, at least temporarily, McCarthy's next salvo came in early June when he announced that he "had reason to believe" there were over one hundred communists on the CIA's payroll, a number he seemed to pull out of thin air and that Allen Dulles derided. The senator and his investigators were finally given at least a little something to work with the following month when Dulles announced he was hiring William Bundy, a prominent New York lawyer, to serve as his chief of staff in the Office of National Estimates, the CIA branch tasked to providing comprehensive security briefs to the president and National Security Council. Given Bundy's FBI background file, Roy Cohn came upon a nugget that, by the standards of the Red Scare, amounted to pure gold: several years earlier, Bundy had contributed to the defense fund of a law firm colleague, the accused spy and now disgraced Alger Hiss. On the morning of July 9, Cohn called the CIA and demanded Bundy appear before the investigative subcommittee within the hour to answer his questions. CIA officials instead spirited Bundy out of Washington and then sent him on vacation, well beyond the reach of McCarthy's young investigator. An incensed McCarthy retaliated by issuing a subpoena for the CIA's congressional liaison and accusing Dulles of a "blatant attempt to thwart the authority of the Senate."

But Allen Dulles now clearly appreciated the deepening peril the CIA faced. The perpetual scheming and backbiting of J. Edgar Hoover could be parried, but the knifework of McCarthy and his committee was having a deeply corrosive effect on the Agency, breeding intrigue and dissension. Disgruntled CIA employees or those looking to topple a bureaucratic rival had taken to secretly passing information to McCarthy's investigators. Others were being blackmailed into doing so by the so-called McCarthy Underground. "Within the CIA," wrote Lyman Kirkpatrick, the CIA inspector general at the time, "we had cases where individuals would be contacted by telephone and told it was known that they drank too much, or were having an 'affair,' and that the caller would make no issue of this if [the recipient] would come around [to McCarthy's office] and tell everything they knew about the Agency."

With the Bundy affair, Allen Dulles took the fight into the open. Going up to Capitol Hill the day after the controversy broke, he met with McCarthy and other Republican members of the Government Operations committee. After an exchange of pleasantries, Dulles calmly turned to the Wisconsin senator and said: "Joe, you're not going to have Bundy as a witness." The CIA director then called the White House and threatened to resign if the president didn't back him up. Seeking to avoid an embarrassing resignation just six months into his term, Eisenhower dispatched Vice President Nixon, a fellow Red-baiter who had a good rapport with McCarthy, to convince him to drop the Bundy matter. McCarthy grudgingly did so. As a face-saving gesture to the senator, Dulles agreed to a compromise protocol that allowed for the questioning of CIA officials in certain circumstances, but he also made sure that official Washington knew he had won. Given the inside scoop, columnist Joe Alsop, who also happened to be an Allen Dulles friend, crowed that "McCarthy has just suffered his first, total, unmitigated, unqualified defeat."

Dulles sought to drive home his advantage. A week later, he assembled a group of some six hundred CIA officials in a government auditorium— the size of the gathering seemed designed to ensure word of it would spread—and announced that any CIA employee caught passing information to McCarthy's committee without approval would be summarily fired.

The effect of Dulles's victory over McCarthy was electric. At CIA headquarters, Peter Sichel sensed an immediately rejuvenated atmosphere. "It was probably the greatest thing Allen ever did as director," he said. "He had lots of flaws, but to his eternal credit, he told McCarthy to go to hell, and he was the first one in the administration to do that. It marked a real turning point—not just for the Agency, but I think for the entire government."

Which wasn't to suggest that the American Red Scare hysteria was ending anytime soon. As Peter Sichel steadily came to realize, much of the virulence and lasting power of the Red Scare stemmed from it having been conjoined in most Americans' minds to the even more pernicious antigay scare. Somewhat mirroring Joe McCarthy's own waxing and waning fortunes, the Lavender Scare had enjoyed a brief heyday at the end of the 1940s, with Carmel Offie being one of its more prominent victims, before falling out of the spotlight with the onset of the Korean War. In the Eisenhower presidency, however, the Lavender Scare was headed for a revival, one that both Hoover and McCarthy helped stoke.

In 1952, the American Psychiatric Association had for the first time classified homosexuality as a mental illness—specifically, a "sociopathic personality disorder." In veiled language, tabloids and right-wing newspapers issued dark warnings about the prevalence of homosexuals in all walks of life, with the more strident publications drawing a direct link between homosexuality and communism, how the acceptance of one often led to adoption of the other. As if this weren't enough, fastening it all into place was President Eisenhower's Executive Order 10450 of April 1953. Ostensibly meant to identify potential security risks, among other fireable offenses the order summarily banned from employment in the federal government anyone who engaged in "notoriously disgraceful conduct" or "sexual perversion," code for homosexuality. Since this ban also extended to government contractors, it meant that some twelve million American workers, or 20 percent of the national labor force, were affected.

"So it became a self-fulfilling prophecy," Sichel explained. "If you say some human trait is a security risk—it could be homosexuality or red hair or whatever—and you start firing people because of it, then naturally those people will try to conceal it. As soon as they do that, voilà, they're security risks."

And even truer than with the Red Scare, given the sexual mores of the time, once "accusations" of homosexuality were leveled in the Lavender Scare, there was virtually no viable defense for the victim. Indeed, their only options were to surrender and go quietly, or to fight back and be forced out anyway, as was the fate of thousands of federal workers.

In response, Peter Sichel took it upon himself to try to protect those CIA colleagues that he could. "This was around the time they brought in the lie detector tests as part of your background investigation," he recalled, "and one of the main questions they asked was about any homosexual conduct. So my first idea was to say to everyone, 'anything of that nature in your background, just tell us. Write it up, and we'll lock the paper away in a vault somewhere. You do that, you can't be blackmailed, so you're no longer a security risk.'" Novel though the idea was, it didn't survive an airing with Sichel's superior, Richard Helms. "Dick said, 'Peter, are you smoking pot? There's no way with our government that you could get away with this.' He felt as I did about the ban, but there was no way around it."

Sichel next came up with a different solution—a particularly radical one.

"I went around to people in the Agency that I suspected were homosexual—no one talked about it openly back then, but you usually knew—and I told them very diplomatically, 'I don't think you have the chance of a long-range career at CIA, better to do something different and get out now.' Because with the lie detectors, even if they got past the first test, they were eventually going to be caught, so why waste the next four or five years of their lives before being forced out or never promoted? I didn't mention homosexuality. I didn't mention anything. I just spoke to them as a friend, and I think most were very grateful for what I said."

While acutely aware that his counsel effectively perpetuated a cruel system, Sichel saw little alternative. "It's easy now to say, 'no, stay and fight,' but that would have gone absolutely nowhere back then, and these were people's lives you're talking about."

To Sichel's surprise, one person who agreed with his actions was Frank Wisner. Somewhat awkwardly, the topic came up while the two stood at adjacent urinals in a CIA headquarters bathroom.

"I hear you're telling people to quit the Agency," Wisner said.

After a brief hesitation, Sichel replied, "Yes, I am."

He then proceeded to outline his reasons, fully expecting it might pre-cipitate an argument; after all, Frank Wisner's reputation was that of a zealot, a true believer who deemed the anti-communist struggle worth any sacrifice—even one's career or future advancement if it came to that. This wasn't Wisner's reaction, however. "People have this idea of Frank being an archconservative—which he was in some respects, I suppose, but not when it came to social issues. And he was also very fair-minded."

After pondering Sichel's explanation, Wisner said he fully agreed with him, then turned and walked away.

At the same time that Peter Sichel watched the renewed Red Scare play out in the hallways of official Washington, Michael Burke was afforded a front-row seat to one of its more bizarre manifestations at his post in West Germany. It occurred shortly after the lunch hour of Wednesday, April 8, 1953, when Roy Cohn and David Schine, now both twenty-six years old and clad in business suits, strode purposefully through the entrance doors of Amerika Haus in downtown Frankfurt. They were trailed by a small horde of radio and print journalists.

For the previous five years, the Amerika Haus building at No. 12 Tau-nusanlage had served as one of Frankfurt's preeminent cultural gather-ing spots, an early prototype of a State Department initiative designed to present and subtly promote the American way of life to foreign audi-ences. This "Marshall Plan of Ideas" had struck an especially responsive chord among the citizens of Frankfurt. So popular was Amerika Haus that, by 1953, its staff of librarians had swelled to over two dozen, while its program of live events, everything from readings by writer Thornton Wilder to concerts by the Juilliard String Quartet, played to standing-room-only crowds.

But to a newly empowered Joe McCarthy, all of this was a boondoggle at best, a Trojan horse for the dissemination of Red propaganda at worst. Even before launching his abortive attacks on the CIA, the senator had zeroed in on his favorite whipping boy, the State Department, and espe-cially its cultural, or soft power, components, a realm where both victory and headlines were assured. The department made for an especially easy target with an acquiescent John Foster Dulles at the helm.

At McCarthy's behest, Cohn and Schine set out for Europe in late March. Their target this time was a little-known State Department ini-tiative known as the Overseas Library Program. It was this that brought the pair to Amerika Haus in Frankfurt, although by then their venture

After Stalin's death in 1953, Churchill urged the new American president, Dwight Eisenhower, to make a peace overture to the Soviets. The idea was vetoed by Eisenhower's right-wing Secretary of State, John Foster Dulles (left). Churchill was appalled by the sway Dulles had over Eisenhower, calling the president "no more than a ventriloquist's doll."

With John Foster Dulles's brother, Allen, heading up the CIA, the Agency's "golden age" of covert operations was born. Known around CIA headquarters as "the great white case officer," part of Dulles's fondness for covert action stemmed from the high cost involved and the effect this had on Congress. "I know the way they think up there," he told a deputy. "If there's no real money involved, it can't be that important, and they just won't pay much attention to us."

Trying to blend in: Peter Sichel (right) and two other CIA officers relaxing on a lake in West Berlin, early 1950s. When Sichel was transferred back to CIA headquarters in 1952, his penchant for shutting down dubious espionage operations won him the enmity of some case officers—and an FBI investigation into rumors he might be a Soviet spy.

The doomed 1953 East German uprising against the communist regime ended with the deaths of scores of demonstrators and the imprisonment of thousands more. The following year, Secretary of State Dulles pressured Michael Burke to provoke another revolt, figuring that the resulting bloodbath would embarrass the Soviets.

Magsaysay with Frank Wisner and Lansdale's chief deputy in the Philippines, Charles "Bo" Bohannon, left. After "Our Man Magsaysay" crushed the communist insurgency as Philippine defense secretary, Lansdale, Wisner and the CIA helped propel him into the presidency in 1953.

French soldiers marching into captivity after their humiliating defeat at Dien Bien Phu, May 1954. The victory by Ho Chi Minh's Viet Minh fighters appeared to herald the end of Western intervention in Indochina—until the Americans stepped into the breach.

Shifty-eyed stare-down: Vice President Nixon awarding Edward Lansdale a medal as Lansdale's wife, Helen, looks on. The Eisenhower administration adjudged Lansdale a miracle-worker for his success in the Philippines, and in 1954 sent him to Vietnam to "do the same thing." Marking the United States' first unilateral military intervention in Indochina, Lansdale's Saigon Military Mission consisted of a mere twelve junior officers.

Just as with Magsaysay in the Philippines, Lansdale grew extremely close to the leader of South Vietnam, Ngo Dinh Diem, right, with the two men even vacationing togethe When the Eisenhower administration decided to overthrow Diem in 1955, the coup was thwarted at the last minute by Lansdale's urgent appeal.

Diem with Eisenhower and John Foster Dulles in Washington, 1957. Despite having plotted his overthrow two years earlier, Diem was now "our man in Saigon" in the eyes of the president and secretary of state. Both resolutely looked the other way as Diem assumed ever greater dictatorial powers, helping fuel the communist insurgency in Vietnam and escalating American military involvement.

Soviet First Secretary Nikita Khrushchev electrified the world with his 1956 "De-Stalinization" speech in which he denounced the brutality and crimes of his predecessor. This was followed up by a series of economic and political reforms, and the release of tens of thousands of political prisoners. The Eisenhower administration, and most especially Secretary of State Dulles, were not at all impressed.

Although the CIA had been trying to provoke an anti-communist insurrection in one of the Soviet satellite states for years, the Agency—and much of the rest of the world—was caught completely off-guard by the spontaneous Hungarian Revolution in October 1956.

Even as Budapest fell to the Soviet army onslaught, Hungarian rebels clung to the belief that the Eisenhower administration would come to their aid. That aid never came. With the revolution crushed, some 200,000 Hungarians fled into the West.

Hungarians of all ages joined in the failed 1956 revolt, but the involvement of youth, like the boy pictured here, led to a particularly cruel sidenote. With the execution of minors legally barred, Hungarian officials had to delay carrying out death sentences given to young rebels until they were of legal age. As a result, state executions continued until 1960.

Wisner in the library of his Maryland farmhouse, late 1950s. Wisner felt personally betrayed by the administration's refusal to help the Hungarian rebels, helping spur a mental collapse that would lead to his hospitalization, shock therapy and, ultimately, early retirement from the CIA. He would take his own life in 1965, on the ninth anniversary of the Hungarian Revolution.

Michael Burke at the retirement ceremony for New York Yankees star Mickey Mantle, 1969. After leaving the CIA, Burke briefly managed Ringling Brothers circus, before becoming a media executive and New York sports venue president. He is best known to a generation of New York sports fans as the Angel of Death: during his tenure, the fortunes of the Yankees, the Knicks and the Rangers all abruptly plummeted.

In happy retirement, Peter Sichel with Gina Swainson, Miss World 1979, promoting the Sichel family's Blue Nun wine label. "It was a crusade," Sichel says today of his earlier career with the CIA, "a romantic crusade."

was already generating considerable publicity. In Paris, journalists had trailed the two investigators as they embarked on a shopping spree in the city's most fashionable salons, and also took note when they skipped out on their hotel bill. Coyly playing to rumors that Cohn and Schine were lovers, a German reporter observed them playfully roughhousing in their Frankfurt hotel lobby, before "both of them disappeared into Mr. Schine's room." The same journalist then collared a chambermaid who could report that "their contents were strewn throughout the room. The furniture was completely overturned."

In the Amerika Haus lobby, the pair were met by its director, a soft-spoken academic just a few years their senior named Hans Tuch. Cohn got right to the point: "We understand you have a lot of communist books in your library. We want to see them."

Nonplussed, Tuch replied that he didn't think there were any communist writers represented in the library at all.

"Do you have any books by Dashiell Hammett?" Cohn asked.

When the library director conceded that he did, in fact, have the American novelists' two most famous books, *The Maltese Falcon* and *The Thin Man,* a triumphant Cohn turned to the band of journalists. "See! Nothing but communist books in this library."

Setting the Hammett novels to one side, McCarthy's advance men spent the next half-hour or so scouring the Amerika Haus bookshelves for more offending volumes.

From his office at CIA Germany headquarters just down the road from the Frankfurt library, Michael Burke might have found all of this slightly amusing if actual lives and careers weren't at stake. Like most everyone else at the CIA, Burke had been appalled by McCarthy's sudden rise in 1950, and was now increasingly alarmed that the Red-baiting senator seemed to be flourishing anew with the help of an acquiescent White House. Most ominous of all, to Burke's mind, was the clear connivance of J. Edgar Hoover's FBI with McCarthy. Already by the time of Cohn and Schine's arrival in Frankfurt, Burke had been witness to the professional destruction of one close friend through this tag-team arrangement, a man named Charles Thayer.

A Foreign Service officer who had served at the American embassy in Moscow during the 1930s, Thayer had been with the OSS during the war, and then rejoined the State Department in its aftermath. Brilliant if somewhat brusque, in 1948 Thayer was chosen to head the State Department's Voice of America broadcasting system, arguably the United States' most potent weapon in its Cold War propaganda arsenal.

It was there that Thayer first ran afoul of Hoover; his original offense, by most all accounts, was having the temerity to complain about FBI delays in completing background checks of VOA employees. An enraged Hoover ordered his men to conduct a full investigation of the agitator. By working their network of government moles, FBI agents stumbled upon an old State Department report that offered a most eclectic rap sheet on Thayer, alleging both that he'd had an illegitimate child with his secretary and that he was a closeted homosexual. Among the "evidence" for this latter charge was testimony that, during his OSS service in war-time Yugoslavia, Thayer had frequented a restaurant at which he'd been served by a gay waiter named Marko, despite other dining options being available. Although Truman had repeatedly rebuffed Hoover's efforts to have Thayer dismissed, it was at least in part to escape the FBI director's relentless pursuit that Thayer left the VOA in 1949 for a succession of lower-profile diplomatic postings in Germany.

But once on the hunt, Hoover didn't give up easily. Shortly after McCarthy's splashy 1950 debut, the senator received an anonymous letter laying out a roadmap of investigative avenues to pursue to bring down a State Department official named Charles Thayer; the remarkably specific details in the letter were lifted straight from FBI files. Once again, though, and despite McCarthy's best efforts, Thayer had survived.

It was while Thayer was serving as U.S. consul general in Munich in March of 1953 that Hoover finally got his man; he personally sent a thirty-eight-page, single-spaced report on the diplomat to Eisenhower's chief of staff, noting that it was a mere "summary" of allegations against Thayer, some of which had to do with "moral conduct." That was quite enough for the new administration. Just three days later, Thayer was informed that he was being dismissed from the State Department on morals charges, a judgment that he could either publicly contest or keep under wraps by voluntarily resigning. Like virtually all other Red/Lavender Scare victims, he chose the latter course, resigning from the Foreign Service after nineteen years of service and effectively blacklisted.

It was the rapidity of Thayer's fall that shocked Burke. During Truman's presidency, there had at least been an element of institutional resistance to McCarthy's attacks, with both agencies and individuals under assault occasionally able to mount stout—and, at times, successful—defenses. With the advent of the Eisenhower presidency, it was suddenly every person and every agency for himself. While that might translate to a degree of protection for Burke and his colleagues in Allen Dulles's CIA, it was a very different story for anyone in John Foster's Department of State.

Unbeknownst to Burke at the time, on the day that the Cohn & Schine roadshow turned up in Frankfurt, another of his State Department comrades in Germany was in imminent danger of being purged. This was Theodore Kaghan, the deputy director of public affairs for the U.S. High Commission in Germany, and the overall administrator of the very soft power mediums—radio stations and publishing houses, cultural centers and fellowship programs—that Joe McCarthy was constantly railing against and had sent his young minions to Europe to expose.

Kaghan had already come to McCarthy's attention. Several weeks earlier, his investigators had been shown enough of Kaghan's civil service file from a source in the FBI to discover that, as an undergraduate at the University of Michigan in the late 1930s, Kaghan had penned a play about the Spanish Civil War that received positive attention from the communist newspaper, the *Daily Worker*. Around that same time, Kaghan signed a nominating petition for a communist to win placement on a local ballot. Despite the passage of fifteen years, during which Kaghan had fought in World War II and edited anti-communist newspapers in Germany and Austria, these "sins" had come back to haunt him; twice that March, he was made to answer long questionnaires from McCarthy's subcommittee detailing his youthful transgressions.

Still, there was a chance that Kaghan might have survived were it not for an unfortunate sequence of events at the Frankfurt Amerika Haus that day. As McCarthy's young investigators continued their hunt through the library shelves for offending volumes, a trailing UPI reporter baited Cohn by asking when he would start the book-burning—"you know, just like Hitler did in 1933."

"We're not here to burn books," an annoyed Cohn replied, "we're here to find communist books."

"Well, Mr. Cohn," the reporter shot back, "if you're not going to burn any books here, you don't interest me," and then promptly left.

McCarthy's investigators were still seething over that slight when it came over the newswire that Theodore Kaghan had just nicknamed the pair "the junketeering gumshoes," a label gleefully passed on to them by the attendant press and one that would haunt Cohn and Schine for the rest of their star-crossed European tour. It was probably at that very moment, standing amid the shelves of the Frankfurt library, that Roy Cohn decided to get his revenge by destroying Ted Kaghan.

Within days, Kaghan was ordered back to Washington to testify before McCarthy's subcommittee. At that hearing, the senator's investigators trotted out more "incriminating" evidence gleaned from FBI investigative files. The State Department official fiercely defended himself, but to little avail; hastening to do McCarthy's bidding, John Foster Dulles reportedly ordered Kaghan's termination papers drawn up even before he had finished testifying. Upon returning to Germany, Kaghan followed Charles Thayer's example of a few weeks earlier and announced his resignation.

But it was with the purging of Theodore Kaghan that State Department officers in the field finally made a stand against their agency's own cowardice. On the evening of May 28, a grand going-away party was held for Kaghan at the La Redoute club outside Bonn, a gathering that drew American diplomats from across northwestern Europe, as well as the senior ranks of the American political, military and intelligence establishment in Germany. Among the attendees, some 250 in all, were Michael and Timmy Burke.

In its own decorous way, the gathering at La Redoute was something altogether remarkable, a collective act of protest by high-level American officials—generals and admirals; ambassadors and CIA station chiefs—against an administration too craven to stand up to a demagogue, or to limit the damage he was inflicting. But if any of those gathered in Bonn that night imagined the vendetta might end with Ted Kaghan, they would soon be set right. In fact, even at La Redoute, rumors circulated about who might be next on the McCarthy hit list.

As it turned out, this was to be Samuel Reber, the acting U.S. High Commissioner to Germany, and another close friend of Michael Burke's. Given unfettered access to State Department personnel files, McCarthy's investigators had already trained their sights on Reber as a possible closeted homosexual, and he had been compelled to take two polygraph tests on the matter. In true witch hunt style, however, what finally sealed Reber's fate was his refusal to support Roy Cohn's denunciations of Kaghan.

One of the most unseemly aspects of the Red and Lavender Scares—and an aspect that obviously helped perpetuate them—was the phenomenon by which the friends and work associates of those targeted would desert them lest they, too, come under suspicion.

In response to the churnings of the gossip mill about Reber's fate in the early summer of 1953, Michael and Timmy Burke did the opposite, and arranged to have dinner with Reber at his home in Bonn. "We three sat alone at one end of a long table built to seat twenty," Michael Burke recounted, "all knowing that Sam too would get the chop in a day, a week, but we dined quietly, intimately as good friends will, saying nothing of what we all knew was in the offing." Sure enough, within days of that dinner, Samuel Reber was gone, too.

For Burke, as for so many other Americans of the political center or left or even mainstream right, the dramatic resurgence of Joseph McCarthy and his allies in the early months of the Eisenhower administration was bitterly ironic: anti-communist inquisitors like McCarthy and his toadies had adopted the tactics and mind-set of the communists they vilified. But every society has its would-be demagogues; in Burke's view, what made matters infinitely worse in this instance were those powerful government officials who, whether due to cowardice or because they saw the Wisconsin senator as a useful fool, were enabling McCarthy to do his worst, men like John Foster Dulles.

Despite the ridicule heaped upon Cohn and Schine for their assault on the Overseas Library Program, Dulles ordered the State Department to comply with their dictates. So zealous was this compliance that, by the summer of 1953, some thirty thousand books and magazines had been removed from the shelves of American cultural centers abroad, including works by Jean-Paul Sartre, Henry David Thoreau and, of course, Dashiell Hammett. In some centers, so many books were removed that librarians simply ran out of storage space for them all. In those instances, and not-withstanding Roy Cohn's outrage when the suggestion was put to him, the offending books were burned.

21

WHITE KNIGHT

I t was a preposterous cover story: Edward Lansdale, Air Force colonel, CIA contract officer and most recently psy-war advisor to the Philippines president, had been appointed to the lowly position of resident historian of the U.S. Thirteenth Air Force—and "assistant historian" at that. No longer was his theater of operations the jungles of Luzon or the barrios of Manila, but rather a government-issue metal desk in the archives room of Clark Air Base. Preposterous, but that was part of its charm; it appealed to Lansdale's sense of the absurd, the material it provided for a good yarn.

Lansdale "earned" this new job title in March 1953 as a result of his escapades of recent months. After orchestrating Ramon Magsaysay's triumphant tour of the United States and Mexico in the summer of 1952, he had accompanied the defense minister back to the Philippines and there set to work to make his friend the nation's next president. His efforts were aided by the fact that, with the communist Huk insurgency all but snuffed out, a large stockpile of CIA counterpart funds was suddenly freed up for other purposes, and Lansdale quietly used a good portion of it toward building a political infrastructure for "Monching" Magsaysay. Where this got a bit ticklish was that Lansdale was still technically attached as an advisor to the sitting Philippine president, Elpidio Quirino, who would be opposing Magsaysay in the November 1953 elections. Loath to ever stand up to the Americans, Quirino publicly suffered this indignity in silence, while complaining bitterly about it in private. When Lansdale went on leave to the United States in early 1953, Quirino saw his opportunity to strike and made plans to bar his return.

While the Eisenhower administration officially professed neutrality in the Philippine presidential contest, that stance fooled no one—least of all the American embassy in Manila who were all in for "Our Guy" Magsaysay. Sensing the Magsaysay campaign beginning to drift in Lansdale's extended absence, in early March the ambassador put in an urgent request for his return. John Foster Dulles didn't need to be asked twice. Figuring that Quirino wouldn't have "the guts" to expel Lansdale if he once reached the Philippines, the secretary of state called up Lansdale and ordered him to get back to Manila as quickly as he could and "by the least obvious way." Two days later, Lansdale was in the Philippines.

What hadn't been worked out, though, was any plausible rationale for his return in the face of Quirino's opposition. The head of the American Military Assistance Advisory Group, or MAAG, had long resented the CIA man's encroachments onto his turf, and wasn't about to provide him with a MAAG cover assignment. In lieu of any more credible explanation for his presence, Lansdale was seconded to the American military archives office at Clark as an assistant historian. This was only the starting point of the American shell game. On orders to keep a low profile, Lansdale would sneak out of Clark to confer with Magsaysay in a variety of Manila safe houses, while staying one step ahead of the local press who wanted to expose him, and two steps ahead of the Quirino goon squads who hoped to kill him.

Some observers found Washington's flagrant boosterism of Magsaysay and bare-knuckle approach to toppling Quirino unseemly. But far more importantly for administration officials back in Washington watching all this unfold, it worked. At the same time that Lansdale endeavored to stay in the background—he no longer appeared onstage at Magsaysay political rallies, for instance—he drew from his advertising background to build the kind of populist campaign machinery only recently becoming a mainstay of American politics. In the Philippine version, this manifested as a gaudy and exuberant display of Monching supporters taking to the streets with posters and floats and balloons, their progress marked by firecrackers and whistles and blaring loudspeakers. Always highly attuned to the power of music, Lansdale helped refashion a campaign song, "The Magsaysay Mambo," into a tune so catchy it became a national hit. With that, he was finally convinced "Our Guy" would win.

He was right. When the votes were tallied in November 1953, Magsaysay had swamped Quirino by over a 2-to-1 ratio. In celebration, and in play to his populist image, Monching threw open the gates of Malcañang Palace to his supporters, to be immediately swarmed by tens of thousands of well-wishers.

With Magsaysay's election, Lansdale's work in the Philippines was effectively finished, and he flew back to Washington in early January 1954. He intended to put in a request for an extended leave to spend time with his family—he had scarcely seen his two young sons in the past several years—before taking on any other long-term assignment. It wasn't to work out that way for, soon after his arrival, he was called into Allen Dulles's office.

To the CIA director, what Ed Lansdale had achieved in the Philippines made him a kind of Cold War white knight, an exemplar of the gentler face of covert operations and of what might be achieved by sensitivity and subtle coercion rather than by guns and sheer force alone. By January 1954 another trouble spot was emerging in Asia, one in which the Eisenhower administration also hoped to expend as little blood or treasure as possible, and it surely wouldn't hurt to have a known problem-solver take a look. What did Ed Lansdale think about going to Vietnam?

"Not to help the French!" Lansdale glowered.

No, the CIA director assured him, not to help the French; rather, to assist the Vietnamese people in navigating their way to independence while also dealing with a communist insurgency. Put in its simplest terms, Dulles explained to his visitor, "we want you to do the same thing in Vietnam that you did in the Philippines."

None of this came as a surprise to Lansdale. The previous summer, he had been temporarily pulled off his Magsaysay-for-president campaign to join a military fact-finding mission to Vietnam headed by Lieutenant General John "Iron Mike" O'Daniel. By then, French rule in its Southeast Asian colony was becoming increasingly threatened by a communist guerrilla war that had raged since 1946. For six weeks, the O'Daniel mission had crisscrossed Vietnam in the escort of French military advisors, observing the colonial government's counterinsurgency operations. O'Daniel had urged a far more aggressive approach on the French and, with its adoption, predicted they would have their communist problem licked within two years' time.

Lansdale wasn't so convinced. Indeed, many of the characteristics of the French military machinery in Vietnam—its nationwide network of fortresses, its ponderous reliance on heavy weaponry, the murderous depredations of its hit-and-run commando units in the countryside— reminded him of nothing so much as the failed strategies the Philippine army had employed against the Huks in the early years. But the French had an added problem the Philippine army, even on its worst days, never faced: to all Vietnamese, even those on their payroll, the French were viewed as occupiers, invaders—and no one is ever truly loyal to an invader. As Lansdale wrote in his own report, Vietnam was likely to stay in ferment so long as the French remained on the scene and maintained the status quo.

And the French campaign against the Viet Minh guerrillas was radically different from the Philippine example in at least one other crucial aspect. Once Ramon Magsaysay became defense minister, the Philippine army proved highly receptive to new ideas, whereas with the French in Vietnam there was simply no mechanism for a Magsaysay to emerge. To the contrary, from the moment Lansdale had arrived in Saigon, he was made aware of the contempt with which the French army held their local hirelings, a disdain reflected by the dearth of Vietnamese officers in any sort of command position. That disdain also transferred to the American fact-finding commission, and most especially to one of its junior members, Colonel Ed Lansdale. A number of French officers had studied Lansdale's counterinsurgency ideas put into practice in the Philippines but, appalled by his egalitarian approach with the locals, mainly took away what *not* to introduce in Vietnam lest the colonial system be upset. According to Lansdale, some French officers had been so aghast at seeing him come off the plane at Saigon airport as part of the O'Daniel mission that they petitioned the French commander in chief to deny his entry.

Exaggerated or not, that episode reflected the resentment the French military in Vietnam held for the American interlopers, an antipathy that extended from senior commanders to foot soldiers in the field. The French were very happy to be bankrolled by the Americans—since 1950, the U.S. had borne much of the cost of the war effort in Indochina—but that didn't mean they had to like them or listen to anything they might say. In true Gallic tradition, and despite their rather spotty record when it came to such outings in recent decades, the French army was going to fight the war in Vietnam their way.

Having observed French intransigence in Vietnam firsthand in 1953, Lansdale initially wasn't sure what to make of Allen Dulles's proposal the following year. What role was there for an American counterinsurgency specialist on a French battlefield in Southeast Asia?

The short answer was that Vietnam was no longer merely a French concern, that conditions had so rapidly deteriorated in the months since Lansdale's first visit they were approaching a crisis. On January 8, just a few days before Lansdale's meeting with Allen Dulles, Vietnam had been the main topic of discussion at a meeting of the National Security Council. At that session, President Eisenhower had railed against French incompetence in Indochina, but also made clear that he had no intention of sending American troops into the breach. "If we did so," the NSC recorder quoted the president, "the Vietnamese could be expected to transfer their hatred of the French to us. I can not tell you, said the President with vehemence, how bitterly opposed I am to such a course of action." Instead, he appointed a special working group drawn from the Defense Department and the CIA, the President's Special Committee on Indochina, to analyze the situation and come up with possible solutions. It was probably right about then that Allen Dulles, a member of the special committee, began thinking of Ed Lansdale.

As the CIA director assured Lansdale at their meeting, none of this meant he had to go rushing off to the war zone. Instead, the colonel could use the next several months to spend time with his family as he gained a thorough grounding on the Southeast Asia situation, perhaps even took some Vietnamese language classes.

The leisurely pace being promised was made possible because, in fact, the news out of Vietnam in January 1954 wasn't uniformly bad. Two months earlier, the French had unveiled a new battlefield stratagem called the hedgehog, or *hérisson*. It consisted of swiftly seizing control of a vital point on the map—a key crossroads, perhaps, or a commanding mountain ridge—and then erecting a network of heavily fortified and interlinked firebases that the Viet Minh would eventually have to attack. The French had first employed the *hérisson* in a valley called Na San in late November and it proved a spectacular success, with a series of futile enemy frontal assaults producing as many as six thousand Viet Minh casualties while leaving the valley firmly in French hands. That same month, French troops had begun setting up an even more elaborate *hérisson* in a remote mountain valley called Dien Bien Phu. By that January, Dien Bien Phu was studded with a constellation of firebases manned by some ten thousand troops; now the French were just waiting for the Viet Minh to repeat their Na San mistake and come in to be slaughtered.

Though no one seemed to have a problem with it at the time, the code name chosen for the Dien Bien Phu campaign, Operation Castor, would seem a puzzling one for a military operation that involved establishing a fortress in an isolated valley without the means to watch for an approaching enemy. In Greek mythology, Castor was acting as a lookout when he chose a highly vulnerable position—in his case, up a tree—where he was caught by surprise by an enemy and slain.

Not that such a fate appeared in store for the French in January 1954. On the last day of that month, the American ambassador reported that it now appeared the Viet Minh, having learned their lesson at Na San, were not planning to attack the Dien Bien Phu garrison after all. This development, the ambassador noted, came as "a great disappointment to French command."

———

For three years, Michael Burke's palatial home in Bad Homburg was a hive of cheery activity, a favored gathering spot of the expatriate community in central Germany. At No. 2 Viktoriaweg, Timmy Burke "entertained with gracious good taste," her husband wrote, playing host to an ever-varying guest list of diplomats and journalists, high-ranking CIA officials and friends visiting from the States. And should the couple ever feel the need for a break from Bad Homburg, all of Western Europe beckoned, cheap and inviting and only lightly touristed. "We listened to opera in Berlin and Munich and attended the Salzburg Music Festival," Burke recalled. "On holidays we drove to Spain or Switzerland or France."

This idyll didn't extend to Burke's professional life. While much of his supervisory work could technically be conducted from CIA headquarters, the string of fiascoes that had marked the infiltration missions caused him to increasingly check over their preparations in person. This meant a constant shuttling between CIA stations and safe houses across Germany, interspersed with tense huddles in the Wiesbaden air command center as he decided whether to approve or abort a spy plane's flight behind the Iron Curtain.

As exciting as it might sound to the outsider, by the close of 1953, this existence was beginning to pall for Michael Burke. Part of his dissatisfaction simply came with the territory, those pedestrian workplace frustrations that, if not as exotic as Burke's, are common to most any office worker. The merger of the OPC and OSO the previous year had translated into new layers of both bureaucracy and oversight. No more those freewheeling days in Rome when Burke had run Operation Fiend—and his bogus Imperial Pictures—as a virtual one-man show. As an added aggravation, he was frequently at odds with other senior CIA officials posted to Germany. After butting heads with his OSO counterpart, Gordon Stewart, Burke had fared even worse when a new CIA country director was brought in, a retired four-star war-hero general named Lucian Truscott. As near as Burke could tell, his fatal faux pas with Truscott was his failure to be waiting on the tarmac when the general had first arrived in Germany in 1951, a slight that Truscott apparently held against his deputy ever afterward.

But along with job burnout and office politics, Burke felt a deepening despair over the political direction the United States was taking. For most Americans, even those to the political left of center, the Red Scare was largely an intellectual affront. More than the actual numbers of lives destroyed was the atmosphere of fear and distrust the Red and Lavender hysterias engendered, the sense that the most innocent association might somehow come to the attention of the loyalty boards or one's employer. For a CIA officer like Michael Burke there was the added insulation of belonging to an organization that stood in defiance of Joe McCarthy.

Except in a place like Germany—and perhaps especially in Germany—there really wasn't any insulation. There, the small community of American diplomats who lived and worked in the frontline nation were people that Burke dealt with most every day, and who he knew to be selfless and decent and loyal. Within this tightly knit group, just as among the larger group of State Department employees in Washington, so great were the numbers being dismissed that one could be forgiven for believing McCarthy was doing the Soviets' dirty work for them, eliminating much of the senior American foreign policy community that opposed them. A dark joke circulating through diplomatic circles at the time held that the most successful Soviet agent of the age was not Kim Philby or Donald Maclean, but rather the junior senator from Wisconsin.

There was also more generalized fallout, like that which had followed the tawdry little spectacle at the Frankfurt Amerika Haus. Burke had found it embarrassing to try to explain the antics of Cohn and Schine to German friends, an embarrassment turned to humiliation as books disappeared from library shelves and the wildly popular cultural programs sponsored by the State Department were slashed one after another due to congressional budget cuts. For a man like Burke—erudite, cultured, liberal, but also engaged in a war where ideas themselves were weapons—it was all enough to call into question just what sort of nation and society he was fighting to defend. It was a question that came into even sharper relief on that day in early February 1954 when Burke was summoned to Berlin, there to meet with the man he increasingly held responsible for setting the United States on such a ruinous path: Secretary of State John Foster Dulles.

The meeting took place at a comfortably appointed guesthouse in West Berlin on the morning of Sunday, February 7, 1954. Besides Burke and Dulles, only two other people were in the room: the chief of CIA Germany, Lucian Truscott, and President Eisenhower's psychological warfare advisor, C. D. Jackson.

In Burke's memory, the gathering got off to a very awkward start. Dulles, slouched in a stiff-back armchair and gazing out a window at the grounds beyond, didn't speak or even acknowledge his visitors' arrival for a long time.

While Burke had never held John Foster's politics in high regard, that view now extended to his person. "He was dour and cold," he would recall. "Studying him, words like harsh, unbending, intolerant came to mind. I imagined him dressed in sixteenth century robes, an ally of Thomas Cromwell, condemning Sir Thomas More to the headsman."

Dulles and Jackson were in Berlin to attend a meeting of the Council of Foreign Ministers (CFM) that had begun two weeks earlier. Established at the Potsdam Conference in 1945, the council was comprised of the foreign ministers of Great Britain, France and the Soviet Union, along with the American secretary of state, with the idea that these "Big Four" representatives would regularly meet to discuss and hopefully resolve issues of global concern. For a time, these semiannual meetings had proven surprisingly effective—a number of postwar peace treaties were resolved at CFM conferences, as was the Berlin Blockade—but then all collapsed in 1949 over the issue of German reunification. Ironically, in light of what was to transpire, the council had been resurrected at the instigation of John Foster Dulles as a way to sidestep calls for a summit meeting between the American and Soviet heads of state. Contending that such a top-level summit would play into Soviet hands, Dulles suggested a meeting of foreign ministers instead. Still, since this was to be the first CFM session in nearly five years, many had approached it with high hopes, an opening act that might lead to an easing of East-West tensions in the post-Stalin era.

But not if John Foster Dulles had any say in the matter. While a number of very weighty issues were on the council agenda—the worsening war in Indochina between France and Viet Minh nationalists; the future status of Austria, still under four-power occupation almost a decade after war's end—Dulles had been utterly unyielding in his talks with his Soviet counterpart, to the growing frustration of the British and French delegations. On that Sunday morning, Dulles was contemplating taking the initiative in the talks, but in a very different manner than his European allies might have hoped. It was to this end that he had sent for Truscott and Burke.

Still staring out the guesthouse window, John Foster finally intoned: "It would be interesting to have a disturbance in East Berlin."

Another uncomfortable silence followed. Burke, for one, wasn't at all sure for whom the comment was meant. "Perhaps he was saying it to

CD Jackson, or aloud to himself. He certainly did not direct it to Truscott or me. It was, I assumed, his way of introducing the reason for our summons."

Dulles held a pencil in his right hand and, in the extending quiet, he raised its sharpened end to his mouth and began rhythmically tapping its lead point against his upper front teeth. Burke watched, transfixed. "It made little black dots," he remembered. "I was so riveted by this strange habit—the imperceptible click of the pencil's point against his teeth and the accumulating black dots—that I was slow in answering his specific question."

That question mirrored Dulles's initial statement: "Can you create a disturbance in East Berlin?"

Burke finally understood that, as CIA head of covert operations in Germany, this question was meant for him. Caught off guard, he replied that, yes, provoking a disturbance in the communist zone was probably possible, but precisely what did the secretary have in mind?

"Something that would embarrass the Russians," Dulles replied, "demanding they get out."

Burke still didn't fully grasp where all this was going. "Are you suggesting a city-wide riot?" he asked. "Or some local disturbance? I'm trying to get a fix on the dimension, so I can give you an accurate answer."

Dulles was growing impatient. "What could you do?" he snapped.

"In what space of time, sir?"

"While the conference is on. While we're sitting with the Soviets. Say in the next two or three days."

It now dawned on the CIA officer exactly what Dulles wanted. Seven months earlier, East Berliners had marched through the streets asking for free elections and better living standards, and been machine-gunned for their trouble. Now, the American secretary of state was fantasizing about provoking another demonstration, one sure to draw another violent response from the state, as a way to embarrass the Soviets at the CFM meeting.

Too stunned to form a reply, Burke merely watched the secretary, still slouched in his armchair, still staring out the window. "The room fell silent again," he recalled, "except for the pencil point tapping almost inaudibly against Dulles' front teeth. I had an urge to brush mine."

Anxious to get away, Burke offered that he would see what he could work up but that it was very short notice. Once out of John Foster's presence, he cornered C. D. Jackson.

Burke surely knew that, in Jackson, he was appealing to the very man who had wanted weapons to be rushed to the East Berlin demonstrators the previous June, who blithely talked about the need for martyrs—but C. D. Jackson was all Burke had.

"Does he really want this?" he asked.

"Of course he does," Eisenhower's psy-war advisor replied.

"People are going to get hurt, you know?" Burke pushed. "They're willing, but just to make sure everyone knows this kind of thing has a price."

Jackson didn't need to be told there was a price—a price well paid, in his view, if it might further tarnish the Soviets' image. "You've made your point," he said brusquely, then turned and walked away.

With the collusion of Lucian Truscott, Burke simply played beat-the-clock for the next several days, steering clear of the secretary of state and his retinue until it was safe to report back that there wasn't enough time to organize a riot. But that encounter with John Foster proved a kind of breaking point for the CIA man. Shortly after the close of the ministers' meeting, Burke was the apparent author of a secret cable sent to the director of the CIA, John Foster Dulles's brother, Allen. Even in an agency where candor was theoretically welcomed, the critique of John Foster's thwarted scheme was blunt, bordering on contemptuous. "There will not be another 17 June," the cable stated. "Western efforts to promote repetition or even minuscule demonstrations would abort dismally and produce severe condemnation in both GFR and GDR [West and East Germany]."

But rather than let it go at that, Burke expanded his remarks to include German reaction to the latest tempest involving Joe McCarthy. In a recent round of Lincoln Day speeches, McCarthy and his acolytes had adopted the theme of "twenty years of treason" for their escalating attacks on the Democratic Party, accusations so incendiary that even the timorous Eisenhower had been moved to issue a vague warning against "extreme partisanship." As the cable concluded: "Lincoln Day antics [of] McCarthy, [Senator William] Jenner and Co. have caused renewing [sic] loathing and contempt among all classes." The reaction to Eisenhower's gentle rebuke fared little better. "President's fine sentiments received very cynically in absence decisive action [to] dissociate or discipline right-wing demagogues."

For a man long known for his unfailing charm, Michael Burke was growing bitter.

———

To begin to grasp the broad contours of the Vietnam conflict that would come to dominate the third quarter of the twentieth century—as well as to be given a taste of its mind-bending complexity—a sufficiently bewildering place to start is in the immediate aftermath of World War II.

Following France's surrender to Germany in 1940, her beleaguered colonies in Indochina swiftly came to terms with Germany's Asian ally, an advancing imperial Japan. In return for making Indochina's natural resources available to the Japanese war machine, the French colonialists, or *colons,* were allowed to maintain a collaborationist government similar to that established by Vichy France. That cozy arrangement prompted the communist party of Vietnam, led by a nationalist leader named Ho Chi Minh, to wage guerrilla war against both occupiers, until the Japanese violently ousted their French puppet ally outright in the closing days of the war. Despite the efforts of Ho's Viet Minh guerrillas, Japanese soldiers were still in control of Vietnam at the time of Japan's official surrender in August 1945.

In order to facilitate their surrender—some 65,000 Japanese soldiers were scattered along the one-thousand-mile length of the country—at Potsdam the victorious Big Three powers had agreed to temporarily split Vietnam at the 16th parallel, with the Chinese Nationalist forces of Chiang Kai-shek given the mandate of restoring order in the North, while some twenty thousand British troops were brought in to do the same in the South. Conspicuously left out of this stopgap solution were the two forces most determined to control the future of Vietnam: the French and the Viet Minh.

But not absent for very long. In late August 1945, Ho Chi Minh got the jump on the approaching Chinese forces by marching his troops into Hanoi, the North's principal city. On September 2, he took to Hanoi's main square to proclaim the independent Democratic Republic of Vietnam, and to repudiate any future French administration for Vietnam. This repudiation also didn't last long. In order to force out the Nationalist Chinese "peacekeepers" who were pillaging their way across northern Vietnam, Ho invited the French back in as part of a temporary power-sharing arrangement. In the South, the situation was even more confusing. Taking advantage of the arrival of the British troops who had come to disarm the Japanese, the French *colons* took control of Saigon, the south's principal city, and restored the French colonial government. With the Viet Minh renewing their attacks on the government, the thinly stretched French troops turned to help from both the British and the surrendered Japanese. Thus, in a mere five months, the Japanese-French *colon* relationship had gone from one of collaboration, to a war in which Japanese troops had suddenly either slaughtered or interned their erstwhile French allies, to a peace in which the surviving French prisoners of war were released to help round up the defeated Japanese, to another war in which the French freed their Japanese prisoners of war to fight alongside them against the Viet Minh—and 1945 wasn't even over yet.

To try to make sense of all this, Allen Dulles had promised Ed Lansdale that he would have several months to methodically study the region and its conflicts before venturing to Vietnam in person. That didn't happen. Instead, soon after arriving in Washington, Lansdale started being besieged with plaintive late night telephone calls from now-President Magsaysay imploring his return to the Philippines to advise him on his fledgling administration. To placate his friend, Lansdale offered to arrange a stopover in Manila when finally he headed to Vietnam, but that wasn't good enough for Magsaysay. Going over Lansdale's head, the Philippine president put a call through to his American counterpart, petitioning Eisenhower to send Lansdale on quickly. So it was that in early April, Lansdale once again left his long-suffering family and headed back to Manila.

The revised plan was that, once things calmed down with Magsaysay, Lansdale would return to Washington for intensive orientation sessions before finally going on to Vietnam—but this didn't happen either. Instead, at the end of May, the lieutenant colonel received terse orders to make for Saigon by "first available transportation." As the laconic Lansdale explained: "I gathered that events in Indochina were moving toward a climax and that the U.S. wanted me on the spot for whatever occurred next."

This was an understatement. Rather than a slaughter pen for Viet Minh guerrillas, the French encampment in Dien Bien Phu had become a trap for its builders. Inexplicably, in building their fortress in the small, remote valley, the French had made no effort to command or even monitor the surrounding mountain ridges. It was from there that the Viet Minh, having disassembled dozens of artillery pieces to haul them piece by piece along jungle paths, had revealed their presence to the enemy with a devastating barrage in mid-March. The only way to supply the stranded force of some ten thousand troops was by air, and after the Viet Minh knocked out the only runway, by parachute. By early May, the starving garrison was overrun.

Not at all coincidentally, the siege of Dien Bien Phu overlapped with peace talks in Geneva between the world's principal powers, along with the Viet Minh, to decide Vietnam's future. With the sitting French government brought down by the shocking humiliation taking place in the Vietnamese jungle, its replacement accelerated those talks by abruptly announcing that French troops would be withdrawing from Indochina entirely; to be decided in Geneva now was merely the timetable for this withdrawal, and who or what would take their place. All of which meant that when Ed Lansdale flew into Saigon on June 1, 1954, he wasn't coming in as some gadfly irritant to the French authorities, but rather as a kind of first explorer in a country about to experience a massive power vacuum.

Which also meant his brief had dramatically changed since his meeting with Allen Dulles four months earlier, now less to figure out how to work around the French, than to help the Vietnamese prepare for their coming departure.

That was much easier said than done in light of how France had administered her colony over the previous seven decades. In that time, Paris had managed Vietnam, along with its neighboring colonies of Cambodia and Laos, as a virtual plantation, with the indigenous populations virtually shut out from most all political, social and financial levers of power. "The French issued and controlled Vietnam's currency," Lansdale noted, "ran the national bank, customs, foreign affairs, armed forces, and police, and had a host of French officials placed throughout the administrative system. . . . Was the shock of Dien Bien Phu and the conference at Geneva causing a change of status? I simply didn't know."

Nor were those Americans already in Saigon in any hurry to help him learn. While Lansdale was attached to the CIA for the duration of his Vietnam tour, the resident CIA station chief was so incensed at the sight of this arriviste that he barred everyone in his office from having anything to do with him. Lansdale's official cover as an assistant Air Force attaché went little better, with the bona fide air attaché all but refusing to acknowledge his existence. "The son of a bitch wouldn't even give me a chair to sit in," Lansdale recalled. Out of desperation, Lansdale took over one corner of a desk and two drawers of a filing cabinet in the office of a friendly embassy official.

Just as he had done upon reaching the Philippines in 1945, Lansdale set out on a fact-finding mission. For most American officials, such missions usually meant roundtable discussions with government and business leaders and briefings at the embassy, but for Lansdale it meant taking to the countryside. For the next three weeks, he crisscrossed the nation in a "tin-can" Citroën 2CV sedan, meeting with local French and Vietnamese administrators as well as striking up impromptu conversations with Vietnamese from all walks of life. While he wouldn't have been so bold as to say he "got" Vietnam as a result, his travels and endless curiosity undoubtedly gave him a far more nuanced view of the situation than was obtained by those foreign diplomats and advisors who rarely left the capital.

One of the first conclusions he came to was that, from a traditional military standpoint, Vietnam was essentially indefensible. While the island archipelago of the Philippines had created its own challenges in fighting the Huks, control of the seas had made it a relatively simple matter to isolate the rebels from receiving any outside help. Vietnam, by contrast, was a narrow strip of land stretching along the coastline of Southeast Asia for over one thousand miles but which, save for a fan of land at its northern end, was rarely more than one hundred miles wide. Worse, most of its long western border was thick jungle, meaning that any attacker coming from that direction was apt to enjoy the element of surprise and able to split the country in two by reaching the coast before a viable defense could be mustered. Theoretically, the French had inoculated themselves against this threat by also taking possession of Vietnam's two western neighbors, Laos and Cambodia, but their legacy of misrule throughout Indochina instead meant that a rebellion in any one of the three colonies could be supported by and spread to the other two.

On top of this was Vietnam's polyglot character, a jumble of different ethnic groups, cultures and religions. Whereas in the Philippines, the government had been able to promote its anti-Huk message through the Catholic Church, the faith of over 90 percent of the population, Vietnam had large communities of Buddhists and Christians and folk religionists, along with animists and adherents to a scattering of regional faiths that defied traditional categorization. Still an overwhelmingly rural nation, the social structure of an isolated fishing village in the Mekong Delta, for instance, bore scant resemblance to that of a farming community in the Central Highlands. The trick, then, was to somehow convert Vietnam's internal divisions into unifying strengths. If that seemed oxymoronic, Ed Lansdale was fond of pointing to the existing example of the United States "melting pot"—and if it could be done there, why not in Southeast Asia?

On the other hand, the notion of the United States having the foresight to assume such a thoughtful mentorship role was to ignore pretty much the entire history of American involvement with Vietnam up to that time. It was a history of missed opportunities and remarkably poor choices—and in 1954, it was still very early days.

The first missed chance had been at the Paris Peace Conference at the end of World War I when a young Vietnamese nationalist, taking at face value Woodrow Wilson's grand talk of self-determination for "small nations," beseeched the American delegation for help in gaining independence for his homeland. The Americans didn't even dignify the petitions of twenty-nine-year-old Ho Chi Minh with a response, and Vietnam remained a French vassal.

Ho Chi Minh came nearer in the closing days of World War II. So ghastly was French misrule in Indochina, that at the Yalta Conference Franklin Roosevelt, the confirmed anti-imperialist, announced his adamant opposition to continued French rule there at war's end. But then Roosevelt had died, and all changed in an instant. Within days of becoming president, and against the advice of most foreign policy advisors, Harry Truman signed a position paper recognizing a continuing French role in postwar Indochina. Within two months, that future role had transformed into acceptance of restored French sovereignty. It was a crucial turning point in American policy in Southeast Asia, and it set up the United States' second snub of Ho Chi Minh. Shortly after proclaiming Vietnamese independence in September 1945, Ho repeatedly wrote Truman asking for diplomatic recognition and promising close relations. Just as with his overtures to President Wilson twenty-five years earlier, Ho was ignored.

Still, the Truman administration tread gingerly in the region, aware that French intransigence on loosening their imperial grip was adding fuel to the anticolonial fervor in the region—and it was Ho and his communists who were turning that fervor to their advantage. Forced to choose sides with the outbreak of the First Indochina War in late 1946, the United States steadily provided an impoverished France with ever more financial and military aid, while still lobbying behind the scenes for Paris to come to a political solution. Then came the Korean War and, with it, an end to all delicacy. With the low-grade brushfire in the backwaters of Southeast Asia recast as a primary East-West battlefield, the Truman administration agreed to fund most of France's military costs in fighting the Viet Minh, a financial windfall soon augmented by the arrival of American military technicians and advisors.

Thus was completed a stunning turnaround. In five years, the United States had gone from urging an end to colonial rule in Southeast Asia, to being colonialism's paymaster and protector. By the time Ed Lansdale was touring the Vietnamese countryside in June 1954, the transformation had hit another milestone: now the French were at last preparing to depart the scene, but leaving the Americans to fill the void.

But during Lansdale's three-week ramble, even more dramatic changes for the region were in the offing. After months of mediation in Geneva, negotiators were soon to agree to the "temporary" partition of Vietnam into North and South until national elections could be held in two years' time. This, of course, was an eerie replay of the "temporary" partition of

Korea, and would ultimately play to the same disastrous result, giving the in-place powers on either side of the divide time to consolidate their hold. In North Vietnam, this meant Ho Chi Minh and his Viet Minh followers, but it was a far hazier situation in the South. There, the French had restored a puppet emperor first placed on the throne by the Japanese, but a puppet who, having spent most of his life in comfortable exile in France, had little interest in actually relocating to Vietnam. After being dragged home by his French handlers long enough to attend his 1949 re-coronation, Emperor Bao Dai had speedily returned to the more regal furnishings of his life in France, accoutrements that included one of the Mediterranean's largest private yachts.

Obviously, with the French scheduled to depart the South, someone had to run the country, and the choice finally settled on a soft-spoken former interior minister named Ngo Dinh Diem. From a prominent Catholic family of high-ranking mandarins, or senior civil servants, the fifty-three-year-old Diem had impeccable anticolonial credentials, having opposed French rule for decades. He had also adroitly avoided Bao Dai's earlier entreaties to serve as his prime minister at a time when, like Bao Dai himself, Diem would have been tainted as a French stooge. By June 1954, the situation was very different, and now a real government, as opposed to a figurehead one, needed to be installed; on June 25, Diem flew into Saigon as Vietnam's new prime minister.

Having just returned to Saigon from his countryside tour, Lansdale made plans to go out to the airport to observe the welcoming ceremony for Diem. That plan was thwarted because so many Saigon residents lined its streets for a glimpse of their new prime minister that travel was impossible. Instead, Lansdale joined the expectant throng on a downtown street corner.

When at last Diem's motorcade came into view, however, it raced down the boulevard at such high speed, with the new prime minister invisible behind its tinted windows, that all was just a quick blur. As the disappointed crowds dispersed, the public relations instinct in Lansdale was aroused: "Whoever was advising him," he wrote of Diem, "had clearly misread the mood of the people. Diem should have ridden into the city slowly in an open car, or even have walked, to provide a focus for the affection that the people so obviously had been waiting to bestow on him. . . . I wondered aloud what further errors of judgment Diem's advisers might be making."

Lansdale returned to his bungalow and began making a list. The process consumed him for the rest of that day and most of the night, but by the end of it he had compiled a comprehensive, multi-page set of recommendations for Diem. As he noted in his memoir with his trademark tinge of false humility: "The thought occurred to me that perhaps he needed help."

———

At one stage during the CIA's infiltration missions into Eastern Europe in the early 1950s, a senior Czech partisan leader was brought across the border into West Germany to confer with the head of OPC Germany, Michael Burke. Joined by the Czech fighter's CIA case officer, the three men sat in the elegant living room of Burke's Bad Homburg home, exchanging pleasantries over brandy and coffee by a roaring fire, until Burke finally suggested they get down to business. This drew a puzzled look from the Czech. Up until that moment, the aging, grizzled warrior had assumed he was there to meet a much older man—perhaps Burke's father—it apparently not having occurred to him that his fate and those of his followers back in Czechoslovakia might be decided by a smooth-faced man less than half his age.

In his memoir, Burke recounted this meeting as a humorous anecdote, but he then struck a somewhat doleful note. Appreciating the "desperately difficult" odds the Czech resistance fighter faced, he wrote: "I wondered if at his age and in his place, I would have finessed the struggle, withdrawn to some quiet anonymous sideline, made peace with the system, minimized the risk."

Spurring such thoughts by 1954 were Burke's ever-growing doubts about the most fraught aspect of his job in Germany: overseeing the airdrop, or overflight, missions behind the Iron Curtain. These had continued—and in many sectors, increased—since the rollout of the Eisenhower administration's New Look policy.

Going all the way back to his first involvement with the CIA infiltration missions, Operation Fiend in 1949, Burke had recognized the unforgiving, crapshoot nature of these undertakings. Back then, he had fortified himself with the thought that these were the early, shakeout days, that as the Agency learned what methods worked and what didn't, success rates would improve. They had not improved. Instead, by the close of 1952, the list of known failures of such missions over the previous two years, failures confirmed by eyewitness reports or Soviet bloc press accounts, was so long and so uniform across so many different countries as to lead Burke to estimate that, in some sectors, over half the commandos he had helped send across were already dead or captured.

And perhaps even this estimate was wishful thinking. Like every other

CIA officer involved with the infiltration schemes, Burke had been profoundly shaken by the revealing of the Polish WiN hoax in December 1952. Soviet intelligence agencies and their Eastern Europe understudies had long proven adept at turning individual commandos or luring penetration teams into traps, but the WiN hoax had been a playback of a wholly different order: the creation of an entire make-believe guerrilla army, a colossal deception that the enemy had managed to maintain for over two years. Given the extraordinary complexity of that con—scores, if not hundreds, of people had to have played some role in perpetuating it—how to be sure that any of the CIA's infiltration "successes" were actually that? The lone wireless operator in Ukraine who continued to send out his optimistic reports; the partisan team still running through the forests of Lithuania; even the Albanian commando coming back across the frontier after a sabotage mission—who was to say these weren't all KGB manufactures? And if this was paranoia, Burke had company. As early as the beginning of 1952, nearly a full year before the exposure of WiN, the CIA chief of operations for the Russia desk had become so convinced that all the agents dropped into the Soviet Union were neutralized—either captured and turned by the KGB, or executed and replaced with doubles—that he called for shutting down the Russian effort entirely. By then, though, the mission had developed what the official called a "mindless momentum" of its own, the airdrops continued.

True, mechanisms had been belatedly put in place to scuttle or wind down the worst initiatives—oversight committees called murder boards—but against this was the constant imperative to come up with something, anything, that might work against the enemy. That, and the peculiar human resistance to cut one's losses amid a losing streak, to ever admit that maybe it was all for naught.

And then there was the most cold-blooded rationale of all. The United States and the Soviet Union were at war and, just as in any war, there were casualties. Most of the people engaged on the front lines of this struggle were, like Michael Burke, veterans of World War II. In that conflict, an intelligence lapse or a communications breakdown or a poorly conceived operation hadn't meant the deaths of one or two or a half-dozen foot soldiers, but hundreds, frequently thousands. What's more, those doing the dying in this war weren't eighteen-year-old draftees from Iowa, but foreigners who enlisted in full appreciation of the dangers they faced, many of whom already had blood on their hands from their past war-making days. Rarely was it explicitly stated in such callous terms, but with World War II as a backdrop—and few would argue that the stakes of the Cold War were any lesser—who could afford to get all weak-kneed at the prospect of a few hundred martyrs, of men and women who gambled and lost?

Where this unsparing logic frayed, though, was in contemplation of the intimacy of this conflict for those on its front lines. For Michael Burke, as for just a small handful of his peers, the men and women chosen for espionage chains or airdrop missions weren't faceless strangers but people that he knew, whose odds for success or death he had personally weighed, soldiers to whom he had given a last word of encouragement as they climbed aboard the unmarked transport planes that were to carry them into the darkness.

As a consequence, the foreign policy directives that issued forth from the Eisenhower administration spurred only a deepening gloom in Burke. As if determined to learn nothing from the WiN deception—and the timing of its reveal just weeks before Eisenhower assumed the presidency was obviously intended to send a message—the new administration set to work to expand these "firestarter" missions to spark revolt in the "captive nations." In July 1953, the month after the East German uprising, the CIA opened up a new front in Eastern Europe by airdropping thirteen Romanian commandos into their homeland. Almost instantly, all were caught, all executed. Soon after came word of the capture of Hamit Matjani, the legendary Albanian commando who had survived over a dozen missions into his native country, fallen victim to a classic *Sigurimi* dangle operation. But Matjani's demise caused no one in Washington to rethink Operation Fiend, already earmarked for expansion in that fiscal year. On the Baltic front, by the close of 1953 plans were being drawn up to infiltrate more commando teams into Latvia and Estonia.

But quite beyond the specifics of these missions, beyond the ledger of successes matched against failures, was a nagging question that Michael Burke had never found a satisfactory answer to: just what were they meant to accomplish? In World War II, the reason behind the risks couldn't have been plainer—to help win the war—but what was the ultimate goal in this contest? Not the high-blown, flag-waving rhetoric about freedom and liberty and enslaved nations that the politicians trotted out, but the actual nuts-and-bolts, tangible results that would show it was all worth it.

It was a question that applied to both types of operatives being sent across, both those meant to merely gather intelligence and sneak back out again, and those meant to foster revolution. When it came to the first group, forget the movie-house portrayal of a secret agent creeping through the forests to get a look at some hidden Soviet missile base. In reality, the entire Soviet bloc was so heavily policed and so battened down through its system of internal passports and travel permits, or *propiskas,* that the security perimeter around important military installations started dozens, even hundreds, of miles away. Realistically, operatives sent across by the CIA weren't going to get anywhere near these "sensitive areas," so just what information were they collecting in the field, and was it valuable enough to warrant the risks they were taking?

As for the would-be revolutionary infiltrator, the question was even more basic: what would happen if it actually worked? By 1953, Michael Burke and every other CIA officer involved in the missions had a firm grasp on what failure looked like, but what about winning? To put the question in concrete form, as Michael Burke did in his memoir: "Even if underground movements had succeeded in gaining enough strength in numbers and arms to rise up, what armies of the West would intervene to ensure their success?"

An answer to that question had been delivered in East Germany on June 17, 1953: none at all. Yet, in Eisenhower's Washington this was an answer that either went unheard or ignored. Instead, the events of June 17 were just one more sign that the Soviet empire was coming apart at the seams, and that meant more covert operations, more infiltration missions, more Eastern European volunteers jumping from airplanes, with no thought to what came next. Worse, it appeared no one cared. This was the ultimate realization Burke took away from his meeting with John Foster Dulles in Berlin, that the president's closest foreign policy advisor was not only willing to trade lives for propaganda points, but wished to create more situations where this could happen. Whatever else such cold-bloodedness said about the administration, it certainly didn't suggest an alarm would be raised over a climbing body count.

Despite all this, Burke found a certain psychological solace by telling himself that he was a mere foot soldier in this great contest, that his role was to minimize the risks and losses however he could. Starting with Operation Fiend and extending to his tour in Germany, he had often tied himself in knots over the missions he was tasked to sanction or scrub. Given their point-of-no-return aspect, this was especially true of the overflights. With each, he had asked himself, is the objective realistic? Is it worth the danger? Is there a good chance the agent will get out alive? As time went on and the litany of disaster grew, these questions became harder and harder to answer in the affirmative, but even then, Burke fortified himself with the belief that somewhere there was a greater plan, that while it was his burden to watch the game play out on the ground level, back in Washington there were people carefully considering how it all fit on the larger chessboard.

Still, after his meeting with John Foster Dulles, Burke was shaken enough to put this conviction to the test. His chance to do so came in April 1954, when he returned to Washington for consultations at CIA headquarters and was invited to a working lunch at the Georgetown home of his ultimate superior in the Directorate of Plans, Frank Wisner. They were joined there by CIA director Allen Dulles.

"We talked of a number of things," Burke recalled, "but one issue that I was most concerned about was the overflights. I said, in essence, that sitting in the Air Intelligence officer's office in Wiesbaden and making a decision on whether or not to go, I had no idea what considerations at the Washington, even presidential, level should be factored into the decision." From the blank stares of Wisner and Dulles, Burke gathered he wasn't explaining himself well. "I suppose I was looking for some reassurance that on the day and hour that I was in an operational briefing, making what seemed a lonely decision, the people in Washington would be synchronized with us and alert us in good time to scrub the mission for reasons unknown to us on the ground."

But the blank stares of Wisner and Dulles remained, and all at once Burke realized he had fooled himself: there was no master protocol, there was no synchronicity. The whole venture was just as slapdash and speculative as it appeared on the ground, a seat-of-the-pants scheme to see what worked and what didn't, and at the cost of men's lives.

That luncheon provoked a bout of intense soul-searching in Burke when he returned to Germany. Most every practical consideration dictated that he remain precisely where he was, that with a wife and two young children to care for—and with a third on the way, he would soon discover—it was only by staying with the Agency that he was guaranteed the means to support them. He surely remembered those lean, desperate days in New York when he'd been forced to borrow money to care for his family. There was also the question of what else he was qualified to do. When pondering his future at the end of his military service, he had counted two sets of work skills to draw on—football and guerrilla warfare—but nine years on, his skill set was down to one.

But against this was all the continuing tragedy, the continuing loss, that had come to define his daily existence. And something else as well. In his memoir, Burke recalled being at a party at a CIA colleague's apartment in Frankfurt when he noticed the man's wife staring meditatively out at the lights of the city. "I wonder what people in the real world are doing tonight?" she said softly, as if to herself. After five years of living a dual life—which was another way of saying a hidden life—Michael Burke wanted out of the shadows. He had had enough.

In early 1955, he resigned from the CIA and, with his family, boarded the SS *United States* in Bremerhaven bound for New York. Waiting for him at voyage's end was only uncertainty: no home, no job and—a condition common to retired spymasters when working up their résumés—no simple way to tout himself as he searched for one.

The matter wasn't resolved until Burke met up for lunch in Manhattan with John Ringling North, the brother of his best friend from back in his OSS days, Henry North. The meal ran long, Burke recalled. "We had a drink or two, ate lunch, and talked, drank, and talked through the afternoon, through the comings and goings of the cocktail hour, through dinner and the after-theatre crowd. By three o'clock in the morning we were alone."

North's income came from a family-operated business, a clue to which was contained in his middle name: the Ringling Brothers Barnum & Bailey Circus. At some point over the course of that long boozy night, North decided it would be a swell idea if Burke became the circus's new general manager. When Burke pointed out that he didn't have a clue about running a circus, North demurred. "You've been training for it all your life," he said. "You just haven't known it."

A bit later into their "lunch," and presumably after a number of more drinks had been consumed, Burke began to see the wisdom of North's idea. Shortly before dawn, on a deserted 52nd Street, the two men shook hands. With that handshake, Burke had traded in the shadow world for the Big Top.

———

In the mid-morning of June 26, 1954, two American men approached the front gates of Gia Long Palace in downtown Saigon. Waved through by the guards, they crossed the manicured lawns and climbed the steps leading to the entrance of the two-story stone building, the offices and official residence of the prime minister of Vietnam.

Stepping into the broad corridor that ran the length of the building, Ed Lansdale and George Hellyer saw a few government bureaucrats going to and fro. When they asked for directions to the prime minister's office, they were pointed to an ornate stone staircase leading to the second floor.

Earlier that morning, Lansdale had met with the American ambassador to go over the list of recommendations he had worked up for Ngo Dinh Diem. With the ambassador's approval, he had then set out for Gia Long in hopes of gaining an audience with the prime minister. Knowing that Diem spoke French but uncertain of his command of English, Lansdale brought along Hellyer, an embassy public affairs officer and fluent French-speaker, in case an interpreter was necessary.

On the second floor, the two Americans came to an empty hallway, at the end of which stood a door slightly ajar. Poking their heads through, they saw a short, pudgy man in a white suit sitting behind a desk piled with papers. The man was so short, in fact, that Lansdale noticed his feet didn't touch the floor; he was reminded of one of Snow White's Seven Dwarfs. Apologizing for the intrusion, Hellyer explained in French that they were looking for the new prime minister.

"I am Ngo Dinh Diem," the man replied.

From that awkward beginning, the meeting became steadily more so. Politely taking Lansdale's list of recommendations, Diem put on his reading glasses and pulled out a small French-English phrasebook to help in translation. Lansdale suggested that perhaps Hellyer could translate and read the document aloud to him—except that Hellyer had forgotten his reading glasses. The Vietnamese prime minister proffered his and, in this ungainly way, the three men spent the next several hours going over ideas that might help Diem save his country.

From this first meeting, Lansdale came to a couple of salient conclusions. First, Diem didn't even have enough advisers to advise him badly; to an astounding degree, he was quite on his own. Second, without the counsel of someone he could implicitly trust, the chances of this unassuming and apparently guileless man surviving in the cutthroat swirl of Vietnamese politics were slim at best.

Diem seemed to sense this, too. In the Philippines, Ramon Magsaysay had moved into Lansdale's house as they charted a path to save the nation from a communist insurgency. In Vietnam, Ngo Dinh Diem suggested that Lansdale move into Gia Long Palace so that he might have the benefit of his counsel at all hours. By all appearances, Edward Lansdale, the "miracle-worker" of Asia, was on the path to his next triumph.

22

OPERATION SUCCESS

O n the first Friday of September 1953, CIA officer Kermit Roosevelt had gone to the White House to give the president and his closest advisors a blow-by-blow account of the coup he'd helped orchestrate in Iran. Roosevelt had picked up on a curious energy in the room, one he would later describe as "almost alarmingly enthusiastic." It may have been that the CIA officer helped amplify that atmosphere by exaggerating his close-call exploits in the streets of Tehran, by reminding his spellbound audience of what a very near thing the coup had been. If so, it was effective; when he finished his tale, President Eisenhower exclaimed that it all sounded more "like a dime novel" than real life.

But of the half-dozen men in the Oval Office, Roosevelt had taken special note of John Foster Dulles. As the CIA man spun his story, the secretary of state sat stock-still, but "with a catlike grin on his face" and a gleam to his eyes. As Roosevelt would recount: "My instincts told me he was planning [something] as well."

Indeed he was, as the CIA officer had discovered a few days later when he was summoned to the secretary of state's office on 21st Street. Joining them was John Foster's younger brother and Roosevelt's ultimate superior at the CIA, Allen Dulles.

As the secretary of state explained, for quite some time the United States had been having difficulties with the elected president of the Central American nation of Guatemala, Jacobo Árbenz Guzmán. An avowed liberal, Árbenz had shaken up the almost feudalistic culture of his nation through a sweeping land reform initiative. In John Foster's view, land reform was often the herald of communism. A proposal to overthrow the Guatemalan president had first been broached during the Truman administration, only to be quashed, but in the wake of the gladdening news from Iran, John Foster was ready to resurrect the idea. As for how such a coup might be executed, the secretary had a simple plan: Roosevelt should just do the same thing he did in Iran.

Although trying hard not to show it, Roosevelt was aghast. At the White House gathering, he had stressed that the conditions that made Operation Ajax a success were peculiar to Iran, and if the CIA was "ever going to try something like this again, we must be absolutely sure the people and the army want what we want." It was a point John Foster took little notice of in the Oval Office, and his interest had not increased in the interim. Diplomatically replying that he would study up on the Guatemala situation and report back, Roosevelt took his leave, then begged off taking command of the mission shortly after. Perhaps in recognition of the fact that Árbenz had been democratically elected with two thirds of the vote, Roosevelt archly told an interviewer later, "I didn't think the Guatemalan people, the Guatemalan farmers, wanted what Foster Dulles wanted for them."

This failed to dissuade the Dulles brothers. Instead they looked around for someone else qualified to oversee the Guatemala operation, and settled on what might seem an odd choice: Frank Wisner.

With many of the CIA's Guatemala files still classified or heavily redacted, it is not clear whether Wisner volunteered to take leadership of the Guatemala plot or was leaned on to do so by Allen Dulles. Either way, it was a puzzling development considering that the deputy director of plans was hardly known for his organizational skills. He also had little experience directly overseeing CIA field operations, and the Guatemala mission promised to be especially complex.

Most likely, Wisner saw in Guatemala the opportunity to recast himself. In the eight months since Eisenhower had assumed the presidency, the CIA deputy director had frequently assumed the role of killjoy in the foreign policy arena, a voice of caution when it came to pursuing adventures abroad. But while such temperance was understandable when contemplating the obstacles in a "captive" nation in Eastern Europe, recent history had proven the rest of the world far more fluid, that there existed opportunities for bold action. And if regime change worked in Iran, why not in Guatemala?

By the start of 1954, the CIA scheme to overthrow President Árbenz geared up in earnest. The agency's confidence was reflected in its code name: Operation PBSuccess.

Ed Lansdale was growing increasingly anxious about the composition of the CIA advisory team he was meant to lead. Under the terms of the Geneva Accords dictating the future administration of Vietnam, no new foreign military advisors were to be sent into the country after August 11, 1954. It was now early August, and thus far his Saigon Military Mission (SMM), conceived as an assemblage of military officers trained in psychological and counterinsurgency warfare, consisted of himself and just one other man. Granted, this was only one fewer than the "team" he'd gone into the Philippines with in 1950, but Lansdale had already pegged Vietnam as a thornier problem.

After a series of steadily more insistent pleas to Washington, mission members at last began to trickle into Saigon. Most were drawn from the Army or Navy and seconded to the CIA. Ten others came in that first wave, a number that would fluctuate over the next two years what with rotations and transfers, but the mission's total complement would rarely rise above a dozen. They represented one of the United States' first deployments of military advisors to Vietnam.

One of the arrivals, beating the Geneva deadline by a mere three days, was a strapping, twenty-four-year-old Army second lieutenant and Yale graduate named Rufus Phillips III. Thus far, Phillips's CIA career had been dispiriting. Having joined one of the CIA's Eastern Europe infiltration programs, only to see that program shut down before he could get there, he was then attached to a political warfare unit in South Korea sending propaganda balloons across the DMZ. Unfortunately, no sooner did Phillips reach Korea than this program was terminated, too. After a dreary three or four months in Korea, in late July 1954 he received orders to proceed to Saigon. Phillips was given no details on what his duties there would be. "And to be honest," he said, "I'm not sure I could've found Vietnam on a map at that point. But nothing was happening in Korea so, 'sure, I'll go.'"

Upon arrival, Phillips made for the Saigon Military Mission gathering point to await further instructions: the Hotel Majestic on Rue Catinat. Built in the 1920s in French Colonial style, the once grand five-story hotel had sufficiently suffered the ravages of the tropics that its name now seemed more ironic than descriptive, and it was here that Phillips first met some of the other newly arrived mission members. Most were junior officers like himself, but with such an eclectic array of backgrounds and specialties that it was quite impossible to discern a pattern to their selection. As the days of waiting dragged on and the men got to know each other, most concluded there was really no pattern at all, that they simply comprised whoever their mysterious new commander, a certain Air Force colonel named Edward Lansdale, had managed to scrounge up from various commands. Certainly, none had been chosen for their grasp of Southeast Asian politics or a familiarity with the Vietnamese language—none of them spoke it—as became clear when, observing the groups of protesters who regularly marched down Rue Catinat, they debated amongst themselves just what the locals' grievances might be. "There we were," Phillips recalled, "working for the Agency, and we couldn't decipher a street demonstration."

With their wait having dragged into a second week, team members were at last told to assemble in one of the Majestic rooms to meet their new commander. As Phillips recounted in his memoir, in walked a man in his mid-forties of average height and build "dressed in khaki shorts, knee socks, and a short-sleeved uniform shirt with an air force officer's hat worn at a slightly rakish angle." Ed Lansdale's most arresting feature, Phillips noted, was the peculiar intensity of his gaze.

Lansdale apologized for having kept the men waiting so long; the situation in Saigon was quite unsettled at the moment, he offered, and he had a lot of things to do. After brief introductions were made, he explained that he would be meeting with each of them individually in the coming days and, based on their aptitudes and interests, start handing out assignments. This was hardly illuminating to the assembled officers, since they still had no idea of their mission's objective. When queried on that point, Lansdale gave a short reply: "Whatever we can do to save South Vietnam." With that, he left the room.

"'Save South Vietnam?'" Phillips recalled thinking. "We just sat there looking at each other: 'how the hell are we going to do that?'"

The slapdash nature of the mission was reaffirmed when Phillips was summoned to Lansdale's rented four-room bungalow—mission headquarters—a few days later for his job assignment interview. Brought before Lansdale, the second lieutenant snapped a crisp salute and, per Army protocol, barked that he was reporting for duty. "[Lansdale] smiled and waved me informally into an easy chair," Phillips remembered. "It was the first and last time I ever gave him a formal salute."

After a few minutes of casual conversation, Lansdale mentioned that a senior Vietnamese army general was asking for help with the G-5, or psychological warfare, units under his command. The problem was that the units were desperately short of equipment, Lansdale explained, and from looking over Phillips's background, he seemed just the person to render an assessment of the situation. Phillips pointed out a second problem: he didn't know anything about psychological warfare.

"So Ed kind of stared at me," Phillips recounted during an interview, "and then he went over to his bookshelf, pulled down a book, and tossed it to me. 'Here; read this.'"

The book, helpfully titled *Psychological Warfare,* was written by a man named Paul Linebarger and, in the mid-1950s, considered the bible on the topic. "Bible because at the time it was pretty much the *only* book on it. So I took it back to the hotel, read it, and that was my training."

Within weeks, the second lieutenant in his mid-twenties was creating psychological warfare training courses for the South Vietnamese military and serving as the chief American advisor to two entire Vietnamese army divisions, a position typically occupied by a brigadier general.

This looseness with job responsibilities found reflection in the Saigon Military Mission's placement on an organizational flow chart—although here the muddying seemed deliberate. For cover, the SMM fell under the umbrella of the preexisting U.S. Military Assistance Advisory Group (MAAG) in South Vietnam, headed by Ed Lansdale's friend General "Iron Mike" O'Daniel. This arrangement offered the ring of authenticity since most SMM members were active military officers, except the unit actually operated under the aegis of the CIA. But not of the official CIA Saigon station that was housed at the American embassy, but rather as a completely separate unit taking its orders directly from the most senior echelons of CIA headquarters in Washington. In essence, the SMM resembled nothing so much as a miniature version of the bureaucratic whack-a-mole that had been the early OPC, with Ed Lansdale enjoying an autonomy similar to that which Frank Wisner had experienced at the larger organization.

Along with several apartments, the SMM soon took over two rented homes located a short distance apart in downtown Saigon, both two stories and surrounded by high walls. The house on Rue Duy Tan became the office and residence of Ed Lansdale, along with his chief deputy, Navy lieutenant Joe Redick, while the larger one at Rue Taberd housed most of the other mission members. With Lansdale reviving the coffee klatsch arrangement he'd established in Manila, the principal gathering spots for team members were the living room of the Duy Tan house and, inevitably in light of Saigon's staggering heat and humidity, beside the swimming pool of the Taberd house. At both places, any semblance of military hierarchy or formality quickly vanished. One curious detail is that, while SMM members normally wore their uniforms in public, making them quite conspicuous, most moved about in civilian vehicles and employed cover names.

It took many of the SMM officers, including Rufus Phillips, some time to adjust to Lansdale's freewheeling leadership style; as junior military officers, they weren't accustomed to being told to "figure it out yourself." Striving to maintain at least a semblance of military structure was Joe Redick. Fluent in French, the professorial Redick became Lansdale's chief translator at meetings with both French and Vietnamese officials, and also positioned himself as something of a gatekeeper to his perpetually overextended commander. His fastidious, slightly fussy, manner earned him the nickname of "Mother Joe" among his colleagues, a moniker somewhat at odds with his status as the team's best marksman.

By far the most intriguing—and intimidating—member of the mission was a thirty-four-year-old Army major named Lucien Conein, better known as "Lou," "Lulu," "Luigi" or, in Ed Lansdale's case, "The Thug." (There was also the sub-nickname of "Three Fingered Luigi" since Conein was missing the ends of two fingers on his right hand, the result—depending on which version listeners were told or chose to believe—of a fan belt accident, a barroom fight, or an unfortunate mishap during a tryst with another man's wife.) Lithe and powerfully built, the cigarette that perpetually dangled from Conein's lips gave him a sneering expression that nicely complemented the sense of menace—some insisted it was more mockery—that radiated from his gray-blue eyes. It's probably safe to say that no one who ever crossed paths with Lucien Conein ever forgot him.

Included in that group was Peter Sichel. At the first mention of Conein's name during an interview, Sichel involuntarily winced. "Of course I knew Lou," he said. "Everyone knew Lou. And everyone loathed him."

For nearly Sichel's entire tenure in Berlin, Conein served with CIA Germany's "disposal" team, sneaking defectors and high-value operatives out of the Soviet bloc. In West Berlin, Conein shuttled the escapees between safe houses until he could arrange their further escape, often with false identity papers identifying them as American officials, out to western Germany and parts beyond.

"He was a horrible man," Sichel said, "but he had this immense power, you see? He used it to seduce women, to demand money—just a total gangster. I tried to get rid of that son of a bitch at least four or five times." That the Berlin station chief was unable to do so spoke to Conein's unique talents. "When it came to getting someone out, there was no one as good as Lou. He was just too valuable."

He was also uniquely suited for the Saigon Military Mission. Born in

Paris, at the age of five Conein's destitute and widowed mother had put him on a ship to New York, unaccompanied but with an explanatory note pinned to his coat, to be raised by an aunt in Kansas City. Frequently suspended from school for fighting, once out of high school Conein appeared headed for a prosaic existence, landing a job as a typesetter at a local printing press for the princely sum of $20 a week—but then World War II came along. Taking advantage of his dual citizenship, he returned to France and joined the fight as an infantryman (not, as he would often later claim, as a member of the French Foreign Legion). When France fell, Conein made a desperate bid to escape back to the United States, a journey that *may* have involved temporary membership in a Nazi youth group, a crossing of West Africa, and a tramp steamer voyage to South America (Conein also cautioned listeners not to believe anything he said because, "it's probably not the truth"). When the United States came into the war in 1941, he reenlisted, this time in the American army.

With his fluency in French and brief combat experience, Conein was inducted into the OSS and selected as one of the Jedburghs parachuted behind German lines just after D-Day. As part of Jedburgh Team Mark, Conein's three-man squad carried out demolitions and sabotage against German forces in southern France. A year later, he was part of an OSS unit dropped into Southeast Asia to assist the Viet Minh in their fight against the occupying and still warring Japanese. In that capacity, Conein became one of the very first Americans to get to know both Ho Chi Minh and the Viet Minh commander in chief, Vo Nguyen Giap. It was an experience that left him both awed by the communist leaders' brilliance, and traumatized by their verbosity. "I didn't talk to [Giap], nor did I talk to Ho Chi Minh; they talked *to me*," Conein told an interviewer. " 'When are they going to get done so I can get myself a beer?' . . . I was going to die of thirst. Goddamn bastards gave me tea!"

After the shuttering of the OSS in late 1945, Conein had finagled a transfer into the Strategic Services Unit. It was when he moved over to the CIA's "disposal" unit in West Germany that he came to the attention of Peter Sichel. "Where the man really belonged was prison," Sichel said.

But one man's degenerate criminal, another's invaluable sidekick. Due both to his French lineage and his brief military service under the Tricolor, Lou Conein had a natural entree to the French military and civilian communities that still dominated most every aspect of South Vietnam society, communities that despised the American interlopers in general and Ed Lansdale in particular. As a dedicated drinker, Conein's links were especially strong with the Corsican bar owners and bartenders who presided over much of Saigon's nightlife. Like barmen everywhere, those in Saigon had unparalleled knowledge of what was happening beneath the surface of the city, and since Corsicans tended to be regarded by their fellow Frenchmen in much the same way that Lou Conein had always been regarded—that is, as uncouth, unpleasant and primitive—a natural rapport developed. This made "The Thug" an invaluable member of Lansdale's team, his conduit into Saigon's extraordinarily powerful underworld. It was a status Conein didn't hesitate to exploit.

"We'd all be sitting around the living room at Duy Tan," Rufus Phillips recalled, "and Ed would be talking about something, and Lou would just sort of snort: 'Ed, you're full of shit, you don't know what the fuck you're talking about; get your head out of your ass and let me tell you what's really going on.' And this is a major talking to a colonel! And then the two of them would just go at it, they argued all the time. But that was the thing about Ed. He didn't give a damn about military protocol. He wanted to hear people's ideas, he knew Lou often had a better sense of what was going on than anyone else, so he put up with it."

Beginning in that summer of 1954 and continuing until late 1956, the dozen or so men who would gather in the Duy Tan living room or loll about the pool at Rue Taberd in between their forays into the Vietnamese countryside represented a unique experiment in American history, a tiny vanguard of untrained advisors set to the task of helping build a foreign nation. If those men ever felt overwhelmed by the enormity of their work—and they did, often—their principal guide was the easy, not to say glib, aphorisms of their leader. As Ed Lansdale once told a frustrated Rufus Phillips when pressed on the ultimate purpose of their mission: "At its heart, it's pretty simple. Our job is to find out what the Vietnamese people want and then help them get it."

———

In a carefully synchronized wave of attacks, on the morning of June 18, 1954, four rebel formations crossed into Guatemala at four different points along its eastern frontier, and began their advance on the nation's capital. On that same day, airplanes belonging to the rebel force, the Guatemalan Army of Liberation, flew over Guatemala City to bomb and neutralize strategic government-held installations.

This was the plan anyway. Instead, one of the rebel formations, numbering about 130 men, encountered a Guatemalan army unit of some thirty soldiers and was immediately pinned down. Another was met by an angry crowd of policemen and dockworkers, and fled back across the border to Honduras. At least these rebel units saw "combat" of sorts;

another detachment never made it into Guatemala at all, but was intercepted and detained by a squad of border agents in El Salvador. The situation was little better when it came to the "air campaign." While the rebel planes did manage to drop a few small bombs and sticks of dynamite on the capital over the next several days, the effort was so scattershot and ineffectual as to spur more excitement than fear among the residents.

Time didn't much improve the outlook. Within forty-eight hours, several of the dilapidated planes that comprised the Army of Liberation air force had been grounded or shot down by the bona fide Guatemalan air force, while the rebel ground troops had barely moved from their frontier outposts. To the few in the outside world who took note of these curious goings-on in Central America, it appeared the whole episode was headed for a quick and embarrassing close. Then again, that had been the consensus in the first days of the Iranian coup, too.

Officially, the Army of Liberation was the handiwork of a former Guatemalan colonel named Carlos Castillo Armas, living in exile after attempting an earlier coup against his nation's elected government. In reality, the "army" was a largely mercenary force of some four hundred bankrolled by the CIA, while the planning for their "invasion" had been conducted in Washington and at a secret CIA field headquarters at a military airfield in Opa-locka, Florida. Involved in every aspect of that planning had been Frank Wisner.

Despite their shaky start, recent trends in Latin America seemed to favor the rebels. Since the end of World War II, one democratically elected government after another in the region had been overthrown, with autocratic—and in some cases, murderous—right-wing dictatorships taking their place. So sweeping was this march into totalitarianism that, by 1954, fully eleven of the eighteen independent nations comprising South and Central America were under military rule.

This rise of anti-communist dictatorship in the Western Hemisphere hadn't appeared to bother the Truman administration in the slightest—indeed, it may have come as something of a relief that, in the ever-widening struggle with the Soviet Union, there was at least one corner of the globe it needn't pay much attention to—and the Eisenhower administration even less. To the contrary, even before coming into office, some of Eisenhower's closest advisors were looking to bring down one of Latin America's remaining democracies, that in Guatemala. Urging them on was the United Fruit Company of Boston.

Over the previous half-century, United Fruit had turned vast tracts of Guatemala into essentially a privately owned plantation, one worked by landless peasants. The company orchestrated a bitter political and legal counterattack when President Árbenz initiated agrarian reform in 1951, largely spearheaded by their onetime legal counsel in New York, John Foster Dulles. Árbenz certainly did himself no favors when, in 1953, he appointed several communist ministers to his coalition government, enabling United Fruit and Dulles, now secretary of state, to claim he was dragging Guatemala into the Soviet camp. President Eisenhower was convinced; that autumn, he approved the CIA's proposal to begin planning for the overthrow of Árbenz in Operation Success.

With Wisner at the helm, PBSuccess became increasingly complex. Early on in the planning, Joseph Caldwell ("J.C.") King, the chief of the CIA's Western Hemisphere division, suggested that the Agency simply pay off the Guatemalan generals to withdraw their support of Árbenz. Wisner dismissed the idea. "J.C., you've had four years to try that approach," he replied. "Now the situation is worse than ever."

Wisner obviously felt something grander was needed, and to deliver it, he pushed King to the sidelines and brought in a swashbuckling Army colonel named Albert Haney. Most recently the CIA station chief in Korea, Haney's scheme was rather clever: not to build up a rebel force of a size that could actually overrun Guatemala, but to merely create the appearance of one sufficient to undermine Árbenz's support within the military and cow his supporters. To this end, the gung ho Haney wrote out a forty-foot-long to-do list along one wall of his headquarters at the Opa-locka airfield, and then set out to complete it.

One aspect was the creation of secret training camps in Honduras and Nicaragua—both military dictatorships and American allies—where the miniature "army" of Castillo Armas would be trained, armed and kept under wraps until D-day. A far more potent weapon, if all went according to plan, was Haney's clandestine rebel radio station, *La Voz de la Liberación*. When *Voz* went on the air in May 1954 with its anti-Árbenz broadcasts, it claimed to be transmitting from somewhere in the Guatemalan jungle along with the vanguard of the "liberation army." In fact, there was no vanguard and the *Voz* broadcasts were taped in a Miami studio but, much like Operation Ajax in Iran, Operation Success was envisioned to be a war of bluff in which the enemy's nerves would eventually crack.

But only if Frank Wisner's nerves didn't crack first. Throughout the weeks and months of planning, he endlessly fretted over the details, worried that leaks or rash actions might upend the mission or, perhaps worse, expose it to the outside world. The biweekly meetings devoted to Guatemala became daily, and so consumed did Wisner become with PBSuccess that he relegated most all other Directorate of Plans administrative work to his deputy, Richard Helms. He even began having second thoughts about Albert Haney, concerned that his field director was moving too fast and not keeping him informed.

Until he was overruled, Wisner balked at the idea of giving the rebels airplanes, figuring this would too flagrantly display the American hand in the overthrow scheme. On that score, he floated a memo suggesting that perhaps the right-wing government of Argentina could be induced to take "credit" for the upcoming attacks on Guatemala, an idea that presumably foundered on the fact that the two countries were three thousand miles apart. Borrowing a page from his past habit in OPC of giving the same job to several different people, Wisner dispatched a number of intermediaries and monitors to watch over things at Opa-locka, but it wasn't long before he was sending new monitors to monitor the monitors.

Quite aside from all this planning, what the CIA still needed was some sort of pretext to launch the attack on Árbenz. They finally found one in the spring of 1954 when the Guatemalan president, his military withering from an ongoing American arms boycott, arranged to buy a shipment of light weapons from communist Czechoslovakia. As John Foster Dulles and others loudly proclaimed, here was final proof that Árbenz intended to create a Red fortress in Central America. Amid the increasingly energetic hand-wringing, even liberal media outlets like *The New York Times* clamored for the administration to do more to meet the communist threat in America's backyard. On June 15, Eisenhower obliged by giving final approval for the launch of PBSuccess and, right on cue, there materialized Castillo Armas's Army of Liberation on Guatemala's frontier.

Despite Kermit Roosevelt's seemingly obvious comment that Iran and Guatemala were not analogous, there were actually to be some uncanny similarities between Operations Ajax and Success. That extended to their initial haplessness. With most of Castillo Armas's militiamen bogged down at Guatemala's border, it was left to the Voice of Liberation to broadcast fables of their great victories and steady march on the capital. When a rebel plane mistakenly bombed a Honduran border town, repercussions were avoided when John Foster Dulles held a hasty press conference to claim the bombing was actually done by the Guatemalan air force. Amid the turmoil, the Árbenz government appealed to the United Nations Security Council to investigate who was behind the attacks on their nation, even though the answer was obvious; after all, as Frank Wisner had rightly pointed out, what rebel group has an air force? That investigation was thwarted when John Foster Dulles personally lobbied the British and French delegates to abstain from the Security Council vote.

What Ajax and Success also shared was a moment when all appeared lost. For the orchestrators of the Guatemala conspiracy, it came on the afternoon of June 27, as Frank Wisner and his principal lieutenants huddled in Allen Dulles's office on E Street. By then, well over a week into the "revolution," the Liberation Army had barely advanced from the border, and while the rebel air sorties were beginning to fray some nerves, Árbenz remained in firm control of the capital. The coup effort was clearly dying on the vine but, incredibly, there was no contingency plan for what to do next. In desperation, Dulles and Wisner now talked of withdrawing the rebel troops on the ground and switching over to an amphibious assault; a bewildered deputy was ordered to start calling New York shipping companies to find a suitable ship to lease.

It was at this very moment, however, with the collapse of Operation Success all but complete, that everything suddenly swung the other way. The Guatemalan military command, having long since figured out that the beleaguered rebels were backed by the United States and Guatemala's neighbors, increasingly feared that crushing them might lead to a regional war, even an American invasion. Thus convinced the walls were closing in, the generals urged Árbenz to resign; with his refusal to do so, they began withdrawing their support. As a last-ditch gambit, on June 26 Árbenz had called for a "popular army" of armed workers to confront the mercenaries, but when that effort fizzled, the exhausted president knew he was through. The following evening, and shortly after the doomsday meeting in Allen Dulles's office, Árbenz announced his resignation and sought asylum in the Mexican embassy. A few days later, a victorious Castillo Armas arrived in the capital.

For an ecstatic Eisenhower administration and CIA, it was the second against-all-odds win in just one year. In contrast to the dreary stasis along the Iron Curtain in Eastern Europe, in Iran and Guatemala there had been bold action and sweeping triumph, not the half-measure of containment but liberation. What's more, it had been accomplished at no cost in American blood and virtually none in terms of treasure. For President Eisenhower, as for his secretary of state, the United States had turned a new page, and was now on the advance against international communism. So expansive was John Foster's mood after Guatemala—"the biggest success in the last five years against communism," he proclaimed—that he began hatching plans for a second coup in the region, this time in Costa Rica, the only democracy remaining in Central America but one that had committed the cardinal sin of staying neutral in the East-West Cold War standoff.

But to remain in this state of exultancy required overlooking several crucial details. Foremost among them was the fact that neither Iran nor

Guatemala had been communist states, let alone likely candidates for joining the Soviet bloc. Much to the contrary; just as they took little notice of Mossadegh before his fall, so the Soviets were so oblivious to their alleged Guatemalan fellow traveler that they didn't even have diplomatic relations with Árbenz. Instead, both coups had the unintended consequence of bringing to the Kremlin's attention that there were new and previously untrammeled regions of the Cold War world to be explored.

Another factor to ignore was the effect these coups had on America's allies, and on world opinion in general. In quick succession, the United States had overthrown two democratically elected governments, and done so for barely discernible reasons. In Guatemala's case, political leaders across Western Europe expressed shock and disgust as the extent of American authorship of the coup became ever more apparent. The appalled reactions from London must have been especially galling for the Eisenhower administration, considering that Washington had essentially done Britain's bidding in knocking over Mossadegh the year before. It was even worse in Latin America, where most every capital city saw impassioned anti-American demonstrations; a senior CIA official who toured Latin America two years after the Guatemala coup encountered continuing bitterness over "Yankee imperialism" at every stop. With more resonance than Soviet propaganda could ever muster, by its own hand the United States had cast herself into the role of imperial and anti-democratic power in the eyes of much of the Third World.

Nor could it be argued that the coup in any way benefited the Guatemalan people. Within weeks of taking office, Castillo Armas banned all political parties except his own. He then annulled Árbenz's land reform initiative, using soldiers to evict small farmers from land they'd just been given title to, and to crush all dissent by arresting tens of thousands and "disappearing" the most troublesome among them. So brutal was Castillo Armas's rule that it would ultimately help spark the Guatemalan civil war in 1960, a scorched-earth struggle between the nation's leftists and a succession of right-wing death-squad dictatorships that would last for thirty-six years and take an estimated quarter-million lives.

But from the standpoint of cold-eyed realpolitik, perhaps the greatest downside of the Guatemalan coup for the American government was that it produced more and hardier enemies. One of these was a twenty-six-year-old Argentine doctor who had been living in Guatemala City at the time of the coup, and who joined Árbenz in seeking asylum in Mexico. A few months later, the doctor would pen a vivid account of those hectic last days in Guatemala entitled "I Witnessed the Coup Against Arbenz," in which he proclaimed that the United States had now become the enemy; as he wrote in his prophetic closing: "the struggle begins." The doctor's name was Ernesto Rafael Guevara, but he was soon to become better known to the world by his nom de guerre: Che.

═══

The official mandate of the Saigon Military Mission, as worked out at a National Security Council meeting in early 1954, was for a select unit of American military advisors to carry out paramilitary operations against the Viet Minh enemy, and to discreetly train the Vietnamese armed forces in the fine art of psychological warfare. Discreetly, because this effort was to be conducted at arm's length from Vietnam's despised French colonial administration.

By the time Lansdale and his mission teammates set up shop in Saigon that summer, most every salient point of this mandate was obsolete. Following the French defeat at Dien Bien Phu, the Geneva Accords had imposed a cease-fire on the warring sides—meaning there was now technically no enemy to wage paramilitary operations against—Vietnam had been partitioned in prelude to future national elections, and a timetable for a phased French withdrawal established. After a hasty rework, the mandate for the Saigon Military Mission now was to help consolidate the rule of the government of southern Vietnam ahead of the impending French departure and the future reunification elections.

This new directive had a problem as well, however, for it presupposed that an indigenous South Vietnamese government actually existed. It did not. Instead, virtually every function of the civil administration in Vietnam's southern half was still officiated over by the French. Lansdale was given a stark illustration of this when, shortly after his arrival, he convened a meeting of provincial Vietnamese officials to discuss security issues. "They were practically all Frenchmen as [sic] province and district chiefs," he recalled. Indeed, whatever natives were to be found in a Vietnamese government office building tended to be glorified errand boys. "They sat at the door when visitors came in," Lansdale explained. "Sometimes they had experience stamping things—the French system of doing any business of the government—to stamp something with a rubber stamp."

This pattern extended all the way to the newly installed prime minister's cabinet members. "The ministries had been run by the French, and suddenly the doorman was brought in. 'You are the minister.' All he knew was to sit at a desk. What does he do now?"

On the other hand, since Lansdale and his mission colleagues didn't have to answer to the French—their mandate remained to steer clear of them as much as possible—it meant they could largely sidestep Vietnam's cumbersome bureaucracy and make up their own rules as they went along. In sum, much like the autonomy the SMM members enjoyed from other American players in Saigon, the embassy and the "real" CIA, so they needn't tolerate local interference in pursuing whatever operations they saw fit. That was a good thing, because already by the summer of 1954 Vietnam's crises were piling on top of one another.

Under the terms of the Geneva Accords, the national elections leading to the nation's reunification were to take place in the summer of 1956. Of much more immediate interest to Ed Lansdale was the clause which called for a three-hundred-day window in which any Vietnamese wishing to relocate to the other partition zone could do so (an astute observer might have questioned how such a population transfer was meant to aid in the country's future reunification, but such an observer would probably have also divined that the main function of the Geneva agreement was simply to kick Vietnam's problems down the road). Initially, this clause was seen as a way to separate the warring factions—the Viet Minh soldiers who controlled regions in the South were to relocate to the Viet Minh–administered North, while the anti–Viet Minh forces in the North would go south—but already by the time of Lansdale's arrival, it had sparked a miniature exodus of northern civilians, with several thousand gathered into squalid refugee camps on Saigon's outskirts. By midsummer, relief workers were growing concerned as to how they might handle the growing influx, which some estimated might reach as high as fifty thousand before the three-hundred-day window shut.

To these concerns, Lansdale offered a startling counterproposal: open the floodgates. "I felt that plans should be made for moving and settling at least a million refugees, perhaps even two million." When Diem blanched at this idea, Lansdale forcefully drove his point home. "I asked him point-blank if he thought it prudent to force a million or so Vietnamese to remain under Communist control when they wanted to move out, just because of travel difficulties and poor prospects at journey's end."

Instead, Lansdale saw the opportunity to both bolster Diem's fledgling government by increasing the South's anti-communist population, and to score a propaganda victory by showing the world a people voting against communism with their feet. Starting that August and continuing until the spring of 1955, Lansdale and his SMM team worked to expand the population transfer effort—given the tired if predictable name of Operation Passage to Freedom—and lure as many northern Vietnamese to the South as possible.

They did so with both the carrot and the stick. Augmenting the French effort, American naval ships and transport planes were pressed into service to move a flood of northerners and their possessions south, while Vietnamese army units were deployed to build new settlements for the refugees. With Lansdale enlisting the help of Ramon Magsaysay, teams of Filipino doctors and nurses gathered under the banner of Operation Brotherhood—another Lansdale coinage—were brought in to provide medical care. It all meshed nicely with a larger effort to reestablish control over those areas of the South being vacated by the Viet Minh through "civic action" projects undertaken by the Vietnamese military—the digging of water wells, the rehabilitation of schools and roads—a scheme that would later be known in counterinsurgency parlance as hearts-and-minds. To some jaded Western journalists, it smacked of a public relations stunt, but to Lansdale it was establishing the most basic precept of counterinsurgency: if you build things the people want, they'll fight to protect them.

The relocation effort also enabled Lansdale to put his adman talents to use. With Vietnam being a highly superstitious society, Rufus Phillips was put in charge of commissioning a mass-market astrological almanac that would tell of the good times lying ahead in the South, and of the much bleaker tidings in the North. Especially targeted was the large Catholic community centered in the Red River Delta below Hanoi. Through coordinating with local priests, natural opponents of atheistic communism, whole communities of northern Catholics were convinced to pack up and leave, answering the exhortation that "the Virgin Mary has gone south." On the flip side, southerners contemplating a move north were liable to come across a flyer reminding them to bring all their jewelry and anything transportable of material value to their embarkation point; there it would be confiscated by North Vietnam officials as payment for their voyage north. Such travelers also needed to prepare for a stressful journey. A leaflet purportedly produced by a Viet Minh relief agency—it didn't actually exist—assured prospective émigrés that they would be locked in the ships' holds during the entirety of their voyage north as protection against strafing warplanes, while sailors on deck kept a watch for the torpedoes of marauding submarines to the best of their ability. So effective was this scare campaign that even many Viet Minh cadre, under orders to journey north, refused to board the evacuation ships.

The public relations effort also played to an external audience. Well into 1955, American readers were buffeted by newspaper and magazine stories telling of the perilous journey so many Vietnamese were making to escape communist savagery, "sustained only by the faith in their heart." The clarion call was picked up by countless American politicians, eager to attach their name to the humanitarian endeavor.

But there was a decidedly darker side to Operation Passage to Freedom that the American public heard nothing about. Under the command of Lucien Conein, about a half-dozen members of the Saigon Military Mission were dispatched north, ostensibly to help coordinate the refugee exodus. Instead, they used the cover of the naval evacuation ships in Haiphong harbor to sneak ashore infiltration agents who had received instruction at a secret CIA training base on Saipan. In their forays through the northern countryside in purported support of the transfer process, Conein and his men organized stay-behind units and hid caches of weapons and ammunition, often burying them in coffins amid bogus funeral ceremonies. In a nighttime raid on the Hanoi municipal bus depot, mission members sabotaged vehicles by pouring acid into their gas tanks, while explosives disguised as coal bricks were scattered amid the legitimate fuel bricks at the Hanoi train terminal, guaranteed to damage a train's engine—or kill its fireman—at some point in the future. As Lansdale would blithely note in a mission report a year later, "U.S. adherence to the Geneva Agreement prevented SMM from carrying out the active sabotage it desired to do against the [Hanoi] power plant, water facilities, harbor and bridge." In fact, all sabotage operations were prohibited under the Geneva agreement but, as Lansdale would later unconvincingly argue, the "dirty tricks" carried out by Conein's team weren't meant to destabilize the Viet Minh regime, only to "give it something to think about."

In any event, there was no arguing with success. When the three-hundred-day window closed on Operation Passage to Freedom, nearly one million northern Vietnamese had come south, dwarfing the estimated ninety thousand southerners who had gone in the other direction.

But here, too, were some troublesome details to overlook. While the addition of one million anti-communist northerners might help bolster the Diem regime, it also meant Ho Chi Minh's regime had shed itself of one million potential dissidents; neither development seemed an aid toward reunification. And just as Lansdale's Saigon Military Mission had used the population transfer to establish stay-behinds—about three hundred operatives by best estimate, almost all of whom either quickly defected or were captured—so the Viet Minh laced the refugees heading south with communist sleeper agents, there to join thousands of Viet Minh stay-behinds. Most ominously, during their official withdrawal from the South, Viet Minh forces had taken—kidnapped, in the eyes of many—some ten thousand boys between the ages of eight and twelve to be trained as future cadre. In a few years' time, the first of these "lost boys of Vietnam" would return to their home villages as the vanguard of a new guerrilla formation: the Viet Cong.

While other SMM members were stretched to the breaking point by the demands of the transfer operation, Ed Lansdale's primary task was one many would have found equally challenging: listening to Ngo Dinh Diem. From their very first meeting at Gia Long Palace when Lansdale and an American embassy official simply walked into his office, Diem had taken a special fondness to Lansdale, a personal bond that, much as with Ramon Magsaysay in the Philippines, led to the CIA officer becoming the ruler's main outside confidant and sounding board. Just as with Magsaysay in Manila, so within a very short time Lansdale was a regular presence at Gia Long, he and Diem spending countless hours in conference while drinking tea and chain-smoking cigarettes. There the similarities ended, however. In Magsaysay, Lansdale had found a charismatic and down-to-earth populist. Diem, by contrast, was a remote and diffident ruler, an aristocrat with little sense of the common touch. And while conversation with Magsaysay was a two-way street, with Diem it usually consisted of a monologue that could go on for many hours, an interminable meandering between topics with no discernible pattern. Many years later, Joe Redick, Lansdale's chief translator at these sessions—Diem spoke in French—could still recall extended Diem soliloquys on banana tree cultivation, the mechanics of road building, and the peculiarly penetrating call made by ethnic Chinese street vendors, while conceding he was merely scratching the surface. "You name it, it was probably talked about."

Journalist Stanley Karnow wrote of meetings with Diem where, "pausing only to light one cigarette from another, he would talk tirelessly in a high-pitched voice, recalling his life in excruciating detail." On one occasion, having finally escaped from Diem's office, Karnow felt "bewildered by the fact that, with his country in crisis, [Diem] could devote half a day to a reporter. Outside, on the veranda, a crowd of officials, army officers and politicians were waiting impatiently, their urgent business delayed by my lengthy audience."

And it's not as if visitors might find safe haven among the extended Ngo family, some of whom lived in the palace with Diem. Famous in Saigon expatriate circles was the story of a visiting congressman, just arrived from Washington, who paid a courtesy call on Diem's younger brother, Ngo Dinh Nhu, and his wife. "The Nhus talked from 8 PM until four o'clock in the morning," recounted writer Frances Fitzgerald, "whereupon the congressman, felled by whiskey and jet lag, had to be carried out of the palace." As Fitzgerald acidly put it, "the Ngo family seemed to have only one great talent, and that was for inducing a state of profound, indeed vertiginous, boredom in almost everyone."

What made Lansdale's patience more remarkable was that, even in the summer of 1954, there seemed little chance that Ngo Dinh Diem would survive in the shark tank that was Saigon politics for very long at all. Indeed, by most any measure, the communists to the north ranked among the least of his problems.

Technically, Diem served at the pleasure of the emperor of Vietnam, Bao Dai, himself a highly unpopular figure for having been a puppet of both imperial Japan and imperial France. It was the French, however, who remained the true power behind the throne, and despite the recent agreement in Geneva setting a timetable for their withdrawal, they appeared in no hurry to abandon that role. Already deeply distrustful of Diem for his past anti-French pronouncements, it would be an easy matter for Paris to have Bao Dai dismiss Diem should he further offend. For that matter, the French could sidestep Bao Dai and employ the forces of the criminal syndicate that controlled Saigon, the Binh Xuyen, and its uniformed "army" of several thousand militiamen. But that was only if the private religious armies floating around Vietnam didn't get to Diem first. As a Catholic in a predominantly Buddhist country, Diem's base of support may have been marginally expanded by the Catholics who came south in the population transfer, but that was more than offset by the deepening distrust of two powerful Buddhist sects, the Cao Dai and the Hoa Hao, who maintained militias of tens of thousands of soldiers, and whose salaries were partly paid by the French. Then there were the regional warlords and tribal chieftains and political kingpins, all of whom had carved out their own spheres of authority under the French colonial system and were sure to resist any attempt at change. Topping it all off was a scheming army chief of staff who regarded the new prime minister as little more than a pest to be tolerated—at least for the time being—and who also happened to be a standing senior officer in the French military.

With the official end of French control in September 1954, Diem crossed the street from Gia Long to the far grander former French governor general's mansion, which he renamed Doc Lap (Independence) Palace. The name held a certain irony, for the move seemed only to make the prime minister more beleaguered. In recalling this period, William Colby, a future Saigon station chief and CIA director, observed that Diem "only controlled the space of his palace grounds," but even this appraisal was overly generous. An American embassy official recounted how Diem's Doc Lap telephone was tapped by so many different third-party spy agencies that it often interfered with transmission. At one point, Lansdale took it upon himself to instruct palace guards on how best to protect Diem in the event of an attempted military coup. The guards found the talk so alarming that, by the following morning, all had fled. No wonder, then, that even by the late summer of 1954, a hot topic of debate among officials at the American embassy was whether Diem's downfall would come in a matter of weeks or of months.

Against all this, Diem had but one trump card: Edward Lansdale. To a degree that even his closest confidants found mystifying, the CIA officer was determined to stand by the plump little man in the white sharkskin suit toiling—or at least talking—away on the second floor of Doc Lap Palace. "Ed saw something in Diem that others just didn't see," Rufus Phillips explained. "Or maybe more accurately, he looked around at all the other players in Saigon and saw that there was no one else to turn to. Diem wasn't corrupt. He couldn't be bought. He was an absolutely committed Vietnamese patriot. That may not seem like an awful lot to work with, but I think Ed saw that it was all we had."

But Lansdale's support of Diem was undoubtedly born of more strategic calculation, as well. So fractured were the politics of southern Vietnam, and so entrenched and diffuse its power blocs that, in a perverse way, it almost required an outsider, a person with no personal power base, to lead it. As both a Catholic and an exile, Diem was just such an outsider, and Lansdale reasoned that the very aspects of his personal story that now seemed so disadvantageous might actually shield him from the oppositional forces that would swiftly overwhelm someone else. Put in more cunning terms, there might be a way to maneuver Diem's enemies to consume one another and leave him standing. For any chance of that happening, though, Diem needed to take on his enemies in a carefully considered order.

In this calculus, Lansdale may have also seen a reflection of his own situation in Saigon, that of the consummate underdog. Like Diem, he had but one powerful ally in the city—in his case, the head of the Military Assistance Advisory Group, General Mike O'Daniel—while most everyone else in the local American power structure regarded Lansdale as a nuisance at best, a dangerous interloper at worst. This disapproval extended from most of the State Department diplomats at the embassy, down through the middle ranks of MAAG, and on over to nearly every member of the official CIA station. In this last camp, friction was exacerbated by an intense personality clash between Lansdale and the station chief, Emmett McCarthy, and the fact that SMM had no independent communication link to CIA headquarters; all was routed through the station. That gave McCarthy endless opportunities for mischief.

"He was lying about me in cables to Washington," Lansdale told a journalist. "He kept other incoming cables addressed to me, and wouldn't give them to me." For his interference, Lansdale finally challenged the younger and more muscular McCarthy to a fistfight, but the station chief wouldn't take the bait. "Oh, he was terrible."

To complete the circle, there were the French. Within the still powerful expatriate community, Lansdale had been an object of loathing from the moment he arrived, a sentiment that gained intensity the more prominent an actor on the Saigon stage he became.

"That was probably one of the few things that most of the Americans and French in Saigon could agree on at that time," Phillips said. "They pretty much all hated Ed."

In light of their precarious status, the opening move that Diem and Lansdale made against their common enemy was a remarkably bold one. It came in mid-September 1954, just two months after Diem's return to Vietnam, and seemed almost designed to infuriate the French. If that was the intent, it worked; where previously French attitudes toward the odd couple on the second floor of Doc Lap Palace had been merely obstructionist, they would eventually turn murderous.

═══

As chief of operations for Eastern Europe, much of Peter Sichel's work at CIA headquarters came to feel routine: interminable staff meetings, the constant sifting through status reports from CIA stations abroad, the long-distance analysis of intelligence. "It was quite removed from the day-to-day of fieldwork," he explained, "and more about taking a longer view on matters. You could even say it was a little dull at times—although dull wasn't necessarily a bad thing after Berlin."

It was also a position that provided Sichel with a unique perspective on how things functioned at the top rungs of the early CIA. Under Allen Dulles, perhaps the Agency's most defining characteristic was its lack of a rigid command structure—or at least of adherence to one—an improvisational streak not normally associated with a government agency. Part of this undoubtedly stemmed from the kind of entrepreneurial, whatever-it-takes culture inherited from William Donovan's OSS, but it was accentuated by Dulles's habit of ignoring organizational convention. If, for example, the CIA director had questions about a particular project, he was likely to call or drop in on the specific case officer involved rather than go through the four or five layers of supervisors that might, on paper, stand between them. While this informality irritated many CIA supervisors, including at times Frank Wisner, it could also make the CIA remarkably responsive to sudden crises or opportunities. The plot to overthrow Iran's prime minister Mossadegh was a case in point; from presidential approval of the plan to final resolution, Operation Ajax had taken a mere six weeks.

On the other hand, this freewheeling quality made the CIA an intensely political place to work, for it helped inculcate the idea that a junior officer with a pet project might work his way around a balky supervisor and find support further up the chain of command. For the same reason, killing an operation gone bad could be incredibly difficult. It was for this that the murder boards had been established but, as Peter Sichel well knew from his years in Berlin, officers in the field had myriad ways to circumvent headquarters and keep their more dubious ventures on life support almost indefinitely. But now Sichel was the one at headquarters casting a skeptical eye over field reports, he the one being stonewalled or lied to. "When you're in the field," he explained, "it's very easy to fall in love with your operations and your agents. And just as with love, you can become blind to their faults. This is why you must have outside oversight—the field officers can't do it—but it's also why completely worthless operations can continue on for years."

Beyond a case officer's loss of objectivity, Sichel appreciated there was often a more complicated dynamic at work, a problem with no easy solution: once an operation was up and running and a chain of agents put on the Agency payroll, how to ever drop them off? For the case officer, there was the legitimate fear that a dismissed operative might compromise another mission out of spite, or even flip to the Soviets. As a result, shutting down an operation was at least as delicate as initiating one, for it required coming up with just the right combination of rewards and threats to ensure a cashiered agent's silence. Far easier, in fact, to simply let a dead-end mission limp along indefinitely.

"They should have made it a rule at the outset," Sichel said, "that if you propose an operation, you also have to explain how you're going to shut it down." He gave a sardonic smile. "Oh, how we envied the Russians; when they were done with their agents, they could just shoot them."

One operation that particularly rankled Sichel was a stay-behind in central Germany code-named Kibitz. Sichel had never been a big believer in the stay-behind programs, and once at headquarters he sought to curtail or phase them out wherever he could. Like other covert operations, however, the stay-behinds had a way of developing a life of their own.

Heading up one part of the Kibitz network was a former German Abwehr colonel named Walter Kopp. Given the code name Kibitz 15, Kopp was so right-wing that even his CIA case officer characterized him as "an unreconstructed Nazi." From Sichel's perspective, far worse was Kopp's persistent refusal to accept directions from the Agency, or to maintain even a modicum of operational security.

Against this, though, Walter Kopp was making life much easier for the CIA station in Karlsruhe. While other local stay-behind team leaders had only managed to bring in a recruit or two, Kopp had methodically built out his own net until it consisted of over seventy operatives. As CIA Karlsruhe had noted in a secret report as far back as 1951, Kibitz 15 "has shown remarkable ability as a staybehind organizer."

To Sichel's way of thinking, this "remarkable ability" in comparison to other local hires should have, in itself, set off alarm bells. Through the closing months of 1952 and into early 1953, Sichel repeatedly commanded Karlsruhe to shut down Kopp's stay-behind chain or, at the very least, get rid of Kopp. Except by now Kopp had so insinuated himself into a position of prominence that his agency handlers were clearly worried what he might do if terminated. On February 17, 1953, Karlsruhe informed Sichel that, in answer to his demands, they were meeting with Kopp the next day; as a way to finally sever him from the stay-behind program, they intended to offer him a transfer into a larger CIA intelligence-gathering mission known as Operation Redcap.

The news sent the normally decorous Sichel into a rage. After first lashing Karlsruhe for imagining the obdurate Kopp would be any more manageable in Redcap than he had been in Kibitz, Sichel homed in on the fact that the station hadn't sought his counsel first. To the contrary, fully aware that he would oppose Kopp's transfer, they had waited until the last possible minute to inform him of the plan. "Since no cable request for permission to take this step was received," Sichel fired back, "we are left to ponder whether Headquarters was purposely circumvented in this matter."

Finally, the operations chief made clear, Kopp was to be terminated—and immediately. "How to work out the problem of discontinuing him after you so recently offered him another job," Sichel wrote, "is quite honestly your own problem. You thought of that idea, and now I think it is up to you to think of a remedy. Nevertheless, we would be interested to hear of the remedy you find."

With that, Walter Kopp's tenure with the CIA at last came to an end, but not the headaches he would cause the Agency. In 1953, Sichel had noted that Kopp's neo-Nazi sympathies posed "a distinct and continuing hazard to American interests in Germany if Kubark [CIA] sponsorship of his activities should ever be subject to publicity," a warning that was borne out in 2006 when the CIA was made to declassify documents detailing the Agency's links with alleged Nazi war criminals in the postwar era. Among the nearly thirty thousand pages released, the name of Walter Kopp figured prominently.

But if the case of Kibitz 15 ultimately played out as embarrassment to the CIA, infinitely worse was the damage inflicted by another agency asset that Sichel tried to shed. His name was Alexander Orlov and his tale would serve as a sterling example of how both bureaucratic inertia and case officer myopia could keep a dubious operation running for years. It would also provide Alexander "Sasha" Orlov with one of the more astonishing life stories of anyone to emerge from the Cold War shadow world.

From a provincial town in western Russia, in World War II Orlov had served as a lieutenant in Soviet military intelligence and been given the near suicidal mission of parachuting behind German lines; sure enough, he was almost immediately wounded and captured by the enemy. Faced with the prospect of slow starvation in a German POW camp, Orlov instead switched sides. After first being attached to a German intelligence unit operating on the front lines, in 1944 he was transferred into the Vlasov Army, an auxiliary force of anti-communist Soviet prisoners and deserters hastily organized by the retreating Germans to slow the Red Army advance. Orlov's first lucky break came in the closing days of the war when, fleeing west to avoid the approaching and vengeful Red Army, he managed to surrender to American troops. His second came the following year when he was hired on by the Gehlen Organization, thus escaping the ongoing repatriation of Vlasov Army members to the Soviet Union.

Eventually, Orlov resettled in Munich, a city rapidly becoming the émigré headquarters of Western Europe. Falling in with a group of like-minded anti-communist Soviet exiles under the banner of SBONR, the Union of the Struggle for the Liberation of the Peoples of Russia, Orlov had been one of the SBONR cadres recruited by the CIA in 1951 and brought to Berlin by William Sloane Coffin.

While most of those SBONR operatives were soon returned to Munich, CIA Berlin case officers saw something special in Sasha Orlov. Obviously clever and possessed of consummate survival skills, there was a slightly standoffish quality about the twenty-eight-year-old Russian that stood very much in contrast to most of his eager-to-please fellow exiles. This may have been because, having married a German woman, the daughter of a former SS officer, Orlov was already putting down roots in his adopted country and didn't need to scrabble for a CIA paycheck to survive. This aloofness understandably had the effect of making him more attractive to agency recruiters.

And there was something else about the man, too. Though married and rather plain-looking, during his time in Berlin Orlov had proven to be an especially adroit seducer of women. Watching him in action, CIA Berlin got the idea of running the sort of honey trap operation for which the Soviets had long been famous, with Orlov cast in the role of recruitment officer—or, less decorously, pimp. While Soviet authorities had no issue with their men consorting with prostitutes, for security reasons long-term assignations were strictly forbidden, and those who transgressed were subject to punishments that began with an immediate transfer home. The goal, then, was for the smooth-talking Orlov, working in tandem with another recent CIA hire, an Estonian refugee named Vladimir Kivi, to find Berlin women who were the mistresses of Soviet officers—or to recruit women willing to become so—and through them, blackmail the officers into passing information to the West. All of that sounded just fine to Orlov when the CIA made the offer, and he signed on to the project in the autumn of 1951.

But almost immediately, disaster struck. In early November, just weeks after the operation was launched, Orlov's partner, Vladimir Kivi, vanished. After several days with no sign of him, CIA officers slipped into Kivi's apartment to find all his possessions still there, the place undisturbed. It led them to a grim conclusion: like so many operatives before him, Vladimir Kivi had been kidnapped and taken over to the Soviet sector, most likely to never be seen or heard from again. For all those who worked out of 19 Föhrenweg, a number that then still included Peter Sichel, Kivi's disappearance served as another reminder of just how deadly the game they were playing could be.

Despite the loss of Kivi, Orlov forged ahead with the honey trap. By the next summer, and shortly after Sichel had left for Washington, he ensnared his first victim in the form of a Soviet lieutenant colonel named Nikolai Svetlov. Working through Svetlov's German mistress, Orlov lured the Soviet officer into the American sector and straight into a CIA net. Under the threat that his superiors would learn of his illicit romance, a panicked Svetlov agreed to pass on to his new CIA handlers whatever classified information he could get his hands on.

This wasn't much, unfortunately, since the unit Svetlov worked for at Karlshorst, the Soviet headquarters in East Berlin, had little access to sensitive material. What he did have access to, though, were all those permits and *propiskas* necessary for internal travel in the Soviet Union and which the authorities constantly changed to thwart counterfeiters; if Svetlov could pass on the latest versions, the CIA could produce new forgeries to give to their infiltration agents.

It wasn't to be. Three days later, Svetlov returned with nothing more interesting for the CIA than a standard-issue and easily obtained military leave ticket. Soon after, Nikolai Svetlov disappeared from Karlshorst altogether, presumably transferred to a new Soviet base or, if his treasonous association with the Americans had been detected, to a gulag.

A disappointed Orlov quickly got to work on a couple of new marks—but then came more bad news. A belated and more thorough CIA background check had turned up some troubling questions about Orlov's past, questions serious enough to cause the headquarters of CIA Germany to recommend he be cut loose. This prompted Orlov's Berlin case officers to immediately rush to his defense. In the spring of 1954, Peter Sichel, now the head of Secret Intelligence's Eastern Europe desk in Washington, was brought in to take a closer look at Orlov's background and resolve the dispute.

No sooner had Sichel glanced at Orlov's file than a startling detail jumped out at him. In his long campaign to lure the wary Nikolai Svetlov into the CIA trap awaiting him in West Berlin, Orlov had grown so frustrated that he'd finally crossed into the Soviet sector himself to track Svetlov down at his Karlshorst apartment. Posing as the cousin of Svetlov's mistress, Orlov had concocted a story about why the Soviet officer needed to meet her in the American sector right away. This was the first Sichel had heard of the brash move, one that even Orlov's apologist case officer acknowledged was a "breach of procedure," but apparently any thoughts of reprimanding Orlov had evaporated when Svetlov did, in fact, come across and fall into the CIA net.

Then, of course, there was the unexplained disappearance of Vladimir Kivi, Orlov's erstwhile partner. In July 1954, Sichel composed a long dispatch to CIA Germany listing the reasons why Orlov and his wife should be immediately cashiered. Again, though, Berlin base resisted, arguing that at the very least Orlov should see out the entrapment operations he had in the works. Berlin's pleading won out.

Over the next five months, two more of Orlov's honey traps followed the frustrating example of Nikolai Svetlov's—and for oddly similar reason. Like Svetlov, a blackmailed Sergeant Alexander Smirnov lacked access to classified information, but agreed to smuggle across an array of Soviet passes and permits for the CIA to counterfeit. When Smirnov returned, though, he brought only two unclassified and obsolete Red Army service manuals, along with some postal money order forms, before he also fell from sight. In his next sting, Orlov convinced a young Soviet officer to become a CIA "agent-in-place" following his upcoming transfer home, but over the course of their subsequent sporadic communication, the officer passed on virtually nothing of substance. As noted by David Murphy, the former CIA Munich station chief, in his book, *Battleground Berlin,* these three operations comprised the sum total of Alexander Orlov's successful missions for the CIA, a track record so poor and Orlov by now so well known to local officials that by early 1955 even Berlin base agreed he should be let go.

Except he wasn't. Incredibly, due to bureaucratic delays in the relocation process, Orlov was kept on CIA Germany's payroll for two more years before he and his family were finally resettled in Alexandria, Virginia. Even then, Orlov was kept on as a CIA contract officer. It wasn't until 1960, fully six years after Sichel's recommendation that Orlov be fired, that the Agency finally severed ties with the unlucky honey trap operator.

But maybe not unlucky at all. Tips provided by a high-ranking KGB defector in 1961 ultimately led to the revelation that Orlov had been a KGB double agent from the very start: not just when he was recruited by CIA Germany, or when he had joined the SBONR émigré group, but perhaps even before he was brought into the Gehlen Organization, maybe as far back as his wartime service with the German army. In this capacity, he had apparently first arranged the 1951 abduction and disappearance of his partner, Vladimir Kivi, and then ensured that his honey trap "victims"—all presumably KGB officers fully briefed on the roles they were to play—provided absolutely nothing of value. Even the one potentially ruinous misstep Orlov made, his foolhardy 1952 visit to the Karlshorst compound, had worked in his favor; rather than suggestive of treachery, his CIA handlers evidently interpreted the act as one of bravery and dedication to the cause.

But in the early 1960s, the information provided by the KGB defector was too sketchy to bring charges against Orlov, or even to deport him. Instead, it wasn't until the mid-1990s, when the KGB's file on him was partially opened to researchers, that a fuller picture of Orlov's extraordinary infiltration became known. As noted by Christopher Andrew and Vasili Mitrokhin in *The Sword and the Shield,* Orlov was probably the most important double agent the Soviets ran anywhere in the West during the 1950s. "By taking an active part in the [Berlin] station's attempt to recruit Soviet personnel and encourage defections, he was able to find numerous opportunities to sabotage its operations. Among the wealth of intelligence which [he] provided were the identities of more than a hundred American intelligence officers and agents in East Germany; some were arrested while others were turned into double agents."

But this disclosure also came too late to ensnare Orlov: he had died in 1982. Up until then, he and his wife ran a picture-framing gallery in Alexandria, just a few miles from CIA headquarters. Perhaps to capitalize on the notoriety of her late husband after his unmasking, in the late 1990s his widow added a retail merchandise section to Gallery Orlov, one "specializing in Soviet and Cold War memorabilia."

In recounting the saga of Sasha Orlov, Peter Sichel gave a weary sigh. "It was a classic example of case officers falling in love with their agents. I tried to tell them they were being played. Unfortunately, in this case they refused to listen."

But of course, everything in the intelligence shadow world can be interpreted from at least two different angles, because everything has the potential of being the precise opposite of what it first appears. So it was with the Orlov affair. Back in 1954 when Sichel first reviewed Orlov's case, and long before his damning conclusion would be supported by the 1961 defector, there were others in the intelligence community who viewed the case quite differently. That's because on the very day that Sichel submitted his report on Orlov—July 21, 1954—there occurred one of the more puzzling side stories of the Cold War, one that centered on a German government official named Otto John, but that also cast a shadow over Peter Sichel.

"You see," Sichel explained, "because of my negativism and wanting to shut down some of these useless operations, there had been these different rumors about me over the years. The Army had looked into them—nothing—but the stories started again after the Otto John affair, and that's what finally brought in the FBI." When asked to which rumors he was referring, Sichel gave a slow shrug. "Well, they put in the charge that I was KGB."

On the morning of September 15, 1954, Ed Lansdale and five other members of his Saigon Military Mission team piled into several cars and headed northwest out of Saigon in the general direction of Tay Ninh, a town close to the border with Cambodia. They were clad in casual sports clothes, "as though for a day's outing," as Lansdale described it. That image was somewhat undercut by the palpably nervous demeanor of one of their traveling companions, a Vietnamese government official in a white sharkskin suit and black tie. The image was further compromised by the pistols most of the SMM men carried in their waistbands, and by the loaded guns Lansdale kept at his feet.

They were actually on their way to meet a legendary guerrilla fighter named Trinh Minh Thé. Although only thirty-two, Thé fairly exemplified the complexities of the Vietnamese warscape of the past decade. First recruited and trained by the Japanese occupation forces, Thé had battled both the French and the Viet Minh during World War II, before realigning with the Viet Minh to fight the reimposition of French rule in the postwar era. Turning against Viet Minh excesses, in 1947 he had taken command of the private army of the Cao Dai religious sect and, bankrolled by the French, gone back to war against the Viet Minh. Eventually rediscovering his antipathy for French rule, Thé then led the Cao Dai into revolt against their *colon* paymasters, before forming his own breakaway militia, the Lien Minh. By 1954, the Lien Minh stood ready to wage battle against all comers from its base camp on the flanks of Nui Ba Den, or Black Lady Mountain, just outside Tay Ninh. While enjoying a Robin Hood reputation among local residents, Thé's image in Saigon was that of a brilliant and fearless fighter. It was for this reason that a beleaguered Ngo Dinh Diem entertained hopes of bringing Thé and his highly trained militia into a reconstituted—and Diem-loyal—national army. One indication of Diem's isolation was that to deliver a secret letter to Thé proposing such a deal, he had turned to one of the few advisors he completely trusted: CIA officer Edward Lansdale.

It's doubtful that Lansdale needed much coaxing for the venture. Carrying the old maxim "know thy enemy" to its logical conclusion, in the Philippines, Lansdale had repeatedly tried to meet the Huk leader, Luis Taruc; Trinh Minh Thé seemed a man cut from similar cloth. After clearing Diem's request with the American ambassador and CIA officials back in Washington, the SMM commander put together a small traveling party for the sixty-mile journey up Highway 1 to Black Lady Mountain. The one discordant note was the overdressed Vietnamese official they'd brought along to facilitate contact, his jumpiness so apparent that some SMM members feared they were driving into a trap.

As for which among South Vietnam's myriad armed factions were most likely to lay such a trap, the most obvious answer was the French. When still the commander of the Cao Dai army, Thé had waged a pitiless terror campaign against the French military, with his crowning success being the assassination of the French commander in chief of southern forces by a suicide bomber. For that and other attacks carried out by Thé's cadres, the French very much wished to kill the guerrilla leader on Black Lady Mountain, and the farther Lansdale's small convoy traveled down Highway 1 toward that mountain, the more obvious their destination.

Following instructions, just outside Tay Ninh, the group turned off the highway onto a rough dirt road before coming to a stop outside a small village. Within minutes, a band of Lien Minh guerrillas emerged from the jungle. Lansdale pegged one member of the party as its leader, a tiny, rail-thin boy in tennis shoes who appeared to be of high school age, and assumed he would be leading them to Thé. "He had a broad, infectious smile on his face," Lansdale recalled, "which brought one to mine as he reached out and shook my hand in welcome. He introduced himself. He was Trinh minh Thé."

Following Thé into the jungle and up the mountain slope, Lansdale and the others came to a small clearing. With two interpreters, Lansdale and Thé crowded into a tiny thatched hut where the CIA officer handed the guerrilla leader Diem's letter. Then, for the next several hours, the two discussed the future of Vietnam.

The meeting with the fugitive Thé was only the most dramatic of a number of such clandestine meetings Lansdale held in the closing months of 1954. Both in quiet backrooms in Saigon and during quick forays into the countryside, the SMM commander met with an array of local warlords, as well as militia leaders from both the Cao Dai and Hoa Hao sects, part of a concerted effort to wean the private armies away from their French paymasters and to Diem's side. If appeals to nationalism or anticolonialism didn't do the trick, Lansdale was more than ready to turn to the cash dispenser. While the precise amount remains in dispute, tens of millions of dollars flowed from secret CIA accounts to the sect armies in late 1954 and early 1955. A crucial first convert was Thé and his Lien Minh militia. Following protracted negotiations and the transfer of at least $1 million in CIA funds into the group's coffers—payroll costs or bribery, depending on one's perspective—Trinh Minh Thé would ultimately lead some 2,500 of his soldiers in a triumphant march through downtown Saigon to mark their formal integration into the South Vietnamese military.

By then, Lansdale had also moved to eliminate one of Diem's most powerful enemies, army chief of staff Nguyen Van Hinh. Time and again, Hinh had flouted Diem's commands, and talked freely of the day he would overthrow the prime minister and install himself as Vietnam's ruler. In a quintessentially Vietnamese touch, the general once sought to humiliate Diem by racing his motorcycle through the gardens of Gia Long Palace and shouting insults up at the resident prime minister, daring Diem or anyone in his retinue to stop him. To Lansdale, the idea that Hinh, long regarded as a bought-and-paid-for creature of the hated French, could generate any kind of popular support for his rule was absurd. "I could only conclude," he wrote, "from the remarks of disgruntled French colonialists and military adventurers, that some of them probably had put Hinh up to planning a coup. Perhaps they thought that they could turn back the clock with such a move. Crazy!"

Just in case, though, upon hearing that Hinh planned to launch his coup on a particular day in late October, Lansdale persuaded several of the general's closest aides to go on a visit to the fleshpots of Manila, a junket that left them out of the country at the crucial moment. "General Hinh told me ruefully that he had called off his coup," Lansdale later claimed. "He had forgotten that he needed his chief lieutenants for key roles in the coup and couldn't proceed while they were out of the country." While Lansdale credited this ruse for thwarting the revolt, it's far more likely that Hinh's French handlers grasped the disastrous consequences of such a move; for weeks beforehand, and also at Lansdale's prompting, the Eisenhower administration had warned the French that a coup in Saigon would bring an immediate end to American aid. In any event, Hinh was soon bundled out of the city to enjoy a golden exile in France where he would eventually be promoted to deputy chief of staff of the French air force.

And if Lansdale could be employed to take down Diem's rivals, there was no reason the arrangement couldn't work in reverse. In his memoir, Lansdale maintained that he enjoyed a good working relationship with the American ambassador to Vietnam, Donald Heath, but he also chafed under the diplomat's tendency to try to rein in or water down his initiatives. With Diem's stock rising in the eyes of official Washington by mid-October 1954—a rise largely attributable to Lansdale's own laudatory reports—the SMM commander sent a new cable to Allen Dulles relating that Diem had lost confidence in the ambassador, and suggested it would "be constructive [to] replace Heath soonest." Whether it spoke to the growing clout of Lansdale or of Diem or of the two of them in partnership, within a matter of weeks Donald Heath was gone.

Even if Lansdale's role in Heath's recall remained veiled, in the uppermost corridors of power in Washington—as well as in Saigon—it was becoming increasingly clear who was now calling the shots in the unfolding American adventure in Vietnam.

23

THOSE BASTARDS OUT THERE

Just as he had following Operation Ajax in Iran, a few weeks after the coup in Guatemala President Eisenhower held a celebratory reception for its principal architects at the White House. Frank Wisner attended, as did Allen Dulles. With the aid of maps and slides, the chief field commander gave the captivated president a blow-by-blow account of the ten-day operation that culminated in the overthrow of President Árbenz and the installation of Colonel Castillo Armas. At the end of the presentation, Eisenhower asked how many of Castillo Armas's men had been killed in the coup.

"Just one," the field commander said. This was a lie. Despite barely budging from their nation's borders before Árbenz fell, the inept Guatemalan rebels had managed to lose at least forty-five fighters, but no one present thought to correct the record. Afterward, a grateful president shook the hands of his guests. "Thanks to all of you," he said. "You've averted a Soviet beachhead in our hemisphere."

Since the coup, some of Wisner's CIA colleagues had noticed he seemed unusually subdued, preoccupied. Most attributed it to exhaustion—even compared to his usual unsparing pace, the CIA deputy director had toiled relentlessly to bring the Guatemalan operation to fruition—but exhaustion mixed with relief. "Wisner was so glad it was over," recalled Frank Holcomb, one of those CIA officers that Wisner had dispatched to the operations base in Florida to keep an eye on things. "He was very happy to be rid of this thing, the nightmare was over."

But not truly over, of course. For Frank Wisner, as for the CIA, there was always another crisis, another battlefield.

With the successful coup in Guatemala building on that in Iran, the CIA now entered what has been called the "golden age" of covert operations. As noted by historian John Ranelagh, "using the total arsenal of the Directorate of Plans—sabotage, propaganda, paramilitary actions, political action," the Agency had proven itself to be "the most effective instrument in the secret brinkmanship of the cold war." In the years just ahead, the CIA would take its fight and clandestine missions to countries on five continents, to nations that were allies or foes or those just wishing to stay neutral. The branch of the Agency that would play a preeminent role in this escalating mission was Wisner's directorate.

There was an air of inevitability about this expansion, and much of it could be attributed to President Eisenhower's personal preferences. In contrast to many of his more tradition-minded colleagues in the American military, Eisenhower had been a strong advocate of covert operations throughout World War II, and saw even greater application for them in the postwar era. Part of the lure was simple economics. When compared to conventional war, engaging the enemy through covert action cost a pittance—the coups in Iraq and Guatemala had amply proved that— which meant the CIA could pursue many more such missions at a fraction of the cost. Such operations also offered plausible deniability. While Eisenhower personally approved every major CIA covert operation conducted during his administration, he was careful to stay ignorant of their details—at least until after the fact.

With the CIA the primary beneficiary of this outlook, Director Allen Dulles paid attention to economics of a different sort: call it the law of bureaucratic self-perpetuation. By that law, the more covert operations the Agency undertook, the more funding it could extract from Congress, and the greater the funding, the more the Agency's standing rose in relation to its bureaucratic competitors. This naturally translated into even more influence with lawmakers, influence that transmuted into greater funding to launch more covert operations. A consummate political animal, Dulles played this game with utter deliberation, purposely funneling the Agency's resources toward those projects that cost the most—covert operations—and away from those that didn't, namely intelligence gathering. As he once breezily explained to Richard Helms, the dean of intelligence collection, the very inexpensiveness of intelligence gathering was a problem when he went to Congress asking for money. "They're accustomed to dealing in billions. What kind of impression can it make when

I come along and ask for a few hundred thousand dollars and a bag of pennies? Believe me, I know the way they think up there. If there's no real money involved, it can't be important, and they just won't pay much attention to us."

An even more cynical explanation was offered by a senior CIA official of the time, Miles Copeland, using the analogy of an arsonist fireman. As Copeland rhetorically asked, once Washington power brokers had created this elite strike force to deal with the world's problems, "didn't they see it as inevitable that we would *seek* fires to put out, even if we had to light them ourselves?"

Theoretically, the federal government's system of budgetary oversight meant that a congressional watchdog committee was likely to catch on to this pattern and demand an audit of the Agency—except for that to happen, there had to be a watchdog. Instead, much like the president himself, Congress figured out that not asking questions of the CIA also meant not having to take responsibility for its actions. As a result, as CIA historian Richard Immerman observed, "the Eisenhower years were the centerpiece of an era of 'congressional undersight.'"

Of course, there was still one actor with the potential to disrupt this cozy arrangement: What should happen if the new Soviet leadership made a peaceful overture so compelling that it called into question the need for—or at least the prevalence of—CIA covert operations? Such a development might result in a "peace dividend" for the American taxpayer in the form of reduced funding for the Pentagon and CIA. This threat had been largely neutralized, however, both by the Eisenhower administration's unyielding stance toward the Soviet Union in the wake of Stalin's death, and by its continuing blanket hostility to most any Kremlin initiative.

That hostility was codified in a remarkable CIA document sent to the president in September 1954, just three months after the coup in Guatemala. Officially known as National Intelligence Estimate 11-4-54, the top secret paper was entitled "Soviet Capabilities and Probable Courses of Action Through Mid-1959."

While the authors of NIE 11-4-54 believed the Soviets wished to avoid outright war with the United States, they also believed "that the USSR will continue to pursue its expansionist objectives and to seek and exploit opportunities for enlarging the area of Communist control." While Moscow was always capable of a change in methods, "for the time being, the Kremlin seems to feel that its foreign objectives will be best served by a generally conciliatory pose in foreign relations, by gestures of 'peaceful coexistence' and proposals for mutual security pacts." The Kremlin goal, the 11-4-54 authors concluded, was "to create the impression that there has been a basic change in Soviet policy, and thereby to destroy the incentive for Western defense and to undermine US policies."

In sum, according to NIE 11-4-54, even the most conciliatory of gestures by the Soviets were really just further proof of their ultimate world-conquering intent, an intent that showed no signs of abating (although it might be asked just what signs were possible within such circular reasoning) for at least the next five years of its projection.

Within those five years of Soviet aggression, the CIA as vanguard of American power abroad could accomplish a very great deal. In addition to its growing involvement in brush wars around the world, Eisenhower was so enamored of the Agency that by the close of 1954 he took the unusual step of entrusting it with the development of a new generation of spy plane, the U-2. With the goal of achieving high-altitude surveillance of the Soviet Union and its nuclear arsenal, the U-2 project would logically seem an Air Force program, but the president wanted to stretch the CIA's charter of plausible deniability to even this most overt of initiatives. On a darker note, by that time, the CIA's Technical Services Staff was conducting a host of experiments using "biological and chemical materials," including psychotropic drugs, that might be used as truth serums or brainwashing aids to control human behavior. Eventually, the CIA's MKUltra project would encompass nearly 150 such dubious experiments and cause at least one fatality, a scientist who leapt to his death from a hotel window after being used as a guinea pig in LSD trials.

Yet, and as paradoxical as it might seem, it may have been this very golden age of covert action looming on the horizon that had cast Frank Wisner in his peculiar mood after the Guatemalan coup. Something rather more than exhaustion seemed to be at work for, according to some in the CIA, Wisner's subdued manner didn't appreciably change in subsequent weeks; it was almost as if he were anticipating some kind of trouble. Or perhaps rather than trouble, it was the burden of responsibility, that in the "golden age" then descending on his directorate, Frank Wisner was already contemplating the setbacks and deaths and recriminations sure to come.

A hint of this was revealed at a CIA gathering that he attended in Vienna in early 1955. The occasion was a meeting of CIA station chiefs from across Europe, brought together for a few days to discuss strategy and compare notes. During a break in the proceedings, Wisner busied himself by flipping through a tall stack of documents, status reports on some of the operations the Agency was conducting in the region. "For Christ's sake," he finally muttered to no one in particular, "will you look at these things we started as emergency, temporary operations, and then got stuck with."

To those at the meeting who hadn't recently observed Wisner at close quarters, that statement surely registered as shocking; the deputy director had once been regarded as a virtual rubber stamp for most any covert action proposal that crossed his desk. This was no longer true, though. In the last two years, there had been the WiN hoax in Poland, the disappearance of agents in Romania and Estonia and Lithuania. These were joined to the earlier deaths or disappearance of agents in Albania and Korea and Byelorussia and most anywhere else the CIA tried to pierce the Iron Curtain. All this changed Wisner.

Given his often brusque manner, one facet of Wisner's personality that subordinates may have overlooked was how emotionally involved he became in the operations he approved, how intently he followed their progress. A close colleague recalled that Wisner had remained confident of the ultimate success of Operation Fiend long after most others in the office had pegged it as a lost cause. That confidence gave way to crushing disappointment when Wisner learned that Hamit Matjani, the legendary Albanian partisan fighter, had fallen into a *Sigurimi* trap. It's unlikely that Wisner ever even met Matjani, but he had clearly become strongly attached to his story and his cause. For someone who was essentially a field marshal on the Cold War landscape, directing his "soldiers" across dozens of battlefields and routinely suffering casualties on most of them, this level of personal involvement must have been both exhausting and distressing to sustain. Peter Sichel once commented that in the East-West spy wars it was important to never take things personally—Frank Wisner took things personally.

Clearly also gnawing at the deputy director was the same question that had come to plague Michael Burke: what would happen if any of this actually worked? In March 1954, Wisner raised the matter with C. D. Jackson, Eisenhower's psychological warfare advisor and a leading proponent of fomenting revolt in the Soviet bloc: "Suppose that our efforts are successful and that there comes to pass an outbreak of violence of large proportions and of a magnitude which would pose the kind of challenge to the Russians that would require them to move in on the situation with massive (military) repressive measures. The question is—what do *we* do then?" Wisner called this the "Number One question thus far unanswered," but there's no record that Jackson provided one.

By the time of that Vienna meeting, Wisner might have buoyed himself with the thought that he was at last in a position to stanch some of the bleeding, since one side effect of the Agency's spectacular successes in Iran and Guatemala was to remind everyone of just how meager the returns in Eastern Europe. This proved only partially true. While Operation Fiend was finally slated to be shut down after five fruitless years, other missions just as futile continued apace. In that spring of 1955, the CIA overseers of the Ukrainian infiltration scheme, Operation Aerodynamic, urged that the mission extend through the rest of the year, despite their having lost all contact with resistance units inside the country for almost two years. That April, those managing the three-year-old penetration scheme into Estonia, Operation Root, conceded that "so far no positive intelligence reports have been produced." Nevertheless, plans were under way to drop two more agents into the Baltic country in 1956, this time by balloon. All this and more, despite the fact that over all those years and all those deaths—a toll that certainly numbered in the hundreds, if not thousands—the CIA had never managed to place an agent anywhere near even a provincial locus of power in the Soviet bloc, nor to stir up anything at all in the way of a true rebellion.

Instead, triumph in Iran and Guatemala simply meant the battlefield was expanded to the rest of the world. Indeed, for every Eastern European operation curtailed or closed out in the mid-1950s, another took its place in the more inviting climes of Asia and Africa and Latin America.

Once again, the deputy director often found himself cast in the role of brakeman—albeit a largely failed one when going up against the Dulles brothers. Despite having been a strong supporter of Ed Lansdale and his actions in the Philippines, Wisner was far less enthusiastic about sending him to Vietnam; the Dulles brothers sent him anyway. With growing frequency, Wisner tried to shelve covert operations he deemed impractical or counterproductive, but the Dulles brothers almost as frequently overruled him. It seemed that at the very moment the multifarious anticommunist apparatus known as "the Mighty Wurlitzer" was becoming truly mighty, its creator was growing apprehensive of it.

In this, there may have been an element of self-protection, as well. By now, there clung to Wisner a sense of aggrievement, the feeling that, no matter what he did or didn't do, his enemies and detractors were always close at hand to leap to the attack. Given the trajectory of his professional life in recent years, the feeling was quite understandable.

Going all the way back to his selection as OPC chief in 1948, the knives had been out for Frank Wisner, and they'd only grown more numerous and sharper since. Especially wounding had been the behind-the-scenes machinations of William Donovan, the former OSS chief and a man Wisner once greatly admired. In hoping to be chosen as Eisenhower's new CIA director in 1952, Donovan had tried to tarnish Wisner's reputation among officials of the incoming administration. That hadn't helped Donovan win the directorship in the end, but it may have ensured that, once again, Wisner was passed over in favor of Allen Dulles. As Polly Wisner diplomatically put it: "Frank turned from having liked General Donovan enormously to being rather unhappy with him."

In 1954, Eisenhower had asked James Doolittle, the famous World War II air commander, to conduct a study on the covert activities of the CIA. Doolittle's report, handed in close on the heels of the Guatemalan coup, scored Wisner for being a poor organizer and filling sensitive positions "with people having little or no training for their jobs." This sense of being constantly disparaged, and Wisner's attempts to defend himself, occasionally led to unintended dark humor: the chief criticism noted in one of Wisner's annual fitness reviews was his sensitivity to criticism.

Certainly, in one sphere, the CIA deputy director was not being overly sensitive at all: the perpetual scheming of J. Edgar Hoover to bring about his downfall. Those efforts had not stopped with the FBI's thwarted investigation in late 1952. Instead, the bureau had launched a new inquiry into Wisner's past in late 1953, and then again in March of 1954. It was in this last effort, a laundry list of twenty-one different allegations of wrongdoing, almost all having to do with Wisner's tenure in wartime Romania, that the secret tag-team arrangement between Hoover and Joe McCarthy was most nakedly revealed. In investigating the charges, the head of the CIA's internal security office determined that at least two of the FBI's allegations "have come from an investigator with a Senate investigating subcommittee, who has been attempting to build a case for Congressional hearings on CIA operations." This clearly referred to Roy Cohn, McCarthy's chief legal counsel, but Cohn likely could have only formulated his accusations with information passed on by his principal source: the FBI. In a letter Wisner wrote to his mother that June, however, with the latest round of inquiries into his past just under way, he chose to focus his ire, as so many others at the time did, on Hoover's front man: "I have no doubt that McCarthy and his people have it in for me personally since my views about his entire performance are well known."

In May 1955, over a year after the FBI had reopened its investigation, Wisner was finally cleared of all twenty-one accusations made against him. As the CIA security chief noted in an eleven-page report to Hoover, most all the claims had been "based on fabrication, distortion of fact and Rumanian refugee gossip," and this included the charges leveled by Joe McCarthy's toady.

By then, Joe McCarthy was no longer a threat to Wisner or to any-one else—his censure by the Senate in December 1954 had precipitated a decline as swift as had been his ascent—but Wisner may have already begun to suspect that the senator had never been his true antagonist any-way. It had always been Hoover and, despite his latest exoneration, Wis-ner surely knew that a new letter from the FBI director announcing yet another investigation of him could come at any time. Certainly, Hoover hadn't given up the hunt. Five months after Wisner's exoneration, he sent a memorandum to his deputies commanding that "in the event that you have any contact with Wisner, you should make certain that you are most circumspect with him. The results of any contact with Wisner should be reported to the Bureau."

In the interim, the CIA deputy director had been buffeted on a wholly new front. In July 1955, yet another outside evaluation of the CIA, the Clark Committee report, was handed in to the president. Once again, Wisner's Directorate of Plans came in for criticism, but in his angered response to those detractors who had hoped for harsher treatment was the trace of a bunker mentality. "The time has now come when this Agency can and should go over onto the attack against its irresponsible critics," Wisner wrote. "We should let it be understood that the 'open sea-son' on CIA is closed, and that it is no longer a fashionable or profitable pursuit to sling mud at our people."

In that missive, Wisner might have unconsciously been speaking of his own travails as much as the Agency's, his words less an exhortation than a plea.

———

Answering Diem's summons, Ed Lansdale set out for Doc Lap Palace at shortly after noon of April 28, 1955; accompanying him was his translator and assistant, Joe Redick.

They found the prime minister, clad in his customary white suit, pac-ing over the marble stones of the broad second floor veranda outside his office. Normally, after brief pleasantries, Diem would have ushered his visitors to the arrangement of armchairs in his alcove office just off the veranda, there to begin one of his discursive monologues, but on this day he drew up to ask Lansdale a blunt question. He had just heard that President Eisenhower had agreed to his overthrow and his replacement by a coalition government; was this true?

"Diem looked at me intently when he asked this," Lansdale recalled in his memoir. "I said firmly that I didn't believe the report." Lansdale offered to make inquiries of Washington to confirm this, but pointed out that, as it was then right around midnight on the American East Coast, it might be some hours before he had an answer.

This appeared to mollify Diem, although on that afternoon any disenchantment on Eisenhower's part seemed a secondary problem. On their way to Doc Lap Palace, Lansdale and Redick had been approaching an intersection when the crackle of machine gunfire had sent them and others scrambling for cover, a clear sign that the government's fragile month-old truce with the Binh Xuyen crime syndicate was coming apart. Lansdale was given further confirmation of this while standing with Diem on the palace veranda. With an incongruously impish grin, the prime minister explained that, according to intelligence reports, the Binh Xuyen had already sighted the palace with their newly acquired long-range mortars, and had pinpointed the very spot where they were now standing. "We might get blown up even as we stood there talking to each other." Meanwhile, reports of shooting were coming in from all over Saigon.

After counseling Diem to get off the veranda, Lansdale said he would return to his Duy Tan home, just eight blocks away, and start calling Washington. No sooner had he and Redick reached the house than there came a steady roar of explosions from the direction of the palace. Moments later, Diem called. He already had the French commander on the line, and he wanted both men to hear the sound of the mortar rounds falling on Doc Lap; after angrily insisting that the Binh Xuyen had started the fight, Diem abruptly hung up. The long-anticipated second battle for Saigon was under way.

This, at least, was Lansdale's version of events. In fact, though, the salient details of his account were almost certainly a fiction, crafted to mask the pivotal role he played in provoking a battle that would forever change the course of American involvement in Vietnam.

The seeds for that battle had been planted several months earlier, and arose from a fight that Diem had picked. Something of a moral crusader, Diem had frequently talked of launching a crackdown on the varied houses of vice for which Saigon was notorious—gambling parlors, bordellos, opium dens—and which also happened to be the lifeblood of the extremely powerful Binh Xuyen crime syndicate. That syndicate bore scant resemblance to the Western conception of a mafia. Instead, having effectively purchased control of Saigon's police force from the Emperor Bao Dai, the Binh Xuyen racketeers wore uniforms, drove marked vehicles, even operated gunboats with which they patrolled the surrounding waterways. The French colonial regime had supported this arrangement, since the Binh Xuyen—like gangsters everywhere, committed capitalists—could be relied on to augment their battle against the communist Viet Minh.

An early bid by Binh Xuyen leaders to forge a compromise with Diem was rejected by the Catholic moralist. Instead, in mid-January 1955, Diem had further alienated the syndicate by revoking their license to operate the Grand Monde casino, the city's largest and most lucrative. In response, the Binh Xuyen gangsters donned a political mask, and reached out to the militia leaders of the Cao Dai and Hoa Hao religious sects. It was propitious timing for the overture came just as the subsidies the sects received from the French administration were slated to end, leaving thousands of militiamen without an income. It had presented sect militia leaders with a stark choice: either throw their lot in with the fragile Diem regime or ally with the powerful and French-supported Binh Xuyen. The result was a so-called United Front that, on March 22, had given Diem a five-day ultimatum to accept a new power-sharing arrangement or face the combined wrath of the Binh Xuyen and an array of sect armies. Instead of heeding the ultimatum, Diem sent the Vietnamese army against his opponents, sparking the first battle for Saigon.

As the contest was joined, there had occurred two rather surprising developments. The first was the army's standing by Ngo Dinh Diem. The smart money had bet that the army would side with the United Front—or stage their own coup—but instead, Diem had been able to salt the armed forces with just enough supporters to ensure the loyalty of most units. And it was when those loyal units closed on the Binh Xuyen gunmen that a second surprise was revealed: the hidden hand of the French.

It had been obvious for some time that within the French colonial administration and resident military were a host of diehards who wished to scuttle the Geneva Accords mandating an end to French rule in Indochina; in observing their endless eleventh-hour intrigues, a frustrated Frank Wisner had once thundered: "What shall we do about those bastards out there?" Somewhat less apparent was that these revanchists had looked to achieve this goal by using the Binh Xuyen to knock out Diem. When that didn't happen, when instead the army attacked the outgunned Binh Xuyen, the French were forced to intervene, blocking off key intersections with tanks and armored cars to stop the fighting and impose a cease-fire. Ostensibly they did so to prevent greater bloodshed, but to most anyone who observed the French troops in the streets of Saigon in late March, a group that included Ed Lansdale, it was clear they were protecting their Binh Xuyen allies.

By then, however, both Lansdale and Diem had another powerful antagonist: American presidential envoy General J. Lawton Collins. A no-nonsense, by-the-book career Army officer, Collins had arrived in Saigon in November to temporarily take the place of the ambassador, Donald Heath, whose departure Lansdale had helped engineer. For Lansdale, it was an object lesson in the maxim, "be careful what you wish for." While Collins took a very dim view of Lansdale's freewheeling approach to policymaking—he made clear there was only one U.S. commanding officer in Saigon, and he was it—he thought even less of Ngo Dinh Diem. As he reported in a cable to Washington soon after arriving in Saigon: "Diem is a small, shy diffident man with almost no personal magnetism. . . . I am by no means certain he has [the] inherent capacity to manage [the] country during this critical period." Collins's estimation of the prime minister hadn't improved with time. He was soon warning Washington that "a possible successor must be sought."

Neither John Foster nor Allen Dulles immediately bought into Collins's view of Diem, buoyed as they were by the far more positive dispatches of Ed Lansdale, but matters had reached a turning point in that first March showdown with the Binh Xuyen. Where Lansdale had wanted the fight to continue, convinced that Diem's forces were defeating the crime syndicate, Collins had joined with the French army commander in arranging for a cease-fire. Thereafter, the envoy's Diem-must-go missives to Washington only grew more insistent—and soon had the desired effect. "In light of your reiterated conviction that Diem cannot gain adequate Vietnam support to establish an effective government," John Foster Dulles wrote Collins on April 11, "and that other men are available whose designation as Premier would improve the existing status, you are authorized to acquiesce in the plans for Diem's replacement." To work out the details for that "replacement," Collins was instructed to temporarily return to Washington.

Collins's abrupt recall had aroused Lansdale's suspicions. As the envoy prepared to leave Saigon on April 20, Lansdale tried to pin him down, pointing out that his sudden departure was likely to make Diem nervous that plans were being made to oust him; if Diem asked, what should Lansdale say? With a straight face, Collins replied: "If he asks, tell him the United States continues to support him."

As Collins made the rounds of senior administration officials in Washington in late April, his bid to get rid of Diem received almost unanimous endorsement. There was one notable exception, however: Frank Wisner. At the beginning of the month, *Time* magazine had run a long and laudatory cover story on Diem, and the CIA deputy director wondered how Collins's estimation of the situation in Saigon was so at odds with journalists who had spent far more time on the ground, and with the dispatches of Colonel Lansdale. What Wisner surely didn't know was that much of the information in the *Time* article had been planted by Ed Lansdale, but it still spoke to Wisner's newly found cautious streak to question why the U.S. should overthrow an ally, flawed though he was, for a politician or general of unknown reliability. On this matter, though, as on so many others, Wisner's reticence was overridden by the more action-oriented Dulles brothers. On the evening of April 27—seven in the morning of April 28 in Vietnam—John Foster Dulles sent a cable to the embassies in Paris and Saigon alerting them to prepare for Diem's removal. Allen Dulles sent a similar cable to Lansdale.

When Lansdale received the news, he jumped to the fray. Within two hours, he had fired back an impassioned defense of Diem to Allen Dulles. "Failure to support Diem," he wrote, "would cause great damage to American prestige and would doom any successor government to Diem's to failure." Clearly knowing his audience, he added: "The only winners would be the [communist] Viet Minh." This was bracing news to the Dulles brothers. Shortly after being shown Lansdale's message, John Foster Dulles sent a second cable to the embassies in France and Vietnam instructing them to place his earlier message on temporary hold. Lansdale was also instructed to prepare a more detailed report outlining his defense of Diem, one that, if it arrived in time, would be taken up at a meeting of the National Security Council scheduled for the following morning. Lansdale had presumably been preparing to write that report when, as noted in his memoirs, he received Diem's summons to the palace and discovered, courtesy of the crossfire he drove into, that the truce with the Binh Xuyen had fallen apart.

Except a couple of nagging questions. Why, when meeting Diem, did Lansdale feign ignorance about the American decision to overthrow him, when he'd already sent a cable to Washington trying to rescind the decision? One can think of a number of reasons why Lansdale might withhold this information from Diem at that moment, but why maintain the fiction when writing his memoirs nearly twenty years later? And then there was Diem's curious behavior, as related by Lansdale, as the Binh Xuyen attack on the palace got under way; when under a mortar attack, is it really one's first instinct to get on the phone to tell someone the other side fired first?

An answer to these questions would seem to rest in answering a different one: who had the stronger motive for breaking the truce on April 28, the Binh Xuyen or Diem? Certainly not the Binh Xuyen. They had been mauled in the fighting in March and, while still enjoying the tacit backing of the French, had little reason to think they would fare better a second time around. Further, given General Collins's close relationship with the French commander, they surely also knew that Collins was in Washington to arrange Diem's demise. The winning move, then, was for the Binh Xuyen to do nothing.

Diem, on the other hand, having heard rumors that Washington was plotting his end, had every motive for launching a preemptive attack on the enemy, a last-chance bid to show his foreign benefactors that he had the ability and the mettle to act decisively. Indeed, an American embassy press officer serving in Diem's inner circle at the time stated flatly that "Diem had ordered his army to move against the sects."

But if Diem acted on these rumors to launch a first strike, who had been their source? Logically, it could only have been a Diem loyalist with knowledge of the top secret deliberations then taking place in Washington, a criterion that narrowed the pool of suspects down to one: Colonel Ed Lansdale. With all of official Washington lined up against the Vietnamese prime minister, joined to virtually every American official in Saigon, it appears that Lansdale decided there was nothing to lose by trying one last gambit. To keep these machinations under wraps, however, meant creating a web of lies—Lansdale didn't know Washington was plotting Diem's overthrow; the Binh Xuyen attacked first—that would never be uncovered so long as the paper trail contradicting them remained under seal.

After his meeting with Diem on the palace veranda, Lansdale sped back to the Duy Tan house to write his report for the National Security Council meeting. Amid constant interruptions, the SMM commander received fragmentary reports of the fighting taking place across Saigon, but all was contradictory, shrouded in the fog of war. That evening, he raced through the deserted and dangerous streets of Saigon for the secure transmission room at the American embassy, there to send off his dispatch to CIA headquarters.

Considering the distractions he'd faced, Lansdale's report was a remarkable feat. While greatly exaggerating the prowess of Diem's loyalist troops—he suggested they were putting the Binh Xuyen to flight throughout the city when, at that early stage, the outcome was still highly in doubt—he emphasized again the point most likely to strike a chord with his audience. "No nationalist aspirant for power in Vietnam has as much to offer as Diem," he wrote, "and no pro-French leader could succeed against the Viet Minh."

Allen Dulles and Frank Wisner received Lansdale's dispatch in the early morning hours, and so compelling did they find his arguments that they descended on John Foster Dulles at his home to implore him to cancel the coup directive. After getting the president's approval, the secretary issued another stay-of-execution order. "The developments of last night," he wrote, "could either lead to Diem's utter overthrow, or his emergence from the disorder as a major hero. Accordingly, we are pausing to await the results."

Over the next few days, Lansdale frantically worked to ensure the latter outcome. A crucial ally in this was Trinh Minh Thé, the baby-faced guerrilla leader Lansdale had met with on Black Lady Mountain. On April 29, he arrived in Saigon at the head of over one thousand of his Lien Minh fighters and rushed into the fight against the Binh Xuyen. Thé was also instrumental in persuading the new army chief of staff, a man of unsteady loyalties, to go on live national radio to denounce the United Front plotters and swear allegiance to Diem. As a former adman, Lansdale was undoubtedly intrigued by the incentive tool employed to win over the wavering officer: throughout the broadcast, Thé held a loaded Colt .45 pistol to the general's temple.

Gradually but inexorably, the battle of Saigon turned in Diem's favor. By the time it was over, at least five hundred citizens were dead, and whole swaths of the city burned to the ground; especially hard hit were some of its poorer neighborhoods. It was a defeat not only for the Binh Xuyen, but for all those who had cast their lot with them. Chief among these were the French *colons,* their desperate last bid to overturn the Geneva Accords now finished. Imperial powers had long used religious or ethnic minorities to serve as their local proxies, but rarely had one turned to the services of an outright crime syndicate. With the squalidness of their failed endgame appalling even to many French citizens, the Paris government reiterated its pledge to leave Vietnam on the timetable agreed to at Geneva.

With the Binh Xuyen brought to heel, the following month Diem turned his attention to the Hoa Hao sect leaders who had joined them, sending his army into the cult's southwestern stronghold to dismantle its private militias. Another whose stock had precipitously fallen was Emperor Bao Dai. In the midst of the battle for Saigon, the emperor had laid bare his French toady status by demanding that Diem relinquish his office. Diem had ignored the command and now, emboldened by victory, set his sights on getting rid of Bao Dai. For a man who just weeks earlier had seemed all but certain to be overwhelmed by his myriad rivals, Ngo Dinh Diem was steadily knocking down those rivals one by one.

As was his chief benefactor, Edward Lansdale. At the end of 1954, the Saigon Military Mission commander had played a behind-the-scenes role in orchestrating the dismissal of ambassador Donald Heath, and he now did the same with presidential envoy Lawton Collins. With administration officials rushing to board the Diem bandwagon—they suddenly remembered they had been huge supporters all along—Collins's position in Vietnam was plainly untenable. Within days of his return to Saigon, his envoy status was revoked and he was packing up for the trip home. "Collins had defeated Japanese and German armies," noted military historian Max Boot, "but in South Vietnam he had been bested by a former advertising man with a colonel's wings on his collar."

Surely most pleasing of all to Lansdale was the downfall of his chief nemesis within the American community in Saigon, CIA station chief Emmett McCarthy. While he had stealthily tried to engineer McCarthy's removal ever since arriving in Vietnam, with his star turn after the battle of Saigon, Lansdale could dispense with subtlety. "Fire that son of a bitch," he reportedly told Allen Dulles. "Get him out of here." In very short order, McCarthy was gone, too.

Those who observed Ed Lansdale in Manila at the beginning of the 1950s had been astounded by how quickly he became a pivotal player in the inner circles of Philippine politics. In Vietnam, he had outdone himself. By June 1, 1955, the one-year anniversary of his having walked off the plane at Saigon's Tan Son Nhut airport, Lansdale was not only a chief advisor to yet another foreign head of state, but he had helped forge the identity of a new nation by exerting his will at a moment of maximum crisis. As an official CIA history noted, Lansdale was "the largest single influence on deliberations in Washington at the most critical point of Diem's tenure." In his seminal book on the Vietnam conflict, *A Bright Shining Lie,* journalist Neil Sheehan would go one better: "South Vietnam, in all honesty, was created by Ed Lansdale."

But in Diem's triumph in the spring of 1955 rested a couple of cautionary notes. One of the very last victims of the battle of Saigon was the guerrilla leader Lansdale had made a pact with on Black Lady Mountain, Trinh Minh Thé, shot in the head while leading his men into battle in Saigon's western suburbs. Except Thé's bullet wound indicated he had been shot from behind. Had he been felled by a French sniper, the *colons* finally getting their revenge on the "terrorist" who had killed their general? Or on orders of a lieutenant vying for control of the Lien Minh militia? Or perhaps by a Viet Minh sleeper agent, determined to be rid of a clever enemy, or by someone in Diem's inner circle, anxious to eliminate a charismatic leader who could become a rival? These were questions for which there would never be an answer, but they spoke to the murky snakepit that was Vietnamese politics.

And there was another legacy of the battle of Saigon. By having helped extinguish any hope for a continued French presence in Indochina, by transforming Ngo Dinh Diem into the "savior" of a nation that had never previously existed, the Americans had inherited South Vietnam. It was their snakepit now.

———

Late into a balmy night in June 1954, Peter Sichel sat out on the patio of his home in northwest Washington, talking and drinking wine with a visitor named Otto John. The director of West Germany's domestic intelligence agency, the Office for the Protection of the Constitution (BfV), the forty-five-year-old John had arrived in Washington on an official visit some days earlier, and his time had largely been taken up with meetings at the FBI and CIA. With his own German lineage, Sichel had acted as John's escort to many of these meetings, and the two had hit it off well enough that Sichel thought to invite the German to his own home for a more relaxed evening. After having dinner with Sichel's wife, Cuy, the two men had repaired to the garden to talk and drink wine. "Too much wine," Sichel recalled, "but John was a drinker, and I was a wine expert, so it was rather inevitable."

Otto John's personal story was a tragic and peculiarly German one. A lawyer from a middle-class background, during the Nazi era he had somehow managed to straddle his opposition to Hitler while remaining the legal director of Lufthansa airlines. After delicately forging ties to high-ranking dissidents in military and business circles, both Otto and his younger brother, Hans, had joined the anti-Hitler conspiracy that culminated in the July 20, 1944, assassination attempt on Hitler at his Wolf's Lair headquarters. While a very close thing, Otto John had managed to stay one step ahead of Gestapo investigators and make his escape to Spain and then on to London. Not so his brother. Arrested along with thousands of other alleged conspirators, Hans John endured months of torture before finally being executed by the Nazis in the closing days of the war.

As he tried to rebuild his professional life in the postwar era, Otto John had carried a double burden: grief over his brother's ghastly death obviously, but also the ostracism of many of his countrymen for having joined in the July 20 plot. Despite a reputation for increasingly intemperate behavior—he became known for his fondness of both alcohol and prostitutes—John was appointed head of the BfV, effectively West Germany's FBI, after much prodding by the British, with whom he had collaborated during the war.

The German security chief clearly felt at ease with Peter Sichel. "He became quite emotional," Sichel said, "and the more he talked, the more I saw he was a very troubled man. He wanted to see a reunified Germany, and he was especially angry about all the former Nazis being brought into the [West German] government. He felt as if the country was being betrayed, that what he had fought for and what his brother had died for, it had all been for nothing. It was probably made worse because the tenth anniversary [of the Hitler assassination attempt] was coming up."

Sichel found himself in a rather odd position for a German Jew, defending the idea of bringing former Nazis into the postwar German power structure as necessary for the nation's reconstruction. "I asked him, 'how can the country function without some of these former bureaucrats running it?' But he didn't want to hear it. He had suffered through the times, and could not look at reality. A sad case, he had lost so much, but he should never have been appointed head of internal security."

At the end of that night, Sichel called a taxi to take John back to his hotel. Within a few days, the BfV chief returned to Germany and Sichel thought little more about their conversation until the following month—until July 21, 1954, to be exact. By coincidence, that very morning, Sichel had turned in his report urging that Alexander Orlov be dismissed, but at both CIA Berlin and CIA headquarters in Washington, any discussion of Orlov was soon eclipsed by startling news out of Germany: Otto John had disappeared.

On the evening of July 20, John had attended a Berlin ceremony marking the tenth anniversary of the Hitler assassination plot, but he had then fallen from sight without a word to anyone; he didn't show up for work the next day, and he was not at home. The mystery deepened over the next several days until finally the BfV chief announced from East Germany that he had defected.

The news triggered a full-blown panic in the West German capital of Bonn, as officials scrambled to determine if John's defection was genuine, if he was being held against his will, or—the most appalling scenario of all—he had been a communist mole all along. In the absence of clear answers, security firewalls started to go up throughout the West German security apparatus—as well as in the foreign intelligence agencies that had been instrumental in creating that apparatus, MI6 and the CIA. Just as with the defections of Donald Maclean and Guy Burgess three years earlier, damage assessment teams immediately set to work to try to gauge what John might have handed over to the Soviets.

For Sichel, the concerns were more immediate and personal. At the same time that he was being bombarded with questions from CIA colleagues about his evening with John, Sichel recalled that he and his wife, Cuy, had spent some time chatting with their guest about Cuy's elderly parents, who lived in Potsdam, then part of East Germany; the BfV chief had promised to look them up the next time his work took him to the East. With no one sure of what anything meant at the moment, a CIA extraction team was swiftly sent into Potsdam to bundle up Cuy's parents and whisk them into West Berlin. Within days, the couple was resettled in a West German city and given temporary aliases on the off chance that an East German Stasi team might come looking for them. At the same time, their American son-in-law, Peter Sichel, was one of the CIA officers detailed to investigate John's defection.

The mystery over the Otto John affair was to linger for the next seventeen months, and to then take an even more bizarre turn. In December 1955, John resurfaced in West Berlin, claiming that he had never defected, but rather had been drugged and taken into the communist zone against his will. This account strained credulity—there were any number of times over the previous year when John could have "re-defected" or alerted someone he was being held hostage—and he was soon brought up on charges of treason. The comparatively light four-year prison sentence he was ultimately given reflected the enduring confusion of German authorities over precisely what had occurred.

Sichel had long since come to his own conclusions. "He wasn't a defector," he said. "I'm quite sure of that. He lacked that kind of personality. He was an unhappy man, an unstable one who drank too much, and I think he did something to draw attention to what he saw as the German problem. He wanted the country reunified, and maybe he saw the East Germans as the ones who would work for that to happen, but he wasn't a defector."

But if Otto John wasn't a defector in the classic sense, his case had caused some within the American intelligence community to focus their fears of a mole within the Western camp on a wholly new suspect: Peter Sichel.

In the immediate aftermath of World War II, a senior U.S. Army intelligence officer in Berlin, Walter Sudymont, had repeatedly clashed with Sichel due to the latter's impolitic habit of pointing out that much of the intelligence Sudymont was collecting came from con men and intelligence mills. In retaliation, the G-2 officer reported to investigators that "there must have existed in the OSS Berlin Office a person or persons deliberately withholding intelligence reports on Soviet activities." While Sudymont furnished no evidence for this assertion, nor named a suspect, suspicion naturally fell on the young upstart who headed the offending office, Peter Sichel. No action was taken on Sudymont's accusation, but over the years, other CIA officers had grumbled about Sichel's proclivity for scrubbing operations that didn't meet his exacting standards. As was typical in the McCarthyist era, these wisps of complaint were duly noted in Sichel's personnel file, there to coalesce into a potential time bomb should someone decide to target Sichel in the future.

In the wake of the Otto John affair, someone opened that file and felt it raised serious questions. Just why had the Berlin station chief been so eager to abort missions that case officers felt were destined for great success? And why Sichel's efforts to get rid of Alexander Orlov, an operative that many CIA officers still strongly vouched for? To top things off, now there was his coziness with the traitor Otto John. Was it possible that Peter Sichel was KGB? In the summer of 1955, the FBI launched an investigation into "Sichel's association with questionable individuals," with a special focus on "his and his wife's families' association with Otto John, his business interests in foreign commercial concerns, and the connection of certain relatives with foreign intelligence services." This last point apparently referred to a deceased British second cousin whom Sichel had never met but who had once worked for Britain's MI6. Along with the decade-old Sudymont accusation, these bits of trivia were to be examined to determine if Sichel held "any lack of sympathy with or qualification of his loyalty to this Government or the intelligence objectives of the Central Intelligence Agency."

By the summer of 1955, however, the Red Scare and the hysterias and witch hunts that accompanied it had finally begun to lose their death grip on the nation following the censure of Senator Joe McCarthy the previous December. For a CIA leadership that had long pushed back against both McCarthy and J. Edgar Hoover's FBI, the frail innuendoes now directed at Sichel were scarcely worth acknowledging. Pointedly, Allen Dulles refused to suspend Sichel's security clearance, standard procedure when a CIA employee was under investigation, and demanded the FBI inquiry be finished quickly.

"One of the things the FBI liked to do," Sichel said, "was to leave people twisting in the wind by dragging the investigation out for as long as possible—years, sometimes. They couldn't do that with me because I was a friend of both Allen Dulles and Frank Wisner, and they made wrapping it up a priority."

Within a few months, Sichel was absolved of any wrongdoing. That judgment also cleared the way for him to take up what many considered the most prized assignment to be had in the CIA: Hong Kong station chief. In early 1956, Sichel and his wife boarded the USS *President Wilson* for the eleven-day voyage, via Japan, to one of the world's most entrancing cities. Sichel would remember his time in Hong Kong as among the best years of his life, a dramatically more relaxed posting than Berlin, and a dramatically more interesting one than Washington. In a romantic splurge, he commissioned the building of a Chinese junk, which he and friends took on long slow sails around Hong Kong harbor.

But as Sichel soon discovered, even Hong Kong came with its unique set of pressures. Residing in a city renowned for having some of the best tailors in the world, the station chief was forever peppered with requests from CIA colleagues similar to the one he received from Frank Wisner in July 1958. After apologizing for burdening Sichel with an errand that was undoubtedly "painfully familiar," Wisner wrote, "I would like to have you procure from the Ying Tai silk shop in Kowloon <u>nine</u> men's dressing gowns of dimensions as set out on the attached sheet."

═══════

As history has repeatedly shown, a special kind of menace attaches to a defeated army, and the dwindling French military contingent in Vietnam in 1955, slated to leave the country altogether before the end of the year, was most certainly that.

Much of their bitterness was naturally directed at the Viet Minh, that army of barefoot soldiers who had humiliated them at Dien Bien Phu, but with few ways to lash out at their enemy in a partitioned Vietnam, their anger was redirected to those they viewed as agents of their ruin closer to hand. Chief among these was Ngo Dinh Diem and Ed Lansdale.

The French desire to bring down Diem didn't end with his victory in the battle of Saigon; if anything, the destruction of their local proxies only whetted a thirst for revenge, for now there was absolutely nothing left to lose, no turning back of the imperial clock. Assassination plots blossomed. While none appear to have been officially sanctioned—they were the handiwork of small cabals of officers, or squads of French Foreign Legionnaires—the conspirators may very well have succeeded in getting Diem if not for the moonlighting intelligence work of Major Lucien Conein.

Working his contacts in the Corsican underworld, Conein was able to track and thwart many of the various schemes afoot—at least when the mood struck him. Rufus Phillips recalled one gathering in the Duy Tan living room when Lansdale was discussing the arrangements for a trip

Diem was about to take into the countryside. The SMM commander had discussed the itinerary at some length before Conein, never a big fan of Diem, thought to break in: "Maybe he better not."

"How's that?" Lansdale asked.

"The trip," Conein replied. "Maybe he should skip it."

When Lansdale asked why, the major casually let slip that he'd heard from his Corsican bartender friends that plotters had planted a bomb along the route Diem would travel.

"So Ed frantically gets on the phone to the palace," Phillips recalled, "and he manages to stop the trip at the last minute. He comes back into the living room: 'Lou, when did you hear about this?' 'Yesterday.' 'Yesterday?! And you're just telling me now?! For Christ's sake, they could've killed the prime minister.' And Lou just sort of shrugs: 'yeah, sorry, I forgot.'"

But at least Diem had bodyguards. Far more vulnerable was Ed Lansdale and, by extension, his SMM teammates.

The list of grievances the French had against Lansdale was long, and dated back almost to the moment of his arrival in Vietnam. In their eyes, Lansdale's open embrace of Trinh Minh Thé, a man Paris regarded as a murdering terrorist, had been an outrage bordering on the criminal. Added to that was the key role he'd played in neutering General Hinh, and in crushing the United Front in the battle of Saigon. Quite understandably, the cocky colonel with the pencil mustache had become the embodiment of everything the French in Vietnam loathed about their erstwhile American ally.

For his part, Lansdale often seemed to go out of his way to tweak French sensibilities, to remind them that theirs was an empire in decline. Certainly the poodle mix that Lansdale had adopted shortly after arriving in Saigon—he named the dog Pierre—was unlikely to win him any Gallic friends. For some strange reason, the normally friendly dog took to biting the ankles of most any Frenchman who came too close. Lansdale professed to be totally mystified by Pierre's ability to detect who was French, only theorizing that maybe "there was an odor about them or something."

Beginning shortly after the battle of Saigon, the Saigon Military Mission became the target of increasingly more serious attacks. Anonymous death threats were delivered to the houses on Rue Taberd and Duy Tan. Stepping out the gate of the Rue Taberd house one morning, an SMM member narrowly escaped being gunned down in a drive-by shooting. A Frenchman who bore a strong resemblance to Lansdale and drove a similar car was shot to death a few doors down from the Duy Tan house in what was clearly a planned ambush. After grenades were thrown over the walls of the SMM houses, team members took to checking the undercarriages of their cars each morning for bombs.

Once again working his contacts in the Corsican netherworld, Lou Conein determined that the grenade attack had been sanctioned by a group of French officers headed up by a colonel. After confronting the Frenchman, who heatedly denied any involvement, Lansdale decided a corrective was in order. Calling a meeting of the SMM team, he announced that things had gone far enough, that the French problem was about to be resolved.

Walking into the kitchen of the Rue Taberd house that night, Rufus Phillips found Conein cutting bricks of C3 plastique into baseball-sized chunks with a butcher knife; alongside were all the accoutrements—primacord, friction tape, a fuse roll—needed for bomb-making. When Phillips asked what he was doing, Conein had a ready answer: "None of your goddamned business; what the hell does it look like?" The major eventually softened enough to allow Phillips to take over the plastique-cutting chore, but declined the younger man's offer of further aid. "You didn't see any of this; now get the hell out of here."

As an assistant, Conein instead chose his girlfriend, a part-French, part-Vietnamese twenty-six-year-old named Elyette Brochot. Late that night, the couple headed out into the streets of Saigon in Conein's car. Pulling up to the house of the French colonel he had identified as the ringleader of the grenade attacks, Conein took up one of the homemade bombs from the pile in Brochot's lap, lit its fuse with his cigarette lighter, and threw it over the wall. A satisfying boom sounded as the pair drove off, en route to the house of their next victim. After a subsequent bombing mission with Conein, Brochot was sufficiently shaken to cause her to question her choice in men. "I had seen a lot of things in my life," she said, "but I was a very proper person. Lou was very exciting, though . . ."

Denials of French complicity notwithstanding, the attacks on the Saigon Military Mission abruptly ended after the nighttime drive of Conein and Brochot. Asked about it later, Conein was uncharacteristically modest in taking any of the credit. "I was just a go-fer for Lansdale, a liaison with people he wanted me to talk to."

Those attacks might have soon ended anyway for, by the summer of 1955, the French had begun closing up their bases in and around Saigon and moving to the coast as their withdrawal from Indochina got under way. By that October, the last contingents had departed for France, bringing to an end its seventy-year rule—or misrule, depending on one's perspective—of Indochina. As for Elyette Brochot, she ultimately chose excitement over good manners; shortly after their partnership in the Saigon bombing campaign, she and Conein married.

At the same time that Lansdale was parrying the last of the French attacks, he and Diem were settling into an easier rhythm with one another. Past—at least for the time being—was the seemingly endless series of crises and foreign and domestic threats that had marked Lansdale's first year in the country and kept him on constant edge. For his part, Diem had come to rely on the American colonel's counsel and companionship more than ever. The CIA officer had stood beside him when most every other American would-be advisor who trooped into his office had given Diem up for dead, with some even actively working to that end. Now, no foreigner was more trusted, more valued, so much so that Diem urged Lansdale to move into Doc Lap Palace with him. Lansdale politely declined the offer—officials at the American embassy felt it would fuel talk of Diem being an American puppet—but his regular meetings with the prime minister took on a more leisurely quality, conversations between friends.

"Our talks that summer were long," Lansdale recalled. "Diem would usher interpreter [Joe] Redick and me into his office, where three heavy chairs had been placed for a tête-à-tête. . . . We then would settle into talk over innumerable cups of tea and packs of cigarettes."

These talks often went so late that Lansdale stayed on to have dinner with the extended Ngo family, gatherings that gave him a glimpse into some of the curious internal dynamics of the Ngo clan. While Diem normally sat at the head of the table, as only befitting a head of state, it was his eldest brother, Thuc, a Catholic bishop, who was the clear patriarchal figure of the family, the one who most often commandeered the dinner conversation and held forth. Lansdale also observed that the strikingly handsome younger brother, Nhu, while regarded as the family intellectual and a political force in his own right, rarely spoke. Instead, and highly unusual in an Asian family in the 1950s, one of the most forceful personalities at the table was Nhu's equally attractive wife, Tran Le Xuan, soon to become known to most all Vietnamese simply as Madame Nhu. While Lansdale had a hard time getting a handle on Nhu—there was a wary, watchful quality to the man—he became a favorite playmate of Nhu's three young children, who had the run of the palace; on many occasions, the marble halls of the palace rang with their excited squeals as Lansdale chased them in a game of tag or cowboys and Indians.

Lansdale took note of something else slightly odd about these dinners. With the exception of himself and Redick, very rarely were nonfamily members in attendance. Instead, most every night was a reprise of the same extended family repast that had occurred the night before. This was not unusual among traditional Asian families but to Lansdale it spoke to an insularity and isolation that was troubling in a head of state. On the other hand, as one of the sole outsiders routinely invited into this closed world, it gave the SMM commander even greater influence at the palace.

Just as Diem's odds of survival in Saigon had improved by that summer of 1955, so, too, had South Vietnam's security situation. Joined by Rufus Phillips and just a tiny handful of American and Filipino military advisors, the Vietnamese army had launched a so-called pacification offensive into the southern Ca Mau Peninsula that spring in hopes of establishing government rule and eliminating the last groups of holdout Viet Minh fighters. Employing tactics that had previously been used against the Filipino Huks—hearts-and-minds infrastructure projects to win over the civilian population; psy-war dirty tricks to wear down the enemy—Operation Liberty had resulted in the consolidation of government control at virtually no cost of life to the Vietnamese army. The success of that offensive had been followed by an even more ambitious one in central Vietnam, Operation Giai Phong (Breaking Chains), in which newly emboldened villagers turned on Viet Minh hiding in their midst. To Phillips's mind, proof of the success of these operations was the hero's welcome Diem received when he paid a visit to a provincial capital just one week after its "liberation" from Viet Minh rule. "The people were absolutely thrilled to see him," Phillips said, "honored that he'd come out there. There's no way the emotion of it could have been orchestrated. It was absolutely genuine."

But along with the expanding peace in the countryside and the growing stability of Diem's rule, by that autumn Lansdale began to sense a growing malignancy within Doc Lap Palace. It centered on Diem's younger brother, Nhu. The CIA man was becoming alarmed by the nature of the political party that Nhu had helped found, the Can Lao, which looked to be taking on the trappings of a personality cult. Members had to swear fealty to Diem—according to rumors, the initiation rite included kissing a photograph of the prime minister—and more and more government posts were being handed out to Can Lao members. Knowing of the extremely close bond between the two brothers, Lansdale delicately warned Diem about the maneuverings of his younger brother, the tilt toward dictatorship he seemed to be pursuing. Even when Lansdale steadily ratcheted up his criticism, though, it appeared to have little effect.

Incredibly, one reason for this was that Ngo Dinh Nhu had his very own CIA advisor, the head of the covert action unit at the embassy, Paul Harwood. Nhu had been deeply involved in Saigon politics during his brother's exile, and it was the view of Harwood, who predated Lansdale's arrival in Vietnam, that any hints of autocracy emerging from the brothers in Doc Lap Palace were of far less concern than using Can Lao to build a stable power base for Diem. Not surprisingly, this neatly dovetailed with Nhu's own thoughts on the topic.

For Lansdale, one of the first signs that he was losing influence came when Diem announced that he wouldn't abide by the Geneva Accords proviso on the holding of national elections in the summer of 1956. In the cynical political circles in which he traveled, Ed Lansdale may have been the only person left in either Saigon or Washington to believe that those elections could and should be held. This was rooted in his belief—and again, Lansdale appeared to be a quorum of one on this point—that Diem could actually beat Ho Chi Minh at the ballot box, an argument he pressed on the prime minister. "I started to describe the improving factors that could mean a victory for the free Vietnamese nationalists in the plebiscite," Lansdale wrote, "but Diem admonished me for underrating the dirty-trick capability of the Communists."

What the SMM commander apparently didn't grasp was that in rejecting elections, Diem was heeding the counsel of Nhu's CIA advisor, Harwood, as well as most every American diplomat up to and including John Foster Dulles with an opinion on the matter.

Which wasn't to say that Diem was opposed to *all* elections; that September he announced plans to hold a national referendum on who should be South Vietnam's official leader, himself or that last great pretender, the Emperor Bao Dai.

The outcome of such a referendum was hardly in doubt. To most every Vietnamese, the Riviera-based Bao Dai was the very definition of a puppet monarch. Diem, on the other hand, had always stood in opposition to the reviled French and, as much as his Catholicism might make some Buddhists nervous, he was regarded as something of a hero for having helped secure Vietnam's full independence. In short, Lansdale counseled, there was absolutely no need for Diem to pad the voting returns; just as with the clean elections that had brought Ramon Magsaysay to the Philippine presidency two years earlier, here was the chance for Diem to consolidate his authority and legitimacy in a fair contest.

That advice was not taken. To the contrary, with brother Nhu in charge of the election commission, Diem won the national referendum in October 1955 with a Soviet-style 98.2 percent of the vote. If that tally seemed unlikely, so, too, did the tens of thousands of votes Diem received in Saigon in excess of the city's number of registered voters. While Lansdale was appalled by the charade, the Eisenhower administration swiftly recognized the returns and congratulated Diem, now the president of the Republic of Vietnam, on the outcome.

If Lansdale hoped that, in the aftermath of the referendum, the Diem brothers might move to expand their political base, he was soon set right. With Nhu now pushing a governing concept that he called "personalism," but which looked an awful lot like dictatorship with a fancy name, the Can Lao secret police became even more powerful and ubiquitous. Matters finally came to a head one night that autumn when Can Lao goons rounded up a number of prominent former government officials and threw them in jail. Upon hearing the news, Lansdale rushed over to Doc Lap Palace and gave Diem a stern lecture. "The Can Lao was going to force the other nationalist parties to go underground in order to survive," he told Diem. "It would leave the body politic in South Vietnam deeply divided, in a covert and deadly game of nationalists struggling against nationalists, at the very time that thoughtful patriots needed to come out into the open to write a constitution and found a new political system to rival the Communist system in the North." Despite his impassioned appeal, Lansdale recalled, "Diem said little after my outburst."

The SMM commander learned why when he met with the new American ambassador, Frederick Reinhardt, to relate his conversation with Diem. As he talked, Lansdale noticed an odd look come over Reinhardt's face, a trace of discomfort. "After a pause, he informed me softly that a U.S. policy decision had been made."

That decision was to aid Diem in building up a strong nationalist party, with concerns like human rights or democratic principles left to the wayside. Far from urging Diem to clamp down on the excesses of Can Lao, the American administration wanted more of it. For Edward Lansdale, super-patriot, advance man for the American Dream, the sell-out was complete.

———

A change had come over Frank Wisner, a certain fevered quality. At first, most of his friends and colleagues attributed it to simple overwork. Whereas his deputy, Richard Helms, left the office promptly at six each evening, and Allen Dulles often even earlier, the deputy director of plans routinely toiled away in his dingy office in L Building until ten or eleven at night. When those office hours were shortened, it was usually the result of social obligations, dinners or cocktail parties or official receptions that, in their own way, were just more work in a different guise. At these, Wisner was often among the last to leave, always ready to tell one more story, to debate one more point over one more drink. Even his weekend getaways to Locust Hill barely qualified as an escape. The toll of it all showed in Wisner's physical appearance. Although still only in his mid-forties, his premature baldness and expanding waistline, the deepening fret lines around his eyes, gave him the appearance of a man fifteen years older.

One who noticed was Peter Sichel. "There was a new tension about him. Frank had always been a great storyteller, he had a wonderful sense of humor, but you didn't see that much anymore. He seemed preoccupied, always on edge."

To those who knew Wisner, it wasn't as if there had been some radical transformation in the man; instead, everything about him now just seemed *more*. He'd long had a reputation for being curt with subordinates who disappointed, but his office tirades now appeared to happen more frequently and with more heat. In both speech and writing, he'd always had a tendency toward verbosity, but now he sometimes launched into long-winded disquisitions that didn't appear to go anywhere, dictated labyrinthine and multi-page memoranda the thrust of which remained obscure. At staff meetings, he occasionally got lost in discursive stories that had little or no application to the matter at hand, with only the ever-tactful Helms able to coax him back to the topic. And while never noted for good time management, by the spring of 1956, Wisner could spend hours writing out a critique of a *New York Times* editorial or a James Reston column, while stacks of important papers remained unsigned and visitors waited.

But if all this was the result of overwork, Wisner's friends and colleagues undoubtedly told themselves, then surely it would get better if he could just relax a little, take some time off, delegate. Except it didn't get better. Rather, by the summer of 1956, his now mercurial moods seemed to have grown worse. As writer Burton Hersh noted, "there was a ferocity about Wisner that season, something apocalyptic behind many of his utterances."

Lawrence Houston, one of Wisner's closest confidants at the Agency, told Hersh of the day he was called into the deputy director's office and subjected to a long and circuitous soliloquy on a propaganda initiative Wisner wished to pursue. Wisner then asked Houston to discuss the idea with another of his closest colleagues, an assistant secretary of defense named Gordon Gray. Once in Gray's office, though, it dawned on Houston that he couldn't make sense of what Wisner had told him. "I'm really quite puzzled as to what Frank wanted me to come in for," Houston said sheepishly.

Rather than be surprised by this, Gray was silent for a long moment. "I think Frank is in real trouble," he finally said.

———

It was a peculiar meeting. On one side of the room sat the Dulles brothers, Allen and John Foster. Less than a year earlier, they had hatched plans to overthrow the prime minister of South Vietnam, Ngo Dinh Diem. Across from them sat the man who had convinced them not to, Colonel Edward Lansdale. Now, it was almost as if everyone had switched sides.

It was mid-January 1956, and Lansdale had returned to Washington from his Saigon post because he felt the American mission in Vietnam was in crisis. To the Dulles brothers, he expounded on what he regarded as the deepening problems with the Diem government. Chief among them were the increasingly sinister machinations of Diem's younger brother, Nhu, and his Can Lao party. Those machinations had taken on a dramatic new dimension even while Lansdale had been en route to Washington. By presidential decree, Diem had just enacted a law, soon to become known as Ordinance 6, that gave his regime the authority to imprison without trial those deemed "dangerous to national defense or common security." Under this catchall term, Lansdale explained to the Dulles brothers, the Diem brothers could now hunt down and arrest the remnants of the religious secret societies, as well as most any other political opponent they saw fit.

Diem's Achilles' heel, however, was his ever-growing reliance on the United States. Because of that, Lansdale counseled, Washington was in a strong position to force democratic changes on the Diem government, including the revocation of Ordinance 6. At the same time, Lansdale didn't feel he was the person to deliver this message. After a year and a half in Saigon, he told the Dulleses, he felt his usefulness there had come to an end, and he wished to be transferred elsewhere.

When Lansdale finished speaking, he would recall, an awkward silence fell over the office. "Well," Allen Dulles said at last, "I think you're being a bit idealistic here."

What he meant was that there would be no getting tough on Ngo Dinh Diem. Much to the contrary, the following month the United States made its first significant military commitment to the Diem regime with the dispatch of 350 military advisors to complement the few dozen already in-country. To get around the foreign military assistance bans imposed by the Geneva Accords, the Eisenhower administration merely declared the advisors were being sent on a "temporary mission," with no definition of temporary provided.

Further, Lansdale was far too important a component in American policy in Vietnam to allow him to depart from the scene now; his request for a transfer deferred, the colonel was soon on his way back to Saigon.

Where just six months earlier Lansdale and Diem had appeared to be fast friends, a distinct coolness had now settled between them. Time and again through the early months of 1956, Lansdale found himself sidelined by Diem, unable to forestall any of the destructive initiatives urged on him by his brother, Nhu. Of these none were more potentially calamitous than the regime's decision to dismantle the traditional structure of village self-government, in which decisions were made by a consensus of elders, and replace it with a system of appointed "village chiefs." Those chiefs were to be chosen by the provincial governors who, of course, were appointed by Diem. In essence, this meant that the entire system of patronage and cronyism initiated by Nhu's Can Lao, once isolated to political circles in Saigon, would now permeate all the way down to the village level. As Lansdale pointed out, this change also gave communist propagandists "a highly effective argument to turn villagers against the Diem regime," since now "everything that went wrong in a village could be blamed upon the Diem-appointed officials, whether they were responsible for it or not."

As the summer of 1956 approached, though, the SMM commander was increasingly a lone voice of dissent amid a growing chorus of fawning American officials. On June 1, Massachusetts senator John F. Kennedy, already considered a rising star in the Democratic Party, gave a speech lauding Diem's "inspired leadership," and calling Vietnam "the cornerstone of the Free World in Southeast Asia" and "a proving ground of democracy." Just two weeks after Diem had inaugurated his village chieftain decree, Saigon was graced with a visit by Vice President Richard Nixon. "The militant march of Communism has been halted in Vietnam," Nixon announced to the thunderous applause of the Vietnamese National Assembly.

Just in case that march ever showed signs of starting up again, Diem next enacted Ordinance 47, making the crime of assisting a communist organization punishable by death. As for Ordinance 47's definition of a communist organization, this was "any groups who resorted to clandestine political activity or armed opposition to the existing government." By any recognizable measure, by that summer of 1956, South Vietnam had become a police state, with an estimated seven thousand political prisoners in Saigon jails alone.

A police state, if not a very efficient one: amid the dragnet spurred by Ordinance 47, attacks by communist insurgents, the law's ostensible targets, spiked.

By that September, Lansdale had become so marginalized in Saigon, pushed to the curb by both the Diem regime and the ever-expanding American political and military presence, that even the Dulles brothers saw little reason to keep him on; his request to end his Vietnam tour was at last granted. As he prepared to leave, he penned a kind of epitaph, a forlorn one in light of recent events: "I was convinced, more than ever, that the most pragmatic course for Americans serving in Asia was to heed the idealism of our country's political tenets and make them the basis for our acts."

Prior to his departure, Lansdale thought to engage Diem in one last act of friendship. Early in his tenure in Saigon, the CIA officer had discovered a simple government cottage perched on the edge of a beautiful, unspoiled beach outside the coastal village of Long Hai. In early October, he convinced the overworked Diem to join him there for a brief vacation. They were accompanied by brother Nhu and his wife, together with Lansdale's girlfriend, Pat Kelly, who flew over from Manila for the occasion.

In photographs that have survived from that trip, Diem and Lansdale seem to have rekindled something of their old friendship, lounging together on the bungalow's veranda, while others show Madame Nhu and Kelly frolicking in a gentle ocean surf. Even Nhu appears at ease, his broad smile recalling the handsomeness of his face before it took on its severity. In the photographs, everyone looks happy.

24

COLLAPSE

The downfall began with a speech. It was delivered on the morning of February 25, 1956, in the Great Hall of the Kremlin.

For the past eleven days, delegates from across the Soviet Union, along with officials from over fifty "fraternal" communist parties throughout the world, had gathered in the Great Hall to hear speeches and ratify proclamations as members of the Twentieth Congress of the Communist Party of the Soviet Union. The closing ceremony had taken place the previous evening, but delegates preparing to leave Moscow were told to return to the vast assembly hall in the morning, there to hear a last-minute address from Nikita Khrushchev, the Soviet first secretary. This news undoubtedly provoked a good deal of despair; in his February 14 speech opening the congress, Khrushchev had droned on for a stupefying seven hours.

For most delegates, that had been their first glimpse of the new Soviet leader. In the three years since Stalin's death, Kremlin watchers had pegged several different members of his inner circle as his successor, only to be proven wrong each time. It wasn't until the summer of 1955, when Khrushchev took leadership of the Soviet delegation at a summit meeting with Western leaders, that most observers started to be convinced that the former party boss of Ukraine was truly in charge. His appearance may have contributed to the hesitation. Short and overweight, with a great bald head and massive workman's hands, Khrushchev looked more the part of an aging nightclub bouncer than the leader of the communist world. Those who knew the new Soviet leader well described a complex figure: gregarious; unpretentious; ruthless.

When Khrushchev took the podium that afternoon no one save a small group of his advisors knew what he planned to say. Given the turgid, jargon-filled oratory favored by communist party leaders, it took some time for the assembled delegates—some 1,500 men and women—to realize what they were hearing was an unsparing denunciation of the man who had ruled the Soviet Union for nearly thirty years: Joseph Stalin. The former demigod was now not only a scoundrel and murderer, but an incompetent coward, a man who, after first joining forces with the fascist Hitler, then hid away in his dacha when the German invasion came. "Not once did Stalin visit the front," thundered Khrushchev, a man who had risked his own life at the battle of Stalingrad. "Not once did he tour the fields or the factories or talk to the Soviet people who were sacrificing so much." From Stalin's failings in World War II, to the pogroms that had wiped out entire classes of Soviet citizens, Khrushchev's recital of his predecessor's crimes continued for the next three and a half hours.

The initial bewilderment of those in the Great Hall gradually gave way to shock and, in some cases, to fury. At one point an angry delegate interrupted the premier's speech by shouting, "if you knew all this about Stalin, why didn't you move against him?"

Khrushchev paused and gazed out at his audience with a cryptic smile. "Who said that?" he asked. When no one answered, he asked again: "Who said that?" In the continuing silence, Khrushchev's smile slowly broadened. "Now you know why we didn't do anything."

In the days following his February 25 address, soon to become known as the De-Stalinization Speech, Khrushchev embarked on an array of economic and political reforms. Tens of thousands of political prisoners were released from the gulags, while others who had been blacklisted were restored to official favor. Copies of his speech were printed and distributed to the senior leadership of Soviet bloc nations so that they, too, could begin the de-Stalinization process in their countries, the loosening of the rigid state controls that had left their economies in shambles, an end to the personality cults and purges that had led to the deaths of so many innocents.

While Western intelligence agencies heard rumors of Khrushchev's secret speech, it was a testament to the hermetically sealed nature of the Soviet world that it took the CIA nearly two months to finally get their hands on a copy, despite fifteen thousand copies having been distributed in Poland alone. After a brief debate over how best to handle the bombshell document, the Eisenhower administration publicly released it in full at the beginning of June 1956.

The impact was stunning. Newspapers throughout the world carried long excerpts on their front pages and under banner headlines. On June 5, *The New York Times* reported on Khrushchev's speech in three different front-page articles, and ran passages that filled five entire inner pages. At Radio Free Europe headquarters in Munich, staff members feverishly worked on translations into almost every language of Eastern Europe, then endlessly broadcast the most shocking portions into the East.

Within the Soviet bloc, signs of public dissent, of activists testing the limits of the new liberalism, increased after the CIA's airing of Khrushchev's address. In late June came the first serious challenge when industrial workers in the Polish city of Poznań went out on strike demanding better working conditions. The strikers were soon joined by ordinary civilians, and economic grievances gave way to the political. What didn't change, though, was the state's stock response in such matters. The Soviet commander of the Polish army ordered Poznań sealed off from the outside world, then sent in tanks and armored cars; in the two-day "pacification" operation, at least fifty-seven civilians were killed and hundreds more arrested.

Thus far, Poznań looked set to play out as a reprise of the quickly snuffed East German uprising of three years before, except now there was one great difference: the new reformist leadership in Moscow. Appalled by the killings in Poznań, Khrushchev ordered the Polish regime to acquiesce to some of the demonstrators' more reasonable demands.

But as dictatorships throughout history have discovered, reform, once set in motion, is a difficult thing to harness. By mid-October, public discontent had so deepened in Poland that the ruling Central Committee moved to install a party moderate as first secretary. The prospective new leader promised a range of economic and political liberalizations, but then took a giant step further; responding to a groundswell of nationalist fervor, he proposed to vastly diminish the Soviet Union's de facto control of the country. All of a sudden, matters were slipping from Moscow's grip, the reforms going well beyond the sort Khrushchev had been envisioning. On October 19, he along with a delegation of senior Kremlin leaders flew to Warsaw to put the newly appointed Polish leader back in his place. But it was already too late, the genie out of the bottle. By then, protesters were taking to the streets of Hungary and Czechoslovakia and, just as in Poland, their grievances swiftly escalated from demands for better pay or a lowering of work quotas to political reform, even to a dismantling of the communist state. And then in the Hungarian capital of Budapest came an explosion of popular rage as spontaneous as it was violent, and now the Kremlin had a full-blown revolution on its hands. It was the beginning of the downfall.

Yet, it was not the downfall that anyone observing the cascade of events in Eastern Europe that autumn may have predicted, not the collapse of the Soviet Union or the breaking away of those satellite nations in its thrall. Rather it was to be the fall of the United States' moral standing in the world, the extinguishing of whatever claim to a higher degree of honor or altruism it still enjoyed. It was to be the final laying bare of the myth of America as the herald of freedom.

In this, the United States really had no one to blame but herself. By that autumn of 1956, she had shown her preference for dictatorship over democracy in Iran and Guatemala. She had so thoroughly shed her anti-colonialist stance of the Roosevelt years as to aid her European imperial allies in quelling independence movements around the world. Under the leadership of the Dulles brothers, the United States had compiled a hit list of foreign leaders to be removed, by assassination if necessary. All the while, American politicians of both parties had continued with the empty but easy rhetoric of "rollback," the freeing of the "enslaved peoples" of Eastern Europe, while doing nothing in practical terms to actually bring it about.

In an extraordinary confluence of history, these various hypocrisies of the American Cold War government were about to be exposed in bold relief amid two very different but overlapping crises, ones that would leave thousands dead, and forever tarnish any claim the United States may have once made of adhering to its stated ideals. Most shameful of all, in the tumult of that autumn of 1956, America may have lost the best chance it ever had to bring the Cold War to an early close, and to avert all the tragedy that was to come.

On the evening of Saturday, October 20, 1956, Frank Wisner boarded an overnight flight to London. He was embarking on an extensive, five-week trip through Europe, one of his semiannual inspection tours of CIA stations there. In light of the startling news coming out of Eastern Europe, it was either a very good or very bad time for him to go. On the positive side, the tour would enable Wisner to get a more direct sense of how these developments were resonating in Western Europe. On the other hand, it would leave him out of the Washington decision-making loop should something truly dramatic occur.

In recent days, the primary focus had been Poland, where a new and liberal communist leader, Władislaw Gomułka, was promising such a sweeping array of reforms that Nikita Khrushchev and his ministers had rushed to Warsaw to confront him. Instead of submitting, though, it seemed the Polish leader had managed to forge a new compact with Moscow. The first details of that compact were just beginning to trickle out on that Saturday evening, but apparently, in return for remaining within the Soviet bloc military alliance, Gomułka was to have broad autonomy to pursue his own domestic agenda. If these initial reports bore out, it was a development without precedent in the Soviet sphere of nations.

But if tensions were easing in Poland—at least for now—not so in other parts of Eastern Europe. Of growing interest to Wisner was the situation in Hungary.

At the beginning of October—and again in reaction to popular discontent—the regime had "rehabilitated" a former interior minister executed as a "right-wing deviationist" seven years earlier. The somewhat macabre spectacle of the man's funeral—his remains and those of four lesser enemies of the state had been dug up from their execution ground and brought to a proper cemetery for reburial—became a rallying point for Hungarian dissidents, with tens of thousands gathering for the ceremony. This was followed by the reinstatement to the communist party of a popular former reformist prime minister, Imre Nagy, who had been ousted from power a year earlier.

The news from Hungary came as a bit of a surprise to the CIA leadership, for two reasons. As one of the most repressive of the Soviet satellite states, the Hungarian regime had always moved swiftly to crush even the slightest hint of dissent, rendering it an unlikely site for such activism now. It was also a surprise because the CIA simply didn't have a good handle on the place. Given the hyper-vigilance of Hungary's secret police, the *Allamvedelmi Hatosag*, or AVH, joined to the country's geography—a flat, Great Plains landscape—the Agency had never been able to implement a successful infiltration program there. In fact, by the time Wisner set off for London, the Hungarian CIA desk in Washington consisted of a mere six analysts and two clerk/typists, while its spying "network" in-country was virtually nonexistent. Nevertheless, in sifting through the scraps of rumor and news filtering out of the country, Wisner had a strong sense that Hungary bore close watching in the days ahead.

For his first two days in London, Wisner went about his schedule of meetings as planned. The first hint that something big was in the offing came on the afternoon of October 23, when Reuters and Associated

Press reported that massive antigovernment demonstrations were taking place in the Hungarian capital. As could best be determined, the protests in Budapest had been set in motion on the previous day when a group of university students, emboldened by events in Poland, had marched on the national radio station with a list of demands for political reform that they insisted be publicly broadcast. Considering that their sixteen demands included democratic elections and the immediate withdrawal of all Soviet troops from Hungary, it wasn't surprising that the state broadcasters refused. On the morning of the 23rd, several thousand university students had set out on a protest march through Budapest, one that swelled to tens of thousands as Hungarians of all walks of life came out to join them.

By that evening, the news out of Budapest took an even more remarkable turn. According to further wire service reports—the only somewhat reliable source of information out of Hungary—a crowd of as many as 200,000 protesters had filled the plaza before the national parliament building. There they began chanting for the overthrow of the nation's strongman ruler, Ernő Gerő, and his replacement with the rehabilitated Imre Nagy. The most frequent and full-throated chant, however, was a very emphatic one: *"Russkik haza!,"* "Russians go home!"

The first great mistake the regime made was when Gerő took to the airwaves to denounce the demonstrations as the handiwork of "hostile elements" bent on subversion. It was like throwing gasoline on a fire. More residents came out of their homes to join the protest, and other demonstrations started to spontaneously pop up all across Budapest. One mob converged on Heroes Square and began trying to pull down a towering bronze statue of Stalin; construction workers with blowtorches finally arrived to sever the statue at the feet. Another crowd closed on the state-run Radio Budapest station downtown to again demand broadcasters air the students' list of sixteen demands. The regime's second great mistake came when someone inside the broadcasting center, presumably one of the AVH secret policemen who had taken up positions there, opened fire. Within moments, the protesters had their first martyrs.

And just like that, the world tipped. All across Budapest, Hungarian soldiers and police sent to quell the demonstrations instead either joined them or handed over their weapons and returned to barracks. At police stations, weapons storerooms were thrown open to beseeching citizens, with every gun snatched up by eager hands. Faced with the collapse of the Hungarian security forces, Soviet military units were mobilized to confront the protesters—except those protesters were now gunmen intent on attacking any Soviet soldiers they could find. In less than twelve hours what began as a peaceful demonstration had given way to outright insurrection.

It was probably not until the following morning, Wednesday, October 24, that Wisner in London became fully apprised of the astounding events in Hungary overnight. Even then, though, the situation was too fluid, reports too contradictory, to know precisely what to make of them. Like most of his British intelligence colleagues that morning, Wisner probably assumed that the Hungarian authorities, with the chaos of the night now behind them, would soon regroup and gain the upper hand. This seemed especially likely given the carrot-and-stick approach the state was pursuing. Very early that morning, Reuters reported, the Hungarian Politburo had abruptly acceded to the protesters' demands and installed the liberal Imre Nagy as prime minister. In case that didn't suffice, they had also declared martial law and ordered in thousands of Soviet troops, backed by hundreds of tanks, to restore order. Their mission would undoubtedly be augmented by plainclothes members of Hungary's dreaded secret police.

If anything, though, the government's initiatives seemed to only make matters worse, for the fight was no longer about putting a more good-natured communist in charge; it was about casting out the machinery of state entirely and sending the Soviets on their way in the process. Throughout Budapest that morning, small bands of fighters, brought together by ties of neighborhood or workplace or mere chance, launched hit-and-run strikes against the Soviet troops in the streets. In the light of day, those strikes also became more sophisticated, with snipers targeting Red Army infantrymen from rooftops, and ad hoc sapper teams luring Soviet tanks into narrow alleys to be bombarded with Molotov cocktails. "It was the least-organized revolution in history," noted Hungarian journalist Victor Sebestyen, "no leaders, no plans, just groups of armed men and women formed in places that offered a vantage point to strike a swift blow and then hide."

It was also stunningly effective. Caught thoroughly off guard, by midday of October 24, one Red Army unit after another in Budapest had shifted from offensive operations to simple survival mode, blindly trying to find an escape from those now shooting at them.

As Wisner made his rounds of appointments in London that day, he kept abreast of the news out of Hungary as best he could. It must have taken on a fantastic quality, as if he were in the grip of a particularly pleasant but implausible dream. For eight years, he had tried to bring about some spark of rebellion within the Soviet empire, and met only with failure. But now, after so many futile missions and so many deaths, it was finally happening—and happening in a place never expected, on a scale beyond all imagining. There was also a note of personal triumph. It would later be said that the CIA never saw the Hungarian Revolution coming and had no hand in provoking it, but already on October 24, Frank Wisner knew that at least the second part of that assessment wasn't true. By that afternoon, and still less than twenty-four hours since the Budapest protests had turned to revolt, the unrest was already spreading across rural Hungary, with self-appointed "revolutionary councils" taking over from a paralyzed state. And just how had the news spread so rapidly to the hinterlands of a closed-off police state? By the Mighty Wurlitzer that Wisner had helped create, by the Hungarian-language broadcasts that made Radio Free Europe the most listened-to station in the country, and which was now providing a running account to its Hungarian listeners of the incredible events taking place in their nation.

In the chaos of the moment, it was hard to know just what the United States could do to aid the Hungarian insurrectionists, but it was a question that had already begun to animate Wisner. It was on that day that he sent the first of what was to become a torrent of top secret cables to Allen Dulles and CIA headquarters, outlining his ideas for how America should seize this opportunity. A first priority, to the deputy director's thinking, was to activate the group of Hungarian exiles recruited and trained through the Agency's Red Sox program and start infiltrating them back into their homeland.

It was also on that day that Wisner was to have his first brush with a counter-story, an incident the significance of which he wouldn't initially grasp.

Wisner had been invited to have dinner that night with John Lockhart, a British intelligence officer he had known for many years, and Patrick Dean, the head of the CIA/MI6 Joint Intelligence Committee, or JIC, together with their wives. Dean, who was hosting the dinner at his home, had been called away on a quick trip to Paris but was scheduled to return that afternoon, and Wisner's hope was that, once the meal was done and the ladies politely sent on their way, the three men could get down to a serious discussion of Hungary. "We met for dinner at 7:30—no Pat [Dean]," Lockhart told writer Evan Thomas. "By eight-thirty, Frank was becoming visibly agitated." Naturally, things came up at the last minute all the time in the intelligence world, but what Wisner found galling was that the JIC chief didn't have the courtesy to call with an explanation.

Finally, Dean's wife suggested they go ahead and eat without him. "It was a grim meal," Lockhart recalled, "but we did what we could. By eleven, Frank could hardly contain his sense of outrage and he left."

When eventually he learned the reason for Dean's absence and lack of communication, Wisner's view of that evening only worsened. The JIC chief had been delayed in Paris and unable to let his wife or dinner guests know because he was taking part in a highly clandestine meeting of senior British, French and Israeli military officials, one so top secret that its attendees had flown into restricted military airfields and been taken to a secluded private home in the Paris suburb of Sèvres. Their discussions ran long, but with no open-channel communication permitted from the safe house, Dean hadn't been able to alert his wife and guests. The participants had good reason for their secrecy. Worked out at that meeting in Sèvres on October 24 were the final details of a plot by their three governments to overthrow Egypt's president, Gamal Abdel Nasser. That plot, code-named Operation Musketeer, was scheduled to get under way in just five days.

―――――

For John Foster Dulles, the matter couldn't be any simpler. Viewed with the moral certitude of the devout Presbyterian that he was, the Cold War was a titanic struggle between good and evil, between godless communism and the Free World, between the enslavers and the liberators. Granted, "Free World" had a fairly broad definition, what with all the right-wing dictatorships in the American camp, but at least their hearts were in the right place and their people were allowed to worship.

Given this mind-set, it's not surprising that the secretary of state didn't warm to the new Soviet leader, Nikita Khrushchev. Having been instrumental in snubbing both British and Soviet invitations for a summit conference back in 1953, when Soviet leadership was still being contested, Dulles had finally relented to such a meeting in the summer of 1955 when Khrushchev's preeminence was becoming clear. The patrician blueblood didn't much care for what he saw in the former metalworker who had clawed his way up through the communist party ranks, regarding Khrushchev as coarse and unpredictable—which, of course, made him dangerous in a new way. What seemed to especially unnerve Dulles was the first secretary's flair for the grand unanticipated gesture. At one point during the summit in Geneva, Khrushchev opined that, if it was true that NATO's sole purpose was to maintain peace, as the Americans insisted, then perhaps the Soviet Union should join it as well, a suggestion that a flabbergasted Dulles rushed to shoot down once he got alone with Eisenhower. While that summit had ended on a hopeful note—it was the first meeting of American and Soviet heads of state since 1945—once back in Washington, the secretary of state moved to squelch any calls for conciliatory overtures; the Soviets needed to prove they could be trusted, Dulles repeatedly declaimed, and they were still a long way from that.

Such rigidity may not have been insurmountable if Eisenhower allowed within his inner circle a countervailing voice, much as Truman had with his council of hawks and doves. But, much to the contrary, John Foster's views didn't just dominate and permeate down through the State Department but, with his brother as its director, the Central Intelligence Agency, as well. When it came to interpreting Soviet actions, at times it was as if agency analysts were channeling the thoughts, and deepest fears, of the secretary of state. This extended even to the CIA's take on Khrushchev's De-Stalinization Speech.

"There is no indication that the present Soviet leaders have renounced the goal of world domination," the Agency reported in analyzing that landmark document. To the contrary, while the Kremlin might strive for great respectability, including granting its satellite nations greater independence, "all these measures would be designed only to further basic Communist objectives." That, of course, meant that the West, rather than be taken in by such liberalist overtures, needed to be even more vigilant. "We shall be compelled to continue warding off a diabolically clever opponent whose ingenuity and resourcefulness, unfortunately, is growing."

Such thinking mirrored that of John Foster, who had decided in the wake of the De-Stalinization Speech and the tremors it unleashed "that Khrushchev was the most dangerous person to lead the Soviet Union since the October Revolution" since he was prone to "irrational acts." At a National Security Council meeting that June, he wistfully noted that "he would be glad indeed to see Khrushchev go. . . . Unhappily there was no easy means to get rid of him. Death or violence were about the only recourse."

The circle was closed. Virtually anything the new Soviet leader did now, whether it was denouncing Stalin or freeing political prisoners or granting new freedoms to his people, was simply further proof of his and his colleagues' ultimate evil intent.

But if the De-Stalinization Speech failed to impress John Foster Dulles, it obviously had a profound effect elsewhere—and most especially in the Soviet satellites in Eastern Europe. In the wave of protests and civil unrest that swept through those countries in the summer and early autumn of 1956, there had been some in the Eisenhower administration who believed the Soviet empire was starting to fracture, a process that might be hastened by American engagement. Once again, though, the secretary of state urged the president to stand back. Now wasn't the time to extend an olive branch or search for common ground with the Kremlin, but rather to wait and let the erosion continue, to keep up the pressure until the whole Soviet system cracked and then crumbled beneath its own weight.

Part of this obduracy was rooted in Dulles's belief that there was unlikely to be any substantive change in Eastern Europe in the foreseeable future. Instead, his attention was now largely focused on the emerging nations of the Third World in Asia and Africa and Latin America, and if these regions posed opportunities for the United States—witness the successful coups in Iran and Guatemala—they also posed new risks.

The most pernicious of these was the so-called Non-Aligned Movement, that growing group of nations that professed neutrality in the Cold War contest. This movement had reached a kind of high-water mark in April 1955, a few months before the Geneva summit, at a conference of non-aligned nations held in the Indonesian city of Bandung. The brainchild of Jawaharlal Nehru, the prime minister of India, and Sukarno, the president of Indonesia, the Bandung conference had drawn delegates from twenty-nine nations in Africa and Asia comprising over half the world's population. Making it somewhat less than non-aligned, as well as driving up the population numbers, was the inclusion of communist China. Still, the professed goal of the conference was for nations in the Third World, many having only recently gained their independence from their colonial overseers, to work together in navigating a neutral path between the superpowers. In John Foster Dulles's eyes, this made the attendees either the communists' fellow travelers or their useful dupes, for how could any nation stay neutral in a primal clash between good and evil? Defining neutrality as a concept that "pretends that a nation can best gain safety for itself by being indifferent to the fate of others," he lectured that this had become both "an immoral and shortsighted conception."

Rather forgotten in this sermonizing was the United States' own long tradition of neutrality, one that had kept it on the sidelines of World War I until it was nearly too late—as well as Dulles's own strenuous efforts to keep the country out of World War II prior to Pearl Harbor. Never mind; at Bandung, the secretary of state found many more enemies to keep close watch on, including some the CIA would soon try to overthrow.

Of these, none were quite so formidable—or irksome—as Egyptian president Gamal Abdel Nasser. A co-leader of the group of junior mili-

tary officers who had overthrown King Farouk in 1952, by the time of the
Bandung conference, Nasser had emerged as Egypt's undisputed ruler.
An ardent nationalist as well as an eloquent spokesman for the cause
of pan-Arabism, the charismatic Egyptian was winning admiration
throughout the Arab world for his opposition to the state of Israel, and
for his stirring denunciations of those European colonial powers, Great
Britain and France, who continued to dominate much of the region. All
of this was perhaps forgivable in Dulles's eyes, regional issues that didn't
much touch on the East-West contest, but at Bandung, Nasser took a
star turn, electrifying the conference with his call for an end to international military alliances and lashing those Arab leaders who had joined
in defense pacts with Britain and the United States. When Nasser left
Bandung, he was no longer an Arab leader but an international one, and
of the very sort that John Foster Dulles was anxious to be rid of.

What the secretary of state may have found especially stinging was that
the CIA had supported the coup that brought Nasser to power and, in a
1953 meeting of the two, Dulles had professed his admiration of Nasser.
In the wake of the Bandung conference, and with a cuckold's desire for
revenge, he looked to the CIA for a solution.

In the run-up to the 1952 Egyptian coup, the CIA's man in Cairo, Miles
Copeland, had been instructed to get close to Nasser, and the two had
developed an excellent rapport, even a friendship. By late 1955, John
Foster thought to put that relationship to new use. According to Copeland, he received a message from Allen Dulles in which the CIA director,
explaining that he was acting on a request from his brother, wanted to
know just how a foreign power might go about having Nasser assassinated. If Copeland's account is to be believed, he took the question to
Nasser himself and, after bandying about a variety of methods—"'How
about poison?' I asked him"—the two concluded none would work.

In any event, Nasser seemed to quite revel in his growing enfant terrible image, and especially his ability to annoy the West. After the Eisenhower administration tried to exert pressure by holding up a substantial
arms sale to Egypt, Nasser instead took his shopping list to the Soviets.
An equal opportunity offender, the Egyptian president constantly savaged a regional defense treaty put together by the British, the Baghdad
Pact, and demanded France grant independence to their North African
colonies of Algeria, Tunisia and Morocco. By the summer of 1956, Nasser,
increasingly beloved in the Third World for his defiance, was an object of
deep loathing in the West.

But Dulles knew that the Egyptian strongman had a weakness—or at
least, so he thought. Since even before assuming power, Nasser had talked

of building an enormous dam on the Nile in the southern city of Aswan, the better to regulate the river that was his nation's economic lifeline. Egypt had obtained financing for the massive project from both Britain and the United States, but in mid-July 1956, both abruptly announced they were backing out of the deal. Not at all coincidentally, Nasser got the news while flying home from a meeting with Josip Tito, the maverick communist leader of Yugoslavia.

Once again, though, Nasser turned the tables on the West. In short order, he announced he'd received partial alternate funding from the Soviets, and would make up the difference by nationalizing the Suez Canal, still under the control of a joint British-French conglomerate. Kicking and screaming, the British and French took the matter to the U.N. Security Council, only to be told the nationalization was perfectly within Egypt's rights. With Nasser's stock sent soaring even further in the developing world, the Eisenhower administration chose to stay on the sidelines of the Suez tempest, figuring there was little to be gained by joining the fray.

But in one last death rattle of empire, Britain and France were determined that this Nasser outrage could not stand. Early that October, they went into secret negotiations with Israel, another nation eager to see the last of the Egyptian ruler, to launch a joint attack that would snatch back control of the canal and, with any luck, topple Nasser. Those plans, finalized at the same top secret meeting in France that had caused Frank Wisner to be stood up on his London dinner date, called for an initial attack by Israel into Egypt's Sinai Peninsula. Shortly after, Britain and France, masquerading as intermediaries, would demand both sides agree to a cease-fire. When Nasser refused—and steps would be taken to ensure he did—British and French forces would then seize the canal and wage a war of annihilation against the Egyptian military. The Sèvres Protocol was one of those ideas that looked better on paper than in execution—it's hard to imagine anyone would be fooled by Britain and France's professed ignorance of Israeli plans ahead of time—but it wasn't as if the colonial powers were apt to make new friends in the region anyway.

Of much greater concern in London and Paris was the American reaction, but most everyone involved in the plot believed Washington would be in at least tacit support. After all, the Eisenhower administration's antipathy for Nasser was well known, so why not go along with his overthrow? Even so, given the president's equally well-known desire for plausible deniability in such matters, for not knowing the messy details until after the fact, the plotters decided the best course was to lay down a series of hints to what was coming, and to let the Americans ask questions if they wished. By mid-October the CIA had picked up enough of these hints for Allen Dulles to warn the White House that an attack on Egypt appeared to be imminent, but elicited no response. Even today, there is some debate on the degree to which the administration was actually blindsided by the Suez affair. That debate is overshadowed, however, by the fact that, on the very eve of the Suez attack, the administration was *truly* blindsided by an altogether different crisis: Hungary.

———

By the evening of October 27, central Budapest resembled a battlefield abandoned. A particularly ghoulish battlefield, for among the burned-out tanks and shell-blasted buildings were the uncollected and putrefying bodies of Red Army soldiers, some having lain there for days, sprinkled with quicklime against the smell of their decay. From lampposts and tree limbs hung the corpses of AVH secret policemen, some battered beyond recognition by the lynch mobs that had set upon them. Here and there lay the corpses of other AVH to which the vigilantes had added a curious flourish, stuffing money under their bodies or in their mouths: "blood money" that no self-respecting Hungarian should touch.

As usually happens in war, the killing in Budapest had become more indiscriminate and more pitiless as time went on. On the afternoon of October 25, a vastly outnumbered line of Soviet soldiers and AVH men in Parliament Square was pressed and taunted by a massive crowd of demonstrators, some of them armed. While it's lost to history who fired first, what is known is that, in the blink of an eye, the square became a free-fire zone, one in which at least seventy demonstrators were killed and as many as 280 wounded. The Parliament Square massacre seemed to spur the rebels to new rage. All across the city wolf-packs of rebels redoubled their hunt for AVH men or vulnerable Red Army units, as the death toll steadily climbed. By that evening of October 27, well over three hundred Hungarians had been killed in the fighting, and at least that many Red Army soldiers.

It was also on that day that Imre Nagy fully crossed over.

Ever since being thrust back into power, the avuncular and chubby politician with the handlebar mustache had tried to gain his footing amid the violent whirlwind that had become his country. That effort also triggered an intense personal struggle.

Within the Hungarian communist party leadership, the sixty-year-old Nagy had always been viewed as a reformist—even when that label wasn't helpful to anyone's career or life expectancy—but in 1956 he still regarded himself as a proud and loyal communist. As a result, as Hungary descended into violence and then revolution, Nagy seemed to be forever trying to catch up to events, to always be one step behind the latest development.

On October 23, he had stepped out on a parliament building balcony to address the demonstrators who had been chanting his name, only to be jeered when he reflexively addressed them as "comrades." A thousand voices called back: "there are no more comrades here." Likewise his declaration of martial law on the following day, accompanied by a promise of amnesty for those who laid down their weapons, had been openly mocked. "A prisoner of the Politburo," many called him, either in derision or in the belief that he really was being held hostage somehow. Amid his fumbling, it was clear that Nagy hoped to somehow calm the furies that had exploded across the city long enough to find some middle ground, to serve as a bridge between the existing political structure and "the street." By that evening of October 27, however, he seemed to finally understand there was no middle ground, and he cast his lot with the revolution.

The following morning, Nagy took to the airwaves to announce that he and his "national resistance" allies had taken complete control of the government; as one of its first acts, it was abolishing the hated AVH. Most startling of all to Budapest residents were reports that the Hungarian leader was negotiating with the Soviets to withdraw their soldiers from the city, as part of larger discussions on the future military relationship between their countries. Buoyed by the news, as well as by massive demonstrations that had taken place throughout the world in support of the revolution, the rebels largely respected Nagy's new call for a cease-fire that day. Within minutes of the 1 p.m. deadline, the streets of the capital, having reverberated with the sound of gun- and shell fire for nearly a week, fell eerily quiet.

One who took careful note of Nagy's apparent political conversion was Frank Wisner. Having already told Allen Dulles that the United States must come to the aid of the Hungarian insurrectionists—"to do less," he said, "would be to sacrifice the moral basis for U.S. leadership of free peoples"—he flew on to Paris from London on October 28, and convened a meeting of regional CIA station chiefs to brainstorm on what should be done. As those gathered in Paris tried to read the Hungarian tea leaves, to divine what might happen next and why, most all agreed that if the changes sweeping across the nation were to be consolidated, Imre Nagy was probably the only man who could pull it off. No other Hungarian communist enjoyed his reformist, outsider status—the absolute minimum requirement of the increasingly militant insurrectionists—and no non-communist leader was going to be acceptable to Moscow. Instead, Nagy was about the best intermediary that could be hoped for: a Hungarian nationalist who would push to escape the Soviet thrall—"the street" would hold him to that—but a communist who could allay Moscow's fears that his reforms might go too far. The Paris group sent a long cable to Allen Dulles at CIA headquarters urging U.S. support of the new Hungarian prime minister.

But what Frank Wisner and the others gathered in Paris didn't know—and there is no indication that Allen Dulles was in any hurry to tell them—was that Eisenhower had long since decided what he was going to do in Hungary, and that policy could be summed up in a single word: nothing. If the revolt in Hungary succeeded, great, but if it failed, that was too bad; either way, the United States was going to sit on its hands. Indeed, the president had told his closest advisors as much no later than October 25, less than forty-eight hours into the insurrection.

This was a stunning reversal from a new policy that the administration had formulated just three months earlier, as outlined in a document known as NSC 5608/1. In a July 12 meeting of the National Security Council to discuss a draft of that document, John Foster Dulles had taken special umbrage at a paragraph calling for "the satellite peoples" to engage in passive resistance, and for the United States to "avoid incitements to violence" that might lead to the kind of brutal Soviet reprisals that had so recently occurred in Poznań, Poland. The secretary of state found this proposal "rather too negative in character" and offered his version of a more positive one, suggesting the administration "not discourage" such violent actions if they increased pressure on Moscow. As recorded in the top secret minutes of the meeting, John Foster further opined that "we shouldn't necessarily be appalled by the fact that if such uprisings occurred a certain number of people would be killed. After all, one cannot defend or regain liberty without some inevitable loss of life." Among those attendees in strong agreement with the secretary's lawyerly construction—the administration wasn't encouraging mayhem but they weren't discouraging it either—had been Vice President Nixon, and it was duly inserted into the NSC directive that President Eisenhower signed a week later. As a historian for the Department of Defense, Ronald Landa, pointed out, this rider to NSC 5608/1 underscored "a greater willingness to view bloodshed in the satellites as desirable," and, in certain circumstances, "to undertake actions that might precipitate violence."

But now, just three months later, the administration had crashed up against the precise situation it had envisioned and hoped to exploit, and was electing to do nothing.

Although never explicitly acknowledged, a chief reason for this was the very New Look doctrine the United States had initiated at the beginning of 1954. With the Eisenhower administration vowing "massive retaliation"—code for the use of nuclear weapons—should its national security be threatened, and the Soviets naturally parroting that pledge, it meant the European battlefield was now frozen in place. The opponents could only engage at the very low end of the risk scale—the espionage and infiltration operations that both the CIA and KGB had been conducting to small advantage since the late 1940s—or at the very top end: nuclear war. No middle option was possible—no rushing of troops into a conventional war, and no active support of an insurrection that threatened the status quo—because the "massive retaliation" doctrine all but dictated a swift escalation to the nuclear option.

While this calculus became quite obvious to the Eisenhower administration within days of the Hungarian Revolution, it seems that no one had fully thought it through back in 1953 when New Look was being formulated. If they had, they surely would have toned down all the empty but perilous talk of "liberation" and "rollback" in Eastern Europe that Eisenhower and John Foster Dulles had endlessly repeated since. Instead, they had performed a bit of political theater, constantly beating the liberation drum to placate the war-hawk wing of the Republican Party, while doing nothing to actually help bring it about.

But having beaten that drum for the past four years, how to stop now when something very much like liberation appeared a possibility in Hungary? And especially how to stop and expose the charade with presidential elections just two weeks away?

One way was to at least maintain the appearance of concern. On October 25, as he campaigned for the presidential elections now just twelve days off, Eisenhower inserted a short reference to events in Budapest into his standard stump speech, allowing that "at this moment the heart of America goes out to the people of Hungary." Nowhere was there the suggestion of American action; rather, it was the 1950s version of the modern "thoughts and prayers" meme.

But there was another strategy that could be tried, one simultaneously quite clever and profoundly cynical: kick the whole matter over to the United Nations. With that institution already gaining a reputation for toothlessness, its inaction could serve as a shield to mask the administration's own indolence. Better yet, by working through the U.N., the

United States could give the *appearance* of trying to address the Hungarian issue, with the confidence that any resolution taken to the Security Council would be vetoed by the Soviets. In just this way, while the United States did nothing to help the Hungarian revolutionaries—their fate rested solely in the hands of Moscow—the administration stood to reap a propaganda bonanza if and when Moscow moved to crush them.

The U.S. ambassador to the U.N., Henry Cabot Lodge, heartily endorsed the plan in a secret cable he sent to John Foster Dulles on October 25. "Even if final action blocked by Soviet veto," Lodge wrote, "[U.S.] initiative would, in addition to increasing US prestige, add to prestige of UN in eyes of satellite peoples who now hold organization in low esteem because of its past failure to note their plight." If the administration really wanted to get fancy, Lodge added, it could argue for sending U.N. observers into Hungary, an idea the Soviets would also shoot down. "This could be done with a great show of reasonableness and sincerity."

This plan was put into effect, but with a further refinement. Even though a Soviet veto of the U.N. Security Council resolution was a sure thing, if the measure came up for a vote too soon, the burden would be back on the Eisenhower administration to take some action on its own. The work-around was for Lodge to slow-walk the Hungarian issue at the U.N., presenting it as a matter "for discussion" rather than as a full-blown crisis worthy of quick action. In the meantime, the only official communication the administration sent to the Kremlin during the Hungarian crisis was a note of assurance that the United States had no interest in making a breakaway Hungary part of a Western alliance, as if this assurance might be enough to cause Moscow to let Hungary go.

Of all these machinations, Frank Wisner, busy and in a foreign country, probably only imperfectly sensed. To the degree he did grasp them, it wouldn't seem to necessarily negate his urging the administration to support Nagy. What Wisner surely didn't know at this stage, though, was that his advocacy of Nagy was being systematically undercut by an arm of the CIA he'd helped create: the Mighty Wurlitzer's Radio Free Europe.

With its Hungarian broadcasting staff largely composed of right-wing Hungarian exiles, RFE was not only the principal source of information on the revolution for most Hungarians, but a cheerleader for the insurrectionists to demand ever more, to not seek compromise but to hold out for the tearing down of Hungary's political structure altogether. To this end, Imre Nagy was not the solution, but the problem. Day after day, and speaker after speaker, RFE Hungary bombarded its listeners with excoriations of the new prime minister. One speaker claimed it was Nagy who had ordered the Soviet tanks back into Budapest on October 24 (it wasn't) and urged his listeners to fight against the man "whose hands are steeped in Hungarian blood." Even when it became clear on the morning of October 28 that Nagy had fully joined with the rebels, the radio still attacked him as a Moscow stooge, while his call for a nationwide cease-fire provoked an escalation of RFE attacks on him. It was as if, safely ensconced in Munich, the RFE broadcasters didn't want to see an end to the killing, but rather more of it. Incredibly, those CIA officials who comprised the senior, policy-setting staff of RFE seemed to have little sense of what was being broadcast under their watch for the simple reason that none of them spoke Hungarian.

Be that as it may, the RFE's estimation of Nagy meshed nicely with that of the moral absolutist John Foster Dulles; as he counseled the president on October 27, Nagy's government contained a number of "bad people" and wasn't to be trusted. So convinced was the secretary that the Nagy regime wasn't worth dealing with that, as noted by foreign policy analyst Martin Ben Swartz, at no time during the crisis were American diplomats in Hungary "instructed to make contact with him or any of his top advisors in order to try to find out just exactly what Nagy hoped to achieve. Indeed, for the most part the Legation was simply not given any instructions at all."

Amid all this, the most perverse irony of all: at the very moment that the Eisenhower administration was turning its back on Nagy and scurrying to wash their hands of the Hungarian Revolution, the Soviet Union was concluding the revolution was a fait accompli and that they had no choice but to work with Nagy. At a meeting of the Soviet Politburo on the afternoon of October 28, most every member was in favor of withdrawing Soviet troops from Hungary, and beginning negotiations with Nagy on the future relationship of their two countries.

Just as Nagy had intimated, on the morning of October 29, the Soviet commander in Hungary announced his troops would begin leaving Budapest at once. With the previous day's cease-fire still holding, there was virtually no shooting in Budapest that day, even as the first long convoys of departing Soviet military units took to its roadways. In the holding calm, an unfamiliar mood spread over the battle-scarred city: celebration. "The belief spread through the city that the Hungarians had won a victory," noted Victor Sebestyen.

In their euphoria, surely very few Hungarians took note of a stray bit of news that came in from afar that afternoon: at about 3 p.m. on October 29, Israeli forces had launched an air and ground assault against Egyptian forces in the Sinai desert. That news would soon have a profound, and catastrophic, influence on events in Hungary.

Victory. On the morning of October 31, Hungarians woke up to the news that the Soviets had capitulated. And not in the quiet, slinking-away posture they had so recently displayed in Poland, but with astounding candor and for all the world to see.

That morning saw the publication in *Pravda* of a manifesto almost as stunning as Khrushchev's De-Stalinization Speech in February: *On Friendship and Cooperation Between the Soviet Union and Other Socialist States*. In it, Khrushchev made clear that the Soviet Union was now to embark on the same liberalizing effort at the international level as it had begun on the domestic. The Soviet bloc was to become a "commonwealth" of independent socialist states, one built on "respect of territorial integrity, state independence and sovereignty, and non-interference in one another's domestic affairs." With each of those nations, the Soviet Union was prepared to enter into negotiations—like those now under way with Hungary—toward coming to a new economic and military relationship acceptable to both. It was the most progressive policy paper to come out of the Kremlin since the 1917 Revolution, and one the likes of which the world would never see again.

On that morning, the Hungarians were also beginning to learn just what this new era might look like. The previous afternoon, Nagy had announced an end to one-party rule and the release of political prisoners. He also revealed that the Soviets had agreed to negotiate toward a complete withdrawal of Soviet troops, not just from Budapest but from Hungary itself. All of this was made possible because Nagy had somehow managed to reassure Moscow that the loosening of the ties between their two nations wouldn't be too extreme—that, and the reality on the ground. As *Pravda* noted: "the Nagy government has won the support of the people."

Unknown to the Hungarian citizenry was the most shocking aspect of the whole affair. The previous afternoon, the Soviet leadership had gone into conference and heard Nikita Khrushchev give a persuasive argument on why they should let Hungary go, that it was too late now to resort to brute force. Because there remained at least the pretense of collective leadership, Khrushchev then polled everyone in the room: to a man, all eventually agreed with the first secretary.

But then, even as foreign ministries and intelligence agencies around the world were struggling to digest the new Soviet Union as outlined by *Pravda*, everything changed. Following a troubled and largely sleepless night, Khrushchev concluded that he'd made a terrible mistake. On the morning of October 31, and at the very same moment that the Hungarians had begun to celebrate their new freedom, the Soviet leader hastily called for another meeting with members of the Politburo.

As Khrushchev explained to his startled colleagues, he now saw that letting Hungary go would be perceived as weakness by the West, and could mean losing all of Eastern Europe. Just yesterday, he noted, there had been demonstrations in support of the Hungarian counterrevolutionaries in Poland, Czechoslovakia and Romania, a sign the erosion was likely to spread there, and what had been granted to the Hungarians would be demanded by the others. If the Soviet Union ceded ground now, the ceding would never stop. Instead, the Hungarian Revolution had to be crushed—decisively and with severity.

Also contributing to the first secretary's change of heart were events in the Middle East. After launching their attack on Egypt two days earlier, the Israelis had now been joined by Great Britain and France, with those nations' warplanes pounding Egyptian military installations along the Suez Canal; there seemed no doubt that the attackers' ultimate intention was to seize the canal and overthrow Nasser, Moscow's new friend in the Middle East. The Soviets simply couldn't lose two battles to the West in one week. Further, the world's attention was already shifting from Hungary to Egypt. Intelligence reports indicated that Western journalists were already beginning to leave Budapest for the larger story in the Middle East. With the world thus distracted, this was the ideal moment to reverse course and crush the Hungarian counterrevolutionaries.

Khrushchev's reversal was undoubtedly also influenced by the American response to Hungary—or, rather, the lack thereof. Despite Soviet propaganda to the contrary, the United States had done nothing to aid the revolutionaries, and if they hadn't done so by now, a week into the troubles, it seemed a safe bet that they never would. Instead, other than a few feeble denunciations on the Soviets' use of force, the Eisenhower administration had foisted the Hungarian issue on the United Nations, where it had to know nothing would be done. It all pointed to the Americans' tacit understanding that Hungary was in the Soviet sphere, and that to intervene raised the specter of wider, much deadlier, war.

Under the weight of these arguments—and rather giving the lie to the notion of collective leadership—the same Politburo members who had voted for a withdrawal from Hungary the day before, now came around one by one in support of invasion. The name chosen for the operation was a particularly apt one: Whirlwind.

At five in the morning of November 1, Nagy was awoken with the news that an enormous Soviet army had begun coming across the border; over the next three days, and even as the Soviet ambassador in Budapest constantly reassured Nagy that Moscow was sticking to their negotiated deal, that army swelled to some sixty thousand troops backed by thousands of T-54s, the newest and most formidable tank in the Soviet arsenal.

To a remarkable degree, it appears the wily Khrushchev had taken Eisenhower's measure. The British and French attack on Egypt had placed the president in a bind, forcing him to choose between supporting two of his closest allies and winning the enmity of much of the Third World, or doing the opposite and coming out against his allies' adventurism. But if a bind, the Suez Crisis also presented the president with a golden opportunity. Having already opted to do nothing for Hungary, as Khrushchev pointed out, Eisenhower could now divert American and world attention away from his failure in that crisis by redirecting attention to Egypt. This he set out to do, and without much subtlety. At the start of an NSC meeting on November 1, the president announced that he didn't want to hear any discussion about the situation in Eastern Europe, but instead wanted to focus solely on the Suez Crisis. In an irony the Hungarians surely didn't appreciate, both superpowers had now latched on to Suez as a handy fig leaf for their actions—or inactions, in the Americans' case—in Hungary.

For the next three days, with the Red Army noose tightening around the capital, Nagy chose to withhold this information from his own people, fearful of causing a mass panic. At the same time, he frantically continued to barter with the Soviets, hoping against hope that a compromise might be reached and the agreement of October 30 honored. In a last desperate act, he declared Hungary's neutrality and withdrawal from the Warsaw Pact military alliance, and pleaded for U.N. intervention. This only had the effect of moving American betrayal from passive to active. While finally presenting a resolution to the U.N. Security Council on November 3 calling for an end of Soviet intervention in Hungary, the American envoy, Henry Cabot Lodge, then pushed back against efforts to bring his resolution to a quick vote, instead urging that the Council focus on Suez and take up the Hungarian matter "in a day or two." Making this stall tactic even more unconscionable, the administration now knew full well of the Soviet military buildup in Hungary, the CIA having picked up on the massive diversion of Hungarian railway rolling stock to the Soviet border, vital for bringing in heavy weaponry. In any event, the American request for a Security Council delay prevailed.

At almost the same moment that Lodge was performing this odd dance in New York, a sign of what was to come in Budapest occurred when the Hungarian defense minister, cajoled by Soviet military officials into driving onto a Red Army base for peace talks, was instead grabbed by KGB officers. Seven hours later, at precisely 6:15 a.m. on November 4, the Soviet commander of Operation Whirlwind issued the code word— "thunder"—for action to commence. All across Budapest, Soviet tanks and artillery opened fire as one.

With the Hungarian military leaderless without the defense minister, and with Nagy refusing to issue an order for the army to fight back—he concluded, undoubtedly correctly, that any defense thrown up would only lead to greater slaughter—the end came quickly. By the close of that first day, only isolated bands of Hungarian fighters remained, the rest having melted away in the face of such overwhelming force or succumbed to the brutal change in Soviet tactics. Where earlier, Soviet troops had acted with considerable restraint, they now simply obliterated any building suspected of harboring gunmen with tank and artillery fire. Already, advance units of KGB and AVH secret police began combing through Budapest's outlying neighborhoods, working off arrest lists of "counterrevolutionaries" that would eventually number in the tens of thousands. As he campaigned for the election, now just two days away, Eisenhower expressed his "inexpressible shock" at the Soviets' actions. For sheer cynicism, however, it was hard to compete with the words of Henry Cabot Lodge. With the Soviet attack under way, he rushed into an emergency meeting of the U.N. Security Council, the same body that he'd blocked from taking up the Hungarian crisis less than twelve hours earlier, to declare: "If ever there was a time when the action of the U.N. could literally be a matter of life and death for a whole nation, this is that time."

And there was a particularly poignant feature of that terrible day in Budapest. In all their talk of liberating the "captive nations" of Eastern Europe, the people of Hungary had taken the Eisenhower administration at their word. Timothy Foote, a journalist with Time-Life, was in the Hungarian capital that day, and observed the result. "Both the fighters and the ordinary civilians, they kept looking up at the western sky," Foote recalled. "They were looking for the American warplanes that they felt sure were coming to help them. All that week, when people realized I was an American journalist, they would grab at my jacket: 'When are the Americans coming? They told us they were coming.'"

Foote recalled an especially awful moment as the ring of Soviet steel closed on some of the last pockets of resistance in the city center. "There was all this shooting going on, people were in despair, they knew the end was coming, and all of a sudden, this cheer goes up. And it spreads. Even over the gunfire, you could hear this cheering. I finally asked someone what was going on, and they said, 'the Americans have arrived at last, they are on the outskirts, but they're coming this way.' So this rumor had started." Even over the span of nearly sixty years, the emotion spurred by that memory caused Foote to go silent for a long moment. "Well," he said finally, "this was a very difficult thing to hear."

═══════

To all of this, Frank Wisner was an increasingly distraught, if distant, observer. After sending the cable from Paris urging the administration to work with Nagy, he had continued to pepper CIA headquarters with directives on what should be done. These cables grew more frequent as administration inaction continued, and took on a hectoring quality: the United States had urged the Hungarians to rebel, they had been urging that on them for years, and they couldn't abandon them now in their hour of greatest need. As the curtain began to close on Budapest, the deputy director's cables grew increasingly angry, increasingly scattershot.

On November 5, a day that saw the Soviet army continuing its mopping-up operations in Budapest, Wisner arrived in Frankfurt. He had been invited to stay in the home of Tracy Barnes—one of his protégés and now the CIA Germany station chief—but from the moment Wisner arrived, Barnes and his wife, Janet, knew something was seriously wrong. "He made no sense," Janet Barnes related to historian Evan Thomas years later. "He was in awful shape."

If initially the Barneses thought Wisner's odd behavior was the result of exhaustion, they were disabused of that notion on the following day; if anything, he seemed to be even more agitated. As it was November 6, Election Day in the United States, the Barneses stayed up most of that night, ostensibly to listen to the election returns, but really to keep watch over Wisner, who wouldn't sleep. "He couldn't stop ticking," Janet Barnes remembered, "he couldn't stop thinking, whether it was about the Hungarians, whether it was about Suez, whether it was about the United States. He was going around in these very tight, agitated circles. It was very hard to discuss it with him because he never stopped talking."

The next day, Wisner went on to Vienna, where he stayed with another friend, the American ambassador to Austria, Llewellyn "Tommy" Thompson. To Thompson, too, Wisner seemed quite beside himself, talking incessantly. Converting one room of the ambassador's residence into a kind of forward command post, the deputy director ordered the Vienna CIA station to bring over all its cable traffic. William Hood, the CIA officer detailed to the task, watched as Wisner rifled through the great stacks of papers, most dealing with mundane administrative matters, and grew increasingly agitated. "He colored as he read," Hood told Thomas. "There was very little [cable] traffic on the revolution. He felt isolated, out of the loop. He was drowning in junk, in useless cable traffic."

On November 11, Wisner made the forty-five-mile drive from Vienna to the Hungarian border. Despite Khrushchev's decision to end the revolution with overwhelming firepower, the Soviets had deliberately left the Hungarian border with Austria loosely guarded, perhaps as a way to encourage the surviving malcontents to leave the country. If that was the intent, it worked. Beginning soon after the Soviet tanks closed on Budapest on November 1 and continuing until mid-month, a steady flow of Hungarian refugees poured across the frontier, nearly 200,000 in all. On the day of Wisner's visit, there was still the sound of gunfire coming from over the border, and the looks of exhaustion and anguish on the faces of the refugees tore at him. Back in Vienna that evening, he was having dinner with friends at a restaurant when he suddenly flew into a rage, shouting that the United States had let the Hungarians down, that he felt personally betrayed and disgraced. He heaped special scorn on John Foster Dulles, accusing the secretary of state of letting Hungary be destroyed just to win propaganda points.

As Wisner continued on his European trip, most every American official he met with came away troubled and concerned. To William Colby, who dined with him in Rome, Wisner "was rambling and raving all through dinner, totally out of control. He kept saying, all these people are getting killed and we weren't doing anything, we were ignoring it." In Athens, the CIA station chief listened in as Wisner dictated one cable after another to be sent to headquarters, and gradually realized that none of them made sense. Alerted to the problem, Wisner's friend and deputy back in Washington, Richard Helms, intercepted the incoming cables and destroyed them.

As for Hungary, the news never got any better. Having sought asylum in the Yugoslav embassy, Imre Nagy and his top aides were eventually tricked into leaving the building with the promise of immunity, only to be grabbed by the KGB and flown to a castle prison in neighboring Romania. In a secret trial in Budapest in 1958, Hungarian officials sentenced Nagy to death for treason; along with two of his closest allies, he was hung that June, their bodies dumped in an unmarked grave. By then, an estimated 25,000 Hungarians had been arrested for their role in the revolution, with some 300 of them ultimately executed. Those executions continued until 1960 since some of the condemned were as young as fourteen at the time of their "crimes" and couldn't be legally put to death until they reached adulthood.

And it didn't end with Hungary. In those other Eastern European countries that had so recently shown stirrings for liberalization, in Czechoslovakia and Romania, untold thousands were rounded up and cast into prison. Operation Whirlwind did come at a cost, though. At one time, Moscow had hoped that the two most powerful communist parties in Western Europe, those in France and Italy, might one day be voted into power. In the wake of Hungary, the French communist party lost half its membership, while the Italian communists divided into pro- and anti-Soviet factions, a split that never mended.

For its part, the Eisenhower administration, newly elected to a second term, moved to capitalize on the opprobrium directed at the Soviets, as well as to limit the political fallout from their own failure to aid the Hungarians. With a poll of Hungarian exiles showing that, during the revolution, three quarters had believed from listening to Radio Free Europe that American military help was coming, the CIA launched an investigation to see if the RFE broadcasters had made false promises or added to the tragedy by inciting its listeners to violence. Despite broadcasts in which RFE's Hungarian announcers had detailed how to make Molotov cocktails and sabotage rail and telephone lines, the investigation found no wrongdoing, only allowing that there had been a few incidental "deviations from policy." As for any larger role the administration might have played in encouraging the revolt through its incessant talk of liberation, it was quite blameless there, as well. Pressed to explain, John Foster Dulles argued that he and others had always been careful to specify "by peaceful means" when urging Eastern Europeans to strike at their communist oppressors, a bit of oratorical fine print that the Hungarians had clearly failed to pick up on. As for President Eisenhower, he was simply mystified as to how the whole thing got started in the first place. "I just don't know what got into those people," he told a friend. "It's the damnedest business I ever saw."

The judgment of history would not be so kind. Future CIA director William Colby noted that in Hungary "we demonstrated that 'liberation' was not our policy when the chips were down." A more caustic appraisal came from historian Elizabeth Hazard. "Not only had the US held out false hope to those who were willing to risk their lives in a desperate crusade," she wrote, "but its policies had subverted the possibility of an early détente with the Soviet Union." Calling the administration's past rhetoric about rollback a tragic hoax, Hazard argued that, "by abandoning those who had placed their faith in its promises, the United States betrayed the hollowness of its pretense as the champion of liberty and exposed its willingness to exploit the desperate hopes of its clients." For Hazard, that betrayal carried special resonance: she was Frank Wisner's daughter.

As for the toll on Wisner himself, his friend Janet Barnes would remember a particularly sad moment. When Wisner arrived at the Barnes home in Frankfurt on November 5, he was accompanied by a CIA officer, his traveling assistant. Seizing a moment when Wisner was otherwise distracted, the assistant took Janet Barnes aside to ask a peculiar question: might they have an electric train set in the house? By odd chance, they did—it belonged to the Barnes's young son—and it was set up in an upstairs room. Later that evening, the assistant thought to calm an increasingly agitated Wisner, following the worsening news out of Hungary, by leading him up to the room with the train set and settling him in a chair. For a long time, Wisner just sat there, his mind soothed at last, as he watched the little train go around and around on its track.

EPILOGUE

At a meeting of the National Security Council on March 20, 1958, Secretary of State John Foster Dulles made a rather startling admission. Visibly weakened by the terminal cancer to which he would succumb in a little over a year, he allowed that he had been quite wrong in regarding the nationalist and anticolonialist movements he had engaged in battle around the world as fifth columns for communism. As the scribe of the meeting paraphrased him, in looking at the three trouble spots that most concerned the Eisenhower administration at that moment—Indonesia, North Africa and the Middle East—Dulles had now concluded that "the directing forces are not communist, but primarily forces favorable personally to a Sukarno, a Nasser or the like. Developments in these areas had not been initiated by Soviet plots."

While a seemingly remarkable turnaround from the truculent policies Dulles had advocated since the end of World War II—and for the past six years zealously pursued as the secretary of state—it was rather too little, too late. By the end of Eisenhower's second term, the geographical spread of governments that his administration had undertaken to overthrow or otherwise subvert suggested an almost purposeful design, as if it sought to alienate the citizenry of most every region and subregion of the globe: Guatemala, Cuba and British Guiana in Latin America; Egypt and Congo in Africa; Syria, Iraq, Iran and Lebanon in the Middle East; Indonesia and Laos in Asia. In 1944, the people in many of these regions had been stirred by President Roosevelt's talk of an end to the colonial era, of the United States as the deliverer of self-determination and democracy. By

1960, such rhetoric seemed risible to these same people, with the United States now regarded as just one more imperial power bent on their political and economic subjugation. In vast swaths of the world, that estimation remains unchanged today.

That assessment also underscores how one of the greatest victims of the battle against communism in the early Cold War was the cause of anti-communism itself. Invoked to prop up right-wing military dictatorships and topple democratic governments, to allow its self-appointed leaders to spout easy shibboleths about "rollback" and "liberation" but then shirk all responsibility for its consequences, anti-communism became to many just one more political hustle, a sales pitch that sold well to the gullible or frightened or overly trusting. Among the 200,000 Hungarians who fled their homeland in 1956, anti-communists all, how many could ever again hear American politicians trot out the term without a tinge of bitterness?

At the same time, it is hard to conceive of another phraseology that has had such a profound effect on modern American history. Just as Eisenhower was compelled to mindlessly recite the anti-communist "liberation theology" because it is what helped him get elected, so his successors were pinioned by the same rhetoric. Having peddled an even more confrontational anti-communism in his own presidential campaign, John Kennedy proceeded with the disastrous Bay of Pigs assault on Cuba, a scheme he inherited from the Eisenhower administration, because he didn't want to appear a hypocrite or "soft on communism." One of the chief reasons Lyndon Johnson kept doubling down in Vietnam was because, haunted by the early 1950s witch hunt over "who lost China?," he didn't want to be the man "who lost Southeast Asia." In the 1970s, the same anti-communist refrain was used to justify the bloody overthrow of a democratically elected government in Chile, and in the 1980s to justify American support for a string of right-wing death-squad dictatorships in Central America. Indeed, it only ever stopped being used when the communist world itself collapsed in a spectacular act of self-implosion.

One of the most tragic results of this mania was that it fairly blinded successive American administrations to pick up on rapprochement signals from the Soviets that may have led to an early détente. While it's hard to imagine anyone trusting in such an overture from Stalin, many Cold War historians point to three specific moments in the early post-Stalin era when a very different relationship with Moscow might have been possible: just after Stalin's death, when the moderates within the Soviet politburo talked for the first time of "peaceful coexistence" with the West; in the wake of Khrushchev's February 1956 De-Stalinization Speech and the spirit of liberalization and reform it unleashed; and amid the Hungarian Revolution of eight months later, when the Soviet Union appeared poised to release one of its satellites and enter a radically new relationship with those that remained. All three of those moments of opportunity were summarily squandered, and in that squandering insured that the Cold War and all that came with it—trillions of dollars in defense spending; American military engagements from Vietnam to Grenada; an almost countless number of proxy wars over three continents—would continue for thirty-five more years.

The cost was also internal, for the excesses and crimes committed in the name of anti-communism in the early Cold War carved a dividing line through the American body politic, planting the seeds of the blue-state/red-state schism that we grapple with today. Amid the domestic Red Scare, those who embraced the belief that America was under siege from within traveled one divergent path, while those who believed it was largely a cynical myth traveled another, with both paths ultimately so antithetical to the other as to make their travelers all but impervious to contradictory facts. As political scientists have pointed out, by knowing which side of the political divide a person chose during the Red Scare of the late 1940s, it's possible to predict with near certainty their and their offspring's political views on foreign affairs ever after: their support or opposition to the Vietnam War in the 1960s, their children's support or opposition to Ronald Reagan's Star Wars initiative in the 1980s; their grandchildren's support or opposition to the invasion of Iraq in 2003. There is very little sign that this divide, rooted in the Cold War passions of seventy years ago, will narrow anytime soon.

Paradoxically, those Americans who manned the front lines of the early Cold War, the intelligence gatherers and covert action specialists of the CIA, was one group that largely bridged this schism. Most early CIA officers were politically and socially liberal, while fiercely anti-communist. Most regarded the spread of communism as a clear and present danger, fully believed that the Kremlin sought world domination, yet also loathed Joe McCarthy and regarded the domestic Red Scare that he and others traded in as a destructive sideshow. At the same time—and neatly rounding off the paradox—no branch of government has been more castigated, both for its actions and inactions, in the Cold War.

In the autumn of 1956, at the very time of the Hungarian Revolution and the Suez Crisis, analysts were putting the finishing touches on yet another investigation into the inner workings—and failings—of the CIA. The Bruce-Lovett report was the most scathing yet, depicting an organization in which its covert action wing was running amok, and flagrantly interfering in the affairs of other nations with virtually no oversight by anyone. "Should not someone, somewhere in an authoritative position in our government," the report asked, "[be] calculating the impacts on our international position, and keeping in mind the long range wisdom of activities which have entailed our virtual abandonment of the international 'golden rule'[?]"

Those criticisms paled, however, next to those that accompanied the investigation of the Agency in the mid-1970s by a Senate select committee headed by Democratic senator Frank Church. In the Church Committee report was a full airing of much of the CIA's dirty laundry over the years, including its plots to assassinate foreign leaders, as well as its involvement in coups and guerrilla wars and domestic surveillance. In Senator Church's famous phrase, it appeared that the CIA had been "behaving like a rogue elephant on a rampage." Such criticisms didn't end with the Cold War, but in more recent years the Agency has most often been scored for sins of omission: for missing the warning signs of the September 11 attacks, for erroneously concluding that Saddam Hussein possessed weapons of mass destruction.

While not a blanket pardon for the many excesses and lapses of the CIA over the years, much of this criticism requires overlooking the very nature of how a government bureaucracy—indeed, how any office of any kind—actually functions. Despite a mandate to analyze and report without fear or favor, to "speak truth to power" as the tired phrase goes, CIA analysts very quickly figure out that what viewpoints or ideas get promoted tend to be those that most closely conform to the wishes or preconceptions of one's higher-ups, while contrarian analysis and ideas get pushed to the margins. Similarly, covert action specialists get noticed for conducting operations, not for canceling them. If variations of this phenomenon are apparent in any office, it's especially burdensome when those calling for action or cherry-picking information are the president or his senior advisors. As CIA historians have long noted, there *were* agency analysts who warned that the Eastern European infiltration operations were thoroughly compromised and should be shut down; that the Chinese army was about to flood into Korea; that Vietnam was going to be an ungodly quagmire; who were dubious of Saddam Hussein's WMD "arsenal." Because this is not what higher-ups wanted to hear, they were ignored.

Ultimately, though, the endless debates over whether the CIA is to be blamed for this misjudgment or that botched mission is to miss the larger truth: one of the Agency's primary functions is to *be* blamed. A clue to this is to be found in that very first memo penned by George Kennan, the architect of the plausible deniability doctrine, in putting forward Frank Wisner's name to head the Office of Policy Coordination in 1948. Despite traveling in the same small social circle as Wisner, and despite having worked closely with him over the previous two years, Kennan could insist that "I personally have no knowledge of his ability," and that he was putting Wisner's name forward "on the recommendations of people who know him." This, in miniature, is the same essential posture that most every American president since Truman has maintained with the Agency. Far from being the "rogue elephant" of Frank Church's imagination, virtually every major covert mission undertaken by the CIA from its inception until today—from the overthrow of Iran's Mossadegh, to the plots to kill Fidel Castro; from interfering in elections in Italy, to building a mercenary army in Laos; from secretly funding the Nicaraguan contras, to "proving" Saddam Hussein possessed weapons of mass destruction—has been done under the express, if unwritten, orders of presidents. In adherence to the doctrine of plausible deniability, the CIA always has been—and likely always will be—the ultimate fall guy.

═══════

Historians have long noted the extraordinary confluence of events that occurred in late October and early November 1956, of two earth-shaping conflicts—the Hungarian Revolution and the Suez Crisis—taking place at the very moment that the U.S. presidential election was also being held. Naturally, there has been much commentary about the interplay between these three events, how one may have shaped the outcome of the other two.

What isn't generally known is that something else with potentially vast consequences occurred at exactly the same time. It happened in early November in the Nghe An province of northern Vietnam, when thousands of villagers and small farmers staged a spontaneous uprising against the draconian land reform policies being imposed by the communist government. Especially shocking, Nghe An was the very cradle of communist ideology in Vietnam, the birthplace of Ho Chi Minh. Not shocking at all was the regime's response: in the brutal suppression of the uprising, estimates of those executed or exiled range as high as six thousand.

The events in Nghe An cast a light—or, at least, should have, had anyone paid attention—on what was perhaps America's first great mistake in Vietnam. Two years earlier, the Geneva Accords had mandated that, although temporarily partitioning the nation, elections would be held in 1956 leading to its reunification. In the interim, most every American advisor and visiting politician had advised President Diem to renounce the elections, sure that he would be crushed at the ballot box by Ho Chi Minh. Practically the only advisor who argued otherwise, who suggested Diem's star was on the rise and Ho's on the wane, was CIA contract officer Edward Lansdale. The news out of Nghe An in the autumn of 1956 suggested that Lansdale may well have been right, that those under communist rule would have chosen otherwise if ever given the chance to vote. At American insistence, they were not.

After leaving Vietnam at the end of 1956, Lansdale was officially returned to the Air Force from the CIA and given a desk job at the Pentagon. He was miserable there—in typical bureaucratic fashion, his extravagantly long official title spoke to its insignificance—and schemed to find some way to get back overseas. He also soon suffered a deep personal blow when, in March 1957, Philippine president Ramon Magsaysay was killed in a plane crash.

Ultimately, Lansdale was intimately involved in the ill-fated attempts to overthrow Fidel Castro's regime in Cuba. While he regarded the Bay of Pigs scheme as sheer lunacy—and got into a near shouting match with Allen Dulles over the subject—he went on to oversee the equally lunatic Operation Mongoose, in which the CIA concocted a host of bizarre assassination scenarios to eliminate the Cuban leader.

Lansdale's involvement with Mongoose remains the most mystifying chapter in his career. The man who had always advocated policies designed to empower locals, who urged armies to engage in hearts-and-minds campaigns to win over the populace, and who argued that fostering democratic governments responsive to people's needs was the best way to defeat communist insurgencies, was now running an operation designed to murder a foreign leader that Lansdale himself recognized had broad popular support. One explanation for this turnaround is that Lansdale was simply being "a good soldier," that issued an order, he felt duty-bound to carry it out. This explanation doesn't quite square, though, with his long record of bucking both military and civilian authority, and letting his own opinions on matters be loudly known.

What Lansdale really wanted to do was get back to Vietnam. By 1961, he had made three trips back, but always only briefly and kept on a short leash by a resentful American embassy and resident CIA. Short leash or not, on each trip he had been struck by the country's political and social deterioration. By the time of his third visit in October 1961, large stretches of the countryside were under the control of a new communist insurgency, the Viet Cong. What Lansdale found especially alarming on that trip, though, was the growing isolation and dictatorial streak of Ngo Dinh Diem, to which the resident American community seemed completely acquiescent.

Another who saw this was Lansdale's former CIA colleague Rufus Phillips. Returning to Vietnam in 1962 to run the U.S. Agency for International Development's counterinsurgency program, Phillips also became keenly aware of a puzzling paradox, that the greater the American military investment in Vietnam, the worse the security situation was becoming. At the beginning of Kennedy's administration in January 1961, there had been fewer than seven hundred American military advisors in Vietnam. By the summer of 1963, that total stood at over sixteen thousand, and the Viet Cong held greater sway in the countryside than ever before. Certainly not helping the situation was Diem's increasingly harsh crackdown on the religious expression of Buddhist sects. Matters reached a crisis point in June 1963 when a Buddhist monk immolated himself in a Saigon street in protest over the Diem regime's repression, an image captured by photographers and flashed around the world. By then, a growing number of Vietnamese army generals were turning against the president, and there was talk in the streets of Saigon that a coup was imminent.

"That's when you could feel the whole place just coming apart," Phillips recalled, "and if anyone at the [American] embassy had any influence on Diem to change his ways, he sure as hell wasn't listening."

Diem clearly sensed the walls closing in, as well. As the crisis deepened, he repeatedly asked Phillips if Lansdale could return to Vietnam. Phillips carried these messages to the American embassy, which relayed them to Washington, but the appeals were lost in the bureaucratic ether, shot down by Lansdale's many enemies in both the State Department and the CIA.

In Phillips's view, there arose one last chance to save the situation. Briefly back in Washington that September, he was brought into a meeting in the White House with President Kennedy. There, he implored the president to send Lansdale, the only man who might turn Diem in time, back to Saigon.

But the Kennedy administration soon settled on a different course. Through the conduit of the new American ambassador to Vietnam, Henry Cabot Lodge—the same Lodge who had stalled a U.N. response to the Hungarian Revolution in 1956—senior Vietnamese generals were given the green light to overthrow Diem. The liaison between Lodge and the military conspirators was one of Lansdale's other former SMM teammates, Lucien Conein. In a moment of dark comedy, when Conein was instructed to deliver $70,000 in cash to the generals on the eve of the coup, he couldn't find a case large enough to hold it all so the plotters had to make do with the $42,000 he could carry.

The coup got under way on the early afternoon of November 1, 1963, just two days after Phillips's last meeting with Diem. After initially escaping the presidential palace, the two Ngo brothers, Diem and Nhu, arranged to surrender the next day in return for safe passage from the country. Instead, the brothers were led into an armored car, where both were shot to death. Sent to verify their deaths was Lucien Conein. Less than three weeks later, President Kennedy would also be assassinated.

By bizarre coincidence, Edward Lansdale had retired from the United States military on the very day the coup against Diem got under way. In fact, his retirement party at the Pentagon had only just ended when the first news flashes out of Saigon came in. Despite accusations to the contrary, there is no evidence that Lansdale knew of the coup ahead of time, and surely would have opposed it if he did.

South Vietnam finally fell to the communists in 1975. It had been twenty-one years since Lansdale and his twelve-man Saigon Military Mission had pitched up to "save south Vietnam." They had been followed by nearly three million American servicemen in a conflict that took the lives of 58,000 Americans and untold millions of Vietnamese, Cambodians and Laotians.

Of the vast number of people with whom Lansdale corresponded in his retirement, one of the more interesting exchanges was with a Georgia journalism student, Tommy Allen, who wrote to ask if Lansdale felt the United States should have used more force or escalated more quickly in Vietnam. In reply, Lansdale described his feelings in watching how American firepower was used in Southeast Asia. "It was as though I were watching a friend on the operating table for delicate brain surgery and the brain surgeon had picked up a sledgehammer for the operation. If someone, then or now, asked me if the surgeon should use a heavier sledgehammer or use such an implement more quickly, I would have to answer a firm 'no.'"

At this point, it is a tired truism to say that, despite having every advantage of money and firepower and modern technology, the United States managed to lose the Vietnam War, but in Lansdale's sledgehammer analogy is the suggestion that a more revelatory truism emerges if one trades out "despite" for "because." *Because* the United States had every advantage of money and firepower and technology, it lost the war. In essence, so overwhelming was the U.S. advantage, and so limitless its resources, that it never bothered to try to be smart. Instead, and rather than deal with the tedious details of nation-building or the painstaking work of hearts-and-minds political warfare, it could simply bomb its way to a solution, and if a half-million soldiers on the ground didn't solve the problem, then surely another 100,000 would. As history going back to the Persians and Romans clearly attests, even the most powerful armies and empires can be defeated if, in their arrogance, they insist on being stupid.

Although their marriage had seemed a rather loveless arrangement for many years, Ed Lansdale remained with his wife, Helen, until her death of respiratory illness in 1972. The following year, he married Patricia Kelly, the Filipino woman he had been in love with since the 1940s. Their time together as husband and wife lasted fifteen years, ending when an increasingly debilitated Lansdale succumbed to heart disease in February 1987 at the age of seventy-nine.

———

After abruptly resigning from his CIA post in Germany in early 1955, Michael Burke arrived back in New York with no job prospects and only the vaguest sense of what he hoped to pursue as a second career. Once again, though, outrageous good fortune found him.

First there was the job with Ringling Brothers Barnum & Bailey Circus. Settling his family in Washington, the former CIA covert ops specialist spent the next year and a half managing the circus's financial affairs. That lasted until 1956, when Burke was again unemployed and in search of a new profession.

This time, Burke's luck turned on a job interview with a man named Hubbell Robinson, the chief of programming for the fledgling CBS television network. Much like William Donovan fifteen years earlier, Robinson was a fanatical college football fan, and Burke's job interview was so dominated by football talk that he worried the conversation would advance no further. He finally cut to the chase. "You understand I know nothing at all about television," he said.

That was all Robinson needed to hear; Burke was hired on the spot, and at an excellent salary. His job training consisted of sitting in a corner of Robinson's office for the next several months and simply watching what the executive did. Burke must have been an impressive watcher, for the chairman of CBS, William Paley, soon decided he was just the man to head up the network's foreign operations division, leading to an idyllic five-year stint in London. When Burke returned to New York it was to head up the network's new office of diversification. "We want to expand beyond broadcasting and records," his immediate supervisor explained, "to get into new lines of business."

Burke took that directive quite literally, and by the summer of 1964 had helped convince Paley to buy the New York Yankees. Happily, that acquisition also led to Burke being appointed to the team's board of directors and, in 1966, its president. It marked the beginning of a new phase in Burke's life, one for which he would become best known to a generation of traumatized New York sports fans: that of professional sports team kiss of death. The Yankees were terrible throughout his tenure, and when Burke took over the Rangers and the Knicks as president of Madison Square Garden, their fortunes abruptly plummeted, too.

At the same time that he watched his sports teams get run into the ground, Burke was a familiar figure in the glittery upper reaches of New York society, a fixture at exclusive parties and gala events. Having amicably divorced from Timmy, he also drew attention for dating a succession of beautiful and accomplished women. One thing Burke didn't much do was trade on stories of his exploits with the OSS and the CIA. Still, the experience of sending countless young volunteers off to their deaths in the infiltration operations of the early Cold War surely informed his opinions about the Vietnam conflict. With President Johnson's dramatic escalation of American involvement in the mid-1960s, Burke became active with a group called Businessmen Against the War, comprised of corporate executives opposed to the misadventure in Asia. On one occasion, Burke took to the pulpit of a New York City church to take his turn reading off the names of American war dead.

"He saw it as a colossal waste," his daughter Patricia Burke recalled. "Whenever the subject came up, he was just heartsick over Vietnam."

To the surprise of many in his wide circle of friends, who thought of Burke as the quintessential social animal, soon after retiring from the Garden in 1981, he moved to a simple stone cottage set on five hundred acres in Ireland's County Galway, the land of his forebears. There he settled down to pen his memoirs, the first of several books he planned to write.

Shortly after publishing his autobiography in 1984, however, Burke was diagnosed with cancer, to which he succumbed in 1987 at the age of seventy. With that peculiar mix of humility and grandiosity that had been his hallmark, Burke had already written a kind of epitaph to himself in his memoirs, describing a man who, with "an occasional burst of outrageous good fortune, wandered out into a mostly happy life, an improvised life, making a living at things he most wanted to do, and, when instinct signaled it was time to go, moved on, the promise of the new always outdistancing the fear."

Frank Wisner returned to Washington from his extended trip to Europe in late November 1956, just as the last holdouts of the Hungarian Revolution were being hunted down by the Soviet Red Army. Three weeks later, on the afternoon of December 16, the CIA deputy director was driving back to Washington from a week at Locust Hill when he felt a small flush of fever. By the time he reached home, he was so ill he could barely walk. "So hard was I shaking that it was almost impossible to hold onto the [staircase] bannister and I more or less crawled up the steps and fell into bed."

Rushed to a nearby hospital, Wisner was diagnosed as suffering from viral hepatitis. So precarious was his condition that his lengthy hospital stay was followed by a months-long recuperation. Wisner concluded that he had probably contracted the disease from having eaten spoiled mollusks during his stopover in Athens—a reasonable assumption considering the typical gestation period of viral hepatitis—and during his recuperation, he wrote a long and detailed analysis of his illness that he distributed to friends and colleagues. Despite problems with chronology, this became the accepted explanation, both to his associates and to Wisner himself, for his recent erratic behavior in Europe.

Once returned to work in March 1957, Wisner initially seemed fully recovered. At his insistence, Allen Dulles gave him a leadership role in a new CIA mission, Operation Archipelago. With striking similarities to the Operation PBSuccess that had overthrown the Guatemalan government three years earlier, the target of Archipelago was President Sukarno of Indonesia, a charismatic nationalist leader who was flirting with Moscow and who had won John Foster Dulles's undying enmity for having hosted the Bandung conference of nonaligned nations. This time, though, the CIA game of bluff ended in an embarrassing muddle, with Sukarno emerging unscathed.

By the summer of 1958, Wisner's wife, Polly, along with several close family friends, became concerned anew over his increasingly fitful behavior; unable to sleep or sit still, his nonstop talking often took on a stream-of-consciousness quality, it was as if he were stuck in a constant state of hyperactivity. Admitted to a psychiatric hospital in Baltimore that September, he was diagnosed as suffering from "psychotic mania," or what today would be called acute bipolar disorder. With treatment for mental illness still in its infancy in the 1950s, Wisner was counseled by a protégé and close friend in the CIA, Desmond Fitzgerald, to undergo shock therapy. While Wisner never spoke about the severity or frequency of the shock treatments he underwent over the six months of his Baltimore hospitalization, a clue to what he had endured was revealed when, recovered and back at work, he and Fitzgerald fell into conversation one day about his treatment. "Des," Wisner said softly and without rancor, "if you knew what you'd done to me, you could never live with yourself."

One agency that took special note of Wisner's difficulties was the FBI. As a suspicious field officer informed FBI headquarters in September 1958, "there is a possibility that there may be more to this nervous breakdown than meets the eye." After noting that Wisner had long been a "controversial figure" and had associated with such other controversial figures as Carmel Offie, the special agent speculated that perhaps "Wisner has been confronted with some problem stemming from his past life which has precipitated or assisted in bringing about the nervous breakdown."

Recognizing that his deputy was no longer able to fulfill the crushing demands of his job, Allen Dulles tactfully "reassigned" Wisner from the deputy director of plans position at the end of 1958, giving him the title of "special assistant." Shortly after, he appointed Wisner CIA station chief in London, a city he loved and where he had many friends.

For a time, all went well in England, but by the autumn of 1961, Wisner had slipped into another relapse. Wisner's youngest son, Graham, a preteen at the time, remembered being confused by the changes he saw in his father during a visit to London from his American boarding school. "He had always been so energetic, with this tremendous capacity for recall, and all that was suddenly gone. Even in London he was disappearing for long periods of time. I was sort of clueless, but I thought, 'my father is so important, there must be a reason, a good reason, why he's going away so much.' I didn't understand that it was for more shock therapy." In fact, his father underwent a staggering eleven more shock treatments while in London.

Finally returned to Washington in the spring of 1962, the fifty-three-year-old Wisner officially retired from the CIA that summer, although was kept on as a special consultant with undefined duties. During this period, he developed something of an obsession with the idea that Martin Bormann, one of Hitler's top henchmen, had somehow escaped from the ashes of Berlin and was living somewhere in South America as a fugitive. The topic was the subject of scores of Wisner letters, as well as appeals to his former CIA colleagues that they make looking into the matter a top priority; it appears these appeals were politely ignored.

In the autumn of 1965, Wisner's behavior took a different—and with the benefit of hindsight, ominous—turn. It was as if he were psychically closing up shop. For the previous three years, the CIA had renewed his annual consultancy contract, essentially designed to provide the famed workaholic with a sense of purpose, as a matter of course. That September, though, Wisner wrote a terse note to the Agency stating that he didn't wish to renew the contract "for a number of reasons" that he didn't specify. In that same month, he had lunch with his old friend and former deputy Richard Helms, at which he requested of a stunned Helms that there be no further communication between himself and the Agency. Polly Wisner was alarmed enough by her husband's deteriorating condition and occasional dark mutterings that, prior to a visit to Locust Hill late that October, she asked the farm caretakers to remove all the guns from the house, a not insignificant task considering that Wisner had always been an avid hunter. That precaution taken, Frank and Polly Wisner set out from Washington for the farm on the morning of Friday, October 29, in the company of a friend of Polly's.

As soon as they reached Locust Hill early that afternoon, Wisner announced he was going upstairs to change into his farm work clothes. A moment later, the two women downstairs heard a loud blast. When there was no response to her calls, Polly, already suspecting the worst, asked her friend if she would investigate. The friend went upstairs, but quickly returned. "He's gone," was all she said.

"It was my shotgun," Graham Wisner said. "My father had given it to me the previous Christmas. He must've hidden it the last time he was down at the farm because they didn't find it when they took all the guns out, so it seems he'd obviously been thinking about it." The pain of suicide never heals, and even at the age of seventy, Graham Wisner's remembrance of his father's death caused him to well up. "Well," he said, with a hint of apology, "Dad was always a very emotional guy, and I guess I inherited that from him."

At his memorial service at Washington's National Cathedral, Wisner was eulogized as a martyr in the cause of freedom. In his eulogy, Richard Helms glided over his colleague's troubled mental state of the past few years, attributing his death to a lethal combination of hepatitis and "overwork."

Graham Wisner identified a different culprit: Hungary. "I've always thought that his suicide was directly related to his disappointment—and some would say betrayal—over Hungary. I think he felt betrayed. He loved the depths of this country, and 100 percent believed in our protecting democracy against the Soviets, so to have been there and seen what was happening to the Hungarians—not just to the CIA operatives and *his* people, but all of them. . . . Well, I think it cast a shadow over the rest of his days."

Coincidentally or not, the day Frank Wisner took his life—October 29, 1965—was the nine-year anniversary of that day in 1956 when the Hungarian freedom fighters first believed they had won against the Soviet Union, when a sudden peace fell over Budapest as the first Red Army units began to leave. It was the day when, for the very first time since the beginning of the Cold War, it looked like the Soviet empire might come apart at the seams, the day that was the stuff of Frank Wisner's most cherished and impossible dreams.

———

It was a glorious time to live in Hong Kong. In the late 1950s, the city's population was just over two million, less than a third of what it is today, and the terrace of Peter and Cuy Sichel's spacious apartment halfway up Victoria Peak provided a stunning, postcard-perfect view of the thrumming metropolis below. Befitting the "gateway to Asia," the city's tightly knit expatriate community, composed of journalists and businessmen, spies and diplomats, was an accomplished and interesting bunch, and Peter Sichel enjoyed taking the most fascinating of them on day-long excursions on his Chinese junk to Aberdeen Harbor for splendid dinners and swims in the South China Sea. The work, too, was compelling and vital. With the Hong Kong station serving as the CIA's primary listening post into Mao's China, Sichel's days were spent endlessly devising new ways to try to get a handle on that vast and sealed-off nation.

Yet, over time, Sichel's Hong Kong tour began to pall. One of the reasons was that the city increasingly reminded him of Berlin—and not in a good way. With a hostile regime of over 600 million inhabitants perched just miles away, it induced the same feeling of claustrophobia, of living in a frontline enclave that could be swept away at any moment. Of course, that constant undercurrent of tension was part of what gave Hong Kong its verve, but after so many years of living in trip-wire outposts, Sichel could do with a little less verve.

The city was also rapidly becoming another focal point in the East-West struggle that held so much of the world in its grip. By 1956, the CIA was deeply involved in Vietnam, as well as in neighboring Laos. By 1958, those operations were joined to the CIA's clandestine campaign to over-throw Sukarno of Indonesia. In all of these efforts, Hong Kong served as a vital back-base, adding new burdens to the CIA station's primary mission of spying on communist China. There was a personal component to Sichel's growing unhappiness, as well. With their marriage fraying, Cuy began an affair with an Englishman, which, given the closed-in nature of the expatriate community, was not at all discreet.

For Sichel, these disparate disappointments finally coalesced around a singular moment. It came at a meeting of CIA officials in the Philippines in the summer of 1959.

It was one of those routine gatherings of regional station chiefs that the CIA convened with some regularity, but the conclave in Manila that summer had a special visitor in the form of Richard Bissell, Frank Wisner's recently named replacement as CIA deputy director of plans. Before the station chiefs, Bissell outlined a breathtakingly ambitious new operation that would strike at Mao's rule of mainland China. With the Eisenhower administration having finally fully embraced Chiang Kai-shek's Nationalist regime on the island of Taiwan, the massive and costly scheme called for airdropping Nationalist Chinese spies and agent provocateurs deep into the People's Republic of China. Other commandos would link up with those remnants of Chiang's pre-1949 army that had taken refuge in the rugged far southern reaches of China. If all went according to plan, Bissell explained, those remnants would serve as the vanguard of an anticommunist insurgency that would shake, perhaps even topple, Mao's dictatorship. As with all things China-related, Hong Kong would serve as the operation's principal administrative base.

To Peter Sichel, it was almost as if he were back in the Berlin of ten years before, once again observing the futile infiltration missions of the Polish and Ukrainian and Czech volunteers into Eastern Europe. During a break in the proceedings, he cornered Bissell in the hallway. "Dick," he said, "we'd save an awful lot of time and money if we just killed them ourselves." To the deputy director's puzzled expression, Sichel added: "It's a fantasy. It didn't work in Eastern Europe, and it's not going to work here." He then thought to add something more. "I'm out. I'm finished."

Recalling that conversation sixty years later, Sichel could still conjure Bissell's reaction. "He just looked at me for a long moment. He didn't try to debate the point, or get me to change my mind, just that long look and: 'okay.' And that was it."

Sichel had first thought of leaving the spy world back in 1946, only to have his Strategic Services Unit superiors convince him to stay on.

Thirteen years later, there was no argument left that could work. "Part of it was the specifics of what they were planning in China," he explained. "I knew it was going to be a fiasco, and it was. But behind that was this whole business of leading a double life, of never being able to fully confide in anyone around you, not even your spouse. It's a very hard way to live, and I finally just didn't want to do it anymore. Seeing what was coming in China only made the decision that much easier."

Resigning from the CIA, Sichel took up a position in the extended family wine business, eventually buying out his uncle to become the president and CEO of the American branch of H. Sichel Sons Inc. With a knack for promotion, Sichel set himself the task of popularizing the company's Blue Nun wine; by 1980, Blue Nun had become one of the best-selling wine brands worldwide. Simultaneously, Sichel was becoming a familiar figure as one of America's leading wine experts, an image he honed through giving seminars, officiating at wine festivals, and coauthoring a wine guidebook; he even cut an LP for Columbia Records, *Wine with Peter Sichel*. As the *Los Angeles Times* noted in a 1980 article entitled "Ex-Spy Is Man Behind Blue Nun," Sichel was "becoming one of the world's most persuasive wine salesmen."

His years of business success also coincided with a much happier personal life. After he and Cuy separated in 1959 and ultimately divorced, Sichel met and eventually married a Greek woman, Stella Spanoudaki. Together he and Stella had three children, all girls, one of whom has followed her father into the wine business. Today, the couple live in a spacious duplex apartment on Manhattan's Park Avenue, while spending the summer months in the Long Island beach resort town of Amagansett. Still spry and fully cogent at ninety-seven, Sichel maintains that one of the secrets to having a harmonious life is to let people live their own lives and to never offer unsolicited advice—although he occasionally violates that stricture with a favorite admonition: "Never grow old."

Of his years in the CIA, Sichel has few regrets, even as his experiences with the Agency have left him a committed liberal and ever-wary of America's propensity for ill-fated foreign adventures. "We need to get away from this idea that we are always right in the world, and that somehow when we're invading countries or overthrowing their governments, we're doing it to help them. We're not helping them. It is often easier to act, especially with the belief that we are always right, than to wait and let problems solve themselves. This is the disease of empires."

Of his time spent on the front lines of the early Cold War, Sichel, an atheist, framed it in religious terms. "It was a crusade, a romantic crusade. We were young and idealistic, and we were going to defeat communism and liberate the world. You saw that in Frank [Wisner], but I think you saw it in a lot of us in those early days. We were the good guys, and because we were good, we didn't have to think too much about the negative things we did along the way." He paused, folded his hands neatly on the table before him. "And we also didn't think about history. If we had, we would have remembered that crusades always end badly."

Acknowledgments

This book is the result of four years of research that included personal interviews, as well as research in a wide range of governmental and private archives and collections. Foremost among those who I must thank in this first category is Peter Sichel. Over the course of eight long and wide-ranging meetings, Peter very patiently endured my litany of probing—and often uncomfortable—questions when, then in his late nineties, he surely had better things to do with his time. It's something of a cliché for writers to say a book couldn't have been written without the help of a particular person, but that is quite true of Peter Sichel and this book.

With the exception of Peter, all the principals in this story are long since deceased, but in each case, their children kindly submitted to lengthy interviews which helped me gain a deeper and more personal understanding of their fathers. These include Graham, Ellis and Frank Wisner, Jr; Ted and Carol Lansdale; and Patricia Burke. Of enormous help also were the two long meetings I had with Rufus Phillips, the last surviving member of the 1954 Saigon Military Mission. A reminder of how quickly the last witnesses of this period of history are leaving us was my interview with Timothy Foote, a journalist who covered the 1956 Hungarian Revolution for Time-Life, and who met with me shortly before his death in 2016. For so meticulously—and swiftly—transcribing the tapes of these various interviews, I'm very grateful to Kathryn Drury.

For all but the most self-confident researcher—of which I am not one—navigating the National Archives and Records Administration in Washington is an intimidating prospect. For her enormous assistance and uncanny ability to ferret out documents from obscure corners of federal agencies, I thank the extraordinarily skilled and resourceful researcher Peggy Ann Brown. I also wish to thank the curators and administrators of the various archives and private collections where I conducted research, all of whom were very hospitable and helpful. This included staff members at the Howard Gotlieb Archival Research

Center (Boston University); Albert and Shirley Small Special Collections Library (University of Virginia); Seeley G. Mudd Manuscript Library (Princeton); Forsyth Library Special Collections (Fort Hays State University, Kansas); and the Hoover Institution on War, Revolution and Peace (Stanford University).

In writing a book this broad in scope, a writer inevitably turns at times to the pioneering work of others, either because those pioneers examined a certain aspect of the story in extraordinary depth, or because they had direct access to individuals or information no longer available. With this project, I was very fortunate to be able to turn to several outstanding works that highlighted particular areas touched upon in my own, and without which my labors would have been infinitely harder. In this realm, I feel a special debt of gratitude to: Douglas M. Charles (*Hoover's War on Gays*); Cecil B. Currey (*Edward Lansdale: The Unquiet American*); Burton Hersh (*The Old Boys*); Albert Lulushi (*Operation Valuable Fiend*); and Evan Thomas (*The Very Best Men*). Also in this category are Professor Igor Lukes of Boston University for his groundbreaking investigations of the Cold War in Czechoslovakia, and Kevin C. Ruffner of the CIA Historical Staff for his scholarly works on the CIA's association with alleged Nazi war criminals, including his seminal *Eagle and Swastika*.

On a more personal note, as with my previous book, *Lawrence in Arabia*, I strong-armed two dear friends whose opinions I trust, Michael Fields and Frances Shaw, to give *The Quiet Americans* an objective, outsiders' read-through; just as previously, I profusely thank them for their very helpful suggestions. I also want to thank my wife and daughter, Nanette and Natasha, for good-naturedly tolerating (for the most part) the many, many hours I spent holed up in my home office and in my own world. And as always, I feel especially grateful and indebted to the two people who have so patiently shepherded my career over these many years, for both their counsel and their friendship: my agent Sloan Harris, of International Creative Management Partners, and my editor, Bill Thomas, of Doubleday.

Finally, most every writer or researcher who focuses on the American intelligence community feels it necessary to score that community for its excessive and mindless secrecy—to offer a dis-acknowledgment, as it were—and I certainly see no reason to break with that tradition. Others have written eloquently of the gutting of the Freedom of Information Act in recent decades, and of how, especially in the wake of September 11, government agencies routinely withhold documents from the public, or redact them into meaninglessness, under the catchall pretense of "national security." Beyond simply parroting these charges, I'd like to provide one personal example of how insidious and corrupting this tendency has become.

In this book, I describe an incident where Secretary of State John Foster Dulles wished to provoke a civil disturbance in East Berlin, in anticipation that it would lead to bloodshed and embarrass the Soviets. Three other people were present when Dulles promoted this shocking idea, but only one, CIA official Michael Burke, ever disclosed it, describing the incident at some length in his memoir. Except not the memoir made available to the American public. Instead, the CIA's Publications Review Board, the body empowered to prescreen the works of current and former CIA employees for possible breaches of national security, ordered the deletion of all mention of the episode. By what rationale is it a matter of national security to withhold an eyewitness account, written three decades after the fact, of how one of the most powerful secretaries of state in American history tried to provoke an incident in which he knew—indeed, hoped—that innocent people would be killed? There is no adequate rationale, and this becomes no longer the sanitizing of history, but rather its attempted erasure.

Yet, that same example left me hopeful that the censors won't always win out, that the American tradition of candor and intellectual honesty still invites defiance: the individual who first alerted me to the existence and location of Burke's original, pre-CIA-scrubbed manuscript was a CIA official.

Notes

ABBREVIATIONS USED IN NOTES

BU: Boston University
CAMH: Currey Archives of Military History
CREST: CIA Records Search Tool
FRUS: Foreign Relations of the United States
HIWRP: Hoover Institution on War, Revolution and Peace
NARA: National Archives and Record Administration
RG: Record Group
SII: Studies in Intelligence
UVa: University of Virginia

PREFACE

8   "There was no one else": Thompson, "Thoughts Provoked by 'The Very Best Men.'"
     Studies in Intelligence, Vol. 39, No. 5, 1996.

ACT 1: THIS SAD AND BREATHLESS MOMENT

11   "Now, at this sad": Winston Churchill, "Iron Curtain speech," March 5, 1946.

1. OPERATION DOGWOOD

13   He was in his mid-forties: NARA, RG 226, Box 471, Folder: Macfarland, Lanning.
13   He was also clearly: The account of Wisner's encounter with Macfarland at the
     Park Hotel is largely drawn from Frank Lindsay interview by Burton Hersh, June
     6, 1985; Hersh, The Old Boys, p. 183.
14   Located near the sprawling: Rubin, Istanbul Intrigues, p. 44.
14   "Would-be spies": Ibid., p. 165.
14   "Please, please": Ibid., p. 164.
15   Indeed, so calamitous was: Hassell and MacRae, Alliance of Enemies, p. 183.
16   In the early 1890s: Jonathan Odell, Laurel MS: City in a Bubble, website.
16   According to one local: Ibid.
16   "That's when he got": Ellis Wisner interview with author.

17   "And that's where you see": Graham Wisner interview with author.

17   There, he sat on: Arthur L. Jacobs, "A Biographic Sketch of Frank Gardiner Wisner," NARA, RG 263, Entry A1 19, Box 7, Folder: HS/HC 544, p. 3.

17   Moving into a spacious: Wisner, "Application for Commission in U.S. Naval Reserve," Oct. 16, 1940, Wisner Papers, UVa, Box 11, Folder 16.

18   Matters didn't improve: Jacobs, "A Biographic Sketch," p. 5.

18   "He had a joke": Frank Wisner Jr. interview with author.

19   "Exhausting. He was a wonderful": Peter Sichel interview with author.

19   As was still common: Waller, *Wild Bill Donovan*, p. 15.

19   Leaving his Buffalo law practice: Cave Brown, *The Last Hero*, p. 36.

19   "some visible symbol": Ibid., p. 61.

20   Donovan's successful 1935 meeting: Waller, *Wild Bill Donovan*, p. 52.

21   Following Donovan's report: Corey Ford, *Donovan of OSS*, p. 94.

23   "league of gentlemen": Cave Brown, *The Last Hero*, p. 298.

23   "it was easier to train": Corey Ford, *Donovan of OSS*, p. 134.

23   That December: Memorandum from Chief of Naval Personnel to Lt. Frank Wisner, "Temporary Additional Duty," Dec. 10, 1943, Wisner Papers, UVa, Box 11, Folder 16.

24   And even though the Cairo: Roosevelt, *War Report of the OSS*, Vol. 2, p. 125.

24   In early June: Memorandum from Headquarters United States Army Forces in the Middle East to Wisner et al., "Travel Orders," June 5, 1944, Wisner Papers, UVa, Box 11, Folder 16.

24   "successes are unheralded": Kennedy speech at CIA headquarters, Nov. 28, 1961.

26   As a result, the OSS: Roosevelt, *War Report of the OSS*, Vol. 1, p. 36.

28   In very short order: Hassell, *Alliance of Enemies*, p. 167.

28   Those requests grew: Ibid., p. 183.

28   Instead, by the terms: Roosevelt, *War Report of the OSS*, Vol. 2, pp. 271–72.

28   Through a hasty joint investigation: "The Istanbul Mission," report, July 25, 1944, pp. 4–7, NARA, RG 226, Entry 211, Box 33, Folder: WN 19902.

29   Guided by information: Rubin, *Istanbul Intrigues*, p. 198.

29   At the same time, bomber: Memo from Col. John Haskell to Macfarland, May 29, 1944, and memo from William P. Maddox to Macfarland, March 10, 1944, NARA, RG 226, Entry UD 190, Field Station Files, Box 309, Folder 249.

29   In early June 1944: Hersh, *The Old Boys*, p. 184.

29   Instead, just thirteen days: Memo from Buxton to Wisner et al., Aug. 16, 1944, NARA, RG 226, Entry 244, Box 847, Folder: Wisner.

2. A DEMON INSIDE ME

30   "Alors, mes amies": Burke, *Outrageous Good Fortune*, p. 23.

30   It was the predawn: Memo from Capt. Lester Armour to Commander, U.S. Naval Forces in Europe re Recommendation for Navy Cross for Edmund Michael Burke, May 23, 1945, NARA, RG 226, Entry 224, Box 93, Folder: Burke, Edmund M.

30   Dropped into the landing zone: Burke, *Outrageous Good Fortune*, pp. 20, 28.

31   "We kept fit": Ibid., p. 16.

32   The problem, he soon discovered: Roger Ford, *Steel from the Sky*, p. 12; Lulushi, *Donovan's Devils*, p. 155.

33   On September 13: Burke, *Outrageous Good Fortune*, p. 32.

33 "cool and resigned": Ibid., p. 34.

34 "I forced myself": Ibid., p. 36.

34 Some of the other highlights: Burke Application for Employment, Jan. 9, 1943, NARA, RG 226, Entry 224, Box 93, Folder: Burke.

34 During this same period: Burke, *Outrageous Good Fortune,* uncensored manuscript, Burke Papers, BU, Box 1, Chap. 7, p. 254.

34 "the pocket of a trenchcoat": Burke, *Outrageous Good Fortune,* p. 142.

35 "the most charming man": Sichel interview with author.

35 "delightful": Interview with Edmund Michael Burke, Nov. 28, 1944, NARA, RG 226, Entry 224, Box 93, Folder: Burke.

35 "Whenever my father walked": Patricia Burke interview with author.

35 Growing up in an Irish: Burke, *Outrageous Good Fortune,* pp. 52–55, 63.

36 "I didn't know whether": Ibid., p. 64.

37 "Anger and frustration": Ibid., p. 74.

37 Burke would later claim: Craig R. Coenen. *From Sandlots to the Super Bowl: The National Football League, 1920–1967* (Knoxville: University of Tennessee Press, 2005), p. 96.

37 A few months later: Burke, *Outrageous Good Fortune,* pp. 79–80. Application for Employment, January 9, 1943, NARA, RG 226, Entry 224, Box 93, Folder: Burke.

37 With no other immediate: Burke, Application for Employment, January 9, 1943, NARA, RG 226, Entry 224, Box 93, Folder: Burke.

38 "I knew I must go": Burke, *Outrageous Good Fortune,* p. 83.

39 "Why don't you come": Ibid., p. 88.

39 On May 15, 1942: Declaration of Appointee, etc., U.S. Civil Service form, May 15, 1942, NARA, RG 226, Entry 224, Box 93, Folder: Burke.

39 With vastly expanded powers: Waller, *Wild Bill Donovan,* p. 96.

39 "Anxious to do field work": Memo from Burke to Watts Hill, Nov. 13, 1942, NARA, RG 226, Entry 224, Box 93, Folder: Burke.

40 The goal of Operation MacGregor: Burke, *Outrageous Good Fortune,* p. 93.

41 Yet, someone had thought: In *Outrageous Good Fortune,* Burke recounts this meeting as occurring in early June 1944. In fact, the V-1 bombing of the Guards' Chapel occurred on the morning of June 18.

42 "We drank bourbon": Burke, *Outrageous Good Fortune,* pp. 15–16.

43 "[They] bore the look": Ibid., pp. 37–38.

43 "I was grateful": Ibid., p. 48.

44 "Christ, kid": Ibid., p. 11.

44 "I was doing it for myself": Ibid., p. 36.

3. A MAN CALLED TYPHOID

46 On August 29: Hazard, *Cold War Crucible,* p. 40.

47 "establish the intentions": Director to Wisner and Kingsley, Istanbul for Action, Aug. 25, 1944, NARA, RG 226, Entry 88 Overseas Dispatch File, Box 609, Folder: Outgoing Macfarland Istanbul.

47 Bursting into the offices: Russell H. Dorr and Philip H. Coombs, "Report on the OSS (R&A) Bucharest Mission," Oct. 2, 1944, pp. 19–22, NARA, RG 226, Entry 180, Roll 121.

47 "the names and locations": Hazard, *Cold War Crucible,* p. 45.

47   "This place is wild": Ibid., p. 44.
47   "In a word," he wrote: Wisner to Polly Wisner, Sept. 6, 1944, Wisner Papers, Uva, Box 20, Folder 7.
47   As a result, wealthy: Bishop, *Russia Astride the Balkans*, p. 95.
48   "Rumanian tables groaned": Ibid., p. 14.
48   "when you're rich": Evan Thomas, *The Very Best Men*, p. 20.
48   "Eating, working, sleeping": Bishop, *Russia Astride the Balkans*, p. 101.
50   Most punishing of all: Hazard, *Cold War Crucible*, p. 49. Also *Armistice with Romania*, Sept. 12, 1944.
50   "the Russians have apparently adopted": Dispatch Caserta to Donovan, Sept. 17, 1944, NARA, RG 226, Entry 190, Roll 86, Microfilm M1342.
50   "speech or action": Donovan to Glavin, Toulmin and Wisner, Oct. 2, 1944, NARA, RG 226, Entry 180, Roll 121, Cable No. 3974.
50   On October 9: Hazard, *Cold War Crucible*, p. 53.
51   With de facto leadership: Mark, "The OSS in Romania," p. 324.
52   Heading the delegation: Ibid., p. 323.
52   "would depend largely": Hersh, *The Old Boys*, p. 192.
53   Late on a night in mid-September: Montefiore, *Stalin*, p. 67.
53   "Pauker, a Jew himself": Ibid., p. 199.
54   Stalin's 1930 pogrom: Ibid., p. 56.
56   For nearly eight hours: Ibid., p. 367.
56   Within a month: Ibid., p. 378.
57   That goal put him: Manchester and Reid, *The Last Lion*, p. 878.
58   Considering that Greece: Winston Churchill, *The Second World War, Vol. VI, Triumph and Tragedy* (Boston: Houghton Mifflin, 1953), p. 228.
58   Deal in hand: Wolff, *The Balkans in Our Times*, p. 259.
58   It also left Frank Wisner: Wisner (presumed) to OSS Headquarters, Nov. 25, 1944, NARA, RG 226, Entry 190, Roll 86, Microfilm M1342, Dispatch 26594 (frame 560).
58   some 100,000 Romanian citizens: Hazard, *Cold War Crucible*, p. 68.
59   "The victims were driven": Bishop, *Russia Astride the Balkans*, pp. 131–32.
60   In early February 1945: Theater Service Record, Feb. 5, 1945, NARA, RG 226, Entry 244, Box 847, Folder: Wisner.
60   "It was what probably": Hersh, *The Old Boys*, p. 194.

4. THE WUNDERKIND

61   "I ended up": Sichel interview with author.
62   They ultimately made: Sichel, *The Secrets of My Life*, p. 100.
62   "I worked my way *up*": Sichel interview with author.
63   "I am a soldier": Sichel, *The Secrets of My Life*, p. 134.
63   "We were assigned rooms": Ibid., pp. 135–36.
64   "So much money you wouldn't": Sichel interview with author.
65   "a Maltese Jew who": Sichel, *The Secrets of My Life*, p. 142.
65   By the time he was done: David C. Crockett, citation for Legion of Merit, NARA, RG 226, Entry 224, Box 122, Folder: Crockett.
66   "made our lives more pleasant": Sichel, *The Secrets of My Life*, p. 142.
66   "The luxury of that cabin": Ibid., p. 143.
66   "the single most beautiful": *American Heritage*, Nov. 1996, Vol. 47, No. 7.
66   In short order: David C. Crockett, unpublished memoir, p. 177.

67 "I was able to get Frank": Sichel email to author, Jan. 28, 2019.

67 In northeastern France: (Name redacted), "Man, You Must Be Lost or Something," *Studies in Intelligence,* Fall 1985, p. 50.

67 Many of these were from: William Casey, Chief SI ETO, "Final Report on SI Operations into Germany," July 24, 1945, Joseph Persico Papers, Hoover Institution on War, Revolution and Peace (HIWRP).

68 After a search of several: Sichel interview with author.

69 As the author of an official CIA: (Name redacted), "Man, You Must Be Lost or Something," p. 52.

70 "Jack was the most beautiful": Sichel interview with author.

70 Within seconds, both Americans: Hemingway, *Misadventures of a Fly Fisherman,* p. 174.

70 "I saw Jack": Sichel interview with author.

71 "tourist missions": Mark Murphy, "The OSS-German POW Controversy," p. 61.

71 "And those guys knew": Sichel interview with author.

71 "Because they're Germans": Ibid.

72 "Frank took things personally": Ibid.

73 "I was a first": Ibid.

74 "Uranium": Ibid.

76 German city of Oranienburg: Details of the bombing of Oranienburg largely drawn from Higginbotham, "There Are Still Thousands of Tons of Unexploded Bombs in Germany, Left Over from World War II."

76 "the most dangerous city": Ibid.

5. THE MAN WHO COULD DISAPPEAR

78 On board were some 4,500: Currey, *Edward Lansdale,* p. 27.

79 So vast was his impact: William Colby, "The Ten Greatest Spies of All Time," in Richard Whittingham, *Rand McNally Almanac of Adventure.* Chicago: Rand McNally, 1982.

79 On a darker and more exotic: Hank Miller letter to Lansdale, Nov. 23 (year not given), Lansdale Papers, HIWRP, Box 5, Miller correspondence.

79 "I consciously backed"; Silet, ed., *Oliver Stone,* p. 96.

79 "a freedom fighter": Hank Paschal interviewed by Cecil Currey, July 29, 1985, Currey Archives of Military History (CAMH), Box 2.

79 "assassinations and exterminations": Panh Chan Thanh, "The Man Sentenced to Death by Ho," *Thoi Nay Magazine* (translated), Saigon, Sept. 1, 1967, Lansdale Papers, HIWRP, Box 73.

80 "I'm a typical American": Lansdale interviewed by Currey, Feb. 15, 1984, CAMH, Box 1, p. 9.

80 "Lansdale was a handsome": Currey, *Edward Lansdale,* p. 11.

80 "We were both very": Ibid., p. 11.

81 Working against him: Memo from Adjutant General's Office to Lansdale, "Temporary Appointment," Feb. 22, 1943, Lansdale Papers, HIWRP, Box 70.

81 Despite his insistent appeals: Currey, *Edward Lansdale,* p. 17.

82 "He quickly found that": Ted Lansdale interview with author.

82 "a great deal about fishing": Lansdale World War II notebook (undated), Lansdale Papers, HIWRP, Box 72, Folder 7.

83 In Salt Lake City: Ibid., Folder 3.

83 "Maybe they thought": Lansdale interview with Currey, Feb. 15, 1984, CAMH, Box 1.

86 Just days before: Lansdale 201 File, "Physical Examination," Aug. 3, 1945, Lansdale Papers, HIWRP, Box 70.

86 "He could make a friend": Currey, *Edward Lansdale*, p. 45.

87 "He made friends with everybody": Peter Richards interview with Currey, July 23, 1985, CAMH, Box 2.

87 "His manner wasn't flamboyant": Phillips interview with author.

87 "The look in your eyes": Lansdale interview with Currey, Nov. 28, 1984, CAMH, Box 1.

87 "I've had to depend": Lansdale interview, U.S. Air Force Academy Oral History Interview, April 25, 1971, CAMH, Box 2.

87 "Ed operated at a genius": Phillips interview with author.

87 "conversation" . . . "okay": Lansdale interview, U.S. Air Force Academy Oral History, CAMH, Box 2.

88 "It was a long time": Lansdale, *In the Midst of Wars*, p. 10.

6. THE SENTINEL

89 So damp was the underground: Wisner, "Circumstances Surrounding the Discovery of German Aviation Sketchbook—1945," Wisner Papers, UVa, Box 4, Folder 10.

90 "if you have not killed": Lowe, *Savage Continent*, p. 118.

90 "German towns are burning": Werth, *Russia at War, 1941–1945*, p. 965.

90 "if a soldier who has": Applebaum, *Iron Curtain*, p. 32.

91 By some estimates, as many: Lowe, *Savage Continent*, p. 55.

91 "I have always believed": Wisner, "Circumstances Surrounding the Discovery of German Aviation Sketchbook—1945."

92 The ban effectively remained: Gaddis, *The Cold War*, p. 209.

92 These included a sketchbook: Wisner, "Circumstances Surrounding the Discovery of German Aviation Sketchbook—1945."

93 "sort of dead and dug up": Carmel Offie, quoted in Bullitt, *For the President, Personal and Secret*, p. 611.

93 "when they told me yesterday": Dobbs, *Six Months in 1945*, p. 161.

96 "I firmly believe": Brownell and Billings, *So Close to Greatness*, p. 293.

98 "He is honest": Harry S. Truman, *Off The Record: The Private Papers of Harry S. Truman* (New York: Harper & Row, 1980), p. 53.

100 On that same evening of July 24: Dobbs, *Six Months in 1945*, p. 330.

101 Despite working with an ever-shrinking: Penrose, "Recommendation for Oak Leaf Cluster to the Legion of Merit for Frank G. Wisner, Commander, USNR," June 26, 1946, NARA, RG 226, Entry 244, Box 847, Folder: Wisner.

102 In the following month: Memorandum, Rositzke to Wisner, Monthly Report of Steering Division, Sept. 5, 1945, Brill, *Cold War Intelligence* archival website.

102 This view clearly wasn't: Alvarez and Mark, *Spying Through a Glass Darkly*, p. 96.

102 "clandestine operators": Memorandum from the Secretary of State's Special Assistant for Research and Intelligence (McCormack) to the Assistant Secretary of State for Public and Cultural Relations (Benton), Oct. 23, 1945, *FRUS*, Emergence of the Intelligence Establishment, 1945–1950, Doc. 78.

102 "The dilemma was": Graham Wisner interview with author.

103   By late summer, Wisner: Wisner to Shepardson and Penrose, "Miscellaneous Operational Details," Sept. 11, 1945, NARA, RG 226, Entry 1088, Box 70.

103   Wisner also passed word: Memorandum, Rositzke to Distribution List, "Intelligence Requirements on Russian Zone/Germany," Aug. 2, 1945, Brill, *Cold War Intelligence* archival website.

103   On this matter at least: Commander, U.S. Navy Forces, Germany to Wisner, "Change of Duty," Dec. 11, 1945, Wisner Papers, UVa, Box 11, Folder 16.

103   An exception was made: Haslam, *Near and Distant Neighbors*, p. 149.

104   To compensate for J. Edgar: Christopher Lydon, "J. Edgar Hoover Made the FBI Formidable with Politics, Publicity and Results," *New York Times*, May 3, 1972.

105   "As soon as you paused": Lamphere and Schachtman, *The FBI-KGB War*, p. 71.

107   "super Gestapo agency": Cave Brown, *The Last Hero*, p. 627.

107   A furious Donovan never doubted: Waller, *Wild Bill Donovan*, pp. 310–11; Riebling, *Wedge*, p. 60.

107   "a cut-and-paste collection": Waller, *Wild Bill Donovan*, p. 336.

108   "a terrible patience": Gentry, *J. Edgar Hoover*, p. 135.

109   "Jesus H. Christ": Helms, *A Look Over My Shoulder*, p. 65.

110   Returning to New York: Commanding Officer, U.S. Naval Personnel Separation Center, to Wisner, January 8, 1946, Wisner Papers, UVa Library, Box 11, Folder 16.

7. A LUSH LAWLESSNESS

111   shortly before Sichel's arrival: Richie, *Faust's Metropolis*, pp. 612–13.

112   "Everywhere you went": Sichel interview with author.

112   "On the Berlin black market": Alvarez and Mark, *Spying Through a Glass Darkly*, p. 90.

112   "The villa is still owned": Bering, *Outpost Berlin*, p. 37.

112   "You're going to have to": Hersh, *The Old Boys*, p. 149.

112   "He told me he could": Sichel interview with author.

113   Facing off against them: Memorandum, Sichel to Stewart, "Secret Intelligence Activity in Berlin," March 19, 1946, NARA, RG-226, Entry 214, Box 4, File: WN 24600–24605.

113   "lush lawlessness": Anonymous, "Report on Berlin Operations Base," April 8, 1948, in Steury, ed., *On the Front Lines of the Cold War*, p. 59.

114   The same audit noted: Ibid., p. 76.

114   "an American is just": SSU Intelligence Report, "Rumors in Russian Zone," Feb. 12, 1946, NARA, RG 226, Report No. A-65306, LP/5-660, WASH-REG-INT-39, Box 169, Entry 108.

114   "Within two hours after my arrival": Anonymous, "Report on Berlin Operations Base," p. 70.

114   During this same period: Alvarez and Mark, *Spying Through a Glass Darkly*, p. 99.

115   "has greatly helped": Memorandum, Sichel to Stewart, Secret Intelligence Activity in Berlin, March 19, 1946.

116   "Of course, if anyone ever": Sichel interview with author.

117   "hinting at possible arrest": Murphy to the Secretary of State, Dec. 29, 1945, *FRUS*, 1945, European Advisory Commission, Austria, Germany, Vol. III, Doc. 799.

117   "be printed by [the] editor": Ibid.

118   "Their attitude was": Sichel interview with author.

119   "You walked down a Berlin": Ibid.

120 Given the code name: Ruffner, *Eagle and Swastika,* p. 106.
120 "Zig-Zag set about his task": Cutler, *Counterspy,* p. 88.
121 "We considered Kemritz": Ibid., p. 91.
121 "Savoy is the outstanding": Author's name redacted, "CIA and Nazi War Crimi-nals," Draft Working Paper, CIA History Staff, p. 12, footnote 33, footnote heavily redacted.
121 "90 percent of the information"; Cutler, *Counterspy,* p. 91.
121 While the SSU checked over: Arthur Smith Jr., *Kidnap City,* p. 66.
122 "We just couldn't take the chance": Sichel interview with author.
122 That mole then tipped off: Anonymous, "Report on Berlin Operations Base," pp. 3, 59.
122 "We have here": George Kennan, "The Long Telegram," Feb. 22, 1946.
123 "From Stettin in the Baltic": Manchester and Reid, *The Last Lion,* p. 960.
123 At the time, the SSU: Memorandum, Lewis to Acting Chief, Foreign Branch M, Recapitulation of Conference, Sept. 24, 1946, NARA, RG-226, Entry 210, Box 349, Folder 1.
123 "Sutton was a socialist": Sichel interview with author.
125 Discovering that Kemritz: Arthur Smith Jr., *Kidnap City,* p. 68.
125 With his unmasking imminent: Cutler, *Counterspy,* p. 94.
125 He went on to a new: Ibid., p. 99.
126 "He begged me": Sichel interview with author.

8. THE QUIET AMERICAN

127 "see the fun": Lansdale, Journal No. 12, March 30, 1947, Lansdale Papers, HIWRP, Box 72.
128 perhaps indicative of: Ibid.
128 "true disciples of Karl Marx": Lansdale, "The Philippine Presidential Campaign II," March 14, 1946, Lansdale Papers, HIWRP, Box 72.
128 "Agrarian reforms seem to exist": Lansdale, Journal No. 12.
130 "all agricultural, timber and mineral": Currey, *Edward Lansdale,* p. 35.
130 While he had come to know Roxas: Lansdale, Journal No. 21, April 23, 1948, Lans-dale Papers, HIWRP, Box 72.
131 The results weren't pretty: Lembke, *Lansdale, Magsaysay, America and the Philip-pines,* p. 17.
132 alleging voter intimidation: Ibid., p. 35. Also Hedman, "Late Imperial Romance," p. 22.
132 The charges were baldly absurd: Kerkvliet, *The Huk Rebellion,* p. 137.
133 "I had a great time": Pat Kelly interview with Currey, June 23, 1985, CAMH, Box 2.
133 "I wasn't that interested": Ibid.
133 "I knew she was . . . helping": Lansdale interview with Currey, Dec. 17, 1984, CAMH, Box 1.
134 "I was one person sitting there": Ibid.
134 "Gambling is against the law": Lansdale, Journal No. 13, April 11, 1947, Lansdale Papers, HIWRP, Box 72, Folder 1.
135 "public relations was the": Lansdale, Journal No. 19, Jan. 4, 1948, Lansdale Papers, ibid.
135 "Being PIO means that": Lansdale, Journal No. 23, Aug. 3, 1948, Lansdale Papers, ibid.

136 "You're the one person": Boot, *The Road Not Taken*, p. 72.

137 "She didn't want to hurt anybody": Dorothy Bohannon to Currey, July 27, 1985, CAMH, Box 1.

137 One year after her death: Currey, *Edward Lansdale*, pp. 333–35.

137 "now that I've switched to Chesterfields": Lansdale, Journal No. 21, April 23, 1948, Lansdale Papers, HIWRP, Box 72.

137 "The place was a grammar school": Lansdale, Journal No. 22, July 11, 1948, ibid.

138 As the ceremony drew to a close: Ibid.

9. A WORLD BLOWING UP

139 This was not eased: Ellis Wisner interview with author.

139 "He absolutely perceived": Frank Wisner Jr. interview with author.

140 Truman had sat on the stage: Manchester and Reid, *The Last Lion*, p. 962.

140 "The world is about to blow": Gaddis, *The United States and the Origins of the Cold War, 1941–1947*, p. 345.

140 And still, the torrent: Hazard, *Cold War Crucible*, p. 171.

141 "My dear Commander": "Sylvia" to Wisner, Jan. 15, 1947, Wisner Papers, UVa, Box 1, Folder 11.

141 In that same time frame: Ranelagh, *The Agency*, p. 101.

141 "They were both chomping": Sichel interview with author.

141 Backed by the communist governments: Lowe, *Savage Continent*, p. 311.

143 Still, having been burned: Evan Thomas, *The Very Best Men*, p. 24.

143 "the many pitfalls": Wisner to family, Oct. 1, 1947, Wisner Papers, UVa, Box 4, Folder 10.

143 "find an inconspicuous slot": Grose, *Gentleman Spy*, p. 295.

144 "Meaning that we all": Sichel interview with author.

144 General Clay admitted: Anonymous, "Report on Berlin Operations Base," April 8, 1948, in Steury, ed., *On the Front Lines of the Cold War*, p. 4.

144 "a gentlemen's agreement": Memorandum by Maj. Gen. Harold R. Bull, Aug. 15, 1946, *FRUS*, 1946, The British Commonwealth, Western and Central Europe, Vol. V, Doc. 479.

145 "eyes-only": William R. Harris, "March Crisis 1948, Act I," p. 7.

146 "Will the Soviets deliberately": Ibid., p. 20.

146 "It actually isn't that difficult": Sichel interview with author.

146 A snap analysis: Steury, ed., *On the Front Lines of the Cold War*, p. 137.

148 "should stop thinking of": Ruffner, *Eagle and Swastika*, p. 257.

148 "encouraging resistance movements": Ibid., p. 225.

148 "remove present deterrents": Ibid.

148 "a euphemism for covert": Christopher Simpson, *Blowback*, p. 100.

149 "CIA has sufficient evidence": DCI to the Executive Secretary, NSC, "Utilization of the Mass of Soviet Refugees," April 19, 1948, in Ruffner, *Eagle and Swastika*, p. 228.

150 "it might be essential": Hoopes and Brinkley, *Driven Patriot*, p. 311.

151 "Up until then, Berliners": Sichel interview with author.

153 On the morning of August: Prados, *Presidents' Secret Wars*, p. 86.

153 "the vicious covert activities": National Security Council Directive on Office of Special Projects, June 18, 1948, *FRUS*, Emergence of the Intelligence Establishment, 1945–1950, Doc. 292.

154 "essentially an instrument": Memorandum of Conversation and Understanding,

Aug. 6, 1948, FRUS, Emergence of the Intelligence Establishment, 1945–1950, Doc. 298.

154   "Because the CIA's work": Sichel interview with author.

155   "I have placed Wisner": Kennan to Lovett, June 30, 1948, *FRUS,* Emergence of the Intelligence Establishment, 1945–1950, Doc. 294.

155   This appraisal surely would: Herken, *The Georgetown Set,* p. 73.

156   "I scarcely paid": Gaddis, *George F. Kennan,* p. 318.

156   "at best, a mixed memory": Frank Wisner Jr. interview with Herken, Oct. 20, 2010, Herken notes, p. 1, Herken Papers, HIWRP, Box 17.

156   "Wisner was accountable": Immerman, *The Hidden Hand,* p. 28.

156   "find an inconspicuous slot": Grose, *Gentleman Spy,* p. 295.

10. AN END TO NORMAL THINGS

157   Four months earlier: Casey to Palmer, May 22, 1945, NARA, RG 226, Entry 224, Box 93, Folder: Burke.

157   There had been signs: Burke, *Outrageous Good Fortune,* p. 114.

157   "Her scheme, she confided": Ibid., p. 122.

158   "I could speak with her": Ibid., pp. 116–17.

158   So meticulous: Ibid., p. 121.

158   In fact, the incoming: Requisition from Robert DeVecchi, Aug. 23, 1945, NARA, RG 226, Entry 224, Box 93, Folder: Burke.

159   "Sleep seemed wasteful": Burke, *Outrageous Good Fortune,* p. 118.

159   " 'Where now?' ": Ibid., p. 123.

160   "From the beginning": Ibid., p. 125.

161   In 1945, he had been: Memo from Capt. Armour to Commander, U.S. Naval Forces in Europe re Recommendation for Navy Cross for Edmund Michael Burke, May 23, 1945, NARA, RG 226, Entry 224, Box 93, Folder: Burke.

162   "the move from Hollywood": Burke, *Outrageous Good Fortune,* p. 135.

163   "He was basically": Patricia Burke interview with author.

163   "I really hate diving": Burke, *Outrageous Good Fortune,* p. 135.

163   "discreet, quiet place": Ibid., p. 139.

164   "rejection slips": Ibid., p. 136.

164   "You knew that": Ibid., p. 141.

164   Finally, the blond asked: Ibid.; uncensored manuscript, Burke Papers, BU, Box 1, Chap. 7.

165   "I gazed into the dark wood": Burke, *Outrageous Good Fortune,* pp. 139–40.

165   The Warner executive: Although Burke may have thought he originated the film-executive-as-cover ruse, credit actually belongs to a British intelligence officer named Andrew King. Recruited in 1936 into an SIS parallel spy agency known as the Z Organisation, King (code name Z-2) passed himself off in prewar Austria as a representative of Alexander Korda's London Films, and was conspicuous for his habit of driving around Vienna in a green Jaguar in the company of his Pekingese dog.

166   "I could feel my adrenaline": Burke, *Outrageous Good Fortune,* p. 141.

ACT 2: HEARTS AND MINDS AND DIRTY TRICKS

167   "It's not enough": Lansdale, "Military Psychological Operations," lecture given at Armed Forces Staff College, Norfolk, Virginia, March 29, 1960. Lansdale Papers, Hoover Institution, Box 73.

11. THE MIGHTY WURLITZER AND THE ROYAL DWARF

169   On the evening of April 13: The account of the Prosvic family is drawn from Igor Lukes's extraordinary research on Czechoslovakia during the Cold War, especially "Kamen: A Cold War Dangle Operation with an American Dimension, 1945–1952."

172   "enabled the KGB": Mikoyan, "Eroding the Soviet 'Culture of Secrecy.'"

172   Even when that proposal: Hansen, "Soviet Deception in the Cuban Missile Crisis."

173   At the time of East Germany's: Childs and Popplewell, *The Stasi*, p. 82.

173   "Frank Wisner was the key": Salisbury, *Without Fear or Favor*, p. 569.

173   "doing some very interesting": Lindsay interview with (name redacted), July 26, 2000, CIA Oral History Project, p. 15.

173   "I suspect they": Ibid.

174   The shabbiness extended: Evan Thomas, *The Very Best Men*, pp. 179–80; Hersh, *The Old Boys*, p. 361.

174   Lindsay also discovered: Weiner, *Legacy of Ashes*, p. 32; Herken, *The Georgetown Set*, p. 99.

174   "He designated me": Lindsay interview, CIA Oral History Project, pp. 15–16.

174   "cool yet coiled": Tom Braden, "The Birth of the CIA," *American Heritage*, February 1977.

174   The former lawyer tended: Evan Thomas, *The Very Best Men*, p. 39.

175   "perpetually smiling to himself": Hunt, *American Spy*, p. 40.

175   By Lindsay's account: Lindsay interview, CIA Oral History Project, p. 16.

175   "undertake the full range": Kennan, "The Inauguration of Organized Political Warfare," May 4, 1948, *FRUS*, Emergence of the Intelligence Establishment, 1945–1950, Doc. 269.

175   "preventive direct action": National Security Council Directive on Office of Special Projects, June 18, 1948, *FRUS*, Emergence of the Intelligence Establishment, 1945–1950, Doc. 292.

175   After reading over Wisner's: While this document is missing, it almost surely bore a close resemblance to an earlier Wisner draft on OPC projects that was circulated on October 29, 1948. Memorandum from the Assistant Director for Policy Coordination to Director of Central Intelligence, Oct. 29, 1948. *FRUS*, ibid., Doc. 306.

175   "In my opinion": Memorandum from the Director of the Policy Planning Staff (Kennan) to Assistant Director for Policy Coordination (Wisner), Jan. 6, 1949, *FRUS*, ibid., Doc. 308.

175   "a cardinal consideration": Memorandum from the Director of the Policy Planning Staff (Kennan) to the Under Secretary of State (Lovett), Oct. 29, 1948, *FRUS*, ibid., Doc. 305.

175   "intelligence was about doing": Corera, *The Art of Betrayal*, p. 57.

176   "There was nothing else": Graham Wisner interview with author.

176   "political aspirations contrary": Anonymous (Gerald Miller), "Office of Policy Coordination, 1948–1952."

177 "the CIA's tastes": Wilford, *The Mighty Wurlitzer*, p. 106.

177 "A trial project took place": *The Story of Radio Free Europe and Radio Liberty*, HIWRP, 2001, p. 3.

178 To remain as the unseen: Wilford, *The Mighty Wurlitzer*, p. 107.

178 These accounts gave OPC: Hersh, *The Old Boys*, p. 220.

178 "[The CIA] could do exactly": Ranelagh, *The Agency*, p. 194.

179 Within another three years: Ibid., p. 135.

179 "exceptionally witty, wonderful": Philip Gehelin, quoted by Hersh, *The Old Boys*, p. 277.

179 "Periodically, our parents": Frank Wisner Jr. interview with author.

179 "That sort of summed up": Hersh, *The Old Boys*, p. 278.

179 "He was very well known": Sichel interview with author.

180 A small and exceedingly: 1920 U.S. Census.

180 In 1926, the seventeen-year-old: Shaw to Selective Service System, Supplement to Federal Government Request for Occupational Classification, March 9, 1944, NARA, RG 59, Box 538, Folder: 123 Offie.

180 There, coworkers marveled: Hersh, *The Old Boys*, p. 249.

180 As Bullitt informed the president: Brownell and Billings, *So Close to Greatness*, p. 178.

180 "Offie was the guest": Bullitt, *For the President, Personal and Secret*, p. 172.

181 "More than ever": Ibid., p. 453.

181 "I merely want to drop you": Offie to Tully, Sept. 9, 1939, Grace Tully Collection, FDR Library.

181 Somewhat incongruously: Kirk to Secretary of State, May 7, 1945, NARA, RG 59, Box 654, Folder: 123 Offie.

182 Wisner's timing was impeccable: Barrett, *The CIA and Congress*, p. 71; Hersh, *The Old Boys*, p. 229.

182 By happy coincidence: Hersh, *The Old Boys*, p. 361.

182 "either he was going": Ibid., p. 143.

183 "The Donovan days are over": Riebling, *Wedge*, p. 66.

183 So enraged was Hoover: Ranelagh, *The Agency*, p. 114.

183 "Wisner's weirdos": Herken, *The Georgetown Set*, p. 107.

184 For the past seven years: Gentry, *J. Edgar Hoover*, p. 340; Lauren Kessler, *Clever Girl*, p. 53.

184 As the outline of the alleged: Schrecker, *Many Are the Crimes*, p. 173.

184 For all their massive: Haynes and Klehr, *Early Cold War Spies*, p. 70.

185 In the spring of 1946: Theoharis, ed., *From the Secret Files of J. Edgar Hoover*, p. 110. Also Theoharis, "A Creative and Aggressive FBI," p. 323.

185 But Hoover had argued: Richard Gid Powers, *Secrecy and Power*, p. 287.

185 "I do fear": Ibid., pp. 288–89.

186 The Republican-controlled Congress: Gentry, *J. Edgar Hoover*, p. 356; Richard Gid Powers, *Secrecy and Power*, p. 291.

186 Never mind that the end: Gentry, *J. Edgar Hoover*, p. 355; Sibley, *Red Spies in America*, p. 207; Schrecker, *Many Are the Crimes*, p. 298.

186 In that same period: Schrecker, *Many Are the Crimes*, p. 211.

186 So absurdist did: Ibid., p. 154.

187 "svelte striking blonde": Lauren Kessler, *Clever Girl*, p. 159.

187 In the late 1940s: Haynes and Klehr, *Venona*, p. 163; Weiner, *Enemies*, p. 143.

12. OPERATION RUSTY

189 "It is not something": Sichel interview with author.

190 In the last days: Wolfgang Krieger, "US Patronage of German Postwar Intelligence," in Loch Johnson, ed., *Handbook of Intelligence Studies*, p. 92.

191 With their informant networks: Ruffner, *Eagle and Swastika*, p. 298.

191 "I was adamantly": Sichel interview with author.

192 Instead, the Org shared: Alvarez, *Spying Through a Glass Darkly*, p. 131.

192 For his part, CIA director: Ruffner, *Eagle and Swastika*, p. 317.

193 "between them, the Nazi": Snyder, *Bloodlands*, p. 379.

193 "He's on our side": Mosley, *Dulles*, p. 275.

194 At no point: Critchfield, *Partners at the Creation*, p. 78.

194 "Dana was all right": Sichel interview with author.

194 "it was a job": Critchfield, *Partners at the Creation*, p. 78.

194 "I had every reason": Ibid., p. 79.

195 "it has been agreed": From (name redacted) to Wisner, Memorandum on "Meeting of 27 December 1948," pdf, p. 63, NARA, RG 263, Second Release of Name Files Under the Nazi War Crimes and Japanese Imperial Government Disclosure Acts, File Unit: Hilger.

195 "Dear Frank": Kennan to Wisner, Oct. 19, 1948, pdf, p. 56, NARA, RG 263, Second Release, ibid.

196 As much as this strained: Simpson, *Blowback*, p. 103.

197 "I do not recall": Ibid., p. 116.

197 Once Hitler came to power: Feigin, "The Office of Special Investigations: Striving for Accountability in the Aftermath of the Holocaust," Department of Justice, Criminal Division report, in *New York Times*, Nov. 13, 2010, p. A1.

198 "not to use subject": Ruffner, *Eagle and Swastika*, pp. 333–35. Also Ruffner, "The Case of Otto Albrecht Alfred von Bolschwing," but no record of release date on CIA website.

198 "We are convinced": Ruffner, *Eagle and Swastika*, p. 337.

198 Given the intriguing code: Ruffner, "The Case of Otto Albrecht Alfred von Bolschwing," p. 64.

198 "He is unquestionably": Ruffner, *Eagle and Swastika*, p. 338.

199 Shortly after his move: Carter, *American Intelligence's Employment of Former Nazis During the Early Cold War*, p. 103.

199 "negative file": Ruffner, *Eagle and Swastika*, p. 339.

199 "At the end of the war": Ibid., p. 340.

199 Suspecting the CIA: Ruffner, "The Case of Otto Albrecht Alfred von Bolschwing," p. 65.

200 led the CIA to request: Ruffner, *Eagle and Swastika*, p. 341.

200 "should admit membership": Ibid., p. 351.

200 Destined to be: Feigin, "The Office of Special Investigations," p. 266.

201 "In its quest for information": Ruffner, *Eagle and Swastika*, p. 147.

13. RIPE FOR REVOLT

203 "was more difficult to conceal": Burke, *Outrageous Good Fortune*, p. 142.

204 "I liked him from the start": Ibid., p. 142.

205 "a ripe peach hanging": Bethell, *Betrayed*, p. 30.

205 "we had only to shake": Ibid., p. 112.

205 In early spring of 1949: Heuser, *Western 'Containment' Policies in the Cold War*, p. 78; Dorril, *MI6*, p. 109.

205 "This operation is not": Wisner, "Revaluation of Project BGFIEND," May 15, 1950, p. 1, NARA, RG 263, Second Release of Name Files Under the Nazi War Crimes and Japanese Imperial Government Disclosure Acts, Box 57, Location 230-86/23/01.

206 "Albania is ripe for revolt": Ibid., pp. 4, 12.

207 "originally established for the": Bethell, *Betrayed*, p. 46.

207 "not particularly inspiring": Lulushi, *Operation Valuable Fiend*, p. 69.

208 "If the results were positive": Burke, *Outrageous Good Fortune*, p. 143.

208 "That would take longer": Ibid., p. 142.

209 Making use of the OPC's: Burke, *Outrageous Good Fortune*, uncensored ms., Burke Papers, BU, Box 1, Chap. 7.

209 "Often a number of us": Burke, *Outrageous Good Fortune*, p. 144.

210 their trainers called them "pixies": Lulushi, *Operation Valuable Fiend*, p. 78.

210 In October 1949: Ibid., p. 80. Also Dorril, *MI6*, p. 384.

210 One four-man team: Dravis, "*Storming Fortress Albania*," p. 432; Peebles, *Twilight Warriors*, p. 26.

210 The news provoked Frank: Lulushi, *Operation Valuable Fiend*, p. 90.

211 As a remedy: Ibid., p. 91.

211 "to reduce and eventually": NSC-58 "United States Policy Toward the Satellite States in Eastern Europe," October 5, 1949. *FRUS, 1949*, Vol. V.

211 "has as its objective": O'Rourke, *Secrecy and Security*, p. 170.

211 Although Michael Burke: Lulushi, *Operation Valuable Fiend*, p. 93.

212 Horace "Hod" Fuller: In *Outrageous Good Fortune*, Burke conceals Hod Fuller's identity—he is called "Ben"—but mentions that he was a Marine who saw action in France in 1940, was wounded in the South Pacific, and then airdropped into southern France in 1944 on a Jedburgh mission. Of all OSS veterans, only Horace "Hod" Fuller meets these criteria.

212 "to pick one": Burke, *Outrageous Good Fortune*, p. 144.

213 Unfortunately—and this was: Crockett unpublished memoir, pp. 177–79.

213 "Afterward," Burke recalled: Burke, *Outrageous Good Fortune*, uncensored ms., Burke Papers, BU, Box 1, Chap. 7, p. 262.

213 "Keeping the two lives": Burke, *Outrageous Good Fortune*, p. 147.

214 So frequent did these: Burke, *Outrageous Good Fortune*, uncensored ms., Burke Papers, BU, Box 1, Chap. 7.

214 "Given the black-and-white": Burke, *Outrageous Good Fortune*, p. 143.

214 "The shutters of the tall": Burke, *Outrageous Good Fortune*, uncensored ms., Burke Papers, BU, Box 1, Chap. 7.

216 "He had a stammer": James McCargar interview with Charles Stuart Kennedy, April 18, 1995, Foreign Affairs Oral History Project, Association for Diplomatic Studies and Training, p. 82.

216 "whiskered and habitually": Philby, *My Silent War*, p. 155.

217 "His considerable charm": Burke, *Outrageous Good Fortune*, p. 145.

14. FINDING "OUR GUY"

218 " 'I'd like to be in' ": Lansdale interview with Currey, May 16, 1984, CAMH, Box 1.

219 "After preparing and giving": Lansdale, *In the Midst of Wars*, p. 12.

220   "These months away": Boot, *The Road Not Taken,* p. 92.
220   "exceptionally capable": Lansdale 201 File, Lansdale Papers, HIWRP, H Box 70.
220   "Looks more than ever": Currey, *Edward Lansdale,* p. 52.
221   In his small, dingy: Ibid., p. 67.
221   "Most of my staff colleagues": Lansdale, *In the Midst of Wars,* p. 12.
221   "a poor man's war": Ibid., p. 13.
222   "There were a lot of": Lansdale interview with Currey, May 16, 1984, CAMH,
       Box 1.
223   "The more I got into": Currey, *Edward Lansdale,* p. 68.
223   "It was filled with": Lansdale, *In the Midst of Wars,* p. 13.
223   "We had no funds": Ibid., p. 14.
225   "They discussed problems": Currey, *Edward Lansdale,* p. 70.
225   "The sequence [of priorities]": Lansdale interview with Currey, Dec. 17, 1984,
       CAMH, Box 1.
226   This was hardly coincidental: Currey, *Edward Lansdale,* p. 72.
226   "to provide Magsaysay": Ibid., p. 72.
226   "I decided he should": Lansdale interview with Currey, Nov. 12, 1985, CAMH,
       Box 1.

15. WITCH HUNT

228   The bureau's investigation of Wisner: Wisner FBI investigative file, Wisner Papers,
       UVa, Box 18, Folder 12.
229   McCarthy leapt to national: Precisely what number McCarthy uttered that night
       has been argued over by historians ever since, with McCarthy detractors tending
       to choose 205 while his defenders almost always cite the number he gave in his
       subsequent speeches that week: 57. The reason for the political divide on the point
       is fairly obvious: one suggests erratic recklessness, while the other suggests reliable
       consistency. The reason I have chosen the 205 figure is that this is the number cited
       in an article about McCarthy's speech that ran in the local newspaper, *The Wheel-
       ing Intelligencer,* the following morning. McCarthy spent the night of February 9 in
       Wheeling, and almost certainly read the *Intelligencer* article; if the newspaper had
       made such an egregious error, multiplying the senator's number almost fourfold,
       one would reasonably expect that McCarthy would ask for a correction. He did
       not do so. What's more, even one of McCarthy's staunchest defenders, M. Stanton
       Evans, notes that McCarthy acknowledged using the larger number "from time to
       time" (Evans, *Blacklisted by History,* p. 180).
229   Through the first few days: Oshinsky, *A Conspiracy So Immense,* p. 120.
230   "Joe never had any names": Ibid., p. 117.
230   Within days, Surine: Ibid., p. 117; Gentry, *J. Edgar Hoover,* p. 379.
230   By mid-March, McCarthy's: Oshinsky, *A Conspiracy So Immense,* p. 120; Gentry,
       J. Edgar Hoover, p. 379.
230   "McCarthy lied about his information": Ronald Kessler, *The Bureau,* p. 103.
231   With passage of the 1947: Schrecker, *Many Are the Crimes,* p. 271.
232   "Where are the 205 card-carrying": Tydings, *Congressional Record,* Proceedings
       and Debates of the 81st Congress, Second Session, Senate, April 25, 1950, p. 5703.
232   "This man has now been": McCarthy, ibid., pp. 5703–4.
232   As for Offie's "complete": John Ford, Director of Office of Security, Department of
       State to J. Edgar Hoover, July 8, 1953, FBI investigative file on Offie, File No. 65-

32871, p. 1. Although Offie was arrested on Vermont Avenue according to official police records, most published accounts cite his place of arrest as Lafayette Park, another popular gay meeting spot in 1940s Washington. The misidentification appears to stem from the fact that in his denunciation of April 25, Joseph McCarthy described Offie as a man who "spent his time hanging around the men's room in Lafayette Park."

233   In fact, though, Offie's police report: Charles, *Hoover's War on Gays*, p. 83.

233   "McCarthy was considering charging": Barrett, *The CIA and Congress*, p. 74.

233   "whether a certain homosexual": Ibid.

234   "I don't think my father": Graham Wisner interview with author.

234   "I think a lot of it": Frank Wisner Jr. interview with author.

235   "Offie embodies a mind": Letter from Murphy, U.S. Political Advisor for Germany, Aug. 20, 1948, NARA, RG 59, Box 654, Folder: 123 Offie.

235   the "Agency's friends would": Barrett, *The CIA and Congress*, p. 75.

235   "spent his time hanging": McCarthy, *Congressional Record*, Proceedings and Debates of the 81st Congress, Second Session, Senate, April 25, 1950, p. 5703.

235   "within the last 30 minutes": Wherry, *Congressional Record*, ibid., p. 5712.

235   Drawing on his prodigious: Charles, *Hoover's War on Gays*, p. 102.

236   "increasingly difficult for a gay": Adkins, "These People Are Frightened to Death," p. 10.

236   Though he left the OPC: In response to an anonymous request for information on Offie made on June 13, 1972, an FBI official replied on June 16 that "Carmel Offie is the subject of current investigation by the FBI." FBI investigative file on Offie, File No. 65-32871, Folder 3, pdf., p. 164. Offie was killed in a plane crash two days later.

237   While the cables' codes: Haynes and Klehr, *Venona*, p. 33.

237   The true breakthrough: Ibid., p. 36.

238   "the defensive response": Powers, *Intelligence Wars*, p. 108.

238   The argument loses some: Haslam, *Near and Distant Neighbors*, p. 160.

238   "the fulfillment or destruction": "A Report to the National Security Council by the Executive Secretary (DeLay)," NSC 68, April 14, 1950, *FRUS*, National Security Affairs; Foreign Economic Policy, Vol. 1, Doc. 85.

239   Even by hugely ramping up: Memorandum by the Assistant Director for Policy Coordination of the Central Intelligence Agency (Wisner), May 8, 1950, *FRUS*, The Intelligence Community, 1950–1955, Doc. 8.

16. OPERATION FIEND

241   On the 12th: Lulushi, *Operation Valuable Fiend*, p. 113.

242   "I hurried from one": Burke, *Outrageous Good Fortune*, p. 149.

242   A hidden motive: Burke, *Outrageous Good Fortune* uncensored ms., Burke Papers, BU, Box 1, Folder 16.

244   "The Americans wanted it": Bethell, *Betrayed*, p. 148.

244   "they were also told to collect": Ibid., p. 151.

244   "operate as small guerrilla": Memorandum, "Evaluation of Project Fiend," May 15, 1950, NARA, RG 263, Entry ZZ-19. Second Release of Name Files Under the Nazi War Crimes and Japanese Imperial Government Disclosure Acts, Box 12, File: Hoxha.

245   For communicating: Lulushi, *Operation Valuable Fiend*, p. 54.

245 At the Athens safe house: Ibid., p. 112.

246 Opting to infiltrate: Burke, *Outrageous Good Fortune*, uncensored ms., Burke Papers, BU, Box 1, Chap. 7, p. 281.

247 "I will not reproduce": Hanrahan, "An Interview with Former CIA Executive Director Lawrence K. 'Red' White," p. 10.

248 "do something, even if": Corson, *The Armies of Ignorance*, p. 308.

248 "it is obviously impossible": Memorandum from the Deputy Special Assistant (Howe) to the Secretary of State's Special Assistant for Research and Intelligence (Armstrong), Sept. 8, 1949, FRUS, Emergence of the Intelligence Establishment, 1945–1950, Doc. 398.

249 "What's your problem?" Hanrahan, "An Interview with Former CIA Executive Director Lawrence K. 'Red' White," p. 11.

249 "if you bring one more": Lawrence Houston, quoted by Evan Thomas, *The Very Best Men*, p. 64.

249 "I expect the worst": Crosswell, *Beetle*, p. 31.

250 "would probably in time": ORE 3-49, "Consequences of US Troop Withdrawal from Korea in Spring 1949," Feb. 28, 1949, in Warner, *The CIA Under Harry Truman*, Doc. 51.

250 "does not have, of itself": Ibid.

250 Pressing home the point: Wisner, Memorandum for Director of Central Intelligence, "Interpretation of NSC 10/2 and Related Matters," Oct. 12, 1950, in Warner, *The CIA Under Harry Truman*, Doc. 64.

251 "Frank," Smith said: Lawrence Houston interview with Grose, undated, Grose Papers, Princeton, Box 3, Folder 9.

251 "Wisner was always shaken": Montague, *General Walter Bedell Smith as Director of Central Intelligence*, p. 92.

251 "rather than coherent": Prados, *Presidents' Secret Wars*, p. 34.

252 "There was never any sense": Hersh, *The Old Boys*, p. 287.

252 Over the next two years: Corson, *The Armies of Ignorance*, p. 320; Ranelagh, *The Agency*, p. 220.

252 "almost impossible for anyone": Corson, *The Armies of Ignorance*, p. 314.

252 "Why don't we round that": Powers, *The Man Who Kept the Secrets*, p. 315, footnote 12.

253 Lending further credence: Peebles, *Twilight Warriors*, p. 46.

254 With a well-established: O'Rourke, *Secrecy and Security*, p. 185.

254 "In view of the extent": Ibid., p. 186.

254 "an intellectual smoothie": Burke, *Outrageous Good Fortune*, uncensored ms., Burke Papers, BU, Box 1, Folder 11, p. 179.

255 "It shall be your responsibility": Memorandum for Randolph R. Northwood (Burke) from Whiting (Wisner), March 16, 1951, Burke, Burke Papers, BU, Box 1, Folder 17.

255 "Looking back," he later wrote: Burke, *Outrageous Good Fortune*, pp. 155–56.

255 The "largest, jolliest and wettest": Ibid., p. 152.

256 "Downs, still carrying one": Ibid.

256 On May 3, his Albanian: Burke, *Outrageous Good Fortune*, uncensored ms., Burke Papers, BU, Box 1, Chap. 7, p. 289.

258 "Beetle Smith, I just don't": Hersh, *The Old Boys*, p. 285.

258 "Between trusted colleagues": Grose, *Gentleman Spy*, p. 308.

258 "a million warm acquaintances": Hersh, *The Old Boys*, p. 348.

258   "learned to deal comfortably": Cited by Evan Thomas, *The Very Best Men*, p. 73, from Grose pre-published manuscript of Dulles biography.

259   "maximum strain": Corke, *US Covert Operations and Cold War Strategy*, pp. 117–18.

259   "would end by Wisner": Mosley, *Dulles*, p. 281. The cited quotation is a good example of Philby's ability to slyly besmirch reputations by grammatical sleight of hand. There is no evidence that Wisner ever kept a bar in his office, but by attributing this feature to "Wisner or whoever," Philby craftily implies that he did, a detail repeated by some subsequent writers as established fact.

259   " 'Well,' said Hoover in reply": Philby, *My Silent War*, p. 162.

260   "How soon? How late?" Ibid., p. 168.

260   Over the course: Newton, *The Cambridge Spies*, p. 16.

260   "a young Englishman": Macintyre, *A Spy Among Friends*, p. 54; Andrew, *Defend the Realm*, p. 267.

260   MI5 hadn't immediately pressed: Newton, *The Cambridge Spies*, p. 25.

261   At a follow-up meeting: Ibid., p. 90; Haslam, *Near and Distant Neighbors*, p. 151.

261   As would only be confirmed: Macintyre, *A Spy Among Friends*, p. 100.

261   "What is Philby doing here?": Corera, *The Art of Betrayal*, p. 62.

263   "I knew his people": Seale and McConville, *Philby*, p. 135.

263   At a subsequent press conference: Macintyre, *A Spy Among Friends*, p. 277.

263   "I can't recall him": Ellis Wisner interview with author.

17. WAR AS A PRACTICAL JOKE

265   "the interfering bastard": Lansdale, *In the Midst of Wars*, p. 44.

266   "Well, all I can say": John Melby interview with Charles Kennedy, June 16, 1989, Foreign Affairs Oral History Project, Association for Diplomatic Studies and Training, p. 33.

267   "to provide counsel and support": Currey, *Edward Lansdale*, p. 78.

267   Not that Lansdale anticipated: Lembke, *Lansdale, Magsaysay, America and the Philippines*, p. 71.

268   This view was seconded: Lansdale, *In the Midst of Wars*, p. 22.

268   As Lansdale soon determined: Currey, *Edward Lansdale*, p. 83.

268   "I had alarmed him": Lansdale, *In the Midst of Wars*, p. 25.

269   "Of course the people were joining": Ibid., p. 28.

270   "Each night we sat up": Ibid., p. 37.

270   Once that confusion: Lansdale interview, U.S. Air Force Academy Oral History Interview, April 25, 1971, p. 38, CAMH, Box 2.

270   "The early fall days": Lansdale, *In the Midst of Wars*, p. 42.

271   Under Quirino's restructuring: Ladwig, "When the Police Are the Problem," in Fair and Ganguly, eds., *Policing Insurgencies*, pp. 5–6.

272   So confident were the rebels: Lansdale, *In the Midst of Wars*, pp. 63–64.

272   "We tried to be quiet": Ibid., p. 46.

273   "to see thousands of": Tierney, "Can a Popular Insurgency Be Defeated?," p. 3.

274   One officer was to remember: Lembke, *Lansdale, Magsaysay, America and the Philippines*, p. 93.

274   For years, the starting salary: Ibid., p. 74.

275   Word of the initiative: Lansdale, *In the Midst of Wars*, p. 57.

275   "all-out friendship": Currey, *Edward Lansdale*, p. 97.

275   A bounty was placed: Ladwig, "When the Police Are the Problem," p. 14.

275   "Conventional military men": Lansdale, *In the Midst of Wars,* p. 71.

276   "Two nights later": Ibid., pp. 72–73.

276   "it's not enough to be *against*": Currey, *Edward Lansdale,* p. 111.

277   "secretly placed into Huk propaganda": Lansdale, *In the Midst of Wars,* p. 92.

278   "excessive humanism": Kerkvliet, *The Huk Rebellion,* p. 232.

278   "There was a time": Karnow, *In Our Image,* p. 350.

278   "to the people, Magsaysay": Lansdale, *In the Midst of Wars,* p. 10.

278   "They are quite mischievous": Lansdale letter to Abueva, Nov. 5, 1962, pp. 3–5, CAMH, Box 5.

279   "did need some hand-holding": Lansdale letter to Shaplen, May 30, 1965, p. 4, CAMH, Box 5.

280   "I slugged him real hard": Lansdale interview with Currey, Nov. 12, 1985, CAMH, Box 1.

18. TOSSING THE DICE

281   "If this was the prelude": Sichel interview with author.

282   Adding to this opaqueness: Andrew, *For the President's Eyes Only,* p. 182.

283   "It was quite haphazard": Sichel interview with author.

284   "NTS agents did not despair": Murphy, Kondrashev and Bailey, *Battleground Berlin,* p. 110.

284   OPC Munich had started: Ibid., p. 111.

284   "That was when": Sichel interview with author.

284   One of its finest homes: Burke, *Outrageous Good Fortune,* p. 167.

285   "an uncommonly agreeable place": Ibid.

285   "I inherited a large disparate": Burke, *Outrageous Good Fortune,* uncensored ms., Burke Papers, BU, Box 1, Chap. 8, p. 293.

286   From its various stations in Germany: Ibid., Box 1, Folder 11, p. 182.

286   "Mine was a command function": Ibid., Box 1, Chap. 8, p. 302.

287   "Finger feel," Burke replied: Ibid., Box 1, Folder 11, pp. 180–81.

288   Beginning in November 1950: Grose, *Gentleman Spy,* p. 355.

288   "to drive the Red Army": Peebles, *Twilight Warriors,* p. 46.

288   Under the Red Sox mantle: Ruffner, *Eagle and Swastika,* p. 237.

288   "to harass and counter": Burke, *Outrageous Good Fortune,* p. 154.

289   "He was extremely impressive": Sichel interview with author.

290   As the unit's sole Russian: Coffin, *Once to Every Man,* p. 65.

290   By the time the process: Ibid., p. 77.

290   "the Americans returned": Nikolai Tolstoy, *The Secret Betrayal* (New York: Charles Scribner's Sons, 1977), p. 360.

290   "He was very gung ho": Sichel interview with author.

290   "had little sense of operational": Murphy, Kondrashev and Bailey, *Battleground Berlin,* p. 111.

291   "Although poorly educated": Coffin, *Once to Every Man,* pp. 95–96.

292   "With only three of us": Ibid., p. 105.

293   But there were precious few: Burke, *Outrageous Good Fortune,* p. 160.

293   "I listened very carefully": Ibid.

295   Indeed, many of the pixies: Dravis, "Storming Fortress Albania," p. 434.

295   Just two months before: Bethell, *Betrayed,* p. 168.

295   In early 1951, OPC teams: Weiner, *Legacy of Ashes*, p. 59; Corke, *US Covert Operations and Cold War Strategy*, p. 113.

296   "I sat quietly for a few": Burke, *Outrageous Good Fortune*, pp. 160–61.

296   "Yes, it's okay now": Ibid., pp. 161–62.

297   In Washington, Sichel: Sichel, *The Secrets of My Life*, p. 223.

298   "This became a big subject": Sichel interview with author.

299   "One boasted of intelligence": Ranelagh, *The Agency*, p. 219.

300   "I very bluntly told Bill": Sichel interview with author.

301   By then, it was determined: Lulushi, *Operation Valuable Fiend*, p. 161.

301   "the apparent ease with which": Anonymous, "CIA/OPC 1952 Albanian Operations," NARA, RG 263, Entry ZZ-19, Box 46, Vol. 2, p. 6.

301   As for the missing commandos: Lulushi, *Operation Valuable Fiend*, p. 121.

302   "I guess that was sort of": Lindsay interview with (name redacted), July 26, 2000, CIA Oral History Project, pp. 29–30.

302   "criminal, anti-Polish activity": Dorril, *MI6*, p. 266.

303   As for Stefan Sieńko: Cable 340, Warsaw to Secretary of State, Dec. 28, 1952, NARA, RG 59, Central Decimal Files 1950–1954, Box 3126, File: 711,5248/12-2852.

303   That occurred ten months *before:* O'Rourke, *Secrecy and Security*, p. 187. Also, Memorandum, Wisner to DCI, Joint OSO/OPC Report on the Ukrainian Resistance Movement, Jan. 4, 1951, NARA, RG 263, Entry ZZ-19 Subject Files, Second Release of Name Files Under the Nazi War Crimes and Japanese Imperial Government Disclosure Acts, Box 9, Aerodynamic Vol. 9 Operations (1 of 2).

304   That same month, a Red Army: Costa, "The CIA and the Ukrainian Resistance, 1949–1954," p. 19.

304   By the time Operation Fiend: Dorril, *MI6*, p. 401.

304   "Although stunned": Coffin, *Once to Every Man*, p. 112.

305   "It destroyed him": Sichel interview with author.

305   "I thought a memorandum": Lindsay interview with (name redacted), July 26, 2000, CIA Oral History Project, p. 30.

305   "The consolidated Communist state": Lindsay, "A Program for the Development of New Cold War Instruments," Oct. 8, 1952, Grose Papers, Princeton, Box 3, Folder 8.

306   Rather to Lindsay's surprise: Wisner to Gordon Gray, Nov. 11, 1952; ibid.

306   "He went over it, line-by-line": Lindsay interview with (name redacted), July 26, 2000, CIA Oral History Project, p. 30.

ACT 3: CROWDING THE ENEMY

307   "This is the kind of time": Hoopes, *Devil*, pp. 179–80.

19. AN ALARMING ENTHUSIASM

309   Nichols then suggested: Memorandum from L. B. Nichols to Tolson, subject redacted, May 9, 1952, Wisner FBI investigative file, Wisner Papers, UVa, Box 18, Folder 12.

310   At that meeting: Memorandum from V. P. Kedy to A. N. Belmont, "Central Intelligence Agency," May 29, 1952, Wisner FBI investigative file, Wisner Papers, UVa, Box 18, Folder 12.

310   "informant of known reliability": J. E. Hoover memorandum to Walter Bedell

Smith, Nov. 28, 1952, Wisner FBI investigative file, Wisner Papers, UVa, Box 18, Folder 12. While the subject of Hoover's inquiry remains completely redacted, it is clear from Smith's Dec. 22, 1952, reply that it was Wisner's purported links to Tanda Caragea.

310 "knowledge of espionage activities": Walter B. Smith to J. Edgar Hoover, Dec. 22, 1952, NARA, CIA Records Search Tool (CREST) Collection, Document No. 0005382735.

310 Yes, Wisner was a lousy administrator: Thomas Powers, *The Man Who Kept the Secrets,* p. 77.

311 Dulles was so enamored: Ibid., p. 83.

311 he also wanted to leave the CIA: Corson, *The Armies of Ignorance,* pp. 333–34; Andrew, *For the President's Eyes Only,* p. 201.

311 "It is outrageous": Weiner, *Enemies,* p. 169.

313 "his speech was slow": Kinzer, *The Brothers,* p. 125.

313 "He was a terrible man": Sichel interview with author.

313 The call came in at about two: Grose, *Gentleman Spy,* p. 349.

314 Without a source anywhere near: CIA Intelligence Report, March 1953, "Intelligence on the Soviet Bloc," in Haines and Leggett, eds., *CIA's Analysis of the Soviet Union, 1947–1991,* p. 35.

314 It was emblematic of the early Cold War: CIA, Office of Current Intelligence, Caesar-2, "Death of Stalin," July 16, 1953, Brill, *Cold War Intelligence* archival website.

315 "[Wisner] was convinced": Mosley, *Dulles,* p. 331.

315 "At this moment in history": Ibid., pp. 330–31.

315 This was reflected: Hixson, *Parting the Curtain,* pp. 88–89.

316 Despite its soaring rhetoric: Ranelagh, *The Agency,* p. 257.

316 "I feel that we should not": DDE to Churchill, April 25, 1953, cited by John Lukas, "Ike, Winston and the Russians," *New York Times,* Feb. 10, 1991.

316 "I can say we have evaluated": Hoopes, *The Devil and John Foster Dulles,* pp. 171–72.

316 "it appears the president is no more": Manchester and Reid, *The Last Lion,* p. 1028.

317 "I don't recall anyone": Sichel interview with author.

318 Wisner had first expressed doubts: Landa, *Almost Successful Recipe,* p. 18.

318 "the brutal efficiency of the Soviet security": Wisner to Deputy Director, Intelligence, "FI Statement for Possible Inclusion in New NSC 50 Progress Report," Jan. 5, 1953, NARA, CREST Collection, Document No. CIA-RDP80R01731R003500120004-1.0.

319 By the time the crowd converged: Lucas, *Freedom's War,* p. 180.

319 Despair was spurring a staggering exodus: Zubok, *A Failed Empire,* p. 85; Childs and Popplewell, *The Stasi,* p. 52.

319 The first intelligence agency in East Germany: Childs and Popplewell, *The Stasi,* p. 53; Popplewell, "The KGB and the Control of the Soviet Bloc," p. 264.

320 By 1953, well over half: Hixson, *Parting the Curtain,* pp. 74–75.

320 Aghast at the prospect: There is enduring historical confusion over both the scope and the author of the cable sent from CIA Berlin to headquarters on June 16. Over the course of a number of interviews, John Bross consistently stated the cable came from Henry Hecksher and that he requested the distribution of small arms; this is the version most often cited by writers. Bayard Stockton, a CIA officer stationed in Berlin at the time, insists the author was William Harvey, the Berlin base chief, and that while he requested some kind of Western "show of force," it did not extend to the distribution of weapons. To complicate matters further, in their sem-

inal book *Battleground Berlin,* Murphy, Kondrashev and Bailey insist there is no record of such a cable being authored by anyone. What is indisputable, however, is that Wisner was strongly opposed to any course of action that would inflame the East German situation, a stance that placed him very much at odds with the Dulles brothers and C. D. Jackson.

320   At last getting hold of Wisner: John Bross interview with R. Harris Smith, undated, Grose Papers, Princeton.

320   "[issuing guns] was the same as murder": Hersh, *The Old Boys,* p. 350.

321   Over the following week: Hixson, *Parting the Curtain,* p. 71.

321   "hit pretty close to the right line": Murphy, Kondrashev and Bailey, *Battleground Berlin,* p. 170.

321   "It was the one time that I saw Allen": Grose, *Gentleman Spy,* p. 357.

321   "undoubtedly the ablest and shrewdest": Memorandum of Discussion at the 150th Meeting of the National Security Council, June 18, 1953, *FRUS,* 1952–1954, Germany and Austria, Vol. VII, Pt. 2, Doc. 715.

321   "This is the kind of time": Hoopes, *The Devil and John Foster Dulles,* pp. 179–80.

323   Now they had a potent new card: Andrew, *For the President's Eyes Only,* p. 203; McMurdo, "The Economics of Overthrow," p. 15.

324   "He was opinionated": Thomas, *The Very Best Men,* pp. 108–9.

325   For his part, Kermit Roosevelt: Ibid., p. 109.

325   At least that was the official story: Rositzke, *The CIA's Secret Operations,* p. 188.

326   "He seemed to be purring": Thomas, *The Very Best Men,* p. 110.

326   "exactly as you would use a bullet": Gaddis, *The Cold War,* p. 66.

326   "the capability of inflicting massive retaliatory": Report to the National Security Council by the Executive Secretary (Lay), Oct. 30, 1953, *FRUS,* 1952–1954, National Security Affairs, Vol. II, Pt. 1, Doc. 101.

328   In the estimation of President Eisenhower's: Kovrig, *Of Walls and Bridges,* pp. 62–63.

330   When Dwight D. Eisenhower took office: U.S. Department of Defense, "Declassified Nuclear Stockpile Information," Department of Energy Office of Public Affairs, Aug. 1995.

330   "was to make the United States progressively": Hoopes, *The Devil and John Foster Dulles,* p. 201.

20. RED SCARE REVIVED

332   On J. Edgar Hoover's: Theoharis, *Chasing Spies,* p. 201.

332   Where even Cohn's detractors: "Roy Cohn, Aide to McCarthy and Fiery Lawyer, Dies at 59," *New York Times,* Aug. 3, 1986.

332   A *Harvard Crimson* reporter: J. Anthony Lukas, "Schine at Harvard: Boy with the Baton," *Harvard Crimson,* May 7, 1954.

333   "the worst human being": Tony Kushner, *Angels in America: A Gay Fantasia on National Themes* (New York: Theatre Communications Group, 1993).

333   "nothing interested him more": Barrett, *The CIA and Congress,* pp. 179–80.

333   "This was really when Dick Helms": Sichel interview with author.

334   There, he was handed a list: Barrett, *The CIA and Congress,* p. 180.

334   As an internal FBI memo: Memorandum from V. P. Kedy to A. N. Belmont, "Central Intelligence Agency," April 28, 1953, Wisner FBI investigative file, Wisner Papers, UVa, Box 18, Folder 12.

334 McCarthy's next salvo came in early June: Ranelagh, *The Agency,* p. 238.
335 "blatant attempt": "M'Carthy Strikes at Allen Dulles," *New York Times,* July 10, 1953, p. 1.
335 "Within the CIA": Kirkpatrick, *The Real CIA,* p. 136; Ranelagh, *The Agency,* p. 238.
335 "Joe, you're not going to have": Grose, *Gentleman Spy,* p. 345.
335 The CIA director then called: Barrett, *The CIA and Congress,* p. 180.
336 "McCarthy has just suffered": Ibid., p. 185.
336 A week later, he assembled: Kirkpatrick, *The Real CIA,* p. 139; Ambrose, *Ike's Spies,* p. 175; Barrett, *The CIA and Congress,* p. 190.
336 "It was probably the greatest thing": Sichel interview with author.
336 Since this ban also extended: Baxter, *Eradicating This Menace,* pp. 549–50.
336 "So it became a self-fulfilling": Sichel interview with author.
338 It occurred shortly after the lunch: "Aide of McCarthy Scored on Charge," *New York Times,* April 9, 1953, p. 17.
338 So popular was Amerika Haus: History of the Amerika Haus, https://de.us embassy.gov.
339 In Paris, journalists had trailed: Oshinsky, *A Conspiracy So Immense,* p. 279.
339 "both of them disappeared": Von Hoffman, *Citizen Cohn,* p. 150.
339 "their contents were strewn": Morgan, *Reds,* p. 444.
339 "We understand you have": Hans Tuch interview with G. Lewis Schmidt, Aug. 4, 1989, Foreign Affairs Oral History Project, Association for Diplomatic Studies and Training, p. 32.
339 It was there that Thayer: Dean, *Imperial Brotherhood,* p. 101.
340 By working their network: Charles, *Hoover's War on Gays,* p. 77.
340 Among the "evidence" for this: Finlator report, July 22, 1948, cited in ibid., pp. 77, 381, footnote 23.
340 It was while Thayer was serving as U.S. consul: J. Edgar Hoover to Sherman Adams, March 4, 1953, cited in ibid., pp. 127, 389, footnote 186.
341 Around that same time, Kaghan: Von Hoffman, *Citizen Cohn,* p. 149.
341 "We're not here to burn books": Hans Tuch interview with G. Lewis Schmidt, p. 34.
341 "Well, Mr. Cohn": Hans Tuch, "Roy Cohn's Descent on the Libraries of Europe," *New York Times,* Aug. 17, 1986, p. A22.
342 On the evening of May 28: Burke, *Outrageous Good Fortune,* uncensored ms., Burke Papers, BU, Box 1, Folder 11.
342 "We three sat alone": Ibid.

21. WHITE KNIGHT

344 Where this got a bit ticklish: Currey, *Edward Lansdale,* p. 119.
345 Sensing the Magsaysay campaign: Spruance to the Department of State, March 6, 1953, *FRUS, 1952–1954,* East Asia and the Pacific, Vol. XII, Pt. 2, Doc. 327.
345 Figuring that Quirino wouldn't: Lansdale interview with Currey, Nov. 12, 1985, CAMH, Box 1. Also Lansdale, *In the Midst of Wars,* p. 107.
346 "Not to help the French!": Currey, *Edward Lansdale,* p. 136.
346 "we want you to do": Both in his memoir and in numerous interviews, Lansdale attributed this exchange to a conversation he had with Secretary of State John Foster Dulles at the January 29, 1954, meeting of the President's Special Committee on Indochina; he further recalled that he was caught off guard by John Foster's recommendation that he be sent to Vietnam. Lansdale was in error—perhaps

intentionally—on both points. First, John Foster Dulles didn't attend the pivotal January 29 meeting, as he was in Berlin for the Council of Foreign Ministers meeting, which had begun four days earlier; instead, Lansdale attended as a representative of the CIA and in the company of Allen Dulles. The official minutes of that meeting also have Allen Dulles as the originator of the proposal to send Lansdale to Vietnam. It also strains credulity that Lansdale would have walked into a meeting with the chairman of the Joint Chiefs of Staff without knowing why he was there, indicating that he and Allen Dulles surely had a meeting on the topic of Vietnam ahead of time. Lansdale may have misremembered this anecdote because he'd repeated the wrong story so often or, as historian Max Boot theorizes, because he first provided the account at a time when he was still denying his CIA links, and his insistence that he received his marching orders from the State Department Dulles rather than his CIA sibling aided this fiction.

346 O'Daniel had urged: Logevall, *Embers of War,* p. 356.

347 According to Lansdale, some French: Lansdale, *In the Midst of Wars,* p. 110; Currey, *Edward Lansdale,* p. 128.

348 "If we did so": Memorandum of Discussion at the 179th Meeting of the National Security Council, Jan. 8, 1954, *FRUS,* 1952–1954, Indochina, Vol. XIII, Pt. 1, Doc. 499.

348 The French had first employed the *hérisson:* Logevall, *Embers of War,* pp. 328–29.

349 "a great disappointment to French": The Ambassador at Saigon (Heath) to the Department of State, Jan. 31, 1954, *FRUS,* 1952–1954, Indochina, Vol. XIII, Pt. 1, Doc. 528.

349 "entertained with gracious": Burke, *Outrageous Good Fortune,* p. 168.

349 As near as Burke could tell: Burke interview with R. Harris Smith, undated, Grose Papers, Princeton.

350 The meeting took place: Burke, *Outrageous Good Fortune,* uncensored ms., Burke Papers, BU, Box 1, Chap. 8, p. 325.

351 "He was dour and cold": The entirety of Burke's account of his 1954 meeting with John Foster Dulles is to be found in ibid., beginning on p. 325.

353 "There will not be another 17 June": Cable No. 6526, (name of writer redacted) to DCI, Feb. 23, 1954, NARA, RG 263, File Unit, Gehlen, Reinhard, Vol. 2, Second Release of Name Files Under the Nazi War Crimes and Japanese Imperial Government Disclosure Acts, pdf, pp. 88–89. Since the name and title of the sender of this cable have been redacted, it can't be definitively established as authored by Michael Burke. However, the reference to Western efforts to provoke demonstrations is so pointed that the writer must have known such actions had been proposed, essentially narrowing the field to the two CIA officers who met with John Foster Dulles earlier in the month, Burke and Truscott. The tone and swipe at McCarthy and Eisenhower aligns with Burke's known political views far more than with Truscott's.

354 In order to facilitate their surrender: Logevall, *Embers of War,* p. 90. A source of frequent confusion is that the victorious World War II powers elected to temporarily divide Vietnam at the 16th parallel, while the more famous Geneva Accords demarcation line was the 17th parallel.

355 Instead, soon after arriving: Lansdale to CIA director, March 21, 1954, Lansdale Papers, HIWRP, Box 97.

355 "I gathered that events": Lansdale, *In the Midst of Wars,* p. 128.

356 "The French issued and controlled": Ibid., p. 129.

356   "The son of a bitch": Currey, *Edward Lansdale*, p. 140.

359   "Whoever was advising him": Lansdale, *In the Midst of Wars*, p. 157.

360   "I wondered if at his age": Burke, *Outrageous Good Fortune*, uncensored ms.,
      Burke Papers, BU, Box 1, Folder 11.

361   As early as the beginning of 1952: Peebles, *Twilight Warriors*, p. 56.

362   In July 1953: Hazard, *Cold War Crucible*, p. 232.

362   Soon after came word of the capture: Lulushi, *Operation Valuable Fiend*, p. 202.

362   On the Baltic front: CIA, Project Outline: AECOB—Jan. 27, 1954, NARA, RG 263,
      Entry ZZ-19 Subject Files (2nd Release), Box 2, File: AECOB/ZRLYNCH Vol. 1
      (2 of 2). Also Memorandum to SR/COP Plans for AEBasin/Redsox Spring 1954
      Operation, Dec. 28, 1953, NARA, RG 263, Entry ZZ-19 Subject Files (2nd Release),
      Box 23, AEROOT/AEBASIN (1 of 2).

363   "Even if underground movements": Burke, *Outrageous Good Fortune*, p. 166.

364   His chance to do so came in April: Ibid., p. 162.

364   "I wonder what people in the real world": Ibid., p. 167.

365   "We had a drink or two": Ibid., p. 174.

366   "I am Ngo Dinh Diem": Lansdale, *In the Midst of Wars*, p. 159.

22. OPERATION SUCCESS

367   "almost alarmingly enthusiastic": Ambrose, *Ike's Spies*, p. 213.

367   "like a dime novel": Andrew, *For the President's Eyes Only*, p. 205.

367   "My instincts told me": Schlesinger and Kinzer, *Bitter Fruit*, pp. 100–101.

368   "ever going to try something": Immerman, *The CIA in Guatemala*, p. 26.

368   "I didn't think the Guatemalan people": Hersh, *The Old Boys*, p. 313.

369   Ten others came in that first wave: Redick interview with Currey, Dec. 18, 1984,
      CAMH, Box 2.

369   "And to be honest": Phillips interview with Ted Gittinger, March 4, 1982, Rufus
      Phillips Collection, Vietnam Center and Archive, Texas Tech University, Folder
      29, Box 3, p. 2.

370   "There we were": Rufus Phillips, *Why Vietnam Matters*, p. 15.

370   " 'Save South Vietnam?' ": Ibid., p. 13.

371   "So Ed kind of stared at me": Phillips interview with author.

371   Within weeks, the second lieutenant: Phillips interview with Charles Kennedy,
      July 19, 1995, Association for Diplomatic Studies and Training, Foreign Affairs
      Oral History Program, p. 12.

372   His fastidious, slightly fussy: Rufus Phillips, *Why Vietnam Matters*, p. 16; Lansdale,
      In the Midst of Wars, p. 162.

372   There was also the sub-nickname: Taylor Branch, "Raising a Glass to Beau Geste,"
      Esquire, Aug. 1976, p. 30.

372   "Of course I knew Lou": Sichel interview with author.

373   Frequently suspended from school: Application for Employment and Personal
      History Statement, June 7, 1943, NARA, RG 226, Entry 224, OSS Personnel Files,
      Box 138, Folder: Conein.

373   "it's probably not the truth": George Crile, "The Colonel's Secret Drug War," *Wash-
      ington Post*, June 13, 1974, p. C4.

373   "I didn't talk to [Giap]": Conein interview with Lydia Fish, July 30, 1989, CAMH,
      Box 10.

373   "Where the man really belonged": Sichel interview with author.

374   "We'd all be sitting around": Phillips interview with author.

374   "At its heart, it's pretty simple": Rufus Phillips, *Why Vietnam Matters*, p. 24.

374   In a carefully synchronized wave: Schlesinger and Kinzer, *Bitter Fruit*, p. 171; Gleijeses, *Shattered Hope*, p. 326.

374   Another was met: Gleijeses, *Shattered Hope*, p. 327.

375   In reality, the "army" was: Schlesinger and Kinzer, *Bitter Fruit*, p. 170.

375   The company orchestrated: Mosley, *Dulles*, p. 347.

376   "J.C., you've had four years": Schlesinger and Kinzer, *Bitter Fruit*, p. 112.

376   To this end, the gung ho: Ibid., p. 113.

376   The biweekly meetings: Notes of Bissell interview by R. Harris Smith, undated, Grose Papers, Princeton.

377   He even began having: Gleijeses, *Shattered Hope*, p. 288; Schlesinger and Kinzer, *Bitter Fruit*, p. 117.

377   On that score, he floated: "Frank G. Wisner's Memorandum of 28 April 1954 Regarding Cover and Deception," May 3, 1954. Released by CIA but no citation information available.

377   On June 15, Eisenhower obliged: Ambrose, *Ike's Spies*, p. 139.

378   For the orchestrators: Gleijeses, *Shattered Hope*, p. 347.

378   In desperation, Dulles and Wisner: Ibid., p. 375; Schlesinger and Kinzer, *Bitter Fruit*, p. 178.

378   "the biggest success in the last": Immerman, *The CIA in Guatemala*, p. 179. On plans to attack Costa Rica: Ranelagh, *The Agency*, p. 276.

379   It was even worse in Latin America: Powers, *The Man Who Kept the Secrets*, p. 88.

380   "the struggle begins": Ambrose, *Ike's Spies*, p. 234.

380   "They were practically all Frenchmen": Lansdale interview with Currey, May 16, 1984, CAMH, Box 1.

381   "I felt that plans should be made": Lansdale, *In the Midst of Wars*, pp. 166–67.

382   To some jaded Western: Lansdale interview with Currey, May 16, 1984, CAMH, Box 1.

382   A leaflet purportedly produced: Lansdale, undated handwritten draft of *In the Midst of Wars*, HIWRP, Box 76. Also Boot, *The Road Not Taken*, p. 225; Currey, *Edward Lansdale*, pp. 158, 161.

382   "sustained only by the faith": Jacobs, *Cold War Mandarin*, p. 45.

383   Instead, they used the cover: Currey, *Edward Lansdale*, p. 161; Boot, *The Road Not Taken*, p. 228.

383   In a nighttime raid: Currey, *Edward Lansdale*, p. 164.

383   "U.S. adherence to the Geneva": Sheehan, ed., *The Pentagon Papers*, p. 60.

383   Most ominously: Lansdale interview with Gittinger, p. 22.

384   "You name it, it was probably": Redick interview with Currey, Dec. 18, 1984, CAMH, Box 2.

384   "pausing only to light one": Karnow, *Vietnam*, p. 230.

384   "The Nhus talked from 8 PM": FitzGerald, *Fire in the Lake*, p. 98.

385   "only controlled the space of": Colby interview with Currey, June 24, 1985, CAMH, Box 1.

385   An American embassy official: Boot, *The Road Not Taken*, p. 220.

386   The guards found the talk so alarming: Ambrose, *Ike's Spies*, p. 247; Gravel, ed., *The Pentagon Papers*, Vol. 1, p. 578.

386   "Ed saw something in Diem": Phillips interview with author.

386   friction was exacerbated: Currey, *Edward Lansdale*, p. 141.

387   "He was lying about me": Grant, *Facing the Phoenix*, p. 119.

387   "That was probably one of the few": Phillips interview with author.

387   "It was quite removed": Sichel interview with author.

388   One operation that particularly: Memorandum, Chief of Station Karlsruhe to Chief, Foreign Branch "M" Kibitz Progress Report, Oct. 24, 1949, in Brill, *Cold War Intelligence* archival website.

389   "an unreconstructed Nazi": From EE/FI/C to STC/SPB "Clearance of Kibitz 15," March 6, 1953, NARA, RG 263, Entry ZZ-19 Subject Files, Second Release of Name Files Under the Nazi War Crimes and Japanese Imperial Government Disclosure Acts, Names Kopp, p. 95.

389   "has shown remarkable ability": "Staybehind Operations in Germany," Oct. 9, 1951, pdf, p. 43. No citation information available.

389   "Since no cable request": Memo from Sichel to Chief of Mission, Frankfurt, Re "Kibitz 15 and his network," March 27, 1953, p. 3, CREST Doc. No. 519b7f92993294098d512659.

390   From a provincial town: Murphy, Kondrashev and Bailey, *Battleground Berlin*, p. 111.

391   Though married and rather plain-looking: Ibid., p. 111; Andrew and Mitrokhin, *The Sword and the Shield*, p. 149.

391   The goal, then, was for the smooth-talking: Murphy, Kondrashev and Bailey, *Battleground Berlin*, p. 241.

391   For all those who worked: Many of the details of Orlov's activities in Berlin are taken from ibid., starting on p. 241.

392   This was the first Sichel: Ibid., p. 485.

393   "By taking an active part": Andrew and Mitrokhin, *The Sword and the Shield*, p. 176.

394   "It was a classic example": Sichel interview with author.

395   After clearing Diem's request: Lansdale, *In the Midst of Wars*, p. 186.

396   Both in quiet backrooms: Boot, *The Road Not Taken*, p. 202; Howard Simpson, *Tiger in the Barbed Wire*, p. 116.

396   While the precise amount remains: Boot, *The Road Not Taken*, p. 257; Howard Simpson, *Tiger in the Barbed Wire*, p. 139.

396   Following protracted negotiations: Currey, *Edward Lansdale*, p. 172; Lansdale, *In the Midst of Wars*, p. 199.

396   In a quintessentially Vietnamese: Phillips, *Why Vietnam Matters*, p. 31.

397   "I could only conclude": Lansdale, *In the Midst of Wars*, p. 174.

397   "General Hinh told me": Ibid., p. 175.

397   In any event, Hinh was soon: Howard Simpson, *Tiger in the Barbed Wire*, p. 136.

397   "be constructive [to] replace": Boot, *The Road Not Taken*, p. 237.

23. THOSE BASTARDS OUT THERE

398   Despite barely budging: Cullather, *Secret History*, p. 109.

398   "Thanks to all of you": David Attlee Phillips, *The Night Watch*, p. 51.

398   "Wisner was so glad": Hersh, *The Old Boys*, pp. 320, 328.

399   "using the total arsenal": Ranelagh, *The Agency*, p. 259.

399   When compared to conventional war: Daugherty, "Covert Action," p. 133.

399   While Eisenhower personally approved: Ibid., p. 132; Andrew, *For the President's Eyes Only*, p. 202.

399 "They're accustomed to dealing": Helms, *A Look Over My Shoulder*, p. 105.

400 "didn't they see it as inevitable": Copeland, *The Game Player*, p. 125.

400 "the Eisenhower years were": Immerman, *The Hidden Hand*, p. 46.

400 "that the USSR will continue": Haines and Leggett, eds., *CIA's Analysis of the Soviet Union, 1947–1991*, p. 48.

401 Eventually, the CIA's MKUltra project: Ranelagh, *The Agency*, p. 206.

401 Something rather more than exhaustion: Evan Thomas, *The Very Best Men*, p. 124.

401 "For Christ's sake": McCargar, quoted in ibid., p. 136.

402 That confidence gave way: Prados, *Safe for Democracy*, p. 51; Hersh, *The Old Boys*, pp. 301–2.

402 "Suppose that our efforts": Memorandum, Wisner to DDI (Charles Cabell), Aug. 8, 1953, cited by Landa, *Almost Successful Recipe*, pp. 59–60.

403 In that spring of 1955: Memorandum, Chief, SR Division to Chief, Foreign Intelligence, An Evaluation of the AERODYNAMIC Operation. NARA, RG 263, Entry ZZ-19 Subject Files, Second Release of Name Files Under the Nazi War Crimes and Japanese Imperial Government Disclosure Acts, Box 8, File: Vol. 2, Aerodynamic Development & Plans.

403 "so far no positive intelligence": CIA, SR Division, AEROOT Project Outline, April 5, 1955, Top Secret, NARA, RG 263, Entry ZZ-19 Subject Files (2nd Release), Box 23, AEROOT/AEBASIN.

403 Nevertheless, plans were under way: Memorandum, Chief, SR Division to DDP/COP, REDSOX Mission to Estonia with Support of DIS, Aug. 1, 1955, NARA, RG 263, Entry ZZ-19 Subject Files (2nd Release), Box 23, AEROOT/AEBASIN.

403 Wisner tried to shelve: Hersh, *The Old Boys*, p. 350.

404 "Frank turned from having liked": Ibid., p. 292.

404 "with people having little or no": "Report on the Covert Activities of the Central Intelligence Agency," Sept. 30, 1954, better known as the "Doolittle Report," p. 31.

404 This sense of being constantly: Hersh, *The Old Boys*, p. 357; Evan Thomas, *The Very Best Men*, p. 137.

404 "have come from an investigator": Memo from [Sheffield Edwards], CIA Director of Security, to Sam Papich, FBI, Re: Result of Investigations," May 24, 1955, CREST Doc. No. 0005382737.

404 "I have no doubt that McCarthy": Letter from Wisner to his mother, June 4, 1954, Wisner Papers, UVa, Box 4, Folder 11.

404 "based on fabrication": Memo from [Sheffield Edwards], to CIA Director of Security, to Sam Papich, FBI, Re: Result of Investigations," May 24, 1955, p. 1.

405 "in the event that you": Memorandum, Hoover to (names redacted), Oct. 14, 1955, Wisner FBI investigative file, Wisner Papers, UVa, Box 18, Folder 12.

405 "The time has now come": Barrett, *The CIA and Congress*, p. 214.

405 "Diem looked at me intently": Lansdale, *In the Midst of Wars*, p. 283.

406 "We might get blown up": Ibid., p. 284.

406 Instead, having effectively purchased: Currey, *Edward Lansdale*, p. 145.

406 The French colonial regime: Howard Simpson, *Tiger in the Barbed Wire*, p. 138.

407 It was propitious timing: Ahern, "The CIA and the Government of Ngo Dinh Diem," p. 41.

407 "What shall we do about those bastards": Ranelagh, *The Agency*, p. 428.

407 When that didn't happen: Boot, *The Road Not Taken*, p. 263; Lansdale, *In the Midst of Wars*, p. 262; Currey, *Edward Lansdale*, p. 174.

408 "Diem is a small, shy": Logevall, *Embers of War*, p. 640.

408 "a possible successor must": *The Pentagon Papers* (Gravel edition), Part IV.A.3, "Evolution of the War: US and France's Withdrawal from Vietnam, 1954–56," p. A-21.

408 "In light of your reiterated conviction": Revised Draft Telegram from the Secretary of State to the Embassy in Saigon, April 11, 1955, *FRUS, 1955–1957*, Vietnam, Vol. I, Doc. 113.

408 "If he asks, tell him": Lansdale, *In the Midst of Wars*, p. 277.

408 At the beginning of the month: Ahern, "The CIA and the Government of Ngo Dinh Diem," p. 45.

409 On the evening of April 27: Miller, *Misalliance*, pp. 122–23; Boot, *The Road Not Taken*, p. 265.

409 "Failure to support Diem": Miller, *Misalliance*, p. 123; Boot, *The Road Not Taken*, p. 265. Also Editorial Note, *FRUS, 1955–1957*, Vietnam, Vol. I, Doc. 145.

410 "Diem had ordered his army": Howard Simpson, *Tiger in the Barbed Wire*, p. 146; Boot, *The Road Not Taken*, p. 266; Shaplen, *The Lost Revolution*, pp. 122–23.

410 "No nationalist aspirant": Boot, *The Road Not Taken*, pp. 268–69.

410 Allen Dulles and Frank Wisner: Ahern, "The CIA and the Government of Ngo Dinh Diem," p. 48.

411 "The developments of last night": Memorandum of Discussion of the 246th Meeting of the National Security Council, April 28, 1955, *FRUS, 1955–1957*, Vietnam, Vol. I, Doc. 148.

411 As a former adman: Howard Simpson, *Tiger in the Barbed Wire*, p. 148.

411 By the time it was over: Boot, *The Road Not Taken*, p. 272; Karnow, *Vietnam*, p. 239.

412 "Collins had defeated Japanese": Boot, *The Road Not Taken*, p. 274.

412 "Fire that son of a bitch": Currey, *Edward Lansdale*, p. 142.

412 "the largest single influence": Ahern, "The CIA and the Government of Ngo Dinh Diem," p. 48.

412 "South Vietnam, in all honesty": Sheehan, *A Bright Shining Lie*, p. 138.

413 "Too much wine": Sichel interview with author.

413 A lawyer from a middle-class: De Graaff, "The Stranded Baron and the Upstart at the Crossroads," p. 688.

413 Despite a reputation for increasingly: Trimble, "The Defections of Dr. John," p. 2.

414 "He became quite emotional": Sichel interview with author.

414 The mystery deepened: Trimble, "The Defections of Dr. John," p. 19.

415 "there must have existed": PAB Files, Inv of Sichel, 0002.png. No citation information available.

416 "Sichel's association with questionable": PAB Files, Inv of Sichel, 0003.png. No citation information available.

417 In early 1956, Sichel: Sichel, *The Secrets of My Life*, p. 236.

417 "painfully familiar": Wisner letter to Sichel, July 3, 1958, Wisner Papers, UVa, Box 9, Folder 1.

418 "So Ed frantically gets on the phone": Rufus Phillips, *Why Vietnam Matters*, p. 56; Phillips interview with author.

418 "there was an odor": Lansdale interview with Currey, May 16, 1984, CAMH, Box 1.

418 Anonymous death threats: Rufus Phillips, *Why Vietnam Matters*, p. 77.

419 Walking into the kitchen: The account of Conein's nocturnal bombing mission is drawn from ibid., pp. 77–78, and Phillips interview with author.

419 "I had seen a lot of things": Grant, *Facing the Phoenix*, p. 126.

419 "I was just a go-fer": Zalin Grant, *Facing the Phoenix*, p. 126.

420 "Our talks that summer": Lansdale, *In the Midst of Wars*, p. 328.

420 While Diem normally sat: Ibid., p. 160; Boot, *The Road Not Taken*, p. 212.

420 While Lansdale had a hard time: Lansdale, *In the Midst of Wars*, p. 160.

421 "The people were absolutely thrilled": Phillips interview with author; Phillips interview with Gittinger, p. 18.

421 Incredibly, one reason: Miller, *Misalliance*, p. 81.

422 "I started to describe": Lansdale, *In the Midst of Wars*, p. 325.

422 To the contrary, with brother Nhu: Howard Simpson, *Tiger in the Barbed Wire*, p. 151; Currey, *Edward Lansdale*, p. 180; Boot, *The Road Not Taken*, p. 288.

423 "The Can Lao was going to force": Lansdale, *In the Midst of Wars*, p. 342.

424 "There was a new tension": Sichel interview with author.

424 At staff meetings: Hersh, *The Old Boys*, p. 358.

424 And while never noted: Thomas Powers, *The Man Who Kept the Secrets*, p. 73.

424 "there was a ferocity": Hersh, *The Old Boys*, p. 356.

425 "I think Frank is in real trouble": Ibid., p. 356.

425 "dangerous to national defense": Miller, *Misalliance*, p. 197.

425 "I think you're being a bit": Paraphrased from Lansdale, *In the Midst of Wars*, p. 344.

426 "a highly effective argument": Ibid., pp. 144, 356.

426 On June 1, Massachusetts senator: Logevall, *Embers of War*, pp. 665–66.

426 "The militant march of Communism": "Nixon Hails Diem on Visit to Saigon," *New York Times*, July 6, 1956, p. 4.

426 "any groups who resorted": *The Pentagon Papers* (Gravel edition), Part IV.A.5, "Evolution of the War: Origins of the Insurgency."

427 "I was convinced": Lansdale, *In the Midst of Wars*, p. 369.

24. COLLAPSE

428 This news undoubtedly provoked: Kalb, *The Year I Was Peter the Great*, p. 62.

429 "Who said that?": Ibid., p. 69.

429 While Western intelligence agencies: Landa, *Almost Successful Recipe*, p. 75.

431 On the evening of Saturday: Wisner, memorandum labeled "Personal and Confidential," Jan. 9, 1957, Wisner Papers, UVa, Box 10, Folder 4, p. 2.

432 In fact, by the time Wisner: Gati, *Failed Illusions*, pp. 73, 94.

433 According to further wire service: Ibid., p. 145.

433 The most frequent and full-throated: Sebestyen, *Twelve Days*, p. 111.

434 "It was the least-organized revolution": Ibid., p. 127.

435 A first priority: Ambrose, *Ike's Spies*, p. 238. Also Hazard, *Cold War Crucible*, p. 236.

435 "We met for dinner at 7:30": Evan Thomas, *The Very Best Men*, p. 143.

437 "There is no indication that the present": "The 20th CPSU Congress in Retrospect: Its Principal Issues and Possible Effects on International Communism," CIA Senior Research Staff Report 1, June 1956, in Haines and Leggett, eds., *CIA's Analysis of the Soviet Union, 1947–1991*, pp. 60–66.

437 "he would be glad indeed": "Memorandum of Discussion at the 289th Meeting of the National Security Council," June 28, 1956, *FRUS*, 1955–1957, Soviet Union, Eastern Mediterranean, Vol. XXIV, Doc. 55.

438 "pretends that a nation can best": Hoopes, *The Devil and John Foster Dulles*, p. 317.

439 " 'How about poison?' ": Copeland, *The Game Player*, p. 165.

441 While it's lost to history: Sebestyen, *Twelve Days*, p. 145; Gati, *Failed Illusions*, p. 157. While estimates of casualties in the massacre vary wildly, most reliable estimates are between 60 and 80 killed, with between 150 and 280 wounded.

442 Within minutes of the 1 p.m. deadline: Sebestyen, *Twelve Days*, p. 178.

442 "to do less ... would be to sacrifice": Weiner, *Legacy of Ashes*, p. 149; Hersh, *The Old Boys*, p. 369.

443 Indeed, the president had told his closest: Kovrig, *Of Walls and Bridges*, p. 90.

443 In a July 12 meeting: Memorandum of Discussion, 290th NSC Meeting, July 12, 1956, NSC Series, Whitman File, Box 8, cited by Landa, *Almost Successful Recipe*, p. 89.

443 "a greater willingness to view": Landa, *Almost Successful Recipe*, p. 92.

444 "at this moment the heart of America": Sebestyen, *Twelve Days*, p. 140.

445 "Even if final action blocked by Soviet": Lodge, Oct. 25, 1956, as cited in ibid., p. 147.

445 The work-around was for Lodge: Sebestyen, *Twelve Days*, pp. 169, 192.

445 One speaker claimed it was Nagy: Ibid., p. 170.

446 Incredibly, those CIA officials who comprised: A. Ross Johnson, *Radio Free Europe and Radio Liberty*, p. 110; Leebaert, *The Fifty-Year Wound*, p. 199.

446 Be that as it may: Memorandum of a Conference with the President, Oct. 27, 1956, *FRUS*, 1955–1957, Eastern Europe, Vol. XXV, Doc. 124.

446 "instructed to make contact": Swartz, *A New Look at the 1956 Hungarian Revolution*, p. 329.

446 "The belief spread": Sebestyen, *Twelve Days*, p. 184.

447 That morning saw the publication: Editorial Note, *FRUS*, 1955–1957, Eastern Europe, Vol. XXV, Doc. 141.

447 The previous afternoon, Nagy: Sebestyen, *Twelve Days*, p. 207. Also Editorial Note, *FRUS*, 1955–1957, Eastern Europe, Vol. XXV, Doc. 141.

447 He also revealed that the Soviets: Gati, *Failed Illusions*, p. 179.

447 "the Nagy government has won": Sebestyen, *Twelve Days*, p. 200.

448 Just yesterday, he noted: Ibid., pp. 217–18.

448 At five in the morning of November 1: Gati, *Failed Illusions*, p. 191; Granville, "In the Line of Fire," p. 14.

449 At the start of an NSC meeting: Memorandum of Discussion at the 302nd Meeting of the National Security Council, Nov. 1, 1956, *FRUS*, 1955–1957, Eastern Europe, Vol. XXV, Doc. 152.

449 While finally presenting a resolution: Editorial Note, *FRUS*, 1955–1957, Eastern Europe, Vol. XXV, Doc. 160.

449 Making this stall tactic even more: John Mapother interview with Swartz, March 23, 1987; Swartz, *A New Look at the 1956 Hungarian Revolution*, p. 562.

450 "If ever there was a time": Editorial Note, *FRUS*, 1955–1957, Eastern Europe, Vol. XXV, Doc. 164.

450 "Both the fighters and": Timothy Foote interview with author.

451 "He made no sense": Evan Thomas, *The Very Best Men*, p. 144.

451 "He colored as he read": Ibid., p. 145.

452 To William Colby, who dined with him in Rome: Ibid., pp. 147–48.

452 By then, an estimated 25,000 Hungarians: While estimates of those arrested and/ or executed for their involvement in the Hungarian Revolution vary widely, the most authoritative numbers appear to be those of historian Csaba Békés. In his article "New Findings on the 1956 Hungarian Revolution" for the *Cold War Inter-*

national History Project Bulletin, p. 3, Békés states that approximately 26,000 were tried, resulting in 22,000 sentences, 13,000 imprisonments, and 350–400 death sentences, of which between 280 and 300 were carried out.

452 Those executions continued until 1960: Henry Kamm, "The Lasting Pain of '56: Can the Past Be Reburied?," *New York Times,* Feb. 8, 1989, p. A-4.

453 With a poll of Hungarian exiles: Ferguson, *American Policy Toward Eastern Bloc Countries Influencing the Hungarian Revolution of 1956,* p. 65. Also Sebestyen, *Twelve Days,* p. 296.

453 Despite broadcasts in which RFE's: A. Ross Johnson, *Radio Free Europe and Radio Liberty,* p. 93; Granville, "Radio Free Europe's Impact on the Kremlin in the Hungarian Crisis of 1956," p. 530.

453 "I just don't know what got into those people": Sebestyen, *Twelve Days,* p. 294.

453 "we demonstrated that 'liberation'": Colby, *Honorable Men,* p. 135.

453 "Not only had the US held out false": Hazard, *Cold War Crucible,* p. 237.

454 For a long time, Wisner just sat there: Herken, *The Georgetown Set,* pp. 225–26; Evan Thomas, *The Very Best Men,* p. 144.

EPILOGUE

455 "the directing forces": Memorandum of Discussion at the 359th Meeting of the National Security Council, March 20, 1958, *FRUS,* 1958–1960, National Security Policy; Arms Control and Disarmament, Vol. III, Doc. 12, p. 54.

458 "Should not someone": As cited by Grose, *Gentleman Spy,* p. 447.

459 "I personally have no knowledge": Kennan to Lovett, June 30, 1948, *FRUS,* Emergence of the Intelligence Establishment, 1945–1950, Doc. 294.

461 "That's when you could feel": Phillips interview with author.

462 In a moment of dark comedy: O'Rourke, *Secrecy and Security,* p. 251.

462 "It was as though I were watching": Lansdale to Tommy Allen, Jan. 30, 1973, CAMH, Box 5.

463 "You understand I know nothing": Burke, *Outrageous Good Fortune,* p. 212.

464 "He saw it as a colossal waste": Patricia Burke interview with author.

464 "an occasional burst of outrageous": Burke, *Outrageous Good Fortune,* p. 7.

465 "So hard was I shaking": Wisner, memorandum labeled "Personal and Confidential," Jan. 9, 1957, Wisner Papers, UVa, Box 10, Folder 4, p. 1.

466 "Des," Wisner said softly: Thomas Powers, *The Man Who Kept the Secrets,* p. 77.

466 "there is a possibility": Memorandum from R. R. Roach to A. H. Belmont, "Frank Wisner," Sept. 13, 1958, Wisner FBI investigative file, Wisner Papers, UVa, Box 18, Folder 12.

466 "He had always been so energetic": Graham Wisner interview with author.

467 "for a number of reasons": "A Biographic Sketch of Frank Gardiner Wisner," NARA, RG 263, Entry A1 19, Box 7, Folder: HS/HC 544.

467 In that same month: Hersh, *The Old Boys,* p. 409.

467 "It was my shotgun": Graham Wisner interview with author.

468 Befitting the "gateway to Asia": Sichel, *The Secrets of My Life,* p. 244.

469 "Dick," he said, "we'd save an awful lot": Sichel interview with author.

470 As the *Los Angeles Times* noted: Carl Cannon, "Ex-Spy Is Man Behind Blue Nun," *Los Angeles Times,* Sept. 15, 1980, p. C-1.

470 "It was a crusade, a romantic crusade": Sichel interview with author.

Bibliography

GOVERNMENT RECORDS AND ARCHIVES

Library of Congress Literature Search
Biography and Genealogy Master Index
Biography in Context
ProQuest Dissertations & Theses
ProQuest Historical Newspapers

National Archives
State Department Records, Record Group 59
    Central Decimal Name Index
Records of the Foreign Service Posts of the Department of State, Record Group 84
Records of the John F. Kennedy Assassination Records Collection Related to Cuba and
    Vietnam, Record Group 218
Records of the Office of Strategic Services, Record Group 226
    OSS Personnel Files
    OSS Personal Names Index
    OSS Code Names Index
Records of the Central Intelligence Agency, Record Group 263
    History Staff Source Collection
    CREST (CIA Records Search Tool)
Records of the Office of the Secretary of the Army, Record Group 335

Foreign Relations of the United States (FRUS)
Retrospective Volumes:
- Emergence of the Intelligence Establishment, 1945–1950
- The Intelligence Community, 1950–1955
- Iran, 1951–1954
- Iran, 1951–1954, Second Edition
- Guatemala, 1952–1954

Regular Volumes:
- 1945, European Advisory Commission, Austria, Germany, Vol. III
- 1946, The British Commonwealth, Western and Central Europe, Vol. V

- 1951, Asia and the Pacific, Vol. VI, Pt. 2
- 1952–1954, National Security Affairs, Vol. II, Pt. 1
- 1952–1954, Germany and Austria, Vol. VII, Pts. 1 and 2
- 1952–1954, Eastern Europe; Soviet Union; Eastern Mediterranean, Vol. VIII
- 1952–1954, East Asia and the Pacific, Vol. XII, Pts. 1 and 2
- 1952–1954, Indochina, Vol. XIII, Pts. 1 and 2
- 1955–1957, Vietnam, Vol. I
- 1955–1957, United Nations and General International Matters, Vol. XI
- 1955–1957, Suez Crisis, July 26—December 31, 1956, Vol. XVI
- 1955–1957, Eastern Europe, Vol. XXV
- 1955–1957, Soviet Union, Eastern Mediterranean, Vol. XXIV
- 1958–1960, National Security Policy; Arms Control and Disarmament, Vol. III

AUTHOR INTERVIEWS

Avis Bohlen, Washington, DC; Feb. 12, 2019.
Patricia Burke, New York, NY; June 23, 2016.
Timothy Foote, Margaretville, NY; Oct. 16, 2015.
Ted and Carol Lansdale, Garden City, NY; Feb. 15, 2017.
Rufus Phillips, Arlington, VA; Oct. 7, 2016; Feb. 9, 2017.
Peter Sichel, New York, NY; June 23, 2016; May 3, May 12, June 9, Oct. 16, 2017; May 21, 2018; Jan. 24, 2019.
Ellis Wisner, Washington, DC; Feb. 11, 2019.
Frank Wisner Jr., New York, NY; June 30, 2016.
Graham Wisner, Washington, DC; Feb. 13, 2019.

ARCHIVES AND COLLECTIONS

Michael Burke Papers. Howard Gotlieb Archival Research Center, Boston University, Boston, MA.
Chisholm Foundation Collection on Frank Gardiner Wisner. Albert and Shirley Small Special Collections Library, University of Virginia, Charlottesville, VA.
Cold War International History Project. Woodrow Wilson International Center for Scholars, Washington, DC.
Cecil B. and Laura G. Currey Archives of Military History. Forsyth Library Special Collections, Fort Hays State University, Hays, KS.
Allen W. Dulles Papers. Seeley G. Mudd Manuscript Library, Princeton University, Princeton, NJ.
Foreign Affairs Oral History Project (FAOHP). Association for Diplomatic Studies and Training, Washington, DC.
Peter Grose Papers. Seeley G. Mudd Manuscript Library, Princeton University, Princeton, NJ.
Gregg Herken Papers. Hoover Institution on War, Revolution and Peace, Stanford University, Palo Alto, CA.
Edward G. Lansdale Papers. Hoover Institution on War, Revolution and Peace, Stanford University, Palo Alto, CA.
Franklin Lindsay Papers. Hoover Institution on War, Revolution and Peace, Stanford University, Palo Alto, CA.

National Security Archives. George Washington University, Washington, DC.
Joseph Persico Papers. Hoover Institution on War, Revolution and Peace, Stanford University, Palo Alto, CA.
R. Harris Smith Papers. Hoover Institution on War, Revolution and Peace, Stanford University, Palo Alto, CA.
Frank Gardiner Wisner Papers. Albert and Shirley Small Special Collections Library, University of Virginia, Charlottesville, VA.

BOOKS, ARTICLES, AND INTERVIEWS

Adams, Jefferson. "Crisis and Resurgence: East German State Security." *International Journal of Intelligence and Counterintelligence,* Vol. 2, No. 4, 1988.
———. *Historical Dictionary of German Intelligence.* Lanham, MD: Scarecrow Press, 2009.
Adkins, Judith. "'These People Are Frightened to Death: Congressional Investigations and the Lavender Scare." *Prologue,* Vol. 48, No. 2, Summer 2016.
Ahern, Thomas L. "The CIA and the Government of Ngo Dinh Diem." *Studies in Intelligence.* No publication date available, but approved for release August 2014.
———. *CIA and the House of Ngo: Covert Action in South Vietnam, 1954–63.* Washington, DC: CIA History Staff, 2000.
———. "'A Road Not Taken': But a Road to Where?" *Studies in Intelligence,* Vol. 62, No. 2, 2018.
———. *Vietnam Declassified: CIA and Counterinsurgency in Vietnam.* Lexington: University Press of Kentucky, 2009.
Albanese, David C. S. *In Search of a Lesser Evil: Anti-Soviet Nationalism and the Cold War.* PhD diss., Northeastern University, 2015.
Albats, Yevgenia. (trans. by Catherine Fitzpatrick.) *The State Within a State: The KGB and Its Hold on Russia—Past, Present and Future.* New York: Farrar, Straus & Giroux, 1994.
Alcorn, Robert Hayden. *No Bugles for Spies: Tales of the OSS.* New York: D. McKay, 1962.
Aldrich, Richard J. *British Intelligence, Strategy and the Cold War, 1945–51.* New York: Routledge, 1992.
———. *The Clandestine Cold War in Asia, 1945–65: Western Intelligence, Propaganda and Special Operations.* London: Frank Cass, 2000.
———. *The Hidden Hand: Britain, America, and Cold War Secret Intelligence.* Woodstock, NY: Overlook Press, 2002.
———. "Intelligence, Anglo-American Relations and the Suez Crisis, 1956." *Intelligence and National Security,* Vol. 9, No. 3, July 1994.
Aldrich, Richard J., Rory Cormac, and Michael Goodman, eds. *Spying on the World: The Declassified Documents of the Joint Intelligence Committee, 1936–2013.* Edinburgh: Edinburgh University Press, 2014.
Allen, George W. "Covering Coups in Saigon in the Early 1960s." *Studies in Intelligence,* Vol. 59, No. 3, 2015.
———. *None So Blind: A Personal Account of the Intelligence Failure in Vietnam.* Chicago: Ivan R. Dee, 2001.
Allen, Susan Heuck. *Classical Spies: American Archaeologists with the OSS in World War II Greece.* Ann Arbor: University of Michigan Press, 2011.
Alsop, Stewart. *Sub Rosa: The OSS and American Espionage.* New York: Harcourt, Brace & World, 1964.

Alvarez, David, and Eduard Mark. *Spying Through a Glass Darkly*. Lawrence: University Press of Kansas, 2016.

Ambrose, Stephen E. *Ike's Spies: Eisenhower and the Espionage Establishment*. New York: Doubleday, 1981.

Anderson, Elizabeth E. "The Security Dilemma and Covert Action: The Truman Years." *International Journal of Intelligence and Counterintelligence*, Vol. 11, No. 4, Winter 1998–99.

Andrew, Christopher. *Defend the Realm: The Authorized History of MI5*. New York: Alfred A. Knopf, 2009.

———. *For the President's Eyes Only: Secret Intelligence and the American Presidency from Washington to Bush*. New York: HarperCollins, 1995.

———. *Her Majesty's Secret Service: The Making of the British Intelligence Community*. New York: Viking, 1986.

Andrew, Christopher, and Oleg Gordievsky. *KGB: The Inside Story of Its Foreign Operations from Lenin to Gorbachev*. London: Hodder & Stoughton, 1990.

Andrew, Christopher, and Vasili Mitrokhin. *The Sword and the Shield: The Mitrokhin Archive and the Secret History of the KGB*. New York: Basic Books, 1999.

———. *The World Was Going Our Way: The KGB and the Battle for the Third World*. New York: Basic Books, 2005.

Angevine, Robert G. "Gentlemen Do Read Each Other's Mail: American Intelligence in the Interwar Era." *Intelligence and National Security*, Vol. 7, No. 2, April 1992.

Anonymous (Gerald Miller). "Office of Policy Coordination, 1948–1952." *Studies in Intelligence*, Vol. 17, No. 2-S, Summer 1973.

Anonymous. "Soviet Use of Assassination and Kidnapping." *Studies in Intelligence*, Vol. 19, No. 3, Fall 1975.

Anonymous. "The Tangled Web." *Studies in Intelligence*, Spring 1987.

Anonymous. *A Woman in Berlin: Eight Weeks in the Conquered City*. New York: Metropolitan Books, 2005.

Aparaschivei, Sorin. *American Service Information in Romania, 1944–1948*. PhD diss., Faculty of History, University of Bucharest, Romania, 2012.

Applebaum, Anne. *Iron Curtain: The Crushing of Eastern Europe, 1944–1956*. New York: Doubleday, 2012.

Ashley, Clarence. *CIA Spy Master*. Gretna, LA: Pelican Publishing, 2004.

Baclawski, Joseph A. "The Best Map of Moscow." *Studies in Intelligence*, Semiannual Edition, No. 1997.

Bacon, Edwin. *The Gulag at War: Stalin's Forced Labour System in the Light of the Archives*. New York: New York University Press, 1994.

Bagley, Tennent H. *Spymaster: Startling Cold War Revelations of a Soviet KGB Chief*. New York: Skyhorse Publishing, 2013.

———. *Spy Wars: Moles, Mysteries and Deadly Games*. New Haven: Yale University Press, 2007.

Baker, Carlos. *Ernest Hemingway: A Life Story*. New York: Scribner, 1969.

Barrett, David M. *The CIA and Congress: The Untold Story*. Lawrence: University Press of Kansas, 2005.

———. "Congress, the CIA, and Guatemala, 1954." *Studies in Intelligence*, No. 10, Winter–Spring 2001.

———. "Glimpses of a Hidden History: Sen. Richard Russell, Congress, and Oversight of the CIA." *International Journal of Intelligence and Counterintelligence*, Vol. 11, No. 3, Fall 1998.

Bartholomew-Feis, Dixee R. *The OSS and Ho Chi Minh: Unexpected Allies in the War Against Japan.* Lawrence: University Press of Kansas, 2006.

Bass, Thomas A. *The Spy Who Loved Us: The Vietnam War and Pham Xuan An's Dangerous Game.* New York: PublicAffairs, 2009.

Batvinis, Raymond J. "The Future of FBI Counterintelligence Through the Lens of the Past Hundred Years." *The Oxford Handbook of National Security Intelligence.* New York: Oxford University Press, 2010.

———. *Hoover's Secret War Against Axis Spies: FBI Counterespionage During World War II.* Lawrence: University Press of Kansas, 2014.

———. *The Origins of FBI Counterintelligence.* Lawrence: University Press of Kansas, 2007.

Baxter, Randolph W. "*Eradicating This Menace: Homophobia and Anti-Communism in Congress, 1947–1954.*" PhD diss., University of California, Irvine, 1999.

———. "'Homo-Hunting' in the Early Cold War: Senator Kenneth Wherry and the Homophobic Side of McCarthyism." *Nebraska History,* 84, 2003.

Bayandor, Darioush. *Iran and the CIA: The Fall of Mossadeq Revisited.* New York: Palgrave Macmillan, 2010.

Beavan, Colin. *Operation Jedburgh.* New York: Viking, 2006.

Behrman, Greg. *The Most Noble Adventure: The Marshall Plan and the Time When America Helped Save Europe.* New York: Free Press, 2007.

Beisner, Robert. *Dean Acheson: A Life in the Cold War.* New York: Oxford University Press, 2006.

Békés, Csaba. "New Findings on the 1956 Hungarian Revolution." *Cold War International History Project Bulletin, No. 2.* Washington, DC: Woodrow Wilson International Center for Scholars, 1992.

———. "The 1956 Hungarian Revolution and World Politics." *Cold War International History Project, Working Paper No. 16.* Washington, DC: Woodrow Wilson International Center for Scholars, 1996.

Békés, Csaba, Malcolm Byrne, and Janos M. Rainer, eds. *The 1956 Hungarian Revolution: A History in Documents.* New York: Central European University Press, 2002.

Benson, Robert L. *The Venona Story.* Fort Meade, MD: Center for Cryptologic History, National Security Agency, 2001.

Benson, Robert Louis, and Michael Warner, eds. *Venona: Soviet Espionage and the American Response, 1939–1957.* Laguna Hills, CA: Aegean Park Press, 1996.

Bergin, Bob. "The Growth of China's Air Defenses: Responding to Covert Overflights, 1949–1974." *Studies in Intelligence,* Vol. 57, No. 2, 2013.

Bering, Henrik. *Outpost Berlin: The History of the American Military Forces in Berlin, 1945–1994.* Chicago: Edition Q, Inc., 1995.

Berman, Larry. *Perfect Spy: The Incredible Double Life of Pham Xuan An.* New York: Smithsonian Books, 2007.

Bethell, Nicholas. *Betrayed.* New York: Times Books, 1984.

Biddiscombe, Alexander P. *Werwolf! The History of the National Socialist Guerrilla Movement, 1944–1946.* Cardiff: University of Wales Press, 1998.

Birstein, Vadim. *SMERSH: Stalin's Secret Weapon; Soviet Military Counterintelligence in WWII.* London: Biteback Publishing, 2011.

Bishop, Robert. *Russia Astride the Balkans.* New York: Robert M. McBride, 1948.

Bissell, Richard M., Jr., with Jonathan E. Lewis and Frances T. Pudlo. *Reflections of a Cold Warrior: From Yalta to the Bay of Pigs.* New Haven: Yale University Press, 1996.

Boghardt, Thomas. "America's Secret Vanguard: US Army Intelligence Operations in Germany, 1944–47." *Studies in Intelligence,* Vol. 57, No. 2, 2013.

Bohlen, Charles. Interviewed by Paige Mulholland, November 20, 1968. Association for Diplomatic Studies and Training: Foreign Affairs Oral History Project.

Boot, Max. *The Road Not Taken: Edward Lansdale and the American Tragedy in Vietnam.* New York: Liveright, 2018.

Borhi, Laszlo. "Rollback, Liberation, Containment, or Inaction? U.S. Policy and Eastern Europe in the 1950s." *Journal of Cold War Studies,* Vol. 1, No. 3, Fall 1999.

Bower, Tom. *Red Web: MI6 and the KGB Master Coup.* London: Aurum Press, 1989.

Boyd, Douglas. *Daughters of the KGB: Moscow's Secret Spies, Sleepers and Assassins of the Cold War.* Stroud, Gloucestershire, UK: History Press, 2015.

Breitman, Richard, N. Goda, T. Naftali, and R. Wolfe. *US Intelligence and the Nazis.* Washington, DC: National Archives and Records Administration, 2004.

Breitman, Richard, and Norman J. W. Goda. *Hitler's Shadow: Nazi War Criminals, U.S. Intelligence, and the Cold War.* Washington, DC: National Archives and Records Administration, 2010.

Brook-Shepherd, Gordon. *The Storm Birds: Soviet Post-war Defectors.* London: Weidenfeld & Nicolson, 1988.

Brownell, Will, and Richard N. Billings. *So Close to Greatness: A Biography of William C. Bullitt.* New York: Macmillan, 1987.

Bruce, Gary. "The Prelude to Nationwide Surveillance in East Germany: Stasi Operations and Threat Perceptions, 1945–1953." *Journal of Cold War Studies,* Vol. 5, No. 2, Spring 2003.

Bukharin, Oleg. "US Atomic Energy Intelligence Against the Soviet Target, 1945–1970." *Intelligence and National Security,* Vol. 19, No. 4, Winter 2004.

Bullitt, Orville. *For the President, Personal and Secret: Correspondence Between Franklin D. Roosevelt and William C. Bullitt.* Boston: Houghton Mifflin, 1972.

Burds, Jeffrey. "Agentura: Soviet Informants' Networks & the Ukrainian Underground in Galicia, 1944–8." *Eastern European Politics and Societies,* Vol. 11, No. 1, Winter 1997.

Burke, Michael. *Outrageous Good Fortune.* Boston: Little, Brown, 1984.

Burkett, Randy. "An Alternative Framework for Agent Recruitment: From MICE to RASCLS." *Studies in Intelligence,* Vol. 57, No. 1, 2013.

Calbos, Paul T. "*Cold War Conflict: American Intervention in Greece.*" Master's thesis, Department of Western European Studies, Indiana University, May 1993.

Calhoun, Ricky-Dale. "The Musketeer's Cloak: Strategic Deception During the Suez Crisis of 1956." *Studies in Intelligence,* Vol. 51, No. 2, 2007.

Callanan, James. *Covert Action in the Cold War: US Policy, Intelligence, and CIA Operations.* New York: I. B. Tauris, 2010.

Campbell, John C. Interviewed by Richard D. McKinzie, June 24, 1974. Truman Library Oral History Project.

Carl, Leo D. *International Dictionary of Intelligence.* McLean, VA: International Defense Consultant Services, 1990.

Carter, John J. *American Intelligence's Employment of Former Nazis During the Early Cold War.* Lewiston, NY: Edwin Mellen Press, 2009.

Catton, Philip E. *Diem's Final Failure: Prelude to America's War in Vietnam.* Lawrence: University Press of Kansas, 2003.

Cave Brown, Anthony. *The Last Hero: Wild Bill Donovan.* New York: Times Books, 1982.

———. *Treason in the Blood: H. St John Philby, Kim Philby and the Spy Case of the Century.* Boston: Houghton Mifflin, 1994.

Chalou, George C. *The Secrets War: The Office of Strategic Services in World War II.* Washington, DC: National Archives and Records Administration, 2002.

Chambers, David Ian. "Edging in from the Cold: The Past and Present State of Chinese Intelligence Historiography." *Studies in Intelligence,* Vol. 56, No. 3, 2012.

Chambers, John Whiteclay. "Office of Strategic Services Training During World War II." *Studies in Intelligence,* Vol. 54, No. 2, 2010.

———. *OSS Training in the National Parks and Service Abroad in World War II.* Washington, DC: National Park Service, 2008.

Charles, Douglas M. *Hoover's War on Gays: Exposing the FBI's "Sex Deviates" Program.* Lawrence: University Press of Kansas, 2015.

Charters, David A., and Maurice A. J. Tugwell, eds. *Deception Operations: Studies in the East-West Context.* London: Brassey's, 1990.

Childs, David, and Richard Popplewell. *The Stasi: The East German Intelligence and Security Service.* New York: New York University Press, 1996.

CIA History Staff. "15 DCI's First 100 Days." *Studies in Intelligence,* Vol. 38, No. 5, 1995.

———. *On the Front Lines of the Cold War: Documents on the Intelligence War in Berlin, 1946 to 1961.* Washington, DC: Center for the Study of Intelligence, 1999.

Clare, George. *Before the Wall: Berlin Days, 1946–1948.* New York: E. P. Dutton, 1990.

Clive, Nigel. "From War to Peace in SIS." *Intelligence and National Security,* Vol. 10, No. 3, July 1995.

Coffin, William Sloane, Jr. *Once to Every Man.* New York: Atheneum, 1977.

Cogan, Charles C. "From the Politics of Lying to the Farce at Suez: What the US Knew." *Intelligence and National Security,* Vol. 13, No. 2, Summer 1998.

Cohen, Eliot A. "'Only Half the Battle': American Intelligence and the Chinese Intervention in Korea, 1950." *Intelligence and National Security,* Vol. 5, No. 1, Jan. 1990.

Colby, William. *Honorable Men: My Life in the CIA.* New York: Simon & Schuster, 1978.

Conquest, Robert. *The Great Terror: A Reassessment.* New York: Oxford University Press, 1990.

———. *Stalin: Breaker of Nations.* New York: Viking, 1991.

Cookridge, E. H. *Gehlen: Spy of the Century.* New York: Random House, 1971.

Copeland, Miles. *The Game Player: Confessions of CIA's Original Political Operator.* London: Aurum Press, 1989.

Corera, Gordon. *The Art of Betrayal: Life and Death in the British Secret Service.* London: Weidenfeld & Nicolson, 2011.

Corke, Sarah-Jane. "The Eisenhower Administration and Psychological Warfare." *Intelligence and National Security,* Vol. 24, No. 2, April 2009.

———. "History, Historians and the Naming of Foreign Policy: A Postmodern Reflection on American Strategic Thinking During the Truman Administration." *Intelligence and National Security,* Vol. 16, No. 3, Autumn 2001.

———. *US Covert Operations and Cold War Strategy: Truman, Secret Warfare and the CIA, 1945–53.* London: Routledge, 2008.

Corson, William R. *The Armies of Ignorance: The Rise of the American Intelligence Empire.* New York: Dial, 1977.

———. *The Betrayal.* New York: W. W. Norton, 1968.

Costa, Chris. "The CIA and the Ukrainian Resistance, 1949–1954." Paper, School of Advanced International Studies (SAIS), November 1991.

Cowden, Robert. "OSS Double-Agent Operations in World War II." *Studies in Intelligence,* Vol. 58, No. 2, 2014.

Cram, Cleveland C. "*Of Moles and Molehunters: A Review of Counterintelligence Literature, 1977–92*" (monograph). Washington, DC: Center for the Study of Intelligence, Central Intelligence Agency, October 1993.

Critchfield, James H. *Partners at the Creation: The Men Behind Germany's Postwar Defense and Intelligence Establishments*. Annapolis: Naval Institute Press, 2003.

Crockett, David. Interviewed by Siegfried Beer, January 16, 1997. OSS Oral History Project.

Crosswell, D. K. R. *Beetle: The Life of General Walter Bedell Smith*. Lexington: University Press of Kentucky, 2010.

Cullather, Nick. "America's Boy? Ramon Magsaysay and the Illusion of Influence." *Pacific Historical Review*, Vol. 62, Aug. 1993.

——. *Secret History: The CIA's Classified Account of Its Operations in Guatemala, 1952–1954*. Stanford: Stanford University Press, 1999.

Cummings, Richard H. *Cold War Radio: The Dangerous History of American Broadcasting in Europe, 1950–1989*. Jefferson, NC: McFarland, 2009.

——. *Radio Free Europe's "Crusade for Freedom": Rallying Americans Behind Cold War Broadcasting, 1950–1960*. Jefferson, NC: McFarland, 2010.

Currey, Cecil B. *Edward Lansdale: The Unquiet American*. Washington, DC: Brassey's, 1998.

Cutler, Richard W. *Counterspy: Memoirs of a Counterintelligence Officer in World War II and the Cold War*. Washington, DC: Brassey's, 2004.

Darling, Arthur B. *The Central Intelligence Agency, an Instrument of Government to 1950*. University Park: Penn State University Press, 1990.

Daugherty, William J. "Covert Action: Strength and Weaknesses." *The Oxford Handbook of National Security Intelligence*. New York: Oxford University Press, 2010.

——. *Executive Secrets: Covert Action and the Presidency*. Lexington: University Press of Kentucky, 2004.

——. "Truman's Iranian Policy, 1945–1953: The Soviet Calculus." *International Journal of Intelligence and Counterintelligence*, Vol. 15, No. 4, Winter 2002–03.

Davidson, Eugene. *The Death and Life of Germany: An Account of the American Occupation*. New York: Alfred A. Knopf, 1959.

Dean, Robert. *Imperial Brotherhood: Gender and the Making of Cold War Foreign Policy*. Amherst: University of Massachusetts Press, 2001.

Dear, Ian. *Sabotage and Subversion: Stories from the Files of the SOE and OSS*. London: Arms & Armour Press, 1996.

Defty, Andrew. "'Close and Continuous Liaison': British Anti-Communist Propaganda and Cooperation with the United States, 1950–51." *Intelligence and National Security*, Vol. 17, No. 4, Winter 2002.

De Graaff, Bob. "The Stranded Baron and the Upstart at the Crossroads: Wolfgang zu Putlitz and Otto John." *Intelligence and National Security*, Vol. 6, No. 4, Oct. 1991.

Deutsch, James I. "'I Was a Hollywood Agent': Cinematic Representations of the Office of Strategic Services in 1946." *Intelligence and National Security*, Vol. 13, No. 2, Summer 1998.

Dobbs, Michael. *Six Months in 1945: FDR, Stalin, Churchill and Truman—from World War to Cold War*. New York: Alfred A. Knopf, 2012.

Dockrill, Saki. *Eisenhower's New-Look National Security Policy, 1953–61*. New York: St. Martin's Press, 1996.

Dorril, Stephen. *MI6: Inside the Covert World of Her Majesty's Secret Intelligence Service*. New York: Free Press, 2000.

Dover, Robert, and Michael S. Goodman, eds. *Spinning Intelligence: Why Intelligence Needs the Media, Why the Media Needs Intelligence*. New York: Columbia University Press, 2009.

Doyle, David W. *True Men & Traitors: From the OSS to the CIA, My Life in the Shadows.* New York: John Wiley & Sons, 2001.

Draitser, Emil. *Stalin's Romeo Spy.* Evanston, IL: Northwestern University Press, 2010.

Dravis, Michael W. "Storming Fortress Albania: America Covert Operations in Microcosm, 1949–54." *Intelligence and National Security,* Vol. 7, No. 4, Oct. 1992.

Dujmovic, Nicholas. "Fifty Years of Studies in Intelligence." *Studies in Intelligence,* Vol. 49, No. 4, 2005.

Dulles, Allen W. *The Craft of Intelligence.* Guilford, CT: Lyons Press, 2006.

———. "William J. Donovan and the National Security." *Studies in Intelligence,* Vol. 3, No. 3, Summer 1959.

Dunlop, Richard. *Donovan: America's Master Spy.* New York: Rand McNally, 1982.

Durning, Marvin B. *World Turned Upside Down: U.S. Naval Intelligence and the Early Cold War Struggle for Germany.* Washington, DC: Potomac Books, 2007.

Ehrman, John. "The Mystery of 'ALES.' " *Studies in Intelligence,* Vol. 51, No. 4, 2007.

———. "What Are We Talking About When We Talk About Counterintelligence?" *Studies in Intelligence,* Vol. 53, No. 2, 2009.

Epstein, Edward Jay. *Deception: The Invisible War Between the KGB and the CIA.* New York: Simon & Schuster, 1989.

Evans, Joseph C. "Berlin Tunnel Intelligence: A Bumbling KGB." *International Journal of Intelligence and Counterintelligence,* Vol. 9, No. 1, 1996.

Evans, M. Stanton. *Blacklisted by History: The Untold Story of Senator Joe McCarthy.* New York: Crown Forum, 2007.

Fakiolas, Efstathios T. "Kennan's Long Telegram and NSC-68: A Comparative Analysis." *East European Quarterly,* Vol. 31, No. 4, Jan. 1998.

Felix, Christopher. *A Short Course in the Secret War,* 4th ed. Lanham, MD: Madison Books, 2001.

Ferguson, Kenneth A. *American Policy Toward Eastern Bloc Countries Influencing the Hungarian Revolution of 1956.* United States Army Command and General Staff College, CreateSpace, 2014.

FitzGerald, Frances. *Fire in the Lake: The Vietnamese and the Americans in Vietnam.* New York: Little, Brown, 1972.

Ford, Corey. *Donovan of OSS.* Boston: Little, Brown, 1970.

Ford, Harold P. *CIA and the Vietnam Policymakers: Three Episodes, 1962–1968.* Langley, VA: History Staff, Center for the Study of Intelligence, Central Intelligence Agency, 1998.

———. "Revisiting Vietnam." *Studies in Intelligence,* Vol. 39, No. 5, 1996.

———. "Why CIA Analysts Were So Doubtful About Vietnam." *Studies in Intelligence,* Semiannual Edition, No. 1, 1997.

Ford, Kirk, Jr. *OSS and the Yugoslav Resistance, 1943–1945.* College Station: Texas A&M University Press, 1992.

Ford, Roger. *Steel from the Sky: The Jedburgh Raiders, France 1944.* London: Weidenfeld & Nicolson, 2004.

Fraser, Andrew. "Architecture of a Broken Dream: The CIA and Guatemala, 1952–54." *Intelligence and National Security,* Vol. 20, No. 3, Sept. 2005.

Freiberger, Steven Z. *Dawn Over Suez: The Rise of American Power in the Middle East, 1953–1957.* Chicago: Ivan R. Dee, 1992.

Friis, Thomas, Kristie Macrakis, and Helmut Muller-Engbergs, eds. *East German Foreign Intelligence: Myth, Reality and Controversy.* London: Routledge, 2010.

Funder, Anna. *Stasiland: Stories from Behind the Berlin Wall.* London: Granta, 2003.

Fursenko, Aleksandr, and Timothy Naftali. *Khrushchev's Cold War: The Inside Story of an American Adversary*. New York: W. W. Norton, 2006.

"G." "Engineering the Berlin Tunnel." *Studies in Intelligence*, Vol. 52, No. 1, 2008.

Gaddis, John Lewis. *The Cold War: A New History*. New York: Penguin, 2005.

——. *George F. Kennan: An American Life*. New York: Penguin, 2011.

——. *The United States and the Origins of the Cold War, 1941–1947*. New York: Columbia University Press, 1972.

Gadney, Reg. *Cry Hungary! Uprising 1956*. New York: Atheneum, 1986.

Gaiduk, Ilya V. *Confronting Vietnam: Soviet Policy Toward the Indochina Conflict, 1954–1963*. Stanford: Stanford University Press, 2003.

Garthoff, Raymond L. *A Journey Through the Cold War: A Memoir of Containment and Coexistence*. Washington, DC: Brookings Institution Press, 2001.

Gati, Charles. *Failed Illusions: Moscow, Washington, Budapest and the 1956 Hungarian Revolution*. Stanford: Stanford University Press, 2006.

Gellately, Robert. *Stalin's Curse: Battling for Communism in War and Cold War*. New York: Vintage, 2013.

Gentry, Curt. *J. Edgar Hoover: The Man and His Secrets*. New York: W. W. Norton, 1991.

George, Roger Z., and Harvey Rishikof, eds. *The National Security Enterprise: Navigating the Labyrinth*. Washington, DC: Georgetown University Press, 2011.

Geraghty, Tony. *Beyond the Front Line: The Untold Exploits of Britain's Most Daring Cold War Spy Mission*. London: HarperCollins, 1996.

Getty, John Archibald, and Roberta Manning, eds. *Stalinist Terror: New Perspectives*. Cambridge: Cambridge University Press, 1993.

Glantz, Mary E. *FDR and the Soviet Union: The President's Battles over Foreign Policy*. Lawrence: University Press of Kansas, 2005.

Gleijeses, Piero. *Shattered Hope: The Guatemalan Revolution and the United States, 1944–1954*. Princeton: Princeton University Press, 1991.

Godson, Roy. *Dirty Tricks and Trump Cards: US Covert Action and Counterintelligence*. Washington, DC: Brassey's, 1995.

Godson, Roy, ed. *Comparing Foreign Intelligence: The U.S., the USSR, the U.K. & the Third World*. Washington, DC: Pergamon-Brassey's, 1988.

Goldstein, Cora Sol. "The Control of Visual Representation: American Art Policy in Occupied Germany, 1945–1949." *Intelligence and National Security*, Vol. 18, No. 2, Summer 2003.

Goldstein, Warren. *William Sloane Coffin Jr.: A Holy Impatience*. New Haven: Yale University Press, 2004.

Goodman, Michael. "The Foundations of Anglo-American Intelligence Sharing." *Studies in Intelligence*, Vol. 59, No. 2, 2015.

——. *The Official History of the Joint Intelligence Committee—Volume 1: From the Approach of the Second World War to the Suez Crisis*. London: Routledge, 2014.

Gorst, Anthony, and W. Scott Lucas. "The Other Collusion: Operation Straggle and Anglo-American Intervention in Syria, 1955–56." *Intelligence and National Security*, Vol. 4, No. 3, July 1989.

Goscha, Christopher E. "Intelligence in a Time of Decolonization: The Case of the Democratic Republic of Vietnam at War (1945–50)." *Intelligence and National Security*, Vol. 22, No. 1, Feb. 2007.

Gould, Jonathan S. "The OSS and the London 'Free Germans.'" *Studies in Intelligence*, Vol. 46, No. 1, 2002.

Gouzenko, Igor. *The Iron Curtain.* New York: E. P. Dutton, 1952.

Granatstein, J. L. "Gouzenko to Gorbachev: Canada's Cold War." *Canadian Military Journal,* Vol. 12, No. 1.

Grant, Zalin. *Facing the Phoenix.* New York: W. W. Norton, 1991.

Granville, Johanna. "Caught with Jam on Our Fingers: Radio Free Europe and the Hungarian Revolution in 1956." *Diplomatic History,* Vol. 29, No. 5, 2005.

———. "Imre Nagy aka 'Volodya'—A Dent in the Martyr's Halo?" *Cold War International History Project,* No. 5. Woodrow Wilson International Center for Scholars, Washington, DC, Spring 1995.

———. "In the Line of Fire: The Soviet Crackdown of Hungary, 1956–58." *Center for Russian and East European Studies,* University of Pittsburgh, 1998.

———. "Radio Free Europe's Impact on the Kremlin in the Hungarian Crisis of 1956: Three Hypotheses." *Canadian Journal of History,* Dec. 2004.

———. "Soviet Archival Documents on the Hungarian Revolution, 24 October–4 November 1956." *Cold War International History Project,* No. 5. Woodrow Wilson International Center for Scholars, Washington, DC, Spring 1995.

Gravel, Mike, ed. *The Pentagon Papers: The Defense Department History of United States Decision-making on Vietnam.* Boston: Beacon Press, 1971.

Greenberg, Harold M. "The Doolittle Commission of 1954." *Intelligence and National Security,* Vol. 20, No. 4, Dec. 2005.

Grose, Peter. *Gentleman Spy: The Life of Allen Dulles.* New York: Houghton Mifflin/A Richard Todd Book, 1994.

———. *Operation Rollback: America's Secret War Behind the Iron Curtain.* Boston: Houghton Mifflin, 2000.

Hack, Karl. "British Intelligence and Counter-Insurgency in the Era of Decolonisation: The Example of Malaya." *Intelligence and National Security,* Vol. 14, No. 2, Summer 1999.

Hadden, John. *Conversations with a Masked Man.* New York: Arcade Publishing, 2016.

Haines, Gerald K., and Robert E. Leggett, eds. *CIA's Analysis of the Soviet Union, 1947–1991: A Documentary Collection.* Washington, DC: Center for the Study of Intelligence, Central Intelligence Agency, 2001.

———. *Watching the Bear: Essays on CIA's Analysis of the Soviet Union.* Washington, DC: Center for the Study of Intelligence, Central Intelligence Agency, 2001.

Halberstam, David. *The Best and the Brightest.* New York: Random House, 1972.

Hall, Roger. *You're Stepping on My Cloak and Dagger.* Annapolis: Naval Institute Press, 1957.

Hanrahan, James. "An Interview with Former CIA Executive Director Lawrence K. 'Red' White." *Studies in Intelligence,* Vol. 43, No. 3, Winter 1999–2000.

Hansen, James H. "The Kremlin Follies of '53 . . . The Demise of Lavrenti Beria." *International Journal of Intelligence and Counterintelligence,* Vol. 4, No. 1, 1990.

———. "Soviet Deception in the Cuban Missile Crisis." *Studies in Intelligence,* Vol. 46, No. 1, 2002.

Harrington, Daniel F. *Berlin on the Brink: The Blockade, the Airlift, and the Early Cold War.* Lexington: University Press of Kentucky, 2012.

Harris, Sarah. *The CIA and the Congress for Cultural Freedom in the Early Cold War.* New York: Routledge, 2016.

Harris, William R. "March Crisis 1948, Act 1." *Studies in Intelligence,* Vol. 10, No. 4, 1966.

Harrison, James P. *The Endless War: Vietnam's Struggle for Independence.* New York: Columbia University Press, 1989.

Haslam, Jonathan. *Near and Distant Neighbors: A New History of Soviet Intelligence.* New York: Farrar, Straus & Giroux, 2015.

———. *Russia's Cold War: From the October Revolution to the Fall of the Wall.* New Haven: Yale University Press, 2011.

Haslam, Jonathan, and Karina Urbach, eds. *Secret Intelligence in the European States System, 1918–1989.* Stanford: Stanford University Press, 2014.

Hassell, Agostino von, and Sigrid MacRae. *Alliance of Enemies: The Untold Story of Secret American and German Collaboration to End World War II.* New York: St. Martin's Press, 2006.

Haynes, John E. *Red Scare or Red Menace? American Communism and Anticommunism in the Cold War Era.* Chicago: Ivan R. Dee, 1996.

Haynes, John Earl, and Harvey Klehr. *Early Cold War Spies: The Espionage Trials That Shaped American Politics.* New York: Cambridge University Press, 2006.

———. *In Denial: Historians, Communism and Espionage.* San Francisco: Encounter Books, 2003.

———. *Spies: The Rise and Fall of the KGB in America.* New Haven: Yale University Press, 2009.

———. *Venona: Decoding Soviet Espionage in America.* New Haven: Yale University Press, 1999.

Hazard, Elizabeth. *Cold War Crucible.* Boulder: East European Monographs, 1996.

Hedman, Eva-Lotta E. "Late Imperial Romance: Magsaysay, Lansdale and the Philippine-American 'Special Relationship.'" *Intelligence and National Security,* Vol. 14, No. 4, Winter 1999.

Helgerson, John L. *Getting to Know the President: Intelligence Briefings of Presidential Candidates, 1952–2004, 2nd ed.* Washington, DC: Center for the Study of Intelligence, Central Intelligence Agency, May 2012.

———. "Truman and Eisenhower: Launching the Process." *Studies in Intelligence,* Vol. 38, No. 5, 1995.

Helms, Cynthia, with Chris Black. *An Intriguing Life: A Memoir of War, Washington, and Marriage to an American Spymaster.* Lanham, MD: Rowman & Littlefield, 2013.

Helms, Richard, with William Hood. *A Look Over My Shoulder: A Life in the Central Intelligence Agency.* New York: Ballantine, 2003.

Hemingway, Jack. *Misadventures of a Fly Fisherman: My Life with and Without Papa.* Dallas: Taylor Publishing, 1986.

Herken, Gregg. *The Georgetown Set.* New York: Alfred A. Knopf, 2014.

Herman, Michael, and Gwilym Hughes, eds. *Intelligence in the Cold War: What Difference Did It Make?* New York: Routledge, 2013.

Hersh, Burton. *The Old Boys: The American Elite and the Origins of the CIA.* New York: Scribner's, 1992.

Heuser, Beatrice. *Western "Containment" Policies in the Cold War: The Yugoslav Case, 1948–53.* London: Routledge, 1989.

Higginbotham, Adam. "There Are Still Thousands of Tons of Unexploded Bombs in Germany, Left Over from World War II." *Smithsonian,* Jan. 6, 2016.

Hill, T. H. E., ed. *Berlin in Early Cold-War Army Booklets.* Scotts Valley, CA: CreateSpace, 2008.

Hitz, Frederick P. *The Great Game: The Myth and Reality of Espionage.* New York: Alfred A. Knopf, 2004.

Hixson, Walter L. *Parting the Curtain: Propaganda, Culture and the Cold War, 1945–1961.* London: St. Martin's Press, 1997.

Hoffman, Bruce, and Christian Ostermann. *Moles, Defectors, and Deceptions: James Angleton and His Influence on US Counterintelligence.* Cold War International History Project, Woodrow Wilson International Center for Scholars, 2014.

Hoffman, David E. *The Billion Dollar Spy: A True Story of Cold War Espionage and Betrayal.* New York: Doubleday, 2015.

Holbrook, James R. *Potsdam Mission: Memoir of a US Army Intelligence Officer in Communist East Germany.* Bloomington, IN: AuthorHouse, 2008.

Holt, Thaddeus. *The Deceivers: Allied Military Deception in the Second World War.* New York: Skyhorse Publishing, 2007.

Holzman, Michael. *James Jesus Angleton, the CIA & the Craft of Counterintelligence.* Amherst: University of Massachusetts Press, 2008.

Hoopes, Townsend. *The Devil and John Foster Dulles.* Boston: Atlantic Monthly Press, 1973.

Hoopes, Townsend, and Douglas Brinkley. *Driven Patriot: The Life and Times of James Forrestal.* New York: Alfred A. Knopf, 1992.

Hopkins, Robert S., III. "An Expanded Understanding of Eisenhower, American Policy and Overflights." *Intelligence and National Security,* Vol. 11, No. 2, April 1996.

Hughes, R. Gerald, P. Jackson, and L. Scott, eds. *Exploring Intelligence Archives: Enquiries into the Secret State.* New York: Routledge, 2008.

Hunt, E. Howard, with Greg Aunapu. *American Spy: My Secret History in the CIA, Watergate, and Beyond.* New York: John Wiley & Sons, 2007.

Immerman, Richard H. *The CIA in Guatemala: The Foreign Policy of Intervention.* Austin: University of Texas Press, 1982.

———. *The Hidden Hand: A Brief History of the CIA.* Chichester, UK: John Wiley & Sons, 2014.

Irwin, Will. *The Jedburghs: The Secret History of the Allied Special Forces, France 1944.* New York: PublicAffairs, 2005.

Isaacs, Stan. "Rebuilding the Monster." *Jock Magazine,* June 1970.

Jacobs, Seth. *Cold War Mandarin: Ngo Dinh Diem and the Origins of America's War in Vietnam, 1950–1963.* Lanham, MD: Rowman & Littlefield, 2006.

Jacobsen, Annie. *Operation Paperclip: The Secret Intelligence Program to Bring Nazi Scientists to America.* Little, Brown, 2014.

Jakub, Jay. *Spies and Saboteurs: Anglo-American Collaboration and Rivalry in Human Intelligence Collection and Special Operations, 1940–45.* London: Macmillan, 1999.

Jeffery, Keith. *The Secret History of MI-6.* New York: Penguin, 2010; revised, 2013.

Jeffreys-Jones, Rhodri. *The CIA and American Democracy.* New Haven: Yale University Press, 1998.

———. "Why Was the CIA Established in 1947?" *Intelligence and National Security,* Vol. 12, No. 1, Jan. 1997.

Jenkins, Peter. *Surveillance Tradecraft: The Professional's Guide to Covert Surveillance Training.* Harrogate, UK: Intel Publishing, 2010.

Johnson, A. Ross. *Radio Free Europe and Radio Liberty: The CIA Years and Beyond.* Stanford: Stanford University Press, 2010.

Johnson, David K. *The Lavender Scare: The Cold War Persecution of Gays and Lesbians in the Federal Government.* Chicago: University of Chicago Press, 2004.

Johnson, Loch. *America's Secret Power: The CIA in a Democratic Society.* Oxford: Oxford University Press, 1989.

Johnson, Loch, ed. *Handbook of Intelligence Studies*. London: Routledge, 2007.

———. *Intelligence: Critical Concepts in Military, Strategic and Security Studies*. New York: Routledge, 2011.

———. *The Oxford Handbook of National Security Intelligence*. New York: Oxford University Press, 2010.

———. *Strategic Intelligence: Covert Action—Beyond the Veils of Secret Foreign Policy*, Vol. 3. Westport, CT: Praeger Security International, 2007.

Johnson, Loch, and James J. Wirtz, eds. *Intelligence and National Security: The Secret World of Spies—An Anthology*, 2nd ed. New York: Oxford University Press, 2008.

———. *Intelligence: The Secret World of Spies—An Anthology*, 3rd ed. New York: Oxford University Press, 2011.

Johnson, William R. *Thwarting Enemies at Home and Abroad: How to Be a Counterintelligence Officer*. Washington, DC: Georgetown University Press, 2009.

Jones, Benjamin F. *Eisenhower's Guerrillas: The Jedburghs, the Maquis, & the Liberation of France*. New York: Oxford University Press, 2016.

Jones, R. V. *Reflections on Intelligence*. London: Heinemann, 1989.

———. "Some Lessons in Intelligence." *Studies in Intelligence*, Vol. 38, No. 5, 1995.

Judt, Tony. *Postwar: A History of Europe Since 1945*. New York: Penguin, 2005.

Kalb, Marvin. *The Year I Was Peter the Great*. Washington, DC: Brookings Institution Press, 2017.

Kalugin, Oleg. *Spymaster: My Thirty-Two Years in Intelligence and Espionage Against the West*. New York: Basic Books, 2009.

Karabell, Zachary. *Architects of Intervention: The United States, the Third World and the Cold War, 1946–1962*. Baton Rouge: Louisiana State University Press, 1999.

Karnow, Stanley. "On Duty, 'Dirty Tricks' and Democracy. A Profile of Maj. Gen. Edward Lansdale, the Original 'Ugly American.'" *Washington Post Potomac Magazine*, December 10, 1972.

———. *In Our Image: America's Empire in the Philippines*. New York: Random House, 1989.

———. *Vietnam: A History*. New York: Viking, 1991.

Katz, Milton. Interviewed by Richard D. McKinzie, July 25, 1975, Truman Library Oral History Project.

Kehoe, Robert R. "1944: An Allied Team with the French Resistance." *Studies in Intelligence*, Vol. 42, No. 5, Winter 1998–99.

Kennan, George F. *Memoirs: 1925–1950; 1950–1963*. Boston: Little, Brown and Company, 1967, 1972.

Kent, Sherman. *Strategic Intelligence for American World Policy*. Princeton: Princeton University Press, 1949.

Kerkvliet, Benedict J. *The Huk Rebellion: A Study of Peasant Revolt in the Philippines*. Quezon City, Philippines: New Day Publishers, 1979.

Kern, Gary. *A Death in Washington: Walter G. Krivitsky and the Stalinist Terror*. New York: Enigma Books, 2004.

———. "How 'Uncle Joe' Bugged FDR." *Studies in Intelligence*, Vol. 47, No. 1, 2003.

Kern, Gary, ed. *Walter G. Krivitsky: MI5 Debriefing & Other Documents on Soviet Intelligence*. Riverside, CA: Xenos Books, 2004.

Kerr, Sheila. "KGB Sources on the Cambridge Network of Soviet Agents: True or False?" *Intelligence and National Security*, Vol. 11, No. 3, July 1996.

Kessler, Lauren. *Clever Girl: Elizabeth Bentley, the Spy Who Ushered in the McCarthy Era*. New York: HarperCollins, 2003.

Kessler, Ronald. *The Bureau: The Secret History of the FBI*. New York: St. Martin's Press, 2002.

———. *The FBI: Inside the World's Most Powerful Law Enforcement Agency*. New York: Pocket Books, 1993.

Kimball, Warren F. "A Different Take on FDR at Teheran." *Studies in Intelligence*, Vol. 49, No. 3, 2005.

Kinzer, Stephen. *The Brothers: John Foster Dulles, Allen Dulles, and Their Secret World War*. New York: Times Books, 2013.

Kirkpatrick, Lyman. *The Real CIA*. New York: Macmillan, 1972.

Knight, Amy W. *The KGB, Police and Politics in the Soviet Union*. Boston: Unwin Hyman, 1988.

Kotek, Joel. "Youth Organizations as a Battlefield in the Cold War." *Intelligence and National Security*, Vol. 18, No. 2, Summer 2003.

Kovrig, Bennett. *Of Walls and Bridges: The United States & Eastern Europe*. New York: New York University Press, 1991.

Kramer, Mark. *New Evidence on Soviet Decision-Making and the 1956 Polish and Hungarian Crises*. Cold War International History Project Bulletin No. 8–9. Washington, DC: Woodrow Wilson International Center for Scholars, Winter 1996.

Kuhns, Woodrow J. *Assessing the Soviet Threat: The Early Cold War Years*. Langley, VA: Center for the Study of Intelligence, Central Intelligence Agency, 1997.

———. "The Office of Reports and Estimates: CIA's First Center for Analysis." *Studies in Intelligence*, Vol. 51, No. 2, 2007.

Ladwig, Walter C., III. "When the Police Are the Problem: The Philippine Constabulary and the Huk Rebellion," in *Policing Insurgencies: Cops as Counterinsurgents*, edited by C. Christine Fair and Sumit Ganguly. Oxford: Oxford University Press, 2014.

Lambridge, Wayne. "A Note on KGB Style." *Studies in Intelligence*, Vol. 15, No. 1, Winter 1971.

Lamphere, Robert J., and Tom Shachtman. *The FBI-KGB War: A Special Agent's Story*. New York: Random House, 1986.

Landa, Ronald D. *Almost Successful Recipe: The United States and East European Unrest Prior to the 1956 Hungarian Revolution*. Washington, DC: Historical Office of the Office of the Secretary of Defense, 2012.

Lansdale, Edward Geary. *In the Midst of Wars: An American's Mission to Southeast Asia*. New York: Harper & Row, 1972.

———. "Viet Nam: Do We Understand Revolution?" *Foreign Affairs*, Vol. 43, No. 1, Oct. 1964.

———. "Viet Nam: Still the Search for Goals." *Foreign Affairs*, Vol. 47, No. 1, Oct. 1968.

Large, David Clay. *Berlin*. New York: Basic Books, 2000.

Laukhuff, Perry. Interviewed by Richard D. McKinzie, July 23, 1974. Truman Library Oral History Project.

Laurie, Clayton D. "A New President, a Better CIA and an Old War: Eisenhower and Intelligence Reporting on Korea, 1953." *Studies in Intelligence*, Vol. 54, No. 4, 2010.

———. "Takes on Intelligence and the Vietnam War." *Studies in Intelligence*, Vol. 55, No. 2, 2011.

Laurie, Clayton D., ed. *CIA and the Wars in Southeast Asia, 1947–75*. A Studies in Intelligence Anthology. Washington, DC: Central Intelligence Agency, 2016.

Leary, William M. "CIA Air Operations in Laos, 1955–1974." *Studies in Intelligence*, Vol. 43, No. 3, Winter 1999–2000.

Leebaert, Derek. *To Dare and to Conquer: Special Operations and the Destiny of Nations from Achilles to Al Qaeda*. Boston: Little, Brown, 2006.

———. *The Fifty-Year Wound: The True Price of America's Cold War Victory*. Boston: Little, Brown, 2002.

Leffler, Melvyn P. *A Preponderance of Power: National Security, the Truman Administration and the Cold War*. Stanford: Stanford University Press, 1992.

Lelyveld, Joseph. *His Final Battle: The Last Months of Franklin Roosevelt*. New York: Alfred A. Knopf, 2016.

Lembke, Andrew E. *Lansdale, Magsaysay, America and the Philippines: A Case Study of Limited Intervention Counterinsurgency*. Thesis, Faculty of the U.S. Army Command and General Staff College. New York: West Point, 2001.

LePage, Jean-Marc, and Elie Tenenbaum. "French and American Intelligence Relations During the First Indochina War, 1950–54." *Studies in Intelligence*, Vol. 55, No. 3, 2011.

Leshuk, Leonard. *US Intelligence Perceptions of Soviet Power, 1921–1946*. Portland, OR: Frank Cass, 2003.

Lilley, James, with Jeffrey Lilley. *China Hands: Nine Decades of Adventure, Espionage and Diplomacy in Asia*. New York: PublicAffairs, 2004.

Lindsay, Frank. Interviewed by (redacted), July 26, 2000. CIA Oral History Program.

Liptak, Bela. *A Testament of Revolution*. College Station: Texas A&M University Press, 2001.

Loftus, John. *The Belarus Secret*. New York: Alfred A. Knopf, 1982.

Logevall, Fredrik. *Embers of War: The Fall of an Empire and the Making of America's Vietnam*. New York: Random House, 2012.

Lombardo, Johannes R. "A Mission of Espionage, Intelligence and Psychological Operations: The American Consulate in Hong Kong, 1949–64." *Intelligence and National Security*, Vol. 14, No. 4, Winter 1999.

Longden, Sean. *T-Force: The Race for Nazi War Secrets, 1945*. London: Constable, 2009.

Lovell, Stanley. *Of Spies & Stratagems*. New York: Prentice-Hall, 1963.

Lowe, Keith. *Savage Continent: Europe in the Aftermath of World War II*. New York: Picador, 2012.

Lowenhaupt, Henry S. "On the Soviet Nuclear Scent." *Studies in Intelligence*, Vol. 11, No. 4, Fall 1967.

Lucas, Scott. *Freedom's War: The American Crusade Against the Soviet Union*. New York: New York University Press, 1999.

Lucas, Scott, and Alistair Morey. "The Hidden 'Alliance': The CIA and MI6 Before and After Suez." *Intelligence and National Security*, Vol. 15, No. 2, Summer 2000.

Lukes, Igor. "The Birth of a Police State: The Czechoslovak Ministry of the Interior, 1945–48." *Intelligence and National Security*, Vol. 11, No. 1, Jan. 1996.

———. "Kamen: A Cold War Dangle Operation with an American Dimension, 1948–1952." *Studies in Intelligence*, Vol. 55, No. 1, 2011.

———. *On the Edge of the Cold War: American Diplomats and Spies in Postwar Prague*. New York: Oxford University Press, 2012.

Lulushi, Albert. *Donovan's Devils: OSS Commandos Behind Enemy Lines—Europe, World War II*. New York: Arcade Publishing, 2016.

———. *Operation Valuable Fiend: The CIA's First Paramilitary Strike Against the Iron Curtain*. New York: Arcade Publishing, 2014.

Luria, Carlos D. *Skating on the Edge: A Memoir and Journey Through a Metamorphosis of the CIA*. Salem, NC: Booksurge Publishing, 2006.

Macdonald, Douglas John. "'Adventures in Chaos': Reformism in U.S. Foreign Policy." PhD diss., Columbia University, 1987.

MacDonogh, Giles. *After the Reich*. London: John Murray, 2007.

Macintyre, Ben. *A Spy Among Friends: Kim Philby and the Great Betrayal*. New York: Bloomsbury, 2014.

MacPherson, B. Nelson. "Inspired Improvisation: William Casey and the Penetration of Germany." *Intelligence and National Security*, Vol. 9, No. 4, Oct. 1994.

Macrakis, Kristie. *Seduced by Secrets: Inside the Stasi's Spy-Tech World*. New York: Cambridge University Press, 2008.

Maddrell, Paul. *Spying on Science: Western Intelligence in Divided Germany, 1945–1961*. Oxford: Oxford University Press, 2006.

Maior, George Cristian, ed. "*Spy for Eternity: Frank Wisner, the Tragic Tale of a CIA Officer Who Tried to Change the World*" (unpublished manuscript). Bucharest, Romania, 2016.

Manchester, William, and Paul Reid. *The Last Lion: Winston Spencer Churchill, Defender of the Realm, 1940–1965*. New York: Bantam, 2012.

Mangold, Tom. *Cold Warrior: James Jesus Angleton: The CIA's Master Spy Hunter*. New York: Simon & Schuster, 1991.

Marchio, James D. "US Intelligence Assessments and the Reliability of Non-Soviet Warsaw Pact Armed Forces, 1946–89." *Studies in Intelligence*, Vol. 51, No. 4, 2007.

Marchio, Jim. "Resistance Potential and Rollback: US Intelligence and the Eisenhower Administration's Policies Toward Eastern Europe, 1953–56." *Intelligence and National Security*, Vol. 10, No. 2, April 1995.

Mark, Eduard. "The OSS in Romania, 1944–45: An Intelligence Operation of the Early Cold War." *Intelligence and National Security*, Vol. 9, No. 2, April 1994.

Marr, David G. *Vietnam 1945: The Quest for Power*. Berkeley: University of California Press, 1995.

Martin, David C. "The CIA's Loaded Gun." *Washington Post*, Oct. 10, 1976.

———. *Wilderness of Mirrors*. New York: Harper & Row, 1980.

Matthias, Willard C. *America's Strategic Blunders: Intelligence Analysis and National Security Policy, 1936–1991*. University Park: Penn State University Press, 2001.

May, Ernest R., ed. *American Cold War Strategy: Interpreting NSC 68*. New York: Bedford Books/St. Martin's Press, 1993.

McCargar, James. Interviewed by Charles Stuart Kennedy, April 18, 1995. Association for Diplomatic Studies and Training, Foreign Affairs Oral History Project.

McCaslin, Leland C. *Secrets of the Cold War: US Army Europe's Intelligence and Counterintelligence Activities Against the Soviets*. Solihull, England: Hellon, 2010.

McCoy, Alfred W. *In the Shadows of the American Century*. Chicago: Haymarket Books, 2017.

McMurdo, Torey L. "The Economics of Overthrow: The United States, Britain and the Hidden Justification of Operation TPAJAX." *Studies in Intelligence*, Vol. 56, No. 2, 2012.

McQuiston, John T. "Michael Burke, Ex-Executive with the Yankees, Dies at 70." *New York Times*, February 7, 1987.

Mecklin, John. *Mission in Torment: An Intimate Account of the U.S. Role in Vietnam*. New York: Doubleday, 1965.

Melby, John F. Interviewed by Charles Stuart Kennedy, June 16, 1989. Association for Diplomatic Studies and Training, Foreign Affairs Oral History Project.

Melton, H. Keith. *Ultimate Spy*. New York: Dorling Kindersley, 2002.

Melton, H. Keith, and Robert Wallace. *The Official C.I.A. Manual of Trickery and Deception*. New York: William Morrow, 2009.

Mendez, Antonio, and Jonna Mendez, with Bruce Henderson. *Spy Dust: Two Masters of Disguise Reveal the Tools and Operations That Helped Win the Cold War*. New York: Atria, 2002.

Methven, Stuart. *Laughter in the Shadows: A CIA Memoir*. Annapolis: Naval Institute Press, 2008.

Mikoyan, Sergo A. "Eroding the Soviet 'Culture of Secrecy.'" *Studies in Intelligence*, Vol. 45, No. 5, Fall–Winter 2001.

Miller, Edward. *Misalliance: Ngo Dinh Diem, the United States and the Fate of South Vietnam*. Cambridge: Harvard University Press, 2013.

Modin, Yuri. *My Five Cambridge Friends*. Toronto: Ballantine, 1994.

Monger, Bradley M. *Stalin's Decision: The Origins of the Korean War*. Thesis, Naval Postgraduate School, Monterey, CA, 2014.

Monod, David. "'He Is a Cripple an' Needs My Love': Porgy and Bess as Cold War Propaganda." *Intelligence and National Security*, Vol. 18, No. 2, Summer 2003.

Montague, Ludwell Lee. *General Walter Bedell Smith as Director of Central Intelligence*. University Park: Penn State University Press, 1992.

Montefiore, Simon Sebag. *Stalin: The Court of the Red Tsar*. New York: Vintage, 2003.

Moran, Christopher R. "The Pursuit of Intelligence History: Methods, Sources, and Trajectories in the United Kingdom." *Studies in Intelligence*, Vol. 55, No. 2, 2011.

Moran, Christopher R., and Christopher J. Murphy. *Intelligence Studies in Britain and the US: Historiography Since 1945*. Edinburgh: Edinburgh University Press, 2013.

Morgan, Ted. *A Covert Life: Jay Lovestone: Communist, Anti-Communist and Spymaster*. New York: Random House, 1999.

———. *Reds: McCarthyism in Twentieth-Century America*. New York: Random House, 2003.

Morley, Jefferson. *Our Man in Mexico: Winston Scott and the Hidden History of the CIA*. Lawrence: University Press of Kansas, 2008.

Mosley, Leonard. *Dulles: A Biography of Eleanor, Allen and John Foster Dulles and Their Family Network*. New York: Dial, 1978.

Murfett, Malcolm H., ed. *Cold War Southeast Asia*. Singapore: Marshall Cavendish Editions, 2012.

Murphy, David E., Sergei Kondrashev and George Bailey. *Battleground Berlin: CIA vs. KGB in the Cold War*. New Haven: Yale University Press, 1997.

Murphy, Mark. "The Exploits of Agent 110." *Studies in Intelligence*, Vol. 37, No. 1, 1994.

———. "The OSS-German POW Controversy," *Studies in Intelligence*, Spring 1988.

Murphy, Robert D. "The Soldier and the Diplomat." *Foreign Service Journal*, May 1952.

Naftali, Timothy J. "Intrepid's Last Deception: Documenting the Career of Sir William Stephenson." *Intelligence and National Security*, Vol. 8, No. 3, July 1993.

Naimark, Norman M. *The Russians in Germany: A History of the Soviet Zone of Occupation, 1945–1949*. Cambridge: Harvard University Press, 1995.

Nashel, Jonathan D. *"Edward Lansdale and the American Attempt to Remake Southeast Asia, 1945–1965."* PhD diss., Rutgers, State University of New Jersey, 1994.

———. *Edward Lansdale's Cold War*. Boston: University of Massachusetts Press, 2005.

Nelson, Michael. *War of the Black Heavens: The Battles of Western Broadcasting in the Cold War*. Syracuse: Syracuse University Press, 1997.

Nelson, Wayne. *A Spy's Diary of World War II: Inside the OSS with an American Agent in Europe*. Jefferson, NC: McFarland, 2009.

Nettl, J. P. *The Eastern Zone and Soviet Policy in Germany, 1945–50*. London: Oxford University Press, 1951.

Newton, Verne W. *The Cambridge Spies: The Untold Story of Maclean, Philby and Burgess in America*. Lanham, MD: Madison Books, 1991.

Ngoei, Wen-Qing. "*The Arc of Containment: Britain, Malaya, Singapore and the Rise of the American Hegemony in Southeast Asia, 1941–1976*." PhD diss., Northwestern University, 2015.

Nitze, Paul H. Interviewed by Richard D. McKinzie, August 5–6, 1975, Truman Library Oral History Project.

O'Brien, Kevin A. "Interfering with Civil Society: CIA and KGB Covert Political Action During the Cold War." *International Journal of Intelligence and Counterintelligence*, Vol. 8, No. 4, 1995.

O'Donnell, Patrick K. *Operatives, Spies and Saboteurs: The Unknown Story of the Men and Women of World War II's OSS*. New York: Free Press, 2004.

Offner, Arnold A. *Another Such Victory: President Truman and the Cold War, 1945–1953*. Stanford: Stanford University Press, 2002.

Ogden, Alan. *Through Hitler's Back Door: SOE Operations in Hungary, Slovakia, Romania and Bulgaria, 1939–45*. Barnsley, UK: Pen & Sword, 2010.

Olmstead, Kathryn S. "Blonde Queens, Red Spiders and Neurotic Old Maids: Gender and Espionage in the Early Cold War." *Intelligence and National Security*, Vol. 19, No. 1, Spring 2004.

———. *Red Spy Queen: A Biography of Elizabeth Bentley*. Chapel Hill: University of North Carolina Press, 2002.

Olson, James M. "The Ten Commandments of Counter-Intelligence." *Studies in Intelligence*, Fall–Winter 2001.

Orlov, Alexander. *Handbook of Intelligence and Guerrilla Warfare*. Ann Arbor: University of Michigan Press, 1963.

O'Rourke, Lindsey A. "*Secrecy and Security: U.S. Orchestrated Regime Change During the Cold War*." PhD diss., University of Chicago, 2013.

Oshinsky, David M. *A Conspiracy So Immense: The World of Joe McCarthy*. New York: Oxford University Press, 2005.

Ostermann, Christian. *New Documents on the East German Uprising of 1953*. Cold War International History Project Bulletin, No. 5. Washington, DC: Woodrow Wilson International Center for Scholars, Spring 1995.

———. *The United States, the East German Uprising of 1953, and the Limits of Rollback*. Cold War International History Project, Working Paper No. 11. Washington, DC: Woodrow Wilson International Center for Scholars, 1994.

Pach, Chester J., ed. *A Companion to Dwight D. Eisenhower*. Malden, MA: Wiley Blackwell, 2017.

Palm, Edward F. *An American Pie: Lansdale, Lederer, Dooley, and Modern Memory*. CreateSpace, 2013.

Parrish, Thomas. *Berlin in the Balance, 1945–1949*. Reading, MA: Addison-Wesley, 1998.

Peake, Hayden B. "Harry S. Truman on CIA Covert Operations." *Studies in Intelligence*, Spring 1981.

———. "OSS and the Venona Decrypts." *Intelligence and National Security*, Vol. 12, No. 3, July 1997.

———. *The Reader's Guide to Intelligence Periodicals*. Washington, DC: National Intelligence Book Center, 1992.

Peebles, Curtis. *Twilight Warriors: Covert Air Operations Against the USSR.* Annapolis: Naval Institute Press, 2005.

Peraino, Kevin. *A Force So Swift: Mao, Truman and the Birth of Modern China.* New York: Crown, 2017.

Perl, Matthew. "Comparing US and UK Intelligence Assessment in the Early Cold War: NSC-68, April 1950." *Intelligence and National Security,* Vol. 18, No. 1, Spring 2003.

Persico, Joseph. *Piercing the Reich: The Penetration of Nazi Germany by American Secret Agents in World War II.* New York: Random House, 1979.

———. *Roosevelt's Secret War: FDR and World War II Espionage.* New York: Random House, 2001.

Petersen, J. K. *Understanding Surveillance Technologies: Spy Devices, Privacy, History & Applications.* Boca Raton, FL: Auerbach Publications, 2007.

Petersen, Martin. "What I Learned in 40 Years of Doing Intelligence Analysis for US Policymakers." *Studies in Intelligence,* Vol. 55, No. 1, 2011.

Philby, Kim. *My Silent War.* New York: Modern Library, 2002.

Phillips, David Atlee. *The Night Watch.* New York: Atheneum, 1977.

Phillips, Rufus. Interviewed by Ted Gittinger, March 4, 1982 (Pt. 1) and May 27, 1982 (Pt. 2). Folder 29, Box 3, Rufus Phillips Collection, Vietnam Center and Archive, Texas Tech University.

———. Interviewed by Charles Stuart Kennedy, July 19 and August 15, 1995. Association for Diplomatic Studies and Training, Foreign Affairs Oral History Program.

———. *Why Vietnam Matters: An Eyewitness Account of Lessons Not Learned.* Annapolis: Naval Institute Press, 2008.

Pipes, Richard. *The Russian Revolution.* New York: Vintage, 1991.

Pisani, Sallie. *The CIA and the Marshall Plan.* Lawrence: University Press of Kansas, 1991.

Plokhy, Serhii. *The Man with the Poison Gun.* London: Oneworld Publications, 2017.

Pollock, Daniel C., Project Director. *The Art and Science of Psychological Operations: Case Studies of Military Application.* Washington, DC: American Institutes for Research, 1976.

Polmar, Norman Allen, and Thomas B. Allen. *Spy Book: The Encyclopedia of Espionage.* New York: Random House, 2004.

Popplewell, Richard J. "The KGB and the Control of the Soviet Bloc: The Case of East Germany." *Intelligence and National Security,* Vol. 13, No. 1, Spring 1998.

Porter, Gareth. *Perils of Dominance: Imbalance of Power and the Road to War in Vietnam.* Berkeley: University of California Press, 2005.

Powers, Richard Gid. *Secrecy and Power: The Life of J. Edgar Hoover.* New York: Free Press, 1987.

Powers, Thomas. *Intelligence Wars: American Secret History from Hitler to Al-Qaeda.* New York: New York Review Books, 2002.

———. *The Man Who Kept the Secrets: Richard Helms and the CIA.* New York: Alfred A. Knopf, 1979.

Prados, John. *Lost Crusader: The Secret Wars of CIA Director William Colby.* New York: Oxford University Press, 2003.

———. *Presidents' Secret Wars: CIA and Pentagon Covert Operations from World War II Through the Persian Gulf.* Chicago: Ivan R. Dee, 1996.

———. *Safe for Democracy: The Secret Wars of the CIA.* Chicago: Ivan R. Dee, 2006.

———. *The Soviet Estimate: U.S. Intelligence Analysis and Russian Military Strength.* New York: Dial, 1982.

———. *Vietnam: The History of an Unwinnable War, 1945–1975.* Lawrence: University Press of Kansas, 2009.

Pringle, Robert W. *Historical Dictionary of Russian Soviet Intelligence.* Lanham, MD: Scarecrow Press, 2006.

———. "The Intelligence Services of Russia." *The Oxford Handbook of National Security Intelligence.* New York: Oxford University Press, 2010.

Ranelagh, John. *The Agency: The Rise and Decline of the CIA.* New York: Simon & Schuster, 1986.

Rathmell, Andrew. "Copeland and Zaim: Re-evaluating the Evidence." *Intelligence and National Security,* Vol. 11, No. 1, Jan. 1996.

Reisman, Arnold, and George Wolf. "Istanbul Intrigue: An Unlikely Quintet." *The Jewish Magazine,* October 2010.

Reynolds, Nicholas. "A Spy Who Made His Own Way: Ernest Hemingway, Wartime Spy." *Studies in Intelligence,* Vol. 56, No. 2, 2012.

Richardson, John H. "My Father, the Spy." *Esquire,* March 1999.

———. *My Father the Spy: An Investigative Memoir.* New York: HarperCollins, 2005.

Richie, Alexandra. *Faust's Metropolis: A History of Berlin.* New York: Carroll & Graf, 1999.

Riebling, Mark. *Wedge: From Pearl Harbor to 9/11.* New York: Simon & Schuster, 2002.

Robarge, David. "Cunning Passages, Contrived Corridors: Wandering in the Angletonian Wilderness." *Studies in Intelligence,* Vol. 53, No. 4, 2009.

———. "Directors of Central Intelligence, 1946–2005." *Studies in Intelligence,* Vol. 49, No. 3, 2005.

———. "Richard Helms: The Intelligence Professional Personified." *Studies in Intelligence,* Vol. 46, No. 4, 2002.

Roberts, Geoffrey. *A Chance for Peace? The Soviet Campaign to End the Cold War, 1953–1955.* Cold War International History Project, Working Paper No. 57. Washington, DC: Woodrow Wilson International Center for Scholars, 2008.

Roosevelt, Kermit. *War Report of the OSS, Vols 1 and 2.* New York: Walker, 1976.

Rose, P. K. "Two Strategic Intelligence Mistakes in Korea, 1950." *Studies in Intelligence,* Vol. 45, No. 5, Fall–Winter 2001.

Rositzke, Harry. *The CIA's Secret Operations: Espionage, Counterespionage, and Covert Action.* New York: Reader's Digest Press, 1977.

Rovere, Richard H. *Senator Joe McCarthy.* New York: Harcourt, Brace & World, 1959.

Rubin, Barry M. *Istanbul Intrigues.* New York: McGraw-Hill, 1989.

Rudgers, David R. *Creating the Secret State: The Origins of the Central Intelligence Agency, 1943–1947.* Lawrence: University Press of Kansas, 2000.

Ruffner, Kevin C. "American Intelligence and the Gehlen Organization, 1945–49." *Studies in Intelligence,* 1997.

———. "The Case of Otto Albrecht Alfred von Bolschwing." *Studies in Intelligence,* 1998.

———. "CIA's Support to the Nazi War Criminal Investigations." *Studies in Intelligence,* 1997.

———. "Cold War Allies: The Origins of CIA's Relationship with Ukrainian Nationalists." *Studies in Intelligence,* 1998.

———. *Eagle and Swastika: CIA and Nazi War Criminals and Collaborators—Secret Draft Working Paper.* Washington, DC: CIA History Staff, April 2003.

———. "Soldiers, Spies and the Rat Line: America's Undeclared War Against the Soviets." *Studies in Intelligence,* 1995.

Salisbury, Harrison E. *Without Fear or Favor.* New York: Times Books, 1980.

Salter, Michael. *Nazi War Crimes, US Intelligence and Selective Prosecution at Nuremburg: Controversies Regarding the Role of the Office of Strategic Services.* New York: Routledge-Cavendish, 2007.

Saunders, Frances Stonor. *The Cultural Cold War: The CIA and the World of Arts and Letters.* New York: New Press, 2000.

Sayer, Ian, and Douglas Botting. *America's Secret Army: The Untold Story of the Counter Intelligence Corps.* London: Collins, 1989.

Schecter, Jerrold, and Leona Schecter. *Sacred Secrets: How Soviet Intelligence Operations Changed American History.* Washington, DC: Brassey's, 2002.

Scheer, Robert. *How the United States Got Involved in Vietnam.* Santa Barbara: Center for the Study of Democratic Institutions, 1965.

Scherer, F. M. "Horst Hesse: A Cold War Military Intelligence Mole." *Intelligence and National Security,* Vol. 21, No. 2, April 2006.

Schiattareggia, M. H. "Counterintelligence in Counterguerrilla Operations." *Studies in Intelligence,* Vol. 57, No. 2, 2013.

Schlesinger, Stephen, and Stephen Kinzer. *Bitter Fruit: The Story of the American Coup in Guatemala.* New York: Doubleday, 1982.

Schrecker, Ellen. *Many Are the Crimes: McCarthyism in America.* Boston: Little, Brown, 1998.

Schroeder, Richard E. "The Intelligence Education of the First Head of CIA: Roscoe Hillenkoetter." *Studies in Intelligence,* Vol. 60, No. 1, 2016.

Scotton, Frank. *Uphill Battle: Reflections on Viet Nam Counterinsurgency.* Lubbock: Texas Tech University Press, 2014.

Seale, Patrick, and Maureen McConville. *Philby: The Long Road to Moscow.* New York: Penguin, 1978.

Searle, Alaric. " 'Vopo'—General Vincenz Muller and Western Intelligence, 1948–54: CIC, the Gehlen Organization and Two Cold War Covert Operations." *Intelligence and National Security,* Vol. 17, No. 2, Summer 2002.

Sebestyen, Victor. *Twelve Days: The Story of the 1956 Hungarian Revolution.* New York: Pantheon, 2006.

Shackley, Theodore, and Finney, Richard. *Spymaster: My Life in the CIA.* Dulles, VA: Potomac Books, 2005.

Shaplen, Robert. *The Lost Revolution: The U.S. in Vietnam, 1946–1966.* New York: Harper Colophon, 1966.

Sharp, Tony. *Stalin's American Spy: Noel Field, Allen Dulles & the East European Show Trials.* London: Hurst, 2014.

Sheehan, Neil. *A Bright Shining Lie: John Paul Vann and America in Vietnam.* New York: Vintage, 1989.

Sheehan, Neil, ed. *The Pentagon Papers.* New York: Quadrangle, 1971.

Sheffy, Yigal. "Unconcern at Dawn, Surprise at Sunset: Egyptian Intelligence Appreciation Before the Sinai Campaign, 1956." *Intelligence and National Security,* Vol. 5, No. 3, July 1990.

Sheinkin, Steve. *Most Dangerous: Daniel Ellsberg and the Secret History of the Vietnam War.* New York: Scholastic, 2017.

Shirer, William L. *Berlin Diary: The Journal of a Foreign Correspondent, 1934–1941.* New York: Alfred A. Knopf, 1941.

Sibley, Katherine A. S. *Red Spies in America: Stolen Secrets and the Dawn of the Cold War.* Lawrence: University Press of Kansas, 2004.

Sichel, Peter M. F. *The Secrets of My Life: Vintner, Prisoner, Soldier, Spy*. Bloomington, IN: Archway Publishing, 2016.

Silet, Charles L. P., ed. *Oliver Stone: Interviews*. Jackson: University Press of Mississippi, 2001.

Silver, Arnold M. "Questions, Questions, Questions: Memories of Oberursel." *Intelligence and National Security*, Vol. 8, No. 2, April 1993.

Simpson, Christopher. *Blowback: America's Recruitment of Nazis and its Effects on the Cold War*. New York: Weidenfeld & Nicolson, 1988.

Simpson, Howard R. *Tiger in the Barbed Wire: An American in Vietnam, 1952–1991*. Washington, DC: Brassey's, 1992.

Smith, Arthur L., Jr. *Kidnap City: Cold War Berlin*. Westport, CT: Greenwood Press, 2002.

Smith, Bradley F. "The American Road to Central Intelligence." *Intelligence and National Security*, Vol. 12, No. 1, Jan. 1997.

———. "An Idiosyncratic View of Where We Stand on the History of American Intelligence in the Early Post-1945 Era." *Intelligence and National Security*, Vol. 3, No. 4, Oct. 1988.

———. *The Shadow Warriors: O.S.S. and the Origins of the C.I.A.* New York: Basic Books, 1983.

Smith, Michael. *SIX: A History of Britain's Secret Intelligence Service, Pt. 1*. London: Dialogue, 2010.

Smith, R. Harris. *OSS: The Secret History of America's First Central Intelligence Agency*. Guilford, CT: Lyons Press, 2005.

Snider, L. Britt. *The Agency and the Hill: CIA's Relationship with Congress, 1946–2004*. Washington, DC: Center for the Study of Intelligence, Central Intelligence Agency, 2008.

Snyder, Timothy. *Bloodlands: Europe Between Hitler and Stalin*. New York: Basic Books, 2010.

Solovyov, Vladimir, and Elena Klepikova. *Behind the High Kremlin Walls*. New York: Dodd, Mead, 1986.

Sorley, Lewis, ed. *The Vietnam War: An Assessment by South Vietnam's Generals*. Lubbock: Texas Tech University Press, 2010.

Sprouse, Philip D. Interviewed by James R. Fuchs, February 11, 1974. Truman Library Oral History Project.

Srodes, James. *On Dupont Circle: Franklin and Eleanor Roosevelt and the Progressives Who Shaped Our World*. Berkeley: Counterpoint Books, 2012.

Stafford, David. *Roosevelt and Churchill: Men of Secrets*. Woodstock, NY: Overlook Press, 2000.

———. *Spies Beneath Berlin*. London: John Murray, 2002.

Stavins, Ralph, Richard J. Barnet and Marcus G. Raskin. *Washington Plans an Aggressive War*. New York: Vintage, 1971.

Stephan, Robert W. *Stalin's Secret War: Soviet Counterintelligence Against the Nazis, 1941–1945*. Lawrence: University Press of Kansas, 2004.

Steury, Donald P. "How the CIA Missed Stalin's Bomb." *Studies in Intelligence*, Vol. 49, No. 1, 2005.

Steury, Donald P., ed. *On the Front Lines of the Cold War: Documents on the Intelligence War in Berlin, 1946 to 1961*. Washington, DC: CIA History Staff, Center for the Study of Intelligence, 1999.

Stevenson, William. *A Man Called Intrepid*. New York: Harcourt Brace Jovanovich, 1976.

Stewart, Brian. "Winning in Malaya: An Intelligence Success Story." *Intelligence and National Security,* Vol. 14, No. 4, Winter 1999.

Stockton, Bayard. *Flawed Patriot: The Rise and Fall of CIA Legend Bill Harvey.* Washington, DC: Potomac Books, 2006.

Stolz, Richard. "A Case Officer's First Tour." *Studies in Intelligence,* Vol. 37, No. 1, 1994.

Stout, Mark. "The Pond: Running Agents for State, War and the CIA." *Studies in Intelligence,* Vol. 48, No. 3, 2004.

Streatfeild, Dominic. *Brainwash: The Secret History of Mind Control.* London: Hodder & Stoughton, 2006.

Stutesman, John H. Interviewed by William Burr, June 22, 1988. Association for Diplomatic Studies and Training, Foreign Affairs Oral History Project.

Sudoplatov, Anatoli, with Jerrold L. Schecter and Leona P. Schecter. *Special Tasks: The Memoirs of an Unwanted Witness.* Boston: Little, Brown, 1995.

Sullivan, William C., with Bill Brown. *The Bureau: My Thirty Years in Hoover's FBI.* New York: W. W. Norton, 1979.

Sulzberger, C. L. *A Long Row of Candles: Memoirs and Diaries (1934–1954).* New York: Macmillan, 1969.

Suvorov, Viktor. *Soviet Military Intelligence.* London: Hamish Hamilton, 1984.

Swartz, Martin Ben. "*A New Look at the 1956 Hungarian Revolution: Soviet Opportunism, American Acquiescence.*" PhD diss., School of Law and Diplomacy, Tufts University, 1988.

Talbot, David. *The Devil's Chessboard: Allen Dulles, the C.I.A. and the Rise of America's Secret Government.* New York: HarperCollins, 2005.

Tarrant, V. E., *The Red Orchestra.* New York: John Wiley & Sons, 1996.

Taylor, Fred. *Exorcising Hitler: The Occupation and Denazification of Germany.* New York: Bloomsbury Press, 2011.

Taylor, Stan A., and Daniel Snow. "Cold War Spies: Why They Spied and How They Got Caught." *Intelligence and National Security,* Vol. 12, No. 2, April 1997.

Thamm, Gerhardt B. *The Making of a Spy: Memoir of a German Boy Soldier Turned American Army Intelligence Agent.* Jefferson, NC: McFarland, 2010.

Theoharis, Athan G. *Chasing Spies: How the FBI Failed in Counterintelligence but Promoted the Politics of McCarthyism in the Cold War Years.* Chicago: Ivan R. Dee, 2002.

———. "A Creative and Aggressive FBI: The Victor Kravchenko Case." *Intelligence and National Security,* Vol. 20, No. 2, June 2005.

———. *J. Edgar Hoover, Sex and Crime: An Historical Antidote.* Chicago: Ivan R. Dee, 1995.

Theoharis, Athan G., ed. *From the Secret Files of J. Edgar Hoover.* Chicago: Ivan R. Dee, 1991.

Theoharis, Athan G., and John Stuart Cox. *The Boss: J. Edgar Hoover and the Great American Inquisition.* New Orleans: Temple University Press, 1988.

Thomas, Evan. *Ike's Bluff: President Eisenhower's Secret Battle to Save the World.* Boston: Little, Brown, 2012.

———. *The Very Best Men: The Daring Early Years of the CIA.* New York: Simon & Schuster, 1995.

Thomas, Gordon. *Secret Wars: One Hundred Years of British Intelligence Inside MI5 and MI6.* New York: St. Martin's Griffin, 2009.

Thomas, Hugh. *The Suez Affair.* London: Weidenfeld & Nicolson, 1986.

Thompson, Nicholas. *The Hawk and the Dove: Paul Nitze, George Kennan and the History of the Cold War.* New York: Henry Holt, 2009.

Tierney, John J., Jr. "Can a Popular Insurgency Be Defeated?" *Military History*, March 2007.

Trahair, Richard C. S., and Robert C. Miller. *Encyclopedia of Cold War Espionage, Spies, and Secret Operations*. New York: Enigma Books, 2012.

Trimble, Delmege. "The Defections of Dr. John." *Studies in Intelligence*, Vol. 4, No. 4, Fall 1960.

Troy, Thomas F. *Donovan and the CIA: A History of the Establishment of the Central Intelligence Agency*. Frederick, MD: University Publications of America, 1980.

Tuch, Hans N. Interviewed by G. Lewis Schmidt, Aug. 4, 1989. Association for Diplomatic Studies and Training, Foreign Affairs Oral History Project.

Tucker, Spencer C., ed. *Encyclopedia of the Vietnam War: A Political, Social, and Military History*. Santa Barbara: ABC-CLIO, 1998.

United States Senate. "Alleged Assassination Plots Involving Foreign Leaders." Interim and Final Reports of the Select Committee to Study Governmental Operations with Respect to Intelligence Activities (Church Committee). Washington, DC: Government Printing Office, 1975 and 1976.

Unsinger, Peter C. "Three Intelligence Blunders in Korea." *International Journal of Intelligence and Counterintelligence*, Vol. 3, No. 4, 1989.

Valero, Larry A. "The American Joint Intelligence Committee and Estimates of the Soviet Union, 1945–1947." *Studies in Intelligence*, No. 9, Summer 2000.

———. " 'We Need Our New OSS, Our New General Donovan, Now . . .': The Public Discourse over American Intelligence, 1944–53." *Intelligence and National Security*, Vol. 18, No. 1, Spring 2003.

Vaughn, Hal. *FDR's 12 Apostles: The Spies Who Paved the Way for the Invasion of North Africa*. Guilford, CT: Lyons Press, 2006.

Verrier, Anthony. *Through the Looking Glass: British Foreign Policy in an Age of Illusions*. London: Jonathan Cape, 1983.

Von Hoffman, Nicholas. *Citizen Cohn: The Life and Times of Roy Cohn*. New York: Doubleday, 1988.

Wallace, Robert, and H. Keith Melton. *Spycraft: The Secret History of the CIA's Spytechs from Communism to al-Qaeda*. New York: Dutton, 2008.

Waller, Douglas. *Disciples: The World War II Missions of the CIA Directors Who Fought for Wild Bill Donovan*. New York: Simon & Schuster, 2015.

———. *Wild Bill Donovan: The Spymaster Who Created the OSS and Modern American Espionage*. New York: Free Press, 2011.

Walton, Calder. *Empire of Secrets: British Intelligence, the Cold War and the Twilight of Empire*. New York: HarperCollins, 2010.

Warner, Michael. *Central Intelligence: Origin and Evolution*. Washington, DC: Center for the Study of Intelligence, Central Intelligence Agency, September 2001.

———. "The CIA's Internal Probe of the Bay of Pigs Affair." *Studies in Intelligence*, Vol. 42, No. 5, Winter 1998–99.

———. "The CIA's Office of Policy Coordination: From NSC 10/2 to NSC 68." *International Journal of Intelligence and Counterintelligence*, Vol. 11, No. 2, Summer 1998.

———. *The CIA Under Harry Truman*. Washington, DC: Center for the Study of Intelligence, Central Intelligence Agency, 1994.

———. "The Creation of the Central Intelligence Group." *Studies in Intelligence*, Vol. 39, No. 5, 1996.

———. "Origins of the Congress of Cultural Freedom, 1949–50." *Studies in Intelligence*, Vol. 38, No. 5, 1995.

———. "Sophisticated Spies: CIA's Links to Liberal Anti-Communists." *International Journal of Intelligence and Counterintelligence*, Vol. 9, No. 4, Winter 1996–97.

Warner, Michael, and Robert Louis Benson. "Venona and Beyond: Thoughts on Work Undone." *Intelligence and National Security*, Vol. 12, No. 3, July 1997.

Warner, Michael, and J. Kenneth McDonald. *US Intelligence Community Reform Studies Since 1947*. Washington, DC: Center for the Study of Intelligence, Central Intelligence Agency, April 2005.

Watts, Larry L. *With Friends Like These . . . The Soviet Bloc's Clandestine War Against Romania, Vol. 1*. Bucharest: Military Publishing House, 2010.

Webb, G. Gregg. "The FBI and Foreign Intelligence: New Insights into J. Edgar Hoover's Role." *Studies in Intelligence*, Vol. 48, No. 1, 2004.

———. "Intelligence Liaison Between the FBI and State, 1940–44." *Studies in Intelligence*, Vol. 49, No. 3, 2005.

Weber, Ralph E., ed. *Spymasters: Ten CIA Officers in Their Own Words*. Wilmington: Scholarly Resources, 1999.

Weiner, Tim. *Enemies: A History of the FBI*. New York: Random House, 2012.

———. *Legacy of Ashes: The History of the CIA*. New York: Doubleday, 2007.

Weinstein, Allen. *Perjury: The Hiss-Chambers Case*. Stanford: Hoover Institution Press, 2013.

Weinstein, Allen, and Alexander Vassiliev. *The Haunted Wood: Soviet Espionage in America—the Stalin Era*. New York: Random House, 1999.

Weintraub, Robert. "Yankee, Executive, Soldier, Spy." *Grantland*, May 6, 2015.

Weisbrode, Kenneth. *The Atlantic Century: Four Generations of Extraordinary Diplomats Who Forged America's Vital Alliance with Europe*. Boston: Da Capo Press, 2009.

Werth, Alexander. *Russia at War, 1941–1945*. New York: Carroll & Graf, 2000.

West, Nigel. *Historical Dictionary of British Intelligence*. Lanham, MD: Scarecrow Press, 2005.

———. *Historical Dictionary of Cold War Counterintelligence*. Lanham, MD: Scarecrow Press, 2007.

Whaley, Barton. *Detecting Deception: A Bibliography of Counterdeception Across Time, Cultures and Disciplines*. Washington, DC: Office of the Director of National Intelligence, National Intelligence Council, 2006.

Wilford, Hugh. *America's Great Game: The CIA's Secret Arabists and the Shaping of the Modern Middle East*. New York: Basic Books, 2013.

———. *The Mighty Wurlitzer: How the CIA Played America*. Cambridge: Harvard University Press, 2008.

Wilson, John D. "At Work with Donovan." *Studies in Intelligence*, Vol. 37, No. 3, 1994.

Winks, Robin W. *Cloak & Gown: Scholars in the Secret War, 1939–1961*. New York: William Morrow, 1987.

Wise, David. *Molehunt: The Secret Search for Traitors That Shattered the CIA*. New York: Random House, 1992.

Wise, David, and Thomas B. Ross. *The Invisible Government*. New York: Random House, 1964.

Wisner, Frank G., Jr. Interviewed by Richard L. Jackson, March 22, 1998. Association for Diplomatic Studies and Training, Foreign Affairs Oral History Project.

Wittner, Lawrence S. *American Intervention in Greece, 1943–1949: A Study in Counterrevolution*. New York: Columbia University Press, 1986.

Wolf, Markus, with Anne McElvoy. *Man Without a Face: The Autobiography of Communism's Greatest Spymaster*. New York: PublicAffairs, 1997.

Wolff, Robert Lee. *The Balkans in Our Times*. New York: W. W. Norton, 1974.

Woods, Randall. *Shadow Warrior: William Egan Colby and the CIA*. New York: Basic Books, 2013.

Yergin, Daniel. *Shattered Peace: The Origins of the Cold War*. Boston: Houghton Mifflin, 1977.

Zegart, Amy B. *Flawed by Design: The Evolution of the CIA, JCS and NSC*. Stanford: Stanford University Press, 1999.

Zervoudakis, Alexander. " 'Nihil mirare, nihil contemptare, Omnia intelligere': Franco-Vietnamese Intelligence in Indochina, 1950–1954." *Intelligence and National Security*, Vol. 13, No. 1, Spring 1998.

Zubok, Vladislav M. *A Failed Empire: The Soviet Union in the Cold War from Stalin to Gorbachev*. Chapel Hill: University of North Carolina Press, 2007.

Zubok, Vladislav M., and Constantine Pleshakov. *Inside the Kremlin's Cold War: From Stalin to Khrushchev*. Cambridge: Harvard University Press, 1996.

Index

Photo Credits